T0190497

Communications
in Computer and Information Science   1770

Rationale

The CCIS series is devoted to the publication of proceedings of computer science conferences. Its aim is to efficiently disseminate original research results in informatics in printed and electronic form. While the focus is on publication of peer-reviewed full papers presenting mature work, inclusion of reviewed short papers reporting on work in progress is welcome, too. Besides globally relevant meetings with internationally representative program committees guaranteeing a strict peer-reviewing and paper selection process, conferences run by societies or of high regional or national relevance are also considered for publication.

Topics

The topical scope of CCIS spans the entire spectrum of informatics ranging from foundational topics in the theory of computing to information and communications science and technology and a broad variety of interdisciplinary application fields.

Information for Volume Editors and Authors

Publication in CCIS is free of charge. No royalties are paid, however, we offer registered conference participants temporary free access to the online version of the conference proceedings on SpringerLink (http://link.springer.com) by means of an http referrer from the conference website and/or a number of complimentary printed copies, as specified in the official acceptance email of the event.

CCIS proceedings can be published in time for distribution at conferences or as post-proceedings, and delivered in the form of printed books and/or electronically as USBs and/or e-content licenses for accessing proceedings at SpringerLink. Furthermore, CCIS proceedings are included in the CCIS electronic book series hosted in the SpringerLink digital library at http://link.springer.com/bookseries/7899. Conferences publishing in CCIS are allowed to use Online Conference Service (OCS) for managing the whole proceedings lifecycle (from submission and reviewing to preparing for publication) free of charge.

Publication process

The language of publication is exclusively English. Authors publishing in CCIS have to sign the Springer CCIS copyright transfer form, however, they are free to use their material published in CCIS for substantially changed, more elaborate subsequent publications elsewhere. For the preparation of the camera-ready papers/files, authors have to strictly adhere to the Springer CCIS Authors' Instructions and are strongly encouraged to use the CCIS LaTeX style files or templates.

Abstracting/Indexing

CCIS is abstracted/indexed in DBLP, Google Scholar, EI-Compendex, Mathematical Reviews, SCImago, Scopus. CCIS volumes are also submitted for the inclusion in ISI Proceedings.

How to start

To start the evaluation of your proposal for inclusion in the CCIS series, please send an e-mail to ccis@springer.com.

Zhiwen Yu · Xinhong Hei · Duanling Li ·
Xianhua Song · Zeguang Lu
Editors

Intelligent Robotics

Third China Annual Conference, CCF CIRAC 2022
Xi'an, China, December 16–18, 2022
Proceedings

 Springer

Editors
Zhiwen Yu
Harbin Engineering University
Harbin, China

Duanling Li
Beijing University of Posts
and Telecommunications
Beijing, China

Zeguang Lu
National Academy of Guo Ding Institute
of Data Science
Beijing, China

Xinhong Hei
Xi'an University of Technology
Xi'an, China

Xianhua Song
Harbin University of Science and Technology
Harbin, China

ISSN 1865-0929   ISSN 1865-0937 (electronic)
Communications in Computer and Information Science
ISBN 978-981-99-0300-9   ISBN 978-981-99-0301-6 (eBook)
https://doi.org/10.1007/978-981-99-0301-6

This Springer imprint is published by the registered company Springer Nature Singapore Pte Ltd.
The registered company address is: 152 Beach Road, #21-01/04 Gateway East, Singapore 189721, Singapore

Preface

As the program chairs of the 2022 China Intelligent Robotics Annual Conference (CCF CIRAC 2022), it is our great pleasure to welcome you to the conference proceedings. CCF CIRAC 2022 was held in Xi'an, China, December 16–18, 2022, hosted by the China Computer Federation, the CCF Intelligent Robot Professional Committee, Northwestern Polytechnical University and Xi'an University of Technology.

With the theme of "human-computer integration and intelligence introduction in the future", the conference focused on key technologies such as robot operating systems and software, perceptual theory and methods, autonomous navigation, human-computer natural interaction and harmonious integration, and robot safety, and promoted interdisciplinary academic exchanges and industry-university research cooperation.

The conference attracted 120 paper submissions. After the hard work of the Program Committee average number of reviews per paper is 3, 35 papers were accepted to appear in the conference proceedings, with an acceptance rate of 29%.

We would like to thank all the Program Committee members for their hard work in completing the review tasks. Their collective efforts made it possible to attain quality reviews for all the submissions within a few weeks. Their diverse expertise in different research areas helped us to create an exciting program for the conference. Their comments and advice helped the authors to improve the quality of their papers and gain deeper insights.

Many thanks should also go to the authors and participants for their tremendous support in making the conference a success.

We thank the team at Springer, whose professional assistance was invaluable in the production of the proceedings. And we sincerely thank the authors and participants for their tremendous support in making the conference a success.

Besides the technical program, this year CCF CIRAC 2022 offered different experiences to the participants. We hope you enjoyed the conference.

December 2022

Zhiwen Yu
Xinhong Hei
Duanling Li
Xianhua Song
Zeguang Lu

Organization

The 2022 China Intelligent Robotics Annual Conference (CCF CIRAC 2022), https://conf.ccf.org.cn/cirac2022, was held in Xi'an, China, December 16–18, 2022, hosted by the China Computer Federation, the CCF Intelligent Robot Professional Committee, Northwestern Polytechnical University and Xi'an University of Technology.

Steering Committee Chair

Xuejun Yang   Academy of Military Sciences, China

Steering Committee

Chunjiang Zhao   National Engineering Research Center for
                                    Information Technology in Agriculture, China
Mengfei Yang   China Academy of Space Technology, China
Yaonan Wang   Hunan University, China
Hong Qiao   China Academy of Sciences, China
Jiansheng Dai   Southern University of Science and Technology,
                                    China
Shimin Hu   Tsinghua University, China

General Chairs

Fuchun Sun   Tsinghua University, China
Xingshe Zhou   Northwestern Polytechnical University, China
Xiaohui Zhang   Xi'an University of Technology, China

Program Chairs

Zhiwen Yu   Harbin Engineering University, China
Xinhong Hei   Xi'an University of Technology, China
Duanling Li   Beijing University of Posts and
                                    Telecommunications, China

Program Vice Chair

Haobin Shi   Northwestern Polytechnical University, China

Organization Chairs

Changhe Tu   Shandong University, China
Junhuai Li   Xi'an University of Technology, China
Gang Yang   Northwestern Polytechnical University, China

Organization Vice Chairs

Xiaogang Song   Xi'an University of Technology, China
Yuan Yao   Northwestern Polytechnical University, China

Forum Chairs

Zengguang Hou   China Academy of Sciences, China
Wenqiang Zhang   Fudan University, China

Forum Vice Chairs

Jun Wang   China University of Mining and Technology,
                                      China
Cheng Shi   Xi'an University of Technology, China

Publicity Chairs

Yuping Wang   Tsinghua University, China
Bin Fang   Tsinghua University, China

Publicity Vice Chairs

Zhenghao Shi   Xi'an University of Technology, China
Sheng Liu   Xi'an University of Technology, China

Paper Chairs

Duanling Li   Beijing University of Posts and
                                     Telecommunications, China
Jing Xin   Xi'an University of Technology, China

Paper Vice Chairs

Wenjuan Gong   China University of Petroleum, China
Jing Luo   Xi'an University of Technology, China

Financial Chair

Haiyan Jin   Xi'an University of Technology, China

Financial Vice Chair

Rong Fei   Xi'an University of Technology, China

Sponsoring Chairs

Shan An   JD Health, China
Bo Shen   Northwestern Polytechnical University, China

Exhibition Chair

Xuesong Mei   Xi'an Jiaotong University, China

Exhibition Vice Chairs

Yichuan Wang   Xi'an University of Technology, China
Jinwei Zhao   Xi'an University of Technology, China

Publication Chairs

Xianhua Song   Harbin University of Science and Technology,
                            China
Zeguang Lu   National Academy of Guo Ding Institute of Data
                            Science, China

Program Committee

Feng Chang   Shandong Sibu Robot Technology Co., Ltd.,
                            China
Renjie Chen   China University of Science and Technology,
                            China
Huadong Dai   National Defense Science and Technology
                            Innovation Research Institute of the Academy
                            of Military Sciences, China
Zhen Deng   Fuzhou University, China
Bin Fang   Tsinghua University, China
Xianping Fu   Dalian Maritime University, China
Wenjuan Gong   China University of Petroleum (East China),
                            China
Yufei Hao   Beijing University of Science and Technology,
                            China
Jie Hao   Luoteng (Hangzhou) Technology Co., Ltd., China
Chenlong He   Shaanxi University of Science and Technology,
                            China
Zhaofeng He   Beijing Zhongke Hongba Technology Co., Ltd.,
                            China
Kai He   Shenzhen Institute of Advanced Technology,
                            China
Xinhong Hei   Xi'an University of Technology, China
Taogang Hou   Beijing Jiaotong University, China
Zengguang Hou   Institute of Automation, Chinese Academy of
                            Sciences, China
Yun Hu   Southeast University, China
Ruizhen Hu   Shenzhen University, China
Qinghua Hu   Tianjin University, China
Hui Huang   Shenzhen University, China
Kai Huang   Sun Yat-sen University, China
Meng Jia   Xi'an University of Technology, China
Xiaoliang Jia   Northwestern Polytechnical University, China
Yongguo Jiang   Ocean University of China, China

Lanju Kong	Shandong University, China
Yankai Li	Xi'an University of Technology, China
Duanling Li	Beijing University of Posts and Telecommunications, China
Minqi Li	Xi'an University of Engineering, China
Yongming Li	Chongqing University, China
Tianrui Li	Southwest Jiaotong University, China
Wei Li	Georgia State University, USA
Yanming Liang	Xi'an University of Technology, China
Shaofu Lin	Beijing University of Technology, China
Xiaohan Liu	Guangzhou Electronic Technology Co., Ltd., Chinese Academy of Sciences, China
Xiuping Liu	Dalian University of Technology, China
Fei Liu	Shanghai Qinglang Intelligent Technology Co., Ltd., China
Yuelei Liu	Chang'an University, China
Xiaoguang Liu	Nankai University, China
Xiaofan Liu	City University of Hong Kong, China
Yang Liu	Henan University of Technology, China
Wenyin Liu	Guangdong University of Technology, China
Hu Lu	Air Force Engineering University, China
Jing Luo	Xi'an University of Technology, China
Na Lv	Xi'an Jiaotong University, China
Xiaomin Ma	Xi'an University of Engineering, China
Xinglu Ma	Qingdao University of Science and Technology, China
Chunguang Maa	HEU, China
Lingxia Mu	Xi'an University of Technology, China
Jianxin Pang	Shenzhen Youbishan Technology Co., Ltd., China
Fei Qiao	Tsinghua University, China
Yanli Ren	Shanghai University, China
Na Ruan	Shanghai Jiao Tong University, China
Liyong Shen	University of Chinese Academy of Sciences, China
Weiwei Shi	Xi'an University of Technology, China
Zhenghao Shi	Xi'an University of Technology, China
Dianxi Shi	National Defense Science and Technology Innovation Research Institute of the Academy of Military Sciences, China
Huyuan Sun	Institute of Oceanography, Chinese Academy of Sciences, China
Yanbin Sun	Guangzhou University, China
Li Tan	Beijing Business University, China

Chaoquan Tang	China University of Mining and Technology (Xuzhou), China
Shaohua Tang	South China University of Technology, China
Youliang Tian	Guizhou University, China
Changhe Tu	Shandong University, China
Zhiguo Wan	Shandong University, China
He Wang	Peking University, China
Peng Wang	Institute of Automation, Chinese Academy of Sciences, China
Shengke Wang	Ocean University of China, China
Shuo Wang	Institute of Automation, Chinese Academy of Sciences, China
Yuping Wang	Tsinghua University, China
Jun Wang	China University of Mining and Technology (Xuzhou), China
Yongjuan Wang	Information Engineering University of Strategic Support Forces, China
Huaqun Wang	Nanjing University of Posts and Telecommunications, China
Yichuan Wang	Xidian University, China
Wei Wang	Beijing Jiaotong University, China
Jianhui Wu	Hunan Institute of Technology, China
Bin Wu	IIE, CAS, China
Min Xian	Utah State University, USA
Jing Xin	Xi'an University of Technology, China
Haixia Xu	CAS, China
Yunzhi Xue	Institute of Software, Chinese Academy of Sciences, China
Jinfu Yang	Beijing University of Technology, China
Shaowu Yang	National University of Defense Technology, China
Xu Yang	Chinese Academy of Sciences, China
Dewei Yang	Chongqing University of Posts and Telecommunications, China
Gang Yang	Northwestern Polytechnical University, China
Zheng Yang	Tsinghua University, China
Yuan Yao	Northwestern Polytechnical University, China
Junfeng Yao	Xiamen University, China
Mao Ye	University of Electronic Science and Technology, China
Lei Yu	Georgia Institute of Technology, USA
Zeguang Lu	National Academy of Guo Ding Institute of Data Science, China

Contents

Robot Safety

Petri Net-Based Attack Modeling for Industrial Control System Networks

Yichuan Wang[1,2], Zhaoqi Lv[1], Yaling Zhang[1(✉)], Yeqiu Xiao[1], and Xinhong Hei[1,2]

[1] School of Computer Science and Engineering, Xi'an University of Technology, Xi'an, China
`ylzhang@xaut.edu.cn`
[2] Shaanxi Key Laboratory for Network Computing and Security Technology, Xi'an, China

Abstract. Industrial control systems have been deeply involved in industrial facilities and infrastructure. With the integrated development of industry and information technology, industrial control systems are tied to the Internet and may be threatened by cyber attacks. Modeling analysis and security evaluation are significant to guarantee industrial control system security. For in-depth research of security in the industrial control network, we first provide a cyber attack strategy for programmable logic controllers with respect to critical nodes in industrial control systems. Then, we explore and validate the viability of attacks based on the proposed strategy through simulations and visualization. Finally, Petri net modeling is utilized to depict both cyber attacks and defensive techniques. The results in this paper demonstrate that the proposed attack strategy gives new ideas for us to investigate industrial control cyber assaults, while the modeling and analytic methodologies in this paper are also useful for system weaknesses analysis.

Keywords: Industrial control systems · PLC security · Petri net modeling · Cyber attacks

1 Introduction

Industrial control system (ICS) is a term that covers numerous control systems, including supervisory control and data acquisition (SCADA) systems, distributed control systems (DCS), and other control hardware such as programmable logic controllers (PLCs). ICSs are mainly responsible for real-time data acquisition, system monitoring, and automatic control and management of industrial processes [1]. They play an important role in a country's critical infrastructure and directly affect a country's economy. With the increasing integration with computer and network technologies (IT), ICSs have become more intelligent and open. In recent years, the security of ICS has attracted widespread public attention and the number of cyber attacks against ICS is rapidly increasing [2]. In 2022, the international hacking group Anonymous carried out cyber attacks on Russian critical infrastructure, such as industrial gas control systems.

Traditionally, ICS have operated in a closed nature. With the development and functional requirements of information and communication technologies (ICT), more and more ICSs have moved from isolated network environments to public networks for

© The Author(s), under exclusive license to Springer Nature Singapore Pte Ltd. 2023
Z. Yu et al. (Eds.): CIRAC 2022, CCIS 1770, pp. 3–19, 2023.
https://doi.org/10.1007/978-981-99-0301-6_1

remote control and supervision of the infrastructure [3]. The communication between remote control components is carried out through the internal network of the ICS and some hardware devices with proprietary protocols [4], such as Modbus RTU, Modbus TCP, etc. The convergence of industrial control networks with the Internet leads to the risk of industrial control systems from traditional network attacks. Infrastructure as a Service (IaaS) is a service provided by cloud providers and some enterprises can benefit from this cloud-based service [5]. However, connecting ICS components to the cloud and the Internet can expose ICS to most cyber attack scenarios. Moreover, ICS devices are inherently less secure against such advanced attacks compared to traditional attacks such as misuse.

Industrial networks are primarily concerned with communication within and between these components and systems. Even though the boundaries between industrial networks and the Internet have begun to blur with the development of industrial networks, in essence they have fundamentally different development needs. Industrial networks connect to system edge devices via bus technology for controlling and monitoring the operation of the devices. Industrial networks usually have a deeper architecture than the Internet has [6] (see Fig. 1). Each layer usually uses a different protocol and requires the use of gateway devices for communication.

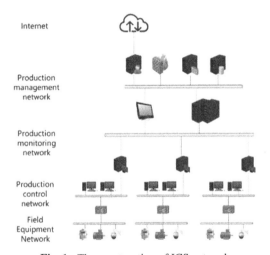

Fig. 1. The construction of ICS network

In view of the frequent occurrence of cyber attacks on industrial control systems, a formal analysis model needs to be established for the attack behavior of extranet penetration into the intranet to provide a research basis for defending against such attacks and to help managers effectively analyze the potential network security problems of industrial control systems. There are still relatively few studies related to the proposal and analysis of attack modeling methods for industrial control networks. The main contributions of this paper are as follows.

- A cyber attack approach for crucial equipment in industrial control systems is proposed.
- Petri net modeling rules are defined, and the attack behavior is formally analyzed and modeled by Petri net modeling method to establish a formal model combining source code and system state.
- Using Petri net modeling rules and methods to analyze the system runtime state changes is important for exploring the modeling methods of cyber attacks on industrial control systems.

The rest of the paper is organized as follows. In Sect. 2, the main academic research works on industrial control network attack modeling are discussed. In Sect. 3, an industrial control system hypothesis model is proposed, attack and defense behaviors are defined, and a cyber-attack model against Siemens PLC is developed. Section 4 provides a fine-grained analysis of the model constructed in Sect. 3. In Sect. 5, the attack verification scenarios are presented and compared with the current research work. Finally, the work related to this paper is summarized.

2   Related Work

A programmable logic controller (PLC) is an industrial computer system that continuously monitors the state of input devices and controls the state of output devices according to customized programs. PLCs are widely used in industrial control systems (ICS) to handle sensors and actuators, mainly because of their robustness and ability to withstand harsh conditions.the reasons for the existence of security vulnerabilities in PLCs are as follows [7].

1) PLCs are similar to the von Neumann architecture and their programmability provides an environment for attackers to write attack codes to run their programs.
2) PLC, as a lower computer, has a flawed communication protocol with the upper computer, which makes it easy for malicious programs to gain access to PLC operations.
3) PLC's memory read and write is weakly protected, making it easy for malicious programs to gain access to PLC's operation.

2.1   PLC Cyber Attacks

Dustin Berman [8] et al. present a device that uses Gumstix technology to simulate ICS field devices in an attempt to describe a cyber attack on ICS. Stephen McLaughlin [9] et al. present an automation tool, SABOT: The main purpose is to recover the semantics of PLC memory locations mapped to physical devices. This allows an attacker to automatically instantiate an attack against a specific PLC in the control system. Klick [10] et al. demonstrate the injection of malware into a Siemens S7–300 PLC with no interruption in the PLC's operation.Wael Alsabbagh [11] discusses a replay attack against the s7–300 PLC, combining the replay attack with the injection method Naman Govil [12] et al. introduced a ladder logic bomb malware written in ladder logic or compatible language in which this malware runs successfully in the PLC. Anastasis Keliris [13] proposed a modular industrial control system reverse engineering framework (ICSREF), which automates the process of reverse engineering ICS binaries and it can automatically generate malicious payloads against the target system to infiltrate a specific PLC.Henry Hui [14] et al. demonstrated a series of attacks against a Siemens S7–1200 PLC by using Windbg and Scapy software to exploit potential vulnerabilities in the Totally Integrated Automation (TIA) software.

2.2 System Vulnerability Model Construction Methods

Xu yue et al. [15] analyzed the architecture and interactions of power cyber-physical systems and used temporal petri nets as a modeling approach to model the attack means and attack information transmission paths in power cyber-physical systems.Radoglou-Grammatikis [16] et al. studied SCADA system security and focused their research on IEC 60870–5-104 protocol security issues, proposed a Petri net-based SCADA threat model, and simulated cyber attacks.Sridhar Adepu [17] et al. proposed a cyber-physical system (CPS) attacker model. The attack model derived from the attacker model is used to generate parametric attack processes and functions for a specific CPS.Raphael Fritz [18] et al. introduced two possible attacks against Discrete Event Systems (DES) that operate on a running process controlled by a PLC without being detected and modeled Petri nets for this attack process.K. Labadi [19] modeled the corresponding petri net for a pharmaceutical manufacturing and packaging system and performed a formal analysis. xu lijuan [20] et al. proposed a PLC security event forensic framework PLC- seiff by modeling attacks against PLCs from the perspective of security event forensics.

2.3 Basic Concepts of Petri Networks

Petri nets (PNs) are formal graphical and mathematical modeling tools suitable for defining and analyzing the operational behavior of complex, concurrent, distributed systems. Petri nets are composed of 4-tuples $N = \{P, T, A, M_0\}$ [21]:

- $P = \{p_1, p_2, p_3, ..., p_n\}$ is a finite set of libraries: a library is represented by a circle.
- $T = \{t_1, t_2, t_3, ..., t_n\}$ is a finite set of variants: a variant is represented by a square.
- $A \subseteq (P \times T) \cup (T \times P)$ is a finite set of arcs denoting a variation from one depot to another.
- $M_0 : P \rightarrow \{1, 2, 3, ...\}$ is the initial tokens of the PN model, indicating the number of tokens contained in each library in the model.

Petri nets can be used to represent the flow of activities in a complex system. Modeling, formal analysis and design of discrete event systems can be implemented by Petri nets [22]. In this study, the modeling and formal analysis of operating system vulnerability, vulnerability patch PLC under attack state are modeled and analyzed respectively based on Petri net modeling technique.

3 A PLC Cyber Attack Model Based on Petri Net Theory

3.1 ICS Environmental Model Assumptions

Cyber Attack Model. The main functions of industrial control networks are data monitoring, sending commands, and communication [23]. When the office network is interconnected with the Internet, it indirectly causes a potential threat to the control network within the enterprise. A network attack is launched against the office network by sending malicious packets, and then the internal industrial control network of the enterprise is attacked through the office network. This kind of attack by penetrating the intranet through the external network may leave the industrial control system in an insecure state, leading to economic losses and human casualties (see Fig. 2).

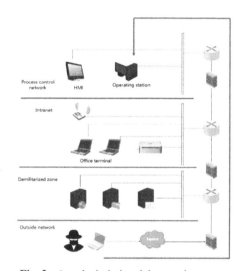

Fig. 2. Attacks in industrial control systems

Definition of Attack and Defense Behavior. The attack is carried out through the external network of the industrial control network, intercepting the communication packets between the PLC and the programmer and modifying the values in the registers of the PLC. The attack is successful: the value of the control output register in the PLC is changed from 1 to 0. Defensive behavior definition: 1) Patching the system vulnerability of the operator station where the programmer is deployed to eliminate the power extraction attack using the operating system vulnerability. 2) Detection of PLC communication process and interception of malicious packets. Successful defense: Data changes normally during PLC operation, no abnormal behavior.

Among the methods implemented for attacks on PLCs focus on random attacks and false data injection attacks.

1) Random attack: This attack can be performed on the sensor to make the sensor reading different from the actual value. When the control system is subject to random

attacks, Eq. (1) can be written as

$$\alpha_p = C\beta_p + \theta_p^{ra} \tag{1}$$

where θ_p^{ra} denotes the random attack, β_p, α_p is the system state and measurement when the control system is subjected to a random attack. C denotes the factor affecting the system.

2) False data injection attack: This attack affects the sensors so that the sensor readings do not match the actual signal. Unlike the random attack, the attacker knows the system structure, so it can affect a subset of sensors. When the control system is subjected to a false data injection attack, Eq. (2) can be expressed as

$$\alpha_p = C\beta_p + \mu\theta_p^{fda} \tag{2}$$

$\mu = diag(\mu_1, \mu_2, \mu_3)$. If the sensor i is affected by the attack, $\mu_i = 1$; otherwise, $\mu_i = 0$. θ_p^{fda} represents the system is under a false data injection attack.

ICS Operating Environment Assumptions. This study is based on the PLC of Siemens S7–1500 model for network attack. Siemens' PLC has two operating modes, run state and stop state. In the run state, the PLC implements the control function by executing the program programmed by the user in advance. Users can work through the supporting PLC programming software for ladder programming, and then the program has been programmed to download the PLC hardware device, in order to make the PLC output can respond to the changing input signal, the user programmed program is usually not only executed once, but repeatedly and repeatedly until the PLC stops working or switch to the stop state.

3.2 Attack Method

The attack is to use the PLC self-scanning cycle, the function of establishing communication with the host computer, and propose a method of attacking the host computer through the network, complete control of the system authority of the host computer, intercepting the communication between the PLC and the host computer and monitoring the data during normal operation of the PLC, and rewriting the status bits of the registers in the running PLC. This leads to abnormal operation in the PLC and achieves the purpose of network attack on the PLC. The specific process is shown in Table 1 below.

3.3 Petri Net Model for PLC Network Attacks Based on Bluekeep Vulnerability Exploitation

An attacker can exploit the cve2019–0708 vulnerability to remotely execute malicious code on the target system without user authentication by sending constructed special malicious data. And because the PLC then needs to interact with the programmer for data in time during the scan cycle, it only needs to hijack the data interaction between the PLC and the programmer and forge instructions to reach the attack purpose. According

Table 1. Attack flow chart

Steps	Process
1	Scanning for operator vulnerabilities
2	Exploit operator system vulnerabilities to attack
3	Upload the script and execute
4	Intercepting data between PLC and programmer
5	Forge communication data
6	Modify PLC specific register states

to the petri net modeling rules, the whole PLC cyber attack behavior is divided into two parts, the first part is to deploy the programmer's machine authority acquisition, and the second part is to portray the state change when the PLC is attacked (see Fig. 3).

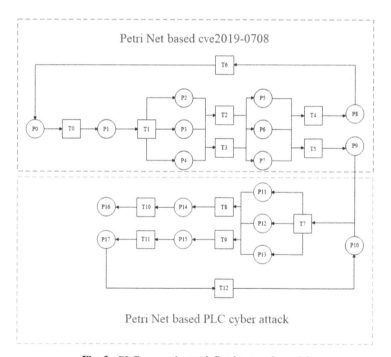

Fig. 3. PLC network attack Petri network model

The meaning of each node is shown in Table 2.

Table 2. PLC cyber attack petri network model node meaning table

Place	Meaning
P0	The target machine keeps the port open
P1	Target machine RDP protocol initialization
P2	Legal secondary binding in RDP protocol
P3	Secondary Binding in RDP Protocol
P4	Illegal secondary binding in RDP protocol
P5	Legal operation state
P6	RDP protocol termination state
P7	Illegal attack state
P8	Target security state
P9	Target machine controlled state
P10	PLC normal operation
P11	Illegal communication with programmer
P12	Communication with programmer established
P13	Normal communication with programmer
P14	Communication hijacked state
P15	Communication normal state
P16	PLC attacked state
P17	PLC operation security state
T0	Creating components
T1	Receiving malicious constructed packets
T2	Legally releasing memory blocks
T3	Illegal release of memory blocks
T4	Pointer reclaimed
T5	Pointer exploited
T6	Reclaiming system resources
T7	PLC auto-scan
T8	Illegal establishment of second data communication
T9	Failure to establish a malicious communication link
T10	Illegal modification of PLC register status
T11	PLC executes command cyclically
T12	Recycle system resources

4 Model Analysis

4.1 Principle of Vulnerability Exploitation

The process of cve2019–0708 vulnerability exploitation belongs to the category of system vulnerability UAF (Use After Free), The process of triggering UAF is as follows:

1) RDP connection is established, RDP Server calls IcaCreateChannel() by default to create MS_T120 static virtual channel and bind to 0x1F(31) channel number, which is the first time the channel is bound.
2) The RDP Client tells the RDP Server to bind the channel with the name MS_T120 to the specified channel number during the Channel Connecttion phase of communication, at which time the Server uses the IcaFindChannelByName() function to search for the MS_T120 channel created by default and bind the channel object to the to the channel number specified by the user. This is the second binding of the MS_T120 channel.
3) The RDP Client informs the RDP Server to disconnect the second bound channel, which will trigger the RDP Server to call IcaFreeChannel() to release the channel and free the space occupied by the object.
4) The RDP Client will inform the RDP Server to close the RDP connection, and this operation will trigger the Server to call the SingalBrokenConnection() function to free the MS_T120 channel object with channel number 0x1F. As the object space has been freed, here again call the IcaFreeChannel() function to perform cleanup operations, where ExDeleteResourceLite() will refer to the object's member data and trigger the UAF vulnerability.

4.2 Defense Patch Model for PLC Network Attacks

According to the vulnerability exploitation model diagram, the attack should be defended against the patch model, and the important patch node lies in the process of operating system vulnerability exploitation, and the network attack is well defended when the cve2019–0708 vulnerability is invalidated (see Fig. 4). The patch defense mechanism is required to make the channel name determination when calling the binding channel-related functions, and when the communication component name is MS_T120, it should be forced to bind to the prefabricated 31 virtual channel. After the initialization of the RDP protocol, before the UAF, add the code for judging the binding channel and add the state of judging the virtual channel number to avoid the UAF vulnerability of the system. The node meanings are shown in Table 3.

According to the above model, we can find that P10, P11, P12, P13 are new library states, T7, T8 are new changes. T7 is the system to determine whether the MS_T120 binding channel number is equal to 31, the attacker sends the packet without the illegal secondary binding of the channel to MS_T120, then it will enter the P10 state, that is, the channel number matches, and the vulnerability cannot be exploited. When the attacker sends a packet to the communication component for illegal secondary binding, it enters the P12 state, and the system is in an insecure state. T8 is the judgment to detect the execution of the abnormal function, when the abnormal data flow is detected and passes

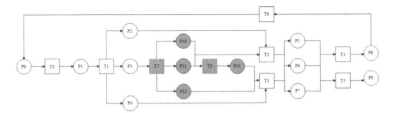

Fig. 4. CVE2019–0708 vulnerability patch Petri net model diagram

Table 3. Node meanings of the defense patch model for PLC network attacks

Place	Meaning
P10	Virtual channel number equal to 31
P11	Channel number judgment status
P12	The virtual channel number is not equal to 32
P13	Exception function execution
T7	Determine if the channel number is equal to 31
T8	Detect exception constructor

through the path, the library capacity of P13 is 0, which will generate blocking when it encounters the inflow of resources, resulting in the subsequent library cannot reach, and instead flows to the P9 secure state, thus ensuring the system This ensures the security of the system.

5   Experiment

5.1   Industrial Control Cyber Attack

For the construction of the industrial control system scenario proposed in this paper, the experimental environment consists of two parts: the attacking machine and the target machine. The experimental configuration is shown in Table 4. Attack scenario deployment diagram (see Fig. 5).

The PLC ladder is programmed through the TIA software as shown in Fig. 6. The industrial control scenario established can be described as follows: infrared motion sensors are installed at two end points on a section of the conveyor belt controlled by the engine, the button is activated and the object moves from left to right, when it touches the right sensor, the engine is reversed, so the object moves from right to left, when it touches the motion sensor at the left end, the engine is reversed once again and the object moves from left to right. The cycle is repeated to keep the object in continuous motion. In order to visualize the PLC programming with the Factory-io software, it is necessary to establish communication between the TIA programming software and the PLC simulation software. The programming is downloaded into the PLC so that the PLC

Table 4. Experimental configuration

Configuration	Attack machine	Target machine
CPU	3 GHz CPU	3 GHz CPU
Memory	4 G	16 G
Operating system	Kali linux 2020	Windows 7 sp1
Software	Metasploit	TIAv15.1, PLCSIM advanced2.0, Factory-IO
Programming ecology	Shell	Python
Communication with PLC	No	Yes
Network	Bridge	Bridge

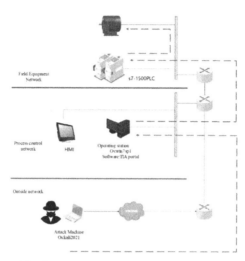

Fig. 5. Attack scenario deployment diagram

is programmed to control the engine and the sensor according to the ladder diagram. The simulation scenario is shown in Fig. 7.

The target machine cve2019–0708 vulnerability is used to achieve a power raising attack on the target machine. After the successful attack, you can get the highest authority of the target machine, and then you can upload and run the attack script to the target machine through the attack machine remote upload function, intercept the upload data of PLC and perform abnormal command injection. The experimental results are described as: a wooden box that does round-trip motion cyclically and stops running after the attack.

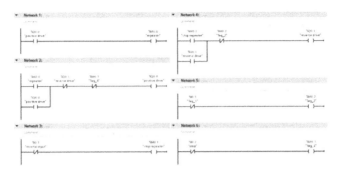

Fig. 6. PLC programming ladder diagram

Fig. 7. The wooden box round trip simulation experiment diagram

5.2 Compare with the Actual Attack Process

This section performs quantitative evaluation of the attack Petri net model. The runtime is set to 1 ms, 10 ms, and 100 ms for the token emitted by the initial library. as the emitting time increases, the model runs slower. The average time for the number of tokens in the model of 10 is used as a reference to compare the real network attack implementation and the Petri net simulated attack running time. The comparison table of the attack time is shown in Table 5.

Table 5. Actual vs. model attack runtime

	Actual Attack	Firing Duration = 1 ms	Firing Duration = 10 ms	Firing Duration = 100 ms	Firing Duration = 1000 ms
Time (s)	54.34	3.86	4.38	16.43	95.76

As shown in Table 5, the Petri net attack model running time is significantly shortened, and the longer the model running time is with the gradual increase of the launch time setting. When the launch time is 1s, the model runs slower and the running time is longer, which is conducive to observing the details of the attack and facilitating the establishment of the patch model. When the firing time is shorter, the attack can be simulated with shorter running time than the actual attack to achieve fast prediction of the attack. Several experiments were conducted on the Petri net model established in this study in the following aspects.

1) Comparing the actual attack time with the Petri net attack model running time at different firing rates. (see Fig. 8).

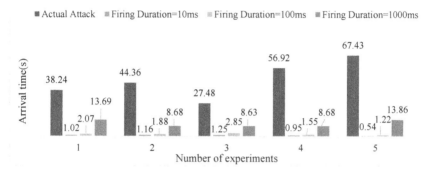

Fig. 8. Petri net model run experiment 1

2) Set the launch time to 1s and record the time when the attack model reaches the critical node. (see Fig. 9).

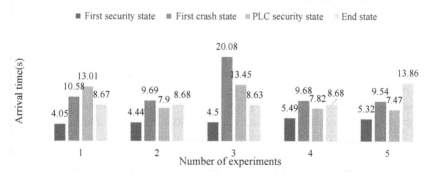

Fig. 9. Petri net model run experiment 2

3) The launch times were set to 1 ms, 10 ms and 100 ms. The attack times were quantitatively compared for 5, 10, 15, 20, 25 and 30 attacks in the attack model (see Fig. 10).

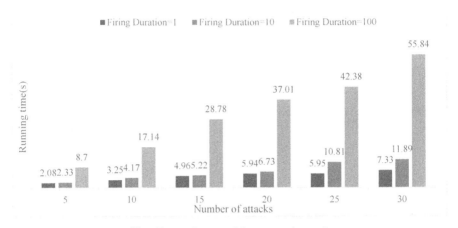

Fig. 10. Petri net model run experiment 3

5.3   Comparison with the Current Study

In this section, the Petri network model established in this paper will be evaluated. More research has been conducted for cyber-attack modeling, but the diversity and multi-level nature of cyber-attacks make it difficult to study cyber-attack modeling in depth, and there is still relatively little modeling for heterogeneous system security. In this paper, the PLC network attack model established by using Petri nets is more microscopic in portrayal compared with the related network attack models, and the vulnerability patch map is also constructed, as shown in Table 6.

In Table 6, A detailed qualitative comparison is made for several typical models. The attack model proposed by Xu yue [15] et al. does not have a fine-grained portrayal of the attack method principle and attack information, and does not have the function of automated operation. Radoglou-Grammatikis [16] et al. study the SCADA system security problem, the model is for system process modeling, without in-depth code The model proposed by Sridhar Adepu [17] et al. does not describe the running state of the PLC in the system under attack, provides the framework idea of the attack process, and does not implement specific attack behavior and attack modeling; the attack model built by Raphael Fritz [18] et al. also does not describe the running state of the lower machine, and does not go deeper into the code level to portray the attack behavior. The corresponding petri net model established by K. Labadi [19] for a pharmaceutical manufacturing and packaging system was formalized and analyzed. However, an industrial process is described and no cyber attack method is proposed for this system. The model proposed by Xu lijuan [20] et al. does not involve the description of cyber attack methods, while

Table 6. Qualitative comparative analysis

Model	In-depth code level	Patch Model	Automatic operation	Formal Analysis	PLC state modeling	Simulation experiments
Xu Yue[15]	×	×	×	✓	×	×
Radoglou-Grammatikis[16]	×	×	×	×	×	✓
Sridhar Adepu[17]	×	×	×	✓	×	✓
Raphael Fritz[18]	×	×	×	✓	✓	×
K. Labadi[19]	×	×	×	✓	×	×
Xu lijuan[20]	×	×	×	✓	✓	✓
This paper	✓	✓	✓	✓	✓	✓

the model does not have the ability to run automatically. And this paper proposes a cyber attack method based on an industrial control system, completes the verification of simulation experiments, and analyzes the principle of vulnerability and the state of operation when PLC operation is hijacked in depth at the code level, and also proposes a defense patch model diagram for this cyber attack, which makes up for the shortcomings of the current research method.

6 Conclusion

In this research, we present a strategy for industrial control cyber assaults, build attack scenarios, and display the attack effect. A Petri net-based attack modeling method for industrial control networks is proposed based on Petri net modeling rules, which analyzes the causes of the cve20190708 vulnerability and can depict the process of vulnerability exploitation at a fine-grained level, deeply analyzes the source code and model of the vulnerability, and establishes a corresponding patch model. The model in this study is quantitatively compared to the real assault runtime and qualitatively compared to models produced by previous research, and the findings demonstrate that the work is relevant for examining the modeling approach of industrial control system network attacks.

Acknowledgments. This research work is supported by the National Natural Science Founds of China (62072368, U20B2050), Key Research and Development Program of Shaanxi Province (2021ZDLG05–09,2022GY-040).

References

1. Conti, M., Donadel, D., Turrin, F.: A survey on industrial control system testbeds and datasets for security research. IEEE Communications Surveys & Tutorials **23**(4), 2248–2294 (2021)
2. Huong, T.T., Bac, T.P., Long, D.M., et al.: Detecting cyberattacks using anomaly detection in industrial control systems: a federated learning approach. Comput. Ind. **132**, 103509 (2021)

3. Yu, H., Zeng, P., Xu, C.: Industrial wireless control networks: from WIA to the future. Engineering **8**, 18–24 (2021)
4. Liang, W., Zheng, M., Zhang, J., et al.: WIA-FA and its applications to digital factory: a wireless network solution for factory automation. Proc. IEEE **107**(6), 1053–1073 (2019)
5. Manvi, S.S., Shyam, G.K.: Resource management for Infrastructure as a Service (IaaS) in cloud computing: a survey. J. Netw. Comput. Appl. **41**, 424–440 (2014)
6. Galloway, B., Hancke, G.P.: Introduction to industrial control networks. IEEE Communications Surveys & Tutorials **15**(2), 860–880 (2012)
7. Dawei, C.H.E.N., Ruzhi, X.U.: Research on security vulnerabilities and control flow integrity of PLC in industrial control system. Electronic Science Technol. **34**(2), 33–37 (2021)
8. Berman, D.J., Butts, J.: Towards characterization of cyber attacks on industrial control systems: Emulating field devices using Gumstix technology. In: 2012 5th International Symposium on Resilient Control Systems, pp. 63–68 (2012)
9. McLaughlin, S., McDaniel, P.: SABOT: specification-based payload generation for programmable logic controllers. In: Proceedings of the 2012 ACM Conference on Computer and Communications Security, pp. 439–449 (2012)
10. Klick, J., Lau, S., Marzin, D., et al.: Internet-facing PLCs-a new back orifice. Blackhat USA, pp. 22–26 (2015)
11. Alsabbagh, W., Langendörfer, P.: A stealth program injection attack against S7–300 PLCs. In: 2021 22nd IEEE International Conference on Industrial Technology (ICIT), Vol. 1, pp. 986–993. IEEE (2021)
12. Govil, N., Agrawal, A., Tippenhauer, N.O.: On ladder logic bombs in industrial control systems. In: Computer Security, pp. 110–126. Springer, Cham (2017). https://doi.org/10.1007/978-3-319-72817-9_8
13. Keliris, A., Maniatakos, M.: ICSREF: A Framework for Automated Reverse Engineering of Industrial Control Systems Binaries. arXiv preprint arXiv:1812.03478 (2018)
14. Hui, H., McLaughlin, K.: Investigating current PLC security issues regarding Siemens S7 communications and TIA portal. In: 5th International Symposium for ICS & SCADA Cyber Security Research 5, pp. 67–73 (2018)
15. Xu, Y., Fu, R.: Petri net-based power CPS network attack and impact modeling. In: 2018 5th IEEE International Conference on Cloud Computing and Intelligence Systems (CCIS), pp. 1107–1110. IEEE (2018)
16. Radoglou-Grammatikis, P., Sarigiannidis, P., Giannoulakis, I., Kafetzakis, E., Panaousis, E.: Attacking iec-60870–5–104 scada systems. In: 2019 IEEE World Congress on Services (SERVICES), Vol. 2642, pp. 41–46. IEEE (2019)
17. Adepu, S., Mathur, A.: Generalized attacker and attack models for cyber physical systems. In: 2016 IEEE 40th annual computer software and applications conference (COMPSAC), Vol. 1, pp. 283–292. IEEE (2016)
18. Fritz, R., Schwarz, P., Zhang, P.: Modeling of cyber attacks and a time guard detection for ICS based on discrete event systems. In: 2019 18th European Control Conference (ECC), pp. 4368–4373. IEEE (2019)
19. Labadi, K., Darcherif, A.M., El Abbassi, I., Hamaci, S.: Petri Net-Based Approach for "Cyber" Risks Modelling and Analysis for Industrial Systems. In: E3S Web of Conferences, Vol. 170, p. 02001. EDP Sciences (2020)
20. Xu, L., Wang, B., Wang, L., et al.: PLC-SEIFF: a programmable logic controller security incident forensics framework based on automatic construction of security constraints. Comput. Secur. **92**, 101749 (2020)
21. Kabir, S., Papadopoulos, Y.: Applications of Bayesian networks and Petri nets in safety, reliability, and risk assessments: a review. Saf. Sci. **115**, 154–175 (2019)

22. Shailesh, T., Nayak, A., Prasad, D.: A study on performance evaluation of computer systems using Petri Nets. In: 2018 International Conference on Computational Techniques, Electronics and Mechanical Systems (CTEMS), pp. 18–23. IEEE (2018)
23. Akerberg, J., Furunas Akesson, J., Gade, J., et al.: Future industrial networks in process automation: goals, challenges, and future directions. Appl. Sci. **11**(8), 3345 (2021)

Intelligent Robot Sensing

CRRNet: Channel Relation Reasoning Network for Salient Object Detection

Shuyong Gao[1,2], Haozhe Xing[2], Chenglong Zhang[1,2], and Wenqiang Zhang[1,2,3,4(✉)]

[1] Shanghai Key Laboratory of Intelligent Information Processing, Fudan University, Shanghai 200433, China
{sygao18,clzhang20,wqzhang}@fudan.edu.cn
[2] School of Computer Science, Fudan University, Shanghai 200433, China
hzxing21@m.fudan.edu.cn
[3] Academy for Engineering and Technology, Fudan University, Shanghai 200433, China
[4] Yiwu Research Institute of Fudan University, Chengbei Road, Yiwu City, Zhejiang 322000, China

Abstract. Channel map matters for salient object detection. Effectively exploring the relationship between channels can enhance the relevant channel maps and infer a better saliency map. The existing channel map enhancement methods focus on learning the weights to re-weight the channel maps or using the similarity between the channels to combine the channel maps and enhance them. We propose a Channel Relation Reasoning Module (CRRM) based on graph convolution, inferring the semantic relations between channels and enhancing the channel maps according to the mutual relations. First, we carefully designed a multi-level complementary feature extraction module, which is used to extract multi-level edge and salient object internal features simultaneously. Then, the rich multi-level edge and salient features are fed to CRRM which projects the features into the hidden space and uses the graph convolution to establish the semantic relationship between the channels to enhance the feature expression. Finally, two stacked convolution layers can produce high-quality saliency maps. Extensive experiments on multiple datasets show the effectiveness of our model.

Keywords: ·Salient object detection · Graph convolution · Multi-level feature

1 Introduction

Due to the widespread usage of fully convolutional networks (FCN), salient object detection (SOD) has recently made quick progress. The FCN-based methods [7,8,12,18,19,21,24,29,39,40] have reached cutting-edge performance. Additionally, the pre-trained backbone [11,25] is frequently employed as an encoder network, enhancing the model's capacity to extract semantic information.

Z. Yu et al. (Eds.): CIRAC 2022, CCIS 1770, pp. 23–38, 2023.
https://doi.org/10.1007/978-981-99-0301-6_2

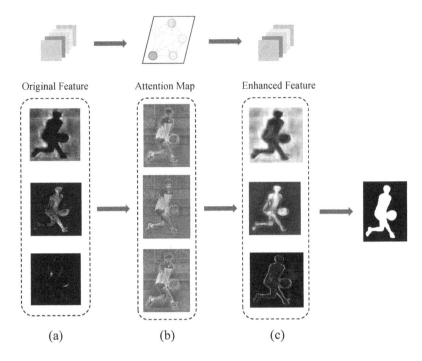

Original Feature   Attention Map   Enhanced Feature

(a)   (b)   (c)

Fig. 1. Illustration of the feature changes of the corresponding channel before and after the feature passing through CRRM. (a) represents the original feature. (b) represents attention map obtained by crrm based on background, foreground and edge features. (c) represents features after CRRM.

SOD models often encounter incomplete interiors and blurring boundaries. Because at the edges of the salient object, the feature extraction function ought to be selective to minor appearance changes to distinguish the objects from the background, while inside the salient object, the function should be invariant to severe appearance changes to get complete object [26], which makes it difficult to directly extract a complete salient object with a clear boundary. We develop a Multi-Level Complementary Feature Extraction module (MLCFE) to extract multi-level edge and salient object internal features separately. The high-level features containing substantial semantic clues are used to produce the internal of the salient object. The low-level features containing abundant details can supplement edge features for the salient object, so they are used to extract edge information. Then we merge these features to get the multi-level edge and salient object internal features.

However, due to the semantic gap between features of different levels [4], simply combining features are inefficient. To mitigate this problem, we propose two solutions. Firstly, in the feature extraction stage (i.e., MLCFE), we propose the Cross-Level Feature Adaptation Module (CLFAM), which provides the transition from high-level to low-level for features. Second but most importantly, in the multi-level feature fusion stage, we propose a channel relation reasoning module (CRRM) to enhance channels based on the semantic relation between channels.

The features output by MLCFE in our network clearly contain rich multi-level edge and salient object features. Moreover, the channel map can be considered as an expression or response to a characteristic, and the features are correlated [9]. We can use the relation between the channel maps to improve the feature expression ability of each channel. But existing methods for enhancing channel features mainly focus on channel attention. SENet [14] is a representative method that uses the global features to learn the importance of each channel, and re-weights them. Some researchers improve the SE block by integrating spatial attention method [9,13,23,33]. But the ways to generate channel attention are similar to SENet. These methods are weak in combining and enhancing features based on the relationship between channels. In DANet [9], the channel attention module uses the non-local method to establish the similarity between channels, and linearly combines the original channels according to the similarity. However, we realize that channel correlation can only show the similarity between channels, but cannot establish the relationship between dissimilar features. For example, eyes and ears have great differences in color and shape, but their semantic connection is obvious. The combination of eyes, ears and other features can enhance facial expression. Employing the powerful relational reasoning ability of graph convolution, we propose a channel relational reasoning network. In summary, our main contributions can be summarized as follows:

- Based on the fact that it is difficult to directly extract a complete salient object with a clear boundary, the multi-level complementary feature extraction module (MLCFE) is proposed to extract multi-level edge and salient object internal features simultaneously.
- To make full use of multi-level edge and salient object features, we propose a channel relation reasoning module using graph convolution to establish a relationship between channels and enhance the features according to the relationship.
- We compare our method with 15 state-of-the-art (SOTA) saliency models on five benchmark datasets in terms of six evaluation metrics. The experimental results show that our proposed method outperforms the previous SOTA methods by a large margin.

2   Related Work

Traditional salient object detection models usually extract manual features (e.g., contrast [6], color difference [1]). They work well on simple images but perform poorly in complex scenarios.

FCN [20] have greatly improved the performance of the SOD models. And recent works have shown that the fusion of multi-level features can obtain better results [5,32,35,40]. Many researchers try to optimize the feature fusion methods to get fine saliency maps. Hou et al. [12] uses short connections in FCN to

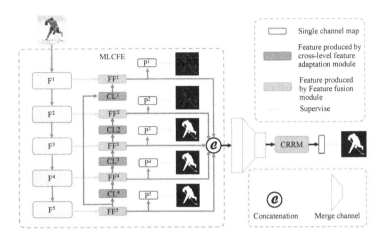

Fig. 2. The overall pipeline of the CRRNet. ResNet-50 is taken as the backbone encoder which is represented by the solid green box. The module in the dashed box on the left represents the MLCFE module. For the features in MLCFE, we use ground truth and its edges to constrain it. CRRM represents the proposed channel relation reasoning module. The features output by MLCFE are sent to CRRM after simple channel merging. (Color figure online)

connect features in different layers. Wu et al. [35] proposes a cross-refinement module to refine multi-level features of edge and salient objects simultaneously. [39] aggregates multi-level features into multiple resolutions to predict multiple resolution saliency maps. Zhao et al. [40] explicitly models complementary salient object and edge information and jointly optimizes the two complementary tasks. Deng et al. [7] alternatively employs low-level and high-level integrated features of FCN to learn the residual between the saliency map and ground-truth. Wu et al. [35] proposes a cross refinement unit that contains direction-specific integration operations to refine multi-level features. These methods make full use of the multi-level features extracted from the backbone network to improve the performance of salient object detection. But they ignore that even a single-stream decoder can still extract both multi-level edges and salient object internal features. We use a single-stream decoder to simultaneously extract multi-level edge and saliency features, which can greatly simplify the model design.

Recently graph-based models are widely used in various tasks relying on their powerful relational reasoning capabilities. Graph Convolution Networks [15] are proposed for semi-supervised classification. Chen et al. [3] proposes to use GCN to establish the relationship between disjoint spatial locations in an image. Zhang et al. [38] uses GCN to capture the long-range interactions between two image spatial positions to predict co-saliency maps.

SENet [14] uses the global features of all channels to acquire the importance of each channel and then weights these channels. GENet [13] is similar to SENet, but in the stage of collecting global information, it performs depth-wise convolution on each channel instead of using global average pooling, which allows

GENet to get spatial attention at the same time. BAM [23] and CBAM [33] both generate spatial attention and channel attention, and its ways to generate channel attention are similar to SENet. Wang et al. [28] proposes a lightweight SE-like module based on the observation of SENet. Fu et al. [9] propose a channel combination method by calculating channel similarity. These channel map enhancement methods focus on learning the weights to reweight the channels or use the similarity between the channels to combine them. Taking into account the complementary characteristics between channels, leveraging graph convolution to model the relationship between nodes, we propose a Channel Relation Reasoning Module (CRRM) which can infer the relationships between channels and enhancing the channel maps according to the mutual relations.

3 Proposed Method

3.1 Common Feature Extraction

In our CRRNet, ResNet-50 [11] is employed as backbone network for transfer learning, since the backbone is independent of the model. The last fully connected layers are removed, leaving only the five convolutional residual blocks as shown in Fig. 2. Specifically, we take the conv1, conv2-3, conv3-4, conv4-6, conv5-3 in ResNet-50 as the basic feature. They are reduced by 1×1 convlayers and transformed into $F = \{F^i | i = 1, 2, 3, 4, 5\}$. Given an image with size of $H \times W$, the size of each feature is $\{C \times \frac{H}{2^i} \times \frac{W}{2^i} | i = 1, 2, 3, 4, 5\}$, and we set C to 64 for simplicity.

3.2 Multi-Level Complementary Feature Extraction

The deeper features of the decoder can generate complete salient object internal features, but its edges are blurring. Nevertheless, the shallow features of the decoder preserve fine edge information (i.e., Fig. 4 (d) and (e)). Considering that it is difficult to directly extract a complete salient object with a clear boundary [26], we employ the deeper feature of the decoder to generate multi-level internal features and shallow features to generate multi-level fine edge features. The multi-level features enhance the network's ability to recognize objects at different scales, and these two features complement each other to generate higher quality saliency objects. Unlike the previous U-Net-like structures [32,40,42], we only use a single-stream encoding and decoding architecture to simultaneously obtain these two multi-level complementary features.

Cross-Level Feature Adaptation Module. In the process of merging features, semantic gaps between different level features will result in ineffective fusion. We design a Cross-Level Feature Adaptation Module (CLFAM). To fuse features F^i and FF^{i+1} (FF^{i+1} is the fused feature in a certain layer, and we will describe in detail below), we designed two convolution layers with different kernel size as shown in Table 1. The large kernel is used for the deep layers, which allows the network to get a larger receptive field and obtain more context information to help shallower layers to eliminate semantic ambiguity. To avoid semantic dilution, we directly merge FF^5 and F^1. So we did not design CLFAM between FF^2 and F^1, but designed CLFAM between FF^5 and F^1. The detailed configuration are shown in Table 1. We denote the features passing through CLFAM as $CL = \{CL^1, CL^2, CL^3, CL^4\}$. For $i = 2, 3, 4$, CL^i can be represented as:

$$CL^i = \sigma(f^i_{cl_2}(\sigma(f^i_{cl_1}(FF^{i+1})))), \tag{1}$$

where $\sigma(\cdot)$ refers to the stacked $ReLU(\cdot)$ and batch normalization layer, $f^i_{cl_1}(\cdot)$ and $f^i_{cl_2}(\cdot)$ refers to the first and the second convolution layer in $CLFAM$ respectively. For $i = 1$,

$$CL^1 = \sigma(f^1_{cl_2}(\sigma(f^1_{cl_1}(FF^5)))). \tag{2}$$

Table 1. Detailed parameters of CLFAM. CLFAM include two convolution layers: CLFAM_P1 and CLFAM_P2. We show the kernel size of each convolution layer.

Name	Stage	CLFAM_P1	CLFAM_P2
$CLFAM^1$	S5-S1	7	3
$CLFAM^2$	S3-S2	5	3
$CLFAM^3$	S4-S3	5	3
$CLFAM^4$	S5-S4	7	3

Feature Fusion Module. After obtaining CL, multiple convolution layers are used to fuse features. As in the same setting of CLFAM, large convolution kernels in the deeper layers are used to obtain more global context information and provide robust semantic information. And small kernels are used in the shallow layers to allow the layer to focus on extracting details. These features are employed to generate salient internal features and edge features. We denote the fused feature as $FF = \{FF^1, FF^2, FF^3, FF^4, FF^5\}$.

For $i = 1, 2, 3, 4$, the feature FF^i can be represented as:

$$FF^i = F_{ff_i}(inter(CL^i) + F^i), \tag{3}$$

where $F_{ff_i}(\cdot)$ refers to three stacked convolution layers followed by the $ReLU(\cdot)$ and batch normalization layer in the i-th decoding stage, and $inter(\cdot)$ refers to bilinear interpolation function. For $i = 5$,

$$FF^5 = F_{ff_5}(F^5). \tag{4}$$

Multi-level Edge and Saliency Feature Constraint. To obtain the multi-level edge and salient object internal features, we constrain different stages based on multi-level edges and salient objects. For the output FF, we use one 3×3 convolution layer to merge the channels and generate coarse maps at different scales, and bilinear interpolation $interp(\cdot)$ is leveraged to convert the map to the original image size. We use $P = \{P^1, P^2, P^3, P^4, P^5\}$ to represent the single-channel map at the corresponding level (Fig. 4):

$$P^i = interp(Conv(FF^i)) \tag{5}$$

For the shallow decoder layer $i = 1, 2$, they are used to extract multi-level edge features. We use the edges of salient object to constrain the corresponding features, and the cross entropy loss function is employed:

$$\mathcal{L}_{edge} = -\sum_{i=1}^{2}\sum_{j=1}^{L}\sum_{c\in\{0,1\}}[\delta(E_j = c)log(P_j^i = c)] \tag{6}$$

where L represents the number of pixels, E refers to the edge of the salient object, P refers to the predicted edge map, δ is the indicator function. For the deeper layers $i = 3, 4, 5$, we leverage them to generate multi-level salient internal features:

$$\mathcal{L}_{sal} = -\sum_{i=3}^{5}\sum_{j=1}^{L}\sum_{c\in\{0,1\}}[\delta(G_j = c)log(P_j^i = c)] \tag{7}$$

where G denotes the ground truth annotation of the salient object, P denotes the predicted saliency map. We explored the best depth of edge constraints for different layers. The experimental analysis is shown in Table 3.

3.3 Channel Relation Reasoning Module

Obviously, the feature FF contains the multi-level salient features and edge features. The channel map can be considered as an expression or response to characteristics, and the features are related [9]. We can use the relationship between these channel maps to improve the semantic expression of each channel. As graph convolution [15] has been proven to have a powerful relationship modeling ability, we use GCN to infer the relationship between channels to enhance the feature expression (Fig. 3).

Pixel Space to Hidden Space. For input $X \in \mathbb{R}^{C \times H \times W}$, the i-th channel is $X^i \in \mathbb{R}^{H \times W}$, which can also be expressed as $X^i \in \mathbb{R}^{1 \times L}$, where $L = H \times W$. And the corresponding X can also be expressed as $X \in \mathbb{R}^{C \times L}$. For convenience, we will use X in the form of a two-dimensional matrix bellow. In our model, L varies with the size of the input images. We transform $X^i \in \mathbb{R}^{1 \times L}$ to $Y^i \in \mathbb{R}^{1 \times N}$, in which N is independent of H and W. And all Y^i forms $Y \in \mathbb{R}^{C \times N}$. We call the space $\mathbb{R}^{C \times L}$ where X is located pixel space Ω and call $\mathbb{R}^{C \times N}$ where Y is located hidden space Ψ. In hidden space Ψ, all input images are converted to the same size. In order to convert X from Ω to Ψ, we make network learn a function $\varphi(\cdot)$:

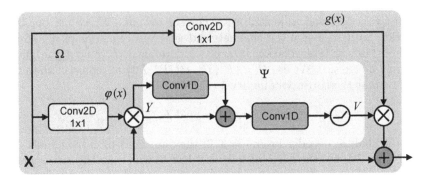

Fig. 3. Illustration of proposed channel relation reasoning module. The $\varphi(x)$ on the left is the space transformation function that can transform the input feature X from pixel space Ω to hidden space Ψ to get Y, and its parameters are learned by one 1×1 convolution layer. The function of $g(x)$ with parameters learned by one 1×1 convolution layer at the top is to transform V from hidden space Ψ back to pixel space Ω.

$$Y = \varphi(X; W_\varphi) = XW_\varphi, \tag{8}$$

where $Y = [Y^1; \cdots ; Y^C] \in \mathbb{R}^{C \times N}$, $W_\varphi \in \mathbb{R}^{L \times N}$, $X = [X^1; \cdots ; X^C] \in \mathbb{R}^{C \times L}$. N represents the node dimension of each channel in the hidden space, and we set $N = 2 \times C$ in our model. W_φ is a projection matrix, and we use one 1×1 convolution layer to model W_φ to make it learnable: $W_\varphi = Conv(X)$.

Channel Relation Reasoning. In the hidden space Ψ each Y^i represents a node corresponding to the channel map X^i in Ω. After getting all the node Y^i, we get a graph, in which we can use graph convolution to infer the relation between the graph nodes to establish the relationship between the channels.

In our model, we established a fully connected graph, so the information contained by each node can be diffused to all nodes. We use A to represent the adjacency matrix and W_h to represent the status update function. Follow [15], the single-layer graph convolution can be defined as:

$$V = \sigma((I - A)YW_h). \tag{9}$$

where $V = [V^1; \cdots ; V^C] \in \mathbb{R}^{C \times N}$, I serves as a identity matrix which is often used to alleviate the optimization difficulties.

The adjacency matrix A is initialized randomly at the beginning of training. Concretely, the first step is Laplacian smoothing, which can spread the information of the node to the neighbors. During the training process, A can automatically learn the strength of the connection between any two channels with gradient updating. Each node receives information from all other nodes and the information is weighted according to the strength. After receiving information from other nodes, the second step is executed, in which the state of all node are updated through a linear transformation. The linear transformation matrix W_h is a learning parameter, which can also be learned through gradient descent.

Specifically, we use two 1D convolution with kernel size 1 to complete the above two steps (Fig. 3), which can be expressed by Eq. (10).

$$V = ReLU(conv((Y - conv(Y; W_A); W_h)), \qquad (10)$$

where W_A and W_h denotes the parameters of adjacency matrix and status update function respectively.

Hidden Space Returns Pixel Space. After reasoning the relation in hidden space Ψ, we need to find a map function $g(\cdot)$ to map $V = [V^1; \cdots; V^C] \in \mathbb{R}^{C \times N}$ back to the original pixel space Ω to obtain the feature $\widehat{X} = [\widehat{X}^1; \cdots; \widehat{X}^C] \in \mathbb{R}^{C \times L}$, where $\widehat{X}^i \in \mathbb{R}^{1 \times L}$ can complement and enhance X^i. Like the way to convert X from Ω to Ψ, we leverage linear transformation to transform V from Ψ to Ω as follows:

$$\widehat{X} = g(V; W_g) = VW_g. \qquad (11)$$

We use a single-layer 2D convolution with kernel size 1 to learn the parameter W_g of the linear transformation $g(\cdot)$:

$$W_g = conv(X), \qquad (12)$$

where $W_g \in \mathbb{R}^{N \times H \times W}$ can also be expressed as $W_g \in \mathbb{R}^{N \times L}$. This indicates that each pixel of $\widehat{X}^i$ is a linear combination of all the features of the node V^i according to the relationship learned by graph convolution. A detailed representation is given in Fig. 3. The features $\widehat{X}$ in the pixel space are returned and added to X as the output of Channel Relation Reasoning Module (CRRM):

$$CRRM(X) = \widehat{X} + X. \qquad (13)$$

After CRRM(X) is obtained, we add two stacked convolution layers with kernel size 5 and 3 respectively after it to generate the final saliency map S:

$$S = Conv(Relu(Conv(CRRM(x)))). \qquad (14)$$

Binary cross entropy loss and IoU loss function are employed to supervise S as follow:

$$\mathcal{L}_{iou} = 1 - \frac{\sum_{j=1}^{L}[G_j \times S_j]}{\sum_{j=1}^{L}[G_j + S_j - G_j \times S_j]}, \qquad (15)$$

$$\mathcal{L}_{bce} = -\sum_{j=1}^{L} \sum_{c \in \{0,1\}} [\delta(G_j = c)log(S_j = c)] \qquad (16)$$

where L represents the number of pixels, G refers to the ground truth of the salient object, δ is the indicator function. So the final loss function is defined as:

$$\mathcal{L}_{total} = \mathcal{L}_{edge} + \mathcal{L}_{sal} + \mathcal{L}_{iou} + \mathcal{L}_{bec} \qquad (17)$$

4 Experiments

4.1 Implementation Details

Our model is trained on DUTS-train dataset. The ResNet-50 network [11] is used as our backbone network , which is pre-trained on ImageNet and the last fully connected layers is removed. SGD is used as the optimizer. Horizontal flip and random crop input are data augmentation methods. During testing stage, we resized images to the resolution of 352×352 and feed it to the network.

4.2 Datasets and Evaluation Metrics

Datasets. We test our model on five benchmark datasets, including ECSSD [36], PASCAL-S [17], DUT-OMRON [37], and HKU-IS [16], DUTS [27].

Evaluation Metrics. The precision-recall (PR) curve, the F-measure curve, the highest F-measure ($F_\beta^m ax$), the mean F-measure (mF), the mean absolute error (MAE), and the S-measure (Sm) are the six metrics we use to assess the performance of our model. F-measure is defined as follow:

$$F_\beta = \frac{(1 + \beta^2) \times Precision \times Recall}{\beta^2 \times Precision + Recall} \tag{18}$$

where β^2 is 0.3. S-measure focuses on analyzing the structural information of saliency maps, that calculated as $S = \gamma S_o + (1 - \gamma)S_r$, where γ is 0.5.

4.3 Comparison with Other SOTA Methods

Compared with 15 models: R³Net [7], RAS [2], DGRL [30], PiCANet-R [19], BASNet-R [24], PoolNet-R [18], MLMS-R [34], AFNet-R [40], EGNet-R [40], GateNet-R [41], MINet-R [22], GCPANet-R [5], F³Net-R [31], DSNet-R [10], our model achieve a better performance. We download the saliency maps provided by the authors and evaluation with the same code for a fair comparison, and they are based on the ResNet-50 backbone.

Table 2. Performance compared with 15 SOTA models on 5 benchmark datasets.

Method	ECSSD $F_\beta^{max}\uparrow$	$mF\uparrow$	$S_m\uparrow$	$MAE\downarrow$	DUT-OMRON $F_\beta^{max}\uparrow$	$mF\uparrow$	$S_m\uparrow$	$MAE\downarrow$	PASCAL-S $F_\beta^{max}\uparrow$	$mF\uparrow$	$S_m\uparrow$	$MAE\downarrow$	HKU-IS $F_\beta^{max}\uparrow$	$mF\uparrow$	$S_m\uparrow$	$MAE\downarrow$	DUTS-test $F_\beta^{max}\uparrow$	$mF\uparrow$	$S_m\uparrow$	$MAE\downarrow$
R³Net₁₈ [7]	0.9248	0.9027	0.9028	0.0555	0.7882	0.7532	0.8172	0.0711	0.8374	0.8155	0.8102	0.1026	0.9096	0.8807	0.8918	0.0478	0.8244	0.7872	0.8354	0.066
RAS₁₈ [2]	0.9211	0.9006	0.8929	0.0564	0.7863	0.7623	0.8141	0.0617	0.8291	0.8125	0.799	0.1013	0.9128	0.8877	0.8874	0.0454	0.8312	0.8025	0.8387	0.059
DGRL₁₈ [30]	0.9224	0.9130	0.9027	0.0407	0.7742	0.7659	0.8059	0.0618	0.8486	0.8355	0.8358	0.0721	0.9103	0.8998	0.8946	0.0356	0.828	0.8181	0.842	0.0495
PiCANet-R₁₈ [19]	0.9349	0.9023	0.9168	0.0484	0.8029	0.7630	0.8301	0.0653	0.8573	0.8228	0.8537	0.0756	0.9185	0.8808	0.9041	0.0433	0.8598	0.8152	0.868	0.05
BASNet-R₁₉ [24]	0.9425	0.9274	0.9163	0.037	0.8053	0.7906	0.8362	0.0565	0.8539	0.8344	0.838	0.0758	0.9284	0.9113	0.909	0.0322	0.8595	0.8422	0.866	0.0472
PoolNet-R₁₉ [18]	0.9415	0.9197	0.9173	0.0417	0.8058	0.7822	0.8322	0.0561	0.8648	0.8480	0.8518	0.0716	0.9305	0.907	0.907	0.033	0.8764	0.8453	0.8785	0.0413
MLMS-R₁₉ [34]	0.9284	0.9007	0.9111	0.0445	0.7741	0.7455	0.809	0.0636	0.8552	0.8254	0.8442	0.0736	0.9207	0.8891	0.9065	0.0387	0.8515	0.8142	0.8615	0.0484
AFNet-R₁₉ [40]	0.9351	0.9157	0.9135	0.0416	0.7972	0.7766	0.8253	0.0574	0.8629	0.8409	0.8494	0.0700	0.9226	0.8998	0.9051	0.0358	0.8629	0.8346	0.8666	0.0453
EGNet-R₁₉ [40]	0.9474	0.9288	0.9245	0.0374	0.8155	0.7942	0.8379	0.0529	0.8653	0.8437	0.8519	0.0740	0.9352	0.9122	0.9178	0.0310	0.8887	0.8603	0.8854	0.0386
GateNet-R₂₀ [41]	0.9454	0.9197	0.9197	0.0401	0.8181	0.7915	0.8374	0.0549	0.875	0.8518	0.857	0.0676	0.9335	0.9097	0.915	0.0331	0.8876	0.8557	0.8847	0.0396
MINet-R₂₀ [22]	0.9475	0.925	0.925	0.0335	0.8099	0.7893	0.8325	0.0555	0.8726	0.852	0.8558	0.0635	0.9380	0.911	0.9189	0.0285	0.8839	0.8603	0.8841	0.0369
GCPANet-R₂₀ [5]	0.9485	0.9261	0.9267	0.0348	0.8118	0.7879	0.8375	0.0563	0.8752	0.8508	0.864	0.0619	0.9380	0.911	0.9202	0.0309	0.8881	0.8582	0.8901	0.0374
F³Net-R₂₁ [31]	0.9453	0.9242	0.9242	0.0333	0.8133	0.7944	0.8381	0.0526	0.8776	0.8588	0.86	0.0616	0.9366	0.9187	0.9171	0.028	0.8913	0.8678	0.8885	0.0351
LDF-R₂₀ [32]	0.9501	0.9379	0.9245	0.0335	0.8199	0.8015	0.8389	0.0517	0.8801	0.8636	0.8624	**0.0596**	0.9393	0.9224	0.9195	0.0275	0.8975	0.8786	0.8921	0.0336
DSNet-R₂₁ [10]	0.9498	0.9350	0.9259	0.0335	0.819	0.7993	0.8405	0.0544	**0.8841**	0.8636	**0.8648**	0.061	0.9406	0.923	0.9238	0.0276	0.8955	0.873	0.8944	0.0341
CRRNet	**0.9531**	**0.9389**	**0.9304**	**0.0317**	0.833	0.8146	0.8505	0.0518	0.8828	0.8649	0.8639	0.0635	**0.9448**	**0.9281**	**0.9252**	**0.0265**	**0.9034**	**0.8838**	**0.8994**	**0.032**

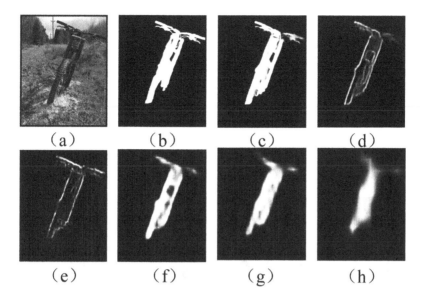

Fig. 4. Illustration of multi-level edge and salient object feature. (a) Input image. (b) GT. (c) saliency map. (d)(e)(f)(g)(h): P^1, P^2, P^3, P^4, P^5.

Quantitative Evaluation. We use F_β^{max}, mF, S_m, MAE on 5 commonly used data sets to compare with 15 typical models. The best results are bolded. It can be found that the performance of our model on all evaluation indicators across all datasets exceeds the performance of the SOTA methods as shown in Table 2. Especially, our method outperforms the best baseline by 1.3%, and 1.3% on the relatively challenging dataset DUT-OMRON [37] in terms of F_β^{max}, mF and S_m. For overall comparisons, Fig. 5 presents the precision-recall curves and F-measure curves on five benchmark datasets. It can be seen that the thick red line which refers to our CRRNet consistently lie above others, which proved that our method has a good ability to detect the salient regions.

Qualitative Evaluation. As shown in Fig. 6, our approach can pop-out the whole salient object under extremely challenging and complex scenes, include the salient object with huge differences in internal visual characteristics (row 1,2,3), images with low contrast (row 3–8), small fine object with discrete distribution (row 7), large object touching image boundaries (row 3,4,8), cluttered foreground and background (row 4,5).

Since we extract the overall and detailed features separately, the model does not focus too much on the details and boundaries and fails to complete the extraction of the overall body, which leads to the extraction of incomplete significant targets. We would like to mention that our method can not only highlight the salient region but also generate clear boundaries benefiting from the multi-level edge and saliency feature constraint module and channel relation reasoning module.

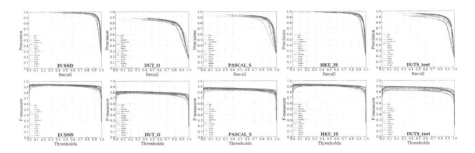

Fig. 5. Illustration of PR curves and F-measure curves on five datasets.

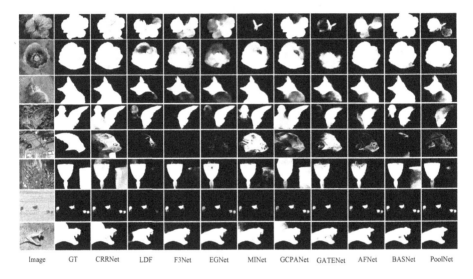

Image   GT   CRRNet   LDF   F3Net   EGNet   MINet   GCPANet   GATENet   AFNet   BASNet   PoolNet

Fig. 6. Qualitative comparison with different SOTA saliency detection methods. Our model (CRRNet) produces more accurate and coherent saliency maps in challenging scenarios, which are the closet to the GT.

4.4   Ablation Studies

The Effectiveness of MLCFE. We take U-Net-like architecture to obtain multi-level features which are then merged by 1×1 convolution layer as our baseline. Here we verify the effectiveness of the multi-level edge and saliency feature constraint method and the cross-layer feature adaptation module in MLCFE on four datasets: ECSSD, DUT-OMRON, HKU-IS, DUTS-test in terms of F_{β}^{max}, mF, S_m and MAE.

To prove the effectiveness of the multi-level edge and saliency feature constraint method in the deep supervision strategy, we design a number of comparative experiments as shown in Table 3. We always use the salient object to constrain the deepest features of the network as the deepest layer of the network contains semantic features, and the detailed features are scarce (Fig. 4 (h)), and

Table 3. Ablation study with different edge supervision. 1,2,3,4 represent different stages of the decoding layers. G and E represent ground-truth supervision and edge supervision, respectively.

1	2	3	4	ECSSD				DUT-OMRON				HKU-IS				DUTS-test			
				F_β^{max} ↑	mF ↑	S_m ↑	MAE ↓	F_β^{max} ↑	mF ↑	S_m ↑	MAE ↓	F_β^{max} ↑	mF ↑	S_m ↑	MAE ↓	F_β^{max} ↑	mF ↑	S_m ↑	MAE ↓
G	G	G	G	0.9513	0.9329	0.9293	0.0321	0.8273	0.7947	0.8384	0.0666	0.9423	0.9215	0.9241	0.0278	0.8939	0.8653	0.8901	0.0393
E	G	G	G	0.9512	0.936	0.9269	0.0332	0.8247	0.8056	0.846	0.0533	0.945	0.9275	0.9256	0.0262	0.9019	0.8799	0.8984	0.0332
E	E	G	G	0.9531	0.9389	0.9304	0.0317	0.833	0.8146	0.8505	0.0518	0.9448	0.9281	0.9252	0.0265	0.9034	0.8838	0.8994	0.032
E	E	E	G	0.9529	0.9355	0.9286	0.0321	0.8197	0.7949	0.8374	0.0614	0.9435	0.9231	0.9228	0.0279	0.8942	0.8702	0.8893	0.039
E	E	E	E	0.9511	0.9385	0.9285	0.031	0.8226	0.8033	0.8423	0.0553	0.9441	0.929	0.9258	0.0256	0.9005	0.8811	0.8968	0.0342

Table 4. The effectiveness of channel relation reasoning module (CRRM) and cross-level feature adaptation module (CLFAM).

CRRM	CL	ECSSD				DUT-OMRON				HKU-IS				DUTS-test			
		F_β^{max} ↑	mF ↑	S_m ↑	MAE ↓	F_β^{max} ↑	mF ↑	S_m ↑	MAE ↓	F_β^{max} ↑	mF ↑	S_m ↑	MAE ↓	F_β^{max} ↑	mF ↑	S_m ↑	MAE ↓
✗	✗	0.9487	0.9341	0.9292	0.0319	0.8208	0.7957	0.8391	0.0619	0.9431	0.9247	0.9268	0.0265	0.8922	0.8691	0.8919	0.0378
✓	✗	0.9543	0.9401	0.9286	0.0318	0.8236	0.8044	0.8456	0.0566	0.9437	0.9275	0.9266	0.0266	0.9005	0.8807	0.8976	0.035
✗	✓	0.9517	0.9376	0.9277	0.0325	0.8308	0.8112	0.8489	0.0535	0.9443	0.9277	0.9249	0.0268	0.8974	0.8779	0.8957	0.0344
✓	✓	0.9531	0.9389	0.9304	0.0317	0.833	0.8146	0.8505	0.0518	0.9448	0.9281	0.9252	0.0265	0.9034	0.8838	0.8994	0.032
Non-Local+CL		0.9513	0.9355	0.9295	0.0326	0.8259	0.803	0.8445	0.0589	0.9423	0.9241	0.9239	0.0275	0.897	0.8746	0.8933	0.0361

it is unreasonable to use edge constraint on the deepest layer. As shown in Table 4, the best performance (row 3) of the network can be obtained when multi-level edge features are obtained with the first and second layer features and multi-level internal features are extracted with the remaining layers. In our model, the shallow layer can focus on extracting edge detail features, while the deep layer focuses on extracting salient internal features as shown in Fig. 4. This avoids being sensitive to boundaries (often with large contrast variations) and not being able to pip-out the salient object as a whole [26]. The first and second rows of Fig. 6 are typical examples in which the interiors of the salient object have strong appearance change, but our model can extract the salient object well. And as can be seen in Table 3, as cross-layer feature adaptation module provides a transition for deeper features and mitigates the differences between features at different level, row 4 (with CLFAM) outperforms row 2 (without CLFAM) in all indicators, which verify the effectiveness of the cross-layer feature adaptation module.

The Effectiveness of CCRM. Figure 1 visually demonstrates the ability of CRRM to accurately model attention. Quantitatively, the results in Table 3 signify that our proposed CRRM greatly improves performance. The commonly used u-shape architecture without the cross-layer feature adaptation module and CRRM is used as our baseline (row 1). In the training process, edge constraints are used for the first and second layers, and salient object constraints are used for the remaining layers. The model using CRRM (row 2) has better performance than the baseline model (row 1) in all four datasets. And after CRRM and cross-layer feature adaptation module are both assembled, the network achieved more excellent performance. The reason is that CRRM leverages the complementarity between the channels to complement each other. To further illustrate the superiority of CRRM, we compared CRRM with the similarity-based method. We use the standard non-local method in the channel dimension as shown in the fifth row of Table 4. The results show that the similarity-based method cannot bring significant performance improvement to the model. The results show that the approach based on similarity in channel dimension is not suitable for the architecture of our model, because MLCFE obtains multi-level internal features and edge features, and establishing and exploiting the complementary relationships between channels can produce better saliency maps.

5   Conclusion

In this paper, we propose a novel network for SOD tasks, called CRRNet which is mainly composed of MLCFE and CRRM. The MLCFE can extract multi-level edge and salient internal features. And considering complementarity between channels, our CRRM uses graph convolution to establish relationships between channels and enhance channel features. The effectiveness of our proposed CRRNet is proved by extensive experiments.

References

1. Achanta, R., Hemami, S., Estrada, F., Susstrunk, S.: Frequency-tuned salient region detection. In: CVPR, pp. 1597–1604 (2009)
2. Chen, S., Tan, X., Wang, B., Hu, X.: Reverse attention for salient object detection. In: Ferrari, V., Hebert, M., Sminchisescu, C., Weiss, Y. (eds.) ECCV 2018. LNCS, vol. 11213, pp. 236–252. Springer, Cham (2018). https://doi.org/10.1007/978-3-030-01240-3_15
3. Chen, Y., Rohrbach, M., Yan, Z., Shuicheng, Y., Feng, J., Kalantidis, Y.: Graph-based global reasoning networks. In: CVPR, pp. 433–442 (2019)
4. Chen, Z., Xu, Q., Cong, R., Huang, Q.: Global context-aware progressive aggregation network for salient object detection (2020)
5. Chen, Z., Xu, Q., Cong, R., Huang, Q.: Global context-aware progressive aggregation network for salient object detection. In: AAAI (2020)
6. Cheng, M.M., Mitra, N.J., Huang, X., Torr, P.H., Hu, S.M.: Global contrast based salient region detection. IEEE Trans. Pattern Anal. Mach. Intell. **37**, 569–582 (2014)
7. Deng, Z., et al.: R3net: recurrent residual refinement network for saliency detection. In: IJCAI, pp. 684–690 (2018)
8. Feng, M., Lu, H., Ding, E.: Attentive feedback network for boundary-aware salient object detection. In: CVPR, pp. 1623–1632 (2019)
9. Fu, J., et al.: Dual attention network for scene segmentation. In: CVPR, pp. 3146–3154 (2019)
10. Gao, S., Guo, Q., Zhang, W., Zhang, W., Ji, Z.: Dual-stream network based on global guidance for salient object detection. In: ICASSP 2021–2021 IEEE International Conference on Acoustics, Speech and Signal Processing (ICASSP), pp. 1495–1499. IEEE (2021)
11. He, K., Zhang, X., Ren, S., Sun, J.: Deep residual learning for image recognition, pp. 770–778 (2016)

12. Hou, Q., Cheng, M.M., Hu, X., Borji, A., Tu, Z., Torr, P.H.: Deeply supervised salient object detection with short connections. In: CVPR, pp. 3203–3212 (2017)
13. Hu, J., Shen, L., Albanie, S., Sun, G., Vedaldi, A.: Gather-excite: exploiting feature context in convolutional neural networks. In: NIPS, pp. 9401–9411 (2018)
14. Hu, J., Shen, L., Sun, G.: Squeeze-and-excitation networks. In: CVPR, pp. 7132–7141 (2018)
15. Kipf, T.N., Welling, M.: Semi-supervised classification with graph convolutional networks. In: ICLR (2016)
16. Li, G., Yu, Y.: Visual saliency based on multiscale deep features. In: CVPR, pp. 5455–5463 (2015)
17. Li, Y., Hou, X., Koch, C., Rehg, J.M., Yuille, A.L.: The secrets of salient object segmentation. In: CVPR, pp. 280–287 (2014)
18. Liu, J.J., Hou, Q., Cheng, M.M., Feng, J., Jiang, J.: A simple pooling-based design for real-time salient object detection. In: CVPR, pp. 3917–3926 (2019)
19. Liu, N., Han, J., Yang, M.H.: PiCANet: learning pixel-wise contextual attention for saliency detection. In: CVPR, pp. 3089–3098 (2018)
20. Long, J., Shelhamer, E., Darrell, T.: Fully convolutional networks for semantic segmentation, pp. 3431–3440 (2015)
21. Luo, Z., Mishra, A., Achkar, A., Eichel, J., Li, S., Jodoin, P.M.: Non-local deep features for salient object detection. In: CVPR, pp. 6609–6617 (2017)
22. Pang, Y., Zhao, X., Zhang, L., Lu, H.: Multi-scale interactive network for salient object detection. In: CVPR, pp. 9413–9422 (2020)
23. Park, J., Woo, S., Lee, J.Y., Kweon, I.S.: Bam: Bottleneck attention module (2018)
24. Qin, X., Zhang, Z., Huang, C., Gao, C., Dehghan, M., Jagersand, M.: Basnet: boundary-aware salient object detection, pp. 7479–7489 (2019)
25. Simonyan, K., Zisserman, A.: Very deep convolutional networks for large-scale image recognition (2015)
26. Su, J., Li, J., Zhang, Y., Xia, C., Tian, Y.: Selectivity or invariance: Boundary-aware salient object detection, pp. 3799–3808 (2018)
27. Wang, L., et al.: Learning to detect salient objects with image-level supervision. In: CVPR, pp. 136–145 (2017)
28. Wang, Q., Wu, B., Zhu, P., Li, P., Zuo, W., Hu, Q.: ECA-net: efficient channel attention for deep convolutional neural networks. In: CVPR, pp. 11534–11542 (2020)
29. Wang, T., Borji, A., Zhang, L., Zhang, P., Lu, H.: A stagewise refinement model for detecting salient objects in images. In: ICCV, pp. 4019–4028 (2017)
30. Wang, T., et al.: Detect globally, refine locally: a novel approach to saliency detection. In: CVPR, pp. 3127–3135 (2018)
31. Wei, J., Wang, S., Huang, Q.: F^{3}net: fusion, feedback and focus for salient object detection, pp. 12321–12328 (2020)
32. Wei, J., Wang, S., Wu, Z., Su, C., Huang, Q., Tian, Q.: Label decoupling framework for salient object detection, pp. 13025–13034 (2020)
33. Woo, S., Park, J., Lee, J.-Y., Kweon, I.S.: CBAM: convolutional block attention module. In: Ferrari, V., Hebert, M., Sminchisescu, C., Weiss, Y. (eds.) ECCV 2018. LNCS, vol. 11211, pp. 3–19. Springer, Cham (2018). https://doi.org/10.1007/978-3-030-01234-2_1
34. Wu, R., Feng, M., Guan, W., Wang, D., Lu, H., Ding, E.: A mutual learning method for salient object detection with intertwined multi-supervision. In: CVPR, pp. 8150–8159 (2019)
35. Wu, Z., Su, L., Huang, Q.: Stacked cross refinement network for edge-aware salient object detection, pp. 7264–7273 (2019)

36. Yan, Q., Xu, L., Shi, J., Jia, J.: Hierarchical saliency detection. In: CVPR, pp. 1155–1162 (2013)
37. Yang, C., Zhang, L., Lu, H., Ruan, X., Yang, M.H.: Saliency detection via graph-based manifold ranking. In: CVPR, pp. 3166–3173 (2013)
38. Zhang, K., Li, T., Shen, S., Liu, B., Chen, J., Liu, Q.: Adaptive graph convolutional network with attention graph clustering for co-saliency detection. In: 2020 IEEE/CVF Conference on Computer Vision and Pattern Recognition (CVPR), pp. 9047–9056 (2020)
39. Zhang, P., Wang, D., Lu, H., Wang, H., Ruan, X.: Amulet: Aggregating multi-level convolutional features for salient object detection. In: ICCV, pp. 202–211 (2017)
40. Zhao, J., Liu, J., Fan, D., Cao, Y., Yang, J., Cheng, M.: EGNet: edge guidance network for salient object detection, pp. 8779–8788 (2019)
41. Zhao, X., Pang, Y., Zhang, L., Lu, H., Zhang, L.: Suppress and balance: a simple gated network for salient object detection. In: Vedaldi, A., Bischof, H., Brox, T., Frahm, J.-M. (eds.) ECCV 2020. LNCS, vol. 12347, pp. 35–51. Springer, Cham (2020). https://doi.org/10.1007/978-3-030-58536-5_3
42. Zhou, H., Xie, X., Lai, J.H., Chen, Z., Yang, L.: Interactive two-stream decoder for accurate and fast saliency detection. In: Proceedings of the IEEE/CVF Conference on Computer Vision and Pattern Recognition, pp. 9141–9150 (2020)

Visual Object Tracking with Adaptive Template Update and Global Search Augmentation

Lu Zeng$^{(\boxtimes)}$, Wei He, and Wenqiang Zhang

Fudan University, Shanghai, China
20110860044@fudan.edu.cn

Abstract. The realization of human-machine-environment intimate interaction by intelligent robots is the research direction of cutting-edge exploration in the field of robotics. One of the important tasks is to realize active target tracking on the robot platform. Single-target tracking is subject to data changes such as target position and size in the video sequence, and is prone to target drift or loss when the environment changes drastically or is occluded. This paper aims at the application background of the intelligent foot robot platform, where deep learning technology is used to adopt adaptive multi-target tracking. The frame detection template updated Shuffle net V2–0.5 convolutional neural network builds a deep tracking model, which speeds up the model calculation. At the same time, the multi-template input ensures that the required target information can be located in a larger search image and a global search module is added. The target position re-detection is carried out, and the background enhancement training is integrated to significantly strengthen the discrimination ability of the global search network. The target tracking accuracy of the improved visual object tracking algorithm reaches 64.7%, and the accuracy of the target located at the center point of the marker frame reaches 86.8%, which is significantly improved compared with the traditional algorithm.

Keywords: Multiple template input · Shuffle net V2–0.5 · Global search · Background enhancement training

1 Introduction

As a key technology in the field of computer vision, single-target tracking has received more and more attention. Single-target tracking needs to predict the state of the target in subsequent video frames given the initial target state. The single target tracking algorithm generally includes three parts: feature extraction [1, 2], state estimation [3] and search strategy [4, 5]. During the tracking process, the appearance of the target will change, and the target template or tracking model needs to be updated according to the change of the target. The method of not updating the model will lead to the offset problem [6]. Therefore, the adaptive model update method needs further research and improvement.

Nam [7] built the MDnet algorithm to introduce deep learning into single target tracking in 2015. Tao [8] proposed the SINT twin network tracking algorithm in 2016,

© The Author(s), under exclusive license to Springer Nature Singapore Pte Ltd. 2023
Z. Yu et al. (Eds.): CIRAC 2022, CCIS 1770, pp. 39–46, 2023.
https://doi.org/10.1007/978-981-99-0301-6_3

which sent the candidate frame data containing the target and a series of candidate frame data together. In the twin network, the template matching function is used for target positioning, but the large number of candidate boxes affects the calculation time.

Luca [9] published the algorithm SiamFC tracker in 2016, which is the first end-to-end twin network. It successfully achieved offline pre-training of single-target tracking on large-scale data sets, but it could not perceive target changes, which was not conducive to target positioning. Li [10] proposed the SiamRPN++ algorithm to apply the deep feature extraction network to the target tracking based on the Siamese network in 2019, but the convolutional padding will destroy the strict translation invariance. Chen [11] built the SiamBAN algorithm in 2020, which has no need for pre-defined candidate boxes, but target tracking and positioning is achieved by outputting the offset between the predicted box and the real box through the regression branch. Voigtlaender [12] proposed that the SiamR-CNN algorithm adopts a re-detection design in 2020, which achieves better results in long-term tracking tests, however, the speed is far from meeting the real-time response requirements.

Occlusion and dramatic changes in the target background are one of the key difficulties in single-target tracking. When the features of the target are occluded or replaced by the background environment, the algorithm will use the occluded image as the target image to update the model, which will lead to the inaccuracy of the tracking model. Predicting the location of the target leads to the loss of the target.

The traditional single target tracking mainly includes two steps: classification task and estimation task. The classification task refers to determining the initial position of the target to be tracked by labeling the first frame in the given video. Since only the first frame is used, it cannot adapt to the target. Therefore, it is very easy to lose the target when encountering a drastic change in the appearance of the target. The estimation task is to provide an accurate feature through the Siamese network, and find the most similar candidate region in the frame of the subsequent video to the standard frame. The traditional twin network will use multi-scale filtering or SiamFC algorithm. Since the set scale is fixed, the accuracy of the algorithm will be reduced when the scale of the video frame changes, which will affect the calculation efficiency. In addition, when the SiamFC algorithm extracts feature objects, there is overlap between different proposals, which is easy to confuse the categories between pixels.

In order to improve the tracking accuracy, this paper uses the Shufflenet0.5 convolutional neural network updated with adaptive multi-frame detection templates to build a deep tracking model to speed up the calculation of the model. At the same time, multi-template input is used to ensure that the desired target information can be located in a larger search image. The discrimination ability of the global search network can be significantly enhanced by redetecting the target position and incorporating the background to enhance the training.

2 Algorithmic Framework

The algorithm decomposes single-target tracking into three sub-tasks: classification based on adaptive multi-frame detection template update, state estimation based on score judgment, and target relocation based on global search enhancement. Specifically, use multiple templates to input the location information of the labeled target. In addition to labeling the target in the first reference frame, the target is also labeled in the previous frame of the current search map. Since the previous frame is constantly changing, this method can adapt to the video The appearance of the target in the sequence changes. Secondly, shufflenet0.5 convolutional neural network algorithm [13] is adopted in the special name extraction link for single target tracking. Multi-scale feature fusion is used to make the extracted target adapt to multi-scale changes and achieve a high-speed, stable and accurate single target tracking model. In addition, a global search part is added to the algorithm, and background enhancement training is used to improve the discriminative ability of the global search network.

2.1 Network Backhone

Single-target tracking has strict requirements on the computing power of the device, and the computing power on the mobile robot platform is relatively limited. In order to achieve dynamic tracking, the backbone network architecture adopts the highly computationally efficient CNN architecture shuffle net v2–0.5, that is, the scale factor is 0.5. The best balance between high precision and low cost can be achieved by two new operations, point-by-point block convolution and channel shuffle.

Conventional point-by-point convolution is usually used in traditional convolutional neural networks, which will result in a limited number of channels that satisfy the complexity constraints, and to affect the computational accuracy. In order to reduce the computational complexity of convolution, point-by-point grouped convolution is used to reduce the convolution density and computational cost. However, when grouping is used, the output of a channel can only come from a small part of input channels, which will prevent the information flow between channels and weaken the expression ability of neural network. Channel shuffling is introduced, and packet convolution is allowed to obtain input data from different families, so as to realize the association between input channels and output channels.

The second is the batch normalization layer. The basic way to build a convolutional neural network is a convolutional layer followed by a non-linear activation function.

The backbone network is shown in Fig. 1. It adopts four stages of shuffle net v2, in which stage1 includes a 3×3 convolutional layer and a 3×3 pooling layer. Stage2-stage4 is composed of Shuffle Unit, the basic component unit of Shuffle NET, which includes residual structure and channel shuffle operation. In addition, the stride of stage2-stage4 is changed from 2 to 1. Finally, in order to combine the semantic features of different stages, the multi-stage feature fusion operation is adopted to obtain the feature CONCAT of stage2-stage4, which can be used for the subsequent tracking features.

2.2 Siamese Network

The algorithm framework is shown in Fig. 2. The Siamese network consists of a template branch and a search branch, and the single-target classification task and state estimation task are realized through offline training. The template branch takes the first frame in the video and the target block in the previous frame of the current search map as input, and the search branch takes the target image frame enhanced by the global search as input,

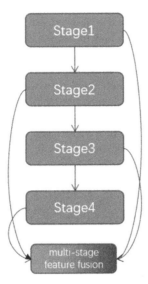

Fig. 1. The frame of Shuffle net V2–0.5

and performs the same transformation in the input image frame. Parameter extraction for subsequent state estimation. Set the input of the template branch to m and the input of the search branch to n, and the cross-correlation operation between the template branch and the search branch in the same feature space:

$$f_i(m, n) = \psi_i(\phi(m)) \star \psi_i(\phi(n)), i \in \{cls, reg\} \tag{1}$$

$\star$ denotes the cross-correlation operation relationship, $\psi_i()$ denotes the task-specific layer, $\phi()$ denotes the backbone of the adopted Siamese network, i denotes the subtask type, 'cls' denotes the subtask for feature classification extraction, 'reg' identifies the subtask used for regression estimation. Two convolutional layers are employed for ψ_{cls} and ψ_{reg} after common feature extraction using shuffle net V2–0.5 to adjust the common features into the task-specific feature space.

The classification branch and regression branch are designed after the cross-correlation calculation in the feature space. For the classification branch, each pixel in the image represents an input image corresponding to a region block, and ψ_{cls} will be used as the input target to calculate the score relationship of the corresponding image, thereby judging the classification relationship of the corresponding image. When the coordinate position (x, y) corresponding to the pixel in the image is within the real bounding box, this pixel is called a positive sample block. When the corresponding coordinate position (x, y) is outside the real bounding box, this pixel is called a negative sample piece. For the regression branch, ψ_{reg} will be used as the input target to predict the positional relationship of the real bounding box and the relationship between the bounding box and the image boundary, and use S* to represent the boundary relationship:

$$S^* = (o^*, p^*, q^*, r^*) \tag{2}$$

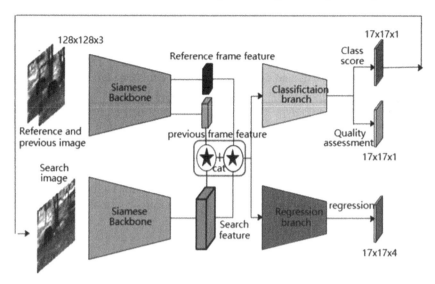

Fig. 2. Overall algorithm framework

The relationship of each parameter can be represented by the following regression branch formula:

$$o^* = (\frac{s}{2} - xs) - x_0 \tag{3}$$

$$p^* = (\frac{s}{2} - ys) - y_0 \tag{4}$$

$$q^* = x_1 - (\frac{s}{2} + xs) \tag{5}$$

$$r^* = y_1 - (\frac{s}{2} + ys) \tag{6}$$

where 's' is the total span of the set backbone network, point (x, y) represents the conners of the true bounding box, point (x_0, y_0) represents the upper left corner of the true bounding box, and point (x_1, y_1) represents the true bounding box bottom right.

In the classification branch, in order to better balance the relationship with its target position, the quality score PSS* is introduced, and the final bounding box score is obtained by multiplying the quality score and the prediction score. The definition formula of the quality score PSS* is:

$$PSS^* = \sqrt{\frac{min(o^*, p^*)}{max(o^*, p^*)} \times \frac{min(q^*, r^*)}{max(q^*, r^*)}} \tag{7}$$

By combining the two scores, the center of the bounding box can be moved closer to the center of the object, which improves the accuracy of the predicted bounding box.

2.3 Global Search Enhancements

We build a memory to dynamically update the template, so that the network can adapt to the changes of the entire video sequence target. As shown in Fig. 2, the memory stores the first frame and a dynamic template, and then sends the search region and these templates to the backbone to extract features respectively to obtain f_x, f_z, and f_{zd}. Then, f_z and f_{zd} are linearly correlated with f_x to obtain two response maps. Then, the two corresponding maps are combined and sent to the tracking head to predict the target. In addition, we use the confidence score of the tracking to judge the correctness of the tracking results. If the confidence score is higher than a certain threshold, we think it is a more accurate tracking result. The bounding box will be trimmed to the current frame to get a new dynamic template to replace the previous dynamic template. Based on the above operations, our method can well adapt to the appearance variation of the target.

3 Algorithmic Test

The OTB2015 dataset is a video target detection dataset [15]. The constructed manually annotated dataset allows different algorithms to have a fair comparison platform through the developed toolkit. The dataset includes video attributes of occlusion, blur, and fast motion. The target image and the corresponding search image can be cropped according to the annotation, which provides a test standard for the performance test of the algorithm.

The algorithm is compared with the internationally representative SiamRPN [16], ECO [17], SiamFC [9] algorithms, and the success rate and the accuracy of the center point of the target frame are used as measurement indicators. The results are shown in Table 1.

Table 1. Comparison of test results.

Method	Success	Precision
SiamRPN	63.6	85.0
ECO-HC	64.3	85.6
SiamFC	58.2	X
Ours	64.7	86.8

As can be seen from Table 1, under the comparison of the success rate and the accuracy of the center point of the target frame, the algorithm has a success rate of 64.7% and an accuracy of 86.8%, which are higher than the internationally recognized algorithms. The effectiveness of the algorithm is improved, and it is improved for single-target tracking.

4 Conclusion

In this paper, the accuracy of target labeling during single target tracking is improved by using multi-template input, so as to avoid target loss caused by target appearance changes. Secondly, the shufflenet0.5 convolutional neural network with faster speed and higher computational efficiency is adopted to realize the high-speed and accurate calculation of the single target tracking model, which improves the actual utilization rate of the algorithm. The success rate and accuracy of the algorithm on OTB2015 dataset reached 64.7% and 86.8%, which verified the effectiveness of the algorithm. How to achieve the balance of accuracy and speed in long-term tracking is still the direction of further research and exploration.

References

1. Bao, H., Lu, Y., Wang, Q.:Single target tracking via correlation filter and context adaptively. Multimedia Tools and Appl. **79**, 27465–27482 (2020). https://doi.org/10.1007/s11042-020-09309-3
2. Wang, D., et al.: Online single target tracking in WAMI: benchmark and evaluation. Multimedia Tools Appl. **77**(9), 10939–10960 (2018)
3. Xiao, J., et al.: Dynamic multi-level appearance models and adaptive clustered decision trees for single target tracking. Pattern Recognition **69**.(2017). https://doi.org/10.1016/j.patcog. 2017.04.001. Author, F.: Contribution title. In: 9th International Proceedings on Proceedings, pp. 1–2. Publisher, Location (2010)
4. Yanqing, W., Liang, Z., Cheng, X.: Fast target tracking based on improved deep sort and YOLOv3 fusion algorithm. Abstracts of the 7th International Conference of Pioneering Computer Scientists, Engineers and Educators (ICPCSEE 2021) Part I.Ed.. Springer, pp. 107–109 (2021). https://doi.org/10.1007/978-981-16-5940-9_27
5. Kwa, H.L., et al.: Optimal swarm strategy for dynamic target search and tracking. Autonomous Agents and MultiAgent Systems.Ed., pp. 672680 (2020)
6. Yıldırım, S., Jiang, L., Singh, S.S., Dean, T.A.: Calibrating the Gaussian multi-target tracking model. Stat. Comput. **25**(3), 595–608 (2014)
7. Nam, H., Han, B.: Learning multi-domain convolutional neural networks for visual tracking. Computer Vision and Pattern Recognition IEEE (2015)
8. Tao, R., Gavves, E., Smeulders, A.: Siamese instance search for tracking. In: IEEE Conference on Computer Vision and Pattern Recognition (CVPR), pp. 1420–1429 (2016)
9. Bertinetto, L., et al.: Fully-Convolutional Siamese Networks for Object Tracking. CoRR abs/1606.09549 (2016)
10. Li, B., et al.: SiamRPN++: Evolution of siamese visual tracking with very deep networks. In: 2019 IEEE/CVF Conference on Computer Vision and Pattern Recognition (CVPR) IEEE (2020)
11. Chen, Z.D., Zhong, B.N., Li, G.R., et al.: Siamese box adaptive network for visual tracking. In: Proceedings of 2020 IEEE/CVF Conference on Computer Vision and Pattern Recognition.Seattle: IEEE, pp. 6667–6676 (2020)
12. Voigtlaender, P., Luiten, J., Torr, P.H.S., et al.: Siam R-CNN:Visual tracking by re-detection. In: Proceedings of the 2020 IEEE/CVF Conference on Computer Vision and Pattern Recognition. Piscataway: IEEE, pp. 6577–6587 (2020)
13. Zhang, X., et al.: ShuffleNet: An Extremely Efficient Convolutional Neural Network for Mobile Devices. CoRR abs/1707.01083 (2017)
14. Grimaldi, M., et al.: Dynamic ConvNets on Tiny Devices via Nested Sparsity. arXiv e-prints (2022)
15. Sharma, S.: Ermenegildo Zegna OTB Process Analysis. (2015)

16. Bo, L., et al.: High performance visual tracking with siamese region proposal network. In: 2018 IEEE/CVF Conference on Computer Vision and Pattern Recognition (CVPR) IEEE (2018)
17. Folberth, J., Becker, S.: Efficient Adjoint Computation for Wavelet and Convolution Operators (2017)

UAV Autonomous Navigation Based on Multi-modal Perception: A Deep Hierarchical Reinforcement Learning Method

Kai Kou$^{(\boxtimes)}$, Gang Yang, Wenqi Zhang, Chenyi Wang, Yuan Yao, and Xingshe Zhou

School of Computer Science, Northwestern Polytechnical University, Xi'an 710072, China
kaikou@mail.nwpu.edu.cn

Abstract. Autonomous navigation is a highly desirable capability for Unmanned Aerial Vehicle (UAV). In this paper, the problem of autonomous navigation of UAV in unknown dynamic environments is addressed. Specifically, we propose a visual-inertial multi-modal sensor data perception framework based on a hierarchical reinforcement learning paradigm. This model consists of a high-level behavior selection model and a low-level policy execution model. The high-level model learns a stable and reliable behavior selection strategy. The low-level model decomposes the UAV navigation task into two simpler subtasks, which respectively achieve obstacle avoidance and goal approximation, which effectively learns high-level semantic information about the scene and narrows the strategy space. Furthermore, extensive simulation results are provided to confirm the superiority of the proposed method in terms of convergence and effectiveness compared to state-of-the-art methods.

Keywords: Unmanned Aerial Vehicles (UAV) · Autonomous navigation · Multi-modal · Hierarchical reinforcement learning

1 Introduction

In the past few decades, UAV have been widely used in various fields due to their excellent maneuvering characteristics, such as emergency rescue [1], military reconnaissance [2], air logistics transportation [3], and other challenging tasks. The prerequisite for performing these tasks is that the UAV has a stable and reliable autonomous navigation system. In free environments, UAV navigation mainly relies on the Global Positioning System (GPS). However, in complex electromagnetic environments or GNSS-denied conditions, due to the limitations of UAV communication and perception capabilities, it is not easy to accurately perceive the surrounding environment and thus cannot work correctly. The limited autonomous navigation capability hinders the application of UAV seriously. Therefore, UAV need other auxiliary or alternative means of environmental perception to achieve accurate and reliable autonomous navigation [4].

Z. Yu et al. (Eds.): CIRAC 2022, CCIS 1770, pp. 47–56, 2023.
https://doi.org/10.1007/978-981-99-0301-6_4

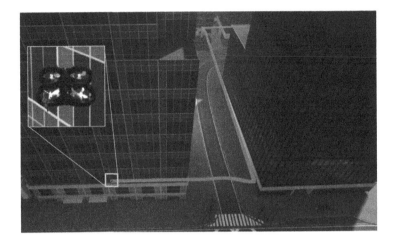

Fig. 1. The UAV navigate autonomously in dense buildings.

The traditional UAV autonomous navigation methods establish accurate mathematical models based on obtaining sufficient sensor information to realize the autonomous flight of a UAV. However, in some particular scenarios, the performance requirements of UAV are more stringent. As shown in Fig. 1, the UAV traverses a dense building to detect the internal situation. On the one hand, due to severe occlusion, when approaching obstacles, the reflection will make the GPS signal particularly weak or even disappear. On the other hand, the interior space of the building is small. Therefore, the volume of the UAV cannot be too large, and the load and power of the UAV are also limited, which limits the advanced depth sensors, such as lidar. At the same time, if conducting military reconnaissance, in order to ensure concealment, the use of active sensors should be avoided, such as radar.

Benefiting from the development of electronic technology and machine learning, the navigation methods that use airborne sensors have become mainstream, for instance, inertial sensors, lidar, and visual cameras *etc.* The visual features in the environment extracted by the UAV's visual sensor contain detailed information about the surrounding environment of the current location, including the location of obstacles, relative heights, and types of obstacles. However, the monocular image data does not contain information about the UAV's motion state, which needs to be obtained by other methods. The UAV uses the Inertial Measurement Unit (IMU) to collect the acceleration and angular velocity. It calculates the position, speed, attitudes and other information of the UAV through integration, which can provide reliable information and state estimation information in a short time. Moreover, the IMU is a passive sensor, and its application scenarios are not restricted by the environment. Compared with single-modal sensor data, the fusion of multi-modal information can better reflect the current state of UAV. Therefore, under the premise set in this paper, the UAV is equipped with a monocular camera and an IMU sensor to obtain accurate environmental perception information.

Currently, UAV autonomous navigation methods based on deep neural networks have made significant progress. However, these methods learn heuristic strategies, which are more focused on environmental perception in nature, and are challenging to meet the navigation needs in dynamic and complex environments of the real world. In contrast, reinforcement learning (RL) directly learns the policy of the current environment through a reward mechanism, which formulates policy through interaction with the surrounding environment. It directly adjusts the policy model through trial and error based on the immediate reaction of the environment. Actually, RL is more in line with the human policy-making process.

In this paper, we describe the learning process of deep reinforcement learning for the UAV autonomous navigation task. Specifically, a UAV autonomous navigation algorithm based on hierarchical reinforcement learning is proposed, which combines the knowledge learned from RGB images and IMU data to better characterize the current state of the UAV and achieve a closed-loop control. Finally, the effect of the algorithm is verified by simulation experiments in Airsim [5], which proves that the convergence speed and training cost of the proposed method is significantly improved compared with the existing algorithms.

2 Related Works

2.1 Hierarchical Reinforcement Learning

Reinforcement learning (RL) is a classic theory in the field of artificial intelligence, received extensive attention in recent years. RL emphasizes the interaction between the agent and the environment, in order to obtain the maximum environmental reward to guide the learning behavior and realize the optimization of the strategy. However, In a large-scale and high-dimensional environment, the state and action of RL grow exponentially with the dimension of its variables, which leads to the problem of dimensional disaster.

Hierarchical reinforcement learning (HRL) is a branch of reinforcement learning research [6]. Building on RL, HRL addresses the sparse reward problem by taking advantage of time-expanded actions, aka options, to make decisions from a higher-dimensional perspective. It introduces a hierarchical structure to reinforcement learning algorithms, so that algorithmic models can be trained on continuous high-dimensional temporal abstractions of the environment, often referred to as sub-goals in practice. This divide-and-conquer strategy enables HRL to avoid the Curse of Dimensionality, that is, the number of parameters required for task training will increase exponentially with the increase of the system state dimension, which will consume A lot of computing and storage resources. Since each subtask has a more minor complexity than the overall task, and the solution strategies of different subtasks are reusable, HRL has a high learning rate and efficiency in solving large-scale complex problems. HRL is the current research focus and application hotspots in many fields, such as complex control and intelligent robot.

2.2   Autonomous Navigation of UAV

The purpose of the autonomous navigation system is to control the UAV to reach the destination of navigation autonomously without collision, which is one of the core components of the UAV flight control system. With the wide application of UAV in all walks of life, the oriented scenarios are becoming more and more complex. The UAV with autonomous navigation capabilities has gradually become a new focus of current researchers.

Nowadays, deep learning shines brightly in the field of artificial intelligence. Some researchers try to apply deep learning technology for UAV autonomous control. The main innovation of these works is to transform control problems into a series of classifications or regression problems, so that the information obtained by the sensor is directly mapped to the high-level behavioral instructions [7]. Gandhi et al. [8] collected a UAV collision dataset, including images and corresponding actions, then used CNN to extract features and predict whether the UAV would collide in a specific direction, thus realizing the UAV collision-free flight indoors. Maciel et al. [2] proposed a model for UAV navigation and exploration in the densely occluded forests, which is based on an end-to-end multi-task regression-based learning method capable of defining flight commands. Jung et al. [9] proposed a visual-inertial navigation approach and the key idea is to introduce an optimal intensity gradient to directly minimize the photometric error and reduce the calculation time.

Deep reinforcement learning uses deep neural networks to process various input sensor data to perceive and understand information about the environment, in which the agent is located. Then, the parameters of the deep neural network are updated according to the feedback signal of the environment to the agent, so that the deep neural network is used to learn the optimal strategy to solve the control problem in complex scenes. Giusti et al. [10] used a GoPro Hero3 camera to collect decision-making data on a UAV crossing the forest, trained the UAV to follow the forward trajectory, and successfully controlled the UAV to travel through the forest. Huang et al. [11] proposed a local autonomous navigation model for ground vehicles. The navigation system directs policy learning to generate flexible actions to avoid collisions with obstacles in navigation by replacing raw RGB images with semantic segmentation maps as input and applying a multi-modal fusion scheme. Finally, the trained model in the simulation environment is generalized to real devices. Theile et al. [12] adopted the structured map information of the environment to train dual-deep Q-networks with the same architecture, and proposed a UAV autonomous path planning method for different task scenarios.

3   Proposed Method

3.1   Background

In this paper, we define the UAV autonomous navigation task as a Partially Observable Markov Decision Process (POMDP). Then, inspired by hierarchical reinforcement learning, the autonomous control strategy of UAV is decomposed into multiple parallel subtasks, such as environment perception, obstacle avoidance, and position estimation, and a visual-inertial multi-modal approach based on hierarchical reinforcement learning, named VI-HRL, is proposed, which attempts to decompose a complex task into a series of consecutive subtasks, so that the UAV-Agent obtains dense intrinsic rewards. Finally, according to the actual situation, setting the state, action, and reward function. The state is replaced by observation, the action is continuous control amount, and the reward function is set as a comprehensive evaluation index, such as safe flight distance and completion time.

3.2   Framework Overview

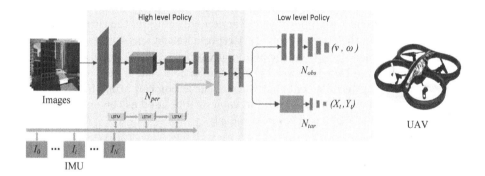

Fig. 2. The model architecture of the proposed method, VI-HRL.

The network architecture of the proposed method is shown in Fig. 2, which consists of a high-level multi-modal perception module N_{per}, two low-level obstacle avoidance control N_{obs}, and a target-drive module N_{tar}. Specifically, the multi-modal perception module maps the observation data obtained by the UAV into low-dimensional information, so that the UAV can produce two behaviors of practical obstacle avoidance and target-driving, and then stores the experience data of the two behaviors in the experience pool of the obstacle avoidance control model, in which the empirical data of the target-driven behavior can be used to optimize the obstacle avoidance strategy. On this basis, the off-policy learning method is used to optimize the training of the obstacle avoidance control model, which can make the learned obstacle avoidance strategy more applicable for autonomous navigation.

According to the needs of the task, In the multi-modal perception module N_{per}, we take monocular images and IMU data as environmental observations and map them to different feature subspaces. The monocular image is processed by the Vgg16 convolutional layer to obtain a feature map, and then passes through a multi-layer fully connected layer to obtain a 100-dimensional image feature vector. The frequency measured by the IMU is typically an order of magnitude higher (about $100 \sim 200Hz$) than the visual data (about $10 \sim 30Hz$). LSTM exploits the temporal dependencies of input data by maintaining hidden states to process batches of IMU data between two consecutive image frames, and outputs 100-dimensional inertial feature vectors. Finally, the two vectors are combined to obtain a 200-dimensional feature vector, which represents all the input information.

The obstacle avoidance control model N_{obs} takes the multi-modal representation as input, and obtains seven continuous actions $a_{(0)}^l, \ldots, a_{(5)}^l, a_{(6)}^l$ by multiple fully connected layers. The target-driven control model N_{tar} first obtains the real-time coordinates of the UAV, then calculates the deflection angle between the forward direction and the target direction at the current moment according to the geometric relationship between the target point and the UAV, and controls the UAV to approach the target point.

In this way, we get the state value and action advantage of the current action, respectively, where the state value $V\left(s_t^l\right)$ represents the long-term benefit that the current state can bring, and the action advantage value $V\left(s_t^l, a_t^l\right)$ is used to measure the relative pros and cons of different action, and is used to estimate The maximum long-term benefit that the current action can bring, in which the action with the most considerable action value will be used as the output of the model to control the UAV to fly autonomously.

3.3   Reward Function

The experimental task scenario designed in this paper is that the UAV navigates autonomously to the destination through a complex terrain areas. The target area is directly in front of the UAV. In order to reach the destination as soon as possible and avoid detection, the UAV needs to perform high-speed flights and avoid obstacles during the flight. According to this idea, the reward function is designed as follows:

$$r_t = \begin{cases} 1 - \varepsilon V & 0 < t < T \quad and \quad not \quad collision \\ -50 - \varepsilon V & if \ collision \\ 20 - \varepsilon & t = T \end{cases} \tag{1}$$

where T represents the number of max episode iterations for each training step, and ε is the penalty coefficient, which needs to be adjusted manually.

4   Experiments

4.1   Simulation Environment

In this paper, the UAV simulator selected is the Airsim simulation platform developed by Microsoft Corporation [5]. This platform provides a variety of functional services including flight control system, UAV 3D fuselage, various sensor information and 3D digital scenes. The provided virtual sensor monoculars, GPS, IMU, *etc.* In addition, this simulator also provides multiple 3D scenes, as shown in Fig. 3, The City, Suburban, and Forest are selected as experimental scenarios to truly reflect the running effect of the algorithm.

(a) City   (b) Suburban   (c) Forest

Fig. 3. Multiple dynamic flight environments in Airsim.

In addition, a virtual quad-rotor UAV, named ARDrone, provided by the Airsim simulation platform is used as an experimental model. The ARDrone features a fixed monocular camera and IMU, which meets our experimental needs. The chosen deep learning training framework is Pytorch. The hardware platform is a desktop computer with an Nvidia GTX 3060 GPU and an Intel i7 4790 CPU. During the training process, the GPU is used to maintain the operation of the simulation scene and the training of the neural network; the CPU is used for general program operation.

4.2   Comparison Methods

In order to objectively evaluate the effectiveness of the proposed method in UAV autonomous navigation tasks. The specific definition of the comparison method is as follows: 1) PPO method: use the PPO model to directly learn autonomous navigation strategies; 2) Two-State DQN method: The two-state input model proposed by Maciel *et al.* [13], which combines knowledge obtained from raw images and maps containing location information, is used for autonomous flight and exploration of UAV in 3D dense spaces.

4.3 Result

A series of objective experiments are adopted to test the effectiveness of the proposed method. The corresponding results are shown in Table 1. Among them, the success rate, the collision rate and the timeout rate represent the proportion of the number of successful navigation rounds, the number of collision rounds and the number of timeout rounds to the total number of test rounds, respectively. From the statistical results of the success rate, it can be seen that although the comparison methods can also complete the autonomous navigation task, the PPO method has the worst performance, which is because it models the UAV control system as a deep neural network to estimate its autonomous navigation. Flight control parameters and guide the UAV to approach the target point while avoiding obstacles, ignoring that the navigation strategy essentially consists of multiple parallel subtasks. The two-stage input strategy adopted by Two-State DQN results in a much larger state space, which is always tricky to converge during training. At the same time, the proposed method exhibits apparent advantages, which indicates that it has better stability and safety in autonomous navigation tasks.

Table 1. The results in multiple environments.

AirSim environment	Baselines	Success rate (%)	Timeout rate (%)	Collision rate (%)
City	PPO	52	62	33
	Two-State DQN	65	57	46
	VI-HRL	85	31	25
Forest	PPO	43	76	35
	Two-State DQN	58	66	49
	VI-HRL	80	40	31
Suburban	PPO	50	46	37
	Two-State DQN	59	42	36
	VI-HRL	82	36	25

In addition, from the statistical analysis of collision rate and timeout rate, the proposed method also achieves the best performance, which indicates that multi-modal perception learns high-level semantic information about the scene, and the hierarchical model effectively reduces the state-action space to speed up the convergence process. The complexity of multiple test environments varies significantly, and the statistics of all test methods fluctuate to some extent. However, the proposed method still achieves the best results in various indicators, indicating that the proposed navigation method can effectively learn navigation strategies in complex environments, and has a good generalization ability to different environments.

5   Conclusion and Discussion

This paper mainly studies the UAV autonomous navigation task in complex scenarios. Aiming at the problem of a single source of input data for existing methods, a multi-modal network is proposed, which fuses data from a monocular camera and IMU, which not only tends to preserve spatial information, but also learns high-level semantics about the scene. Aiming at the difficulty of training convergence caused by the large state and action space of the reinforcement learning model, a hierarchical model is proposed, which significantly improves the real-time performance, and a better autonomous flight effect is achieved.

In the future, we will develop an autonomous navigation system for swarms of UAV, where multi-modal information sharing between different UAV improves the perception range of each UAV. Therefore, this research is of great significance for the further development of UAV swarm navigation capability.

Acknowledgements. This work was supported in part by the National Natural Science Foundation of China under Grants (No. 62032018, 62141220, and 61876151).

References

1. Ye, Z., Wang, K., Chen, Y., Jiang, X., Song, G.: Multi-UAV navigation for partially observable communication coverage by graph reinforcement learning. IEEE Trans. Mob. Comput. 1 (2022). https://doi.org/10.1109/TMC.2022.3146881
2. Maciel-Pearson, B.G., Holder, C.: Breckon: multi-task regression-based learning for autonomous unmanned aerial vehicle flight control within unstructured outdoor environments. IEEE Robot. Autom. Lett. 4(4), 4116–4123 (2019)
3. Fatemidokht, H., Rafsanjani, M.K., Gupta, B.B., Hsu, C.H.: Efficient and secure routing protocol based on artificial intelligence algorithms with UAV-assisted for vehicular ad hoc networks in intelligent transportation systems. IEEE Trans. Intell. Transp. Syst. 22(7), 4757–4769 (2021)
4. Guo, H., Huang, Z., Ho, Q., Ang, M., Rus, D.: Autonomous navigation in dynamic environments with multi-modal perception uncertainties. In: IEEE International Conference on Robotics and Automation, pp. 9255–9261 (2021). https://doi.org/10.1109/ICRA48506.2021.9561965
5. Shah, S., Dey, D., Kapoor, A.: AirSim: high-fidelity visual and physical simulation for autonomous vehicles. In: Field and Service Robotics, pp. 621–635 (2018)
6. Eppe, M., Gumbsch, C., Kerzel, M., Nguyen, P.D., Butz, M.V., Wermter, S.: Intelligent problem-solving as integrated hierarchical reinforcement learning. Nat. Mach. Intell. 4(1), 11–20 (2022)
7. Wang, S., Clark, R., Wen, H., Trigoni, N.: DeepVO: towards end-to-end visual odometry with deep recurrent convolutional neural networks. In: IEEE International Conference on Robotics and Automation, pp. 2043–2050 (2017)
8. Gandhi, D., Pinto, L., Gupta, A.: Learning to fly by crashing. In: IEEE International Conference on Intelligent Robots and Systems, pp. 3948–3955. IEEE (2017)
9. Jung, J.H., Choe, Y., Park, C.G.: Photometric visual-inertial navigation with uncertainty-aware ensembles. IEEE Trans. Robot. 38, 1–14 (2022). https://doi.org/10.1109/TRO.2021.3139964

10. Giusti, A., Guzzi, J., Cireşan, D.C., He, F.L., Schmidhuber, J., Di Caro, G., et al.: A machine learning approach to visual perception of forest trails for mobile robots. IEEE Robot. Autom. Lett. **1**(2), 661–667 (2015)

11. Huang, X., Deng, H., Zhang, W., Song, R., Li, Y.: Towards multi-modal perception-based navigation: a deep reinforcement learning method. IEEE Robot. Autom. Lett. **6**(3), 4986–4993 (2021)

12. Theile, M., Bayerlein, H., Nai, R., Gesbert, D., Caccamo, M.: UAV path planning using global and local map information with deep reinforcement learning. In: International Conference on Advanced Robotics, pp. 539–546 (2021)

13. Maciel-Pearson, B.G., Akcay, S., Atapour, A., Garforth, J., Breckon, T.P.: Online deep reinforcement learning for autonomous UAV navigation and exploration of outdoor environments. arXiv preprint arXiv:1912.05684 (2019)

Design and Control of an Intelligent Robot System for Metro Bottom Inspection

Wei Zhou[1,2], Juntai Zhang[1,3], Yuan Ji[1,3], Qiyang Zuo[1,3], and Kai He[1,3(✉)]

[1] Shenzhen Institute of Advanced Technology, Chinese Academy of Sciences, Shenzhen 518055, China
kai.he@siat.ac.cn

[2] College of Mechanical Engineering, Yanshan University, Qinhuangdao 066004, China

[3] Shenzhen Key Laboratory of Precision Engineering, Shenzhen 518055, China

Abstract. To replace the manual work on the daily inspection of critical components of the metro bottom, such as the loose bolts, cracks, foreign bodies, and bogies. We propose a design and control method for an intelligent inspection robot that has been developed. The paper mainly introduces the technical approach from the overall structure design and system software and hardware design of the inspection robot and emphasizes the system integration method of the robot system design and control. The designed inspection robot can autonomously move between the inspection trenches according to the planned path, conduct the autonomous inspection of the metro bottom with a lateral guide and return exceptional conditions and positions, and purge the dust on the inspection location. In addition, users can view the running status and inspection results of the inspection robot in real-time through the remote control center.

Keywords: Metro bottom inspection · Autonomous localization and navigation · Deep learning · Mobile robot

1 Introduction

The bottom structure of the metro vehicle is complex, and there are many small parts. Therefore, it is inspected in the factory, which consumes more human and material resources, and there may be missed inspections. Manual inspection mainly relies on the inspectors to complete by seeing, listening with ears, touching with hands, and hammering. Therefore, the efficiency is low, and the labor intensity is high. The experience level of the train inspector and the degree of fatigue during the test will impact the test results of the bottom of the vehicle.

Supported by NSFC-Shenzhen Robot Basic Research Center project (U2013204) and SIAT-CUHK Joint Laboratory of Precision Engineering.

Corresponding inspection robots have appeared for the bottom maintenance of metro vehicles [1–5], but most are still in the experimental stage, and the relevant functions and technologies are not very mature. In addition, the existing metro bottom inspection robot is mounted with only one mechanical arm with vision detection module. Hong Kong metro introduced the operation and maintenance inspection robot developed by China's high-speed railway to carry out the daily maintenance work of metro vehicles [6]. However, in practical applications, the inspection robot still has many shortcomings and needs to be improved. For example, the inspection robot used the track for positioning and navigation, and the inspection robot can only detect on the track. On the one hand, the layout of the rails is complicated, and the existing environment needs to be retrofitted. On the other hand, the track is arranged in the middle of the detection trench so that the arm span cannot be extended to the two sides of the metro vehicle, resulting in a detection blind spot. The detection accuracy of the current inspection robots is not high, and the maintenance efficiency is also relatively low, which cannot meet the expectations of the bottom inspection of metro vehicles. In addition, the bottom of the metro vehicle is often covered with the dust during maintenance, as shown in Fig. 1. No matter how high-definition the camera is or how excellent the algorithm is, it is impossible to accurately identify and judge its fault. The dust must be removed first, as shown in Fig. 2, to ensure the normal operation of the inspection robot. And this kind of manual pre-wiping method will greatly reduce the practical application value of intelligent inspection.

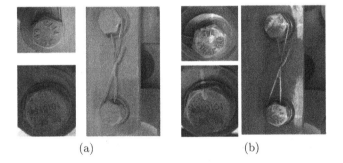

(a)   (b)

Fig. 1. Bolts at the bottom of the metro vehicle. (**a**) Before dusting. (**b**) After dusting.

In view of the mentioned problems faced by the bottom inspection of metro vehicles, the paper proposes and designs a dual-manipulator cooperative intelligent inspection robot with lateral guide. The robot can not only inspect and cover the bottom of metro vehicles in a full range, but also clean up dust to reduce missed inspections caused by dust. In addition, the developed robot system has an autonomous positioning and navigation system, a deep learning detection system and a remote monitoring system, which improves the intelligence and operability of the inspection robot. This paper is organized as follows:

Sect. 2 mainly introduces the structural characteristics of the intelligent inspection robot system at the bottom of the metro vehicle. Section 3 mainly introduces the hardware platform and intelligent control system. Section 4 mainly introduces the experiments of the inspection robot positioning and navigation system and visual recognition system. Finally, we draw conclusions and discuss future work in Sect. 5.

2 Inspection Robot Mechanical Structure

According to the on-site investigation on the bottom of the vehicle, many screws have much dust whose adsorption is tight on the surface. It needs to wipe hard, which seriously affects visual recognition. Therefore, according to the actual application requirements, the inspection robot structure is mainly divided into three parts: dust cleaning structure, vision inspection structure, and lateral movement structure, as shown in Fig. 2.

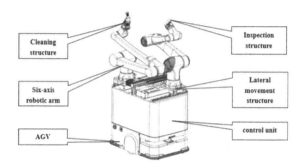

Fig. 2. Mechanical structure of intelligent inspection robot for metro vehicles

2.1 Dust Cleaning Structure

The dust cleaning structure mainly uses to clean the dust before the visual inspection, as shown in Fig. 3. It consists of a six-axis robotic arm, a force sensor, and an electric brush. The electric brush connects with the force sensor that fixes on the mechanical arm. During operation, it is judged whether the area inspected needs clean the dust by visual positioning. If necessary, the robotic arm moves to the area that needs clean, and determines whether it is in the correct place by vision feedback. When cleaning the dust, set the appropriate force according to the actual needs. After cleaning, it is going to identify the defects.

2.2 Visual Inspection Structure

Visual inspection structure can locate key components and detect anomalies, as shown in Fig. 4. This structure is mainly composed of a six-axis robotic arm and 3D vision. The position and angle of the camera can adjust by moving the robotic arm to locate and detect different features.

Fig. 3. Cleaning structure

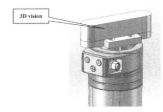

Fig. 4. Structure of visual inspection

2.3   Lateral Movement Structure

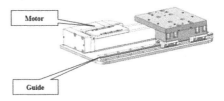

Fig. 5. Mechanical arm lateral movement structure

Lateral movement structure mainly realises the lateral movement of the mechanical arm to increase the dust cleaning and visual inspection range, as shown in Fig. 5. This structure consists of a linear motor that fixes on mechanical arm and a moving guide track. The linear motor drives the mechanical arm to move laterally, and cleans and detects the dust at the edge position.

The designed inspection robot for the bottom of the metro vehicle has a decoupled modular structure, which makes the robot system easy to maintain and manage. Furthermore, these modular mechanisms make the control and kinematics of the robot easy.

3   Inspection Robot Hardware Platform and Intelligent Control System

The hardware system of the inspection robot is showed in Fig. 6. Multiple hardware modules interconnect without interfering, which can expand in a network. The process can be automated and intelligently called according to functional needs. It can load multiple collaborative robot arms and automatically change the end effector structure. It can autonomously perceive the environment through cameras and laser lidars to automatically complete maintenance operations. The system has good reliability and maintainability, and can adapt to complex market demands.

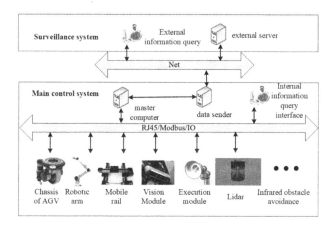

Fig. 6. System hardware platform

The hardware system mainly includes:

- Linux-based host computer control platform with rich expansion interfaces and mature function packages.
- Control scheme of AGV chassis and multi-cooperative manipulator based on TCP network, easy to expand.
- Real-time image acquisition hardware based on 2D and 3D cameras, through image processing technology to achieve high-precision, high-efficiency, high-performance defect detection of key components of the vehicle bottom.
- In addition to the above-mentioned core components such as industrial control motherboards, collaborative robot controllers, chassis motherboards, and camera hardware, it also includes peripherals such as displays, switching power supplies, guide, vision cameras, actuators, and lidars.

On the basis of hardware, develop a host computer platform integrating perception, decision-making and control. It mainly includes real-time perception layer, such as visual perception, laser ranging perception. Real-time decision-making layer includes perception data access, process analysis and prediction.

For example, the control layer controls the movement of the collaborative robot and the chassis according to the decision information, and completes the detection operation, interface interaction, abnormal monitoring. The software structure is showed in Fig. 7.

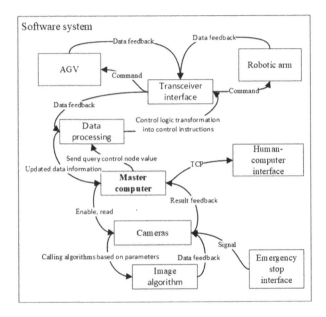

Fig. 7. Modular and intelligent software structure

4   Intelligent Control System Experiment

On the basis of the developed inspection robot hardware platform, positioning and navigation system, visual recognition detection system and inspection robot debugging system. Experiments are carried out on the positioning accuracy, path tracking and speed control. In addition, the recognition accuracy of the deep learning-based visual inspection system is verified. The interface of the remote control system used during the experiment is showed in Fig. 8.

In practical applications, the maintenance trench for metro vehicles is relatively narrow, which is a straight channel. Therefore, the positioning and navigation experiment is carried out in the aisle of the laboratory, mainly to verify the positioning accuracy and linear path tracking of the inspection robot. The experimental equipment and experimental scene are showed in Fig. 9. By manually controlling the inspection robot, the environment 2D map is built. Then the inspection robot moves to the aisle and mark the robot's current pose on the established map. There are four points that include the position and orientation

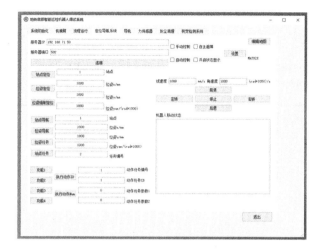

Fig. 8. Debugging system of intelligent inspection robot for metro vehicles

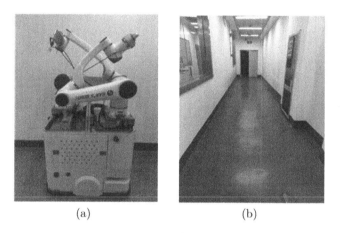

Fig. 9. Experimental equipment and experimental scene. (**a**) Rail vehicle bottom inspection robot. (**b**) Experimental environment.

of the robot to label the map in the aisle. The marked points are the target point of the inspection robot's navigation, and the connections between two adjacent target points are the target driving path of the robot.

The autonomous navigation of the inspection robot is started by the remote debugging system, navigating to four marked points respectively. A sampling frequency 3 Hz is used to collect the estimated pose and robot velocity values during navigation. Nine repeated experiments are carried out, and the path tracking results of the inspection robot were obtained from the pose estimation values, as shown in Fig. 10. In the aisle, the robot moves in the x direction of the map. According to the position estimated value in the y direction and the estimated value of the yaw angle, the straight-line driving effect of the robot is obtained, as shown in Fig. 11. After the robot reaches the target point, the positioning accuracy of the robot according to the comparison between the position estimate and the actual target value is showed in Fig. 12. The speed control of the robot is showed in Fig. 13.

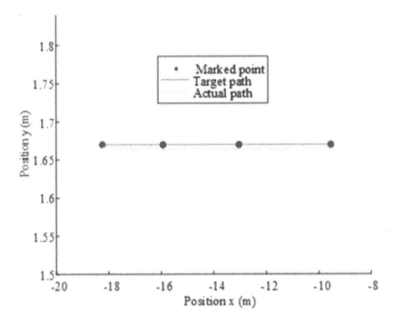

Fig. 10. Robot path tracking.

From the experimental results, the average position error of the yaw angle of the inspection robot is $-0.2°$, the average position error of the position x is 2.65 mm, and the average position error of the position y is -5.35 mm. Therefore, compared with the target path, the maximum error is 7 mm on the bottom of the target path of the inspection robot. According to the actual application requirements of the bottom of the metro vehicle, the positioning accuracy, path tracking and the ability of the inspection robot to walk in a straight line in the inspection trench can be well satisfied (Fig. 14).

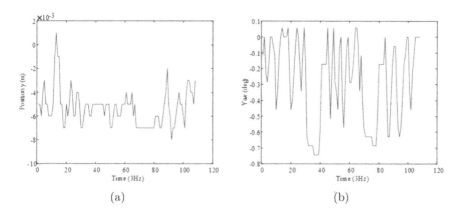

Fig. 11. Inspection robot travels in a straight line. (**a**) y-direction position fluctuation. (**b**) Yaw angle fluctuation.

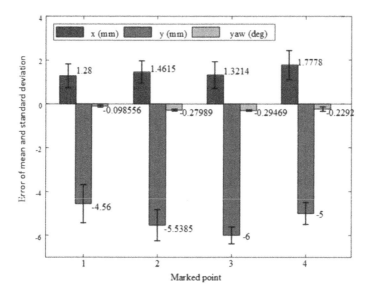

Fig. 12. Pose positioning error of mean and standard deviation.

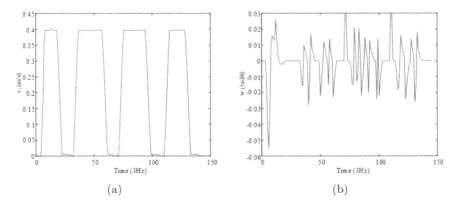

Fig. 13. Inspection robot speed control. (a) Linear velocity in the x direction. (b) Angular velocity.

For the bolt looseness detection project, based on the developed visual detection system and the following operation steps, the paper verifies the recognition accuracy of bolt looseness.

– Collect bolt data:
  1. On the tightened bolt, use a marker to mark the lock line as a reference line.
  2. Two-dimensional images of bolts with different angles, different distances and different lighting conditions are taken with a multi-eye camera, and the images of the bolts collected at this time are the images in the tightening state. Loosen the bolts at different angles, and take two-dimensional images of various situations again. The bolt images collected at this time are the images in the loosened state.
  3. Annotate the obtained bolt data set, and annotate different categories according to the bolt state: tightening state, loosening state, and unmarked line state.
  4. Divide the dataset into training set, test set, and validation set.
– Train a deep learning detection network with the training set.
– According to the loss curve of the training set and the loss curve of the validation set, judge whether the training is under-fitting, over-fitting, appropriate training, and adjust the training parameters.
– Test the model's detection rate, missed detection rate, correct recognition rate and false recognition rate of screw and bolt states and other indicators with the test set.

Based on the above steps, after identification and judgment by the visual inspection system, the inspection result is showed in Fig. 11 is finally obtained. As can be seen from the inspection results, the vision inspection system identifies almost all the bolts within the visual range, and has a fairly high accuracy rate in determining whether the bolts are loose or not.

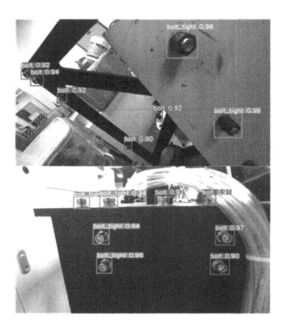

Fig. 14. Bolt detection renderings.

5   Conclusion and Future Work

Inspection requirements for key components such as loose bolts, cracks, foreign bodies, and bogies at the bottom of metro vehicles. The paper proposes and designs an intelligent inspection robot for the bottom of metro vehicles. The development of the prototype and the development and experiment of the control system have proved the feasibility, practicability and innovation of the scheme. The designed intelligent inspection robot has the following contributions:

- Double collaborative robotic arm with guide and dust cleaning structure.
- Advanced vision algorithm detection based on deep learning.
- Using a variety of sensor fusion perception, safe and efficient automatic inspection function.

In fact, system integration is very important for real robot application and commercialization, so later research will focus on algorithm and software design, and further research work is as follows:

- Optimize the visual recognition detection system, increase the training samples, improve the learning model, and improve the recognition accuracy.
- Solve the path planning problem of dual robotic arms in the process of robot vision detection and dust cleaning.
- Perfect system integration and remote monitoring software design.

References

1. Yue, S., Haishan, Z., Hao, Y., Zhen, J., ShenTao, J.: Research and design of a multi track daily inspection robot for urban rail transit. In: 2022 14th International Conference on Measuring Technology and Mechatronics Automation (ICMTMA), pp. 528–531(2022)
2. Shixi, S., Chao, Z.: Application of robot technology in metro vehicle maintenance. Mod. Urban Rail Transit. **08**, 105108 (2020)
3. Wang, J.: Design and research of intelligent inspection robot for railway locomotive and vehicle bottom. Res. Eng. Technol. **08** (2018)
4. Cheng, C.: Research on metro vehicle maintenance strategy based on Intelligent train inspection robot. Railw. Surv. Des. **02** (2020)
5. Zikai, Y., et al.: Inspection of exterior substance on high-speed train bottom based on improved deep learning method. Measurement **163**, 108013 (2020)
6. https://www.shenzhou-gaotie.com/gtszgt/gsdt/gsxw/webinfo/2020/11/160646279350124431.html

Autonomous Robot Navigation

An Improved Algorithm of Multi-robot Task Assignment and Path Planning

Yanming Liang and Haiyang Zhao[✉]

School of Automation and Information Engineering, Xi'an University of Technology,
Xi'an 710048, P.R. China
hanochzhao@qq.com

Abstract. For robots to operate effectively and swiftly in complicated environments, task assignment and path planning must be reasonable. However, many of the present algorithms distribute tasks to many robots without considering the surroundings, which results in arbitrary task allocations and interferes with path planning. To address the multi-robot task allocation and path planning (MRTA-PP) issue in complicated environments, this paper proposes an enhanced algorithm of the MRTA-PP based on the integration of the improved genetic algorithm (IGA) and the improved A* algorithm (IA*). First, the multi-robot task assignment (MRTA) problem was transformed into the multiple traveling salesman problem (MTSP) in this paper. Secondly, the IA* was proposed and used to solve the distance matrix consisting of the distances between task points. Then, the IGA was proposed, and the MTSP was solved based on the distance matrix using the IGA. Finally, the overall route of each robot was planned according to the solution using the IA*. The results demonstrate the efficacy of the enhanced algorithm of the MRTA-PP based on the integration of the IGA and the IA* (IGA-IA*), as proposed in this paper, in solving the MRTA-PP issue in complex environments.

Keywords: Multi-robot · Task assignment · Path planning · Multiple traveling salesman problem · A* algorithm · Genetic algorithm

1 Introduction

Robotics has advanced along with technology and culture, and more and more robots are being deployed in challenging circumstances. For instance, service robots were extensively deployed following the COVID-19 epidemic to limit human interaction and the potential for secondary transmission and cross-infection. Examples include interior delivery robots, restaurant service robots, and others. However, most interior service robots [1, 2] still operate alone at this moment, resulting in low efficiency and the inability to complete duties on schedule. Therefore, cooperation between several robots is crucial. However, there are still a lot of issues with robot cooperation [3–5], such as arbitrary duty distribution and path planning. Studying multi-robot work allocation and path planning techniques in complicated situations is crucial.

Map creation, task allocation, and path planning are the three primary components of multi-robot work allocation and planning in complicated situations. Methods for

Z. Yu et al. (Eds.): CIRAC 2022, CCIS 1770, pp. 71–82, 2023.
https://doi.org/10.1007/978-981-99-0301-6_6

assigning tasks can be categorized into two categories: centralized and distributed. The centralized approach requires a central processor to generate the task plan for the whole system and then pass the results to each robot. Centralized intelligent optimization algorithms such as the ant colony optimization [6], the particle swarm optimization [7], and the gray wolf optimization [8] have superior solutions to the MRTA problem. Although centralized methods yield better results globally, they rely on a large communication load and computational effort. In addition, the centralized approach is less robust, the robot is prone to a single point of failure, and it responds slowly to dynamically changing communications [9]. Distributed approaches do not require a central processor; each robot generates a list of tasks internally and then resolves conflicts with surrounding robots through communication. Distributed systems are able to respond quickly to changes in the external environment and are less dependent on communication bandwidth. Although the optimization results are not as good as centralized, the algorithm is more efficient and robust, and the impact of a single point of failure is smaller, which can cope well with the uncertainty of complex environments in the field. Game theory-based mechanisms and market-based mechanisms are the two primary categories of distributed methods. Game theory takes a comparatively longer convergence time, but the market-based auction algorithm is currently a popular and effective method.

Many researchers have done extensive research on task assignment. A multi-robot task assignment strategy based on an improved Gray Wolf optimizer (IGWO) was proposed in the literature [10]. The method first converts the MTSP into multiple TSPs and then solves the TSPs using the IGWO. The ideas are then combined to create the best solution for the MTSP. In order to analyze the task assignment issue in purposely cooperative multi-robot systems, the literature [11] suggests an axiomatic framework based on social choice theory. It is based on the well-known impossibility theory of Kenneth J. Arrow [12]. The proposed framework is analyzed using the Arrovian perspective in this literature to examine whether the implemented MRTA architecture is feasible. The literature [13] develops a decentralized job assignment algorithm based on submodule maximization that can be used in the practice of large-scale MRS. The primary goal is to provide optimal mathematical guarantees for monotonic submodular functions and non-monotonic functions with low processing complexity. A distributed strategy for solving the multi-robot task assignment problem has been described in the literature [14] by merging consensus-based bundling algorithms and ant colony systems. Consensus and inclusion are the two phases of the process. Each UAV creates a group of survivors during the inclusion phase utilizing an ant colony system. The UAVs use an appropriate coordination approach to settle disagreements in their survivor bundles during the consensus phase.

The above-mentioned literature focuses on the minimum time to complete the task as the objective function but does not consider the complexity of the paths and simply plans according to the Euclidean distance between nodes, leading to complex environments containing obstacles in some practical application scenarios, such as restaurants and libraries. Therefore, an enhanced algorithm based on the IGA-IA* is proposed in this paper to address the issue of MRTA-PP in complicated scenarios. The enhanced algorithm first transforms the MRTA problem in a complex environment into the MTSP. Secondly, it calculates the distance matrix consisting of the distances between task points and solves the MTSP based on the distance matrix. Finally, the overall route of each robot was planned according to the solution. The enhanced algorithm based on the IGA-IA* can successfully address the issue of MRTA-PP in complicated situations, as demonstrated by simulation results.

2   Mathematical Model

In order to maximize overall income, reduce task completion time and robot loss, many tasks must be assigned to various robots in the system to perform, and each robot's movement route must be planned. This is known as the problem of the MRTA and PP. The following restrictions on task simulation are made in this article, which focuses on single task, single robot, and delayed task allocation:

1) All robots move in a two-dimensional plane, regardless of height.
2) The robots all travel at the same speed.
3) The robot is capable of completing all duties that have been given to it.
4) When accomplishing the prescribed work, the robot only worries about the distance it must go in order to finish the assignment; it gives no thought to how long it will take to complete the task.

The MTSP takes a_0 as the starting point and $A = \{a_1, a_2, \ldots, a_n\}$ as the task points, which requires m individuals $(b_1, b_2, \ldots, b_m)$ to access and return to the initial point a_0. Define variables.

$$x_{ij}^k = \begin{cases} 1, b_k \text{ from } a_i \text{ to } a_j \\ 0, \text{ otherwise} \end{cases} \tag{1}$$

$$y_i^k = \begin{cases} 1, b_k \text{ visit } a_i \\ 0, \text{ otherwise} \end{cases} \tag{2}$$

The robot b_k moves from task point a_i to task point a_j when $x_{ij}^k = 1$. The robot b_k does not go from task point a_i to task point a_j when $x_{ij}^k = 0$.

The condition $y_i^k = 1$ indicates that the robot b_k has arrived at task point a_i and has been given the task at that moment. Similar to this, $y_i^k = 0$ indicates that robot b_k is not given the task point a_i task.

The expression of the distance matrix C is found in Eq. (3), which is consisted of the distances between of task points.

$$C = \begin{bmatrix} c_{11} & \cdots & c_{1j} \\ \vdots & \ddots & \vdots \\ c_{i1} & \cdots & c_{ij} \end{bmatrix}_{n \times n} \quad i, j = 1, 2, \ldots, n \tag{3}$$

$$z_k = \sum_{i=0}^{n} \sum_{j=0}^{n} c_{ij} x_{ij}^k \quad k = 1, 2, \ldots, m \tag{4}$$

c_{ij} is the distance between a_i and a_j. In the MTSP model, c_{ij} is generally the Euclidean distance between two points. However, in a complex environment, the robot cannot move to the task point in a straight line, so the actual moving distance of the robot from a_i to a_j should be taken as the distance c_{ij} between a_i and a_j. z_k is the distance that the robot b_k needs to move to complete all the assigned tasks. The objective function and constraints are as follows:

$$Z_D = \sum_{k=1}^{m} z_k \tag{5}$$

$$\sum_{k=1}^{m} y_i^k = \begin{cases} m, i = 0 \\ 1, i = 1, 2, \ldots, n \end{cases} \tag{6}$$

$$\begin{cases} \sum_{i=0}^{n} x_{ij}^k = y_j^k \\ \forall j = 0, 1, \ldots, n, k = 1, 2, \ldots, m \end{cases} \tag{7}$$

$$\begin{cases} \sum_{j=0}^{n} x_{ij}^k = y_i^k \\ \forall i = 0, 1, \ldots, n, k = 1, 2, \ldots, m \end{cases} \tag{8}$$

In this model, Eq. (5) shows the minimum and average distances traveled by each traveler; Eq. (6) shows that a particular traveler strictly visits each city from a_0 only once; Eq. (7) shows that each arc's end city has only one starting city connected to it; and Eq. (8) shows that each arc's beginning city has only one ending city connected.

3 Problem Solving

An analysis of formulas (3), (4), and (5) in the mathematical model of the MRTA issue shows that the necessary conditions for solving the objective function are the known distances between the task points. As a result, the distance matrix C is known. The distance between two places is no longer relevant in complicated situations, though. Assuming that the Euclidean distance between the task locations can solve the objective function, the robot does global path planning in accordance with the results of the task assignment produced by the solution. Because there are unusual circumstances in complicated settings, the minimal moving distance needed for the robot to perform all jobs will not be achieved; hence, the task assignment outcome will not be optimum. In the real world, however, the distance that the robot travels from task point a_1 to task point a_2 is greater than the distance from the task point a_1 to the task point a_3. For instance, the Euclidean distance between task points a_1 and a_2 is smaller than the Euclidean distance between task points a_1 and a_3. . When the MTSP is solved, this unique scenario may produce inferior task allocation outcomes. Therefore, the enhanced algorithm based on the IGA-IA* successfully integrates the IA* with the IGA in order to tackle the problem of MRTA-PP in complicated environments.

3.1 The Improved A* Algorithm (IA*)

The A* algorithm [15] employs a heuristic function akin to the breadth-first search algorithm to analyze pathways and uses it to evaluate the predicted cost of the current node to the desired end point as well as the cost of the initial node to the current node. This combines the advantages of the breadth-first search technique and the D algorithm [16]. The output of the evaluation function, whose expression is as follows, is used to evaluate each node's input in a certain region around the current node.

$$f(\alpha) = g(\alpha) + h(\alpha) \tag{9}$$

$g(\alpha)$ is for the consumption cost already incurred from the starting node to the current node α; $h(\alpha)$ stands for the consumption cost anticipated to be required from the current node to the goal endpoint; and $f(\alpha)$ stands for the global surrogate value integrating the two separate costs. In Eq. (9), the variables $g(\alpha)$ and $h(\alpha)$ are mutually constrained, with $h(\alpha)$ being the heuristic function, one of the most significant variables impacting the temporal complexity of the A* algorithm.

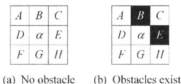

(a) No obstacle   (b) Obstacles exist

Fig. 1. Schematic diagram of adjacent nodes of node α

The traditional A* algorithm finds accessible nodes in two ways. The first method is horizontal and vertical search, whereas the second method is horizontal, vertical, and oblique search. Using the first search strategy to find the path may assure the mobile robot's safe journey. The second search strategy, on the other hand, does not, for the following reasons. The current node is considered to be α in Fig. 1, and the second search technique is utilized to discover accessible nodes. When there are no obstacle nodes near node α, as shown in Fig. 1(a), the robot can move safely from node to any of A, C, F, and H when doing an oblique search. When there are obstacle nodes near node α, as shown in Fig. 1(b), the robot can only move safely from node to node F when executing an oblique search. Because the robot is a volumetric entity, it will come into contact with nodes B or E when moving from node α to nodes A, C, or H. As a result, IA* is proposed in this paper, which avoids the aforementioned issues during the oblique search for nodes and can plan a better path. The pseudocode of the IA* is represented by algorithm 1.

Algorithm 1: the IA*
Input: *start, end, Map*
Output: *path, pathLength*

1:	$Checked \leftarrow \emptyset$, $Blocks \leftarrow \{start\}$
2:	**while** $Blocks \mathrel{!=} \emptyset$ **do**
3:	$\alpha \leftarrow Min(Blocks)$;
4:	**if** $\alpha == end$ **then**
5:	**return** *path, pathLength*;
6:	**end**
7:	$X_{near} \leftarrow GetNear(\alpha, Checked)$
8:	**for** each $x_{near} \in X_{near}$ **do**
9:	**if** x_{near} in $Blocks$ and $f(x_{near}) < f(Blocks[x_{near}])$ **then**
10:	$f(Blocks[x_{near}]) = f(x_{near})$;
11:	**else**
12:	$Blocks \leftarrow Blocks \cup \{x_{near}\}$;
13:	$f(\alpha x_{near}) = g(x_{near}) + h(x_{near})$;
14:	**end**
15:	**end**
16:	**if** $\alpha \mathrel{!=} start$ **and** $\alpha \mathrel{!=} end$ **then**
17:	$Checked \leftarrow Checked \cup \{\alpha\}$;
18:	**end**
19:	**end**

- *Map*: It represents a raster map.
- *start*: It represents the initial coordinates of the robot.
- *end*: It represents the coordinates of the robot's end point.
- *path*: It represents the movement path of the robot.
- *pathLength*: It represents the length of the robot's movement path.
- *Checked*: It represents the set of checked nodes.
- *Blocks*: It represents the set of nodes whose cost has been calculated.
- *GetNear*: It returns the surrounding passable nodes.

3.2   The Improved Genetic Algorithm (IGA)

The IGA initializes two populations during the population initialization procedure, in contrast to the classical genetic algorithm [17]. The first population's gene length is n, which represents a randomly distributed set of n task points. The second population's genes have an expanding array and a gene length of $m - 1$, therefore n may be allocated to m robots.

| 6 9 10 19 15 20 17 3 7 1 2 8 11 14 12 13 5 18 16 4 |

(a) Mission gene sequence

| 3 9 11 15 |

(b) Interrupt gene sequence

Fig. 2. Task gene sequence and interrupt gene sequence

For example, in Fig. 2, the analysis shows that $n = 20$ and $m - 1 = 4$. The interrupt gene sequence divides the task set into five parts and assigns them to robots in sequence. Thus, the task set of the first robot is [6, 9, 10], the task set of the second robot is [19, 15, 20, 17, 3, 7], the task set of the third robot is [1, 2], and the task set of the fourth robot is [8, 11, 14, 12], the task set of the fifth robot is [13, 5, 18, 16, 4].

Algorithm 2: the IGA

Input: C

Output: *TaskResult, TotalDis*

1: *popSize, Iter, minTask*;

2: *MissionGeneList* ← *InitMissionGene(popSize)*;

3: *InterruptGeneList* ←*InitInterruptGene(popSize, minTask)*;

4: *DisList* ← {}, *globalMinDis* = *Inf*;

5: **while** *iter = 1:Iter* **do**

6: *DisList* ← *CalDis(MissionGeneList, InterruptGeneList, C)*;

7: [*minDis, minIdx*] ← *Min(DisList)*;

8: **if** *minDis* < *globalMinDis* **then**

9:   *globalMinDis* = *minDis*;

10: *MissionGene* = *MissionGeneList[minIdx]*;

11: *InterruptGene* = *InterruptGeneList [minIdx]*;

12: **end**

13: *MissionGeneList* ← *CreateNewMissionGeneList(popSize)*;

14: *InterruptGeneList* ←*CreateNewInterruptGeneList(popSize, minTask)*;

15: **end**

16: *TotalDis* = *globalMinDis*;

17: *TaskResult* ← *AssignTask(MissionGene, InterruptGene)*;

- *nitMissionGene*: Given a population size, it returns the task gene set.
- *InitInterruptGene*: Given a population size, it returns the interrupt gene set.
- *CalDis*: Given *MissionGeneList, InterruptGeneList* and *C*, it returns a distance set.
- *CreateNewMissionGeneList*: It uses the method shown in Fig. 3 to generate a new set of task genes.
- *CreateNewInterruptGeneList*: It randomly generates a set of interrupted genes that meet the requirements.
- *AssignTask*: Given *MissionGene* and *InterruptGene*, it returns the corresponding task assignment result.

Algorithm 2 represents the pseudocode of the IGA, and Fig. 3 shows the method of generating new task genes in the IGA.

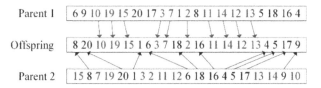

Parent 1 | 6 9 10 19 15 20 17 3 7 1 2 8 11 14 12 13 5 18 16 4

Offspring | 8 20 10 19 15 1 6 3 7 18 2 16 11 14 12 13 4 5 17 9

Parent 2 | 15 8 7 19 20 1 3 2 11 12 6 18 16 4 5 17 13 14 9 10

Fig. 3. Location-based crossover process

3.3   The Enhanced Algorithm Based on the IGA-IA*

The enhanced algorithm based on the IGA-IA* recognizes that in complicated situations, the Euclidean distance between task locations cannot be regarded as the actual distance between task locations. It successfully handles the MRTA-PP problem in complex situations by effectively integrating the IGA and the IA*. Algorithm 3 is the pseudocode of the enhanced algorithm based on the IGA-IA*.

Algorithm 3: The enhanced algorithm based on the IGA-IA*

Input: *TaskList, RobotList*
Output: *TaskResult, TotalDis, Path*
1:   **for** ecah *task* ∈ *TaskList* **do**
2:     **for** ecah *robot* ∈ *RobotList* **do**
3:       $C \leftarrow C \cup$ Algorithm1(*task, robot*);
4:     **end**
5:   **end**
6:   [*TaskResult, TotalDis*] ← Algorithm2(*C*);
7:   **for** ecah *robot* ∈ *RobotList* **do**
8:     **for** ecah *task* ∈ *TaskResult*{*robot*} **do**
9:       *Path* ← *Path* ∪ Algorithm1(*task, robot*);
10:   **end**
11: **end**

---

4   Experimental Study and Simulation Results

The enhanced algorithm based on the IGA-IA* proposed in this paper is intended to reasonably perform work allocation and route planning for multi-robots in complex environments. As a result, we chose to simulate algorithms in the master map environment shown in Fig. 4(a). The grid map is 52 × 52 in size and is rather intricate, making it an appropriate choice for the experimental simulation in this article.

Fig. 4. Raster map

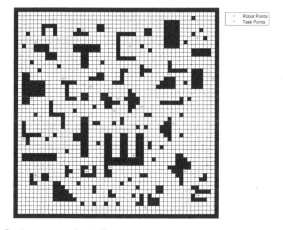

Fig. 5. Raster map including task coordinates and robot coordinates

As illustrated in Fig. 5, 20 randomly selected coordinates are chosen as task locations in the white region of this raster map, and it is assumed that the robots' beginning positions are all in the center of the map and that the robots must return to their initial places after completing the jobs. Two strategies are utilized in this work to perform experiments in order to validate the usefulness of the algorithm provided in this study. The first method assigns tasks using the IGWO, then plans paths using the IA*, and lastly calculates the total distance traveled. The second method is to calculate the overall moving distance using the enhanced algorithm based on the IGA-IA* proposed in this paper for task allocation and route planning. The number of robots in the simulation studies is gradually raised from 3 to 5, and the data is recorded in Table 1. The results of subsequent tests will not show the raster lines to avoid visual fatigue (Figs. 6, 7, 8).

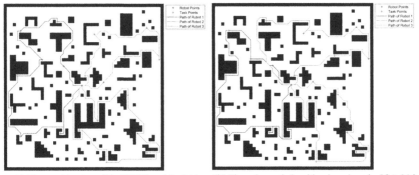

(a) The combination of the IGWO and the IA*   (b) The enhanced algorithm based on the IGA-IA*

Fig. 6. The simulation results with $m = 3$

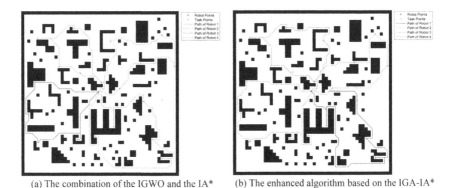

(a) The combination of the IGWO and the IA*   (b) The enhanced algorithm based on the IGA-IA*

Fig. 7. The simulation results with $m = 4$

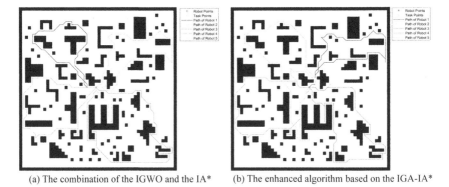

(a) The combination of the IGWO and the IA*   (b) The enhanced algorithm based on the IGA-IA*

Fig. 8. The simulation results with $m = 5$

Table 1 counts the moving distances of robots completing all the tasks for the enhanced algorithm based on the IGA-IA* and the combination of the IGWO and the

Table 1. Comparison of experimental results

Algorithm	The number of robots		
	3	4	5
The combination of the IGWO and the IA*	371.23	386.64	423.03
The enhanced algorithm based on the IGA-IA*	347.61	374.21	402.69

IA*. As shown in Table 1, when the number of robots is three, four, or five, the improved algorithm achieves shorter journey distances than the combination of the IGWO and the IA* for task allocation and route planning for several robots in complicated situations. It shows that the enhanced algorithm proposed in this paper outperforms the combination of the IGWO and the IA* in solving task allocation and route planning issues for several robots in complex environments.

5   Conclusion

In this paper, we improve the search method of the IA* and then propose the IGA to solve the MTSP. Based on these works, we propose the enhanced algorithm based on the IGA-IA* to address the issue of MRTA-PP in complex environments. The improved algorithm first transforms the MRTA problem in a complex environment into the MTSP. Secondly, to address the issue of erroneous usage of Euclidean distance in complex environments, it solves the distance matrix consisting of the distances between task points and solves the MTSP based on the distance matrix. Finally, the overall route of each robot was planned according to the solution. By resolving the problem of MRTA-PP in challenging situations and contrasting the outcomes with the combination of the IGWO and the IA*, the effectiveness of the enhanced algorithm based on the IGA-IA* was verified.

References

1. Hu, B., Yu, Q., Yu, H.: Global vision localization of indoor service robot based on improved iterative extended kalman particle filter algorithm. Journal of Sensors (2021)
2. Zheng, Y., Chen, S., Cheng, H.: Real-time cloud visual simultaneous localization and mapping for indoor service robots. IEEE Access **8**, 16816–16829 (2020)
3. Dong, S., Xu, K., Zhou, Q., et al.: Multi-robot collaborative dense scene reconstruction. ACM Trans.on Graphics (TOG) **38**(4), 1–16 (2019)
4. Lu, W., Zong, C., Li, J., et al.: Bipartite consensus-based formation control of high-order multi-robot systems with time-varying delays. Trans. Inst. Meas. Control. **44**(6), 1297–1308 (2022)
5. Matsui, N., Jayarathne, I., Kageyama, H., et al.: Local and global path planning for autonomous mobile robots using hierarchized maps. J. Robotics Mechatronics **34**(1), 86–100 (2022)
6. Trelea, I.C.: The particle swarm optimization algorithm: convergence analysis and parameter selection. Inf. Process. Lett. **85**(6), 317–325 (2003)

7. Manfrin, M., Birattari, M., Stützle, T., et al.: Parallel multicolony ACO algorithm with exchange of solutions. In: 18th Belgium–Netherlands Conference on Artificial Intelligence, BNAIC, pp. 409–410 (2006)

8. Mirjalili, S., Mirjalili, S.M., Lewis, A.: Grey wolf optimizer. Adv. Eng. Softw. **69**, 46–61 (2014)

9. Kim, K.S., Kim, H.Y., Choi, H.L.: A bid-based grouping method for communication-efficient decentralized multi-UAV task allocation. Int. J. Aeronautical Space Sci. **21**(1), 290–302 (2020)

10. Li, J., Yang, F.: Task assignment strategy for multi-robot based on improved grey wolf optimizer. J. Ambient. Intell. Humaniz. Comput. **11**(12), 6319–6335 (2020)

11. dos Reis, W.P.N., Lopes, G.L., Bastos, G.S.: An arrovian analysis on the multi-robot task allocation problem: analyzing a behavior-based architecture. Robot. Auton. Syst. **144**, 103839 (2021)

12. Campbell, D.E., Kelly, J.S.: Impossibility theorems in the arrovian framework. Handbook of Social Choice Welfare **1**, 35–94 (2002)

13. Shin, H.S., Li, T., Lee, H.I., et al.: Sample greedy based task allocation for multiple robot systems. Swarm Intell. **16**(3), 233–260 (2022)

14. Zitouni, F., Harous, S., Maamri, R.: A distributed approach to the multi-robot task allocation problem using the consensus-based bundle algorithm and ant colony system. IEEE Access **8**, 27479–27494 (2020)

15. AlShawi, I.S., Yan, L., Pan, W., et al.: Lifetime enhancement in wireless sensor networks using fuzzy approach and a-star algorithm. IEEE Sens. J. **12**(10), 3010–3018 (2012)

16. Zhou, R., Hansen, E.A.: Breadth-first heuristic search. Artif. Intell. **170**(4–5), 385–408 (2006)

17. Mirjalili, S.: Genetic algorithm. Evolutionary algorithms and neural networks. Springer, Cham, pp. 43–55 (2019). https://doi.org/10.1007/978-3-319-93025-1

Design and Implementation of a Collaborative Air-Ground Unmanned System Path Planning Framework

Yixuan Sun[1], Lin Li[1], Chenlei Zhou[2(✉)], Shaowu Yang[1], Dianxi Shi[1,2,3], and Haojia An[1]

[1] College of Computer, National University of Defense Technology, Changsha 410073, China
[2] Tianjin Artificial Intelligence Innovation Center(TAIIC), Tianjin 300457, China
zhouchenlei58@126.com
[3] Artificial Intelligence Research Center (AIRC), National Innovation Institute of Defense Technology (NIIDT), Beijing 100071, China

Abstract. This paper proposes an air-ground collaborative unmanned system path planning framework based on a specific search and rescue environment. In recent years, UAVs have been widely used in a variety of scenarios due to their many advantages, including aiding path planning for UGVs on the ground. Most path planning assumes a digital map. However, in situations where a map is not available, especially in search and rescue operations where the operating environment is often a disaster or post-disaster area, it is very difficult for ground-based UGVs to explore the unknown environment. The use of UAVs flying in the airspace above the UGV enables a rapid search of the surrounding environment and guides the rescue operations of the UGV. Ground-based UGVs carrying rescue facilities can enable rescue operations that cannot be completed by UAVs. Therefore, we propose a collaborative air-ground cross-domain unmanned system path planning framework, with the generation of global paths based on the improved A* algorithm. Based on this, path management is used to update the waypoints. The path tracking algorithm PID and collision avoidance method VFH are used to optimise the local paths. A visual guidance method is introduced to ensure that the UAS is as close to the target as possible to complete the mission. Finally, extensive simulation experiments are conducted to verify the feasibility of the approach.

Keywords: Air-ground cooperation · UAVs · UGVs · Path planning · Search and rescue

1 Introduction

Unmanned systems can perform more new and complex tasks for humans in both civil and military applications, such as urban scene reconstruction [1], underground environmental exploration[2], unmanned piloting [3], aerial photography [4] and search and rescue operations [5, 6]. Common intelligent unmanned systems include unmanned aerial vehicles (UAVs), unmanned ground vehicles (UGVs) and unmanned ships. In the case of air-ground cooperation, for example, UAVs work and communicate closely with UGVs to achieve distributed coordination of tasks in the execution of actual missions. UAVs can be seen as an extension of the freedom of UGVs in the airspace. Search and rescue missions are a typical application of air-ground unmanned systems working in tandem. The operational environment for search and rescue operations is usually a disaster or post-disaster area. The exploration of unknown environments by ground UGVs is difficult. UAVs flying in the overhead airspace in conjunction with UGVs enable rapid search of the surrounding environment and guide the UGV's rescue operations. Ground-based UGVs carry rescue facilities to enable rescue operations that cannot be carried out by drones.

We focus on the collaborative movement planning of airspace UAVs and UGVs in a specific search and rescue mission. The aim is to search for and extinguish fires within the scene and to detect surrounding hazards and carry them to a safe location. In other words, we consider a typical fire rescue application scenario, navigated by real-time motion planning. The air-ground collaborative unmanned cluster system is able to reach the vicinity of the fire point and transport hazardous materials to a safe location in the best possible time in an unknown environment. Our main contributions are as follows.

- An improved A* algorithm is proposed as a global path planning method, which is combined with multiple methods to achieve autonomous navigation of unmanned systems. A global path is first planned from the start point to the target point. Based on this, path management is used to update the waypoints. Local paths are optimised using path tracking and collision avoidance. A visual guidance method is introduced to ensure that the UAS is as close to the target as possible to complete the mission.
- Build a complete framework of path planning methods for air-ground cooperative unmanned systems. The method is able to navigate autonomously to a target point in a specific search and rescue scenario, and to complete a collaborative area search task for multiple unmanned systems in an unknown environment.
- The proposed framework approach is validated by simulation on a high-fidelity robotics simulation platform. The experiments fully demonstrate the feasibility of the collaborative air-ground UAS path planning framework in practical scenarios.

The first part of this paper provides the problem background and research significance of collaborative air-ground unmanned system motion planning. The second part introduces the relevant research and important techniques for motion planning of unmanned systems. The third part describes the architecture of our collaborative air-ground UAS motion planning method for search and rescue scenarios and explains the technical details involved in the practical planning of collaborative air-ground UAS. The fourth section presents the simulation experiments and results analysis of the system.

2   Related Work

In recent years, it has become popular for unmanned systems to work together. Many studies have addressed the cooperative problem of collaborative air-ground motion planning. Collaborative autonomous navigation aims to enable unmanned systems to generate a feasible trajectory from origin to destination through motion planning in an unknown environment. The literature [7] has made a seminal contribution to the work on collaborative air-ground autonomous navigation. In this paper, the UAV first generates a map which is then used to design the navigation controller and plan the mission of the UGV on the ground. With a pre-given map of the environment, a distributed and hierarchical approach to path planning is proposed in the literature [8]. In which an aerial UAV performs the aerial task and a ground-based UGV acts as a support to provide a safe landing zone for the UAV. For unknown and complex environments, literature [2] proposes a waypoint planning algorithm for the collaboration of UAVs and UGVs to perform search and rescue missions in underground environments. Through multi-sensor fusion, the UAV can localise the UAV and perform UAV trajectory planning, with the goal of the planning algorithm being to satisfy the mission detection criteria while reducing the error in UAV localisation.

For the path planning of air-ground cooperative unmanned systems, a hybrid path planning method is proposed in the literature [9]. This method uses genetic algorithms for global path planning and continuously uses rolling optimisation algorithms for local paths. This algorithm allows for less costly paths to be obtained. Based on this, the literature [10] uses UAVs as eyes to explore unknown environments, collecting surrounding information in real time and generating trajectories to guide ground-based UGVs around obstacles. The UAV is primarily based on a computer vision approach to identify the location of the obstacle and plan a feasible path from the starting point to the end point. Drones can therefore be seen as an extension of the UGV to spatial freedom.

The literature [11] applies collaborative UAV and UAV path planning to the mission of Mars exploration. A strategic path planner was designed to calculate the paths of the air-ground cooperative unmanned cluster to all exploration target points. The path planning focuses on the energy constraint of the unmanned cluster and models the ground-based UGV as a mobile charging station to sustain the UAV's exploration operations. More recent research results, such as in the literature [12], extend the area coverage task that UAVs cannot perform alone to air-ground collaborative unmanned clusters, with the goal of minimising time to complete a high coverage rate as the path planning goal. First, the UAV and UGV trajectory planning problem is transformed into a large-scale 0–1 optimisation problem. Based on this, a hybrid method combining a distribution estimation algorithm and a genetic algorithm is proposed and validated by simulation experiments.

3   System Design and Technical Details

In this paper, we design autonomous collaborative motion planning for UAVs and UGVs to solve the problem of search and rescue in specific scenarios. The main objective is to navigate autonomously through an unknown environment to reach the point of fire to extinguish the fire and carry hazardous materials to a safe location. The aerial rotary wing UAV has the advantage of hoverability and a global field of view for the detection, identification and localisation of target points or obstacles. Ground-based UGVs have the advantages of long range and accurate target location. We construct the environment map dynamically by laser SLAM algorithm and through the autonomous navigation system based on path planning. The final movement control of the unmanned system to the target point is achieved.

3.1 System Framework

We set the scene for a fire in an area of the city where a number of flammable and explosive materials may be present in the vicinity. The extent of the fire is known, the detailed location of the fire, the exact fire situation and the detailed location of the hazardous materials are unknown. The rescue centre sends an air-ground unmanned cluster system consisting of a ground command console, an aerial patrol drone, an aerial firefighting drone, a ground patrol drone and a ground rescue drone to search and rescue the area and complete the firefighting and hazardous material handling tasks. The search and rescue process is shown in Fig. 1. First, the patrol UAV is instructed to search for the fire in a designated area. The patrol UAV carries sensors that allow it to cover the fire area. It is responsible for obtaining information on the location of the fire spot and converting the coordinates of the fire spot into coordinates available to the UGV. The firefighting UAV receives information about the fire point and navigate autonomously to the fire point to extinguish the fire and assess its status afterwards. Once the ground patrol UGV has received information about the fire point, it starts patrolling the area around the fire point to detect the presence of dangerous goods. If hazardous materials are detected, the patrol UGV sends a signal to the ground rescue UGV. After receiving information about the location of the hazardous materials, the ground rescue UGV goes to the target point and transports the hazardous materials to a safe place.

The prototype system of the air-ground cross-domain collaborative path planning algorithm is shown in Fig. 2. Our work is based on the underlying hardware and robot operating system. The underlying communication and interoperability protocol layer is mainly through DDS distributed communication. This approach enables information sharing of positional information and collaborative reconnaissance targets between unmanned platforms across domains. In the autonomous navigation system layer, the implementation of target detection and localisation, and SLAM map construction all build on previous work. Path planning is the key layer of this system. We use global path planning as the basis and add path management, collision avoidance, path tracking and visual guidance to ensure that the unmanned system reaches the target point location quickly. Collaborative control of the unmanned systems is achieved through behavioural tree scheduling and task allocation.

3.2 Coordinate Transformation

There are multiple heterogeneous sensors in the air-ground collaborative unmanned cluster. The results of the collaborative target detection are in the form of GPS coordinates. In contrast, the autonomous navigation and path planning of the ground-based unmanned system is based on a robotic SLAM map coordinate system. Therefore an interconversion of the two coordinate systems is required. In addition, the fusion of GPS data for SLAM map building requires the conversion of the GPS coordinate system data to the robot SLAM map coordinate system. This is achieved in the middle with the help of the ENU coordinate system. Here, the WGS84 coordinate system is used for GPS. The

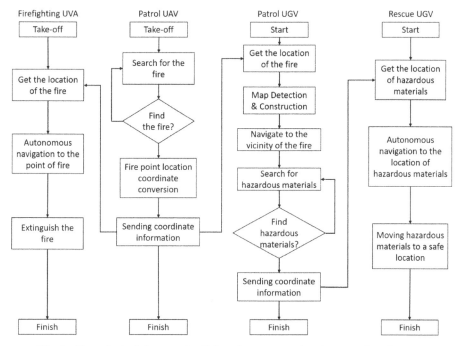

Fig. 1. Flow chart of air-ground collaborative unmanned system search and rescue.

same GPS position of all the air-ground cross-domain unmanned systems is first used as the origin of the ENU coordinate system. Then the standard GIS conversion algorithm is used to transform the GPS coordinates into ENU coordinates $[e, n, 1]^T$. Finally, the GPS coordinates $[a, b, 1]^T$ and the yaw angle θ at the initial moment of the robot are used to obtain the SLAM map coordinate system $[x, y, 1]^T$ through the transformation matrix. This method achieves the conversion of coordinate data between the two coordinate systems. The equation of the transformation matrix is as follows.

$$\begin{pmatrix} x \\ y \\ 1 \end{pmatrix} = \begin{bmatrix} \cos\theta & -\sin\theta & a \\ \sin\theta & \cos\theta & b \\ 0 & 0 & 1 \end{bmatrix} \begin{pmatrix} e \\ n \\ 1 \end{pmatrix} \tag{1}$$

3.3 Global Path Planning and Path Management

Path planning means finding a collision-free path from the start point to the target point in an obstacle-prone environment, subject to certain constraints. The path management processes the track points of the path planning, including track point updates, heading additions and dynamic updates of target points. In order to obtain fast and safe movement paths in an air-ground cross-area collaborative unmanned system emergency rescue scenario, this paper improves on the classical A* algorithm. We propose fast and safe path planning and path management algorithms for ground-based UGVs.

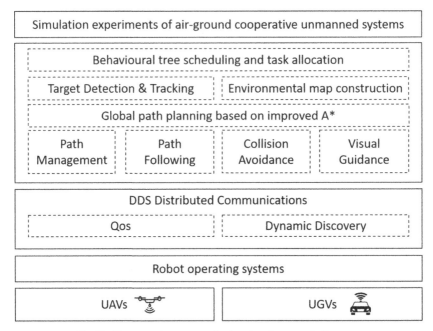

Fig. 2. Unmanned system path planning framework diagram.

Global Path Planning. The traditional A* algorithm performs a search with equal search weights in all directions. It does not consider the current orientation of the UAS and often results in planning the resulting path in the opposite direction to the current orientation of the unmanned system. Therefore, a backward or in-situ rotation must be performed in order to perform path following. This is less efficient for practical applications for unmanned systems where cooperative reconnaissance sensors are located in front or where rotation in place is difficult. To address this problem, we improve the classical A* algorithm. The current orientation of the unmanned system is introduced into the design of the cost function, and the improved A* algorithm cost function is designed as shown in Eq. (2).

$$f(n) = g(n) + w(n) * h(n) \tag{2}$$

where $f(n)$ denotes the cost of reaching the target node from the starting node via n nodes. $g(n)$ denotes the cost from the starting point to the current nth node. $h(n)$ denotes the surrogate value from the nth node to the end point. $w(n)$ is the weight that can influence the cost function and is taken as shown in Fig. 3. The value of $w(n)$ is set to be less than 1 for raster maps within the explored area, where the direction and the direction of the unmanned system are the same, as shown in the yellow area in the figure. For grids where the direction and the direction of the unmanned system do not match, set the value of $w(n)$ to be greater than 1, as shown in the blue area. For grids outside the exploration area, set the value of $w(n)$ equal to 1, equivalent to the normal A* algorithm. After physical and simulation tests, excluding scenes with particularly dense obstacles, the global path planned by the improved A* algorithm can effectively avoid the occurrence of reversing or rotating in place, with a success rate of over 90%.

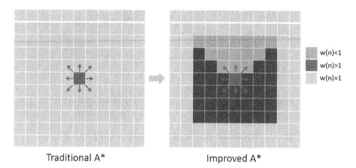

Traditional A*   Improved A*

Fig. 3. Improvement of the A* algorithm.

Path Management. Path management consists of track point updates and target point updates, as shown in Fig. 4. Based on the global paths planned by the improved A* algorithm, path management is achieved by waypoint updates. The update of the waypoints is mainly implemented by means of closures. When the UAS reaches the range of the blue circle in Fig. 4(a), the target point followed by the current path is updated to the next trajectory point. It is important to note that there is no direction information between the two track points, we add the heading information through the path management to achieve the path following. This is shown by the black arrow in Fig. 4(a).

When the target point received by the unmanned system is not reachable, the target point needs to be dynamically updated. As in Fig. 4(b), the coordinates of the fire point or hazmat location sent by the UAV are located right in the centre of the obstacle, at which point the target point is surrounded by the obstacle and is unreachable by the UGV on the ground. The global path planning algorithm fails and the UGV is stuck in a dead loop, unable to reach the target point through path tracking. For this scenario, we use a dynamic update mechanism of the target point to bring the unmanned system as close to the target point as possible. Starting from the target point, a point is taken every certain distance in the direction where the UGV is located, as shown in Fig. 4(b) at points A, B, C and D. Then the obstacle surrogate value of the unmanned system at each point is calculated. If the obstacle surrogate value is less than 0, it means that this target point is not located on an obstacle. We replace the dynamically calculated target point A, which has a non-zero obstacle surrogate value and is closest to the target point, with the new target point.

3.4 Trail Tracking, Collision Avoidance and Visual Guidance

Path tracking is the generation of control commands based on the results of global path planning to control the unmanned system to follow the specified path and keep moving towards the target point. During the unmanned system path tracking process,

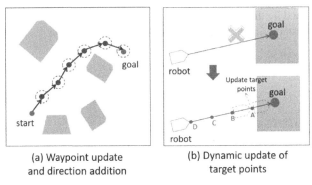

(a) Waypoint update   (b) Dynamic update of
and direction addition   target points

Fig. 4. Illustration of the path management process.

if there are dynamic or static unknown obstacles on the planned global path point, the unmanned system will perform autonomous collision avoidance. When the unmanned system detects a target feature in its field of view, it will no longer use the path tracking algorithm and will directly control the unmanned system to approach the target point through the vision guidance algorithm.

The path tracking algorithm uses the classical PID algorithm [13]. The core of the algorithm consists of a proportional unit, an integral unit and a differential unit. The algorithm characteristics can be adjusted by adjusting the gain weights of these three units. As in Eq. (3), K_p, K_i and K_d are all debugging parameters, K_p is the proportional gain, K_i is the integral gain, and K_d is the differential gain. e is the margin of error, t is the current period time, and τ is the integration variable.

$$u(t) = K_p e(t) + K_i \int_0^t e(\tau)d\tau + K_d \frac{d}{dt}e(t) \tag{3}$$

The collision avoidance algorithm instead uses the VFH algorithm [14], which is a navigation algorithm improved from the artificial potential field method. The core idea is to represent the obstacle occupancy of all grids and the effect on the direction of motion by means of a statistical histogram. Such a representation is ideally suited to the fusion of multi-sensor readings. First, the unmanned system continuously collects information about surrounding obstacles and updates the sensor data. Then, based on the data collected by the sensors, a polar co-ordinate obstacle density histogram is constructed, generating an angle to control the direction. Finally, based on the polar co-ordinate obstacle density histogram and density thresholds, combined with the minimum angle threshold for unmanned platform passage, a safe polar co-ordinate angle interval is selected to determine the direction of subsequent movement.

In order to effectively circumvent the target positioning deviation brought about by path planning, we also introduced a visual guidance algorithm to approach the target. In this scenario, even with precise path planning and path tracking algorithms, the UAS cannot control the maximum approach to the target. This would make subsequent disposal processes such as aerial firefighting and ground handling of hazardous materials impossible. We therefore use a visual guidance algorithm. Based on the PID algorithm, the aerial UAV calculates the linear velocity of the UAV in the X and Y directions towards the target centre point by means of the deviation of the coordinates of the target point pixel position and the image centre point pixel. Combining the X-directional deviation of the pixel position coordinates of the target point, the pixel coordinates of the image centre point and the depth information of the UAV from the target point, the X-directional linear velocity and the rotational angular velocity of the UAV towards the target point are calculated. After testing, the aerial and ground-based unmanned systems can be controlled to have a distance deviation of no more than 0.5m from the target centre point after visual guidance.

4   Experimental Results

This section validates the effectiveness of the air-ground collaborative unmanned cluster search and rescue system through simulation experiments implemented on the high-fidelity simulation platform GAZEBO [15]. We constructed a fire search and rescue scenario on GAZOBO and used two UAVs (a patrol UAV and a firefighting UAV) and two UGVs (a patrol UGV and a rescue UGV) to complete the search and rescue mission. The simulation scenario is shown in Fig. 5. The experimental environment is a 3D scene with known boundaries. Inside the scene are several obstacles of unknown number and shape, a fire point of unknown location and several hazardous chemicals of unknown location.

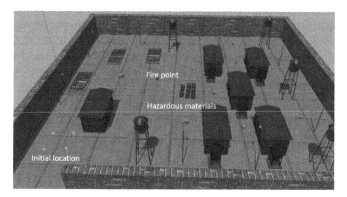

Fig. 5. Simulation scenario of an air-ground collaborative unmanned cluster search and rescue system.

4.1   Experimental Environment Configuration

The experimental configuration is shown in Table 1.

The patrol UAV is a DJI M210 quadcopter UAV with a Jetson Xavier NX development board, an integrated target detection plug-in that can identify fires, an H20 binocular camera cloud platform, a separate battery and a satellite positioning system. The firefighting UAV is also a DJI M210 quadcopter UAV that can be loaded with water

Table 1. Prototype system experimental environment configuration.

Type	Specific configuration
Hardware	CPU: 8-core i7–9700
	Communication: C-band single channel, bandwidth 5.8 GHz
	GPU: NVIDIA GTX-1050Ti
Software	Operating system: Ubuntu 20.04 64bit
	Development platform: micROS
	Simulation tools: Gazebo
	Programming language: Python, C++
Unmanned systems	UAV: M210 Quadcopter Drone
	UGV: HDZ-A
	Cloud Platform: H20
	Communication: GPS

tanks to perform the functional task of firefighting. It uses the Jetson Xavier NX development board as the core controller on board for motor drive and water spray control, and is equipped with the H20 binocular camera cloud platform, a separate battery and a satellite positioning system. The patrol UGV is an HDZ-A model emergency rescue UGV, equipped with a central computing unit with integrated autonomous navigation system, including a 16-line LiDAR sensor, depth camera D435i, RTK sensor, IMU sensor and GPS. It also has a central computing unit with an integrated autonomous navigation system, including a 16-line LiDAR sensor, depth camera D435i, RTK sensor, IMU sensor and GPS, and a robotic arm for handling hazardous chemicals. The ground station command console is a computer with Ubuntu 20.04. The unmanned platforms are all equipped with M110-502B communication boards with C-band single-channel communication and a bandwidth of 5.8 GHz.

4.2   Experimental Results and Analysis

The path of a single unmanned system is shown in Fig. 6. Paths for individual unmanned systems. Both the patrol UAV and patrol UGV follow a lawn mower pattern to search the area. The patrol UGV has a smaller search area than the patrol UAV, searching only within a fixed area near the fire point. The firefighting UAV chooses the shortest path to the fire when there are no obstacles in the air. The rescue UGV follows a planned path obstacle to the point of fire. The global path planning of the unmanned system is implemented on the basis of the improved A* algorithm. The improved A* algorithm plans a global path that effectively avoids reversing or rotating in place, as illustrated in Fig. 7(a), which shows the local trajectory of the UGV at the starting point. Figure 7(b) demonstrates the dynamic update of the target point from the centre of the object to the edge of the object reachable by the unmanned system. Figure 8 shows the visualisation of the polar co-ordinate obstacle density histogram and angular partitioning of the VFH collision avoidance algorithm. The zoning angle is 5°. The obstacle density threshold is set to 2. The angle threshold is set to 45°. Figure 9 shows the UGV view detecting a hazardous material label and the UGV approaching the hazardous material with visual guidance.

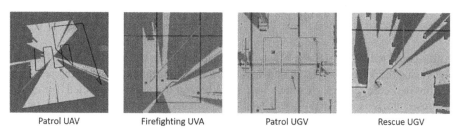

| Patrol UAV | Firefighting UVA | Patrol UGV | Rescue UGV |

Fig. 6. Paths for individual unmanned systems

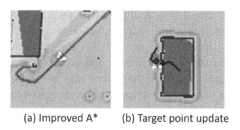

(a) Improved A*   (b) Target point update

Fig. 7. Validation of global path planning and path management

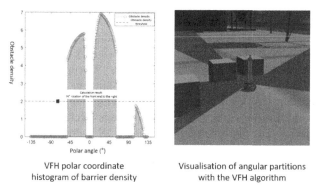

VFH polar coordinate
histogram of barrier density

Visualisation of angular partitions
with the VFH algorithm

Fig. 8. Experimental results of the VFH obstacle avoidance algorithm.

The collaboration between the air-ground cooperative unmanned systems is controlled by a behavioural tree. The complete experiment is shown in Fig. 1. Prior to the start of the search and rescue, the UAVs and UGVs are located on the boundary of the search and rescue scenario, as shown in Fig. 1(a). After receiving the activation signal from the ground station, the patrol UAV uses the existing area coverage method to plan

Fig. 9. Visually guided simulation demonstration.

an area patrol path similar to the "lawn mower pattern". The UAV moves along this path while using the YOLO-v3 [16] based target detection algorithm to identify the presence of a fire in the target area, as shown in Fig. 10(b). If a fire point is detected, the patrol UAV uses the TensorRT and CUDA parallel accelerated DasiamRPN [17] based target tracking algorithm to determine the location coordinate information of the fire point and sends this information to the ground station and other unmanned platforms. The firefighting UAV and patrol UGV receive the information about the fire point and then proceed to the fire point to perform tasks such as firefighting and hazardous material detection. Flying at high altitude, the firefighting drone is at a distance from low-level obstacles on the ground and there is no risk of collision between the two. It can therefore simply follow the closest straight-line path from its current coordinates to the point of fire and then lower its altitude to extinguish the fire, as shown in Fig. 10(c). In contrast, an unmanned ground patrol vehicle on the ground may be surrounded by a large number of obstacles. It needs to use its own loaded computing unit to build an autonomous SLAM map, and then to perform real-time online path planning to create a fast and collision-free path for the UGV. The patrol UGV arrives at the fire and starts patrolling the area following the path of coverage planned in "lawn mower mode". If hazardous materials are detected during the patrol, it sends information about their location to the ground station and other robots. Figure 10(d) shows the moment when the patrol UGV detects dangerous goods. After the ground rescue UGV receives the information on the location of the hazardous materials, it navigates autonomously using the location of the hazardous materials as a target point and travels to the vicinity of the hazardous materials to complete the handling task, as shown in Fig. 10(e). During this process, the patrol UAV and patrol UGV still patrol the area. After patrolling the entire target area, neither the UAV nor the patrol UGV finds any new targets, which means the search and rescue mission is over. At this point, the ground station sends a return command to the four unmanned platforms. The patrol UAV, firefighting UAV, patrol UGV and rescue UGV receive the command and return to their initial positions, as shown in Fig. 10(f).

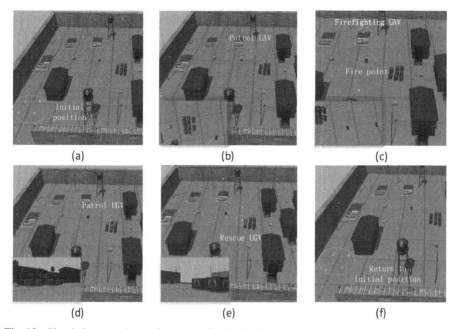

Fig. 10. Simulation experimental process of path planning for air-ground cooperative unmanned systems.

References

1. Kuang, Q., et al.: Real-Time UAV Path Planning for Autonomous Urban Scene Reconstruction. IEEE (2020)
2. Petrillo, M.D., et al.: Search Planning of a UAV/UGV Team with Localization Uncertainty in a Subterranean Environment (2021)
3. Sadat, A., et al.: Jointly Learnable Behavior and Trajectory Planning for Self-Driving Vehicles (2019)
4. Bonatti, R., et al.: Towards a robust aerial cinematography platform: localizing and tracking moving targets in unstructured environments. In: 2019 IEEE/RSJ International Conference on Intelligent Robots and Systems (IROS) IEEE (2019)
5. Haris, et al.: Integrated data management for a fleet of search-and-rescue robots. J. Field Robotics **34**(3), 539–582 (2016)
6. Likhachev, M., Gordon, G., Thrun, S.: ARA*: Anytime A* with Provable Bounds on Sub-Optimality. ibl.liu.se (2004)
7. Adaptive teams of autonomous aerial and ground robots for situational awareness. Journal of Field Robotics 24.11:991–1014 (2010)
8. Arbanas, et al.: Decentralized planning and control for UAV–UGV cooperative teams. Autonomous robots (2018)
9. Li, J., et al.: A hybrid path planning method in unmanned air/ground vehicle (UAV/UGV) cooperative systems. IEEE Transactions on Vehicular Technology (2016)
10. Lakas, A., et al.: A framework for a cooperative UAV-UGV system for path discovery and planning. In: 2018 International Conference on Innovations in Information Technology (IIT) (2018)

11. Ropero, F., Muñoz, P., R-Moreno, M.D.: A strategical path planner for UGV-UAV cooperation in mars terrains. In: Bramer, M., Petridis, M. (eds.) SGAI 2018. LNCS (LNAI), vol. 11311, pp. 106–118. Springer, Cham (2018). https://doi.org/10.1007/978-3-030-04191-5_8

12. Cooperative Path Planning of UAVs & UGVs for a Persistent Surveillance Task in Urban Environments (2021)

13. Misir, D., Malki, H.A., Chen, G.: Design and analysis of a fuzzy proportional-integral-derivative controller. Fuzzy Sets Syst. **79**(3), 297–314 (1996)

14. Borenstein, J., Koren, Y.: The vector field histogram - fast obstacle avoidance for mobile robots. IEEE Trans. Robot. Autom. **7**(3), 278–288 (1991)

15. Chen, L.S.: Gazebo. US, USD591867 S1 (2006)

16. Redmon, J., Farhadi, A.: YOLOv3: An Incremental Improvement. arXiv e-prints (2018)

17. Zhu, Z., Wang, Q., Li, B., Wu, W., Yan, J., Hu, W.: Distractor-aware siamese networks for visual object tracking. European Conference on Computer Vision (2018)

Artificial Intelligence and Cloud Robot

Wishart Deeplab Network for Polarimetric SAR Image Classification

Junfei Shi[1,2,3], Tiansheng He[2,3], Haiyan Jin[2,3(✉)], Hua Wang[1], and Weinan Xu[2,3]

[1] State Key Laboratory of Geo-Information Engineering, Xi'an 710048, Shaanxi, China
[2] School of Computer Science and Engineering, Xi'an University of Technology, Xi'an 710048, Shaanxi, China
jinhaiyan@xaut.edu.cn
[3] Shaanxi Key Laboratory for Network Computing and Security Technology, Xi'an 710048, Shaanxi, China

Abstract. Polarimetric Synthetic Aperture Radar (PolSAR) images have attracted much attention with abundant polarimetric scattering information. In recent years, many deep learning models have been proposed and highly expanded to PolSAR image classification. However, how to learn the complex matrix information is an indispensable problem. To address this problem, a Wishart Deeplab network is developed, which can not only learn the polarimetric matrix structure by designing Wishart network level but also learn multi-scale polarimetric scattering features by incorporating dilated convolution. Specifically, the Wishart-Deeplab based PolSAR classification model is constructed by designing the Wishart convolution operation to learn the statistical information of PolSAR data. Then, a deeplabV3 + network is followed to obtain the multi-scale semantic features by dilated convolution. By this way, statistical distrubtion-based and high-level semantic features are adaptively learned to improve the performance of the network. The experiments are conducted on two sets of real PolSAR data and results show that this method can obtain better classification results.

Keywords: PolSAR · Deeplab network · Wishart distance · PolSAR image classification

1 Introduction

Polarimetric synthetic aperture radar (PolSAR) is a microwave remote sensing detection technology by radar imaging, which is capable of obtaining multi-channel backscattered echo information from the Earth's surface and has the capability of all-weather, all-day imaging to the Earth. PolSAR image classification methods have been given and utilized in agricultural development, military monitoring, and other areas. Previous research approaches [1] have mainly used shallow approaches to classify images, such as artificial neural network-based remote sensing data analysis [2], support vector machine-based classification algorithms [3], and neural network-based Wishart classification algorithms [4]. Later, deep learning models have been widely applied in PolSAR

Z. Yu et al. (Eds.): CIRAC 2022, CCIS 1770, pp. 99–108, 2023.
https://doi.org/10.1007/978-981-99-0301-6_8

image classification[5]. Especially, convolutional neural networks(CNN) are developed for PolSAR classification. Different from traditional methods, deep learning does not command manual selection of image features but can automatically extract deeper features of images. Typical deep learning models include deep Boltzmann machines [6], Stacked Auto Encoders (SAE) [7], Deep Belief Network (DBN) [8], and Convolutional Neural Network (CNN) [9, 10] and so on.

Deep learning has been rapid developed for remote sensing image processing. For example, Saito et al. [11] used CNN for road and building detection, and Bentes et al. [12] used CNN for ship and iceberg recognition. However, the above methods are designed for the regular patch input, which cannot eliminate the discontinuities on the edges of the image. In addition, Jiao et al. [13] utilized the polarimetric coherency matrix into the stacked neural network by designing optimized Wishart metric (W-DSN), which can learn the polarimetric information effectively. However, only single pixel is learned in the stacked network, which ignores the spatial relationship between neighboring pixels. Later, the fully convolutional networks (FCN) framework[14] is proposed for semantic informiration, which is based the image block to achieve semantic segmentation to improve the classification accuracy. To learn semantic information, the deeplab network [15, 16] is proposed, which can obtain more homogeneous semantic segmentation result by using the dilated convolution and Xception model. In short, deep convolutional neural networks can learn deeper features of images.

Although many research results have been obtained for the PolSAR image classification, the deep learning method that performs well in optical images still has large limitations for PolSAR images due to its unique imaging mechanism and characteristics. One is that it cannot learn some inherent polarimetric information and PolSAR data. The other is that the traditional convolutional layer in Euclidean space does not take the relationship among the feature channels into account. Therefore, the existing deep learning-based methods still have some problems, such as insufficient feature representation capabilities and imprecise edge segmentation.

To overcome the above problems, a Wishart deeplab network for PolSAR image classification is proposed. This model uses the Wishart convolutional network to learn the statistical information on the PolSAR data, which improves the ability of feature representation of the PolSAR data. Then, the DeeplabV3 + network is utilized to learn the contextual relationship and multi-scale features in the network. After fusing the Wishart convolution and DeeplabV3 + network, the polarimetric information is enhanced and semantic features are learned to improve the classification performance. Contracted with the traditional classification algorithms, the proposed model is customized for integrative polarimetric feature selection and classification tasks. The end-to-end training mode ensures that polarimetric features that are beneficial to classification can be excited. This is beneficial to improve the accuracy of classification.

2   Proposed Methodology

Inspired by the W-DSN method, a novel Wishart deeplab network model is proposed for classification of PolSAR images. It can learn the polarization matrix structure by designing the Wishart network layer and multi-scale features to realize the classification of ground objects.

The framework of the proposed Wishart deeplab network is given in Fig. 1. It contains Wishart distance and DeeplabV3 + network. Firstly, the vector form of the coherence matrix is used as the input, and the ResNet network is used to calculate the Wishart distance of the category of convolution kernel to obtain the feature map; Secondly, depth separable network, hole convolution network and atrous spatial pyramid are utilized to learn the spatial relationship between pixels; Then, the Wishart feature map and the spatial relationship feature map are fused, and restored to the original image size through 3×3 convolution kernel convolution and upsampling. Finally, the classification layer is used to judge the probability of the target to obtain the final classification result.

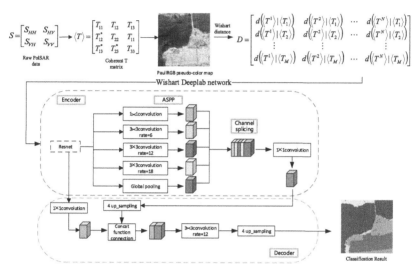

Fig. 1. The framework of the proposed Wishart deeplab network.

2.1 Wishart Convolution Structure

For PolSAR images, the coherency matrix and covariance matrix obey the complex Wishart distribution [17]. Therefore, a maximum likelihood classifier is utilized to classify the PolSAR image and the Wishart distance is derived to describe the distance between two pixels in the PolSAR image. The coherency matrix T of the PolSAR data is expressed as:

$$\langle T \rangle = \begin{bmatrix} T_{11} & T_{12} & T_{13} \\ T_{12}^* & T_{22} & T_{11} \\ T_{13}^* & T_{23}^* & T_{33} \end{bmatrix} \tag{1}$$

where T_{11}, T_{22} and T_{33} are real numbers, the others are complex numbers, and * represents the conjugate operation. The coherency T matrix satisfies the complex Wishart distribution, and a Wishart distance[17] is utilized to measure the distance between each pixel and category centers, and the category corresponding to the smallest distance is labeled to the pixel. The Wishart distance is defined as:

$$d(\langle T \rangle | \langle T_m \rangle) = Trace\left(\langle T_m \rangle^{-1} | \langle T \rangle\right) + ln|\langle T_m \rangle| \tag{2}$$

where $d(\langle T \rangle | \langle T_m \rangle)$ is the Wishart distance between the pixel T and the mth category center, T_m is the coherency matrix of the mth category center, $Trace(\bullet)$ denotes the trace operation of the matrix, $(\bullet)^{-1}$ denotes the inverse operation of the matrix, and $ln(\bullet)$ is the logarithmic operation.

Since the data format of the PolSAR is a complex matrix, it is necessary to add the complex matrix convolution to the neural network, and the computational process is complicated and not easy to implement the derivative for the complex matrix. Besides, the optimation resolving the complex matix network structure is also a challenge.

To solve the above problems, we utilized a Wishart convolutional network structure.to learn the complex matrix. Firstly, the original PolSAR data are filtered by Lee filter, then the filtered coherency matrix T is obtained; Secondly, the T matrix is transformed to $I(T) = [T_{11}, T_{22}, T_{33}, T_{12real}, T_{13real}, T_{23real}, T_{21imag}, T_{31imag}, T_{32imag}]$. Then, the Wishart convolution kernel [13] is used to extract features. In this convolution network structure, the Wishart distance is converted into the linear transformation, and a fast computing method is proposed. The convolution calculation is defined as:

$$y_{w,b}(T) = \sum_{i=1}^{c} T_i * w_i + b \tag{3}$$

where $*$ defines the convolution operation, T_i stands for the ith input data, w_i is the convolution kernel, and y is the computing result. Here, the convolution kernels are initialized as the initial clustering centers. Each convolution kernel calculates the Wishart distance between T and the class center, Besides, a pixel block structure is extracted as the input, and each pixel is a 3×3 real matrix, so that the feature map of Wishart distance can be obtained. Then, the spatial relationship among pixels is learned by the hole convolution layer. Finally, the feature map by the depth convolution network is used as the input of the coding module.

2.2 Wishart Deeplab Network

The proposed Wishart DeepLab network architecture in this paper uses the DeepLabV3 + algorithm [16], which is a semantic segmentation network including encoding and decoding parts. In addition, dilated-separable convolution is adopted to obtain different scale features in this network. The network structure contains two steps: One is the feature extraction process of the down-sampling encoding network, which contains the convolutional and pooling layers. The encoding network uses a Wishart deep residual network (ResNet) [18] to learn semantic information, and utilizes dilated convolution to control the size of the obtained feature map and increase the receptive field by the ratio of the dilated convolution. Different void rates are used to obtain rich semantic information at different scales. The structure of deep residual network is given in Fig. 2.

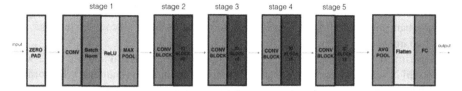

Fig. 2. ResNet network model diagram

The second step is a decoder network composing of a convolution and up-sampling layers. The decoder module gradually restores the spatial information.

The encoding module is composed of 4 convolutional blocks. The 1×1 convolution converts the feature map based on the Wishart deep residual network output into 256 channels. Then the 3×3 convolution with three scales are designed by defining the void ratios of 6, 12, and 18. The kernel performs convolution to obtain 3 feature maps with different scales and receptive fields. With the increase of void rate, the role of the convolution kernel will gradually weaken. Until the void convolution kernel has the same size as that of feature map, the 3×3 convolution kernel is actually a 1×1 convolution kernel, and only the center of the convolution kernel are activated. Therefore, the atrous spatial pyramid pooling(ASPP) module of the DeeplabV3 + network introduces an average pooling layer to pool the characteristic maps along the channel direction. The five characteristic maps output by the ASPP network are merged along the channel direction, and used 1×1 convolution converts channel number to 256, so the output size of feature map is $32 \times 32 \times 256$.

During the decoding module, the result of deeplabv3 + encoder module is utilized as the input, and the number of output channels are reduced by 1×1 convolution kernels. Secondly, the obtained features are upsampled by bilinear interpolation with factor 4. Then, the current features and the learned features from the low-level network are connected directly, since they have the same spatial resolution. After the connection, a 3×3 convolution kernel and a bilinear interpolation up-sampling with a factor of 4 are used. By this way, the obtained feature map is the same size as the original image. At last, the softmax classifier is used to obtain the classification probability, and the final classification map of PolSAR image is completed.

3 Experiments

3.1 Dataset and Experimental Settings

To test the performance of our method, experiments are conducted on two real PolSAR public datasets, AIRSAR Flevoland and AIRSAR San Francisco. One is the L-band fully PolSAR subimage obtained by NASA / JPL laboratory AIRSAR system. It is the agricultural area in the Netherlands. The PauliRGB image is given in Fig. 3 (a), the corresponding label map can be seen in (b). It has 6 crop categories including bare soil, potatoes, beets, peas, wheat, and barley. Another one is from San Francisco Bay, California, obtained by AIRSAR airborne. The PolSAR data is the L-band radar data. The image size is 512×512. The PauliRGB image and its label map are illustrated in

Figs. 4 (a) and (b) respectively. It includes 5 types of land cover: bare soil, mountains, ocean, urban, and vegetation. A refined Lee filtering is used to reduce speckle noises for these two images.

Experiments are operated on the Windows 10 operating system and use a PC with 8GB RAM NVIDIA GeForce GTX 1050. The experimental environment is Tensorflow Gpu 1.9.0. The batch size is fixed to 32 in the experiment, and the whole training process is 2000 epochs. The optimization method uses 0.001 as the learning rate to ensure the network converging as soon as possible.

The comparison methods are CNN [12], FCN [14], and deepLabV3 + [16] methods during experiments. Two quantitative indicators are calculated to evaluate the effectiveness of our method. One is the overall accuracy (OA), which is the percentage of the correct classified pixels in all labeled samples. The other is the Kappa coefficient, which can measure the consistency of the classification results. Larger Kappa coefficient means better consistency in the classification result.

3.2 Flevoland Area

The classification results on Flevoland data by compared and our methods are given in Figs. 3(c)-(f).Among them, Fig. 3(c) is the classification result of CNN, in which some classes are misclassified and region consistency is not well. Although FCN enhances regional consistency, the edge details are lost in (d). The deeplabV3 + method improves the classification result and produces less misclassification in (e). However, some details are still misclassified without considering data distribution. The proposed algorithm can achieve superior performance in both region consistency and edge details in (f).

Table 1. Classification accuracy of Flevoland.

Class/Method	CNN	FCN	DeeplabV3 +	Proposed
Bare soil	91.89	98.72	98.70	**99.03**
Potato	99.17	97.88	98.79	**99.24**
Beet	94.42	**98.53**	98.14	97.81
Pea	99.66	**99.99**	99.90	99.90
Wheat	99.78	99.14	99.53	**99.86**
Barely	97.38	97.23	97.18	**97.42**
OA	97.88	98.92	99.04	**99.16**
Kappa	0.9704	0.9862	0.9878	**0.9903**

The classification accuracies by proposed and other compared algorithms are illustrated in Table 1. It shows our method can obtain best accuracy in both OA and Kappa. The values are 0.12% and 0.25% higher than deeplabV3 + in OA and Kappa respectively. It shows the advantage of the Wishart network structure. Contrasted with other deep learning methods, the deeplabV3 + also obtain higher accuracy than others. It verifies the deeplabV3 + model is a superior deep learning method. The CNN and FCN are also the common used deep learning methods. However, without considering polarimetric information, they still produce some misclassifications.

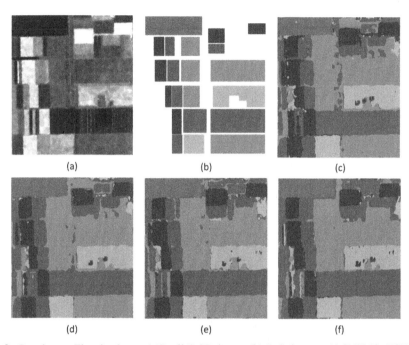

Fig. 3. Results on Flevoland area.(a)Pauli RGB image;(b) Label map; (c)CNN;(d) FCN; (e) DeeplabV3 +; (f) the proposed method.

3.3 San Francisco Area

The experimental results by compared and proposed methods on San Francisco area are given in Figs. 4(c)-(f). Among them, Fig. 4(c) is the classification result by CNN, in which some classes are misclassified and some noisy points are produced. Although FCN reduce the misclassification, region consistency is still not good in (d). The deeplabV3 + method improves the region consistency and produce less misclassification in (e). However, some edge details are misclassified without considering PolSAR data distribution. The proposed algorithm can obtain superior result in both region consistency and edge details in (f).

The classification indicators by proposed and compared algorithms are given in Table 2. It proves that our method can obtain the highest accuracy in both OA and Kappa. The values are 0.6% and 1.0% higher than deeplabV3 + in OA and Kappa respectively. It shows the advantages of the Wishart network structure. Contrasted with other deep learning methods, the deeplabV3 + also obtain higher accuracy than others. It verifies the deeplabV3 + model is a superior deep learning method. The CNN and

Table 2. Comparison of different methods on San Francisco area.

Class/Method	CNN	FCN	DeeplabV3 +	Proposed
Bare soil	**98.97**	95.97	98.11	96.05
Mountain	91.85	96.29	95.54	**96.74**
Ocean	96.05	**98.06**	97.70	97.72
Urban	95.09	94.52	94.31	**95.12**
Vegetation	85.50	85.21	90.39	**93.19**
OA	94.31	95.53	95.87	**96.47**
Kappa	0.9061	0.9253	0.9313	**0.9413**

FCN are also the common used deep learning methods. However, without considering polarimetric information, they still produce some misclassifications.

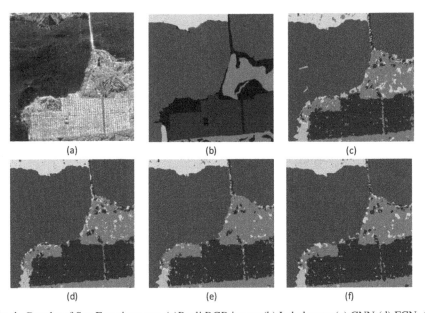

Fig. 4. Results of San Francisco area.(a)Pauli RGB image;(b) Label map; (c) CNN;(d) FCN; (e) DeeplabV3 +; (f)the proposed method.

4 Conclusion

In this paper, the Wishart deeplab network is proposed for PolSAR image classification. Contrasted with the traditional deep learning models, our method designs the Wishart convolution structure to better extract the feature information of PolSAR data. Besides, the Wishart Deeplab network is proposed to further learn the polarimetric contextual information and multi-scale features. This network can enhance the smoothness of the complex terrain objects to improve performance. Besides, experimental results and quantitative index also prove our method shows more advantages than others owing to the structure of Wishart deeplab network. In the future work, a multi-level deep feature fusion method can be developed, which is designed to suppress noise and learn more robust polarimetric features.

Acknowledgement. This work was supported by the National Natural Science Foundation of China under Grant 62006186, the Science and Technology Program of Beilin District in Xian under Grant GX2105, in part by the Open fund of National Key Laboratory of Geographic Information Engineering under Grant SKLGIE2019-M-3-2.

References

1. Shi, J.F., Jin, H.Y., Xiao, Z.L.: A novel multi-feature joint learning method for fast polarimetric SAR terrain classification. IEEE Access **8**, 30491–30503 (2020)
2. Mas, J.F., Flores, J.J.: The application of artificial neural networks to the analysis of remotely sensed data. Int. J. Remote Sens. **29**(3), 617–663 (2008)
3. Taşskın, G.: A comprehensive analysis of twin support vector machines in remote sensing image classification. In: 2015 23nd Signal Processing and Communications Applications, SIU 2015 **3**, pp. 2427–2429. IEEE, Malatya (2015)
4. Pajares, G., López-Martínez, C., Sánchez-Lladó, F.J.: Improving wishart classification of polarimetric SAR data using the hopfield neural network optimization approach. Remote Sensing **4**(11), 3571–3595 (2012)
5. Guo, Y.W., Jiao, L.C., Qu, R., et al.: Adaptive fuzzy learning superpixel representation for PolSAR image classification. IEEE Trans. Geosci. Remote Sens. **60**, 1–18 (2022)
6. Salakhutdinov, R., Hinton, G.: Deep boltzmann machines. In: Artificial intelligence and statistics, AISTATS 2009, pp. 448–455 (2009)
7. Ma, X., Geng, J., Wang, H.: Hyperspectral image classification via contextual deep learning. EURASIP J. Image and Video Processing **2015**(1), 1–12 (2015)
8. Hinton, G.E., Osindero, S., The, Y.W.: A fast learning algorithm for deep belief nets. Neural Comput. **18**(7), 1527–1554 (2006)
9. LeCun, Y., Kavukcuoglu, K., Farabet, C.: Convolutional networks and applications in vision. In: Proceedings of 2010 IEEE International Symposium on Circuits and Systems, ISCAS 2010, pp. 253–256. IEEE (2010)
10. Chen, X., Xiang, S., Liu, C.L., et al.: Vehicle detection in satellite images by hybrid deep convolutional neural networks. IEEE Geosci. Remote Sens. Lett. **11**(10), 1797–1801 (2014)
11. Saito, S., Aoki, Y.: Building and road detection from large aerial imagery. In: Image Processing: Machine Vision Applications VIII. MVA 2015, vol. 9405, pp. 153–164. SPIE, San Francisco (2015)
12. Bentes, C., Frost, A., Velotto, D., Tings, B.: Ship-iceberg discrimination with convolutional neural networks in high resolution SAR images. In: 11th European Conference on Synthetic Aperture Radar, EUSAR 2016, pp. 1–4. VDE, Hamburg (2016)
13. Jiao, L.C., Liu, F.: Wishart deep stacking network for fast POLSAR image classification. IEEE Trans. Image Process. **25**(7), 3273–3286 (2016)

14. Long, J., Shelhamer, E., Darrell, T.: Fully convolutional networks for semantic segmentation. In: Proceedings of the IEEE conference on computer vision and pattern recognition, CVPR 2015, pp. 3431–3440. IEEE, Boston (2015)
15. Chen, L.C., Papandreou, G., Kokkinos, I., et al.: DeepLab: semantic image segmentation with deep convolutional nets, atrous convolution, and fully connected CRFs. IEEE Trans. Pattern Anal. Mach. Intell. **40**(4), 834–848 (2018)
16. Chen, L.-C., Zhu, Y., Papandreou, G., Schroff, F., Adam, H.: Encoder-decoder with atrous separable convolution for semantic image segmentation. In: Ferrari, V., Hebert, M., Sminchisescu, C., Weiss, Y. (eds.) ECCV 2018. LNCS, vol. 11211, pp. 833–851. Springer, Cham (2018). https://doi.org/10.1007/978-3-030-01234-2_49
17. Goodman, N.R.: Statistical analysis based on a certain multivariate complex Gaussian distribution (an introduction). Ann. Math. Stat. **34**(1), 152–177 (1963)
18. He, K.M., Zhang, X.Y., Ren, S.Q., Sun, J.: Deep residual learning for image recognition. In: Proceedings of the IEEE conference on computer vision and pattern recognition, CVPR, 2016, pp. 770–778. IEEE, Las Vegas (2016)

Intelligent Detection of Stratigraphy Boundary Based on Deep Learning

Qin Zhao[1], Tilin Wang[1], Yanming Liu[2]($\boxtimes$), Mingsong Yang[3], Xiaojuan Ning[3], and Xinhong Hei[3]

[1] School of Civil Engineering and Architecture, Xi'an University of Technology, Xi'an, China
[2] State Key Laboratory of Rail Transit Engineering Informatization (FSDI), China Railway First Survey and Design Institute Group Ltd., Xi'an, People's Republic of China
1004474117@qq.com
[3] School of Computer Science and Engineering, Xi'an University of Technology, Xi'an, China

Abstract. Robotic exploration technology is widely used in various fields such as information acquisition and topographic photography. Due to dimensional transformation and data loss in data transmission, an additional manual pre-processing is required, which is very time consuming and difficult to ensure the data accuracy. In this paper, we propose an intelligent recognition method of stratigraphy boundaries of engineering geological images based on the Hough prior deep learning network (HT-LCNN). We annotate geological drawing datasets manually at first. And then improve the binary matrix size of the original network, retrain the network on a self-constructed dataset. Finally we design experiments to compare and analyze model learning capabilities so that the optimal model can be adopted to detect negligible gaps on graphical junctions. Experimental results demonstrate that our method outform HT-LCNN in recognizing strata features. It gives the robot the capability to intelligently recognize geological images and can accurately identify over 96% of stratigraphy boundaries and junctions location, thus improving the fluidity of data in the design process and reducing time costs.

Keywords: Geological images · Deep learning algorithms · Line segment detection

1 Introduction

In recent years, the combination of autonomous robot technology and geological exploration has produced various prototype robots, which is made of navigation instruments and used for geological and topographic surveys in various dangerous and difficult environments. Robotic technology has been applied in exploration path planning, geological information extraction and topographic photography [1–3]. The various geological information collected by the robot are generally used in the design of the geological information model. However, the data still require to be reprocessed. The current mainstream modeling software does not have the ability of automated identification and correction. In most cases, the survey data are processed manually. At present, designers

---

The original version of this chapter was revised: the acknowledgement has been added at the end of the paper. The correction to this chapter is available at
https://doi.org/10.1007/978-981-99-0301-6_36

© The Author(s), under exclusive license to Springer Nature Singapore Pte Ltd. 2023, corrected publication 2023
Z. Yu et al. (Eds.): CIRAC 2022, CCIS 1770, pp. 109–119, 2023.
https://doi.org/10.1007/978-981-99-0301-6_9

follow an area-to-boundary checking process, using the fill command of the drawing software to manually exclude gaps at graphical junctions. This approach is extremely time consuming and is limited by the subjectivity and level of design experience of the designer. Therefore, it is of great significance to study intelligent recognition methods for geological images to automate data preprocessing and speed up the flow of accessible data flow from robot exploration to geological modeling.

In this paper, we propose an automatic geological stratigraphic detection method based on deep learning. This method can directly detect the stratigraphic images and achieve the intelligent processing of geological data, which is of great significance to improve the quality and efficiency of the whole process of survey and modelling.

The main contributions of the paper are as follows:

The Geological Report Stratigraphy Boundary Dataset (GRSBD), which contains more than 4,100 annotated geological boundaries, has been labeled in order to detect geological report maps with higher resolution requirements and closer vertical alignment of line segments.

An intelligent stratigraphy boundaries recognition algorithm is brought forward to accomplish the task of automatic recognition of engineering geological images, which is combined by advanced HT-LCNN [4]. This method can decrease the edge gaps in the raw images effectively.

2   Related Works

The recognition of subgraphic symbols and graphic elements in geological drawings is a hugely important research topic. The workflow for recognizing engineering maps can be broadly summarized in two stages: preprocess the vector drawings, and establish the recognition rules according to the features of the graphic elements of the maps [5]. Many scholars have concentrated on these methods, which can be grouped into the following three categories based on different data processing formats:

Mathematical and Statistical Analysis. This method uses mathematical statistics and computational analysis to identify and extract specific graphic objects. Bahorich et al. presents the C1–C3 classical algorithm, the earliest automatic fault recognition method, which was precisely based on principal component analysis (PCA) and used the data covariance ratio relationship as the correlation coefficient to identify geologic fault [6, 7]. However, the algorithm has a certain degree of mean effect, which makes it difficult to identify small faults. Gibson et al. [8, 9] proposes a fault identification method based on a maximum credibility-first strategy, which firstly uses a mathematical model of the discontinuity to determine the fault location, and then identifies the fault based on a maximum credibility-first strategy. However, such methods cannot yield satisfactory results in terms of the recognition accuracy and generalizability, and are limited by the expertise of the experimental equipment and the theoretical solidity of the researcher.

Traditional Algorithmic Strategies. This method uses a custom rule function to calculate all possible implementations by analyzing data patterns. For example, Wang et al. [10, 11] proposes a fault identification method based on the Hough transform, which can obtain continuous fault lines. The shortcoming is that when multiple faults exist, the straight lines belonging to different faults cannot be separated effectively, resulting in the misidentification of multiple faults. Randen et al. [12] tried to apply an ant colony algorithm on line segment detection in three-dimensional geological body. This method can obtain a 3D fault surface, which takes a long time. However, the weakness of such methods is the relatively large number of control variables, slow convergence, high time complexity and long recognition times, which results in a limited number of situations that the method can handle.

Intelligent Learning Methodology. This method analyzes and processes images through intelligent algorithms such as machine learning and deep learning. As artificial intelligence technology advances rapidly, machine learning approaches have shown great advantages in handling vision tasks. In recent years, this method has been widely applied in the lithology identification domain and stratigraphic structure identification domain with positive results [13, 14]. Arias P et al. [15] proposed to generate the structure of the missing region by searching for the most similar patch from a known region and iterating from outside to inside. Song Y et al. [16] trained convolutional neural networks (CNN) to predict pixels in the absence region, thanks to a large number of training images, and the method can generate semantic image prediction complements for the absence region. Compared with the former two methods, the artificial intelligence learning methods pay more attentions to the implicit feature information between the data rather than the graphical objects on the drawings itself. The results of artificial intelligence learning are strongly related to the annotation of data. This is quite different from the traditional verification work that rely exclusively on the design experience of the surveyors. Therefore, the combination of depth learning algorithm and expert prior knowledge in the pre-processing of geological information model data provides a new approach for intelligent recognition of geological formation image.

In task of stratigraphy boundary identification, the stratigraphic data has no clear data rules and the relationship between map elements, and the gap position of the drawings has great randomness. In traditional solutions, the prior knowledge of human expert is an important basis for determination of the gap location. If the computer attempts to learn from the geometric relationships between line segment representations, thousands of data annotations may be required. However, the regional jurisdictional and confidentiality nature of geological data are not easy to achieve. Most of the current deep learning methods [17] rely heavily on rules and knowledge learned from large manual annotation datasets. It is difficult to directly obtain a large number of samples and generate large-scale datasets. Therefore, the domain-specific prior knowledge becomes one of the important breakthroughs to improve the detection accuracy.

3   GRSBD ImageNet

Neural networks can not be separated from data support. In this paper, we produce the GRSBD (The Geological Report Stratigraphy Boundary Dataset) imageNet [v1.0] based on the Wireframe dataset (as shown in Fig. 1) structure, which can be available in the geological domain and it can better apply deep learning methods in the field of engineering geological images.

Fig. 1. Example images of wireframe dataset [18]

3.1 Data Sampling

The engineering geological image samples labeled in this paper are from the example design drawings that are not disclosed by the local design institutes in the engineering survey and design drawings. Based on the actual engineering requirements and considering the mapping of strata under different working conditions, the stratigraphic lineaments of the images can be divided into straight line and curved strata. It can be divided into dense and scattered strata from the perspective of longitudinal stratigraphic densities. In order to avoid the low proportion of data from a certain category, which leads to the flooding of its features and affects the final model recognition, it is best to collect the images in the proportion of straight line: curve = 1:1 and dense: dispersion = 1:1. The classification of engineering geological stratum images and the number of sample data sets are shown Table 1. The data division is based on the common 8:1:1 ratio. The total sample are randomly selected to the training set and testing set.

Table 1. Number of engineering geological stratum image samples

Stratigraphic linearity	Num of images	Num of training set	Num of testing set	Number of line segments
Straight	66	51	15	10612
Curved	54	45	9	6132
Sum	120	96	24	16744

3.2 Dataset Labeling

Data Structure Analysis. The ShanghaiTech dataset applied to the hough prior based deep learning network framework contains the tagged wireframe_raw folder and the processed wireframe folder adapted to the network. The completed dataset should be based on the structure of wireframe_raw folder, focusing on how to obtain the matching training set, and the verification set of JSON files.

JSON, a lightweight data interchange format, has two forms of array structure. The json file format for individual image annotations is an ordered array structure. By comparing with the parsed train.json file, we found that the JSON file structure is quite different from the former structure (as shown in Fig. 2). In a single image json file, a label is treated as a jsonobj, with { } dividing each jsonobj object structure. The complete set of image annotations is made up of N jsonobj's. In addition, other information about the image is described as a combination of key-value pairs in an ordered json array structure. The author follows the format of the json instance file in wireframe_raw to design the GRSBD dataset labelling algorithm and produce the Geoline_raw file of the dataset.

```
01. json

{
  "version": "4.6.0",                       ...
  "flags": {},                                  }
  "shapes": [                               ],
    {                                       "group_id": 0,
      "label": "polylines",                 "shape_type": "linestrip",
      "points": [                           "flags": {}
        [                                 },
          0.819672131147541,            ],
          48.63387978142077             "imagePath": "01.png",
        ],                              "imageData":
                                        "iVBORw0KGgoAAAANSUhEUgAABQAAAAAc
        [                               ==",
          1279,                         "imageHeight": 1600,
          119                           "imageWidth": 1280
                                      }
```

Fig. 2. File structure of single image

Dataset Labeling Design. In this paper, we create and configure the virtual environment, and applies the labelme as image annotation tool (Fig. 3).

An exemplary operation of the whole labeling process is detailed as follows:

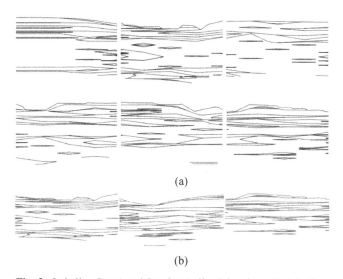

(a)

(b)

Fig. 3. Labeling Step1 and Step2. (a) sliced drawings. (b) labeling.

Step1. determine the output specification information for the drawing. The development of guidelines includes:

1) The wireframe is not less than 20 mm from the Ymax and Ymin endpoints of the stratigraphic line segment.
2) Conformity to CAD print drawings.
3) Avoid dense vertical trends as area boundaries wherever possible.
4) Ensure that all slices are printed to the same size. Dividing the drawings into multiple regional stratigraphic images and exporting them in.png format, in accordance with the specification information (e.g. Table 2).

Table 2. Output specification information of geological drawings of Dingjiawan Bridge

Export information	Value
Slicing pixels	128 * 100
Print size	1600 * 1280
Window offset (default x-direction)	28
Number of slicing	21

Step2. use the labelme tool to label the line segments of the slices. select polyline as the labeling line type and the labeling guidelines are as follows:

1) Setting the x-axis direction as the main direction of the labeling, a standard "polyline" is defined as a continuous marking of all contiguous strata from Xmin to Xmax, with a maximum of two lines joining the same endpoints at the same time.
2) Allow for different label lines to exist junction. (i.e. the number of lines connected by endpoints can be greater than or equal to 2).

Step3. integrate and annotate the sliced image json files to get the train.json, valid.json files, and generate a certain number of test data randomly according to the scale, and place them in the test.txt file.
Step4. synthesize the Geoline-raw labeled dataset.

4 Methods

HT-LCNN [4] is developed based on the L-CNN, which replaces the Hourglass Block in the Hourglass Network with the HT-IHT block to obtain the global geometric line segments predicted in advance by hough transform. It is also combined with the local features of the outer contour of the image to improve the data efficiency of the neural network segment detection model, reduce the amount of training data required and lower the annotation cost. It has been successfully tested on two more common datasets

[18, 19]. Therefore, we propose a method of stratigraphy boundary recognition of engineering geological images based on hough prior deep learning network, and combine the advanced Ht-lcnn algorithm to optimize the model parameters. Then the drawings are preprocessed by layer line condition filtering and imported into the Geo_HT-LCNN model to obtain the detection results.

4.1 Drawing Pre-processing

In order to obtain the stratigraphy boundaries from the drawings to be detected, a filter needs to be established to delete all elements that do not match the following conditions:

(Layer infor is stratigraphic line (Generalized stratigraphy boundary map elements)) ∪ (Object type is polyline) ∪ (Linear is Continuous line type)

The process of the pre-processing drawing method is shown in Fig. 4.

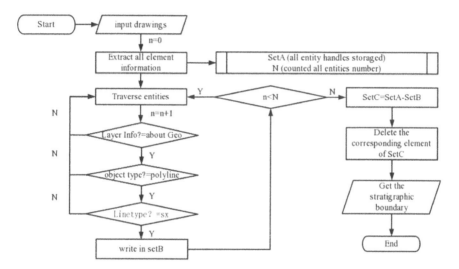

Fig. 4. Framework of pre-process drawings

4.2 Drawing Slicing and Data Augmentation

In order to clearly view of the original engineering geological map, the resolution is mostly around 16000×12800, which is 10 times that of the drawing area division in Fig. 3 of Sect. 3.2. Importing the entire drawing will result in slow calculation and insufficient memory. Therefore, after pre-processing the drawings, the drawings are sliced and the resolution of each slice is set to 1600×1280, and the location of the boundary endpoints is recorded for subsequent return to CAD to enclose the stratigraphy boundary.

In addition, due to the small number of annotated geoengineering maps, random rotation and Gaussian noise are added to enhance the data of the images in order to avoid overfitting of the model. This experiment is performed on our own GRSBD dataset.

First, we rotate the sample image at an angle ($0°$, $90°$, $180°$, $360°$). Since the original image is not square, the size of the image is guaranteed to be the same only when the rotation angle is equal to a multiple of 180. Other values will result in undefined black areas of the image. We solve this problem by constant interpolation and fill the unknown areas with constant values to ensure that each image is the same size. And then, the 0-mean Gaussian noise is added to the image to return the noise image, which can enhance the network learning ability.

4.3 Stratigraphy Boundary Detection

The general framework is shown in Fig. 5. We use CNN to learn local features. ResNet is the backbone, with two convolution layers containing ReLU, and followed by two residual blocks. And then, the improved Ht-IHT block [4] is inserted into each residual block to learn priori knowledge of global line parameterizations, followed by a single one-dimensional convolution layer to reduce computational effort, and finally the detection results are output.

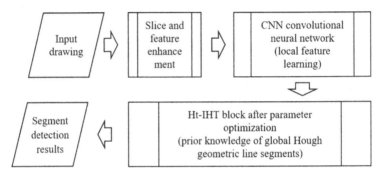

Fig. 5. Framework of stratigraphy boundary detection

The framework of stratigraphy boundary detection proposed in this paper improves the size of the binary matrix in the original network by combining the edge features of the geological image with the slicing parameters. The binary matrix stores the correspondence between the network learned image pixels $(x(i), y(i))$ and the Hough space bin (ρ, θ). We define an image line $1_{\rho,\theta}$ in polar coordinates, any pixel point $(x(i), y(i))$ along this line is given by:

$$(x(i), y(i)) = (\rho \cos \theta - i \sin \theta, \rho \sin \theta + i \cos \theta) \tag{1}$$

For a bin (ρ, θ), exists:

$$HT(\rho, \theta) = \sum_i F_{\rho,\theta}(x(i), y(i)) \tag{2}$$

$\sum_i F_{\rho,\theta}(x(i), y(i))$ is the feature map value of the pixel indexed by i along the (ρ, θ) line in the image, and enters the Hough domain for a pixel vote, which is the binary matrix mentioned above. The binary matrix is an important data for the network and the key to improving the performance of the network and the quality of the detection results. The improved network works better for high-resolution image recognition and can be applied to more complex detection tasks.

5   Experimental Analysis

We evaluate the proposed method in terms of correctness, simplicity and efficiency. Our experiments are based on the NVIDIA Tesla P40 GPU workstation for development and testing. The algorithm uses the PyTorch 1.11.0 deep learning framework and the Adam optimizer for training. Parameters are set in the Table 3.

Table 3. Network parameter setting

Parameters	Value
lr	4e−4
weight_decay	Default
batch_size	5
max_epoch	24
loss_weight	Default
mean	[249.66555, 250.2365, 250.2365]
stddev	[36.4946, 34.5256, 34.5256]

The parameter-optimized Ht-lcnn model is trained on the GRSBD [v1.0]. The stratigraphy boundaries of the pre-processed geological section of the DK528+264 left line Bai Shenjia ditch grand bridge are tested on the basis of the trained model. Figure 6 shows the comparison of the recognition results of drawings after model improvement. It can be seen that the Geo_HT-LCNN model after targeted training outperforms the other one, and the model can basically detection stratigraphy boundary line segments correctly. The original model has features learned from the 3D spatial images of the Wireframe dataset, causing vertical straight lines to appear in the gaps of the results.

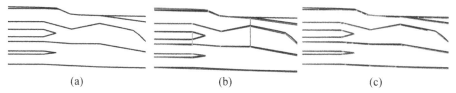

| (a) | (b) | (c) |

Fig. 6. Comparison of the drawing detection results. (a) original Img. (b) detection of Ht-lcnn model. (c) detection of Geo_HT-LCNN model.

We also calculate the precision of stratigraphic image detection at different learning rates shown in Table 4.

Computed objects are based on continuous pixel segments. Accuracy of image recognition is calculated by dividing the number of identical image recognition segments by the number of dataset tagged segments. It demonstrates that the best results are around 0.75.

Table 4. Detection precision of Geo_HT-LCNN model with different learning rates

Learning rate	Precision
0.93	0.7734
0.85	0.8984
0.80	0.9219
0.75	0.9625

6   Conclusions

In order to detect stratigraphy boundaries in engineering geological drawings with high resolution and graphic complexity, we produce the GRSBD imageNet containing 120 images of stratigraphy boundaries from sliced geological drawings of engineering instances under five different working conditions and propose a set of criteria for images labelling of geological stratigraphy boundaries to provide data support for subsequent work. At the same time, we explore the deep learning-based stratigraphy boundary recognition method for engineering geological drawings, optimize the parameters of the Deep-Hough-Transform-Line-Priors network, validate the method with engineering instance drawings, and obtain better recognition results. Further work will focus on the intelligent automation of data pre-processing for geological information models, so that autonomous robotics can be more deeply integrated with geological survey scenarios.

Acknowledgment. The authors wish to acknowledge the support of the National Natural Science Foundation of China (No.51878556), State Key Laboratory Opening Project Research (SKLKZ21-03).

References

1. Zheng, H., Smereka, J.M., Mikluski, D., Wang, Y.: Bayesian optimization based trustworthiness model for multi-robot bounding overwatch. arXiv preprint arXiv:2201.01878 (2022)
2. Zhang, S.: Mine drilling robot with remote control and self-balance. In: 2022 the 3rd International Conference on Artificial Intelligence in Electronics Engineering, pp. 97–103 (2022)

3. Hong, I.S., Yi, Y., Ju, G., et al.: Lunar exploration employing a quadruped robot on the fault of the rupes recta for investigating the geological formation history of the marenubium. J. Space Technol. Appl. **1**(1), 64–75 (2021)

4. Lin, Y., Pintea, S.L., van Gemert, J.C.: Deep hough-transform line priors. In: Vedaldi, A., Bischof, H., Brox, T., Frahm, J.-M. (eds.) ECCV 2020. LNCS, vol. 12367, pp. 323–340. Springer, Cham (2020). https://doi.org/10.1007/978-3-030-58542-6_20

5. Chhabra, A.K.: Graphic symbol recognition: an overview. In: Tombre, K., Chhabra, A.K. (eds.) GREC 1997. LNCS, vol. 1389, pp. 68–79. Springer, Heidelberg (1998). https://doi.org/10.1007/3-540-64381-8_40

6. Bahorich, M.S., Lopez, J., Haskell, N.L., Nissen, S.E., Poole, A.: Stratigraphic and structural interpretation with 3-d coherence. In: SEG Technical Program Expanded Abstracts 1995, pp. 97–100. Society of Exploration Geophysicists (1995)

7. Marfurt, K.J., Kirlin, R.L., Farmer, S.L., Bahorich, M.S.: 3-d seismic attributes using a semblance-based coherency algorithm. Geophysics **63**(4), 1150–1165 (1998)

8. Gibson, D., Spann, M., Turner, J.: Automatic fault detection for 3D seismic data. In: DICTA, pp. 821–830 (2003)

9. Gibson, D., Spann, M., Turner, J., Wright, T.: Fault surface detection in 3-d seismic data. IEEE Trans. Geosci. Remote Sens. **43**(9), 2094–2102 (2005)

10. Wang, Z., AlRegib, G.: Fault detection in seismic datasets using hough transform. In: 2014 IEEE International Conference on Acoustics, Speech and Signal Processing (ICASSP), pp. 2372–2376. IEEE (2014)

11. Wang, Z., Long, Z., AlRegib, G., Asjad, A., Deriche, M.A.: Automatic fault tracking across seismic volumes via tracking vectors. In: 2014 IEEE International Conference on Image Processing (ICIP), pp. 5851–5855. IEEE (2014)

12. Pedersen, S.I., Skov, T., Randen, T., Sønneland, L.: Automatic fault extraction using artificial ants. In: Iske, A., Randen, T. (eds.) Mathematical Methods and Modelling in Hydrocarbon Exploration and Production. Mathematics in Industry, vol. 7. Springer, Heidelberg (2005). https://doi.org/10.1007/3-540-26493-0_5

13. Li, N., Hao, H., Gu, Q., Wang, D., Hu, X.: A transfer learning method for automatic identification of sandstone microscopic images. Comput. Geosci. **103**, 111–121 (2017)

14. He, K., Zhang, X., Ren, S., Sun, J.: Deep residual learning for image recognition. In: Proceedings of the IEEE Conference on Computer Vision and Pattern Recognition, pp. 770–778 (2016)

15. Arias, P., Facciolo, G., Caselles, V., Sapiro, G.: A variational framework for exemplar-based image inpainting. Int. J. Comput. Vision **93**, 319–347 (2010)

16. Song, Y., et al.: Contextual-based image inpainting: infer, match, and translate. In: Ferrari, V., Hebert, M., Sminchisescu, C., Weiss, Y. (eds.) ECCV 2018. LNCS, vol. 11206, pp. 3–18. Springer, Cham (2018). https://doi.org/10.1007/978-3-030-01216-8_1

17. Xue, N., et al.: Holistically-attracted wireframe parsing. In: Proceedings of the IEEE/CVF Conference on Computer Vision and Pattern Recognition, pp. 2788–2797 (2020)

18. Huang, K., Wang, Y., Zhou, Z., Ding, T., Gao, S., Ma, Y.: Learning to parse wireframes in images of man-made environments. In: Proceedings of the IEEE Conference on Computer Vision and Pattern Recognition, pp. 626–635 (2018)

19. Denis, P., Elder, J.H., Estrada, F.J.: Efficient edge-based methods for estimating Manhattan frames in urban imagery. In: Forsyth, D., Torr, P., Zisserman, A. (eds.) ECCV 2008. LNCS, vol. 5303, pp. 197–210. Springer, Heidelberg (2008). https://doi.org/10.1007/978-3-540-88688-4_15

Unmanned Cluster Collaboration

Multi-UAV Path Planning in Complex Obstacle Environments

Li Tan[(✉)], Hongtao Zhang, Jiaqi Shi, Xiaofeng Lian, and Feiyang Jia

Beijing Technology and Business University, Beijing 100048, China
tanli@th.btbu.edu.cn

Abstract. The performance of UAV path planning algorithm is mainly reflected in the convergence time, flight distance and flight time. However, in practical applications, the environment is quite complex, and many interference factors must be considered. In many cases, when the flight path of UAV reaches the global optimum, the convergence time of the algorithm will be affected, that is, the search ability and convergence ability of the algorithm are conflicting. Aiming at these problems, this paper establishes a complex flight environment, uses the Nash equilibrium method to transform the convergence and searchability of the genetic algorithm into two players in the game, and uses the Nash equilibrium method to find a balance between the convergence and searchability of the algorithm, so as to realize path planning of multiple UAVs in complex obstacle environments.

Keywords: Multi-UAV · Complex environments · Nash equilibrium

1 Introduction

In recent years, UAVs have been used in many fields. Firstly, it is used in military fields such as military investigation, attack and surveillance, and then it is gradually used in civil fields such as electric patrol, video and traffic monitoring [1] UAV is equipped with intelligent devices that can simulate the working environment in real time, locate, control flight status, detect obstacles and calculate obstacle avoidance path, so that the UAV can successfully avoid obstacles and complete the set tasks. Path planning capability is a necessary condition for UAV to find flight path, and is the core part of multi UAV path planning.

This paper is organized as follows: The second section introduces the development of UAV path planning, the third section proposes the improved path planning method of this paper, the fourth section uses experiments to verify, and the fifth section summarizes this paper.

2 Related Work

The Swarm intelligence optimization algorithm is one of the main algorithms in UAV research, which has been widely used in various multiple UAV path planning. Saeed et al. [2] summarized the path planning algorithm of UAV, focusing

Z. Yu et al. (Eds.): CIRAC 2022, CCIS 1770, pp. 123–132, 2023.
https://doi.org/10.1007/978-981-99-0301-6_10

on the research of swarm intelligence algorithm. Puente Castro A [3] and others analyzed the path planning problem of UAVs and compared different path planning algorithms. Chen [4] and others based on the ant colony algorithm to obtain a better UAV path and explore all areas as much as possible. Meier [5] et al. put forward a new backup path planning method by reusing ACO's distributed pheromones, which can only obtain feasible paths from available pheromone concentrations. A new method based on the cuckoo optimisation algorithm was proposed by Hosseininejad et al. [6]. To reduce computational complexity, a new method is used to optimize the eigenvectors. Kumar et al. [7] improved the gray wolf optimization algorithm to reduce the convergence time of the algorithm. These methods mainly focus on path distance and execution time and do not consider the possible imbalance of convergence and search capabilities. These methods focus on path distance and execution time and do not pay attention to the possible imbalance of convergence and search capabilities.

John Holland [8] first proposed the genetic algorithm (GA). Genetic algorithm is a natural heuristic algorithm based on Darwin's theory of evolution. The genetic algorithm is a global optimization algorithm with the characteristics of intelligence and parallelism, which is very suitable for large-scale problems. Many scholars have studied and improved it. Geng [9] and others added obstacle avoidance constraints, no-fly zone constraints, task execution time window constraints, task execution order constraints, etc. to the multiprocessor resource allocation problem model for a more real battlefield environment, and established a more complete UAV collaborative task allocation model, which was solTved by integer programming method MIP and genetic algorithm. To settle the problem that genetic algorithms may cause path detours in the process of UAV path planning, Li et al. [10] proposed a hierarchical genetic algorithm, which reduced the cost and enhanced the stability of path planning. Ramirez et al. [11] proposed a new multi-objective genetic algorithm to settle the multi-task planning problem of UAVs, and gave the specific implementation process of the algorithm. To avoid the early convergence of the algorithm, Lamini et al. [12] proposed a new crossover operator and provided a feasible path, which is superior to the fitness value of the parent operator, making the algorithm converge faster, Game theory is often used to solve complex problems and make them tend to be balanced. The method of game theory is also used for the path planning of UAVs. On the basis of game theory and multi-agent reinforcement learning algorithm, Guo [13] et al. studied the multi-agent path planning problem.

To settle the conflict between the searching ability and the convergence ability of path planning for multiple UAVs, this paper improves the genetic algorithm and proposes a path planning method for multiple UAVs that takes both the convergence ability and the search ability into account.

3 The Improvement of Algorithm

3.1 The Genetic Algorithm Structure

The genetic algorithm is a search method by imitating the evolutionary process in nature. Using a mathematical approach, the search is translated into the process of chromosomal gene selection, crossover, and mutation in biological evolution. As a search algorithm for solving global optimization problems, genetic algorithm has the characteristics of wide coverage and robustness and can be widely used in various optimization problems. The operation process of genetic algorithm is shown in Fig. 1.

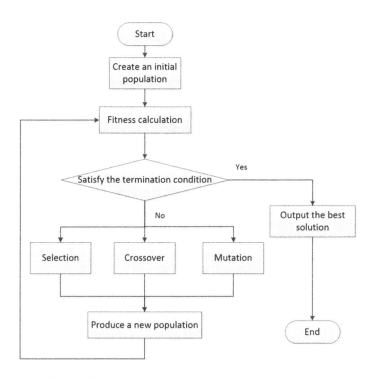

Fig. 1. The operation process of the genetic algorithm

However, the genetic algorithm has shortcomings such as being easy to fall into local optimum, which affects the effect of the algorithm for solving optimization problems. For such problems, the crossover probability and mutation probability are adjusted to balance the convergence ability and search ability of the algorithm.

3.2   Nash Equilibrium

Nash equilibrium is a key strategy combination in game theory. In the game, one side will choose a certain strategy without knowing what the other side will choose. When other participants have determined their choice, if someone chooses the optimal strategy, the strategy combination is defined as Nash equilibrium.

3.3   Balanced Search and Convergence Capabilities

The genetic algorithms undergo an iterative process of selection, crossover and mutation and convergence occurs when the results are optimal. However, if one wants to increase the speed of convergence of the algorithm one may destroy the population diversity and fall into a local optimum. If one wants to obtain a globally optimal solution, one needs in order to enrich the population, which may affect the speed of convergence of the algorithm. Therefore, Nash equilibrium is introduced into the genetic algorithm to obtain a balance between convergence ability and search ability.

In genetic algorithm, convergence speed is related to crossover probability P_c and mutation probability P_m. In a traditional genetic algorithm, fixed crossover probability and mutation probability are selected, but this is not conducive to solving problems in many cases. The convergence capability takes the crossover probability P_c as the strategy, and the search capability takes the mutation probability P_m as the strategy. The payment functions of convergence and search capability are $\pi_1 (P_c, P_m)$ and $\pi_2 (P_c, P_m)$, respectively. The game assumes that there is a unique stable solution to the Nash equilibrium, so its payment function is strictly concave. In this case, $\pi_1 (P_c, P_m)$ and $\pi_2 (P_c, P_m)$ are maximum, and it is found that there is a Nash equilibrium between the convergence capacity and the payment capacity, as shown in Eq. (1).

$$\frac{\partial^2 \pi_1}{\partial p_c^2} = 0, \quad \frac{\partial^2 \pi_2}{\partial p_m^2} = 0 \tag{1}$$

Equation (1) defines two reaction functions at once. P_c and P_m are the optimal strategies for reaction functions indicating the ability to converge and search, respectively, and the intersection of the two reaction functions corresponds to NASH equilibria. The reaction functions R1 and R2 are shown in Eq. (2).

$$p_c = R_1 (p_m), p_m = R_2 (p_c) \tag{2}$$

3.4   Constraints for UAV Flight

To settle the problem of multiple UAVs being prone to collision in complex obstacle environments, various constraints are added to the UAV path planning process, such as area constraints (TC), no-fly constraints (FFC) and multi-UAV collision avoidance constraints (CAC). When the UAV encounters obstacles during flight, it will adjust its path according to the situation, so as to obtain a path with short flight distance and no collision.

TC: When performing flight search, the flight range of the UAV must always be within the restricted area so that collision problems can be avoided, so this constraint is modeled as follows, where Ter(x, y) is the area function to return the Z-axis coordinate value of the (x, y) position as the height value of the place.

$$TC_i = \begin{cases} Q, z_j < \text{Ter}(x_i, y_i) \\ 0, \text{else} \end{cases}$$
$$TC = \sum_{i=1}^{n} TC_i \tag{3}$$

FFC: Set a rectangular area as a no-fly area, the UAV should avoid the area when flying to ensure safety, modeled as follows, l_x, l_y, l_z denote the lower limit of the x, y, z axis of the j_{th} no-fly area Range (x_j, y_j, z_j); u_x, u_y, u_z denote the upper limit of its coordinate axis.

$$FAC_i = \begin{cases} Q, (x_i, y_i, z_i) \in \text{Rang}(x_j, y_j, z_j) \\ 0, \text{else} \end{cases}$$
$$FAC = \sum_{i=1}^{n} FAC_i \tag{4}$$
$$\text{Rang}(x_j, y_j, z_j) = \{l_x \le x_j \le u_x\} \cap \{l_y \le y_j \le u_y\} \cap \{l_z \le z_j \le u_z\}$$

CAC: In the multi-UAV path planning problem, in order to avoid collisions between UAVs, the safe distance d_{sa} is introduced to avoid collisions by making the distance between flight points greater than the safe distance. The modeling is as follows, where d_{ij}^{mn} represents the i_{th} flight point on the m_{th} UAV path and the j_{th} waypoint on the n_{th} UAV path.

$$CAC_i = \begin{cases} Q, d_{ij}^{mn} < d_{sa} \\ 0, \text{else} \end{cases}$$
$$CAC = \sum_{i=1}^{n} CAC_i \tag{5}$$
$$d_{ij}^{mn} = \sqrt{\left(x_j^m - x_i^n\right)^2 + \left(y_j^m - y_i^n\right)^2 + \left(z_j^m - z_i^n\right)^2}$$

4 Experiment Results

4.1 Environment Model

The experiments in this paper were simulated in a Python 3.8 environment with Windows 10 operating platform and AMD Ryzen 7 5800H CPU model due to the need for simulation experiments, environment modelling was first performed. In this section, two simulation environments were designed to evaluate the feasibility and effectiveness of the improved algorithm. The experimental area was set up as a $100 * 100 * 100$ 3D space area with three drones in the area.

The simulation experiment was repeated 15 times independently for each of the two simulation environments. All three UAVs were set to start from a uniform starting point and reach the same end point, with randomly generated coordinates for the starting and end points. The other parameters set in the experiment are shown in Table 1.

Table 1. The parameters of simulation experiments.

Experimental parameters	Value
Number of populations	800
Crossover probability range	[0.4, 0.99]
Variation probability range	[0.0001, 0.1]
Selection operator	2
Maximum number of iterations	8000

4.2   Result Analysis

In this chapter, the effectiveness of the algorithm is examined in three aspects: convergence time of the algorithm, flight distance and flight time of the UAV. The effectiveness of the proposed algorithm is verified by comparing it with a genetic algorithm for multiple UAV path planning in a complex obstacle environment under the same circumstances.

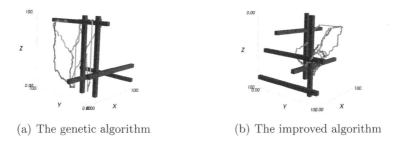

(a) The genetic algorithm   (b) The improved algorithm

Fig. 2. The roadmap of the first case

For the first case, Fig. 2(a) is the UAV flight route map of the genetic algorithm, and Fig. 2(b) is the UAV flight route map of the improved algorithm. The green cube on the way represents the obstacles set, and the three lines in dark pink, yellow and green represent the flight routes of the three UAVs. Figure 2 show some differences between the experimental results of the two algorithms. It can be seen that the performance of the improved algorithm is better than that of the genetic algorithm.

Table 2. The overall data comparison of the first case

No.	Convergence time (s)		Average flight distance (m)		Average flight time (s)	
	GA	IGA	GA	IGA	GA	IGA
1	165.47	114.93	312.06	210.87	157.35	96.39
2	136.85	106.04	259.2	186.84	115.09	92.36
3	165.73	100.68	250.34	203.96	152.28	91.38
4	148.2	114.53	271.78	187.47	133.46	110.2
5	161.31	120.37	287.3	195.64	113.47	102.54
6	189.25	116.32	270.99	207.3	116.24	106.85
7	135.63	116.82	320.52	199.53	107.38	106.11
8	190.98	104.84	242.85	193.89	140.03	118.57
9	172.75	110.77	246.8	246.66	105.07	124.03
10	134.14	99.88	326.38	221.17	138.8	100.84
11	128.32	121.47	242.96	243.83	148.99	115.62
12	125.99	96.28	300.86	233.11	108.24	90.22
13	148.8	123.33	310.16	208.28	154.28	91.31
14	166.4	117.94	315.61	223.1	140.65	110.08
15	141.24	105.13	306.31	185.7	136.07	98.01
Ave	154.071	111.289	284.275	209.823	131.16	103.634

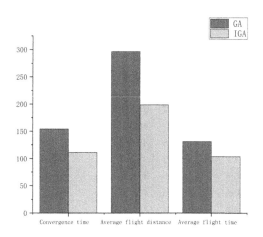

Fig. 3. The overall data comparison of the first case

It can be seen from Table 2 that in 15 groups of experiments, the convergence time of the improved algorithm decreases by about 27.8% on average; The flight distance of the improved algorithm UAV decreases by about 26.2% on average; The average flight time of the improved algorithm UAV decreases by about 21%

on average. It can also be seen from Fig. 3 that the performance of the improved algorithm has been significantly improved.

(a) The genetic algorithm   (b) The improved algorithm

Fig. 4. The roadmap of the second case

In the second case, a more complex flight environment is designed to test the performance of the two algorithms. Figure 4(a) shows the UAV flight route map of the genetic algorithm, and Fig. 4(b) shows the UAV flight route map of the improved algorithm. It can be seen from Fig. 4 that the improved algorithm can be used to find a feasible path with lower cost that meets the requirements of path planning.

Table 3. The overall data comparison of the second case

No.	Convergence time (s)		Average flight distance (m)		Average flight time (s)	
	GA	IGA	GA	IGA	GA	IGA
1	359.4	157.53	538.81	300.63	198.11	149.07
2	323.72	233.15	534.96	332.62	195.51	138.16
3	296.1	200.16	460.57	344.18	205.72	148.12
4	294.21	158.04	506.9	408.7	214.99	143.46
5	392.22	227.16	568.28	352.74	202.32	130.56
6	220.16	251.42	599.68	330.05	204.15	127.33
7	269.26	170.55	565.96	301.5	192.47	143.18
8	214.7	194.06	560.15	408.57	212.61	137.07
9	336.17	188.39	518.57	340.23	198.6	150.48
10	214.93	227.19	577.56	319.11	192.73	152.95
11	345.9	169.36	582.46	377.08	203.28	136.03
12	382.03	135.1	478.41	342.12	202.68	136.9
13	416.12	168.35	530.52	410.29	194.03	140.7
14	245.24	206.04	533.68	388.64	213.16	142.26
15	336.94	146.02	481.17	411.14	202.84	135.81
Ave	309.807	188.825	535.845	357.84	202.213	140.805

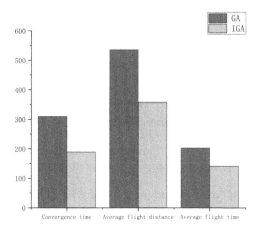

Fig. 5. The overall data comparison of the second case

It can be seen from Table 3 that in 15 groups of experiments, the convergence time of the improved algorithm decreases by about 39.1% on average; The flight distance of the improved algorithm UAV decreases by about 33.2% on average; The average flight time of the improved algorithm UAV decreases by about 30.4% on average. It can also be seen from Fig. 5 that the path planning capability of the UAV is excellent in complex environments with the improved algorithm.

In conclusion, from the above experimental results, it can be seen that the performance of the improved algorithm is better than that of the genetic algorithm.

5   Conclusions

To solve the contradiction between the search ability and the convergence ability of the genetic algorithm, this paper uses the Nash equilibrium algorithm in game theory to improve the genetic algorithm and balance the convergence and search ability in the UAV path planning problem. Experiments show that this algorithm can effectively improve the performance of the algorithm, and has a better performance in UAV path planning.

References

1. Wu, H., Shahidehpour, M.: Applications of wireless sensor networks for area coverage in microgrids. IEEE Trans. Smart Grid **9**(3), 1590–1598 (2016)
2. Saeed, R.A., Omri, M., Abdel-Khalek, S., Ali, E.S., Alotaibi, M.F.: Optimal path planning for drones based on swarm intelligence algorithm. Neural Comput. Appl. **34**(12), 10133–10155 (2022)
3. Puente-Castro, A., Rivero, D., Pazos, A., Fernandez-Blanco, E.: A review of artificial intelligence applied to path planning in UAV swarms. Neural Comput. Appl. **34**, 1–18 (2021)

4. Chen, J., Ling, F., Zhang, Y., You, T., Liu, Y., Du, X.: Coverage path planning of heterogeneous unmanned aerial vehicles based on ant colony system. Swarm Evol. Comput. **69**, 101005 (2022)
5. Meier, D., Tullumi, I., Stauffer, Y., Dornberger, R., Hanne, T.: A novel backup path planning approach with ACO. In: 2017 5th International Symposium on Computational and Business Intelligence (ISCBI), pp. 50–56. IEEE (2017)
6. Hosseininejad, S., Dadkhah, C.: Mobile robot path planning in dynamic environment based on cuckoo optimization algorithm. Int. J. Adv. Rob. Syst. **16**(2), 1729881419839575 (2019)
7. Kumar, R., Singh, L., Tiwari, R.: Path planning for the autonomous robots using modified grey wolf optimization approach. J. Intell. Fuzzy Syst. **40**(5), 9453–9470 (2021)
8. Sampson, J.R.: Adaptation in Natural and Artificial Systems (John H. Holland). MIT Press, Cambridge (1976)
9. Geng, L., Zhang, Y., Wang, J., Fuh, J.Y., Teo, S.: Cooperative mission planning with multiple UAVs in realistic environments. Unmanned Syst. **2**(01), 73–86 (2014)
10. Li, J., Huang, Y., Xu, Z., Wang, J., Chen, M.: Path planning of UAV based on hierarchical genetic algorithm with optimized search region. In: 2017 13th IEEE International Conference on Control and Automation (ICCA), pp. 1033–1038. IEEE (2017)
11. Ramirez-Atencia, C., Bello-Orgaz, G., Camacho, D., et al.: Solving complex multi-UAV mission planning problems using multi-objective genetic algorithms. Soft. Comput. **21**(17), 4883–4900 (2017)
12. Lamini, C., Benhlima, S., Elbekri, A.: Genetic algorithm based approach for autonomous mobile robot path planning. Proc. Comput. Sci. **127**, 180–189 (2018)
13. Guo, Y., Pan, Q., Sun, Q., Zhao, C., Wang, D., Feng, M.: Cooperative game-based multi-agent path planning with obstacle avoidance. In: 2019 IEEE 28th International Symposium on Industrial Electronics (ISIE), pp. 1385–1390. IEEE (2019)

Natural Human-Computer Interaction

Research on Network Traffic Anomaly Detection for Class Imbalance

Zhurong Wang, Jing Zhou, Zhanmin Wang, and Xinhong Hei[✉]

School of Computer Science and Engineering, Xi'an University of Technology, Xi'an 710048, China

{wangzhurong,zhanmin,heixinhong}@xaut.edu.cn

Abstract. It is actually a classification that the anomalistic detection on traffic of network belongs to. The imbalance of data about network traffic, leading to the disability of anomaly model on learning the characteristics of the minority class samples, makes the detection accuracy in the minority samples poor. Aiming at the imbalance of network flow data, a network traffic anomaly detection method combining Deep Convolutional Generative Adversarial Networks (DCGAN) and Vision Transformer is proposed to make the detection accuracy of network traffic data more perfect. The network traffic dataset is sampled, and the sampled imbalanced dataset is class balanced by DCGAN. The class balanced network traffic data is fed into Vision Transformer for prediction. To simplify the model structure, the vision Transformer model is proposed, and only N encoders are included in the vision Transformer, and the decoder structure is removed. Using residual network in encoder to solve the problem of model degradation. The dataset uses CIC-IDS-2017 network intrusion detection data. After experiments, it was enough to hold that the model which was proposed can positively perform class balancing of data and increase the prediction precision of data about network traffic.

Keywords: Class imbalance · Network traffic classification · Deep convolutional generative adversarial networks · Attention · Residual network

1 Introduction

Witnessing a rapid development of Internet and its global using, it has greatly changed people's way of life. While the Internet has brought great convenience, there are also many hidden security problems. In actual network traffic data transmission, normal traffic is much larger than abnormal traffic, and the class imbalance of network traffic data will cause the model prediction results to be biased towards the majority of samples, which also results in the low detection rate of many IDSs. Therefore, it is vital that finding a method which can effectively solve the class imbalance matter of data about network traffic and promote the detection rate of abnormal traffic.

At present, there have been some researches on network traffic anomaly detection at home and abroad, which are mainly divided into methods of artificial experience and prior knowledge, the method of traditional machine learning and deep learning. Xu et al. [1] advance a method that can draw the spatial and time features of network traffic

© The Author(s), under exclusive license to Springer Nature Singapore Pte Ltd. 2023
Z. Yu et al. (Eds.): CIRAC 2022, CCIS 1770, pp. 135–144, 2023.
https://doi.org/10.1007/978-981-99-0301-6_11

data, divide the data samples according to the quantity of data groups, and test them in public data sets. The consequence of his experiment indicate that the suggested method behaves well on accuracy. Yang et al. [2] put forward a detection model, introduced a residual network into multi-head self-attention, and alleviated the long tail effect caused by class imbalance through semi-supervised learning. The accuracy rate is higher than other deep learning models. Li et al. [3] put forward a network traffic anomaly detection model combining autoencoder and Mahalanobis distance. Amount of training was reduced by the reciprocal Mahalanobis distance and the discriminant threshold. The experiments show that it has a good detection effect on the dataset CICIDS2017 and NSL-KDD. However, the deep learning-based methods will produce overfitting and lack the treatment of imbalanced traffic data.

It is actually a classification that the anomalistic detection on traffic of network belongs to. The imbalance of data about network traffic, leading to the disability of anomaly model on learning the characteristics of the minority class samples, makes the detection accuracy in the minority samples poor. As the class imbalance problem has gradually attracted the attention of researchers, a series of excellent results have emerged. Such as the majority class weighted minority class oversampling algorithm [4], A Composed Oversampling and Undersampling Algorithm Originating from Slow Start Method [5], multi-stage Generative Adversarial Networks for fabric defect detection [6] and an improved majority-class weighted minority-class oversampling algorithm [7]. In the long run, network traffic anomaly detection should not only improve the detection accuracy, but also deal with data imbalance.

The major achievements of this paper include: 1) The DCGAN [8] is used to balance the classes of network traffic data, and high-precision network traffic data samples are generated through the convolution process in the generator. 2) A Vision Transformer (VT) model is proposed to calculate the balanced network traffic data, and finally, test it with CICIDS2017 [9] data set.

2 Related Theory

2.1 Deep Convolutional Generative Adversarial Networks

Generative Adversarial Network (GAN) [10] consists of discriminator and generator. The generator's role is to train the generated random noise to be close to the true samples, the discriminator's role is to judge the samples produced by the generator and the real samples. Generative adversarial network is a constant game between the discriminator and the generator, and finally reaches a balance. The optimization function is shown in formula (1):

$$\min_{B} \max_{A} V(A, B) = E_{s \sim p_{data}(s)}[\log A(s)] + E_{r \sim p_r(r)}[\log(1 - A(B(r)))] \quad (1)$$

In formula (1), $B(r)$ denotes the output of the generator, $A(B(r))$ denotes the likelihood that the discriminator discriminates the data produced by the generator as true, $A(s)$ denotes the likelihood of discriminating the data s as true. DCGAN is based on GAN, and the discriminator and generator use convolutional neural networks for data generation and feature extraction. Based on DCGAN, this paper proposes discriminating network and generating network suitable for network traffic. Figure 1 shows the convolution process.

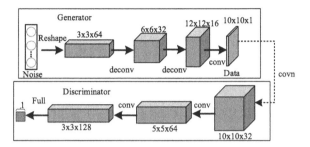

Fig. 1. The convolution process

In Fig. 1, the overall structure consists of a discriminating network and generating network, each of which includes 3 layers. The training goal of the generating network is to convert the input noise (Noise) into the target data, and the discriminant network distinguishes the true and false of the produced data and the real data.

2.2 Vision Transformer

Transformer [11] is composed of a decoder and an encoder. The kernel of this model is attention mechanism.

Each of which includes Feed Forward network and Multi-Head Attention mechanism. Each of which includes Feed Forward network, Masked Multi-Head Attention mechanism and Multi-Head Attention mechanism. To simplify the amount of calculation for the model, the Vision Transformer designed in this paper only includes an encoder, including n Encoders. Key information is extracted through feed forward networks and multi-head attention mechanisms. Figure 2 is the Vision Transformer structure diagram.

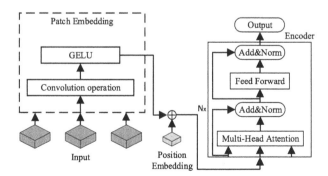

Fig. 2. Vision Transformer structure diagram

To learn the effect of different sequence position features on the prediction consequences, the PositionEmbedding is represented by cosine and sine functions of various
frequencies, as shown in formulas (2)–(3):

$$Pst_{(x,2k)} = \sin(x/10000^{2k/d \, \text{mod} \, el})\tag{2}$$

$$Pe_{(x,2k+1)} = \cos(x/10000^{2k/d \, \text{mod} \, el})\tag{3}$$

Multi-head attention mechanism integrates multiple attention mechanisms internally,
as represented by formula (4):

$$MltH(Q, K, V) = Concat(y_1, y_2, \cdots, y_n)W^o\tag{4}$$

Splicing the self-attention mechanisms, and then performing matrix operations with
the additional weight matrix, compressing the self-attention of different subspaces into
a matrix can extract important features more accurately.

3   Network Traffic Anomaly Detection Model Combining Generative Adversarial Network and Transformer

Obtain the network traffic data set, and classify various abnormal traffic and normal traffic. Since the normal traffic data is much larger than the abnormal traffic, the class with
a small amount of data in the abnormal traffic is regarded as the class imbalanced data.
The class-imbalanced data is transformed into class-balanced data through a deep convolutional generative adversarial network, and the balanced data is input into the Vision
Transformer for prediction. Figure 3 shows the framework of the anomaly detection
model.

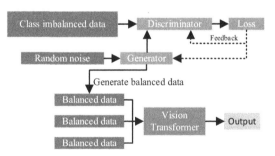

Fig. 3. Anomaly detection model framework

Figure 3 is composed of two parts. Part one adopts DCGAN to balance the class
imbalanced data. First, DCGAN is trained with class-imbalanced data, then the information produced by the trained generator and the original sample are merged into balanced
data. The second part inputs the balanced data into the Vision Transformer for abnormal
traffic detection.

3.1 Network Traffic Anomaly Detection Algorithm Combining Generative Adversarial Network and Transformer

A network traffic anomaly detection algorithm combining deep convolution generative adversarial network and Vision Transformer (DCGAN-VT) as follows.

Algorithm 1 DCGAN-VT Algorithm
Input: network traffic data($x_1,x_2,...,x_n,y$);
Output: prediction results y=($y_1,y_2,...,y_n$);
Begin:
    Statistics on the number of each class m;
    if m < 10000
        Class balancing with deep convolutional generative adversarial network;
    End if
    The balanced data is split up into test set and training set;
    Building a network traffic anomaly detection model of Vision Transformer;
    For 1 to n do
        Training set training model;
        Gradient descent update weight;
    End For
    Input the test set into the trained network traffic anomaly detection model for testing, record the experimental results y=($y_1,y_2,...,y_n$);
    Return y=($y_1,y_2,...,y_n$);
End:

4 Experiment Analysis

4.1 Experimental Data

It is the CICIDS2017 dataset [9] that used in this paper, which is widely used in network anomaly detection research. This data set comes from the network traffic data that collected from Monday to Friday, including normal traffic and abnormal traffic caused by common attacks. The network traffic data caused by these attacks is classified and counted, and 11 types of 10 attack classes and normal class (BENIGN) are selected for experiments. The dataset contains a total of 2,830,608 pieces of data.

4.2 Data Preprocessing

The data preprocessing steps are shown below.
    Step 1: The dataset is cut apart into test set and training set, four fifths of which are training sets, one fifth are test sets.
    Step 2: We delete outliers (Nan and Infinity in the data), and convert all classification labels into numbers according to one-hot encoding.
    Step 3: Fill in the missing values of continuous variables with adjacent mean values.
    Step 4: Finally, standardize all data.

4.3 Evaluation Indicators

The classification evaluation indicators in this experiment include accuracy (A), F1-score (F1-S), recall (R) and precision (P).

In the classification problem, TP represents true positive prediction, FP indicates false positive prediction, TN expresses true negative prediction, FN represents false negative prediction.

4.4 DCGAN Class Balance Experiment

In the experiment, Adam is selected to the DCGAN model's optimizer and the learning rate 0.0001, the loss function selects the cross entropy loss function, besides the iteration number is 14000 times. Use DCGAN to balance less than 10,000 pieces of data. Figure 4 shows the change of the loss of each class of discriminator during the training process. As shown in Fig. 4, it can be found that with the constant change of iteration times, the loss of the discriminator decreases slowly, fluctuates up and down in a small range, and the model training tends to be stable.

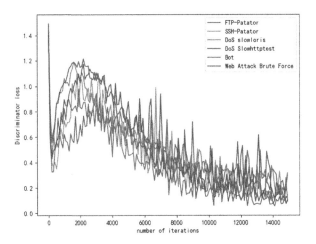

Fig. 4. Discriminator loss change diagram

4.5 Analysis of the Experimental of Vision Transformer

In the experiment, Feed the balanced data into the VT for anomaly detection.

The experimental data is cut apart into one fifth of the test set and four fifths of the training set. Table 1 shows the comparison of the Vision Transformer in the balanced dataset and the imbalanced dataset is shown. After the experimental test, the accuracy of the Vision Transformer iterated 20,000 times in the balanced dataset is 99.24%, and the accuracy in the imbalanced dataset is 92.33%.

Table 1. Performance comparison of Vision Transformer datasets before and after balancing

Class	Before data balance			After data balance		
	P	R	F1-s	P	R	F1-s
BENIGN	79.9%	86.8%	83.2%	99.9%	99.7%	99.8%
DoS Hulk	93.0%	96.1%	94.5%	99.2%	99.2%	99.2%
PortScan	98.1%	99.3%	98.7%	98.4%	99.8%	99.1%
DDoS	94.4%	91.8%	93.1%	99.9%	99.5%	99.7%
DoS GoldenEye	95.1%	95.0%	95.1%	99.5%	99.4%	99.4%
FTP-Patator	98.0%	90.3%	94.0%	99.8%	99.7%	99.8%
SSH-Patator	98.6%	88.7%	93.4%	99.2%	98.4%	98.8%
DoS Slowloris	88.1%	88.3%	88.2%	97.8%	97.7%	97.8%
DoS Slowhttptest	91.1%	94.2%	92.6%	98.2%	98.3%	98.2%
Bot	84.5%	92.1%	88.2%	99.7%	99.8%	99.7%
Web Attack	76.0%	76.6%	76.3%	99.7%	99.7%	99.7%

As could be perceived from Table 1, from the three evaluation indicators of recall, precision and F1-score, after class balanced, the three indicators are improved in 11 classes. The balanced dataset was tested in Decision Tree (DT), Bidirectional LSTM (BiLSTM), CNN combined with Residual Network (CNN-ResNet) and Vision Transformer (VT) methods, and the test accuracy was 92.9%, 96.1%, 97.0% and 99.2% respectively. The contrast of each model on the balanced dataset is shown in Table 2.

Table 2. Performance of each model on the balanced dataset

Class	Model	P	R	F1-s
BENIGN	DT	99.9%	99.9%	99.9%
	BiLSTM	99.3%	99.8%	99.5%
	CNN-ResNet	98.8%	99.5%	99.2%
	VT	99.9%	99.7%	99.8%
DoS Hulk	DT	83.0%	99.8%	90.6%
	BiLSTM	96.9%	98.9%	97.9%
	CNN-ResNet	95.3%	97.8%	96.6%
	VT	99.2%	99.2%	99.2%
PortScan	DT	99.7%	99.9%	99.8%
	BiLSTM	96.7%	96.3%	96.5%

(*continued*)

Table 2. (*continued*)

Class	Model	P	R	F1-s
	CNN-ResNet	98.3%	99.9%	99.1%
	VT	98.4%	99.8%	99.1%
DDoS	DT	99.9%	96.6%	98.2%
	BiLSTM	98.7%	98.1%	98.4%
	CNN-ResNet	99.3%	95.2%	97.2%
	VT	99.9%	99.5%	99.7%
DoS GoldenEye	DT	96.2%	95.4%	95.8%
	BiLSTM	95.3%	98.3%	96.8%
	CNN-ResNet	97.9%	95.7%	96.8%
	VT	99.5%	99.4%	99.4%
FTP-Patator	DT	96.4%	98.2%	97.3%
	BiLSTM	97.0%	95.9%	96.4%
	CNN-ResNet	97.9%	97.2%	97.5%
	VT	99.8%	99.7%	99.8%
SSH-Patator	DT	91.7%	99.5%	95.4%
	BiLSTM	98.1%	93.3%	95.7%
	CNN-ResNet	96.5%	98.2%	97.3%
	VT	99.2%	98.4%	98.8%
DoS slowloris	DT	99.5%	61.2%	75.8%
	BiLSTM	94.3%	94.6%	94.4%
	CNN-ResNet	96.8%	92.4%	94.5%
	VT	97.8%	97.7%	97.8%
DoS slowhttptest	DT	60%	99.8%	74.9%
	BiLSTM	92.0%	89.6%	90.8%
	CNN-ResNet	88.4%	92.3%	90.3%
	VT	98.2%	98.3%	98.2%
Bot	DT	97.6%	96.9%	97.2%
	BiLSTM	91.2%	94.8%	92.9%
	CNN-ResNet	99.1%	98.8%	98.9%
	VT	99.7%	99.8%	99.7%
Web attack	DT	98%	98.9%	98.4%
	BiLSTM	97.4%	97.3%	97.3%
	CNN-ResNet	98.6%	99.8%	99.2%
	VT	99.7%	99.7%	99.7%

In Table 2, the performance of each model in the balanced data is compared. It can be obtained that the contrast of the put forward model is generally preferable, and only the indicators of the two classes of BENIGN and PortScan are all less than or equal to the DT model. The F1-score covers the recall rate and the precision rate, and is more convincing.

In Fig. 5, the accuracy of each model in the data before and after balanced is compared. Although the improvement percentage of the VT model is the least among the four models, its prediction accuracy is the highest among the four models.

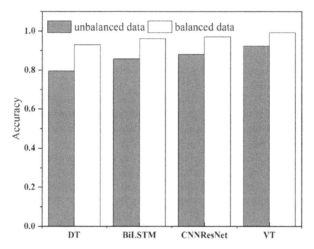

Fig. 5. Comparison of accuracy of each model before and after balancing

5   Conclusion

In this paper, a network traffic anomaly detection method which combine Generative Adversarial Network and Transformer is put forward, which validly solves the problems of existing network traffic data class imbalance and low detection accuracy. In the prediction model of this paper, DCGAN is used for balancing the class imbalanced data, and the Vision Transformer model is used to improve the anomaly detection accuracy. Model detection results are evaluated by accuracy, F1-score and recall. It is obvious from the above that DCGAN can enhance the detection effect after balancing the data, and the VT model can promote the detection accuracy through the attention mechanism. Then, normal traffic and abnormal traffic will be deeply mined, and build a detection model that can identify new abnormal traffic.

Acknowledgments. This work is partially supported by Natural Science Foundation of China (No. U20B2050, 61773313), Key Research and Development Program of Shaanxi Province (2019TD-014), Science and technology research project of Shaanxi Province (2021JM-346).

References

1. Hongping, X., Zewen, M., Hang, Y., et al.: Network traffic anomaly detection technology based on convolutional recurrent neural network. Netinfo Secur. **21**(7), 54–62 (2021)
2. Yue-lin, Y., Zong-ze, B.: Network anomaly detection based on deep learning. Comput. Sci. **48**(S2), 540–546 (2021)
3. Beibei, L., Li, P., Feifei, D.: A method combining Mahalanobis distance and autoencoder to detect abnormal network traffic. Comput. Eng. **48**(4), 133–142 (2022)
4. Barua, S., Islam, M.M., Yao, X.: MWMOTE–majority weighted minority oversampling technique for imbalanced data set learning. IEEE Trans. Knowl. Data Eng. **26**(2), 405–425 (2012)
5. Park, S., Park, H.: Combined oversampling and undersampling method based on slow-start algorithm for imbalanced network traffic. Computing **103**(3), 401–424 (2020). https://doi.org/10.1007/s00607-020-00854-1
6. Liu, J., Wang, C., Su, H.: Multistage GAN for fabric defect detection. IEEE Trans. Image Process. **29**, 3388–3400 (2019)
7. Wang, C.R., Shao, X.H.: An improving majority weighted minority oversampling technique for imbalanced classification problem. IEEE Access **9**, 5069–5082 (2020)
8. Wu, Q., Chen, Y., Meng, J.: DCGAN-based data augmentation for tomato leaf disease identification. IEEE Access **8**, 98716–98728 (2020)
9. Sharafaldin, I., Lashkari, A.H., Ghorbani, A.A.: Toward generating a new intrusion detection dataset and intrusion traffic characterization. ICISSp **1**, 108–116 (2018)
10. Goodfellow, I., Pouget-Abadie, J., Mirza, M.: Generative adversarial nets. In: Advances in Neural Information Processing Systems, vol. 27 (2014)
11. Vaswani, A., Shazeer, N., Parmar, N.: Attention is all you need. Adv. Neural. Inf. Process. Syst. **30**, 6000–6010 (2017)

Dual-Sequence LSTM Multimodal Emotion Recognition Based on Attention Mechanism

Danyang Dong[✉], Ruirui Ji, and Yuan Mei

Xi'an University of Technology, Xi'an, China
ddongooo@163.com

Abstract. This paper presents a multimodal emotion recognition method based on dual-sequence Long Short-Term Memory (LSTM) network with attention mechanism. The ResNeXt50 network and coordinated attention mechanism are introduced to the video sequences to acquire the long-term dependence information in the location and space of video images. CNN with self-attention mechanism is utilized to catch the semantic features of audio sequences. In order to eliminate redundancy, a dual-sequence LSTM cross-modal network embedded with self-attention mechanism is applied for emotion feature fusion, and finally get the emotion output. The experimental results on RAVDESS dataset and eNTERFACE '05 dataset prove that, compared with different baseline methods, the proposed algorithm is more attentive to the correlation between features and can significantly improve the recognition accuracy.

Keywords: Multimodal · Emotion recognition · Attention mechanism · LSTM

1 Introduction

Affective computing was born at the MIT Media Lab to give computers the ability of recognition, understanding, expression and adaption to human emotions [1]. Emotion recognition is an important research direction in affective computing, with a variety of applications such as lie detection, audio-visual monitoring and online conferences. At present, great progress has been made in single mode emotion recognition. However, the emotion is presented by a series of modal, also have a certain correlation among them. At the same time, different modes have different degrees of contribution to emotional outcomes [2].

In general, the performance of multimodal emotion recognition is superior to single mode. Video content analysis is a very hot and challenging direction in the area of machine vision. From the perspective of video emotion analysis, fusion of facial expression and speech information has naturally become the main research focus.

According to the fusion method, current multimodal emotion recognition is segmented into feature layer fusion [3], decision layer fusion [4,5] and model layer

© The Author(s), under exclusive license to Springer Nature Singapore Pte Ltd. 2023
Z. Yu et al. (Eds.): CIRAC 2022, CCIS 1770, pp. 145–157, 2023.
https://doi.org/10.1007/978-981-99-0301-6_12

fusion [6, 7]. Feature layer fusion method firstly fuse multiple single modal emotion features and then classify them. Kim [8] proposed a two-layer Deep Blief Network (DBN) structure, which fused features of video and audio modes in final stage, and then used Support Vector Machine (SVM) to evaluate and categorize them. Atmaja [5] used BiLSTM network to extract and directly merge to learn multi-modal representations. Feature fusion layer method could keep more data information, but easily cause the dimension disaster and redundancy. Decision layer fusion method is to classify and then fuse decision results. Sahoo [9] used Hidden Markov Model (HMM) and SVM to evaluate the audio and video modes respectively, and fused the dual-mode results according to different decision rules. The structural complexity of decision layer fusion is reduced, however the correlation of different modal features is ignored. Model layer fusion method utilize powerful models to improve recognition performance. Huang [10] proposed Transformer model to fuse audio-visual representations. Liu [6] proposed Capsule graph convolutional network for multimodal emotion recognition. Model layer fusion method do not have dependencies on individual learners of audio and video modes.

The better the diversity, the higher the fusion effect. However, the existing methods lack the modeling in the time dimension, and the capturing ability of long-term dependencies is still poor.

The Coordinate Attention mechanism [11] was introduced to let the recognition model to focus on the interest region of the facial expression. The self-attention mechanism [12] was used to grasp the internal correlation of audio sequence features and obtain a more expressive Mel-scale Frequency Cepstral Coefficients (MFCC) feature representation. In order to further reduce feature redundancy in the fusion process, a dual-sequence LSTM network embedded with self-attention mechanism is used to grasp interdependent features in sequence and learn audio and video fusion representation. Adding different attention module could make the network more sensitive to critical information, thus to improve the multi-feature discriminant ability.

The paper is arranged as follows: Sect. 2 recommends dual-sequence LSTM emotion recognition model based on attention mechanism, Sect. 3 describes the experimental process and results analysis, Sect. 4 summarizes the full paper.

2   Proposed Method

The method of this paper includes four modules, multimodal data pre-processing, feature extraction, feature fusion and emotion classification, as shown in Fig. 1. ResNeXt with coordinated attention mechanism aims to obtain the video sequence features. 1D CNN with self-attention mechanism captures the audio features. Then dual-sequence LSTM fusion module embedded with self-attention mechanism computes the emotion output.

2.1   Video Sequence Preprocessing

By means of image preprocessing and enhancement algorithm, the important features in the face are highlighted, also the influence of relatively unimpor-

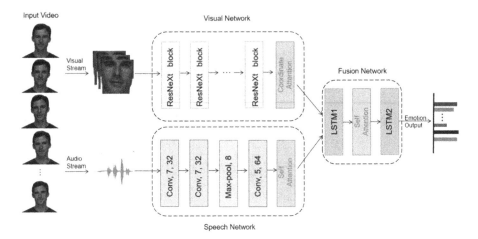

Fig. 1. The proposed framework of multimodal emotion recognition.

tant noise and background is suppressed, so that the network can capture more robust features and lead the model stronger generalization ability. In this paper, 30 consecutive frames are drawed from the video, and 2D face markers are supplied to each image to crop the face region, and the measurement is adjusted to 224×224. The random cropping horizontal flip and normalization method are used to enhance the data.

2.2   Video Sequence Feature Extraction

Considering the video sequences are characterized by spatio-temporal structure, ResNeXt network is used to learn facial expressions and actions, the addition of coordinate attention mechanism enhances the measure of content similarity by selectively focusing on the key information parts of video features, then the key features with attention can be extracted. ResNeXt is the reinforcement of ResNet. The number of group convolutions in ResNeXt is determined by a variable cardinality, which performs better on large datasets and deeper networks. The obtained video sequence features are taken as input, denoted as X_V.

$$\hat{X}_V = ResNeXt50\left(X_V\right) \in R^{C \times S \times H \times W} \tag{1}$$

where C, S, H and W represent the channels number, and the length, height and width of the video sequence respectively.

The output feature $\hat{X}_V$ of ResNeXt network is inputted into the coordinated attention module, and the feature is decomposed into two one-dimensional features along different orientations, which helps networks to target features of interest more precisely. The output is $\hat{Y}_V$. The specific structure of coordinated attention is shown in Fig. 2.

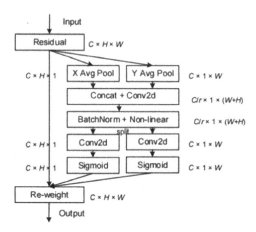

Fig. 2. Coordinate attention.

Coordinated attention takes middle characteristic tensoras $X = [x_1, x_2, ...,$ $x_C] \in R^{C \times H \times W}$ as input, and transform the output tensor with augmented representations $X = [y_1, y_2, ..., y_C]$ as the same size as X.

Firstly, given the tensor X, every channel is coded along the abscissa and ordinate respectively. The output of the c-th channel at high h can be expressed as Z_c^h, at wide W can be expressed as Z_c^w, as the follows:

The Features aggregated horizontally and vertically are transformed by a convolution kernel of size 1. Intermediate feature map is generated to get the spatial information in two directions, where shows the reduction ratio, as the follows:

$$Z_c^h (h) = \frac{1}{W} \sum_{0 \leq i \leq W} x_c (h, i) \tag{2}$$

$$Z_c^w (w) = \frac{1}{H} \sum_{0 \leq i < H} x_c (j, w) \tag{3}$$

The Features aggregated horizontally and vertically are transformed by a convolution kernel of size 1. Intermediate feature map $f \in R^{C/r \times (H+W)}$ is generated to get the spatial information in two directions, where r shows the reduction ratio, as the follows:

$$f = \delta \left(F_1 \left([Z^h, Z^w] \right) \right) \tag{4}$$

In (4), F_1 is the 1×1 convolution transformation function, δ is the a non-linear activation function, f is segmented into f^h and f^w two characteristic mappings along the space dimension, then the characteristic mappings are converted to have the same number of channels as the input X through convolution kernels of size 1, as the follows:

$$g^h = \sigma\left(F_h\left(f^h\right)\right) \tag{5}$$

$$g^w = \sigma\left(F_w\left(f^w\right)\right) \tag{6}$$

In Eqs. (5) and (6), F_h and F_w are respectively (1×1) convolution transformation functions of f^h and f^w. σ is the sigmoid function. Expand the outputs g^h and g^w respectively, then take them as weights of attention. The final output feature formula as:

$$y_c\left(i, j\right) = x_c\left(i, j\right) \times g_c^h\left(i\right) \times g_c^w\left(j\right) \tag{7}$$

2.3   Audio Sequence Preprocessing

In order to avoid audio interference and output errors, the first 0.5 s audio are trimmed and consistent for the next 2.45 s, until the first 0.5 s of audio does not include sound. The top 13 MFCC features of each audio segment are extracted as suggested by speech emotion recognition research [13].

2.4   Audio Sequence Feature Extraction

The speech emotion features are analyzed in the frequency domain. The MFCC characteristics are extracted as the speech emotion features. Considering the temporality of audio features, CNN with self-attention mechanism are used to obtain MFCC characteristics of audio sequences.

The preprocessed audio feature, denoted as input X_A, and the associated features of adjacent audio are extracted through the convolution layer, then the max-pooling is used for downsampling to squeeze features and remove redundant information, the formulas as:

$$\hat{X}_A = BN\left(ReLU\left(Conv1D\left(X_A, k_A\right)\right)\right) \tag{8}$$

$$\hat{X}_A = Dropout\left(BN\left(MaxPool\left(\hat{X}_A\right)\right)\right) \tag{9}$$

In Eqs. (8) and (9), k_A is the convolution kernel size of the audio mode, $\hat{X}_A$ is the learned semantic features, BN is Batch Normalization. The learned features are inputted into 1D timporal convolution again, and then the obtained features are flattened to get the audio high-order semantic features, the output is $\hat{X}_A$.

$$\hat{X}_A = Flatten\left(BN\left(ReLU\left(Conv1D\left(\hat{X}_A, k_A\right)\right)\right)\right) \tag{10}$$

Different from attention mechanism, self-attention mechanism iteratively update its own information. By means of self-attention mechanism, audio modes can learn intramodal representation, so that it can focus more features which have big impact on the weight of results. The self-attention mechanism reflects the effect of adjacent elements on features, and its query Q, key K, and values V share same audio morphological representations in diverse projection spaces.

$$self - attention\,(Q, K, V) = softmax\left(\frac{QK^T}{\sqrt{d_k}}\right)V \qquad (11)$$

Q, K, V are symbols of $Z_A^{[i-1]}$. $Z_A^{[i-1]}$ represents different parameter matrices for different projection spaces. The learned weight coefficients are fed back to the fully connected layer to acquire features adaptive learning result. The formula as:

$$\hat{X}_A = LN\left(Z_A^{[i]} + Feedforward\left(Z_A^i\right)\right) \in R^{d_f} \qquad (12)$$

where, LN represents layer normalization, $Feedforward$ represents the fully connected layer, d_f represents the dimension of the extracted features. This treatment implements feature selection of audio higher-order features to obtain feature output $\hat{X}_A$ which has a greater impact on the result.

2.5 Audio-Video Bimodal Features Fusion

The higher-order semantic features learned from the audio-video are imported the cross-modal block respectively. In order to make more reasonable decision, dual-sequence LSTM network and self-attention module are used to learn the fusion representation of long-term dependent information and higher-level time-domain features.

LSTM network learn the information on which sequence data depends on over time. The specific structure of LSTM is shown in Fig. 3.

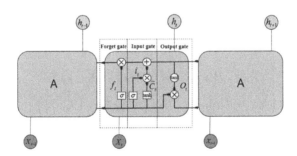

Fig. 3. The structure of LSTM Block.

In Fig. 3, A is the neighboring neuron, h_t is the output of neuron at time t, C is the candidate state. There are also three types of unit gating, input gate i_t, output gate O_t and forget gate f_t.

The addition of layers raises the abstraction level of the input observation time, and the two-layer LSTM stacked together can learn the higher level of time domain feature representation, which makes the network have better expression performance. In order to better improve the model recognition effect, the self-attention mechanism is assimilated into the input sequence to acquire features of long-distance interdependence, as shown in Fig. 4.

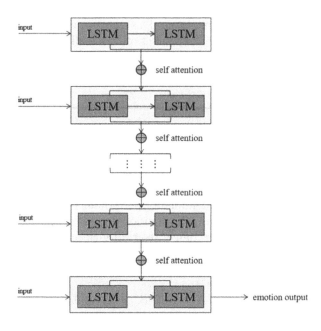

Fig. 4. Dual-sequence LSTM model with embedded attention mechanism.

The model is major made up of dual-sequence LSTM network embedded with a self-attention mechanism, the unit states of the LSTM network are taken as the import X_t of the self-attention mechanism module. In dual-sequence LSTM, different weights are assigned to the network according to the importance of the network, and the attention weight matrix W is obtained.

$$W = softmax\left(\left(QK^T\right)/\sqrt{d_k}\right) \tag{13}$$

where, d_k is the dimension of the key value, $1/\sqrt{d_k}$ is zoom factor, and the scaling factor to prevent the inner product value from affecting the learning of neural network. By multiplying the weight matrix W with the state value V of LSTM, and then using the $softmax$ function to predict emotions, prediction function $\hat{y}$ is shown as (14).

$$\hat{y} = softmax\left(\left(QK^T\right)/\sqrt{d_k}\right)V \tag{14}$$

Optimizing the model with cross-entropy loss, as the follows:

$$L = -\sum_i y_i log\left(\hat{y}_i\right) \tag{15}$$

where, $y = [y_1, y_2, ..., y_n]^T$ is one-hot vector of emotion labels, n is the number of sentiment categories, which is take n as 8 in this paper.

The TOP-1 evaluation index is used as the evaluation criterion, as the network training times increase, loss function gradually decreases, the model achieves the optimal recognition performance, and finally the classification of audio and video emotion recognition is obtained.

3   Experiments

3.1   Datasets

Ryerson Affective Speech and Song Audiovisual Database (RAVDESS) [14] is a multimodal affective recognition dataset, which contains 1440 short speech video clips of 24 actors to record the high quality performance of the actors after they are told to express their emotions. The emotion dataset contains eight emotions: neutral, calm, happiness, sadness, anger, fear, disgust and surprise.

eNTERFACE '05 is an English-language audio and video emotion dataset that records 46 men and women's emotional clips, including anger, disgust, fear, happiness, sadness, and surprise.

The datasets were subjected to 5-fold cross-validation, and actors were divided into training set and testing set in a 5:1 ratio.

3.2   Experimental Setting

This experiment completed the training of the whole model in the system platform Ubuntu 18.02, CPU@3.0 GHZ, CUDA 11.2, NVIDIA RTX 2080.

In the training phase, the face images of the datasets are normalized between $[-1,1]$, the training data can be forced to maintain the same distribution to expedite model convergent speed. In the model with dropout, set the parameter p as 0.2, then each node does not work with the probability of 20%, which can effectively alleviate the occurrence of over fitting. Adam optimizer [15] was used in the overall experimental process, and the total epoch was set to 70, that is, the complete training set passed the network 70 times. Batch size was set to 64, then model training shock was reduced and could converge to a better level. The learning rate is 0.001. With the increase of iteration times, the model loss value decreases continuously, and the model parameters gradually approach a relatively stationary state. The final identification accuracy of the model is determined by the average accuracy of 5-fold cross validation.

3.3   Experimental Design

Three groups of experiments were set up to examine the validity of the model. The specific experimental design is as follows.

(1) To determine the effectiveness of the model, this model adopts the latest multi-mode fusion algorithm. Top-1 evaluation index is used as evaluation criteria, which is the eight emotional categories probability take the highest probability in a category. If the probability is the highest category of this test image categories, it is suggested that predict correctly, whereas forecast fault by mistake.

(2) To test the effect on model precision of added attention mechanism, ablation experiment was carried out to verify whether the self-attention mechanism, coordinated attention mechanism and self-attention mechanism embedded in the dual-sequence LSTM fusion module could enhance the discernment precision of model.

(3) To examine the generalization ability of the emotion recognition model, the experimental comparison of different models is carried out on eNTERFACE '05 dataset.

3.4   Results and Discussion

Experiment 1: By comparing the proposed method with various methods in literature [16–20], the comparison of recognition accuracy between our method and other fusion algorithms is shown in Table 1.

Multiple multimodal fusion algorithms are taken as the baseline, which are divided into the following categories.

1) Early Fusion: Feature fusion in multimodal emotion recognition based on DNN [16] and MCBP [17] are two typical early fusion methods.

2) Late Fusion: Adopt the average and multiplication methods as the baseline.

3) Late Fusion: The multiplication layer [18], which adds a weight reduction factor in CE loss to suppress weak patterns.

4) Modle Fusion: Adopt the average and multiplication methods as the baseline. MMTM [19] module achieves the fusion between modes by adding different feature layers, and realizes the feature fusion of convolutional layers with different spatial dimensions.

5) Modal Fusion: The CFN-SR [20] module completes the transmission of semantic features through cross-modal blocks, ensures the validity and completeness of information transmission.

Table 1. Comparison of multimodal fusion method and the proposed method on RAVDESS dataset.

Modal	Fusion stage	Accuracy	#Params
3D ResNext50 (Vid.)	–	62.99	25.88M
1D CNN (Aud.)	–	56.53	0.03M
Averaging	Late	68.82	25.92M
Multiplicative β = 0.3	Late	70.35	25.92M
Multiplication	Late	70.56	25.92M
Concat + FC [18]	Early	71.04	26.87M
MCBP [17]	Early	71.32	51.03M
MMTM [19]	Model	73.12	31.97M
CFN-SR [20]	Model	75.76	26.30M
(Ours)	**Model**	**76.16**	**28.70M**

From Table 1, the accuracy of the model in this paper is 76.16% when the number of parameters is 28.70M, which is the most advanced level. Compared with the baseline of single mode, the accuracy of the model is improved by more than 10%, which verifies the necessity of multimodal feature fusion. Although the model improvement adds 2.40M parameter, it brings significant performance improvement. The network accuracy have risen by 5% compared with the earlier fusion methods, which shows that it is so difficult to find the correlation between audio and video patterns using the early fusion method. In addition, the proposed model is 0.4% better than the best-performing CFN-SR [20], which indicates that the proposed model fully complements the features of the two modes and reduces the redundancy of features.

Experiment 2: For examining the efficiency of the improved model, the emotion recognition network composed of 3D ResNext50, 1D CNN and two-layer LSTM feature fusion network was used as the basic model. By adding different attention mechanisms to the model for ablation experiments, Table 2 shows the experimental results.

Table 2. Performance comparison of different attention mechanisms added to the model.

Model	Accuracy	#Params
Modal with no attention mechanism	71.50	25.73M
Coordinate attention (Vid.)	75.23	26.55M
Self-attention(Aud.)	73.48	26.03M
LSTM model with self-attention	74.13	26.76M
(Ours)	**76.16**	**28.70M**

Table 2 shows that the capability is usually improved with attention mechanism. For example, when only coordinate attention mechanism is added, the recognition accuracy is 75.23%, which is 3.73% higher than that without any attention. It reflects that the coordinate attention mechanism can catch cross-channel information, spatial and positional information, which is helpful for the model to locate more accurately and learn more distinguishing features. When self-attention mechanism is added to audio characteristic extraction module, the recognition accuracy is increased by 1.98% compared with that without any attention, which indicates that the self-attention mechanism can cut down the redundant features of the audio and improves the recognition accuracy. Using the dual-sequence LSTM embedded with self-attention mechanism only in the model fusion stage, improves the model accuracy by 2.63%, which shows that the model can consider the complementary information of different modes and extract more complex dependencies in time series data. The experiments indicate that different mechanisms of attention perform differently on different network models. The addition of attention mechanisms increases the model parameters, but enhances the multi-feature discrimination ability, which is of extremely vital practical significance to create an emotion recognition system with high recognition rate and better network model.

Experiment 3: For examining the generalization ability of the proposed emotion recognition model, the experimental comparison of different models is carried out on eNTERFACE '05 dataset.

Table 3. Comparative experiments on the eNTERFACE '05 dataset.

Model	Dataset	Accuracy	#Params
CapsGCN [6]	**eNTERFACE '05**	80.23	33.15M
(Ours)	**eNTERFACE '05**	**81.04**	**28.70M**

For the purpose of measuring the generalization performance of the model, this paper increases the diversity of the datasets. The eNTERFACE '05 dataset include accurate emotional videos judged by experts, recording the emotional responses of actors after listening to different short stories. The comparative test in Table 3 shows that the model can still show high recognition ability after changing the data set, which verifies the advantages of strong fitting ability and good network performance of the model.

4   Summary

This paper proposes a dual-sequence LSTM multimodal emotion recognition based on attention mechanism method, through adding different attention mechanism improve the correlation of modal information. ResNeXt network combined with coordinated attention mechanism and convolution network combined with self-attention mechanism feature extraction method of video and audio sequence. The dual-sequence LSTM network embedded with self-attention mechanism is used to fuse features to eliminate redundancy. The results of the experiment on RAVDESS dataset and eNTERFACE '05 dataset show that of the method could get higher accuracy than other multimodal fusion method. The validity of different attention mechanisms in the model is also tested by ablation experiments. How to design multimodal representation learning method to improve the recognition accuracy will be the next research work.

References

1. Korsmeyer, C., Rosalind, W.: Affective computing. Mind. Mach. **9**(3), 443–447 (1999)
2. Chen, L., Wu, M., Pedrycz, W., Hirota, K.: Emotion Recognition and Understanding for Emotional Human-Robot Interaction Systems. SCI, vol. 926. Springer, Cham (2021). https://doi.org/10.1007/978-3-030-61577-2
3. Tripathi, S., Beigi, H.: Multi-Modal Emotion recognition on IEMOCAP Dataset using Deep Learning. arXiv preprint arXiv:1804.05788 (2018)
4. Zhang, S., Zhang, S., Huang, T., Gao, W., Tian, Q.: Learning affective features with a hybrid deep model for audio-visual emotion recognition. IEEE Trans. Circ. Syst. Video Technol. **28**(10), 3030–3043 (2017)
5. Atmaja, B., Akagi, M.: Multitask learning and multistage fusion for dimensional audiovisual emotion recognition. In: ICASSP 2020 IEEE International Conference on Acoustics, Speech and Signal Processing (ICASSP), pp. 4482–4486. IEEE (2020)
6. Liu, J., et al.: Multimodal emotion recognition with capsule graph convolutional based representation fusion. In: ICASSP 2021 IEEE International Conference on Acoustics, Speech and Signal Processing (ICASSP), pp. 6339–6343. IEEE (2021)
7. Sun, L., Liu, B., Tao, J., Lian, Z.: Multimodal cross and self-attention network for speech emotion recognition. In: ICASSP 2021 IEEE International Conference on Acoustics, Speech and Signal Processing (ICASSP), pp. 4275–4279. IEEE (2021)
8. Kim, Y., Lee, H., Provost, E.: Deep learning for robust feature generation in audio-visual emotion recognition. In: 2013 IEEE International Conference on Acoustics, Speech and Signal Processing, pp. 3687–3691. IEEE (2013)
9. Sahoo, S., Routray, A.: Emotion recognition from audio-visual data using rule based decision level fusion. In: 2016 IEEE Students' Technology Symposium (TechSym), pp. 7–12. IEEE (2016)
10. Huang, J., Tao, J., Liu, B., Lian, Z., Niu, M.: Multimodal transformer fusion for continuous emotion recognition. In: ICASSP 2020 IEEE International Conference on Acoustics, Speech and Signal Processing (ICASSP), pp. 3507–3511. IEEE (2020)
11. Hou, Q., Zhou, D., Feng, J.: Coordinate Attention for Efficient Mobile Network Design. arXiv preprint arXiv:2103.02907 (2021)
12. Lin, Z., Feng, M., Santos, C., Yu, M.: A structured self-attentive sentence embedding. arXiv preprint arXiv:1703.03130 (2017)
13. Jin, Q., Li, C., Chen, S., Wu, H.: Speech emotion recognition with acoustic and lexical features. In: 2015 IEEE International Conference on Acoustics, Speech and Signal Processing (ICASSP), pp. 4749–4753. IEEE (2015)

14. Livingstone, S., Russo, F.: The Ryerson audiovisual database of emotional speech and song (RAVDESS): a dynamic, multimodal set of facial and vocal expressions in North American English. PLoS ONE **13**(5), e0196391 (2018). https://doi.org/10.1371/journal.pone.0196391

15. Kingma, D., Ba, J.: Adam: a method for stochastic optimization. arXiv preprint arXiv:1412.6980 (2014)

16. Ortega, J., Senoussaoui, M., Granger, E., Pedersoli, M., Cardinal, P., Koerich, A.: Multimodal fusion with deep neural networks for audio-video emotion recognition. arXiv preprint arXiv:1907.03196 (2019)

17. Fukui, A., Park, D., Yang, D., Rohrbach, A., Darrell, T., Rohrbach, M.: Multimodal compact bilinear pooling for visual question answering and visual grounding. ArXiv preprint arXiv:1606.01847 (2016)

18. Liu, K., Li, Y., Xu, N., Natarajan, P.: Learn to combine modalities in multimodal deep learning. arXiv preprint arXiv:1805.11730 (2018)

19. Joze, H., Shaban, A., Iuzzolino, M., Koishida, K.: MMTM: multimodal transfer module for CNN fusion. In: Proceedings of the IEEE/CVF Conference on Computer Vision and Pattern Recognition, pp. 13289–13299. IEEE (2020)

20. Fu, Z., et al.: A cross-modal fusion network based on self-attention and residual structure for multimodal emotion recognition. arXiv preprint arXiv:2111.02172 (2021)

Learning to Embed Knowledge for Medical Dialogue System

Yuan Wang[1,2], Zekun Li[1(✉)], Panting Chen[1], Leilei Zeng[1], Anqi Liu[1], Ning Xiong[1], Peng Huo[1], and Qi Yu[3]

[1] College of Artificial Intelligence, Tianjin University of Science and Technology, Tianjin 300457, China
963630410@qq.com
[2] Population and Precision Health Care, Ltd., Tianjin 300000, China
[3] College of Management, Shanxi Medical University, Taiyuan 030001, China

Abstract. The medical dialogue system (MDS) is committed to constructing an intelligent platform to complete an automatic medical online consultation. Most previous researchers have focused on using the dialogue history between doctors and patients to yield an accurate and informative response, while neglecting that most patients lack professional medical knowledge, which leads to oral expressions during their self-report period. As a result, there are many medical terms that fail to utter formally in the dialogue, which leads to performance degradation of conventional MDS. In the paper, we propose a learning to embed KnowledGe for Medical Dialogue system (KGMD). We first construct an entity normalized knowledge graph, which intuitively helps to unify the deviation caused by oral expressions. Then, we embed knowledge information into corresponding entities to complete entity alignment. However, additional knowledge incorporation may divert the sentence from its correct meaning, which is called knowledge noise. To overcome knowledge noise, KGMD introduces Knowledge-Masked (*KM*) to complete information hiding. Thus, doctor response is generated within unambiguous entity knowledge. Experimental results show that the knowledge introduced effectively boosts the robustness of dialogue systems. Especially, our proposed model achieves supreme performance on MedDG.

Keywords: Medical dialogue system · Knowledge-embed · Knowledge graph · Dialogue generation

1 Introduction

Task oriented dialogue system is making enormous progress in recent years and the shortage of healthcare personnel is imminent. Previous work on electronic health records (EHRs) has obtained superior results in handling the diagnosis of anxiety disorder [1] and infection detection [2]. However, on the one hand, EHRs usually contain historical information, which fail to commendably appear the current situation of the patients. Contrarily, real-time diagnostic process for doctors and patients provides more valuable threads. On the other hand, collecting electronic health records is expensive and outrageous.

© The Author(s), under exclusive license to Springer Nature Singapore Pte Ltd. 2023
Z. Yu et al. (Eds.): CIRAC 2022, CCIS 1770, pp. 158–170, 2023.
https://doi.org/10.1007/978-981-99-0301-6_13

In summary, most scholars focus on the research of medical dialogue and consultation by the pre-trained Sequence-to-Sequence (Seq2Seq) models to generate instructive responses [7]. TBDS [3] realizes automatic medical diagnosis for the first time. Dependent on patient's self-reporting, the system collects additional symptoms through dialogue with the patient to promote the diagnostic effect. GAMP [4] takes the generator as a policy network and discriminator as part of the reward function to optimize the reinforcement learning model for automatic diagnosis. However, the Seq2Seq approach only using dialogue context is notorious for generating responses that are irrelevant to the medical context.

Additional medical knowledge is important in multiple rounds of medical dialogue diagnosis and decision-making. A senior doctor uses his/her rich medical experience to complete the dialogue process. Therefore, more and more researchers begin to realize the ability of medical knowledge reasoning by introducing and modeling medical entities and their relationships [18, 19]. GEML [5] learns the knowledge graph that can evolve to infer the relevant symptoms of diseases. KRDS [6] integrates a relationship refinement branch to encode the relationship between symptoms and diseases. Above methods all use knowledge information and improve the system performance to a certain degree. However, previous works [22, 23] often use the retrieved knowledge to bluntly concatenate the original information. With the increase of embedded knowledge in the dialogue context, knowledge noise will be generated accordingly, that is, the meaning of the original dialogue context will gradually deviate from the expression of natural language information. For example, the original dialogue context "Doctor, what should I do if my stomach feels bad?", After knowledge-embed (stomach feels bad, symptom, stomachache), it is converted into "Doctor, what should I do if my stomach feels bad symptom stomachache?", which may cause the model to produce inaccurate or even wrong diagnostic response. Unfortunately, how to enrich dialogue semantic without introducing knowledge noise has been hesitating, and an effective way to integrate knowledge information is crucial to the performance of the dialogue system.

We observe that patients lack professional medical knowledge background, there are a full range of entity ambiguities in the process of communication with doctors by oral expressions, which lead to the failure of the model when modeling different expressions of the same medical entities in distinct patients. For example, "When the patient expresses that **my stomach is slightly inflamed/inflamed/inflammation in the stomach**". In fact, "**stomach is slightly inflamed**", "**inflamed**", and "**inflammation in the stomach**" can be aligned as "**gastritis**". If we do not express it uniformly in advance, the model will model three unique entities and fail to detect general relationship. During the real diagnosis, in fact, doctors will internally correct the ambiguity described by the patient according to their medical knowledge, especially for key medical entities. Sometimes, doctors will confirm this with patients, so as to further dialogue and complete the diagnosis. It can be seen that the alignment of medical entities in the process of dialogue plays a decisive role in improving the accuracy of diagnosis.

Inspired by the above observations, we propose a learning to embed knowledge for medical dialogue system. Specifically, we first constructed an entity normalized knowledge graph KgMed, which contains the correspondence between commonly oral expressions and medical professional vocabularies in the medical field. Through the KgMed, we can effectively align the nonstandard medical information in the oral expressions of a patient. As a result, we have successfully unified the standardized description in the self-report of a patient. Just like in the real diagnosis process, doctors use familiar medical knowledge to internally correct the ambiguous expressions. Not yet, how to integrate acquired knowledge information from knowledge graph is the core of KGMD. Previous works [22, 23] often use the retrieved knowledge to bluntly concatenate the original information. However, the lighthearted strategy also produces terrible effects, that is, knowledge noise. To overcome knowledge noise, KGMD introduces *KM* to complete information hiding, which provides a plug and play method to make embedded entities pay attention to knowledge information, while the conventional contents keep its original appearance. Fortunately, the model can better understand the dialogue history and explore the relationship between oral expressions and medical professional vocabularies to further promote the robustness of the model to future self-reporting.

The main contributions of our paper are summarized as follows:

(1) We construct an entity normalized knowledge graph of medical entities to assist the model to align the professional medical entities and oral expressions.
(2) We introduce knowledge-masked matrix to prevent the corruption of the expression of natural language caused by knowledge-embed, which can seamlessly integrate into the dialogue context.
(3) Experimental results on MedDG show that the proposed knowledge embedding enhances the robustness of the model and improves the various evaluation indicators.

2   Related Work

Task oriented dialogue system is making enormous progress in recent years, including ticket booking [9], online shopping [10]. The medical dialogue system is also concerned by massive researchers due to its huge commercial value and potential. TBDS [3] first realizes automatic medical diagnosis. The system collects additional symptoms for diagnosis on the basis of patient self-reporting through dialogue with patients, so as to improve the diagnostic effect. However, the system performs natural language generation based on templates, which is difficult to fully cover the complex natural language patterns and scenarios of medical dialogue. In order to solve this problem, KRDS [6] integrates abundant medical knowledge to assist dialogue management. A doctor with rich medical experience can diagnose disease simply by talking to a patient. In contrast, the above knowledge-based dialogue system models usually demand massive dialogues and examples, because they are difficult to explicitly learn the correlation between diseases.

To fix the problem of modeling for diseases with insufficient data resources, GEML [5] uses the knowledge graph to reflect and infer the correlation between diseases and symptoms. Owing to the advantages of reinforcement learning in modeling sequential decision, GAMP [4] takes the generator as a policy network and discriminator as part of the reward function to optimize the reinforcement learning model for automatic diagnosis.

Recently, knowledge-grounded dialogue plays an import role in dialogue robot, where the knowledge could be acquired from knowledge bases [18, 19], retrieved from unstructured documents [20, 21]. However, they tend to focus on strengthening the understanding of the long dialogue history so as to generate responses with medical background, ignoring the importance of medical entities between dialogues. To this end, we propose a knowledge-grounded model framework to embed knowledge information in related medical entities to enrich entity-representation, which introduces *KM* to complete the information hiding. Thus, knowledge entities can be embedded seamlessly.

3 Model

3.1 Task Definition

The medical dialogue system is committed to generating instructive responses based on multiple rounds of dialogue between doctors and patients. In short, according to the dialogue context $S = <s_1, s_2, ..., s_n>$ between doctors and patients, where $s_1 - s_n$ is a dialogue of system or patients. $s_i = <x_1, x_2, ..., x_n>$, $1 \le j \le n$ is the j_th token in sentence s_i. For the following segment, the system's reply Y is generated to diagnose the patient.

3.2 KGMD

The framework of KGMD is showed in Fig. 1. It is primarily divided into the following modules: knowledge search layer module, embedding layer module, knowledge masked context encoder module and knowledge-grounded dialogue generation decoder module. We will elaborate on each module in the following sections.

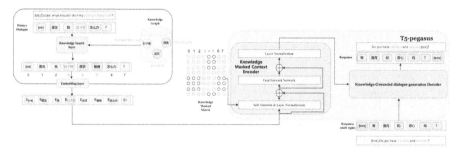

Fig. 1. The overall architecture of KGMD. Knowledge search layer searches relative knowledge triplets from knowledge graph first. Then, embedding layer converts dialogue history and fed it to knowledge masked context encoder to obtain context encoding through the knowledge masked matrix. Finally, the knowledge-grounded dialogue generation decoder generates response one-by-one.

3.3 Knowledge Search Layer

The knowledge search layer is used to embed the normalized entity and entity interpretation triplet into the input information. Specifically, an input sentence $S = <s_1, s_2, ..., s_m>$ and a knowledge graph G, where s_i represents the i_th word of sentence S. Through the knowledge query layer, we will obtain $S^{\sim} = <s_1, s_2, ..., s_k(r_k, t_k), s_{k+1}, s_{k+2}(r_{k+2}, t_{k+2}), ..., s_m>$. This process can be divided into two steps: knowledge search (K-Search) and knowledge embedment (K-Embed).

In K-Search, all the entity names involved in the sentence S are selected out to query their corresponding triples from G. K-Search can be formulated as (1):

$$KS = K\_Search(s, G) \tag{1}$$

where $KS = \{(s_k, r_k, t_k), (s_{k+2}, r_{k+2}, t_{k+2}), ...\}$ is a collection of the corresponding triples.

Next, K-Embedment embed the searched knowledge into the sentence along the corresponding entities. Specifically, suppose the patient says: "Doctor, what should I do if my stomach feels bad?". Due to the lack of medical knowledge of the patient, so the patient makes oral expression "stomach feels bad". With the equipment of knowledge graph, we note that spoken expression corresponds to normalized entity "stomachache" and entity type "symptom". The described process is illustrated in Fig. 1 (Embedding layer) and K-Embed can be formulated as (2):

$$S^{\sim} = K\_Embed(s, KS) \tag{2}$$

where $S^{\sim} = <s_1, s_2, ..., s_k(r_k, t_k), s_{k+1}, s_{k+2}(r_{k+2}, t_{k+2}), ..., s_m>$.

3.4 Embedding Layer

The Embedding layer is responsible for converting the sentence $S^{\sim}$ into a continuous vector representation that can be fed into the knowledge masked context encoder module. The embedding representation is consistent with Transformer, which is the gather of two parts: token embedding and position embedding. The described process is illustrated in Fig. 2:

Fig. 2. The information representation of embedding layer (left). Attention representation between different layers (right), where arrows point out the visible area and dots point out the invisible area.

3.5   Knowledge Masked Context Encoder

With the increase of our embedded knowledge, the meaning of the original sentence S will gradually deviate from the natural information content owing to knowledge noise. Inspired by the construction of relative position representations [11], in order to prevent the change of original semantics, we introduce KM matrix M (Fig. 1) to mask the context content, which will be injected into Scaled Dot-Product Attention [12].

The $S^\sim = <s_1, s_2, ..., s_k(r_k, t_k), s_{k+1}, s_{k+2}(r_{k+2}, t_{k+2}), ..., s_m>$ is first packed into $H^0 = [h_1, ..., h_m]$, and then is encoded hierarchically as $H^l = [h_1^l, ..., h_m^l]$ using knowledge masked context encoder (KMCE). $H^l = KMCE_l(H^{l-1})$, $l \in [1, L]$. For the l_th KMCE block, the self-attention V_{att}^l is computed as:

$$Q^l, K^l, V^l = H^{l-1}W_l^Q, H^{l-1}W_l^K, H^{l-1}W_l^V \tag{3}$$

$$M_{ij} = \begin{cases} 0, & h_i \ attend \ h_j \\ -\infty & h_i \ not \ attend \ h_j \end{cases} \tag{4}$$

$$V_{att}^l = softmax\left(\frac{Q^l K^{l^T}}{\sqrt{d}} + M\right)V^l \tag{5}$$

where Q, K and V represents query and key-value metrics, the injected entities and knowledge entities in M. Are mutually visible merely. Other primary tokens maintain the original state of attention. For example, in "Doctor, what should I do if my stomach feels bad sympm stomachache?", "stomach feels bad" and "symptom stomachache" are mutually visible, but "Doctor, what should I do?" are not visible to "symptom stomachache", vice versa. As shown in Fig. 2. The KM matrix construction algorithm is as following:

Algorithm 1 Knowledge-masked Matrix

Input: Context Information X; Knowledge Graph $\mho$;

1. $Y \leftarrow$ Tokenizer(X)
2. $S \leftarrow$ [];S_mask $\leftarrow$ []
3. **for** token $\in$ Y **do**
4. $S \leftarrow$ token
5.   S_mask $\leftarrow$ 0
6.   **if** token $\in \mho$ **then**
7. $S \leftarrow \mho$[token]
8.   S_mask $\leftarrow$ 1
9. **end if**
10. **end for**
11. KM = np.ones([len(S), len(S)])*-np.inf
12. **for** i $\in$ range(len(S)) **then**
13.   **if** S_mask[i]==1 **then**
14.   KM[i][i-1] $\leftarrow$ 0
15.   KM[i-1][i] $\leftarrow$ 0
16.   KM[i][i] $\leftarrow$ 0
17.   **continue**
18.   **end if**
19.   **for** j $\in$ range(len(S)) **do**
20.   **if** S_mask[j]==0 **then**
21.   KM[i][j] $\leftarrow$ 0
22.   **end if**
23.   **end for**
24. **end for**

3.6 Knowledge-Grounded Dialogue Generation Decoder

Through the above operations, the encoder converts historic dialogue $S^\sim = <s_1, s_2, ..., s_k(r_k, t_k), s_{k+1}, s_{k+2}(r_{k+2}, t_{k+2}), ..., s_m>$ to $H^l = [h_1^l, ..., h_m^l]$. Given H^l, the knowledge-grounded dialogue generation decoder (KGDG) which is a standard decoder based on Transformer to generate a response sequence $[y_1, ..., y_n]$.

More specially, KGDG makes up multiple decoder blocks. Let h_{dt}^l denote the output of $(l-1)\_th$ layer at t step in the decoder. The calculation method in l_th is as follows:

$$h_{dt}^l = LayerNorm\left(USA\left(h_{dt}^{l-1}\right) + h_{dt}^{l-1}\right) \tag{6}$$

$$h_{cross\_t}^l = LayerNorm\left(Cross\_Attention\left(h_{dt}^l, H^l, H^l\right) + h_{dt}^l\right) \tag{7}$$

$$h_{ffn\_t}^l = LayerNorm\left(Feedforward\left(h_{cross\_t}^l\right) + h_{cross\_t}^l\right) \tag{8}$$

where $USA(\cdot)$ denotes unidirectional self-attention, $Cross\_Attention(\cdot)$ is a cross-attention mechanism between encoder and decoder.

In the last layer, a full connection layer is used to get the distribution of the current time step p_t and the optimization object is shown as follows:

$$p_t = softmax\left(W_o h_{ffn\_t}^l + b_o\right) \tag{9}$$

$$L(\varphi) = -\sum_t \log P_\varphi(y_t|x_{1:m}, y_{1:t-1}) \qquad (10)$$

where $x_{1:m}$ represent the input sequence, y_t represents the t_th word generated by the decoder.

4 Experiments

4.1 Datasets

In order to prove the validity of our method, we selected MedDG [8], the authoritative data set in the medical dialogue generation task.

MedDG. An authoritative medical dialogue dataset, which involves 12 gastrointestinal diseases. It contains more than 17000 conversations from medical online website. There are 160 entities and they are divided into 5 categories in the candidate entity set, including diseases, symptoms, attributes, examinations and drugs etc. The specific dialog style is shown in Fig. 3:

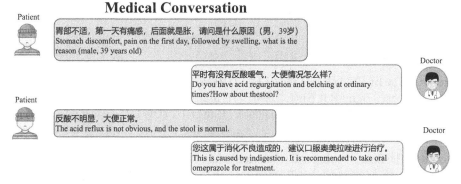

Fig. 3. The dialogue example in the MedDG dataset.

KgMed. The unstructured data are gathered from *Chunyu-Doctor*[1]. By inviting 5 persons with a medical background and leveraging regularization techniques, we constructed 11398 triplets KgMed[2] of symptom normalization and prompt information, which contain three types of hypernym (oral symptoms, prompt type, and normalized symptoms).

---

[1] https://www.chunyuyisheng.com/.

[2] After the paper is accepted, we will open source data.

4.2 Baselines

Seq2Seq [14] is a RNN model based on attention mechanism.

HRED [15] is a hierarchical RNN model, which can model word level and utterance level representation.

DialoGPT [16] is a GPT-2 model, which use maximum mutual information to constrain dull response.

GPT2 [17] is a pre-trained language model based on Transformer.

VRbot [24] summaries states between patient and doctor through variational method.

4.3 Implementation Details

For the infrastructure of the model, in order to produce a decent effect and control the capacity of the model, we adopted T5-Pegasus[3], which is a Transformer-based and language model of Chinese pre-trained. In order to make the model more sensitive in the medical field, we carry out secondary pre-trained on the basis of the original model through a large number of medical dialogue corpus **CMCQA**[4].

In downstream task, the word embedding is set to 768. We use Adam optimizer and set the batch size to 10. The initial learning rate is $2e-4$.The model is trained for 20 epochs and the training time of a single epoch is about 90 min with a NVIDIA RTX3090 graphic card.

4.4 Automatic Evaluation

Metrics. The BLEU-1 (B@1) and BLEU-4 (B@4) [13] reflect the relevance and fluency of the response. Entity-P/R/F1 (E@P/R/F1) is used to check the accuracy of the medical entities involved in the generated response. Distinct-1/2 (D@1/2) evaluate the diversity of generated responses.

Results. The final experimental results are exhibited in Table 1. Our model has finished overwhelming advantages in all indicators almost. Compared with the conventional Seq2Seq model, the model based on pre-trained shows incomparable merits. As for the role played by knowledge embedding module, we will elaborate in the ablation experiments.

Ablation Study. With the introduction of knowledge normalization information, the model has significantly improved various evaluation indicators. When *KM* is removed, the model produces relatively terrible results, which verifies the knowledge noise caused by directly integrating knowledge. On the contrary, the introduction of *KM* fully learns the unified representation of entity normalization (see Fig. 4). The specific ablation comparison results are shown in Table 2.

---

[3] https://github.com/ZhuiyiTechnology/t5-pegasus.
[4] https://github.com/WENGSYX/CMCQA.

Table 1. All comparative dialog systems perform in terms of response quality, diversity, and entity correctness.

Models	B@1	B@4	D@1	D@2	E@P	E@R	E@F1
Seq2Seq [14]	26.12	14.21	0.88	4.77	14.07	11.45	12.63
Seq2Seq_Entity [8]	35.24	19.20	0.75	5.32	12.41	25.65	16.73
HRED [15]	31.56	17.28	1.07	8.43	13.29	11.25	12.18
HRED_Entity	38.66	**21.19**	0.75	7.06	12.01	26.78	16.58
DialoGPT_Entity[16]	34.90	18.61	0.77	9.87	21.16	13.53	16.51
GPT-2 [17]	29.35	14.47	1.26	**13.53**	7.33	12.22	9.17
GPT-2_Entity	30.87	16.56	0.87	11.20	20.76	14.51	17.08
VRBot [24]	32.83	17.48	1.45	8.93	14.73	12.78	13.69
KGMD	**38.78**	17.88	**1.57**	12.11	**25.14**	**27.04**	**26.01**

Note:- Entity suffix indicates the model is used to predict the entities involved in the response

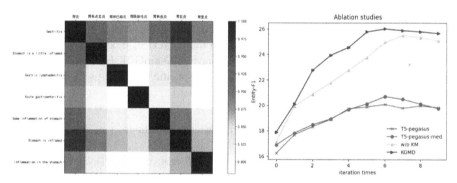

Fig. 4. Through normalization of entities injected by knowledge-embed and introduction of KM, the model preferentially learns the correlation between original entities and knowledge entities, such as Gastritis (1,1) and Gastric lymphadenitis (1,3).

Table 2. Comparison of ablation experiments

Model	B@1	B@4	D@2	D@1	E@P	E@R	E@F1
T5-pegasus	31.62	15.44	10.83	1.12	20.91	19.32	20.08
T5-pegasus-med[*1]	33.17	16.83	11.37	1.32	22.14	19.44	20.70
w/o KM[*2]	38.03	17.44	11.88	1.53	24.81	26.23	25.50

Note: [*1] indicates the use of medical corpus for secondary pre-trained; [*2] indicates that the *KM* module is removed

4.5 Manual Evaluation

For a more thorough comparison, we also conduct human evaluations on four selected dialog models (HRED-Entity/GPT2-Entity/DialoGPT_Entity/KGMD).

We randomly selected 100 test cases from valid datasets. Three annotators with medical background were invited to independently evaluate the generation effect of the model in four levels: knowledge correctness, relevance, informativeness and the doctor similarity. The score is limited from 1 (strongly bad) to 5 (strongly fair). Specifically, knowledge correctness refers to the clinical correctness of the reply, relevance refers to the relevance between the reply and the historical dialogue, informativeness refers to the amount of information that provides medical information and suggestions in the reply, and doctor similarity refers to the similarity between the generated reply and the real doctor's reply.

The evaluation result is summarized in Table 3. On all metrics, KGMD is remarkably higher than other generative models, which is inconsistent with automatic evaluation, which is inconsistent with an automatic evaluation. Thus, the introduction of normalized knowledge can improve the learning of similar entities in the model, so as to improve the accuracy of prediction. From the indicators of the previous three generation models, we can notice that HRED-based models outperform GPT2-based models in terms of informativeness and doctor similarity. It shows that the simple stacked encoder structure is inferior to the hierarchical RNN structure in the context of modeling dialogue. We observe the knowledge correctness and relevance of DialoGPT_Entity is better than the first two models, which shows pre-trained in specific fields helps to improve the understanding of knowledge in the corresponding field.

Table 3. Comparison of manual evaluation

Model	Knowledge correctness	Relevance	Informativeness	Doctor similarity
HRED-Entity	2.78	3.11	**3.25**	3.84
GPT2-Entity	2.83	3.27	3.18	3.47
DialoGPT_Entity	2.97	3.44	3.12	3.76
KGMD	**3.12**	**3.83**	3.22	**4.03**

4.6 Case Study

We demonstrate the effect of different models on the same conversation. As we can see in Fig. 5, the reasoning in the initial stage is relatively straightforward, so all models have made correct responses. As the conversation goes on, the first three models predict intestinal problems, which is basically related to the content. Nevertheless, GPT2-Entity gives an uncertain response, which shows the limitation of model learning. HRED-Entity replenishes a similar sentence "How about your diet recently?" that the patient has already expressed. KGMD full learning through entity normalization, which improves model robustness and predicts the "gastroscope" perfectly.

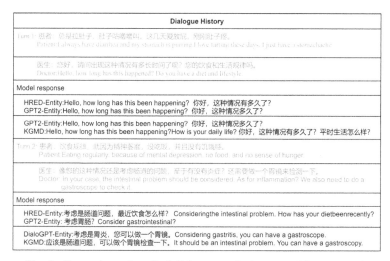

Fig. 5. Comparison of medical dialogue results between different models

5   Conclusion

In this paper, we propose a learning to embed knowledge for medical dialogue system. We first construct an entity normalized knowledge graph, which intuitively helps to unify the deviation caused by oral communication. With the construction of knowledge graph, entity knowledge is integrated into the context to enrich semantics and align oral expressions. Experiments demonstrate that our proposed method is in line with the real medical dialogue background. In the future, we expect to introduce textual knowledge to make the conversation more diverse.

Acknowledgments. This work was supported by the National Natural Science Foundation of China (Grant No. 61976156, No. 11803022 and No. 61702367), Tianjin Science and Technology Commissioner project (No. 20YDTPJC00560), the Natural Science Foundation of Tianjin(Grant No. 19JCYBJC15300), and the Research Project of Tianjin Municipal Commission of Education (No. 2018KJ105 and No. 2018KJ106).

References

1. Trinh, N.-H.T., et al.: Using electronic medical records to determine the diagnosis of clinical depression. Int. J. Med. Inform. **80**(7), 533–540 (2011)
2. Tou, H., Yao, L., Wei, Z., Zhuang, X., Zhang, B.: Automatic infection detection based on electronic medical records. BMC Bioinform. **19**(5), 117 (2018)
3. Wei, Z., et al.: Task-oriented dialogue system for automatic diagnosis. In: ACL, pp. 201–207 (2018)
4. Xia, Y., Zhou, J., Shi, Z.: Generative adversarial regularized mutual information policy gradient framework for automatic diagnosis. In: AAAI, pp. 1062–1069 (2020)
5. Lin, S., Zhou, P., Liang, X.: Graph-Evolving Meta-Learning for Low-Resource Medical Dialogue Generation. arXiv preprint arXiv:2012.11988 (2020)

6. Xu, L., Zhou, Q., Gong, K., Liang, X., Tang, J., Lin, L.: End-to-end knowledge routed relational dialogue system for automatic diagnosis. arXiv preprint: arXiv:1901.10623 (2019)
7. Zeng, G., Yang, W., Ju, Z., Yang, Y.: Meddialog: a large-scale medical dialogue dataset. In: EMNLP, pp. 9241–9250 (2020)
8. Liu, W., Tang, J., Qin, J., Xu, L., Li, Z., Liang, X.: MedDG: a large-scale medical consultation dataset for building medical dialogue system. arXiv preprint arXiv:2010.07497 (2020)
9. Li, X., Chen, Y. N., Li, L., Gao, J., Celikyilmaz, A.: End-to-end task completion neural dialogue systems. In: IJCNLP, pp. 733–743 (2017)
10. Yan, Z., Duan, N., Chen, P., Zhou, M., Zhou, J., Li, Z.: Building task oriented dialogue systems for online shopping. In: AAAI, pp. 4618–4626 (2017)
11. Shaw, P., Uszkoreit, J., Vaswani, A.: Self-attention with relative position representations. In: ACL, pp. 464–468 (2018)
12. Vaswani, A., et al.: Attention is all you need. In: NIPS, pp. 6000–6010 (2017)
13. Papineni, K., Roukos, S., Ward, T.: BLEU: a method for automatic evaluation of machine translation. In: ACL, pp. 311–318 (2002)
14. Sutskever, I., Vinyals, O., Le, Q.V.: Sequence to sequence learning with neural networks. In: NIPS, pp. 3104–3112 (2014)
15. Serban, I.V., Sordoni, A., Bengio, Y., Courville, A., Pineau, J.: Building end-to-end dialogue systems using generative hierarchical neural network models. In: AAAI, pp. 4813–4823 (2016)
16. Radford, A., Wu, J., Child, R., Luan, D.: Language models are unsupervised multitask learners. OpenAI Blog **1**(8), 9 (2019)
17. Zhang, Y., et al.: DialoGPT:Large-Scale Generative Pre-training for Conversational Response Generation. arXiv preprint arXiv:1911.00536 (2020)
18. Zhou, K., Prabhumoye, S., WBlack, A.: A dataset for document grounded conversations. arXiv preprint arXiv:1809.07358 (2018b)
19. Moon, S., Shah, P., Kumar, A., Subba, R.: Opendialkg: explainable conversational reasoning with attention-based walks over knowledge graphs. In: ACL, pp. 845–854 (2019)
20. Dinan, E., Roller, S., Shuster, K., Fan, A., Auli, M., Weston, J.: Wizard of Wikipedia: knowledge-powered conversational agents. In: ICLR (2019)
21. Tuan, Y.-L., Chen, Y.-N., Lee, H.: Dykgchat: benchmarking dialogue generation grounding on dynamic knowledge graphs. In: EMNLP, pp. 1855–1865 (2019)
22. Chen, X., et al.: Bridging the gap between prior and posterior knowledge selection for knowledge-grounded dialogue generation. In: EMNLP, pp. 3426–3437 (2020)
23. Ghazvininejad, M., et al.: A knowledge-grounded neural conversation model. In: AAAI, vol. 32 (2018)
24. Li, D., et al.: Semi-supervised variational reasoning for medical dialogue generation. In: SIGIR, pp. 544–554 (2021)

Robot Learning from Human Demonstration for Playing Ocarina

Junfeng Wei[1,2], Ziang Liu[1], Fuchun Sun[1], and Bin Fang[1(✉)]

[1] Department of Computer Science and Technology, Tsinghua University,
Beijing 100084, China
`liu-za22@mails.tsinghua.edu.cn`, {`fcsun,fangbin`}`@tsinghua.edu.cn`
[2] Beijing University of Technology, Beijing 100086, China

Abstract. Nowadays the field of combining robots with music has received great attention. However, the current work often focuses on how to control the mechanical performance of music with established rules. We hope that the robot can play a musical instrument without being so monotonous and can have playing skills other than regularity as a human being. We designed an anthropomorphic robotic ocarina playing system. The movements and corresponding action parameters when the dexterous hand is playing are designed so that the system can read the digital score and automatically play according to the score. Through our pitch and intensity analysis algorithm, the audio is parsed into the pitch sequence and intensity sequence required for ocarina performance, and the dexterous hand can play the ocarina through these two sequences so that the ocarina can be imitated by only listening to the audio. Furthermore, a granularity method is proposed to evaluate the similarity of performances.

Keywords: Robot learning · Orcarina playing · Imitation

1 Introduction

Playing musical instruments, especially orchestral instruments, has always been a very difficult task that requires the simultaneous operation of multiple senses. It usually takes years or even decades of practice to skillfully complete the performance of musical instruments. One of the main difficulties lies in the accuracy, speed and power control of performance. But for robots, this huge difficulty is what they are good at. Robots are accurate, fast, and good at controlling power. Therefore, more and more researchers participate in the research of robot playing musical instruments. Its purpose is to analyze the principle and operation details of musical instruments from a scientific point of view, and to verify the empirical theory of traditional music [6]. At the same time, it can expand the ability range of artificial intelligence, including emotion analysis and expression ability, fine motion ability and so on [10,15].

Among them, humanoid robot is the top priority in the development of musical instrument playing robot [2,8]. Because the structure of humanoid robot is

Z. Yu et al. (Eds.): CIRAC 2022, CCIS 1770, pp. 171–182, 2023.
https://doi.org/10.1007/978-981-99-0301-6_14

similar to that of human, and human performance skills can be well introduced into the robot through programming. The humanoid robot can better reflect the human performance skills of musical instruments.

However, the biggest difference between human beings and robot players is that human beings can integrate emotion into the expression of music. Today's musical instrument playing robots still play the music score mechanically according to the existing rules, but humans are not. When playing the same music, musicians can express their feelings by changing the playing intensity, rhythm and playing time of each note on the basis of the original score. For example, for the same music, playing slowly and gently can express sadness or calm, and fast rhythm and great power can express passionate emotions. These emotional expressions of human behavior are impossible for the robots. Therefore, we hope that the robot can not only perform mechanically according to the music score, but also imitate the results of human performance, and imitate every softness and every fluctuation as much as possible, so as to complete the emotional performance of musical instruments.

The traditional Chinese musical instrument 6-hole Ocarina is chosen is that it is relatively simple, with only 6 playing holes. At the same time, as a wind instrument, it can express different musical characteristics under different playing dynamics, which is exactly what we need. Even if the same music is played with different dynamics, different music can be played. This is the charm of the ocarina.

We use a dexterous hand and change the air flow through the actuator valve to simulate the breathing control of human blowing. Manipulator and driver are connected with Python based control program through serial port. In the most basic task of reading the digital music score and playing it automatically according to the music score, we set the action of the dexterous hand (the parameters of each degree of freedom) and the parameters of the driver through experiments to complete the performance of the digital music score.

In addition, the robot can complete the imitation and reproduction of music in the audio by "listening" to an audio (learning from the demonstration). The audio processing in this part is mainly divided into two modules. One is the pitch extraction algorithm for obtaining pitch sequences and the other is the intensity extraction algorithm for obtaining intensity sequences. The obtained pitch sequence and intensity sequence are input asynchronously to complete the audio reproduction of the system.

Evaluating the similarity between the robot's copy and the original audio is a problem. It sounds like a very important indicator, but obviously, listening alone is not scientific and specific enough. For this reason, we propose a sub granularity performance audio similarity evaluation algorithm, which can evaluate whether our Ocarina performance system can reproduce this Ocarina audio in terms of single tone and multi note.

2 Related Work

Musical robots have been studied for many years. Some early works [2,8,13] used humanoid robots to realize the basic musical instrument playing function of robots. They applied the algorithm of robot playing musical instruments and achieved relatively good results. The references [3,13,14] have realized the robot playing musical instruments, but these performances have only preliminarily completed the imitation of the musical instrument playing mode, and there is still room for improvement in the accuracy and flexibility of their performance. Some works [7,11,16] have made breakthroughs in the complexity of performance. However, the above works only use the established performance rules (such as the movement angle of the fingers playing the piano), and uses the same method to perform each note on the music score, which is the same without any modifications. Therefore, its essence is the mechanical playing of digital music scores, which is essentially different from the robots that imitate human emotions.

Ref. [11] has developed a violin playing robot system. The author designed a humanoid robot for Violin fingering, because violin fingering plays an important role in determining tone or sound. In addition, the author also puts forward a feedback method to judge whether the sound produced by the robot finger when pressing the violin string is the same as that produced by the human violinist when pressing the string. The researchers suggested using the precedent sound quality rating system to analyze the violinist's performance sound and create the conditions required to produce accurate sound quality. Inspired by this, we also proposed a sub granularity evaluation method to judge the similarity of performance strength with human beings. On this basis, the researchers compared the playing sounds made by robot fingers and human violinists' fingers, and proposed strategies to improve the shortcomings. Ref. [12] uses reinforcement learning and other methods to learn human behavior skills. In the above article, reinforcement learning is used to train the performance skills of robots in the simulated environment, but the instruments they play only stay on the keyboard instruments, which only need to control the movements of the hands, but they rarely play wind instruments, because the physical model required by wind instruments is much more complex than that of percussion instruments, and reinforcement learning and other imitation learning methods based on deep learning rely on the construction of virtual environment. In addition, the essence of their learning goal through reinforcement learning is to play music through existing rules, but in a different form, the established rules originally written in the program are written in the neural network structure, which is completely different from the emotional expression in the robot performance we want to achieve.

The pitch extraction algorithm is widely used in different tasks [9,17], which is similar to our pitch sequence extraction algorithm. However, our work is not only to analyze and extract pitch sequences, but also to analyze and extract performance ability sequences. We extract more diversified music elements, providing more angles to describe and reproduce the audio clips played by the robot.

[12]is similar to the performance intention we want to express, that is, to show performance skills that can express emotions to a certain extent like people. Their work accomplished this goal excellently, but their method was to analyze the performance skills of bright and low voice and write them into the robot performance. The essence of their work is to execute digital music scores in a complex way by mechanically executing written action sequences. Unlike them, we have not written these performance skills in advance in the code. The imitation action of our robot is entirely from the analysis of human playing audio. [5] used audio feedback to change the playing position and playing skills of violin robots. The aim is to improve the robot's violin playing skills and reduce the occurrence of discordant sounds. This is similar to our works. We all want to make the robot play less stiff when playing musical instruments, and reduce the stiffness and monotony of machinery and life. However, its core content is also different from our work. Their work focuses more on performance skills, while our work focuses more on the strength control, rhythm control, that is, emotional expression that robots can imitate human beings' performance in a track. [4] pays attention to the innovation ability of the robot itself, so that the robot can independently expand this music after listening to it. Although this article excellently completes the improvisation ability of the robot, the innovation ability in this aspect is closer to the field of autonomous composition of the robot, rather than letting the robot play its own emotional expression like human beings.

3   System Structure Overview

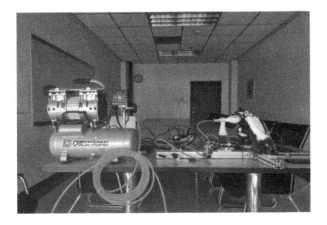

Fig. 1. Overall appearance of the system

The musical instrument we choose to play is the 6-hole ocarina, which is a traditional Chinese musical instrument. It is simple but will have many different musical experiences under different blowing strengths and changes. Therefore, it is suitable for the initial imitation of robot emotional expression. Playing musical instruments. As a substitute for the human hand, we choose two human-like mechanical dexterous hands. Each finger can move freely to press the ocarina playing hole to complete the performance, in which each hand has six degrees of freedom, two thumbs and one for each of the other four fingers, and the control parameters are 0–1000 decimal values. To imitate the different blowing strengths when humans play musical instruments, we installed a driver valve between the air pump and the ocarina as an air valve to adjust the air flow into the ocarina. The different loudness of each note corresponds to the different air volumes. The valve opening size is obtained by interpolation after sampling. The initial size is a decimal value of 0–2000, where 0 means fully closed, and 2000 means fully open (Fig. 1).

4   Methods

4.1   Performance of Reading Digital Music Score

The purpose of reading the digital music score performance part is to realize the music performance design based on the established rules, write the parameters of each part of the robot corresponding to each action, and then play the performance in sequence according to the digital music score on the file. In this part, the ocarina playing system will not imitate human's emotional performance, that is to say, the parameter size of the driver is only controlled by the parameters set when playing each note. We believe that this is the most basic step to realize the robot playing musical instruments, and it is also a crucial part to pave the way for the following text to imitate human playing the ocarina only through the audio of human playing the ocarina.

We have designed a method to digitize the music score, which is very suitable for our Ocarina performance system. It is also very simple and has high scalability.

We use a quarter note as a beat without distinguishing the number of beats in the measurement. Each line in the digital music score has two parameters: the notes to be played (empty beat, C, D, e, F, G, etc.) and the number of beats to be played for each note. At the same time, we need to set the BPM of this song so that the playing duration of each note can be calculated by formula (1)

$$t = \frac{b \cdot 60}{bpm} \tag{1}$$

Therefore, we can get the intensity sequence and pitch sequence and input them to the system for performance. The system then parses the intensity sequence into the numerical value of the driver valve, parses the pitch sequence into the numerical value of the degrees of freedom of the dexterous hand, and performs the performance according to the timing sequence. The control posture of the dexterous hand corresponding to each note is the result of a large number of experiments and adjustments. The degree of freedom value needs to meet that the fingers can just cooperate with the silicone rubber ring to block the performance hole, and the performance will not be affected by the jamming of the dexterous hand or the dislocation of the ocarina due to excessive force. The numerical value of the driver valve corresponding to each note is also the most comfortable numerical value obtained by us through many experiments to adjust the sense of hearing without change. It is worth mentioning that to solve the problem of roaring, we designed a Inlet valve. When waiting for the playing and playing to the stop note, the system will set the bool parameter to 0, and the Inlet valve will be opened to let the gas flow out to prevent the gas from being trapped. Accumulation inside the performance system caused the driver to suddenly open and produce a loud noise.

However, although our performance system has been able to play songs of various difficulty at this time, this way of writing the intensity by ourself still has great drawbacks, which are mainly reflected in the performance of In terms of the mechanical feeling and the bland expression of the music, each sound is controlled by only one strength, and the playing method is very simple, which can be said to be completely different from the real person playing. Therefore, we need a way to make the ocarina playing system play a piece of music more "lively" and more emotionally (we think this is mainly reflected in the change of playing strength), so we make improvements on this basis, proposing the learning from demonstrations part.

4.2   Learning from Demonstrations

In order to make the robot play the ocarina less mechanically and rigidly and more like a real person, we hope that the ocarina robot can learn human playing skills and emotional expression by imitating human playing instruments. We hope that as long as we input the audio of playing ocarina, the system can complete the reproduction of this audio only by "listening". Therefore, the pitch sequence and intensity sequence that can be input into the system can only be obtained by analyzing the audio played by human beings. When human beings play musical instruments, the playing intensity is often not a constant. Therefore, how to use audio only to flexibly analyze it is a problem that puzzles us. Therefore, we apply Yin algorithm [1] to pitch sequence analysis, and propose a strength analysis algorithm to obtain performance strength sequence. This algorithm is used to analyze audio pitch sequence and strength sequence, and immediately transmit them to the ocarina performance system for complex performance (Fig. 2).

For the input Ocarina audio played by human beings, we first divide it into equal length small audio sequence groups with a fixed length. The actual value of this fixed length is the audio sequence length corresponding to the playing duration of 32 diaeresis at bpm80. The reason why the 32 diacritic notes is adopted is that in the wind instruments, few instruments will use this short note, because its duration is too short to be played. Therefore, we believe that for the ocarina instrument, setting the pitch extraction granularity to 32 diaeresis

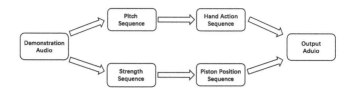

Fig. 2. Flow chart of learning from demonstration

can well complete the task. If the granularity is set too large, such as 16 diaeresis and 8 diaeresis, it may lead to inaccurate extraction of some extreme fast playing situations. If the granularity is set to be smaller than 32 diaeresis, it is bound to increase the amount of calculation and affect the audio parsing speed, This increase in computation is meaningless. The reason why the BPM is 80 is that most songs have a BPM of about 80. When we cannot extract and calculate the BPM of a human playing Ocarina audio, it is a reasonable decision to default to the BPM commonly used in songs.

After the segmented short audio sequence is obtained by the above method, one of the short audio sequences is now called note sequence. Next, Yin algorithm needs to be applied to extract the fundamental frequency of each note sequence in the. We have noticed that for each note sequence, the position of its occurrence may be at the beginning, middle and end of a playing actual note, while the internal value of the note sequence at the beginning and end will inevitably be disturbed by the instrument itself (the instability of the beginning and end of the note), resulting in the periodicity of the single tone and the decline of the stability of the fundamental frequency characteristics. Therefore, when we apply Yin algorithm to extract the fundamental frequency of each note sequence, we will first divide it into four sequences, and then only extract the fundamental frequency of the second sequence, which effectively avoids the inaccurate judgment of pitch caused by the instability of the first and last tones.

We use the Yin algorithm, but the traditional Yin algorithm will cause us to spend too long parsing a piece of audio (in our experiment, an audio is only 10 s, and parsing takes almost 5 min). Therefore, how to make the Yin algorithm run faster is a problem that needs to be solved. We note that applying the algorithm to each audio segment to obtain the fundamental frequency and pitch is essentially an independent event. The process of extracting the fundamental frequency of a note sequence does not need the extraction result of the fundamental frequency of the previous note sequence. Therefore, we use parallel computing to optimize the Yin algorithm, which greatly reduces the time it takes to parse a piece of audio. When we need to parse an audio, if the duration of the audio is less than 5 s, the algorithm will execute normally as described in the above article. If it is longer than 5 s, the task will be placed on multiple CPU cores for parallel operation processing. This greatly reduces the time required to extract the pitch sequence, so that we can obtain the pitch sequence, which is used to control the hand posture of the dexterous hand, so as to block the playing hole of the ocarina to complete the performance of the corresponding note (Fig. 3).

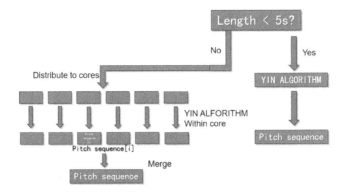

Fig. 3. Parallel algorithm of YIN [1]

Intensity Analysis In terms of extracting intensity sequences, we propose an audio-based intensity sequence extraction algorithm. The core idea is to control the air valve to close -> fully open the performance and record the standard sound mapping waveform (as shown in the figure) (Fig. 4).

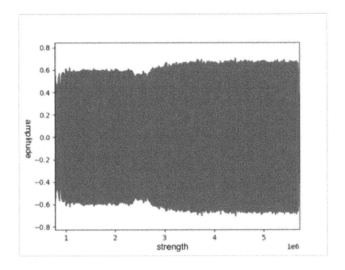

Fig. 4. Sampling image of amplitude and driver value

Then, the data are sampled at 0.1 s intervals, and a mapping relationship table between the amplitude and the driver valve opening size is constructed (the mapping relationship value table here is often affected by factors such as the environment, and its value needs to be fine-tuned in actual use). In this way, for an amplitude of the parsed audio file, we only need to look up the table and then use the interpolation method to obtain the sequence of arbitrary loudness to driver parameters.

$$amplitude \in [amplitude[k], amplitude[k+1]] \tag{2}$$

$$arg = \frac{arg - arg[k]}{arg[k+1] - arg[k]} \cdot (amplitude[k+1], amplitude[k]) \tag{3}$$

Note that the amplitude here is the amplitude, not the value of the sampling point. What we actually sample is the largest number in the amplitude value of the one cycle before and after the sampling point as the amplitude of the sampling point. According to the mapping relationship (numerical table) between the amplitude and the opening size of the driver obtained in the above experiment, when obtaining a new amplitude, we first query the comparison table of the relationship between the driver value and the amplitude that has been obtained and locate the amplitude in the above experiment. In the minimum sampling interval, the interpolation method is used to obtain the corresponding driver value required for the amplitude according to the sampled result. Then, the force sequence is obtained. In the experiments, we used different interpolation methods, such as direct interpolation, linear interpolation, Lagrange interpolation, and b-spline interpolation.

After applying the above two algorithms to obtain the pitch sequence and the intensity sequence, because these two sequences control two independent controls, the pitch sequence controls the playing posture of the dexterous hand, and the intensity sequence controls the size of the driver valve's opening. We designed an asynchronous control, and the two sequences control the two controls. However, this raises a new problem, that is, the transmission delay of the signal in different controls is not the same, which leads to confusion in asynchronous control performance results. To solve this problem, we design a "pair table" algorithm. To solve the difference in the serial communication time between the two modules, we make corrections to the actual holding time of the two parts of the note performance. The actual duration of each part is the duration we set minus the time that the detected signal spends in the execution of the serial transfer. After adding this algorithm, our ocarina playing system will no longer play disorderly in the reproduction performance, which has achieved a very good effect.

4.3 Performance Similarity Evaluation Index

We propose a method to evaluate the similarity of the intensity between the reproduction and the original audio. Our evaluation will refer to two different granularities at the same time namely, the overall difference and the local difference. They respectively represent the overall accuracy of the reproducing playing audio and the reproducing accuracy of each music note in the reproducing playing audio. As the difference value, the smaller they are, the better.

In terms of the overall difference, we simultaneously sample the amplitude of the obtained audio and the original audio at a small interval to obtain an amplitude sequence. In order to minimize the amplitude difference caused by external reasons such as recording position, we compare not the absolute difference of amplitude between the two audio, but the difference of overall amplitude distribution. Therefore, we softmax the two audio sequences, then align them through an alignment function, subtract each element of the sequence and sum the absolute value of the result as the overall difference of two audio.

$$diff = \sum |softmax(x) - align(softmax(x^*))| \tag{4}$$

Among them, align is an alignment function, which is used to align the sequences obtained after two audio parsings during calculation. We designed this function to eliminate the error caused by different playing start time and better reflect the overall difference between the two audio segments. The function method calculates the centroid positions of the two sequences and then aligns the centroid positions.

$$x = \frac{\sum x_i * y_i}{\sum x_i} \tag{5}$$

Specifically, after the centroid coordinates of the two sequences are obtained, the audio obtained by reproducing and playing is transformed by translating and complementing zero, so that the centroid position of the transformed reproducing audio is consistent with that of the original audio.

In terms of local difference, we analyze the pitch and intensity of the audio obtained from the performance and the original audio. The two audio segments are divided according to different notes to obtain two groups of audio sequence groups. The elements in each group are small audio clips corresponding to each note in the original audio. After that, we will correspond the two groups of short audio in order to form a short audio pair. In order to cope with the possibility that the number of notes parsed is not equal to the number of notes in the original audio. We will add empty short sequence audio in the short audio sequence group, so that the short frequency of each audio sequence group can just form a short audio pair. Next, we do the same for each short audio pair as the overall difference. In this way, n difference values will be obtained, and n is the logarithm of the formed short audio. Then, the average value of these n difference values can be used to obtain a fine-grained evaluation index reflecting the accuracy of each note reproduction, that is, local difference. In the next experiment, we will consider and analyze the two differences at the same time.

5   Conclusions

The field of combining robotics and music technology is still a brand new field that requires further exploration. Our work innovatively combines the ocarina, a traditional Chinese musical instrument, with technologically advanced manipulator so that this ancient musical instrument has new vitality and possibilities under the impetus of new technology. At the same time, we also innovatively proposed that the robot should not only play according to the musical score but also imitate the emotional performance of human beings. Let the robot automatically parse and generate the required two types of action sequences by "listening" to the ocarina performance (that is, the input of audio information) and complete the reproduction of this ocarina audio. The experimental results show the effectiveness of our proposed method.

Acknowledgment. This work is supported by Major Project of the New Generation of Artificial Intelligence, China (No. 2018AAA0102900), National Natural Science Foundation of China (Grant No. 62173197) and Tsinghua University Initiative Scientific Research Program 2022Z11QYJ002.

References

1. De Cheveigne, A., Kawahara, H.: Yin, a fundamental frequency estimator for speech and music. J. Acoust. Soc. Am. **111**(4), 1917–30 (2002)
2. Dan, Z., Lei, J., Li, B., Lau, D., CaMeron, C.: Design and analysis of a piano playing robot. In: International Conference on Information and Automation (2009)
3. Han, W.C., Huang, W.H.: Simulation design of gourd flute playing robot based on sound signal feedback. Transducer Microsyst. Technol. **93**, 87–89 (2016)
4. Hoffman, G., Weinberg, G.: Shimon: an interactive improvisational robotic marimba player. Ann. Rheum. Dis. 3097–3102 (2010)
5. Jo, W., Lee, B., Kim, D.: Development of auditory feedback system for violin playing robot. Int. J. Precis. Eng. Manuf. **17**(6), 717–724 (2016). https://doi.org/10.1007/s12541-016-0089-6
6. Li, W., Almeida, A., Smith, J., Wolfe, J.: Tongue, lip and breath study on clarinet playing using a playing machine. In: Music Cognition and Action Symposium (2014)
7. Li, Y.F., Chuang, L.L.: Controller design for music playing robot - applied to the anthropomorphic piano robot. IEEE (2013)
8. Lin, J.C., Huang, H.H., Li, Y.F., Tai, J.C., Liu, L.W.: Electronic piano playing robot. In: International Symposium on Computer Communication Control and Automation (2010)
9. Mauch, M., Dixon, S.: pYIN: a fundamental frequency estimator using probabilistic threshold distributions (2014)
10. Melo, R., Monteiro, R., Oliveira, J., Jeronimo, B., Kelner, J.: Guitar tuner and song performance evaluation using a NAO robot. In: 2020 Latin American Robotics Symposium (LARS), 2020 Brazilian Symposium on Robotics (SBR) and 2020 Workshop on Robotics in Education (WRE) (2020)
11. Park, H., Lee, B., Kim, D.: Violin musical tone analysis using robot finger. Procedia Comput. Sci. **94**, 398–403 (2016)
12. Shibuya, K., Kosuga, K., Fukuhara, H.: Bright and dark timbre expressions with sound pressure and tempo variations by violin-playing robot. In: 2020 29th IEEE International Conference on Robot and Human Interactive Communication (RO-MAN) (2020)
13. Solis, J., Bergamasco, M., Chida, K., Isoda, S., Takanishi, A.: The anthropomorphic flutist robot WF-4 teaching flute playing to beginner students. In: IEEE International Conference on Robotics and Automation (2004)

14. Solis, J., Takanishi, A., Hashimoto, K.: Development of an anthropomorphic saxophone-playing robot. In: Angeles, J., Boulet, B., Clark, J.J., Kövecses, J., Siddiqi, K. (eds.) Brain, Body and Machine. Advances in Intelligent and Soft Computing, vol. 83, pp. 175–186. Springer, Heidelberg (2010). https://doi.org/10.1007/978-3-642-16259-6_14

15. Zahray, L., Savery, R., Syrkett, L., Weinberg, G.: Robot gesture sonification to enhance awareness of robot status and enjoyment of interaction. In: 2020 29th IEEE International Conference on Robot and Human Interactive Communication (RO-MAN) (2020)

16. Zhang, W., Fu, S.: Time-optimal trajectory planning of dulcimer music robot based on PSO algorithm. In: 2020 Chinese Control And Decision Conference (CCDC) (2020)

17. Zhao, F., Li, M., Zhou, C., Chen, G., Lou, Y.: Music melody extraction algorithm for flute robot. In: 2020 IEEE International Conference on Real-time Computing and Robotics (RCAR) (2020)

A Complex Networks Analytics Approach Combining Markov Skeleton Process for Predicting Makespan of Aircraft Overhaul Process

Han Wei[1], Xiaoliang Jia[1]([✉]), Mingjun Huang[2], Bingyang Sun[1], and Xiao Chang[1]

[1] School of Mechanical Engineering, Northwestern Polytechnical University, Xi'an 710072, China
jiaxl@nwpu.edu.cn
[2] State-Owned Wuhu Machinery Factory, Wuhu 241000, China

Abstract. A typical challenge that aircraft overhaul enterprises faced is the lack of dynamically accurate prediction of makespan during aircraft overhaul process (AOP), which allows supervisors to make more informed decisions such as task scheduling and resource optimization. Therefore, in this paper, an approach using Markov skeleton process and complex network analytics is proposed to predict makespan of aircraft overhaul process. Firstly, aiming at the uncertainty characteristics of aircraft overhaul, the complex network model of AOP is established to describe the aircraft overhaul process. Then, the critical process path could be identified by adopting ant colony algorithm, and Markov skeleton process state space could be built according to the critical process path, which would greatly improve the prediction accuracy considering NP-hard in Markov skeleton process. Finally, the proposed approach is applied to predict the makespan of a near-life AOP scenario and support further applications for the control and optimization of AOP.

Keywords: Makespan · Aircraft overhaul · Markov process · Complex network · Critical process path

1 Introduction

Currently, the aviation maintenance, repair and overhaul (MRO) industry is facing the increasing pressure on cost, cycle and quality for aircraft overhaul enterprises [1]. Aircraft overhaul process (AOP) is the most complicated recovery activities among MRO. Aircraft overhaul aims at restoring the original design standards and product performance of the aircraft [2]. With the continuous improvement of modern technologies, the complexity of aircraft have been greatly improved, and the requirements for AOP have become higher and higher [3, 4]. Therefore, it is necessary to realize the effective management for AOP. Aircraft overhaul makespan has great significance for instructing AOP. The accurate prediction of aircraft overhaul makespan can enable the aircraft MRO

© The Author(s), under exclusive license to Springer Nature Singapore Pte Ltd. 2023
Z. Yu et al. (Eds.): CIRAC 2022, CCIS 1770, pp. 183–195, 2023.
https://doi.org/10.1007/978-981-99-0301-6_15

enterprises to reasonably allocate production tasks and improve the MRO effectiveness [5].

Recently, many researchers have done a lot of research in the field of production in the prediction cycle [6]. The existing makespan prediction methods can be divided into three categories, including simulation modeling [7], mathematical analysis [8], and statistical analysis [9, 10]. Despite these progresses, prediction of aircraft overhaul makespan is still facing the following challenges: (1) How to establish an AOP model that considers the uncertainties in terms of process routes and process time to support the AOP makespan control and optimization. (2) How to accurately identify the critical process routes of AOP and perform effective management to reduce the impacts of AOP route uncertainties on makespan prediction. (3) How to analyze the process time and make effective use of it to predict the overhaul makespan.

To address these problems, this paper proposes an analytics approach fusing complex network and Markov skeleton process to predict the aircraft overhaul makespan. Firstly, according to the characteristics of AOP, the complex network model of AOP is established. Then the criticality of the aircraft is combined with the ant colony algorithm to identify the critical process routes of the aircraft overhaul complex network (AOCN). The AOCN Markov skeleton process is constructed based on the critical process routes, which would solve the difficulty of accurately predicting the makespan due to the NP-hard problem in the Markov skeleton process prediction method. Finally, the Markov skeleton process solving algorithm is used to accurately predict the aircraft overhaul makespan.

2   Overall Architecture of AOP Makespan Prediction Approach

To predict the overhaul makespan under uncertainties properly, it is necessary to construct the overall architecture of AOP makespan prediction, as shown in Fig. 1. It consists of four parts, namely, Aircraft overhaul resources, Complex network model, Identification of critical process routes for aircraft overhaul, Makespan prediction based on Markov skeleton process. The details are as follows.

(1) **Aircraft overhaul resources.** It involves a variety of physical resources in AOP, including workers, materials, cars, parts, etc. Based on these physical resources, the overhaul process needs to be considered including process flows, process time, etc. They are important to assist to predict the makespan. The process flows can help find the critical process route. The process time can be used to obtain the distribution of the time. After that, the overhaul tasks should be considered and decomposed. These factors provide a solid foundation for building complex networks and making subsequent cycle forecasts during AOP.

(2) **Complex network model.** It aims describe AOP by using complex networks. Firstly, the characteristics of AOP are analyzed. Due to the uncertainties of AOP routes and the uncertainties of process time, it is necessary to analyze the uncertain sources and expression forms. Then, the tasks of aircraft overhaul are decomposed according to the process characteristics of AOP. Finally, the resources is set as node of network to establish AOCN.

(3) Identification of critical process routes for aircraft overhaul. It aims determine AOCN critical process route. The criticality of the node is set as the initial value of the ant colony pheromone, considering the uncertainties of the process route in AOP. Set the parameters of the ant colony algorithm and use the ant colony algorithm to search the complex network of AOP to obtain the critical path sequence.

(4) Makespan prediction based on Markov skeleton process. Based on the researches on the time calculation method and the critical process route of AOP, the Markov skeleton process was constructed. And then, the aircraft overhaul prediction model was established. After that the backward equation of Markov skeleton process was used to solve the aircraft overhaul makespan prediction model. Finally, the probability distribution of the aircraft overhaul makespan is obtained.

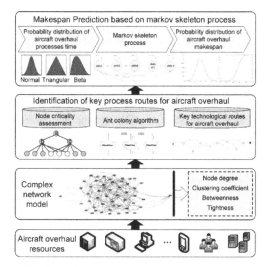

Fig. 1. Makespan prediction approach for AOP.

3 Key Technologies

3.1 AOP Complex Network Model Considering Uncertainties

Each overhaul resource involved in the production activities of the overhaul shop-floor is taken as a resource node (Including equipment, tools, workers, etc.). The overhaul operation process (Such as logistics, information flow, etc.) between the resource nodes is indicated by the directed edges (the process relationship between resource nodes). The strength of the relationship between resource nodes can be seen as the weight of the directed edge, and the entire AOP constitutes a directed weighted complex network. An AOCN G can be represented by a five-tuple, shown as

$$G = (V, E, W, L, RU) \tag{1}$$

where:

$V = \{v_1, v_2, \cdots, v_m\}$ represents a set of aircraft overhaul resource nodes;

$E = \{e_{ij}, i, j = 1, ..., n\}$ represents edge collections between resource nodes. The directed edge E_{ij} represents the overhaul route from the resource node V_i to the resource node V_j. The binary relationship is used to describe the connectivity of the directed edges. $E_{ij} \neq 0$ when two nodes are connected, and $E_{ij} = 0$ when not connected.

$W = \{W_{ij}, i, j = 1, ..., n\}$ represents edge weight set. In the complex network, the edge weight indicates the strength of the relationship between the resource nodes. Once the overhaul process routes are determined, it is necessary to represent the uncertainties of the AOP routes. Here are the definitions: there is no process branch when the value of W_{ij} is 1; while, if there are at least two process branches, the values of W_{ij} would indicate the probability of the process branches, respectively. The probability of a general overhaul route is obtained from the historical data through the ratio of the parts to be repaired in the process route.

$L = \{L_{ij}, i, j = 1, ..., n\}$ represents the load set of resource node (i, j). That is, the duration of a process activity that process on the resource node i.

RU represents the mapping relationship set between overhaul tasks and resources. Usually, each overhaul task requires the cooperation of several kinds of resources, and RU indicates the mapping relationships between overhaul tasks and these resources.

Combined with the characteristics of AOP and the definition of complex network model, the construction steps of the aircraft overhaul complex network model (AOCN-model) are shown in Fig. 2:

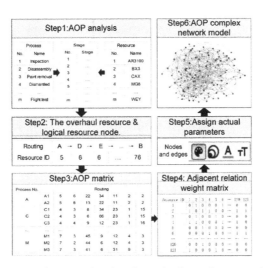

Fig. 2. Construction steps for aircraft overhaul complex network model.

STEP 1: Analyze the AOP and list all possible overhaul routes;

STEP 2: Based on the overhaul process of each station in the shop-floor, extract all the overhaul resources required for each process. Then code the overhaul resources as logical resource nodes;

STEP 3: Networking the resource nodes and the edges between them to construct an AOP matrix;

STEP 4: Analyze the process adjacency relationships between resource nodes in the AOP matrix, and establish the adjacency weight matrix;

STEP 5: Endow actual performance parameters to resource nodes and the edges between nodes;

STEP 6: Based on complex network theory, a complex network model for aircraft overhaul is established based on the adjacency weight relationships between resource nodes.

3.2 Identification of Critical Process Routes for AOP

The process route and process activity time are uncertain during AOP, but the timing relationships between the aircraft overhaul processes (the topology of the AOCN) is determined. Therefore, facing the uncertainties of critical process routes in AOP, this paper transforms the critical process route identification problem into the path search problem with the optimal value in AOCN.

Definition 1: The similarity of the node domain. The index of the importance of the node is measured by obtaining the information of the lower-order neighbor nodes in the two hops of the node, and is recorded as $LLS(i)$.

Definition 2: Node criticality. Synthetically consider the evaluation index of domain similarity and node network efficiency. The criticality of node i is $C_i = I_i \times LLS(i)$. I_i represents efficiency of node i. It can be calculated as follows:

$$I_i = \frac{1}{n} \sum_{k=1, k \neq i}^{n} \frac{1}{d_{ik}} \tag{2}$$

where d_{ik} represents the distance between node i and node k.

By increasing the initial value of the pheromone on the edges of the critical nodes, it is possible to induce the ants to move to the nodes at high frequencies in AOCN. Then the searching efficiency of the ant colony could be improved. The formula for calculating the initial value of the pheromone as follows:

$$Tau(i, j) = Tau\_primary \times \frac{Criticality(j)}{AverageCriticality} \tag{3}$$

where:

$Tau(i, j)$ represents the initial values of all connected pheromone connected to critical node j;

$Tau\_primary$ represents the initial value of the pheromone in the ant colony optimization algorithm. The value is 1 in this paper;

$Criticality(j)$ represents criticality of node j;

$AverageCriticality$ represents the average of the criticality of the entire network nodes.

For the identification of critical process route in AOCN, due to the uncertainties of the time of overhaul processes, this paper only needs to compare the summation of all importance values all nodes in the routes when selecting the critical route. The distances between nodes could be abstracted to the probability of process route. The calculation formula shown as follow when applying ant colony optimization algorithm to search the critical process route of AOCN.

$$P_{ij}^k(t) = \begin{cases} \dfrac{[\tau_{ij}(t)]^\alpha [\eta_{ij}]^\beta}{\sum_{u \in J_k(i)} [\tau_{iu}(t)]^\alpha [\eta_{iu}]^\beta} & \text{if } j \in J_k(i) \\ 0 & \text{else} \end{cases} \tag{4}$$

where:

$\tau_{ij}(t)$ represents the pheromone intensity of the edge between node i and node j at time t;
α represents the pheromone intensity;
β represents relative importance of expected value;
$J_k(i)$ represents the set of points that ant k can access at point i;
η_{ij} represents the probability of choosing process route (i, j).

In the searching process of critical process routes for AOCN, the key step is to update the pheromone of related resource nodes after each generation of ants, so as to guide the next generation of ants. This paper chooses pheromone updating rules with elite strategy. The ant with the best search results from each generation is selected as the elite ant. The increased pheromones are evenly distributed to the route that the ant crawls. At the same time, the pheromones of all nodes volatilize at a certain speed. The situation that other ants search the same route could be avoided so as not to fall into local optimal solution. What's more, it makes better use of global information, making the search process more instructive, making full use of the known optimal solution, and reducing the situations of local optimal.

3.3 Solution of AOCN Model Using Markov Skeleton Process

3.3.1 Construction of AOCN Model

For the AOCN $G(V, E, W, L, RU)$, $V = \{v_1, v_2, \cdots, v_m\}$ represents overhaul resource node set; $E\{e_1, e_2, \cdots, e_n\}$ represents the collection of process activities. For any process activity $e \in A$, its duration is a random variable subjecting to general distribution. Set $\alpha(e)$ as the starting point of process activity e, $\beta(e)$ represents the end point of process activity e, s represents the initial resource node and t represents the termination resource node for aircraft overhaul. An aircraft overhaul process path (s, t) is a sequence of process activities $(e_1, e_2, ..., e_k)$. At the same time, the sequence has the following conditions:

$$\alpha(e_1) = s, \ \beta(e_k) = t, \ \alpha(e_i) = \beta(e_{i-1}), i = 2, 3, ..., k \tag{5}$$

Let $I(v)$ and $O(v)$ represent the whole process activities with resource node V as the end point and starting point respectively, which can be expressed as follows:

$$I(v) = \{e \in E : \beta(e) = v\} \ (v \in V) \tag{6}$$

$$O(v) = \{e \in E : \alpha(e) = v\} \ (v \in V) \tag{7}$$

Set $s \in X \subset V$, $t \in \overline{X} = V - X$, Then the cut set of (s, t) is defined as

$$\left(X, \overline{X}\right) = \left\{e \in E : \alpha(e) \in X, \beta(e) \in \overline{X}\right\} \tag{8}$$

If the cut set $\left(X, \overline{X}\right)$ of (s, t) is an empty set, $\left(X, \overline{X}\right)$ is called uniformly directed cut set (*UDC*). If $\left(X, \overline{X}\right) = M \cup N$, $M \cap N = \emptyset$, and $\forall e \in N$, $I(\beta(e)) \not\subset N$, the (M, N) is called an admissible dichotomy of D.

In the process of aircraft overhaul, each process activity will be in one of three states: active, inactive and idle at t:

(1) Active: If an overhaul process is in operation at time t, the process's state is active.
(2) Inactive: If an overhaul process e has been completed, but not all the processes in parallel with the overhaul process e have been finished. The immediate process of overhaul process e can't start immediately, then the process e is said to be inactive.
(3) Idle: If a process is neither active nor inactive, it is called idle.

It is assumed that the duration of each overhaul process activity is an independent random variable (not limited to a particular distribution). According to the previous definition, here let

$$X(t) = (Y(t), Z(t)) \tag{9}$$

where:

$Y(t)$ represents the set of process activity in active state at t; $Z(t)$ represents the set of process activity in inactive state at t.

At time t (for $Y(t) = (e_1, e_2, ..., e_k)$), we introduce a random variable $\theta_{e_i}(t)$, where $\theta_{e_i}(t)$ represents the operating time of the overhaul process activity e_i from the beginning to time t (the operating time that the overhaul process activity e_i has spent at time t. $\theta_{e_i}(t) \in R^+$, $i = 1, 2, ..., k$.

Define:

$$\overline{X}(t) = \left(Y(t), Z(t), \theta_{e_1}(t), \theta_{e_2}(t), ..., \theta_{e_k}(t)\right) \tag{10}$$

Obviously, $\left\{\overline{X}(t), t \geq 0\right\}$ is a Markov process with continuous time. We can regard Markov process as a special case of Markov skeleton process.

3.3.2 AOCN Model Solution

For the backward equation, if $\{P(x, t, A)\}_{x \in H, t \geq 0, A \in \varepsilon}$ is the minimum nonnegative solution of the equation group shown as follows:

$$q(x, t, A) = P(X(\tau_1) \in A, \tau_1 \leq t | X(0) = x)$$
$$h(x, t, A) = P(X(t) \in A, t < \tau_1 | X(0) = x) \tag{11}$$

where $\{q(x, ds, dy)\}$ is the mixed conditional distribution of $(\tau_1, X(\tau_1))$ with respect to $X(0)$.

Hence, $P(x, t, A) = h(x, t, A) + \int_H \int_0^t q(x, ds, dy) P(y, t - s, A), (x \in H, t \geq 0, A \in \varepsilon)$ can be the backward equation of $X = \{X(t, \omega), 0 \leq t < \infty\}$.

In order to solve the Markov skeleton process of aircraft overhaul critical process route, it is necessary to determine its state set at first. Based on the previous definition, to determine the state set, we need only find out all the generalized admissible dichotomies. Let N represents the number of the allowable bipartitions for AOCN. The state set $\overline{S}$ of $\{\overline{X}(t), t \geq 0\}$ could be divided to N groups, which marked as $S_1, S_2, ..., S_N$. S_N represents the absorbing state $(\emptyset, \emptyset)$. Assumed that the starting resource node of AOCN as s, hence:

$$S_1 = \left(O(s), \emptyset, \theta_{e_1}(t), \theta_{e_2}(t), ..., \theta_{e_k}(t) \right) \tag{12}$$

where $O(s) = (e_1, e_2, ..., e_k)$. In the following chapters, we abbreviate $\theta_{e_k}(t)$ as θ_{e_k} and use asterisks to mark the overhaul processes in inactive state.

According to the backward equation of Markov skeleton process, we can get:

$$P(S_i, t, S_N) = \sum_{S_k \in succ(S_i)} \int_0^t q(S_i, ds, S_k) P(S_k, t - s, S_N), 1 \leq i < N \tag{13}$$

where $succ(S_i)$ represents the direct following-up state set of state S_i. Based on the above formula and the initial condition $P(S_N, t, S_N) = 1(t \geq 0)$, $P(S_{N-1}, t, S_N), ..., P(S_2, t, S_N), P(S_1, t, S_N)$ could be solved. The recursive process is shown in Fig. 3. Aircraft overhaul makespan T is exactly the time when $\{\overline{X}(t), t \geq 0\}$ transfers to absorb state S_N for the first time from state S_1. Therefore, the distribution function of aircraft overhaul makespan is obtained $F(t) = P(S_1, t, S_N)$.

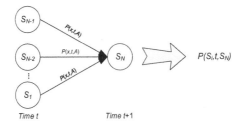

Fig. 3. The recursive process of backward equation

4 Case Study and Analysis

This paper takes the aero engine low-pressure turbine of a certain aircraft type as the main research object. Due to long service time of the aircraft and the complicated damage of parts, the overhaul process is very complicated, and the various processes involved are numerous. It is necessary to obtain the critical process routes and the distribution of overhaul makespan of this specific aircraft type, so as to carry out effective management and control for AOP.

First, The AOCN is established based on process analysis, as shown in Fig. 4. Then, the resource node criticality in the AOCN is evaluated based on the definition of node criticality. Based on node criticality and ant colony algorithm, the critical process routes of aircraft overhaul are analyzed. According to the evaluation results of resource node criticality, the average criticality of resource nodes in AOCN is calculated to be 0.5321. The nodes with the first 25% of the critical value of resource nodes are selected as the critical nodes, and the initial pheromone values of resource nodes are calculated. The results are shown in Table 1.

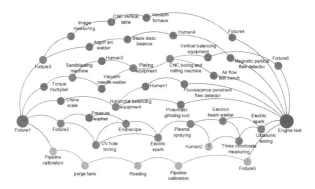

Fig. 4. Schematic diagram of AOCN

Table 1. Initial pheromone values of critical nodes

Node ID	Resource node	Initial pheromone value
36	Fixture 1	1.88
4	Sandblasting machine	1.55
18	Plating equipment	1.52
40	CNC boring and milling machine	1.24
8	UV hole boring	1.51
10	Endoscope	1.52
20	Electric spark	1.59
19	Electron beam welder	1.54
11	Ultrasonic testing	1.59
24	Engine test	1.88

For non-critical nodes, the initial value of pheromone is set to 1. By setting the initial value of pheromone of critical nodes in AOCN, ants can be guided to move to critical resource nodes in AOCN. That is to say, the ants would move to the resource nodes with high probability in critical process routes of AOCN, which would reduce the probability of moving errors due to random migration. This paper applied MATLAB to calculate the critical process routes of aircraft overhaul. The adjacency matrix of AOCN is input into MATLAB. The critical routes are obtained by ant colony algorithm (36, 37, 8, 10, 20, 16, 19, 6, 11, 24) as shown in Fig. 5.

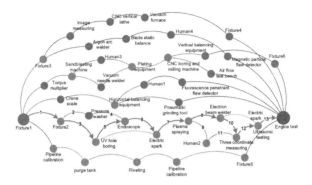

Fig. 5. Critical process routes for aircraft overhaul

Based on the critical process routes of AOCN, the makespan prediction of AOCN can be converted to the prediction of the critical process routes. The Markov skeleton process is constructed for the critical process routes of aircraft overhaul, which reduces the impacts of NP-hard problem on the prediction accuracy of the Markov skeleton process.

The critical process routes are numbered form 1 to 13, and the uniform directed cut set (UDC) for overhaul critical process routes are as follows: (1), (2,3), (4,5), (2,4), (3,5), (6), (7), (8,9), (8,11), (10,11), (9,10), (12), (13). Furthermore, the allowable dichotomy of UDC are: (1), (2,3), (4,5), (4*,5), (4,5*), (2,5), (2,5*), (3,4), (3,4*), (6), (7), (8,9), (10,11), (10*,11), (10,11*), (8,11), (8,11*), (9,10), (9,10*), (12), (13), (∅,∅). According to the analysis, there are 22 kinds of Markov skeleton processes corresponding to the critical process routes of aircraft overhaul, as shown in Table 2.

Set

$$E = [\{1\} \times [0, \infty)] \cup [\{2, 3\} \times [0, \infty)] \cup [\{4, 5\} \times [0, \infty)] \cdots \cup [\{\emptyset\} \times \{\emptyset\}]$$

Assumed that $\overline{X}(t)$ is the stochastic process with E as the state space. Let $\tau_0 = 0$, and $\tau_k (k \geq 1)$ represents the kth discontinuity point of $\overline{X}(t)$. Then $\{\overline{X}(t), t \geq 0\}$ is the Markov skeleton process with (τ_k) as the skeleton sequence.

Based on the backward equation of Markov skeleton process, the distribution function of aircraft overhaul makespan could be solved. When the overhaul activities included in E finished, the state of Markov skeleton process $\{\overline{X}(t), t \geq 0\}$ would be changed. Calculate $P(S_{19}, t, S_{22})$, ..., $P(S_2, t, S_{22})$, $P(S_1, t, S_{22})$ in turn from the back to the front. According to the equations above, we can get that:

$$P(S_1, t, S_{22}) = \int_0^t q((1, \theta_1), ds, (2, \theta_2))P((2, \theta_2), t - s, (\emptyset, \emptyset))$$
$$= \int_0^t \left(1 - G_{\theta_2}^{(2)}(s)\right)F_2(\theta_2, t - s)dG_{\theta_1}^{(1)}(s)$$

Table 2. State set of Markov skeleton process corresponding to critical process routes of aircraft overhaul

No	State	No	State
S_1	$(1, \theta_1)$	S_{12}	$(8, 9, \theta_8, \theta_9)$
S_2	$(2, 3, \theta_2, \theta_3)$	S_{13}	$(10, 11, \theta_{10}, \theta_{11})$
S_3	$(4, 5, \theta_4, \theta_5)$	S_{14}	$(10^*, 11, \theta_{11})$
S_4	$(4^*, 5, \theta_5)$	S_{15}	$(10, 11^*, \theta_{10})$
S_5	$(4, 5^*, \theta_4)$	S_{16}	$(8, 11, \theta_8, \theta_{11})$
S_6	$(2, 5, \theta_2, \theta_5)$	S_{17}	$(8, 11^*, \theta_8)$
S_7	$(2, 5^*, \theta_2)$	S_{18}	$(9, 10, \theta_9, \theta_{10})$
S_8	$(3, 4, \theta_3, \theta_4)$	S_{19}	$(9, 10^*, \theta_9)$
S_9	$(3, 4^*, \theta_3)$	S_{20}	$(12, \theta_{12})$
S_{10}	$(6, \theta_6)$	S_{21}	$(13, \theta_{13})$
S_{11}	$(7, \theta_7)$	S_{22}	$(\emptyset, \emptyset)$

Then set $\theta_1 = \theta_2 = 0$

$$F(t) = P(S_1, t, S_{22}) = \int_0^t \left(1 - G_0^{(2)}(s)\right) F_2(\theta_2, t - s) dG_0^{(1)}(s)$$

Based on historical data of overhaul and probability theory, it can be concluded that the duration distribution of process 1 in the critical process route of aircraft overhaul obeys the Chi-square distribution, and the degree of freedom is 30; The duration distribution of process 3 obeys the Gamma distribution with parameters being (10, 4); The duration distributions of process 2, 4, 5, 6, 7, 8, 9, 10, 11, 12 obeys normal distribution with parameters being (16, 1.78), (36, 2.5), (23, 1.5), (46, 1.78), (136, 4), (34, 5.2), (128, 2), (20, 3), (49, 3.5) and (36, 2.5), respectively. The duration distribution of process 13 obeys Gamma distribution with parameters being (15, 5). Appling the backward equation of Markov skeleton process, with the help of MATLAB 2014a, $P(S_{19}, t, S_{22})$, ..., $P(S_2, t, S_{22})$, $P(S_1, t, S_{22})$ could be calculated in turn. Finally, we can get:

$$E(T) = \int_0^\infty t dF(t) \approx 546$$

$$Var(T) = \int_0^\infty t^2 dF(t) - (E(T))^2 \approx 25$$

Through applying MATLAB for analysis, we can get the probability density distribution curve of aircraft overhaul as shown in Fig. 6. We can see that the overhaul makespan is between 425 h and 675 h, and the overhaul makespan has the highest probability around 540 h.

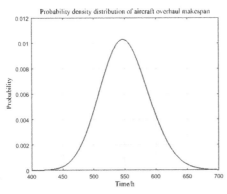

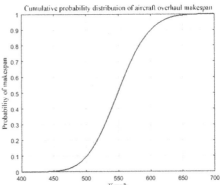

Fig. 6. Aircraft overhaul makespan probability density distribution curve

Fig. 7. Aircraft overhaul makespan cumulative probability distribution curve

Meanwhile, the cumulative probability distribution curve of aircraft overhaul mekespan can be obtained, as shown in Fig. 7. It can see that the probability of makespan of aircraft overhaul in 600 h is 90%. The aircraft overhaul factory can monitor the aircraft overhaul progress according to the probability of completion on time. Calculate the on-time completion rate after each repair progress report, and then compare it with the threshold. If the on-time completion rate is lower than the set threshold, it will alert the aircraft overhaul supervisors.

Applying the prediction model to predict the makespan of five different batches of aircraft low pressure turbine, flaps, slotted wings and elevator, the gaps between the five predictions and the actual overhaul makespan are analyzed. The confidence interval is 90% and the results are shown in Table 3. It can be seen that the differences between the predicted values and the actual values are mostly within the allowable value ranges. The predicted results have high reliability. Generally, the overhaul prediction model can meet the prediction needs of aircraft overhaul enterprises. The prediction results can support further applications for the control and optimization of AOP.

Table 3. Prediction results of aircraft overhaul makespan

No.	Predicting expectations/h	True value/h	Confidence interval	Error
1	512	468	[453, 572]	8.5%
2	72	68	[51, 93]	5.5%
3	116	99	[101, 131]	14.6%
4	56	63	[45, 65]	−12.5%
5	232	241	[204, 265]	−3.8%

5 Conclusions

This paper presented a new method for predicting the overhaul makespan of aircraft. The main contributions of this paper are as follows. The first contribution is the AOP model based on complex network. This paper analyzed the complex process flows and uncertainty characteristics of aircraft overhaul. It is also found that the topological structure of the model has the properties of small-world network and scale-free network. The second contribution is the evaluation model of node criticality of AOCN. Based on the node criticality and ant colony algorithm, this paper analyzed the critical process route of aircraft overhaul. A new method for identifying critical routes is proposed. The third contribution is the aircraft overhaul makespan prediction model based on Markov skeleton process. It reduces the prediction complexity caused by NP-hard problem, improves the prediction efficiency, and provides a new solution for aircraft overhaul makespan prediction.

Acknowledgements. This work was supported by the National Natural Science Foundation of China under Grant 52075452.

References

1. Khan, N., Manarvi, I.: Identification of delay factors in C-130 aircraft overhaul and finding solutions through data analysis. In: The 2011 Aerospace Conference (2011)
2. Lee, S., Ma, Y., Thimm, G., Verstraeten, J.: Product lifecycle management in aviation maintenance, repair and overhaul. Comput. Ind. **59**(2–3), 296–303 (2008)
3. Geng, J., Tian, X., Bai, M., Jia, X., Liu, X.: A design method for three-dimensional maintenance, repair and overhaul job card of complex products. Comput. Ind. **65**(1), 200–209 (2014)
4. Ramudhin, A., Paquet, M., Artiba, A., Dupre, P., Varvaro, D., Thomson, V.: A generic framework to support the selection of an RFID-based control system with application to the MRO activities of an aircraft engine manufacturer. Prod. Plan. Control **19**(2), 183–196 (2008)
5. Lavorato, P., Rodrigues, D.: Maintenance, repair and overhaul (MRO) fundamentals and strategies: an aeronautical industry overview. Int. J. Comput. Appl. **135**(12), 21–29 (2016)
6. Chung, S., Huang, H.: Cycle time estimation for wafer fab with engineering lots. IIE Trans. **34**(2), 105–118 (2002)
7. Bekki, J., Fowler, J., Mackulak, G., Nelson, B.: Indirect cycle time quantile estimation using the Cornish-Fisher expansion. IIE Trans. **42**(1), 31–44 (2009)
8. Shanthikumar, J., Ding, S., Zhang, M.: Queueing theory for semiconductor manufacturing systems: a survey and open problems. IEEE Trans. Autom. Sci. Eng. **4**(4), 513–522 (2007)
9. Backus, P., Janakiram, M., Mowzoon, S., Runger, G., Bhargava, A.: Factory cycle-time prediction with a data-mining approach. IEEE Trans. Semicond. Manuf. **19**(2), 252–258 (2006)
10. Chien, C., Hsu, C., Hsiao, C.: Manufacturing intelligence to forecast and reduce semiconductor cycle time. J. Intell. Manuf. **23**(6), 2281–2294 (2012)

A Cyber Physical System (CPS) Enabled Approach for Aircraft Overhaul Shop-Floor Based on Real-Time Smart Data Analyzing

Bingyang Sun[1], Xiaoliang Jia[1(✉)], Mingjun Huang[2], and Xiao Chang[1]

[1] School of Mechanical Engineering, Northwestern Polytechnical University, Xi'an 710072, China
jiaxl@nwpu.edu.cn
[2] State-Owned Wuhu Machinery Factory, Wuhu 241000, China

Abstract. Typical challenges that aircraft overhaul enterprises faced are the lack of timely, accurate information of operation and inter-operation in shop-floor during the whole overhaul process, resulting in long overhaul cycle, rising cost and labor. Therefore, it is very important to establish quick-response troubleshooting policy incorporating with complex and variable overhaul process flow, long cycle time etc. to improve shop-floor performance. In this paper, a cyber-physical system (CPS) enabled real-time analytical framework for aircraft overhaul process (AOP) is proposed to give a new paradigm through applying the CPS technologies to aircraft overhaul shop-floor. AOP data and information, such as process flow, operation time, disturbances etc. can be perceived, value-added and integrated in real-time status. Considering the complexity of overhaul process variability and disturbances, a decision-making mechanism based on event-rule fusion method is constructed to assist in making better-informed decision for managers that helps to overcome the above-mentioned barriers. A real-time smart data analyzing method was developed to promote AOP improvement. Finally, a proof-of-concept application with a real-life scenario has been developed to illustrate the proposed framework.

Keywords: Cyber-physical system · Aircraft overhaul process · Analytical framework · Real-time

1 Introduction

Currently, the aviation maintenance, repair and overhaul (MRO) industry is facing the increasing pressure on cost, cycle and quality, accompanied with new technologies applied and improved strict legislation. Aircraft overhaul process (AOP) is the most complicated recovery activities among MRO [1]. The aircraft would be typically completely disassembled, and all parts would be inspected and returned to like-new condition for customers [2]. The general characteristics of AOP (e.g., complex, and variable operating process flow, long repair times, high operational flexibility) could lead to typical problems of prolonged overhaul cycle, costs increment, or compromising the features of the

© The Author(s), under exclusive license to Springer Nature Singapore Pte Ltd. 2023
Z. Yu et al. (Eds.): CIRAC 2022, CCIS 1770, pp. 196–207, 2023.
https://doi.org/10.1007/978-981-99-0301-6_16

overhauled aircraft, which reduces the aircraft overhaul shop-floor performance. Therefore, it is necessary to use novel information technologies in AOP to realize continuous and potential methods of process improvement and optimization [3, 4].

Recently, cyber-physical system (CPS) technologies have been received great attention and researched in many areas [5, 6]. CPS technologies can effectively establish the exchange and connection relations of information between different units. A bottom-up highly integrated system could be formed to perform a series of autonomous operations such as perception, transmission, decision making, and execution and so on [7]. Based on this, it can benefit from these five aspects, (1) real-time data has become accessible, (2) production disturbances can be detected timely and responded rapidly, (3) overhaul resources are made 'smart' which can communicate with the management system actively, and adjust their status dynamically [8]. Despite these progresses, the following challenges still exist in and are of our particular interest. Firstly, how to perceive, value-add and integrate the dynamic data of AOP including process operations, tasks, resources etc. to establish a CPS enabled real-time analytical framework through constructing? Secondly, how to construct a mechanism for easily and efficiently processing and integrating the real-time data to emerge high level sematic information for decision-maker during the whole AOP? Thirdly, how to design an effective method based on real-time information combing data-driven prediction is the key to achieve AOP optimization?

Considering the advantages of CPS, in this paper, a CPS enabled real-time analytical framework is presented to provide a novel paradigm by using CPS to AOP [9]. In the context of the framework, problems of long overhaul cycle, rising cost and labor etc. during AOP can be addressed. AOP data, such as process flow, operation time, disturbances etc. can be perceived, value-added and integrated in real-time to assist in making better-informed decision for managers. It will potentially increase the performance of AOP and facilitate the optimal decision during the whole AOP.

2 A CPS Enabled Real-Time Analytical Framework for AOP

To realize the real-time analysis during the overhaul process, it is necessary to construct the analytical framework, which can acquire shop-floor information in real time, transmit mass data efficiently, and then support the real-time supervision by the managers [10]. Under this framework, all the execution processes can be timely perceived, as shown in Fig. 1. The real-time tracking of each operation and the process execution of can be monitored. It can support the decision-making to achieve optimal management of AOP. The proposed framework consists of four components, namely, the configuration of CPS environment, Data perception and value-adding, Quick decision-making, and AOP application services. They are depicted as follows:

(1) The configuration of CPS environment: The most basic component is the configuration of CPS environment. The intelligent sensing devices are helpful for collecting data for individual aircrafts as well as other resources involved. The physical shop-floor has a lot of objects to monitor, including aircraft parts, workers, tools, logistics vehicles and other physical resources. At the same time, the shop-floor temperature,

humidity, pressure, air quality and other necessary environmental information could be acquired. Then the data would be transmitted to the AOP data perception and value-adding component through the shop-floor network for overall calculation.

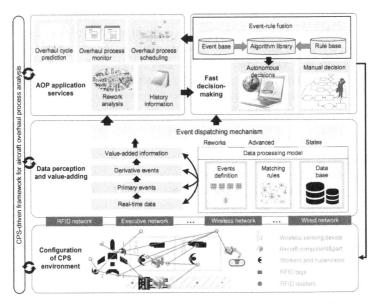

Fig. 1. CPS enabled real-time smart AOP analytical framework.

(2) Data perception and value-adding: It focuses on the processing of information. In the CPS environment, huge amounts of data are generated. And the data need to be transmitted and interacted among various services. Therefore, a powerful network transmission capability of the system is very important. Based on these data, combined with the events models and rules base, lots of events can be identified and the data could be value-added. An event response mechanism can be used to realize the interaction among different levels. The AOP decision-making component and analytical application services could get real-time data through corresponding interfaces.

(3) Quick decision-making: AOP fast decision-making component consists of two main functions: autonomous decision-making and manual decision-making. An important concept of CPS system is highly autonomous. All the events could enter the decision-making component. Based on the event-rule fusion, for simple shop-floor events, some autonomous decisions such as routine distribution of logistics cars could be defined. When a task is about to start, resources information will be acquired. The system could independently order the logistics vehicle or workers to prepare and distribute the materials. There are still many uncertain events in the shop-floor, such as overhaul errors, which cannot be corrected by the predefined decision-making system. Such events require the participation of managers and

they would be uploaded to the application services. The managers could analyze and then work out reasonable and feasible solutions based on application platform.

(4) AOP application services: Large number of data and events have been processed, and meaningful information could interact with application services. Managers can get convenient services from AOP application services, and then better manage the overhaul shop-floor. At present, it mainly includes five types of services: overhaul process monitoring, overhaul cycle prediction, overhaul process dynamic scheduling, overhaul ability analysis, exception management. These services can be applied separately and integrated with some other systems. Real-time information from the shop-floor plays the role of supporter to the application layer. Combining real-time information, the managers can adjust the schedules of the overhaul shop-floor in time.

3   Key Technologies

3.1   Real-Time Perception and Value-Adding of Aircraft Overhaul Shop-Floor Data

Based on the intelligent sensing devices such as Bluetooth, RFID etc., CPS has abilities to perceive the overhaul process under different conditions. As shown in Fig. 2, there are three kinds of wireless devices. The first one is the high frequency RFID reader, which could perceive large scare. It can be equipped on the working area so that the resources could be perceived once they enter the working zone. The second kind is the infrared module, which is placed by the gate in order to monitor the objects who pass by. The data it generates can be used to assist to analyze the behaviors of the resources. The last kind is the low frequency RFID. They can perceive the objects at close quarters. Hence, they can be put on the way the logistics trolleys pass and feedback the location information to the system in real time.

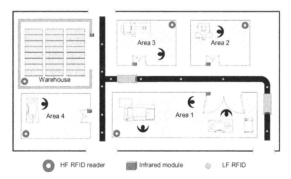

Fig. 2. Shop-floor equipped with perception devices.

Based on these technologies, the data could be collected effectively. But the raw data are mainly numbers and the managers cannot figure out the meanings directly. It is necessary to construct a predefined events and rules base to add values to the data. Events could describe the changes of resources' states. Rule base can support to define multi-level events and even simple decision-making. These event definitions could be abstracted to some rules. These are the basic rules. To consider further and construct the decision-making mechanism, some rules need to be defined based on rich repair experiences to assure the quick decision. A kind of event-rule fusion mode should be designed primarily. Figure 3 shows the classification of rules for AOP.

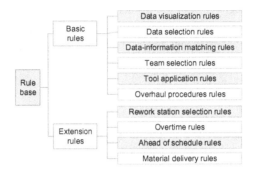

Fig. 3. Rules base for AOP.

Through the predefinition of key devices, based on the rule base, the basic events could be acquired directly to realize real time value-adding for shop-floor data. In this paper, a multi-level event model for overhaul shop-floor is proposed, which includes primitive event, derivative event and complex event. The primitive event represents that a certain tag was detected by a reader at a certain time, which is marked $PE = <Rid, Tid, Time>$. Here, Rid represents the ID of the reader; Tid represents the ID of the tag; and Time is the instantaneous time the tag is retrieved by the reader. Derivative event is the event gathered and filtered from primitive events to describe the important state of a specific tag or group of tags, denoted as $DE = <e, P, t>$. Here, e refers to a specific tag, and $e.type$ is the category of tags; P is the location of the tag; t means that the tag e exists at P at time t. It is also the simplest existence event $OE = <e, P, t>$.

While in the overhaul process, some complex event should be acquired. In order to connect real-time data and these events, derivative and complex events can be defined using some methods. Hence, this paper introduced some event operators, as shown in Table 1.

These operators could be combined to represent a specific event. For example, an aeroengine turbine bearing numbered "E12345" stops at position W154, the event can be marked as:

$$SE_{(e.type = "bearing")} \wedge (e.sn = "E12345") \wedge (P = "W154") \wedge ("T = t_e - t_s") \tag{1}$$

Table 1. Event operators (partial)

Type	Meaning
AND X∧Y	Both event X and event Y occur
OR X∨Y	Event X or event Y occur
NOT ¬X	Event X is not occurred
Constraint XC	C represents a set of constraints
Combination COUNT(X), MAX (X, f), MIN (X, f), AVG (X, f)	Statistics of an attribute in a group of events
Time window XT	Defining the time range of complex events
Time constraint <, > et al	Time logical relationship between different events
Choice XS	All events that conform to keyword S

Lots of events can be expressed in this form, and the information can be traced in real time. Through the event model, we can get large number of original events and complex events. Combined with rule base, we can define a complex pattern. Assume that there are five parts named 'A' and part named 'B' no more than 10 arrived working area 'W154', if the workers 'M' and 'N' arrived here in 20 min, it will report that the repair task has started. Assume that a[] = {'A', 'B'}; b[] = {'M', 'N'}; and the pattern is shown as follows.

PATTERN SEQ (a[ ], b[ ])

WHERE { a[0]=5 ∧

a[0].place='W154' ∧

a[1]<10 ∧

a[1].place='W154' ∧

b[0].place='W154' ∧

b[1].place='W154'}

WITHIN 20 min

RETURN Current time, "Start!"

3.2   Real-Time Information and Data-Driven Prediction of AOP

To make full use of these information, some services such as prediction services, management services et al. need to be designed. The bottleneck and overhaul cycle prediction are two critical issues affecting the overhaul progress in the real-time information and data-driven prediction of AOP. Through the calculation of corresponding data, the bottleneck and overhaul cycle of overhaul process could be obtained at any time. Results of bottlenecks would be generated to support the managers to adjust the resources of the current overhaul shop-floor and try to solve the bottleneck problem caused by uneven distribution of resources. The prediction of overhaul cycle is of great economic value to the overhaul shop-floor. The longer the cycle is, the higher the overhaul cost would be, the lower the availability of the aircraft is.

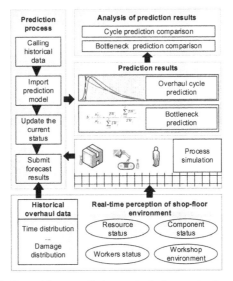

Fig. 4. Data-driven prediction analysis for overhaul process.

Bottleneck prediction mainly includes the following steps: (1) Abstract the overhaul activities as network nodes according to the AOP flow rules, and establish the AOP network diagram based on logical relationships among the overhaul activities. (2) Define the bottlenecks of AOP based on the uncertainty analysis data and historical data of the overhaul process sequences. (3) Use historical data to simulate the bottleneck and get the bottleneck distribution model. (4) Predict the bottleneck of aircraft overhaul combined with real-time information.

For overhaul cycle prediction model, there are also some key steps. (1) Establish the network diagram of AOP; (2) Construct the probability distribution of aircraft overhaul activity duration based on the analysis data and historical data. (3) Solve the model and analyze the performance using PERT and Monte Carlo simulation methods.

The real-time information and data-driven prediction of AOP shown in Fig. 4 mainly includes three parts: overhaul process sequence simulation, overhaul process execution bottleneck prediction, and overhaul cycle prediction. It's of great guiding significance in overhaul shop-floor. For the process simulation modular, it can simulate the repair process of subsequent in accordance with the current overhaul schedule. Through the simulation, the trend of each component, the use of tools, the operation status of logistics trolley and so on can be obtained. Managers could take preventive measures in advance based on the problems found in simulation.

3.3 AOP Decision-Making Model

Based on the real-time information and the analysis results of simulation, the proper decisions should be done. Event and rule base are the fundamental for AOP, it includes managerial implications that generated from hidden knowledge and key findings of expertise which are useful when various department managers are making decisions accordingly. Event-rule fusion is a mechanism mainly for fast decision making. There are some rules stored in the databases based on rich overhaul experience. For example, to perform the decision making for rework, there are several rules here to constraint the behaviors of the shop-floor to lower the effects which caused. Events and rules have "one-to-one", "one-to-many", "many-to-one" and "many-to-many" four kinds of relationships. For one event, a rule or several rules can lead to a specific operation. And for several events, a rule or several rules can determine another complex decision.

Based on event-rule fusion, this paper proposes a decision-making mechanism of AOP based on event-rule fusion, which benefits from its fast acquisition technology, efficient data transmission capability, and high-grade decision-making mechanism. As shown in Fig. 5.

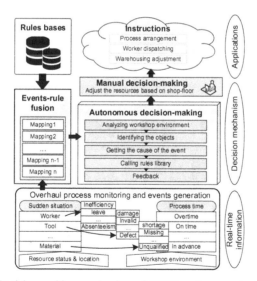

Fig. 5. Decision-making mechanism of AOP based on event-rule fusion.

The decision mechanism is mainly composed of two parts, one is the autonomous decision-making. It initially collects the information including machine type information, parts information, damage form information and damage degree. Benefit from the long history of aircraft overhaul, a great deal of repair experiences could be utilized. Combined with the concept of scientific repair, the process can be directly invoked for different initial inspection results and events. By calling to behavior database, it could timely feedback the corrective operations. If the worker leaves his post when executing a specified task, this modular would call to assign additional workers. If the tool is lost, it would locate and retrieve it for the workers. It could save the time to shorten the overhaul cycle. But some emergencies unavoidably lead to uncontrolled situation. Usually, manual intervention is needed. The processes could be determined by human. This mechanism can promote overhaul efficiency greatly.

4 Case Study

This section describes a proof-of-concept application scenario to demonstrate how to implement the presented framework. Two typical scenarios in AOP related to our business partner company X are discussed. It aims to verify the effectiveness and feasibility of the proposed framework.

4.1 Background

In the traditional overhaul shop-floor, the recording and transmission of the data is mainly carried out manually, which is inefficient. By constructing the CPS environment, data can be perceived by intelligent sensing device and transmitted through powerful networks. The physical shop-floor equipped with sensing devices is the most basic part in the whole CPS system. In order to show the CPS-driven AOP more perfectly, this paper chooses some representative resources to configure shop-floor with CPS sensing devices.

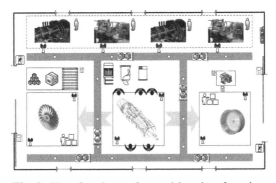

Fig. 6. Shop-floor layout for repairing aircraft engine.

The layout of aircraft overhaul shop-floor in case study is shown in Fig. 6. The middle part is the disassembly and assembly station. The sensing device located in this area senses the resources when they enter the station. Then, the dismantled parts from aircraft engine would be labeled and sent to other repair stations for further repairing. Logistics dollies are responsible for transporting parts and components. The sensing devices are equipped on the dolly. When parts are loaded on the dolly, loading events are obtained. The sensing device on the dolly can sense the location label on the floor of the shop-floor in real time, and then upload the dolly's location. Based on this, the loading and movement of the dolly can be monitored in real time. Sensing devices equipped in each repairing station could acquire the parts and components entering the area. At the same time, the workers in shop-floor are equipped with tags. The workers' position and status can also be monitored. After completing the repair process, the components and parts returned to middle part.

4.2   Implementation of the Proposed Framework

Base on the technological characteristics of the aircraft overhaul shop-floor, this paper develops aircraft overhaul process execution system (AOPES). For better understanding, this section mainly introduces the rework management in AOP. Rework is a typical factor restricting the progress of overhaul.

Rework is the most typical uncertain event in AOP. Usually, an aircraft part should be inspected for second time after repairing. If qualified, it would enter the waiting area to be reassembled. If it is not qualified, it would be judged whether it can be repaired or not. If not, it would be scrapped directly. If it can be repaired again, which would be a rework event. Based on the definition of rework events, the CPS sensing devices placed at each node of the workstation can transmit related data and sequences to the upper layer in real time. When several nodes of the rework event are triggered, the rework event occurs, uploads and reminds managers to pay attention.

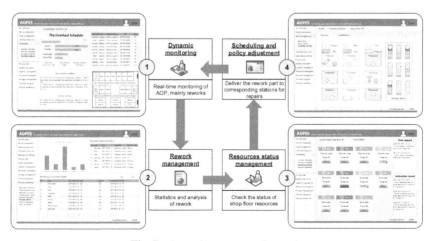

Fig. 7. Operating process of rework.

The operation flow of rework is shown in the Fig. 7. Similar with the processes of cycle prediction, the rework process consists of four steps:

STEP 1: Monitor the overhaul process, obtain the relevant information of the components;

STEP 2: According to the definition of rework, perform the statistical for rework and issue a warning;

STEP 3: Check the statuses of resources in shop-floor, obtain the free work stations;

STEP 4: Reschedule the repair tasks for the rework part. Deliver the part to the corresponding station.

Once the rework events were identified in the shop-floor, the information could be fed back to the system in real time. And then the statistics results can be displayed visually on the system interface. The system would record the latest rework tasks, events, shop-floors and responsible persons in the Rework Event Statistics Table in the interface. By analyzing and combining historical information, the system can generate real-time histogram of causes for rework events. It is intuitive and clear to show managers the major accident factors that should be focused on. Because the rework event has great impacts on the overhaul process, there are real-time overhaul process tables in the rework event service. Through the algorithm, the rework task can be inserted into the repair sequence of a workstation, and managers can modify it manually. The related interface is shown in the Fig. 2, 3, 4, 5, 6 and 7.

5 Conclusion

This paper focuses on a CPS enabled real-time analytical framework for aircraft overhaul process. The main contributions of this paper are as follows. The first contribution is a CPS enabled real-time analytical framework for AOP. AOP information, such as process flow, operation time, disturbances etc. can be perceived, value-added and integrated in real-time status. The second contribution is the constructed decision-making operation mechanism based on event-rule fusion method, which aims to assist in making better-informed decision for managers. The third contribution is a real-time information combing with data-driven prediction method was developed to promote AOP improvement. A proof-of-concept application with a real-life scenario has been developed to illustrate the proposed framework in an aircraft overhaul shop-floor.

Acknowledgements. This work was supported by the National Natural Science Foundation of China under Grant 52075452.

References

1. Bracken, J., Simmons, K.: Minimizing reductions in readiness caused by time-phased decreases in aircraft overhaul and repair activities. Naval Res. Logist. Q. **13**, 159–165 (2010)
2. Khan, N., Manarvi, I.: Identification of delay factors in C-130 aircraft overhaul and finding solutions through data analysis. In: 2011 Aerospace Conference (2011)

3. Mandolla, C., Petruzzelli, A., Percoco, G.: Building a digital twin for additive manufacturing through the exploitation of blockchain: a case analysis of the aircraft industry. Comput. Ind. **109**, 134–152 (2019)
4. Ramudhin, A., Paquet, M., Artiba, A.: A generic framework to support the selection of an RFID-based control system with application to the MRO activities of an aircraft engine manufacturer. Prod. Plan. Control **19**, 183–196 (2008)
5. Windmann, S., Maier, A., Niggemann, O.: Big data analysis of manufacturing processes. In: Journal of Physics: Conference Series, p. 012055 (2015)
6. Wang, L., Torngren, M., Onori, M.: Current status and advancement of cyber-physical systems in manufacturing. J. Manuf. Syst. **37**, 517–527 (2015)
7. Iarovyi, S., Mohammed, W., Lobov, A.: Cyber–physical systems for open-knowledge-driven manufacturing execution systems. Proc. IEEE **104**, 1142–1154 (2016)
8. Wang, W., Zhang, Y., Zhong, R.Y.: A proactive material handling method for CPS enabled shop-floor. Robot. Comput. Integr. Manuf. **61**, 101849 (2020)
9. Wan, J., Tang, S., Li, D.: A manufacturing big data solution for active preventive maintenance. IEEE Trans. Industr. Inf. **13**, 2039–2047 (2017)
10. Leitão, P., Colombo, A., Karnouskos, S.: Industrial automation based on cyber-physical systems technologies: prototype implementations and challenges. Comput. Ind. **81**, 11–25 (2016)

Other Robot-Related Technologies

A Lightweight Algorithm Based on YOLOv5 for Relative Position Detection of Hydraulic Support at Coal Mining Faces

Lihu Pan, Yuxuan Duan[✉], Yingjun Zhang, Binhong Xie, and Rui Zhang

School of Computer Science and Technology, Taiyuan University of Science and Technology, Taiyuan 030024, China
S20202002003@stu.tyust.edu.cn

Abstract. To solve the existing problems that the moving process monitoring method of hydraulic support in comprehensive coal mining faces, such as complex detection equipment and has poor flexibility and maintainability, we propose a method of hydraulic support relative position detection in coal mining faces based on object detection LG-YOLO. To better deploy the deep learning model on end-side devices, the GhostNet convolution module and the Ghost residual module are integrated into the YOLOv5s network to reduce the number of parameters and the occupancy of computing resources. Additionally, the PReLU activation function is integrated to achieve faster inference speed. In the postprocessing stage, DIoU NMS is used to help detect closely aligned targets. The network model is further compressed by channel pruning and knowledge distillation. Experiments show that the improved algorithm can effectively detect the status of hydraulic supports. Finally, the model size is reduced by 73% and the computational amount is reduced by 69%, which can meet the requirements of end-side device deployment and real-time detection.

Keywords: Lightweight · YOLOv5 · GhostNet · Pruning · Knowledge of distillation

1 Introduction

Intelligent construction is an important measure for mines to achieve high-quality development and an effective way to reform and develop the coal mining industry. Influenced by the development of the big data technology, artificial intelligence and Internet of Things, smart mines have a high degree of information integration, automation and intelligence, their goal is to realise the unmanned or less humanised key processes in coal mining [1]. In addition to the improvement of production efficiency, safe production is also an issue that cannot be ignored in the field of coal mining field. The special production environment and equipment of coal mining and the lack of effective management tools have led to a high incidence of coal mine disasters. The coal mining face support is a necessary condition for safe and efficient mining, and hydraulic supports are the core of the mechanised mining system [2]. Ideally, the hydraulic supports are

Z. Yu et al. (Eds.): CIRAC 2022, CCIS 1770, pp. 211–227, 2023.
https://doi.org/10.1007/978-981-99-0301-6_17

aligned with each other on the mining face and move automatically when the shearer cuts coal. However, they may deviate from their proper position due to hydraulic system failure or unfavourable environments. With existing technical facilities, the inspection of the position status of hydraulic supports often relies on manual inspections or a large number of sensors, which is less efficient but safer.

The manual inspection method is gradually eliminated due to poor safety and low inspection efficiency. Sensor monitoring has a good monitoring effect, but its maintenance cost is high, its flexibility is poor, and its coverage area is not large enough [3], and deep learning is still poorly used in this area. To achieve accurate acquisition of hydraulic support positional status, contact measurement methods are now predominantly used worldwide to measure the key posture parameters of hydraulic supports by installing a variety of sensors on each component of the support. Gao K. et al. [4], who used angle sensors and displacement sensors, based on particle swarm optimization (PSO) algorithm, proposed a method to detect the relative position and attitude, and conducted experiments on the position state detection of the hydraulic support. The author also verified that the method can effectively detect the change in the pose of the top beam of the hydraulic support in the working condition. Zhang Y. et al. [5] proposed a sensor measurement method based on the three-point coplanar principle, setting a series of reference points to achieve the monitoring of equipment position status. Zhang S.N. et al. [6] proposed a method for measuring the straightness of hydraulic support using multisensor combination, which mainly derives the position relationship between adjacent support by arranging two stroke displacement sensors at the fixed position of the hydraulic support base plate in combination with three-axis tilt sensors and solves the straightness of the hydraulic support group through the hydraulic support straightness derivation model based on the D-H coordinate system. Wang J.B. et al. [7] proposed a mining hydraulic support moving distance measurement method based on the random circle detection (RCD) algorithm and the fruit fly optimisation algorithm (FOA) to obtain the relative positions of adjacent support by camera according to the changes in the circle centre and the radius on the support. Ren H.W. et al. [8] used the depth vision principle to measure the height and attitude angle of the hydraulic support. RGB-D cameras are deployed on top of equipment, the depth vision technique is used to obtain the colour information and the depth information, and the fast extraction and matching of the base feature points are realised by the ORB algorithm and the FLANN algorithm. In addition, the ICP model is based on the spatial 3D-3D estimation of camera position changes at adjacent moments. Zhang X.H. et al. [9] investigated the image processing and solving by installing an explosion-proof camera and infrared LED marker board on a coal miner and hydraulic support, respectively. They also used a vision algorithm with 4 working feature points to achieve the measurement of hydraulic support base posture status.

Although the above detection methods are improving in accuracy, the detection perspective is relatively singular, the detection surface coverage is small, and the hardware facilities to be deployed are still large, making it difficult to achieve real-time detection. However, the various position sensors may fail after a long time, and the large number of sensors makes maintenance difficult and less reliable. At the same time, the complex geographical environment and harsh working conditions in the coal mine lead to difficulties in deploying some large arithmetic devices, and real-time monitoring basically relies on end-side low arithmetic platform devices.

Based on the current problems faced by the industry, we propose a lightweight model LG-YOLO (Lite Ghost YOLO) to detect the relative position of hydraulic support in coal mine comprehensive mining faces using deep learning object detection. Based on YOLOv5 network model, the Ghost Module of GhostNet is introduced to reduce the calculation cost of neural network, and the optimised model is further compressed by channel pruning. Finally, the detection accuracy is improved by knowledge distillation. By obtaining the target location points of each hydraulic support, the relative position relationship between the adjacent hydraulic support is calculated to determine the status of the hydraulic support group. Experiments have proven that the LG-YOLO algorithm not only maintains a high level of detection accuracy but also greatly reduces the need for arithmetic power and basically meets the requirements of actual industrial production.

2 YOLOv5 Network Model

YOLO [10], one of the masterpieces of one-stage object detection algorithms, was once one of the most popular object detection network models due to its notable performance. Since its introduction in 2016, it has evolved to YOLOv5, which has faster inference speed, as well as smaller size than the previous generation, YOLOv4. Ultralytics gives four versions of the YOLOv5 network model: YOLOv5s, YOLOv5m, YOLOv5l and YOLOv5x.

The network structure of YOLOv5 is mainly composed of four parts: inputs, backbone, neck, and head. YOLOv5 continues the use of the CSP structure in YOLOv4 [11], which borrows the CSPNet network structure, consisting of a CBS convolutional module and several residual structures for concat feature splicing, which enhances the learning performance of the neural network while substantially reducing the computational effort. Among them, the CBS module consists of a convolutional layer Conv, a normalised processing BN layer and a SiLU activation function. In YOLOv5, the authors designed two different CSP structures distinguished by the presence or absence of a residual structure to be applied in the backbone and neck stages. The FPN and PAN structures are used in the neck layer where the FPN layer passes fused strong semantic features from the top down, while the feature pyramid PAN passes strong localisation features from the bottom up with parameter aggregation from different backbone layers to different detection layers. Compared with the previous version, YOLOv5 has considerably improved in speed and flexibility.

3 GhostNet Lightweight Network Model

Deploying convolutional neural networks to embedded devices is often constrained by limited computational and memory resources. GhostNet [12], which originated from Huawei Noah's Ark Laboratory, aims to design a lightweight network that guarantees accuracy and is easy to deploy on mobile devices. Its Ghost module obtains more characteristic graphs with cheaper operation. In convolutional neural networks, there are often some similar characteristic graphs. This phenomenon is also known as feature map redundancy in neural networks, and this redundancy is more beneficial to the network's understanding of the input information. In contrast to the work on network lightweighting by reducing redundancy, the authors propose the Ghost module, which both ensures the redundancy of feature maps and addresses these redundancies in a less expensive way, thus generating more feature maps with cheaper operations to fully reveal the information behind the internal features.

In GhostNet, the Ghost module replaces the traditional convolutional layer. First, the feature map without redundant information is obtained by compressing the feature dimension using ordinary convolution. Then the complete feature map is obtained by the inexpensive linear operation Φ, where Φ is a 3 * 3 or 5 * 5 depth separable convolution. Finally, the identification operation is used to ensure that the output channel number is consistent with the input. The network structure of the Ghost module is displayed in Fig. 1.

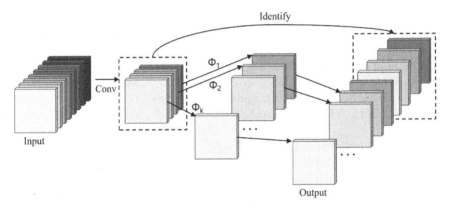

Fig. 1. Ghost module structure

Assuming that C_{in} is the number of input channels, C_{out} is the number of output channels, k is the convolution kernel size, and s is the total number of mappings generated by each channel, then the parameter quantity of ordinary convolution *params* is shown in Eq. (1) as follows:

$$params = k^2 C_{in} C_{out} \tag{1}$$

The parameter quantity of the Ghost module *paramg* is shown in Eq. (2) as follows:

$$params_g = \frac{k^2 C_{in} C_{out}}{s} + \frac{k^2 C_{out}}{s(s-1)} \tag{2}$$

From Eq. (1) and Eq. (2), the compression ratio of the Ghost module's number of parameters compared to the ordinary convolutional module is approximately equal to s.

In terms of computational effort, FLOPs (floating point operations) are usually used to measure the complexity of the algorithm. Assume that c is the number of input feature maps, h is the output feature map size in length and w in width, and n is the number of input feature maps. Then, the computation of the ordinary convolution module is shown in Eq. (3) as follows:

$$FLOPs = hwnk^2c \tag{3}$$

The computation of the Ghost module $FLOPsg$ is shown Eq. (4) as follows:

$$FLOPs_g = hw\frac{n}{s}k^2c + (s - 1)hw\frac{n}{s}k^2 \tag{4}$$

As seen in Eqs. (3) and (4), compared with the ordinary convolution module, the compression ratio of the Ghost module for floating point operations is about to s.

The Ghost Bottleneck, another important module in GhostNet, is shown in Fig. 2. Two Ghost modules constitute the Ghost bottleneck. The role of the two Ghost modules is to increase the number of channels of the input feature map and reduce the number of channels of the output feature map to match the diameter structure in the network.

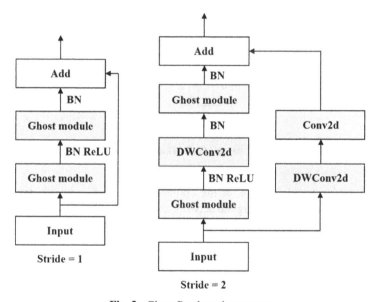

Fig. 2. Ghost Bottleneck structure

4 LG-YOLO Network Model

4.1 YOLOv5s Network Optimisation Based on the Ghost Module

In the study of this paper, the YOLOv5s network structure is modified using the Ghost module structure of the GhostNet to realize the lightweight of the model.

In YOLOv5s, the CBS structure based on the traditional convolutional approach is the basic convolutional unit of each layer of the network. In this paper, by designing the GhostConv module, each input channel is mapped into one intrinsic feature map and one ghost feature map, and the total mapping number s of each channel has a value of 2. The ghost feature map is generated by the depth-separated convolution with a convolutional kernel size of 5. The GhostConv module replaces the original CBS module in the LG-Ghost network, and the structure of the GhostConv module is depicted in Fig. 3.

Fig. 3. GhostConv structure

The Ghost Bottleneck structure replaces the Bottleneck of the CSP module in YOLOv5 and form a new C3Ghost module with three CBS convolutional units. The two Ghost modules are connected by identification or depth-separable convolution, and finally, the residual connection is decided according to the stride of the kernel. The Ghost Bottleneck structure is illustrated in Fig. 4.

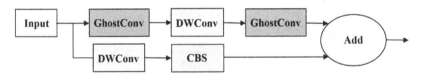

Fig. 4. Redesigned Ghost Bottleneck structure

In the backbone and the neck of the optimised YOLOv5s network, the standard convolutional units CBS in the original network are all replaced by GhostConv modules, and the C3 modules are all replaced by C3Ghost. The structure of the LG-YOLO is depicted in Fig. 5.

4.2   Activation Function Optimisation

In YOLOv5s, the author uses the SiLU as the activation function for each CBL module, which has no upper bound and lower bound, and it is smooth, and nonmonotonic. The advantage is more obvious in deeper networks, but it is computationally intensive due to the inclusion of the sigmoid function. The SiLU function equation is shown in Eq. (5) as follows:

$$SiLU(x) = x \cdot Sigmoid(x) \tag{5}$$

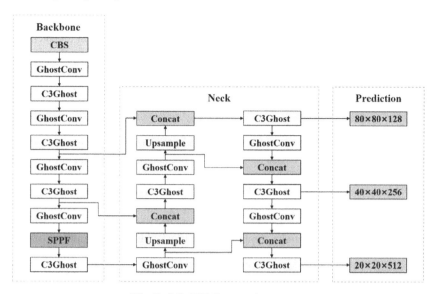

Fig. 5. LG-YOLO network structure

The PReLU [13] activation function is shown in Eq. (6). Compared with the SiLU function, the PReLU activation function has a smaller computational cost and faster computational speed. At the same time, the PReLU activation function has some specific improvements. It assigns coefficients ai to different neurons in the negative range to produce a smaller slope; this solves the "neuron necrosis" phenomenon caused by zero output for any negative value input in ReLU.

$$PReLU(x_i) = \begin{cases} x_i & x_i > 0 \\ a_i x_i & x_i \leq 0 \end{cases} \tag{6}$$

To further shorten the inference time of the model, we chose PReLU activation function instead of SiLU. Compared with the SiLU activation function, using the PReLU activation function has a loss of accuracy, so a relatively balanced approach of inference speed and accuracy is adopted using the SiLU activation function in convolution with a convolution kernel step of 2 the last conv convolution of the C3Ghost module and the SPPF module. The PReLU activation function is used elsewhere.

4.3 Nonmaximum Suppression Method Optimization

In the postprocessing stage of the object detection algorithm, the nonmaximum suppression (NMS) algorithm can exclude duplicate bounding boxes for the same target and keep the best one. YOLOv5 adopts the weighted NMS method. By calculating the corresponding IOU of the bounding box, filter out all the bounding boxes with values exceeding the threshold. However, this method, which takes the intersection of bounding boxes and the ratio of IoU as the only consideration, leads to easy suppression of bounding boxes that obscure objects when there is overlap between targets, which then leads to missed detection.

The DIoU-NMS method uses the DIoU [14] loss function to calculate IOU. On the basis of the original NMS, the distance, overlap rate and scale between the anchor box and the ground truth box are also comprehensively considered. The formula of DIoU is shown in Eq. (7) as follows:

$$DIoU = IoU - \frac{\rho^2(b, b^{gt})}{c^2} = IoU - \frac{d^2}{c^2} \tag{7}$$

b is the centre of the anchor box, b^{gt} is the centre of the ground truth box, $\rho^2(b, b^{gt})$ is the square of the distance between them, and c is the length of diagonal of the smallest rectangular box that contains both the prediction box and the ground truth box. In the DIoU-NMS algorithm, when the overlap of two prediction frames is large but the centre distance between the two prediction frames is large, none of the prediction boxes are filtered. Therefore, we change the original NMS to DIoU-MNS in this study, which are conducive to the detection of closely arranged or blocked hydraulic supports, reducing the missed detection rate and improving the detection accuracy.

5 Model Compression

5.1 Sparse Training

The convolutional neural network model pruning method based on sparse regularisation [15] is an efficacious method to compress the model that maintains good performance of the network model. To perform sparse regularisation on the training model more simply, we first introduce a scaling factor γ [16] for each channel, and multiply it by the output. After that we combine the training network weights with γ and sparsely regularise the latter to identify the insignificant channels. Each CBS convolution unit in YOLOv5 has a BN layer with a channel-level scaling factor, as seen in Eq. (8); z_{in} and z_{out} are the input and output of it. B is the minibatch, μ_B and $\sigma 2 B$ are the squared mean and standard deviation values of the input activation on B, γ are the BN layer coefficients, and β is the bias value. The outputs of each channel z_{out} and γ are positively correlated. Therefore, we can directly use the BN layer coefficients γ as the scaling factors required for sparse training as follows:

$$\hat{z} = \frac{z_{in} - \mu_B}{\sqrt{\sigma_B^2 + \varepsilon}}; z_{out} = \gamma\hat{z} + \beta \tag{8}$$

The L1 paradigm is widely used for sparsification [16], adding the L1 paradigm regularity constraint to the loss function, which constitutes the sparsely trained loss function as in Eq. (9) as follows:

$$L = \sum_{(x,y)} l(f(x, W), y) + \lambda \sum_{\gamma \in \Gamma} g(\gamma) \tag{9}$$

(x, y) is the input and output of sparse training, W is the training weight, and the first summation is the loss function of normal training. γ is the scaling factor, and $g(\gamma)$ is the L1 paradigm for sparsity in this study. λ is the penalty factor.

5.2 Channel Pruning

In the sparsely trained model, the coefficients of some channels in the BN layer γ will tend to be 0. These channels with small coefficients correspond to small BN layer output values, so the loss in accuracy of the network model will be small if these channels are pruned. These losses can be compensated for in the fine-tuning process. In this study, channel pruning is not performed for all BN layers. In the Ghost Bottleneck structure, to avoid the problem of inconsistent dimensionality between the shortcut and the residual layers, the Ghost Bottleneck layer is not pruned in this study. The sparsely trained network as a whole is sorted according to the BN layer coefficients γ in ascending order. According to the set pruning rate θ, a pruning threshold is obtained, and the channels with coefficients γ that are lower than this threshold are deleted for all BN layers that can be pruned in the network model to obtain a denser network model.

The pruned network model may lose precision, but by fine-tuning it, the lost accuracy can be compensated to some extent. After fine-tuning, the accuracy of the model may be higher than that of the unpruned network. [16].

5.3 Knowledge Distillation

Knowledge distillation [17] is one of the methods of model compression in this study, which aims to compensate for the loss of accuracy of the network model due to pruning. This method uses the output of complex models and the true labels of data to train smaller models, and migrate the knowledge of a larger model to a smaller model. The teacher model is a relatively complex model while the student model is the relatively simple model. The process of training is displayed in Fig. 6.

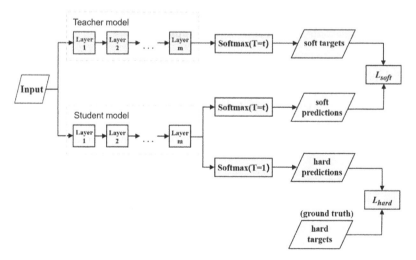

Fig. 6. Knowledge distillation process

First, input the training data set into the two models at the same time. The cross-entropy of the soft targets output from the teacher model under the parameter t and the soft predictions from the student model under the same parameter t constitutes L_{soft}, and L_{soft} is shown in Eq. (10) as follows:

$$L_{soft} = -\sum_{N}^{i} p_i^T log(q_i^T) \tag{10}$$

$pT\ i$ is the output value of the class i target by the complex model when the temperature parameter is t. $qT\ i$ is the output value of the class i by the simple model when the temperature parameter is t.

L_{hard} is the cross-entropy between the output of the student model and the ground truth of the original data set when the parameter is 1. L_{hard} is shown in Eq. (11) as follows:

$$L_{hard} = -\sum_{i}^{N} c_i log(q_i^1) \tag{11}$$

c_i is the target value of class i, $c_i \in \{0, 1\}$, and $q1\ i$ is the output value of class i of the student model when the temperature parameter is 1. Finally, the result of the distillation process is weighted by L_{soft} and L_{hard}, which is shown in Eq. (12) as follows:

$$L = \alpha L_{soft} + \beta L_{hard} \tag{12}$$

We use YOLOV5m as teacher model to participate in the process of knowledge distillation to improve the accuracy of the pruned model.

6 Relative Position Detection of Hydraulic Supports

6.1 Coordinates Collection of Hydraulic Supports

The moving status of the hydraulic support group is judged by its relative position relationship. For the purpose of measurement, we consider the base part of each hydraulic support as the detection target. The coordinate of the target box $xyxy$ is obtained from the detection results of the optimised YOLOv5s network, which contains the coordinates of the upper left vertex (x_i, y_i) and the lower right vertex (x_i', y_i') of the bounding box. The central coordinates of each bounding box are calculated using Eq. (13) as follows:

$$X_i = \frac{x_i + y_i}{2}, \ Y_i = \frac{x_i' + y_i'}{2} \tag{13}$$

The central coordinates of bounding boxes are used as the position information of the detected positioning point of the hydraulic support. A plane rectangular coordinate system is established with this central point as the coordinate origin. The coordinate system is as shown in the Fig. 7.

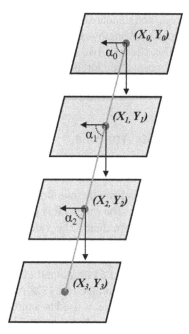

Fig. 7. Coordinate system of hydraulic support position measurement

6.2 Position Status Analysis of Hydraulic Support

After obtaining the positioning points of each support in the hydraulic support group through object detection, the relative position status between the hydraulics support is analysed using the coordinates of each positioning point. First, the information of location point coordinates is sorted in ascending order according to the magnitude of vertical coordinates and is stored in the set of location points P; and the azimuth angle α between the coordinates of adjacent location points is calculated using Eq. (14) as follows:

$$\alpha_i = arctan(\frac{X_{i+1} - X_i}{Y_{i+1} - Y_i}) \tag{14}$$

The calculated azimuths of each locus are stored in the azimuth set Q, and the average angle c is calculated. To reflect the dispersion of azimuths of adjacent positions in the hydraulic support group to better identify outliers with excessive azimuths, it is also necessary to calculate the standard deviation of the azimuths α_i in the azimuth set Q using Eq. (15) as follows:

$$\sigma = \sqrt{\frac{\sum_{i=1}^{n}(\alpha_i - \alpha_{avg})^2}{n}} \tag{15}$$

Using the azimuth mean α_{avg} and standard deviation σ obtained in the above steps, the values in the azimuth set Q are judged one-by-one. If $|\alpha_i - \alpha_{avg}| > \sigma$ and $|\alpha_i - \alpha_{avg}| > d$, it is determined that the position between two adjacent supports corresponding to this azimuth is abnormal, and the abnormal support position is adjusted manually and timely. d is the artificially set threshold value of the allowed deviation degree of the adjacent hydraulic support.

7   Experiments and Results Analysis

7.1   Data Set

The data needed in this experiment is from the monitoring video in the real production environment of the coal mining face. The video clips of the movement process of the hydraulic supports are intercepted from them. The video is extracted frame by frame into 1204 images.

These images are amplified by scaling, horizontal flipping, rotation and other operations, and 1500 images are amplified to 6140. A total of 3384 pieces are taken as the training set, 1228 pieces as the test set, and the rest 1228 pieces as the validation set.

The image annotation tool, LabelImage, is used to annotate the dataset images. The annotation area is the hydraulic support base. The annotated image is delineated in Fig. 8.

Fig. 8. Image dataset annotation diagram

This experiment is based on the Ubuntu operating system. The main computing equipment is NVIDIA GeForce RTX 3090 graphics card and uses the CUDA 11.0 computing architecture to build and train the model through the PyTorch deep learning framework. There are 300 epochs in the training process with the batch size of 64. And the IOU threshold is 0.45. The hardware environment of the improved model test and verification experiment is an AMD Ryzen 7 4800U CPU and 16 GB memory. The size of the input image is 640 * 640, the confidence threshold is 0.25, and the IOU threshold is 0.45.

7.2 Network Model Optimisation Experiment

We take the YOLOv5s network model before optimisation as the reference object and compare the performance changes in the process of network model optimisation with it. The network model performance evaluation indices in the experiment are accuracy (P), recall (R), mean average precision (mAP 0.5), number of parameters (Params), calculation (FLOPs), and model size (size). The mAP 0.5 is the average precision of the mean value for all target categories when the IoU threshold is 0.5. The calculation of mAP is shown in Eq. (16). The experimental results of the network model optimisation process are shown in Table 1.

$$mAP = \frac{\sum_{c=1}^{n} AP_c}{k} \tag{16}$$

Table 1. Experimental results of the model optimisation process

Models	mAP 0.5	Params	FLOPs/G	Size/MB	Time/ms
YOLOv5s	0.957	7022326	6.7	14.1	113.7
Ghost-YOLOv5s	0.939	3884110	4.0	7.4	68.1
Ghost-YOLOv5s-PReLU	0.922	3684542	3.4	7.4	62.7
Ghost-YOLOv5s-PReLU-DIoU	**0.934**	**3684542**	**3.4**	**7.4**	**62.9**

It can be seen from the above table that after using the Ghost module to optimise the network, the number of parameters is reduced by approximately 45%, the size of the model is approximately 48% smaller with approximately 55% less computation, and the inference time is reduced by approximately 40%. However, the loss of model accuracy is not significant. After using the ReLU activation function in some modules of the network, the inference time is further reduced with an acceptable accuracy. After using DIoU-NMS to improve the nonmaximum suppression method, the lost accuracy is partially compensated. In the process of network model optimisation, the calculation and size of the model are considerably reduced, and the accuracy is not considerably reduced.

7.3 Model Compression Experiments

Before channel pruning of the network model, the optimised network model should be sparsely trained to make the BN layer coefficient distribution tend to 0 as much as possible. The BN layer coefficients have very few values of approximately 0 before sparse training. If pruning is done at this time, it will lead to many channel mis-pruning. Setting different penalty factors λ results in different degrees of the sparse effect. When λ is too small, the network sparsity is not enough, and when λ is too large, it leads to excessive sparsity, and too many channels are pruned, causing a large loss of accuracy. In this experiment, the penalty factor λ is set to vary uniformly from 0.001 to 0.009. The distribution of BN layer coefficients and the change in mAP are observed. The histogram of the BN layer coefficients under different penalty factor λ is shown in Fig. 9. The distribution of BN layer coefficients gradually approaches 0 as γ goes from small to large. The change in sparse training performance under different values of scaling factor is shown in Table 2. The mAP gradually decreases as the scaling factor increases, and the mAP gradually stabilises when the scaling factor is greater than 0.007. It can also be seen from the figure that when γ is 0.007, most of the BN layer coefficients approach 0. Therefore, set the scale factor γ 0.007 and sparse training model.

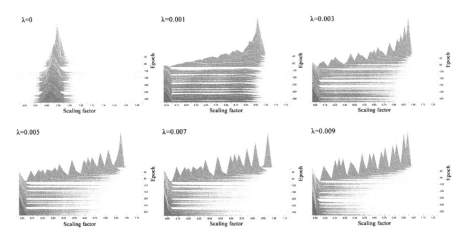

Fig. 9. Distribution of the BN layer scaling factor with different penalty factors

Table 2. Variation in model performance with different penalty factors

Penalty factor (λ)	P	R	mAP 0.5
0	0.916	0.957	0.934
0.001	0.904	0.915	0.927
0.003	0.881	0.877	0.921
0.005	0.868	0.848	0.912
0.007	**0.843**	**0.841**	**0.907**
0.009	0.853	0.840	0.907

After sparse training, different pruning rates are set to prune the channel of the sparse model. The pruning rate determines the threshold value of BN layer coefficients corresponding to the channels to be pruned in the network model. The channels with a BN layer coefficient that is lower than the threshold value will be pruned. Table 3 shows the changes of model performance under different pruning rates.

Table 3. Variation in model performance at different pruning rates

Pruning rate	mAP 0.5	Params	FLOPs/G	Size/MB	Time/ms
0.5	0.905	1041962	2.52	4.4	49.6
0.6	**0.902**	**868302**	**2.1**	**3.7**	**40.2**
0.7	0.872	739374	1.8	2.9	36.9
0.8	0.835	597553	1.43	2.3	35.3

By comprehensively evaluating each evaluation index, the model performance starts to show a substantial decrease when the pruning rate is greater than 0.6. The model compression rate and accuracy reach a relative balance at a pruning rate of 0.6. At this time, the model size is reduced by 50%, 74% reduction in parameters, the inference speed is reduced to 40.2 ms, and the mAP is reduced by 0.032, which is in the acceptable range. Therefore, when the pruning rate is 0.6, the pruned network model is fine-tuned and processed by knowledge distillation. The mAP of the model after knowledge distillation is restored to 0.928, and the model size, calculation are basically unchanged. Overall, after sparse training, channel pruning, fine-tuning and knowledge distillation, the model is well-compressed with a small loss of accuracy. Therefore, it can basically meet the application requirements of deployment and real-time monitoring in end-side devices.

7.4 Model Comparison Experiment

In this experiment, the current mainstream lightweight target detection models are selected for comparison with the models in this paper, which are YOLOv5n, MobileNetV3s-YOLOv5s [18], and ShuffleNetV3-YOLOv5s after replacing the backbone of YOLOv5s with the inverted residual in ShuffleNetV2 [19]. The comparison results are shown in Table 4.

Table 4. Comparison of LG-YOLO and other lightweight models

Models	mAP 0.5	Params	FLOPs/G	Size/MB	Time/ms
LG-YOLO	**0.928**	**868302**	**2.1**	**3.7**	**40.2**
YOLOv5n	0.930	4352842	4.2	7.1	73.5
MobileNetV3s-YOLOv5s	0.933	4641353	4.96	7.3	86.2
ShuffleNetV3-YOLOv5s	0.893	442934	5.9	2.3	102.9

By comparing the experimental results, the LG-YOLO model is close to the YOLOv5n model in terms of mAP, it has obvious advantages over the other three models in terms of the model size and inference speed. In contrast, the LG-YOLO model has better detection performance, which not only substantially reduces the model computation and size, but also maintains better detection accuracy.

7.5 Detection Effect

The monitoring video of a coal mining face is taken as the input data, and the detection results under four different scenarios are shown in Fig. 10. This algorithm can recognise the position of each hydraulic support within the video image and the position relationship between its neighbours. Moreover, when the hydraulic support arrangement deviation angle exceeds the threshold value, it is determined that the hydraulic support is abnormal and not in the place in time, and a prompt is given at the corresponding position in the image.

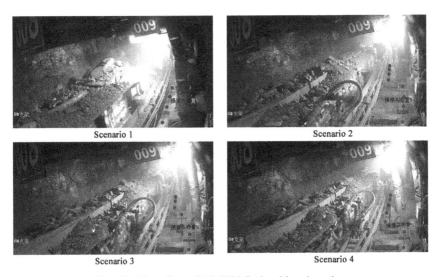

Fig. 10. The effect of LG-YOLO algorithm detection

8 Conclusion

For the current intelligent construction requirements of China's mines, the current monitoring methods for the equipment of integrated mining faces of coal mines are still relatively single, have a high cost and poor maintainability. This paper proposes a lightweight algorithm based on YOLOv5 for the relative position detection of hydraulic support at a coal mining face to find the abnormal status within the video monitoring range of the integrated mining face of coal mines and anomaly detection. Considering the limited computing power and memory resources of the end-side equipment platform, to facilitate the deployment and operation of the model, we combine GhostNet to optimise the YOLOv5 network structure, reduce the computation of neural network, shrink the model size, and further compress the optimised model with pruning and distillation. Through the series of optimization methods mentioned above, in the case of a small loss of accuracy, it maintains a good detection effect on the moving status of the hydraulic support. At the same time, the calculation and model size are greatly reduced, which can meet the needs of end-side equipment deployment and real-time detection.

References

1. Ding, E.J., Yu, X., Xia, B., et al.: Development of mine informatization and key technologies of intelligent mines. J. China Coal Soc. **47**(01), 564–578 (2022)
2. Wang, G.F.: Theory system of working face support and hydraulic roof support technology. J. China Coal Soc. **8**, 1593–1601 (2014)
3. Pei, W.L., Zhang, S.S., Li, J.W.: The design and application of inspection robot for mine. Manuf. Autom. **2**, 73–74 (2017)
4. Gao, K., Xu, W., Zhang, H., et al.: Relative position and posture detection of hydraulic support based on particle swarm optimization. IEEE Access **8**, 200789–200811 (2020)
5. Zhang, Y., Zhang, H., Gao, K., et al.: New method and experiment for detecting relative position and posture of the hydraulic support. IEEE Access **7**, 181842–181854 (2019)
6. Zhang, S.N., Cao, X.G., Cui, Y.Z., et al.: Research on straightness measurement method of hydraulic support based on multi-sensor. Coal Mine Mach. **41**(04), 56–59 (2020)
7. Wang, J., Wang, Z., Xu, J., et al.: Moving distance measurement for hydraulic support based on fruit fly optimization algorithm. Opt. Eng. **56**(1), 013111 (2017)
8. Ren, H.W., Li, S.S., Zhao, G.R., et al.: Research on measuring method of support height and roof beam posture angles for working face hydraulic support based on depth vision. J. Min. Saf. Eng. **39**(1), 72 (2022)
9. Zhang, X.H., Wang, D.M., Yang, W.J.: Position detection method of hydraulic support base on vision measurement. Ind. Mine Autom. **45**(3), 56–60 (2019)
10. Redmon, J., Divvala, S., Girshick, R., et al.: You only look once: unified, real-time object detection. In: Proceedings of the IEEE Conference on Computer Vision and Pattern Recognition, pp. 779–788. IEEE (2016)
11. Bochkovskiy, A., Wang, C.Y., Liao, H.Y.M.: Yolov4: optimal speed and accuracy of object detection. arXiv preprint arXiv:2004.10934 (2020)
12. Han, K., Wang, Y., Tian, Q., et al.: Ghostnet: more features from cheap operations. In: Proceedings of the IEEE/CVF Conference on Computer Vision and Pattern Recognition (CVPR), pp. 1580–1589. IEEE (2020)
13. He, K., Zhang, X., Ren, S., et al.: Delving deep into rectifiers: surpassing human-level performance on imagenet classification. In: Proceedings of the IEEE International Conference on Computer Vision, pp. 1026–1034. IEEE Computer Society (2015)
14. Glorot, X., Bordes, A., Bengio, Y.: Deep sparse rectifier neural networks. Proceedings of the fourteenth international conference on artificial intelligence and statistics. J. Mach. Learn. Res. **15**, 315–323 (2011)
15. Wei, Y., Chen, S.C., Zhu, F.H., et al.: Pruning method for convolutional neural network models based on sparse regularization. Comput. Eng. **47**(10), 61–66 (2021)
16. Liu, Z., Li, J., Shen, Z., et al.: Learning efficient convolutional networks through network slimming. In: Proceedings of the IEEE international Conference on Computer Vision, pp. 2736–2744. IEEE (2017)
17. Hinton, G., Vinyals, O., Dean, J.: Distilling the knowledge in a neural network. Comput. Sci. **14**(7), 38–39 (2015)
18. Chen, Y., Chen, X., Chen, L., et al.: UAV lightweight object detection based on the improved YOLO algorithm. In: Proceedings of the 2021 5th International Conference on Electronic Information Technology and Computer Engineering, pp. 1502–1506. ACM (2021)
19. Ma, N., Zhang, X., Zheng, HT., Sun, J.: ShuffleNet V2: practical guidelines for efficient CNN architecture design. In: Ferrari, V., Hebert, M., Sminchisescu, C., Weiss, Y. (eds.) Computer Vision – ECCV 2018. ECCV 2018. LNCS, vol. 11218, pp. 122–138. Springer, Cham (2018). https://doi.org/10.1007/978-3-030-01264-9_8

Inverter Fault Diagnosis Based on Improved Grey Correlation Analysis

Ying Zhang, Chujia Guo[✉], and Liwen Ma

School of Electrical and Control Engineering, Shaanxi University of Science and Technology, Xi'an 710021, China
guochujia@sust.edu.cn

Abstract. The main component of the robot power system, the inverter, is crucial for maintaining the safety of the robot system. The failure modes and fault current characteristics of the converter switching tubes are analyzed by introducing the grey correlation analysis modeling method, and the main faults are simulated to obtain the system fault state characteristics data and realize the inverter fault diagnosis and location. This helps to solve the problems of various failure modes of inverters, which are easily affected by noise and difficult to diagnose and locate the switching tubes. The results of the model calculation demonstrate that the suggested approach decreases the redundancy of fault current features, extracts effective fault current signals, and completes the identification and localization of inverter fault failure modes in a timely and precise manner.

Keywords: Inverter · Compressed sensing · Gray analysis · Fault diagnosis

1 Introduction

The converter, as the main part of the robot power system, includes features like great resistance to electromagnetic interference, small size, and high output power, and others. To ensure the safe functioning of the entire power system, its operational stability is necessary [1–3]. According to statistics, the switching devices and their control circuits of the main circuit in the inverter are the weakest links that are most prone to failure, accounting for 34% of overall failures [4]. Power device failures are further classified as short-circuit faults and open-circuit faults [5, 6], with short-circuit faults being converted to open-circuit faults by the inverter circuit under certain conditions by their own fuses. When an open-circuit fault occurs, the instantaneous damage is modest, and system goes on to operate malformed under the fault, gradually leading to system breakdowns. Therefore, diagnosing inverter open-circuit faults is critical for the safe running of robot power systems [7–9].

At present, the main fault intelligence diagnosis methods for inverter open-circuit faults appear at domestic and international are neural networks, support vector machines (SVM), rough sets and so on. The paper [10] proposed a fault diagnosis method based on quantum neural network information fusion by conducting local fusion diagnosis for power transformer faults, then introduce each local diagnosis information into the

Z. Yu et al. (Eds.): CIRAC 2022, CCIS 1770, pp. 228–236, 2023.
https://doi.org/10.1007/978-981-99-0301-6_18

decision fusion network for global fusion. The paper [11] proposed a fault diagnosis method based on deep neural networks for multilevel coupled H-level inverters, which improve the fault diagnosis efficiency but ignore the disturbance caused by the system itself. The paper [12] addresses the problems of multiplicity, complexity and low accuracy of the feature information in case of inverter open-circuit faults, proposed a rough set greedy algorithm to perform data discretization and attribute approximation and extract the effective rule table, the method considers the redundancy of fault feature information, but the computation is generally large and the computation process is complicated. Therefore, considering the noisy interference of the inverter, we proposed using compressed sensing theory to compress and reconstruct the sampled fault currents, remove the redundant noise information, and recover the fault current signal effectively. A method of turnout fault diagnosis based on grey correlation is proposed by the change law of action power curve under typical fault of turnout rutting machine in [14]. The grey correlation analysis theory has been introduced in [14–16] to biological, construction and early warning prediction fields, but none of them design to the field of inverter fault diagnosis. In diagnosis for inverter faults, the diagnosis methods based on artificial intelligence learning algorithms such as neural network, support vector machine, etc. need a large number of sample calculations for learning, and the calculation process is more complicated.

To solve the above problems, introduce the gray correlation method, which has the advantage of small computation, without lots of samples, Performing grey correlation analysis on the compressed and reconstructed current fault features to achieve inverter open current fault diagnosis.

2 Inverter Fault Diagnosis Based on Improved Grey Correlation Analysis

This paper uses inverters as the object of study for fault analysis and algorithm verification. Firstly, compressed sensing technique preprocesses the fault signal and extracts the effective fault current characteristics. And then calculates the gray correlation degree between the fault current sequence and the reference current sequence by the gray correlation analysis method to identify the fault and complete the fault diagnosis. The specific flow chart shows in Fig. 1.

2.1 Inverter Fault Classification

A three-phase two-level voltage-source inverter composed of a three-phase full bridge is the object of the fault diagnosis study in this paper, shown in Fig. 2. The inverter uses output pulse width modulation (PWM), and the switches T1–T6 are fully controlled power devices with anti-parallel diodes D1–D6. Ra~Rc and La~Lc are equal three-phase load resistors and inductors, meaning $R_a = R_b = R_c = R$, $L_a = L_b = L_c = L$, N is the neutral point. During normal operation, the upper and lower switches of the three-phase bridge arm stagger the output phase current.

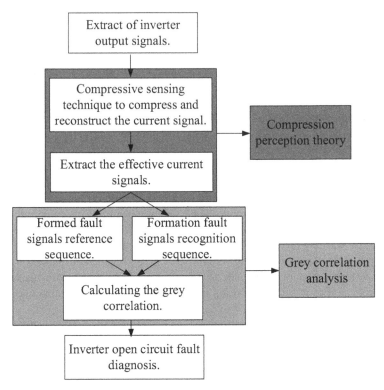

Fig. 1. Flowchart of inverter fault diagnosis based on grey correlation analysis

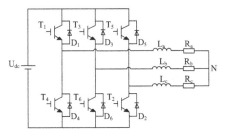

Fig. 2. Voltage source type inverter circuit

Makes the inverter switches faults respectively, set $F_1 \sim F_6$ represent $T_1 - T_6$ switches occurring open circuit faults respectively, F0 represent no switches occurring no faults.

2.2 Compressed Sensing Based Noise Reduction for Fault Signals

Compressed sensing theory is based on the sparsity of a signal or its compressibility in a transform domain, and using an observation matrix uncorrelated with the transform base to project the compressed high-dimensional signal onto another low-dimensional space. Through optimization algorithms the original signals are reconstructed with high probability from projections of compressed signals on a low-dimensional space, where the compression-aware compressed signals are recoverable [18].

Compressed sensing performs the fault current signals processing by knowing the measured value y and the measurement matrix ϕ, by solving the system of underdetermined equations $y = \phi x$, obtain the original current signal x. Each row of the measurement matrix a can be considered as ϕ sensor, which multiplies with the original current signals and retains enough valid information to represent the original current signals. Then, find a suitable optimization algorithm to restore the compressed current signals to the original signals with high probability. Compressed perception has the mathematical expression:

$$y = \phi x = \phi \varphi s \qquad (1)$$

where: φ is the sparse basis matrix and s is the sparse matrix.

Conversion of the measurement matrix ϕ into a sensing matrix θ by sparse basis matrices φ.

$$\theta = \phi \varphi \qquad (2)$$

Then the compressed sensing equation can be rewritten as:

$$y = \theta s \qquad (3)$$

The current signals collected in the actual inverter operating conditions are not the original signals, which contain the own system disturbances (noise), so it is not feasible to process the collected current signals directly. According to the noise signals are not sparse and incompressible, the original current signals will discard the noise signals in the compression process, and the signal reconstruction process cannot recover the lost noise signals and perform noise reduction on the current signals [19, 20]. In order to verify the noise reduction processing of the current signals by the compressed sensing technique, meaning to verify the sparsity of the current signals and the non-sparsity of the noise signals during inverter faults. In this paper, selected the traditional discrete cosine transform (DCT) to compare the fault current signals with the noise signals for sparse representation, the comparison results shown in Fig. 3.

Figure 3(a)(c) shows the results of the original waveform of the fault current and the fault current transformed by DCT, respectively, comparing Fig. 3(a), (c) indicates that the fault current signal is significantly sparse, namely compressible. In Fig. 3(b)(d), which shows the original waveform of Gaussian noise signal and the waveform after DCT transformation, respectively, the noise signal is not sparse, namely incompressible. Thus, the current signals through compressed sensing technique removes redundant noise information during compressed sampling, and the noise signals are not recoverable [19].

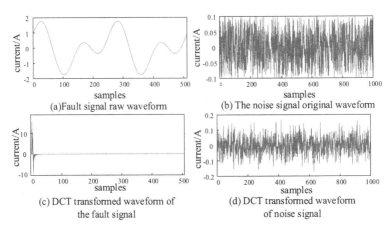

Fig. 3. Signal comparison graphs

2.3 Fault Identification of Inverter Based on Grey Correlation Analysis

For inverter switches open-circuit fault diagnosis, set the current reference sequence as $x_0(k)$, the current comparison sequence $x_i(k)$, whose dimensionless processing yields the sequence $\{x_0(k), x_i(k)\}$, where:

$$X_0 = (x_0(1), x_0(2), \cdots x_0(n))$$
$$X_1 = (x_1(1), x_1(2), \cdots x_1(n))$$
$$\cdots \cdots$$
$$X_i = (x_i(1), x_i(2), \cdots x_i(n))$$
$$\cdots \cdots$$
$$X_m = (x_m(1), x_m(2), \cdots x_m(n))$$

In the grey correlation analysis the general correlation model calculation formula is:

$$\gamma(x_0(k), x_i(k)) = \frac{\min_i \min_k |x_0(k) - x_i(k)| + \xi \max_i \max_k |x_0(k) - x_i(k)|}{|x_0(k) - x_i(k)| + \xi \max_i \max_k |x_0(k) - x_i(k)|} \tag{4}$$

$$\gamma(X_0, X_i) = \frac{1}{n} \sum_{k=1}^{n} \gamma(X_0(k), X_i(k)) \tag{5}$$

Then $\gamma(X_0, X_i)$ satisfies the four axioms of gray correlation, where is the discrimination coefficient, which is usually restricted to the range of (0, 1). The discriminative power depends on the different correlation coefficients, where the smaller the difference between the two correlation coefficients, the stronger the discriminative power. $\gamma(X_0, X_i)$ is the gray correlation between X_0 and X_i. The calculation of the gray correlation degree can be divided into the following steps.

- Step 1: collect the fault current signals of the inverter reconstructed by compressed sensing technique and represent the current sequences in matrix form as follows:

$$(X_0, X_1, \ldots, X_m) = \begin{pmatrix} x_0(1) & x_1(1) & \cdots & x_m(1) \\ x_0(2) & x_1(2) & \cdots & x_m(2) \\ \vdots & \vdots & \cdots & \vdots \\ x_0(n) & x_1(n) & \cdots & x_m(n) \end{pmatrix} \tag{6}$$

In which, represents the reference current sequence of each operating state of the inverter, and n represents the number of samples of fault current collection. $X_i = (x_i(1), x_i(2), \ldots, x_i(n)), i = 1, 2, \ldots, m$

- Step 2: By applying the dimensionless method to the current signals, the dimensionless model is:

$$x_i'(k) = \frac{x_i(k)}{\frac{1}{n}\sum_{k=1}^{n} x_i(k)}, i = 0, 1, \ldots, m; k = 1, 2, \ldots, n \tag{7}$$

The fault current signal sequence after the dimensionless model processing is:

$$(X_0, X_1, \ldots, X_m) = \begin{pmatrix} x_0'(1) & x_1'(1) & \cdots & x_m'(1) \\ x_0'(2) & x_1'(2) & \cdots & x_m'(2) \\ \vdots & \vdots & \cdots & \vdots \\ x_0'(n) & x_1'(n) & \cdots & x_m'(n) \end{pmatrix} \tag{8}$$

- Step 3: Calculate the distance between the reference current and the fault current for each operating state of the inverter as:

$$\Delta_{0ik} = \left\| x_0'(k) - x_i'(k) \right\| \tag{9}$$

- Step 4: Find the maximum and minimum differences between the poles of ($i = 0, 1, 2, \ldots, m$), denoted as:

$$\begin{aligned} \Delta_{\max} &= \max_i \max_k \left\| x_0'(k) - x_i'(k) \right\|, \\ \Delta_{\min} &= \min_i \min_k \left\| x_0'(k) - x_i'(k) \right\|. \end{aligned} \tag{10}$$

- Step 5: Calculate the correlation coefficient between the reference current signal $x_0'(k)$ and the fault current signals $x_i'(k)$ as:

$$\gamma_{0i}(k) = \gamma\left(x_0'(k), x_i'(k)\right) = \frac{\Delta_{\min} + \xi \Delta_{\max}}{\Delta_{oik} + \xi \Delta_{\max}}, \xi \in (0, 1) \tag{11}$$

where is the respective coefficient, usually taken as $\xi = 0.5$.
- Step 6: Calculate the correlation.

$$\gamma_{0i} = \frac{1}{n}\sum_{k=1}^{n} \gamma_{0i}(k), i = 1, 2, \cdots, m \tag{12}$$

Output correlation vector $\gamma = [\gamma_{01}, \gamma_{02}, \cdots \gamma_{0m}]$, if $\gamma_i = \max[\gamma_{01}, \gamma_{02}, \cdots \gamma_{0m}]$, then the correlation between X_0 and X_i is maximum, and the inverter switches a fault of open circuit as the i-th fault.

3 Experimental Verification

Build a three-phase two-level inverter simulation system in Matlab/Simulink to simulate open-circuit faults. After obtaining the current reference sequence of each operation state through simulation, the seven fault states from F_0 to F_6 are simulated. Through compressed sensing technique and simultaneous compressed reconstruction, obtains the inverter fault current signal with valid fault information.

Set the output current signal of the measured inverter as y and the current signal containing fault information as x. By compressed sensing technique, it compresses and reconstructs the output current signal y to remove it contains noise information, and verifies the effectiveness of noise reduction processing based on compressed sensing theory. After reconstruction, the effective fault current feature x is extracted as the sequence of fault currents to be identified in the grey correlation to complete the inverter fault identification.

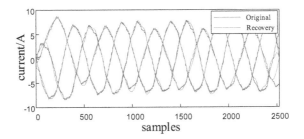

Fig. 4. Inverter output current signal

Figure 4 shows that the current signals at the output of the inverter can be observed that the current signals reconstructed by the compressed sensing technique have relatively less redundant noise information content, which extracts effective fault current features for subsequent fault diagnosis.

After obtaining the reference fault current signals, simulate the various types of faults from F_0 to F_6 of the inverter, and obtain a set of fault current signals from the actual output of the inverter. Using the grey correlation model to calculate the correlation between the actual fault current signals and the reference fault current signals, shown in Table 1.

From Table 1, taking the maximum value of each row $\gamma_i = \max\{\gamma_{01}, \gamma_{02}, \cdots \gamma_{0m}\}$, respectively, such as the inverter state of the first row is T_0(no fault state). And the maximum value of correlation is γ_{00}, so that the inverter can be diagnosed to be working at this time, which is consistent with the actual state of the inverter. Equally the inverter is observed in the fault states of the switches T_1 to T_6 with the maximum correlation of respectively. In Table 1, bold data can be diagnosed that the status of the inverter is $T_1 \sim T_6$ open circuit fault occurred respectively.

Table 1. Grey correlation of inverter switches fault diagnosis

Failure status	γ_{00}	γ_{01}	γ_{02}	γ_{03}	γ_{04}	γ_{05}	γ_{06}
F_0	**0.9558**	0.8102	0.7705	0.6877	0.8145	0.8034	0.7727
F_1	0.7347	**0.9647**	0.6132	0.8373	0.8987	0.7857	0.7777
F_2	0.6841	0.7944	**0.9657**	0.7318	0.8176	0.8322	0.8684
F_3	0.6817	0.6740	0.7377	**0.8651**	0.7058	0.7203	0.7427
F_4	0.7485	0.8954	0.8156	0.6751	**0.9484**	0.8886	0.8462
F_5	0.7143	0.8294	0.8080	0.6694	0.8738	**0.9776**	0.8573
F_6	0.6745	0.7741	0.8169	0.7348	0.7991	0.8090	**0.8997**

4 Conclusion

To solve the problem of high redundancy of current feature information and complex fault modes for inverter open-circuit fault diagnosis, this paper proposes a fault diagnosis method with improved grey correlation analysis method. Compressed sensing technology makes fault current signals less redundant and greatly reduces data processing, extracts a valid current signature containing sufficient fault information. Based on the grey correlation analysis method, complete the inverter open circuit fault diagnosis.

The simulation results verify that the method improves the accuracy of the fault information, reducing the error caused by the own interference of the inverter while having good stability in inverter fault diagnosis, making the diagnosis results more objective and proving the effectiveness of the method for inverter open-circuit fault diagnosis. However, the diagnostic results are still influenced by the reference current signals, thus requiring iterative dynamic adjustment of the reference current signals.

References

1. Zhong, Q.C., Blaabjerg, F., Cecati, C.: Power-electronics-enabled autonomous power systems. IEEE Trans. Ind. Electron. **64**, 5904–5906 (2017)
2. Liu, B., Li, W., Sun, J.J.: A high-frequency isolated dual-stage power converter for electric vehicle fast charging stations. Power Syst. Technol. **41**, 1636–1643 (2017)
3. Chen, G., Cheng, S., Xiang, C.: Non-invasive power tube open circuit fault diagnosis method for inverters. Proc. CSEE **37**, 3854–3862 (2017)
4. Ren, L., Wei, Z., Gong, C., et al.: A review of fault feature parameter extraction techniques for power electronic circuits. Proc. CSEE **35**, 3089–3101 (2015)
5. Li, S., Wu, G., Gao, B., et al.: Interpretation of DGA for transformer fault diagnosis with complementary SaE-ELM and arctangent transform. IEEE Trans. Dielectr. Electr. Insul. **23**, 586–595 (2016)
6. Cheng, X., Huang, H., Li, C., et al.: Loss and efficiency analysis of two-level and three-level inverters using SiC switches. Guangdong Electr. Power **31**, 99–105 (2018)
7. Liu, C., Kan, J., Zhi, Y., et al.: Reliable transformerless battery energy storage systems based on cascade dual-boost/buck converters. Power Electron. IET **8**, 1681–1689 (2015)

8. Zadeh, M.K., Gavagsaz-Ghoachani, R.,Martin, J.P., et al.: Discrete-time tool for stability analysis of DC power electronics-based cascaded systems. IEEE Trans. Power Electron. **32**, 652–667 (2017)
9. Song, G.B., Tao, R., Li, B., et al.: A review of fault analysis and protection of power systems containing large-scale power electronic equipment. Autom. Electr. Power Syst. **41**, 2–12 (2017)
10. Gong, R.K., Ma, L., Zhao, Y.J., et al.: Transformer fault diagnosis based on quantum neural network information fusion. Power Syst. Prot. Control **39**, 79–84+88 (2011)
11. Xu, J.W., Song, B.Y., Gong, M.O.F.: Deep neural network-based fault diagnosis for multilevel inverters. Electr. Meas. Instrum. **56**, 123–128 (2019)
12. Han, S.-M., Zheng, S.-Q., He, Y.-S.: Inverter open-circuit fault diagnosis based on rough set greedy algorithm. Power Syst. Prot. Control **48**, 122–130 (2020)
13. Zhao, L., Lu, Q.: Grey correlation-based turnout fault diagnosis method. J. China Railw. Soc. **36**, 69–74 (2014)
14. Chen, Z., Li, Q.Q., Xu, G.H., et al.: Gray correlation analysis of diesel spray penetration distance influencing factors. J. Jiangsu Univ. (Nat. Sci. Edn.) **38**, 13–17 (2017)
15. Yang, L., Luo, W., Deng, C., et al.: Research on public opinion grading and early warning model based on gray correlation analysis. Inf. Sci. **38**, 28–34 (2020)
16. Zhang, L., Li, Y.A., Liu, X.L.: Research on energy consumption prediction of civil buildings based on grey correlation analysis. Arch. Technol. **51**, 1129–1134 (2020)
17. Chang, F., Zhao, L.P., Feng, J.B.: Application of five-level AC/DC converter in through-phase homogeneous power supply. Proc. CSU-EPSA **27**, 26–31 (2015)
18. Yan, S., Tang, H., Liu, B., et al.: Compression-aware HIFU echo signal noise reduction research. J. Electron. Meas. Instrum. **34**, 19–25 (2020)
19. He, Y., Li, Q.: Noise reduction and reconstruction application of FISTA algorithm in seismic signals based on compressive perception theory. In: Joint Annual Meeting of Chinese Geosciences (2019)

Cross-View Nearest Neighbor Contrastive Learning of Human Skeleton Representation

Xuelian Zhang[1], Zengmin Xu[1,2(✉)], Lulu Wang[1], and Jiakun Chen[1]

[1] School of Mathematics and Computing Science, Guangxi Colleges and Universities Key Laboratory of Data Analysis and Computation, Guilin University of Electronic Technology, Guilin, China
[2] Anview.AI, Guilin Anview Technology Co., Ltd, Guilin, China
`xzm@guet.edu.cn`

Abstract. Traditional self-supervised contrastive learning approaches regard different views of the **same** skeleton sequence as a positive pair for the contrastive loss. While existing methods exploit cross-modal retrieval algorithm of the **same** skeleton sequence to select positives. The common idea in these work is the following: ignore using **other** views after data augmentation to obtain more positives. Therefore, we propose a novel and generic Cross-View Nearest Neighbor Contrastive Learning framework for self-supervised action Representation (CrosNNCLR) at the view-level, which can be flexibly integrated into contrastive learning networks in a plug-and-play manner. CrosNNCLR utilizes different views of skeleton augmentation to obtain the nearest neighbors from features in latent space and consider them as positives embeddings. Extensive experiments on NTU RGB+D 60/120 and PKU-MMD datasets have shown that our CrosNNCLR can outperform previous state-of-the-art methods. Specifically, when equipped with CrosNNCLR, the performance of SkeletonCLR and AimCLR is improved by 0.4%~12.3% and 0.3%~1.9%, respectively.

Keywords: Self-supervised learning · Plug-and-play · Cross-view nearest neighbor contrastive learning · Action representation

1 Introduction

In the research field of robot action planning, the action of joints is an important factor to evaluate the goodness of robot products, which can be associated with human action analysis. As a research hotspot in computer vision, human action analysis plays an important part in video understanding [1]. Early researchers employ supervised learning methods [2–4] to study human action potential dynamics based on RGB frames, e.g., a two-stream network [5], spatial-temporal attention model [6], and LSTM network [7]. However, these visual representations are not robust to various backgrounds and appearances. Therefore, researchers focus on the human skeleton dataset, which offer light-weight

© The Author(s), under exclusive license to Springer Nature Singapore Pte Ltd. 2023
Z. Yu et al. (Eds.): CIRAC 2022, CCIS 1770, pp. 237–256, 2023.
https://doi.org/10.1007/978-981-99-0301-6_19

representations, attracting many people to research skeleton-based action recognition [8–10], e.g., Part-Aware LSTM [11] treats each joint point of each frame of skeleton sequence as an LSTM unit, and performs LSTM operations in both temporal and spatial dimensions. MS-G3D [12] proposes a multi-scale spatial-temporal aggregation scheme to solve the question of biased weighting. Although the recognition accuracy is improved, it requires large volumes of labeled robot body skeletons, which is time-consuming and labor-intensive to annotate in real life.

Given this, self-supervised learning methods are introduced [13,14], which can learn semantic content in large-scale unlabeled samples to provide supervised information for models and algorithms. The early emergence of various self-supervised model building strategies, e.g., jigsaw puzzles [15], colorization [16], prediction mask words [17], etc. With the emergence of the idea of contrastive learning, some self-supervised contrastive learning methods are constructed for 3D skeleton data, e.g., ISC [18] makes exploit of inter-skeleton contrastive learning methods to learn feature representations from skeleton inputs of multimode. Colorization [19] designs a skeleton cloud colorization technology to learn the feature representation of samples from unlabeled skeleton sequences. However, the above self-supervised learning works, ignoring the different views after skeleton augmentation can also be applied as an auxiliary tool to finding positive samples.

Therefore, we propose a self-supervised action representation approach based on Cross-View Nearest Neighbor Contrastive Learning (CrosNNCLR). Firstly, the framework introduces the nearest neighbor search algorithm to look for more semantically similar samples in the latent space by combining different views of the same skeleton sequence skeleton augmentation. Secondly, CrosNNCLR loss is proposed for the network to learn parameters more efficiently and minimize the embedding distribution between nearest-neighbor sample views. Finally, the proposed method is designed in a plug-and-play manner, which is integrated into the traditional and existing self-supervised contrastive learning models to form a new network structure. The main contributions of this paper are as follows:

- A plug-and-play block is designed using different views of each sample data after augmentation, and the close association between similar skeleton sequences, combined with the nearest neighbor search algorithm to find more positive sample pairs from the latent space.
- CrosNNCLR loss is proposed to learn the network model parameters, capture richer semantic information, enable better clustering of same category samples, and obtain a good feature space for 3D actions from unlabeled skeleton data.
- The plug-and-play block is integrated into an existing self-supervised contrastive learning network to form new model structures. We evaluated the model on three benchmark datasets, i.e., NTU RGB+D 60/120, PKU-MMD, and outperforms the mainstreaming methods.

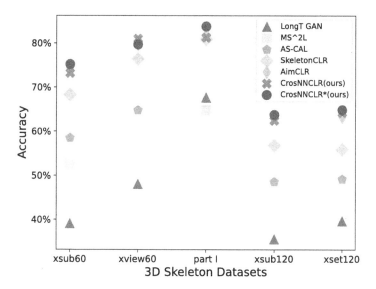

Fig. 1. Comparison of recognition accuracy of different models, which can visually observe the recognition accuracy of each model, where the green cross symbol and the red solid circle respectively indicate the proposed method CrosNNCLR and CrosNNCLR*.

2   Related Work

Skeleton-based Action Recognition. To solve skeleton-based action recognition tasks, previous work is based on manual features [20–22]. In recent years, some approaches avail RNNs to process skeleton data in different time intervals, e.g., VA-RNN [23] proposes a view adaptive neural network to automatically transform skeleton sequences into observation viewpoints, eliminating the effect of viewpoint diversity. Although these approaches have achieved many significant results, researchers shifted their attention to CNNs due to the gradient disappearance question of RNNs, where VA-CNN [23] maps skeleton sequences as RGB frames. HCN [24] automatically learn hierarchical co-occurrence features of skeleton sequences. Considering that CNNs need to transform skeleton sequences into a specific form, which is not conducive to the feature representation of the original skeleton data itself, further proposes GCNs to model the graph structure of skeleton data, e.g., ST-GCN [25] proposes a spatial-temporal GCN to solve the problem of human action recognition based on skeleton data. In this work, we exploit ST-GCN [25] as the encoder.

Self-supervised Learning. Many self-supervised representation learning methods are employed to image and video classification. For RGB image data, MoCo [26] establishes a dynamic dictionary to do the self-supervised representation learning task by momentum contrast. OBow [27] incorporates knowledge distillation technology into the self-supervised contrastive learning model and reconstructs the bag-of-visual-words (BoW) representation of image features. For RGB video data, CoCLR [28] avails complementary information from different modalities of the same data source to obtain positives from one view to another. Similarly, NNCLR [29] proposes the self-supervised image classification method, compatible with skeleton video data, RGB images have fewer actual practical application scenarios, as in real life, long videos are mainly used to record events.

Self-supervised Skeleton-Based Action Recognition. In recent years, researchers have proposed many self-supervised learning approaches of skeleton data, which are mainly divided into two types. The first one proposes encoder-decoder structures, e.g., LongT GAN [30] reconstructs masked 3D skeleton sequences by combining encoder, decoder, and generative adversarial networks. P&C [31] adopt a weak the decoder to discriminate their embedding similarity. The second is the contrastive learning network structures, e.g., CrosSCLR [32] roots a cross-view consistent knowledge mining method, which exploits the feature similarity of one modality to assist another modality for contrastive recognition learning. AimCLR [33] explores the different patterns of movement brought about by extreme augmentations to alleviate the irrationality of positive sample selection. However, these methods rely on obtaining positive samples from different modal data or views after adding skeleton augmentation, and ignoring the different views obtained after random skeleton augmentation can also be used as auxiliary tools to find positives. Therefore, we introduce CrosNNCLR to obtain positive sample pairs from nearest neighbors more concisely.

3   Approach

Although 3D skeleton data has made great progress in self-supervised contrastive learning representation, some algorithms regard different views of each skeleton as positive samples for the contrastive loss, i.e., only one positive sample exists. While other algorithms employ multimodal skeleton data to acquire positive samples of another modal skeleton view from one modal skeleton view, i.e., multiple positive samples exist. Unlike previous approaches [30–33], we apply different views of the same skeleton sequence after skeleton augmentation to increase the number of positive samples without using multimodal skeleton data. We first describe the main approaches of skeleton-based self-supervised representation learning, e.g., SkeletonCLR [32] and AimCLR [33]. Second, we base on the original model, establish a plug-and-play block, namely Cross-view Nearest Neighbor Contrastive Learning framework for self-supervised action Representation (CrosNNCLR). This module exploits the Nearest Neighbor (NN) of original positive samples to obtain more positives and enhance comparative instance discrimination.

3.1   Problem Setting

Given a skeleton sequence x is subjected to the following operations for obtain encoding features $z = \psi_\theta(aug(x))$, $\hat{z} = \psi_{\hat{\theta}}(aug(x))$, where $aug(\cdot)$ denotes the random data augmentation function and x generates different views q, k by

$aug(\cdot)$, ψ denotes the ST-GCN network function with nonlinear projection layer, ψ_θ enotes the Query encoder network whose network parameters are updated by gradient descent method, $\psi_{\hat\theta}$ denotes the Key encoder whose network parameters follow the momentum update.

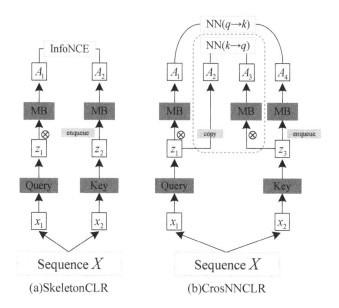

Fig. 2. Comparison between SkeletonCLR and CrosNNCLR, the left figure shows the SkeletonCLR framework and the right figure shows our CrosNNCLR framework. where X is the input N skeleton sequence data, x_1, x_2 are the different views obtained after random skeleton augmentations, **Query**, **Key** are the encoder network, z_1, z_2 are the encoding feature, **MB** is the memory bank, $A_i\,(i \in 1,2,3,4)$ is the positive sample set, **enqueue** indicates that encoding feature enters the MB to update negatives, $\otimes$ indicates the dot product, **copy** indicates the copy function. **InfoNCE**, **NN**$_{q\to k}$ and **NN**$_{k\to q}$ are the loss functions involved in each model.

3.1.1 SkeletonCLR

SkeletonCLR [32] is a single-view contrastive learning method based on skeleton representation. As shown in Fig. 2(a). Firstly, the given sequence of skeletons is randomly transformed into different views q, k that are regarded as positive pairs, the other samples in the memory bank $M = \{m_i\}_{i=1}^{M}$ are considered negative samples, and q, k are embedded into the encoder ψ_θ, $\psi_{\hat\theta}$ to obtain the encoding features z, $\hat z$, θ and $\hat\theta$ are the required parameters for both encoders, $\hat\theta$ following the momentum update: $\hat\theta \leftarrow \alpha\hat\theta + (1 - \alpha)\theta$, α is the momentum coefficient. Secondly, similar to the MoCo [26], SkeletonCLR exploits a FIFO strategy for updating negative samples in its memory bank to eliminate redundant computation. In other words, a certain number of negative sample tensors are randomly generated when the model starts training, with the increase of training iterations, the N-dimensional tensor z is continuously transferred into the memory bank, replacing the previously randomly generated tensor as the negative samples for the next iteration. Finally, SkeletonCLR employs InfoNCE [26] loss to learn model parameter. The formula is as follows:

$$L_{\text{InfoNCE}} = -\log \frac{\exp(z \cdot \hat{z}/\tau)}{\exp(z \cdot \hat{z}/\tau) + \sum\limits_{i=1}^{M} \exp(z \cdot m_i/\tau)}. \tag{1}$$

where $m_i \in M$, τ is a temperature hyperparameter, $z \cdot \hat{z}$ are normalized, and $z \cdot \hat{z}$ represents the dot product of two tensors to find the similarity between them.

SkeletonCLR relies only on one positive sample pair generated by the same sample under random data augmentation, while treating other samples as negative samples. This reduces the ability to discriminate intra-class variations, as semantically similar samples are hard to cluster with other positives in the embedding space.

3.1.2   AimCLR

The model framework of AimCLR [33] is shown in Fig. 3(a). Firstly, the model proposes an extreme skeleton augmentation method and adds a Query encoder branch to the dual branches of SkeletonCLR, which utilizes the method to data amplify for the same sample. Secondly, a data augmentation method based on the EADM is proposed, which can obtain different positives under the new branch after adding the Query encoder branch. Specifically, in the original branch, the same skeleton sequence is amplified by random normal skeleton augmentation, then the sample features z, $\tilde{z}$ are obtained through the encoder and projection layer (ψ_θ, $\psi_{\hat{\theta}}$), respectively. In the new branch, the same skeleton sequence is amplified by extreme skeleton augmentation to form two parallel branches, one of which passes through the encoder and projection layer ($\psi_{\hat{\theta}}$) to form the sample features $\tilde{z}$, then others passes through the encoder, projection layer (ψ_θ) and the EADM module to form the sample features $\tilde{z}_{drop}$. Finally, the Nearest Neighbor Mining (NNM) method with the multi-branch view is utilized to increase the number of positives, and updates the network parameters using D³M loss function. The specific loss function involved in the work is as follows:

$$L_{d1} = -p(z \mid \hat{z})\log p(z \mid \tilde{z}) - \sum_{i=1}^{M} p(m_i \mid \hat{z})\log p(m_i \mid \tilde{z}). \tag{2}$$

$$L_{d2} = -p(z \mid \hat{z})\log p(z \mid \tilde{z}_{drop}) - \sum_{i=1}^{M} p(m_i \mid \hat{z})\log p(m_i \mid \tilde{z}_{drop}). \tag{3}$$

$$L_{\text{D}^3\text{M}} = 1/2(L_{d1} + L_{d2}). \tag{4}$$

$$L_N = -\log \frac{\exp(z \cdot \hat{z}/\tau) + \sum_{i \in N_+} \exp(\hat{z} \cdot m_i/\tau)}{\exp(z \cdot \hat{z}/\tau) + \sum\limits_{i=1}^{M} \exp(\hat{z} \cdot m_i/\tau)}. \qquad (5)$$

where $p(\cdot \mid \cdot)$ is the conditional probability and $m_i \in$ M, N_+ is the index value of the similar samples obtained by NNM method. The numerator of the loss L_N shows that the increase number of positive pairs, prompting a better clustering of more similar samples with high confidence.

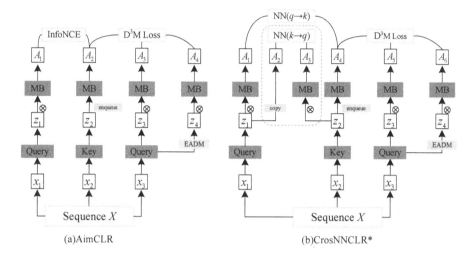

(a)AimCLR   (b)CrosNNCLR*

Fig. 3. Comparison between AimCLR and CrosNNCLR*, the left figure shows the AimCLR framework and the right figure shows our CrosNNCLR* framework. Where $x_i (i \in 1, 2, 3)$ are the different views obtained after random skeleton augmentations, $z_i (i \in 1, 2, 3, 4)$ are the encoding feature, $A_i (i \in 1, 2, 3, 4, 5, 6)$ is the positive sample set, **EADM** is the new skeleton augmentation method. **InfoNCE**, **D³M loss**, **NN$_{q \to k}$** and **NN$_{k \to q}$** are the loss functions involved in each model.

AimCLR employs embedding space that are most similar semantic information to q, achieves better clustering by different views of samples from the same category, but it ignores that view k also can be utilized for nearest neighbor search.

3.2   Our Approaches

To increase the richness of latent similarity representation, beyond single-instance positive samples and multi-instance positive samples generated by view q, we propose a plug-and-play block that combines the cross-view (q, k) nearest neighbor contrastive learning method to obtain more diverse positives. The model construction is similar to MoCo [26], but it obtains not only negative set but also positive sample sets from the memory bank.

SkeletonCLR takes different views obtained by random skeleton augmentations as positive pairs, denoted as $(z, \hat{z})$. AimCLR utilizes the extreme skeleton augmentation, EADM, and NNM approaches to generate three skeleton augmentation pairs, which are paired to form positives, denoted as $(z, \hat{z}), (z, \tilde{z}), (z, \tilde{z}_{drop})$. Instead, we root the nearest neighbor search algorithm to find out multiple positives from the memory bank that is similar to z and $\hat{z}$ semantic information, denoted as $(z, \hat{z}), (z, \hat{z}_1), (z_1, \hat{z})$. In Figs. 2(b) and 3(b), similar to SkeletonCLR and AimCLR, we acquire the negative samples from the memory bank and use the idea of InfoNCE loss (1), we define the loss function as follows:

$$L_{q \to k} = -\log \frac{\exp(z \cdot \hat{z}/\tau) + \exp(\mathrm{NN}(z, M) \cdot \hat{z}/\tau)}{\exp(z \cdot \hat{z}/\tau) + \sum\limits_{i=1}^{N} \exp(z \cdot m_i/\tau)}. \tag{6}$$

where $\hat{z}_1 = \mathrm{NN}(z, M) = \underset{m_i \in M}{\mathrm{argmin}} \parallel z - m_i \parallel_2$ is the nearest neighbor operation, τ is the temperature hyperparameter, the numerator contains 2 positive samples. The denominator contains $N+1$ samples in total, including 2 positives and $N-1$ negatives.

Similarly, the nearest neighbor instances in the feature space of view k can be used as pseudo-labels. Therefore, the loss function equation is as follows:

$$L_{k \to q} = -\log \frac{\exp(z \cdot \hat{z}/\tau) + \exp(\mathrm{NN}(\hat{z}, M) \cdot z/\tau)}{\exp(z \cdot \hat{z}/\tau) + \sum\limits_{i=1}^{N} \exp(\hat{z} \cdot m_i/\tau)}. \tag{7}$$

where $z_1 = \mathrm{NN}(\hat{z}, M)$, and the parameters are expressed the same as Eq. (6). The two views take positive samples from each other to enhance the network model performance and obtain better clustering results.

$$L_{\mathrm{CrosNNCLR}} = 1/2(L_{q \to k} + L_{k \to q}). \tag{8}$$

The cross-view loss function $L_{\mathrm{CrosNNCLR}}$ pulls in more high-confidence positive samples than the single-view loss function L_{InfoNCE}, making it easier to aggregate same category sample features in the embedding space.

3.2.1 CrosNNCLR Based on SkeletonCLR

This section focuses on using Nearest Neighbors (NN) to find out semantically similar samples with view q or view k, and improve contrastive instance discrimination methods. The concrete implementation framework of CrosNNCLR is shown in Fig. 2(b). Firstly, CrosNNCLR is inserted into SkeletonCLR, which compensates for the shortcoming that the original model treats same category samples as negative samples. Secondly, CrosNNCLR loss is proposed to enhance the InfoNCE loss-based approach. Finally, we evaluate the proposed approach

Algorithm 1: CrosNNCLR(plug-and-play block) Pseudocode.

```
# Query, Key: encoder network
# N: batch size
# MB: memory bank(queue)
# t: temperature

for x in loader:
    x1, x2 = aug(x), aug(x) # random augmentation
    z1, z2 = Query(x1), Key(x2) # obtain the encoded features
    h1, h2, mb = normalize(z1), normalize(z2), normalize(MB) # l2-normalize

    NN1 = NN(h1, mb) # cross-view the nearest neighbor index
    NN2 = NN(h2, mb) # cross-view the nearest neighbor index

    loss = L(NN1, h2, h1)/2 + L(NN2, h1, h2)/2 # Loss_CrosNNCLR
    loss.backward() # back-propagate
    update([Query.params, Key.params]) # SGD update
    update_queue(MB, z2)

def L(nn, c, d, t=0.07):
    logits_cd = mm(c, d.T)/t # mm: Matrix multiplication
    logits_nnc = mm(nn, c.T)/t # mm: Matrix multiplication
    logits = concat([logits_cd, logits_nnc], axis=1) # logits_qk, logits_kq
    labels = range(N)
    loss = CrossEntropyLoss(logits, labels)
    return loss

def NN(h, mb):
    simi = mm(h, mb.T) # mm: Matrix multiplication
    nn = simi.argmax(dim=1) # Top-1 NN indices
    return mb[nn]
```

with the linear evaluation protocol, and carry out relevant experimental verification on three benchmark datasets. Algorithm 1 provides the pseudo-code for the pre-training task of CosNNCLR.

3.2.2 CrosNNCLR* Based on AimCLR

This section focuses on using Nearest Neighbors (NN) to find samples that are semantically similar to view k. The feature representation is learned by pulling the distance between different views of each sample and the nearest neighbor samples in the embedding space. The specific implementation framework of CrosNNCLR* is shown in Fig. 3(b). Firstly, CrosNNCLR branch is integrated into the AimCLR, which alleviates the reliance of self-supervised learning on the data augmentation approach. Secondly, CrosNNCLR loss is added to the D^3M loss to improve contrastive instance discrimination methods. Finally, we evaluate the proposed approach with the linear evaluation protocol, and carry out relevant experimental verification on three benchmark datasets.

4   Experiments

In this section, our CrosNNCLR and CrosNNCLR* are compared with other self-supervised skeleton representation learning approaches. The datasets (Subsect. 4.1) and experimental settings (Subsect. 4.2) for CrosNNCLR and

CrosNNCLR* are described. In Subsect. 4.3, the model performance is compared. In Subsect. 4.4, ablation experiments are performed to demonstrate the effectiveness of the proposed methods.

4.1 Datasets

NTU RGB+D 60 (NTU-60) [34]. It consists of 56,880 action sequences. The dataset is captured from different viewpoints, with action samples performed by 40 actors, and contains 60 action categories. Two evaluation benchmarks for this dataset are utilized: Cross-Subject (xsub) and the Cross-View (xview).

PKU-MMD (PKU) [35] . It is a human action analysis benchmark dataset with good annotation information. It specifically consists of 28,000 action sequences, with 51 action classes. PKU-MMD is divided into two parts, the first part (part I) is a large-amplitude action detection task and the second part (part II) is a small-amplitude action detection task.

NTU RGB+D 120 (NTU-120) [36] . It is an extension of the NTU-60 dataset, which contains 120 actions performed by 106 actors, and the total number of action skeleton sequences expanded to 114,480. Similarly, two evaluation benchmarks for this dataset are utilized: Cross-Subject (xsub) and Cross-Setup (xset).

4.2 Experimental Settings

The hardware platform in this experiment includes four TITAN XP graphics cards with 128 GB memory, the software platform includes python 3.6 and the PyTorch 1.2.0 framework. The parameter configuration of CrosNNCLR is consistent with the SkeletonCLR, where the models run 800 epochs and the linear evaluations run 100 epochs. The parameter configuration of CrosNNCLR* is consistent with the AimCLR, where the models run 300 epochs and the linear evaluations run 100 epochs. Specifically, during the training of these models, the Query and Key encoders mainly use the ST-GCN network with a hidden layer dimension of 256, a feature dimension of 128, the batch size is 128, the momentum coefficient $\alpha = 0.999$, $M = 32768$, and the initial lr = 0.1, which becomes 0.01 after 250 epochs, the weight decay is 0.0001, the initial value of the learning rate for linear evaluation is 0.3, which became 0.03 after 80 epochs of evaluation.

4.3 Analysis of Experimental Results

We design a plug-and-play block for enhancing positives, which utilizes CrosNNCLR to identify sample instances in the latent space. It means that sample instances with semantic information more similar to different views will be mined, and take them as positive samples. This subsection mainly gives the experimental results of CrosNNCLR and CrosNNCLR*.

Experimental studies are conducted on different datasets to compare the model performance. As shown in Table 1, on the single mode of skeleton dataset (joint, motion, bone), the action recognition of our CrosNNCLR is higher than the SkeletonCLR, except for the motion modality under the xset benchmark on the NTU-120 dataset, and the bone modality under the xsub evaluation benchmark on the NTU-60 dataset. The performance of our 3s-CrosNNCLR is better than the 3s-SkeletonCLR, when the evaluation effects of these three modalities are fused.

Table 1. Comparison of SkeletonCLR and CrosNNCLR linearity evaluation results on the NTU-60/120 and PKU datasets. "3s" means three stream fusion.

Method	Stream	NTU-60(%)		PKU(%)	NTU-120(%)	
		xsub	xview	part I	xview	xset
SkeletonCLR	joint	68.3	76.4	80.9	56.8	55.9
CrosNNCLR	joint	**73.2**	**81.0**	**81.3**	**62.5**	**64.3**
SkeletonCLR	motion	53.3	50.8	63.4	39.6	**40.2**
CrosNNCLR	motion	**56.7**	**62.0**	**67.4**	**41.4**	36.4
SkeletonCLR	bone	**69.4**	67.4	72.6	48.4	52.0
CrosNNCLR	bone	64.3	**72.9**	**77.0**	**60.4**	**64.3**
3s-SkeletonCLR	joint+motion+bone	75.0	79.8	85.3	60.7	62.6
3s-CrosNNCLR	joint+motion+bone	**76.0**	**83.4**	**86.2**	**67.4**	**68.3**

As shown in Table 2, our CrosNNCLR* is compared with the original Aim-CLR on three modal datasets. On the skeleton single-modal dataset (joint), our CrosNNCLR* is better than the AimCLR. On the other skeleton modal datasets (motion, bone), the effect of our presented model is similar to the original model's performance. When three modalities are fused, the recognition performance of our 3s-CrosNNCLR* is superior to the 3s-AimCLR on the xsub60, PKU part I, and xset120, our model's recognition is similar to the original model on the xview60 and xsub120.

Table 2. Comparison of AimCLR and CrosNNCLR* linearity evaluation results on the NTU-60/120 and PKU datasets. "3s" means three stream fusion.

Method	Stream	NTU-60(%)		PKU(%)	NTU-120(%)	
		xsub	xview	part I	xview	xset
AimCLR	joint	74.3	79.7	83.4	63.4	63.4
CrosNNCLR*	joint	**75.2**	**79.7**	**83.8**	**63.8**	**64.9**
AimCLR	motion	**66.8**	**70.6**	72.0	**57.3**	54.4
CrosNNCLR*	motion	66.1	69.8	**72.8**	56.4	**54.9**
AimCLR	bone	**73.2**	77.0	82.0	62.9	63.4
CrosNNCLR*	bone	72.8	**77.2**	**83.9**	**63.1**	**65.7**
3s-AimCLR	joint+motion+bone	78.9	**83.8**	87.8	**68.2**	68.8
3s-CrosNNCLR*	joint+motion+bone	**79.2**	83.7	**88.6**	68.0	**69.9**

Through the above experiments, the overall results show the model can not only enhance the expression of semantic relevance among different views of the same skeleton sequence, but also learn the low-level semantic information of the skeleton samples, and the recognition of the proposed method with different modalities of the skeleton data is verified through comparative experiments. We explain this result by that the model construction can take advantage of the close correlation among the views of the skeleton data, integrate the idea of CrosNNCLR, find out the semantically similar samples with view q, k as positive sample pairs, change the original model's method of obtaining more positive pairs, and capture richer view information.

4.4   Analysis of Ablation Experiment Results

To verify the effectiveness of our CrosNNCLR and CrosNNCLR* model for representation learning, we compare them with the latest unsupervised action recognition works, including AS-CAL, ISC, Colorization, LongT GAN, MS^{2}L, P&C, SkeletonCLR, CrosSCLR and AimCLR, etc. It is also compared with a small number of fully-supervised action recognition models, including Part-Aware LSTM, VA-RNN, Soft RNN, and ST-GCN, etc. The ablation experiments are mainly carried out on the NTU-60/120 and PKU datasets.

Table 3. Comparison of experimental accuracy on the NTU-60 dataset (joint).

Method	xsub(%)	xview(%)
LongT GAN(AAAI 18)	39.1	48.1
MS^{2}L(ACM MM 20)	52.6	–
P&C(CVPR 20)	50.7	76.3
AS-CAL(Information Sciences 21)	58.5	64.8
SkeletonCLR(CVPR 21)	68.3	76.4
CrosSCLR(CVPR 21)	72.9	79.9
AimCLR(AAAI 22)	74.3	79.7
CrosNNCLR(ours)	73.2	**81.0**
CrosNNCLR*(ours)	**75.2**	79.7

Table 4. Comparison of experimental accuracy on the NTU-60 dataset (joint+ motion+bone).

Method	xsub(%)	xview(%)
3s-Colorization(ICCV 21)	75.2	83.1
3s-SkeletonCLR(CVPR 21)	75.0	79.8
3s-CrosSCLR(CVPR 21)	77.8	83.4
3s-AimCLR(AAAI 22)	78.9	**83.8**
3s-CrosNNCLR(ours)	76.0	83.4
3s-CrosNNCLR*(ours)	**79.2**	83.7

Results of Linear Evaluation on the NTU-60 Dataset. As shown in Table 3, for the skeleton single-modal data (joint), the recognition accuracy of our CrosNNCLR respectively increases 4.9% and 4.6% over the original SkeletonCLR on the xsub and xview benchmarks dataset, then by 0.3% and 0.1% over the cross-modal contrastive learning CrosSCLR on the xview benchmark dataset, respectively. On the xsub benchmark dataset, the recognition accuracy of our CrosNNCLR* is 0.3% higher than the AimCLR. On the xview benchmark dataset, the recognition effect of our CrosNNCLR* is equal to the original AimCLR.

In Table 4, the performance of skeleton multimodal data (joint+motion +bone) is given. We can see that our 3s-CrosNNCLR respectively obtains 76.0% and 83.4% recognition accuracy, the presented 3s-CrosNNCLR* obtains 79.2% and 83.7% recognition accuracy respectively. Compared with the other models, these results further demonstrate the effectiveness of CrosNNCLR.

Table 5. Comparison of experimental accuracy on the PKU dataset (joint).

Method	part I(%)	part II(%)
Supervised:		
ST-GCN(AAAI 18)	84.1	48.2
VA-RNN(TPAMI 19)	84.1	**50.0**
Self-supervised:		
LongT GAN(AAAI 18)	67.7	26.0
MS^{2}L(ACM MM 20)	64.9	27.6
3s-CrosSCLR(CVPR 21)	84.9	21.2
ISC(ACM MM 21)	80.9	36.0
3s-AimCLR(AAAI 22)	87.8	38.5
3s-CrosNNCLR*(ours)	**88.6**	**44.7**

Table 6. Comparison of experimental accuracy on the NTU-120 dataset (joint).

Method	xsub(%)	xset(%)
Supervised:		
Part-Aware LSTM(CVPR 16)	25.5	26.3
Soft RNN(TPAMI 18)	36.3	44.9
Self-supervised:		
P&C(CVPR 20)	42.7	41.7
AS-CAL(Information Sciences 21)	48.6	49.2
3s-CrosSCLR(CVPR 21)	67.9	66.7
ISC(ACM MM 21)	67.9	67.1
3s-AimCLR(AAAI 22)	**68.2**	68.8
3s-CrosNNCLR*(ours)	68.0	**69.9**

Results of Linear Evaluation on the PKU Dataset. Table 5 gives a comparison of the current state-of-the-art approaches. Firstly, our 3s-CrosNNCLR* respectively achieves 88.6% and 44.7% recognition accuracy on the part I and part II datasets, which gains 0.8 and 6.2% points better than the original 3s-AimCLR, respectively, and higher than other algorithms. Secondly, the self-supervised learning approaches achieve higher recognition than some fully-supervised models, e.g., ST-GCN and VA-RNN, demonstrating that CrosNNCLR has a strong discriminatory ability to distinguish the motion pattern caused by skeleton noise.

Table 7. Comparison of linear evaluation results of SkeletonCLR and CrosNNCLR at different epochs on the NTU-60/120 datasets (joint).

Method	Datasets	300ep	400ep	500ep	600ep	700ep	800ep	900ep	1000ep
SkeletonCLR	xsub60	68.3	70.0	70.0	70.4	70.4	69.7	70.6	70.6
CrosNNCLR	xsub60	**70.8**	**71.4**	**71.9**	**72.7**	**73.4**	**73.2**	**73.5**	**73.7**
SkeletonCLR	xview60	76.4	74.9	74.3	74.1	74.0	73.7	73.6	73.1
CrosNNCLR	xview60	**76.5**	**78.4**	**79.4**	**80.0**	**80.7**	**81.0**	**80.7**	**80.9**
SkeletonCLR	xsub120	56.8	56.0	56.1	56.1	56.1	56.3	55.8	55.5
CrosNNCLR	xsub120	**60.7**	**61.8**	**62.0**	**62.1**	**62.4**	**62.5**	**62.7**	**62.7**
SkeletonCLR	xset120	55.9	54.7	54.9	55.2	54.9	54.1	54.6	54.7
CrosNNCLR	xset120	**62.2**	**62.8**	**63.4**	**63.8**	**64.0**	**64.3**	**64.5**	**64.8**

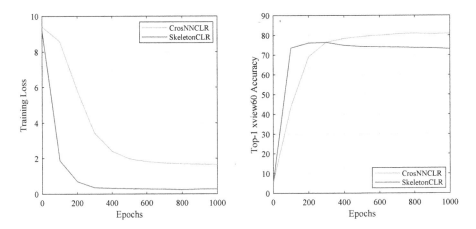

Fig. 4. CrosNNCLR vs SkeletonCLR Training curves and linear evaluation curves for xview60 linear evaluation.

Results of Linear Evaluation on the NTU-120 Dataset. As shown in Table 6, on the xsub benchmark dataset, our 3s-CrosNNCLR* achieves 68.0% recognition accuracy, which is similar to the 3s-AimCLR. On the xset benchmark dataset, our 3s-CrosNNCLR* achieves 69.9% action recognition accuracy, which gains 1.1% improvement over the original 3s-AimCLR. In fully-supervision, the accuracy of the proposed algorithm is better than some methods, e.g., Part-Aware LSTM and Soft RNN, which verifies the validity of the proposed model again.

Selection of Epoch Values for CrosNNCLR. Given the skeleton single-modal data (joint), corresponding experiments are conducted on four datasets from the NTU-60/120 to select the epoch values suitable for our CrosNNCLR. Firstly, Table 7 and Fig. 4 show the performance of CrosNNCLR is superior to SkeletonCLR after 300 epochs on single-modal (joint), while the model does not converge. In contrast SkeletonCLR no longer has a significant increase in loss and accuracy after 300 epoch, proving that the model has reached convergence. Furthermore, the performance of our CrosNNCLR continues to improve when the loss value continues to decrease. At 1000 epochs, the proposed method obtains 73.7%, 80.9%, 62.7%, and 64.8% recognition accuracy respectively, further increasing the gap to 4~8% points. Finally, we select the experimental results at 800 epochs training as the final evaluation results, mainly due to the weak feature expression of the model at the beginning of training, it is unable to learn deeper semantic information. As the number of iterations increases, the network will learn richer semantic representation and promote the convergence of the network model.

Table 8. Performance with only crop augmentation (joint) for xview60 linear evaluation.

Method	SkeletonCLR	CrosNNCLR	AimCLR	CrosNNCLR*
Full aug.	76.4	**81.0**	79.7	79.7
Only crop	51.5($\downarrow$ 24.9)	**63.0**($\downarrow$ 18)	53.3($\downarrow$ 26.4)	54.6($\downarrow$ 25.1)

Table 9. Embedding size (joint) for xview60 linear evaluation.

Embedding size	128	256	512	1024
Top-1	76.8	81.0	77.6	**80.7**
Top-5	96.4	**97.2**	96.8	**97.2**

Table 10. Memory bank size (joint) for xview60 linear evaluation.

Queue size	256	512	1024	2048	4096	8192	16384	32768
Top-1	75.5	74.5	78.2	78.7	74.2	79.0	77.6	**81.0**
Top-5	96.3	95.7	96.8	96.8	96.0	96.9	96.7	**97.2**

Data Augmentation. Both SkeletonCLR and AimCLR rely on multiple data augmentation methods to obtain the best performance. However, CrosNNCLR and CrosNNCLR* do not rely too much on complex augmentation approaches, because a richer real column of similar samples can be obtained from the cross-view nearest neighbors. As shown in Table 8, we remove the complex data augmentation methods and keep only one data augmentation method, random crops. Although the method proposed in this paper also benefits from complex data augmentation operations, CrosNNCLR relies much less on its removed data augmentation operations in comparison.

Embedding Size. As shown in Table 9, four embedding sizes have been selected for comparison, i.e., 128, 256, 512 and 1024, from which we can see that our CrosNNCLR is more robust and finds similar recognition results for different embedding sizes.

Memory Bank Size. Enhancing the number of samples in the memory bank usually improves the model performance, and the experimental results are shown in Table 10, which has a peak value of 32768. Overall, Using a larger memory bank in the cross-view nearest neighbor method increases the probability of capturing similar samples.

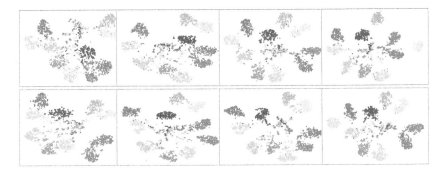

Fig. 5. The t-SNE visualization of the embedding features of SkeletonCLR, AimCLR, CrosNNCLR, and CrosNNCLR* on the xsub and xview dataset of NTU-60, where the first-row visualization results include: t-SNE(SkeletonCLR) and t-SNE(AimCLR) on the xsub and xview datasets. The second-row visualization results include: t-SNE(CrosNNCLR) and t-SNE(CrosNNCLR*) on the xsub and xview datasets.

Qualitative Analysis Results. To verify the effectiveness of inserting CrosNNCLR modules into existing models, the t-SNE [37] dimensionality reduction algorithm visualizes the embedded features distribution of SkeletonCLR, AimCLR, CrosNNCLR, and CrosNNCLR*. As shown in Fig. 5, 10 classes from the xsub and xview datasets of NTU-60 are selected for embedding comparisons. Compared to SkeletonCLR and AimCLR, the proposed method CrosNNCLR and CrosNNCLR* can cluster the embedding features of the same class more compactly, and separate the embedding features of different classes.

Quantitative Analysis Results. To more clearly and intuitively compare the action classification results of SkeletonCLR and CrosNNCLR, we plot the test results into a confusion matrix on the NTU-60 dataset. As shown in Fig. 6, we compare the 10 kinds of actions single-modal (joint) of xsub and xview datasets. In general, our CrosNNCLR is more accurate than SkeletonCLR in most of the actions, e.g., the classification of "eat meal" increased from 48% and 63% to 55% and 73%, respectively. The classification accuracy of CrosNNCLR is similar to SkeletonCLR for a few actions, e.g., 48% and 46% for "clapping" under the xsub evaluation benchmark, respectively. Thus, the conclusion is validated that our CrosNNCLR model can improve the feature representation of each type of action.

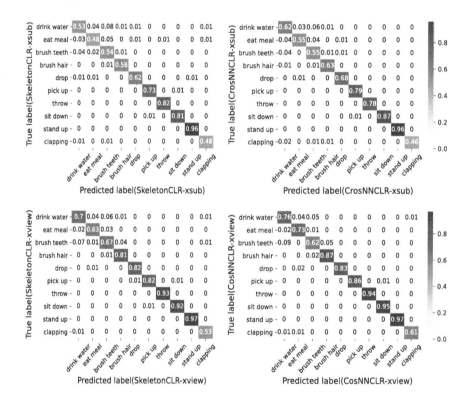

Fig. 6. Comparison of the confusion matrix on NTU-60 datasets

5   Conclusion

In this paper, a generic module called Cross-View Nearest Neighbor Contrastive Learning framework for self-supervised action Representation is proposed to obtain more positives. Our CrosNNCLR, as a view-level block, can be applied to existing contrastive learning architectures in the plug-and-play manner, bringing consistent improvements. Moreover, under various linear evaluation protocols, our method outperforms previous state-of-the-art methods on the NTU-60/120 and PKU datasets, demonstrating that the model has good generalization in low-probability learning scenarios. In future work, we will study the self-supervised action recognition based on robot body skeletons, aiming at active human-robot collaboration and lightweight recognition model with knowledge distillation techniques.

Acknowledgements. This research was supported by the National Nature Science Foundation of China (61862015), the Science and Technology Project of Guangxi (AD21220114), the Guangxi Key Research and Development Program (AB17195025).

References

1. Weinland, D., Ronfard, R., Boyer, E.: A survey of vision-based methods for action representation, segmentation and recognition. Comput. Vis. Image Underst. **115**(2), 224–241 (2011)
2. He, K., Zhang, X., Ren, S., Sun, J.: Deep residual learning for image recognition. In: Proceedings of the IEEE Conference on Computer Vision and Pattern Recognition, pp. 770–778 (2016)
3. Girshick, R.: Fast R-CNN. In: Proceedings of the IEEE International Conference On Computer Vision, pp. 1440–1448 (2015)
4. Chen, L.-C., Papandreou, G., Kokkinos, I., Murphy, K., Yuille, A.L.: DeepLab: semantic image segmentation with deep convolutional nets, atrous convolution, and fully connected CRFs. IEEE Trans. Patt. Anal. Mach. Intell. **40**(4), 834–848 (2017)
5. Li, C., Zhong, Q., Xie, D., Pu, S.: Co-occurrence feature learning from skeleton data for action recognition and detection with hierarchical aggregation. arXiv preprint arXiv:1804.06055, 2018
6. Song, S., Lan, C., Xing, J., Zeng, W., Liu, J.: Spatio-temporal attention-based LSTM networks for 3D action recognition and detection. IEEE Trans. Image Process. **27**(7), 3459–3471 (2018)
7. Liu, J., Shahroudy, A., Xu, D., Wang, G.: Spatio-temporal LSTM With trust gates for 3D human action recognition. In: Leibe, B., Matas, J., Sebe, N., Welling, M. (eds.) ECCV 2016. LNCS, vol. 9907, pp. 816–833. Springer, Cham (2016). https://doi.org/10.1007/978-3-319-46487-9_50
8. Kay, W., et al.: The kinetics human action video dataset. arXiv preprint arXiv:1705.06950, 2017
9. Ke, Q., Bennamoun, M., An, S., Sohel, F., Boussaid, F.: A new representation of skeleton sequences for 3D action recognition. arXiv e-prints (2017)
10. Liang, D., Fan, G., Lin, G., Chen, W., Zhu, H.: Three-stream convolutional neural network with multi-task and ensemble learning for 3D action recognition. In 2019 IEEE/CVF Conference on Computer Vision and Pattern Recognition Workshops (CVPRW) (2019)
11. Srivastava, N., Mansimov, E., Salakhudinov, R.: Unsupervised learning of video representations using LSTMs. In: International Conference on Machine Learning, pp. 843–852. PMLR (2015)

12. Liu, Z., Zhang, H., Chen, Z., Wang, Z., Ouyang, W.: Disentangling and unifying graph convolutions for skeleton-based action recognition. In: Proceedings of the IEEE/CVF Conference on Computer Vision and Pattern Recognition, pp. 143–152 (2020)

13. Gui, L.-Y., Wang, Y.-X., Liang, X., Moura, J.M.F.: Adversarial geometry-aware human motion prediction. In: Ferrari, V., Hebert, M., Sminchisescu, C., Weiss, Y. (eds.) ECCV 2018. LNCS, vol. 11208, pp. 823–842. Springer, Cham (2018). https://doi.org/10.1007/978-3-030-01225-0_48

14. Kundu, J.N., Gor, M., Uppala, P.K., Radhakrishnan, V.B.: Unsupervised feature learning of human actions as trajectories in pose embedding manifold. In: 2019 IEEE Winter Conference on Applications of Computer Vision (WACV), pp. 1459–1467. IEEE (2019)

15. Noroozi, M., Favaro, P.: Unsupervised learning of visual representations by solving jigsaw puzzles. In: Leibe, B., Matas, J., Sebe, N., Welling, M. (eds.) ECCV 2016. LNCS, vol. 9910, pp. 69–84. Springer, Cham (2016). https://doi.org/10.1007/978-3-319-46466-4_5

16. Zhang, R., Isola, P., Efros, A.A.: Colorful image colorization. In: Leibe, B., Matas, J., Sebe, N., Welling, M. (eds.) ECCV 2016. LNCS, vol. 9907, pp. 649–666. Springer, Cham (2016). https://doi.org/10.1007/978-3-319-46487-9_40

17. Zhang, J., Zhao, Y., Saleh, M., Liu, P.: PEGASUS: pre-training with extracted gap-sentences for abstractive summarization. In: International Conference on Machine Learning, pp. 11328–11339. PMLR (2020)

18. Thoker, F.M., Doughty, H., Snoek, C.G.M.: Skeleton-contrastive 3D action representation learning. In: Proceedings of the 29th ACM International Conference on Multimedia, pp. 1655–1663 (2021)

19. Ni, B., Wang, G., Moulin, P.: RGBD-HuDaAct: a color-depth video database for human daily activity recognition. In: 2011 IEEE International Conference on Computer Vision Workshops (ICCV workshops), pp. 1147–1153. IEEE (2011)

20. Vemulapalli, R., Arrate, F., Chellappa, R.: Human action recognition by representing 3D skeletons as points in a lie group. In: Proceedings of the IEEE Conference on Computer Vision and Pattern Recognition, pp. 588–595 (2014)

21. Vemulapalli, R., Chellapa, R.: Rolling rotations for recognizing human actions from 3D skeletal data. In: Proceedings of the IEEE Conference on Computer Vision and Pattern Recognition, pp. 4471–4479 (2016)

22. Wang, J., Liu, Z., Wu, Y., Yuan, J.: Mining Actionlet ensemble for action recognition with depth cameras. In: 2012 IEEE Conference on Computer Vision and Pattern Recognition, pp. 1290–1297. IEEE (2012)

23. Zhang, P., Lan, C., Xing, J., Zeng, W., Xue, J., Zheng, N.: View adaptive neural networks for high performance skeleton-based human action recognition. IEEE Trans. Pattern Anal. Mach. Intell. 41(8), 1963–1978 (2019)

24. Du, Y., Wang, W., Wang, L.: Hierarchical recurrent neural network for skeleton based action recognition. In: Proceedings of the IEEE Conference on Computer Vision and Pattern Recognition, pp. 1110–1118 (2015)

25. Yan, S., Xiong, Y., Lin, D.: Spatial temporal graph convolutional networks for skeleton-based action recognition. In: Thirty-second AAAI Conference on Artificial Intelligence (2018)

26. He, K., Fan, H., Wu, Y., Xie, S., Girshick, R.: Momentum contrast for unsupervised visual representation learning. In: Proceedings of the IEEE/CVF Conference on Computer Vision and Pattern Recognition, pp. 9729–9738 (2020)

27. Gidaris, S., Bursuc, A., Puy, G., Komodakis, N., Cord, M., Perez, P.: OBoW: online bag-of-visual-words generation for self-supervised learning. In: Proceedings of the IEEE/CVF Conference on Computer Vision and Pattern Recognition, pp. 6830–6840 (2021)

28. Han, T., Xie, W., Zisserman, A.: Self-supervised co-training for video representation learning. Adv. Neural. Inf. Process. Syst. **33**, 5679–5690 (2020)

29. Dwibedi, D., Aytar, Y., Tompson, J., Sermanet, P., Zisserman, A.: With a little help from my friends: Nearest-neighbor contrastive learning of visual representations. In: Proceedings of the IEEE/CVF International Conference on Computer Vision, pp. 9588–9597 (2021)

30. Zheng, N., Wen, J., Liu, R., Long, L., Gong, Z.: Unsupervised representation learning with long-term dynamics for skeleton based action recognition. In: AAAI-18 (2018)

31. Su, K., Liu, X., Shlizerman, E.: Predict & cluster: Unsupervised skeleton based action recognition (2019)

32. Li, L., Wang, M., Ni, B., Wang, H., Yang, J., Zhang, W.: 3D human action representation learning via cross-view consistency pursuit (2021)

33. Guo, T., Liu, H., Chen, Z., Liu, M., Wang, T., Ding, R.: Contrastive learning from extremely augmented skeleton sequences for self-supervised action recognition. arXiv e-prints (2021)

34. Shahroudy, A., Liu, J., Ng, T.T., Wang, G.: NTU RGB+D: a large scale dataset for 3D human activity analysis. In: IEEE Computer Society, pp. 1010–1019 (2016)

35. Liu, J., Song, S., Liu, C., Li, Y., Hu, Y.: A benchmark dataset and comparison study for multi-modal human action analytics. ACM Trans. Multimedia Comput. Commun. Appl. (TOMM) **16**(2), 1–24 (2020)

36. Liu, J., Shahroudy, A., Perez, M., Wang, G., Duan, L.Y., Kot, A.C.: NTU RGB+D 120: a large-scale benchmark for 3D human activity understanding. IEEE Trans. Pattern Anal. Mach. Intell. **42**(10), 2684–2701 (2020)

37. Shi, S.: Visualizing data using GTSNE (2021)

Bogie Temperature Detection Method for Subway Trains Based on Dual Optical Images

Kaijie Du$^{(\boxtimes)}$ ⓘ, Shangbin Jiao ⓘ, Yujun Li ⓘ, Wenhao Liu ⓘ, Zhangjie Lei ⓘ, and Jing Xin ⓘ

Xi'an University of Technology, Xi'an 710048, China
{2200321208,2210320097,2210321193}@stu.xaut.edu.cn,
{jiaoshangbin,Leo,xinj}@xaut.edu.cn

Abstract. The bogies of metro trains are key components of the trains. If abnormal conditions of the bogies are not detected and handled in time, the safe operation of the trains will be seriously affected. The temperature of bogie components can visually reflect the bogie status, therefore, it is crucial to detect the temperature of bogie components. To ensure a more comprehensive and effective bogie temperature detection, this paper proposes a bogie temperature detection method based on dual-light images, which has the advantages of non-contact, unattended, high detection accuracy and wide detection range. This method uses both infrared thermal images and visible images to complete the detection. For target positioning, this paper uses Transformer-based component positioning strategy, and after several experiments to calculate the evaluation index, the results prove that this solution has higher detection accuracy and better mastery of the global situation. For dual-light image matching, this paper uses an image matching strategy based on affine transformation, which achieves the mapping of the target position from the visible image to the infrared thermal image. After comprehensive testing, the loss rate of this method reached 1.8%, which has practical application value in the field and can provide a reliable maintenance basis for metro intelligent operation and maintenance.

Keywords: Steering rack · Dual light image · Transformer · Image alignment · Temperature detection

1 Introduction

The bogies of metro trains are the power and load-bearing devices of trains, which directly affect the safety of train operation. Traction motors(An electric motor that generates traction power for a locomotive or locomotive), couplings(An important transmission component of a high-speed train that transfers power from the traction motor to the gearbox to drive the wheelset), axle boxes and gearboxes are the key components of the bogies, and failure of any of them may lead to train operation accidents. The temperature is the most intuitive reflection of the bogie's health status, and even a minor fault will inevitably cause abnormal changes in the temperature rise of the components. Therefore, it is a common inspection method used by major metro companies to detect the temperature rise of bogie components to determine the health of the components.

At present the mainstream detection methods are: manual inspection, contact temperature sensor detection, infrared temperature sensor detection, etc. However, the above detection programs, there are certain shortcomings, among them, manual inspection needs to wait for the train to return to the garage after the use of point temperature gun one by one detection, detection efficiency is low, and the vehicle back to the garage, the temperature has been seriously inaccurate, it is difficult to find abnormalities; contact temperature sensor although can achieve at any time to detect, but it needs to install additional temperature sensors on each part of the bogie, the line is complex, safety can not guarantee; Although the non-contact infrared temperature measurement eliminates the disadvantages of manual inspection and contact sensor detection, it is difficult to accurately locate the parts, especially for the coupling joints, gearboxes and other components that are not easy to detect, and the rate of missed detection and false alarm is high [1–4].

After the actual research of a domestic metro company, we found that the metro operation system would like to visualize the status of the working bogie components and get the temperature information of important components. Therefore, the above traditional detection methods can no longer meet the needs of users. Therefore, this paper proposes to combine the infrared thermal imaging camera and visible light camera, using dual-light image processing technology to complete the inspection of bogie components, to ensure that users can intuitively see the high-definition image of the components and get the temperature data of the components. This inspection method has the advantages of: non-contact measurement, real-time detection, accurate positioning, wide detection range and low temperature distortion, which can provide reliable data support for subway train maintenance.

The dual-light image processing techniques used in this paper mainly include visible image target localization strategy and visible image and infrared thermal image matching strategy. For visible image target localization, due to the large number of bogie components to be detected in each train, a Transformer-based component localization strategy is used to achieve fast response; for image matching, this paper uses the image affine transformation technique to complete the coordinate conversion between infrared thermal image and visible image, which has a better effect.

2   Transformer-Based Part Positioning Strategy

2.1   Transformer Target Recognition Framework

In 2017, Google proposed a deep neural network based on a self-attentive mechanism and applied it to the field of natural language processing. Its superior parallelized processing mechanism has caused significant repercussions in the field, while many Transformer-based approaches have been proposed in the field of computer vision one after another [5].

The Transformer framework proposed by Google is based on the Encoder-Decoder architecture, as shown in Fig. 1 below. Six sets of encoders and six sets of decoders are used in this architecture, where the output of each encoder is used as the input of the next encoder, and each decoder gets the output of the previous decoder along with the output of the whole encoder [6–8].

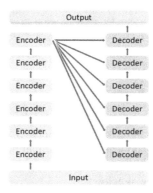

Fig. 1. Transformer encoder-decoder architecture

For each Encoder, it consists of a Multi-head attention and a Feed Forward, as shown in Fig. 2 below. Among them, Multi-head attention is improved on the basis of Self-attention, which makes Self-attention performance more superior and the extraction of features more comprehensive and rich, which is mainly in two aspects:

(1) Improving the ability of the model to focus on different locations of the encoding.
(2) enables self-attention to have multiple "representation subspaces" [5].

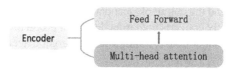

Fig. 2. Encoder internal structure

The structure of Decoder is similar to Encoder, as shown in Fig. 3 below, but it adds an additional layer of Masked multi-head attention on top of Encoder, which masks the unpredicted information and ensures that the prediction results are based on the known information.

Transformer completes feature extraction of the input sequence by the above Encoder-Decoder architecture, which has a better grasp of the global picture and excellent long-range feature extraction capability. If the image is converted into a sequence similar to a sentence, the image can be extracted and processed with features by the Transformer architecture.

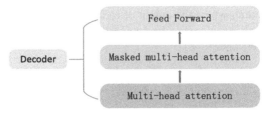

Fig. 3. Decoder internal structure

2.2 DETR Target Detection Framework

Detection Transformer is the first detection framework to apply the Transformer structure to the field of target detection, which combines Transformer and CNN to enable end-to-end automatic training and learning by parallel prediction without the need for specialized libraries and with strong migration properties. The block diagram of the DETR structure is shown in Fig. 4 below:

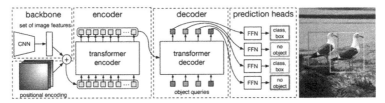

Fig. 4. DETR structure block diagram

The DETR model first extracts feature information of 2D images through CNN network, encodes the features, and sends them to Encoder-Decoder structure of Transformer for processing, and the output of Decoder is sent to FFN to get the final prediction result. DETR innovatively converts the target detection problem into a simple ensemble prediction problem, which effectively simplifies the target detection process.

3 Infrared Image and Visible Image Matching Strategy Based on Affine Transformation

3.1 Affine Transformation

Image affine transformation is a linear transformation of an image from one two-dimensional coordinate system to another two-dimensional coordinate system. It can do a series of transformations on the image, and at the same time can ensure the "straightness" and "parallelism" of the image, [9, 10] so as to facilitate the image processing, mainly: scaling, translation, rotation, flip, etc. The expression of affine transformation is shown in Eq. 1:

$$\begin{cases} u = a_1 x + b_1 y + c_1 \\ v = a_2 x + b_2 y + c_2 \end{cases} \tag{1}$$

The matrix form is expressed as:

$$\begin{bmatrix} u \\ v \\ 1 \end{bmatrix} = \begin{bmatrix} a_1 & b_1 & c_1 \\ a_1 & b_2 & c_2 \\ 0 & 0 & 1 \end{bmatrix} \begin{bmatrix} x \\ y \\ 1 \end{bmatrix} \qquad (2)$$

In the equation, (u, v) is the coordinates of the target point in the infrared thermal image and (x, y) is the coordinates of that target point in the visible image, and the two can be converted by the affine transformation matrix M.

3.2 Dual Light Camera Calibration

In this paper's inspection scheme, an infrared thermal camera in collaboration with a visible camera is used. After the visible camera finishes locating the target, it needs to correspond to the infrared thermal image to extract the temperature of the part. In this paper, we use the tessellation grid calibration method, using an aluminum plate made in the shape of a tessellation grid as shown in Fig. 5. Since the thermal imaging camera is for infrared radiation imaging, the white area in the figure is hollowed out to capture the infrared image after heating.

Fig. 5. Schematic diagram of checkerboard calibration board

4 Bogie Temperature Testing Experiment

4.1 Experimental Environment

Two image processing algorithms are involved in this paper, which are Transformer-based part localization strategy and affine transform-based infrared image and visible image matching strategy. To ensure that the detection system can achieve the expected results after installation, and to verify the processing stability of the above two algorithms, we built an experimental platform for bogie temperature detection in a laboratory environment, as shown in Fig. 6 below.

Fig. 6. Bogie temperature testing experimental platform

4.2   Experimental Procedure

Step1: Model training. During the training process, the data set is divided into training set and test set according to the ratio of 9:1, where the test set is not involved in the model training, and the model is tested during the training process to adjust the parameters in time to reduce the loss and improve the learning rate. The training convergence process is shown in Fig. 7. When small sample training is conducted, the number of iterations is set to 20, and according to the curve, it is known that the curve has basically converged when it reaches 15 iterations.

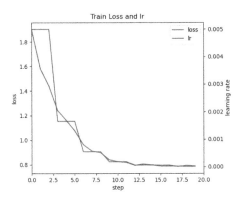

Fig. 7. Model training curve

Step2: Simulation trigger. Using the laboratory bogie to simulate passing a vehicle, the detection system is triggered to work by the wheel sensor, and after the passing is completed, the algorithm processing results can be viewed in the system software, as shown in Fig. 8 below. In the image, the detailed locations of the components are marked using rectangular boxes, and the component temperature information is extracted.

Fig. 8. Passing test results

Step3: Repeat the over-vehicle experiment and artificially set different levels of interference to calculate the algorithm evaluation index and the system leakage rate.

4.3 Evaluation Indicators

The effect of machine learning requires the use of some evaluation metrics to assess the model performance. In the field of target detection, the commonly used model evaluation metrics are: accuracy, precision, recall, AP, mAP, etc. Among them, AP and mAP are the two most used evaluation metrics, which can directly reveal the model performance [11]. The formula for accuracy is shown in Eq. 3:

$$accuracy = \frac{(TP + TN)}{(TP + TN + FP + FN)} \tag{3}$$

The formula for precision is shown in Eq. 4:

$$precision = \frac{TP}{(TP + FP)} \tag{4}$$

The formula for recall is shown in Eq. 5:

$$recall = \frac{TP}{(TP + FN)} \tag{5}$$

AP (Average Precision), which is the average of accuracy at different recall points, is the area enclosed by the PR curve (the curve drawn with recall as the horizontal coordinate and precision as the vertical coordinate) and the two axes, and is an important indicator of model performance.

mAP (mean average precision), which is the average of AP values of multiple categories, measures the performance of the model on all target categories and is the most important indicator of model performance [12]. In this paper we will use AP and mAP to evaluate the performance of the DETR model under a homemade dataset.

4.4 Analysis of Experimental Results

Analysis of Target Localization Detection Results
Four different networks were experimented in this paper, namely Faster RCNN, SDD, YOLOv4, and DETR networks. Through several experiments, the AP and mAP of each network for different components are calculated as shown in Table 1 below.

Table 1. Network AP and mAP metrics.

Method	Traction motor	Coupling joint	Left axle box	Right axle box	Gearboxes	mAP
Faster RCNN	88.14%	85.41%	79.22%	78.52%	82.83%	82.82%
SDD	85.06%	82.15%	76.41%	77.48%	79.36%	80.09%
YOLOv4	86.45%	84.79%	80.67%	78.20%	83.05%	82.63%
DETR	91.87%	88.66%	82.05%	80.32%	85.46%	86.87%

Analysis of the index parameters in the above table shows that the DETR model has a minimum improvement of 3.73% for traction motors, 3.25% for couplings, 1.38% for left axleboxes, 1.8% for right axleboxes, and 2.41% for gearboxes compared to other network models. The network mAP improved by a minimum of 4.05% compared to other networks.

The results demonstrate that using the DETR target detection model based on Transformer structure can significantly improve the detection accuracy rate with the same dataset and targets, especially better grasp of the global picture and higher accuracy for large targets such as traction motors.

Analysis of Image Matching Results
The image matching strategy based on affine transformation is used to convert the coordinates of the target position in the visible image to the coordinates in the infrared thermal image, taking the left axial box as an example, as shown in Fig. 9 below. According to the image, it can be found that after locating the target position in the visible image, the left axial box position is also obtained in the infrared thermal image after affine transformation, and the highest point temperature within the range of the left axial box is extracted, which is the palm surface temperature of 56.32 °C.

The experiments are repeated several times, and the results show that the image matching accuracy can reach 100% in the case that the visible image accurately identifies the part location and the target is present in the infrared thermal image. Therefore, the image matching strategy based on affine transformation is fully applicable to the application scenario of the detection system in this paper.

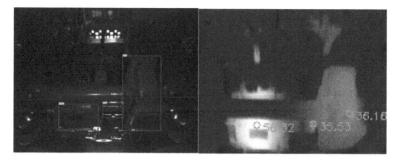

Fig. 9. Image matching results

System Leakage Rate Analysis

In order to verify whether the detection scheme proposed in this paper achieves the requirement that the loss rate is no more than 5%, we have done several simulated over-vehicle experiments, and the detection of each component is statistically shown in Table 2 below.

Table 2. Loss rate statistics.

Parts	Number of experiments	Number of detections	Number of losses	Loss rate
Traction motor	500	491	9	1.8%
Left axle box	500	489	11	2.2%
Right axle box	500	490	10	2.0%
Coupling Joint	500	491	9	1.8%
Gearboxes	500	494	6	1.2%
Totals	2500	1955	45	1.8%

According to the data in the above table, the detection loss rate of the bogie temperature detection method based on dual-light image proposed in this paper reaches 1.8%, which is much lower than the requirement of 5% loss rate, specifically for a single component, of which the left axle box has the highest loss rate of 2.2%, which is still lower than the requirement of 5%, therefore, the method proposed in this paper can fully meet the field inspection requirements.

5 Conclusion

For the problem of subway train bogie temperature detection, this paper proposes a bogie temperature detection method based on dual-light images, which uses a Transformer-based target localization strategy and an affine transform-based image matching strategy. It is experimentally verified that in terms of target localization, the scheme used in this paper is more accurate and has significant superiority compared with other network models. At the global level, the loss rate of the scheme in this paper reaches 1.8%, which is much lower than the requirement of 5% loss rate, and can meet the detection demand in actual operation, which can provide a reliable maintenance basis for metro intelligent operation and maintenance.

References

1. Liu, J., Wang, Z.: Typical fault analysis of locomotive travel monitoring device. Railw. Locomot. Mov. Veh. (02), 46–48+6 (2017)
2. Wang, Z.: The design of bearing monitoring system of running locomotive. Dalian Jiaotong University (2018)
3. Xie, Q.: The design and realize of subway train axle temperature detection based on ZigBee. Southwest Jiaotong University (2017)
4. Wang, B.: Development trends of rolling stock fault diagnosis and monitoring technology. Foreign Rolling Stock Technol. (01), 1–5+13 (2020)
5. Liu, W.T., Lu, X.M.: Progress of Transformer research based on computer vision. Comput. Eng. Appl. **58**(06), 1–16 (2022)
6. Ratsch, G.: Soft margins for AdaBoost. Mach. Learn. **42**(3), 287–320 (2001)
7. Dalal, N., Triggs, B.: Histograms of oriented gradients for human detection. In: 2005 IEEE Computer Society Conference on Computer Vision and Pattern Recognition (CVPR 2005), vol. 1, pp. 886–893. IEEE (2005)
8. Hearst, M.A., Dumais, S.T., Osman, E., et al.: Support vector machines. IEEE Intell. Syst. Their Appl. **13**(4), 18–28 (1998)
9. Peng, Y., Guo, J., Yu, C., Ke, B.: High precision camera calibration method based on plane transformation. J. Beijing Univ. Aeronaut. Astronaut. 1–10 (2022)
10. Bai, Y., Hou, C., Liu, X.Y., Ma, S., Yu, W.S., Pu, L.: Target detection algorithm based on decision-level fusion of visible and infrared images. J. Air Force Eng. Univ. (Nat. Sci. Edn.) **21**(06), 53–59+100 (2020)
11. Felzenszwalb, P., McAllester, D., Ramanan, D.: A discriminatively trained, multiscale, deformable part model. In: 2008 IEEE Conference on Computer Vision and Pattern Recognition, pp. 1–8. IEEE (2008)
12. Russakovsky, O., Deng, J., Su, H., et al.: ImageNet large scale visual recognition challenge. Int. J. Comput. Vis. **115**(3), 211–252 (2015)

Operating Health State Prediction and Evaluation of Excitation Unit Based on GMM and LSTM

Yinxing Ma[1]([✉]) (iD), Peihao Yang[2] (iD), Gang Lv[3] (iD), Shibin Deng[3] (iD), Shangbin Jiao[1] (iD), Yujun Li[1] (iD), Xiaohui Wu[3] (iD), and Jing Zhang[1] (iD)

[1] Shaanxi Key Laboratory of Complex System Control and Intelligent Information Processing, Xi'an University of Technology, Xi'an 710048, China
2200321234@stu.xaut.edu.cn

[2] Xi'an Thermal Power Research Institute Co., Ltd., Xi'an 710054, China

[3] Huaneng Weihai Power Generation Co., Ltd., Wei'hai 264200, China

Abstract. The excitation unit is the weak link in the generator operation since it produces internal deterioration under long-term operation. To evaluate the health condition of the key excitation unit and generate warning information in advance, this work proposes a health assessment method based on the Gaussian mixture model (GMM) and LSTM neural network. Firstly, the weights of each type of data will be determined by obtaining the electrical parameter data of the generator excitation unit from the SIS system, using the infrared image data of carbon brush and excitation transformer based on infrared image acquisition system, and the correlation between each electrical parameter data and temperature on account of the MIC correlation analysis method. On the top of it, LSTM neural network prediction model is established. And establish a GMM-based health benchmark model based on the data collected in the field during healthy operation, and design the health decline index HDI using the Marxist distance for evaluating the health status and deterioration degree of the unit. Finally, the method of this paper is validated by the 2022 operation data of a thermal power plant in Weihai, which proved that this method can provide a basis for regular maintenance and early identification of faults in the power plan and quantifying the degradation degree of the excitation unit under long-term operation and making early warning before the abnormal occurrence of the unit.

Keywords: Excitation system · Correlation analysis · LSTM model · Health assessment · GMM

1 Introduction

The excitation unit is the weak link in generator operation. Due to the harsh operating environment, complex internal structure and fluctuating grid load, the operating state of the unit is constantly changing, resulting in internal deterioration of various components in the whole unit, such as excitation variable and carbon brush, under prolonged

Z. Yu et al. (Eds.): CIRAC 2022, CCIS 1770, pp. 267–279, 2023.
https://doi.org/10.1007/978-981-99-0301-6_21

operation. In practice, it is found that the performance of the control system cannot always be kept in good condition [1], and the operating stability of the power system will gradually decline with the growth of operating time. If reasonable evaluation and maintenance measures are not taken in time, the long-term development may lead to unit shutdown and even damage the key devices in the unit. Therefore, against the background of the increasing installed capacity of electric power equipment in China, it is of great significance to conduct health status assessment research of excitation units, predict the deterioration trend of the units, and take measures to eliminate hidden equipment problems in advance for the safe and stable operation and regular maintenance of the units.

Generally, fault diagnosis is based on feature extraction, analysis, and training of fault data from equipment or unit operation to achieve fault detection, separation, and identification, which is a process of identifying fault states based on fault data [2]. The main methods are model-based and AI based diagnosis methods. In the literature [3], the output voltage Ud is obtained by establishing a simulation model, and the amplitude information is extracted by FFT, normalized and input into a BP neural network, to quickly identify and analyze the fault site and fault point in the circuit, which is a relatively simple algorithm and is widely used in practice. Literature [4] combines rough set and neural network and proposes the RSNN stepwise method and RSNN overall fault diagnosis method, both of which can accurately locate the faulty components, especially the RSNN overall fault diagnosis, by processing the sample data with rough set theory, which makes the network structure size reduced and improves the diagnosis speed and correct rate. Literature [5] proposed a two-dimensional convolutional neural network CNN with multi-source information fusion for synchronous motor turn-to-turn short circuit fault diagnosis, converting the fault signal into a two-dimensional grayscale image for input to CNN and using D-S evidence theory for decision fusion, which eliminates the problem of single signal susceptibility and improves the fault diagnosis accuracy. Literature [6] proposed a MSCNNSA-BiGRU-based method for rolling bearing fault diagnosis of wind turbines under variable working conditions, which directly extracts the timing features from the original vibration signal for fusion, and has a better effect compared with classical MSCNN when tested under variable working conditions. Diagnostic methods based on fault data require fault data, however, the problem of few fault sample data and difficulty to obtain data is common in the field of generator fault diagnosis, and once the unit fails, it may cause the unit to shut down for maintenance or burn up the damaged parts. In the case of a small amount of data, most deep learning algorithms suffer from overfitting, poor diagnostic results, and generalization of the model [7].

Health assessment and prediction essentially also belong to fault diagnosis, which focuses on the information under normal conditions in the operation of the unit, and establishes a health benchmark model to judge the current operating status of the unit based on a large amount of healthy operating data in monitoring with a distribution model. Literature [8] proposed a wind turbine health assessment and prediction method, which divides the variables under normal operation into two parameter spaces for identification and establishes GMM health benchmark models for different operating condition subspaces to accurately assess the generator status and improve the performance of special fault prediction. In the literature [9], according to the structure of WTGU and the working principle of wind turbine, the condition evaluation index of WTGU was established, and the health condition of Wind turbine evaluation using similar cloud computing and fuzzy comprehensive evaluation methods, respectively. The literature [10] proposed a statistical and machine learning model based on the Wind Turbine Health Monitoring System (WTHMS), which classifies the raw sequences by variance range, calculates the gradual changes using long short-term memory (LSTM), and uses a weighted assessment method which combines the health condition of the main components to determine the health of the wind turbine. The method of health assessment because of the data which under normal operation of the generator, which facilitates model building and avoids the problem of difficult to obtain fault sample data to assess the working condition of the generator from the other side.

Through the analysis of the above literature, it is more difficult to realize the condition warning of excitation units using fault data, so this paper, based on a large amount of health data from the operation of excitation units in power plants, firstly performs MIC correlation analysis, analyzes the distribution characteristics of the data and establishes the health benchmark model, after that establishes the evaluation index of HDI health based on the Marxian distance, determines the dynamic HDI alarm threshold, and finally calculates the health index under the condition data of key parts predicted by LSTM neural network to predict the health status of components.

2   Analysis of Data Correlation

The MIC theory was proposed by David N. Reshef in a related article published in Science at 2011 [11]. eqThe MIC theory is based on the mutual information (MI), which is used to measure the nonlinear dependence between variables, and explore the linear or nonlinear relationship between variables as well as characterize the nonfunctional dependence between different variables, so it can measure the mutual influence relationship between variables more accurately than the traditional distance-based correlation measure.

It is an improved method, mainly using mutual information and grid partitioning for calculation, the larger the mutual information, the stronger the correlation between the two variables. Suppose A, B are two variables, x, y are the sample variables in A, B, then the mutual information between them is defined as:

$$I(A; B) = \sum_{y \in \gamma} \sum_{x \in \chi} p(x, y) \log \left(\frac{p(x, y)}{p(x)p(y)} \right) \tag{1}$$

In Eq. 1, $p(x, y)$ represents the joint probability density of the two variables, denoting the marginal probability densities of A and B, respectively.

The computational steps of MIC:

Step 1, Given a and b, grid the scatter graph formed by A and B, and calculate the maximum $I(A; B)$;

Step 2, normalization of the maximum $I(A; B)$ value;

Step 3, MIC value is the maximum value of $I(A; B)$ at different scales.

MIC is calculated as follows:

$$MIC(x, y) = max_{a*b<B(n)} \frac{I(x, y)}{log_2 min(a, b)} \tag{2}$$

In Eq. 2, a, b is the number of grids divided in the x, y direction; B(n) is a variable.

The state parameter data monitored by the excitation unit include: exciter secondary voltage, exciter temperature, active power, reactive power, frequency, stator voltage, power factor, stability, dynamic characteristics, excitation voltage, excitation current, trigger pulse, trigger angle, fan temperature, carbon brush temperature, rotor temperature, demagnetization switch, demagnetization waveform data, etc. The temperature of the key parts of the exciter and carbon brush and other variables are selected for correlation calculation, and the five variables with the highest correlation are taken as input variables for subsequent multi-parameter prediction.

3 Data Pre-processing

Due to equipment failure, bad network, harsh environment and human factors, the raw data collected by sensors will inevitably be missing and abnormal. [12], which can lead to an increase in data processing costs and corresponding time, and require the data to be supplemented with missing values. Temperature is a time-series signal, which is difficult to mutate under normal circumstances, and the data processing uses a method based on time-series relationships for filling, with the following calculation formula.

$$x_{a+i} = x_a + \frac{i \cdot (x_{a+j} - x_a)}{j}, 0 < i < j \tag{3}$$

In Eq. 3, x_{a+i} is the missing data; x_a, x_{a+j} is the original data value;
The data were normalized [13], and the data were normalized by:

$$x_i = \frac{(y_{max} - y_{min})(x_{max} - x_{min})}{x - x_{min}} + y_{min} \tag{4}$$

In Eq. 4, x_{max}, x_{min} are the maximum and minimum values, y_{max} and y_{min} are the default data, -1 and 1, respectively; x_i is the normalized data.

4 Healthiness Prediction Model Construction

The temperature of the critical part of the excitation unit is time series data, which usually grows slowly and does not change abruptly. Through the previous data preprocessing and data correlation analysis, the input data dimension of the neural network has been determined, and LSTM model is constructed next.

LSTM is a temporal recurrent neural network, which differs from RNN in that its repetition module structure consists of 4 layers, by adding memory units and gate units in the hidden layer, in this way, controls the information stored on time series and stores long time series information, which is excellent in time series data prediction like temperature.

LSTM chain structure is shown in Fig. 1, where C_t, h_t denotes the memory of the node, h_{t-1} denotes the input of the previous node, and the input x_t of this node is stitched together to calculate three gating states [15]: f_t, forgetting gate; i_t, input gate; o_t output gate. The addition and removal of information is achieved through the gate structure, which goes through the training process to learn which information should be saved or forgotten.

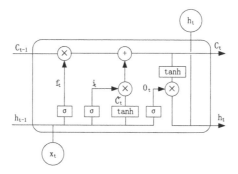

Fig. 1. LSTM chain structure

The equations for each cell in the entire structure in Fig. 1 are shown below:

$$i_t = \sigma\left(W_i \cdot \left[h_{t-1}, x_t\right] + b_i\right) \tag{5}$$

$$o_t = \sigma\left(W_o\left[h_{t-1}, x_t\right] + b_o\right) \tag{6}$$

$$f_t = \sigma\left(W_f \cdot \left[h_{t-1}, x_t\right] + b_f\right) \tag{7}$$

In Eq. 5–Eq. 7 are three gate structures. The input gate i_t is used to update the cell state, the forgetting gate f_t decides to keep or discard the information, and the output gate o_t determines the value of the next hidden state.

$$\tilde{C}_t = \tanh\left(W_C \cdot \left[h_{t-1}, x_t\right] + b_C\right) \tag{8}$$

$$C_t = f_t * C_{t-1} + i_t * \tilde{C}_t \tag{9}$$

$$h_t = o_t * \tanh(C_t) \tag{10}$$

In Eq. 8–Eq. 10, the new candidate node information $\tilde{C}_t$ represents the current input content, and the state of the incoming next node is C_t, which is related to both the input gate and the forgetting gate. The implied transmission state is h_t, it represents the output of the unit at time t.h_t is the implied transmission state. σ is sigmoid activation function, *tanh* is activation function; W is the weight matrix, b is the bias quantity, $*$ is the Hadamar product.

5 Healthiness Evaluation Model

5.1 GMM

Gaussian mixture model (GMM) is a semi-parametric unsupervised learning algorithm. The k submodel is regarded as the hidden variable of the mixed model to better describe the sample distribution of the mixed model, and any continuous distribution can be approximated with arbitrary accuracy by increasing the number of members, and the anti-interference and denoising ability is more outstanding.

The condition monitoring system of the excitation unit has many kinds of data and noise, and the data space distribution of normal and abnormal states has multiple types, which is consistent with the mechanism of GMM, and this work uses GMM to construct the health benchmark model of the excitation variable unit. Assuming a random variable X, the GMM is defined as follows:

$$p(x|\pi, \mu, \Sigma) = \sum_{k=1}^{K} \pi_k N(x|\mu_k, \Sigma_k) \tag{11}$$

In Eq. 11, $N(x|\mu_k, \Sigma_k)$ is the k-th component in the mixture model, which denotes the k-th multidimensional Gaussian distribution function, and π_k is the mixing coefficient of each component, which denotes the weight magnitude of the component.

Assuming that the state data of the excitation variable obeys a mixed Gaussian distribution, the probability distribution model of the GMM can be inferred from the collected state data. The unknown parameters in Eq. 6 are π_k, x_K, Σ_k, and the unknown parameters can be calculated iteratively by using the EM algorithm:

Defining the number of components k, setting the initial values of π_k, x_K, Σ_k for each component k, and then calculating the log-likelihood function in Eq. 6.

E step: compute the posterior probabilities based on the current π_k, x_K, Σ_k:

$$\gamma(z_{nk}) = \frac{\pi_k N(x_n|\mu_n, \Sigma_n)}{\sum_{j=1}^{K} \pi_j N(x_n|\mu_j, \Sigma_j)} \tag{12}$$

M step: compute new π_k, x_K, Σ_k based on the posterior probabilities computed in E step:

$$\mu_k^{new} = \frac{1}{N_k} \sum_{n=1}^{N} \gamma(z_{nk}) x_n \tag{13}$$

$$\Sigma_k^{new} = \frac{1}{N_k} \sum_{n=1}^{N} \gamma(z_{nk})(x_n - \mu_k^{new})^T \tag{14}$$

$$\pi_k^{new} = \frac{N_k}{N} \tag{15}$$

$$N_k = \sum_{n=1}^{N} \gamma(z_{nk}) \tag{16}$$

Calculate the log-likelihood function, check whether the parameters converge or whether the log-likelihood function converges, and return to step 2 if it does not converge, with the following convergence conditions:

$$||\theta_{i+1} - \theta_i|| < \varepsilon \tag{17}$$

In Eq. 17: ϵ is a small positive number, indicating that the parameter changes very little after one iteration, and $\epsilon = 10$–5.

5.2 HDI Health Decline Indicator

This work based on the distribution model under the health state constructed by GMM, the distance between the state feature vector at the time of deterioration and the health benchmark model is used to judge the degree of unit deterioration, and then the prediction data of LSTM can be used to judge the unit health state prediction. The Marxist distance is used to measure the distance between the predicted excitation unit state data and the health benchmark model, which is a distance description based on the sample distribution and, unlike the Euclidean distance, is able to take into account the connection between various features [16]:

$$d_P(x) = \sqrt{(x - \mu)^T C^{-1}(x - \mu)} \tag{18}$$

where x represents a point in the multidimensional space, μ represents the mean of each data point in the distribution P, and C represents the covariance matrix between data points in the distribution P.

Assuming that the state feature vector obtained from the excitation unit prediction is x, the health decline indicator HDI [17] is defined as:

$$HDI(t) = \frac{hi(t) + hi(t-1) + \cdots + hi(t-1+m)}{m} \tag{19}$$

$$hi(t) = \ln\left(\frac{\omega_1 d_1(x) + \cdots + \omega_i d_i(x) + \cdots + \omega_K d_K(x)}{\sum_{i=1}^{K} \omega_i}\right) \tag{20}$$

where m denotes the sliding window; hi(t) belongs to the range (0, 1); K denotes the number of Gaussian distributions in the model; $d_i(x)$ is the martingale distance between the generator real-time parameter vector x and the i-th Gaussian distribution, and ω_i is the weight; the closer the current operating state is to the healthy state HDI(t) the smaller it is.

6 Healthiness Prediction

6.1 Experimental Data

To validate the health assessment model, this paper takes unit #5 of a power plant in Weihai as the object, and collects generator-related operating data from March to July

Table 1. Acquisition data type

	Directly measured quantities	Calculated state quantities
Analog quantities	Stator three-phase voltage, stator three-phase current, excitation current, excitation voltage, secondary line voltage of excitation transformer	Stator voltage RMS, stator current RMS, unit active power, unit reactive power, power factor, frequency
Temperature quantities	Infrared image of excitation variable three-phase winding, fan temperature, infrared image of carbon brush	Excitation variable three-phase winding temperature, carbon brush temperature, generator stator temperature, rotor temperature, excitation chamber temperature
Digital quantities	Circuit breaker status, demagnetization switch status, trigger signal, stator voltage TTL square wave	

2022 based on the SIS system and the infrared temperature monitoring device built on site. Based on expert experience, the selected state parameters are shown in Table 1.

For the LSTM neural network and health evaluation index, the parameters that have a large impact on the state need to be used as input parameters. Using MIC correlation analysis method for each data, carbon brush temperature was selected as the variable for correlation analysis, and correlation was calculated for each data, and the results are shown in Table 2.

According to the correlation calculation results, the variables with low MIC correlation were deleted, and five variables, namely active power, excitation current, excitation variable three-phase winding temperature, rotor temperature, and excitation chamber temperature, were selected as the inputs to the LSTM; in order to avoid the reduction of model accuracy caused by the input of redundant variables, and the effect of the same type of variables on the carbon brush temperature was similar, so one variable of each data type was selected as a parameter.

From the above-mentioned state data set of the excitation unit during normal operation, 50% of the data are randomly extracted, and combined with the results of correlation analysis, weights are assigned to each data, and a health benchmark model is established using the EM algorithm to describe the distribution of the original state space species data. Then 20% of the data are extracted, and the HDI value of all sample points relative to the health benchmark model is calculated with the HDI index designed in this work.

Figure 2 shows the HDI index of carbon brush temperature under normal operation. From the figure, it can be seen that the HDI index is basically stable within a fixed range, while the actual operation state of the unit is complex and variable, and there are differences in the selected data, resulting in the alarm threshold is not a fixed value, but a dynamic changing parameter. It is assumed that the data of HDI index obeys normal

Table 2. Data type correlation calculation results

State parameter	MIC correlation
Active power	0.913
Reactive power	0.897
Power factor	0.889
Stator voltage RMS	0.724
Stator current RMS	0.778
Excitation current	0.953
Excitation voltage	0.934
Frequency	0.445
Secondary line voltage of excitation transformer	0.632
Fan temperature	0.112
Exciter three-phase winding temperature	0.963
Carbon brush temperature	1.000
Stator temperature	0.937
Rotor temperature	0.915
Excitation chamber temperature	0.996

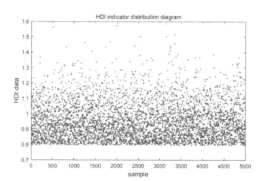

Fig. 2. HDI Indicator Distribution

distribution when the unit operates to a certain state, and the value is taken according to the 3σ principle, thus setting the dynamic alarm threshold as 1.5.

6.2 LSTM Network Prediction

A total of 5233 data from 15 days before the occurrence of the abnormality in the excitation unit is selected as the training sample for the LSTM neural network, and the data from the 16th day is predicted using multi-step prediction. Model validation is performed with the actual day 16 collection data, and the prediction error of the model is calculated.

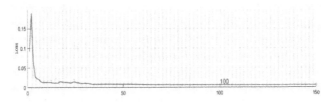

Fig. 3. LOSS curve during training

Figure 3 shows the LOSS curves during the training process, with RSME as the loss function to correct the errors, and the Loss curves gradually converge with the training iterations. The prediction process uses a point-by-point iterative calculation method, and it can be seen that the model adaptation of the generator carbon brush data is good and the model accuracy is all within the accepted range.

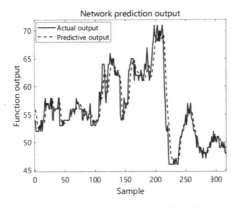

Fig. 4. Comparison graph of actual and predicted results

Figure 4 shows the temperature data of day 16 predicted by using the LSTM model. The LSTM can predict the trend of carbon brush temperature very well, even at the moment of sudden temperature change.

Figure 5 shows the percentage error in the peak time period. Most of the absolute percentage errors in the figure are at a low level value (less than 1%), especially, the LSTM model in the latter period, the percentage error is smaller, and the actual generator carbon brush temperature data matches well with the prediction, achieving a better prediction.

6.3   Results Analysis

Using the A1 carbon brush temperature data three days before the abnormal occurrence of the unit for analysis, first calculate the HDI index of the data before the abnormal

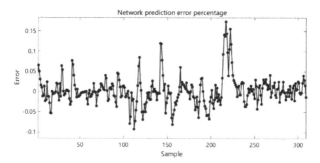

Fig. 5. Relative errors

occurrence, and then use the predicted data to calculate the HDI index. As shown in Fig. 6, The abnormal alarm point of the actual data was at 16:15 pm of the same day, and the HDI index had exceeded the set alarm threshold at 12:03 about 4 h before the abnormal point, indicating that the deterioration of the carbon brush had been detected at that time trend. The above results verified the effectiveness of this prediction algorithm and the healthiness evaluation index.

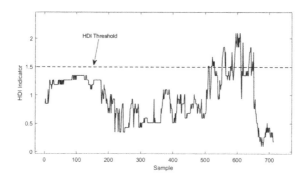

Fig. 6. HDI Health Decline Indicator Forecast

7   Conclusion

This work propose a GMM model and LSTM neural network-based method for predicting and evaluating the operational health of excitation units. The correlation analysis of monitoring variables is first conducted to determine the correlation weights of each variable; the GMM health benchmark model based on EM algorithm and the carbon brush temperature prediction model based on LSTM neural network are established based on the results of the correlation analysis; finally, the relative deterioration trend of the predicted data is analyzed based on the designed HDI health evaluation index based on the Marxian distance. The results of the practical example show that the method can reflect the unhealthy development trend of the unit in the first 4 h of abnormal occurrence, realize the prediction and evaluation of health status, evaluate the deterioration degree of the excitation unit under long-term operation, and make an early warning before the abnormal occurrence of the unit, providing a basis for regular maintenance and early identification of faults in power plants.

Funding. This work was supported by the Collaborative Innovation Center Project of Shaanxi Provincial Department of Education (Approval No. 20JY046), Xi'an City Science and Technology Plan Project (Approval No. 21XJZZ0044), and Huaneng Group Headquarters Science and Technology Project (Approval No. HNKJ21-HF175).

References

1. Zeng, S., Pecht, M.G. Wu, J.: Status and perspectives of prognostics and health management technologies. Acta Aeronautica et Astronautica Sinica (05), 626–632 (2005)
2. Dash, S., Venkatasubramnian, V.: Challenges in the industrial application of fault diagnosis systems. Comput. Chem. Eng. **24**, 785–791 (2000)
3. Wu, D.: The power electronic circuit fault diagnosis based on the neural network. Harbin University of Science and Technology (2017)
4. Xu, X.: The fault diagnosis of power unit of the excited system based on rough set theory and artificial neural network. Xi'an University Of Technology (2007)
5. Ma, M., Hou, Y., Li, Y., He, P., Qi, P., Wu, Y.: Synchronous motor rotor inter-turn short circuit fault diagnosis method based on two-dimensional CNN and multi-source electromechanical information fusion. J. North China Electr. Power Univ. (Nat. Sci. Edn.), 1–14 (2022)
6. An, W., Chen, C., Tian, M., Jin, Y., Sun, X.: Rolling bearing fault diagnosis of wind turbine under variable working conditions based on MSCNNSA-BiGRU. J. Mech. Electr. Eng. 1–9 (2022)
7. Wang, J., Yue, L., Cao, J., Ma, J.: Fault diagnosis of generator bearing based on stochastic variational inference Bayesian neural network. Control Decis. 1–8 (2022)
8. Wang, J., Zhang, J., Jiang, N., Song, N., Xin, J., et al.: Online health assessment and fault prediction for wind turbine generator. Proc. Inst. Mech. Eng. Part I: J. Syst. Control Eng. **236**(4), 718–730 (2021)
9. Li, J., Li, Q., Zhu, J.: Health condition assessment of wind turbine generators based on supervisory control and data acquisition data. IET Renew. Power Gener. **13**(8), 1343–1350 (2019)
10. Sun, Z., Sun, H.: Health status assessment for wind turbine with recurrent neural networks. Math. Probl. Eng. **2018**, 1–16 (2018)
11. Reshef, D.N., et al.: The maximal information coefficient. detecting novel associations in large data sets. Science **334**(6062), 1518–1524 (2011)
12. Barrera, D., Sales, S.: A high-temperature fiber sensor using a low cost interrogation scheme. Sensors (Basel, Switzerland) **13**(9) (2013)
13. Luo, Z., Bu, Y.: Research on price forecast method of building materials based on grey neural network PGNN model. Constr. Econ. **41**(10), 115–120 (2020)
14. Song, H., Dai, J., Luo, L., Sheng, G., Jiang, X.: Power transformer operating state prediction method based on an LSTM network. Energies **11**, 914 (2018)
15. Lei, Y., Karimi, H.R., Chen, X.: A novel self-supervised deep LSTM network for industrial temperature prediction in aluminum processes application. Neurocomputing **502**, 177–185 (2022). ISSN 0925-2312

16. Liu, Q., Zhao, H.F.: Integrated optimization of workshop layout and scheduling to reduce carbon emissions based on a multi-objective fruit fly opti-mization algorithm. J. Mech. Eng. **53**(11), 122–133 (2017)
17. Zhang, J., Li, N., Li, S., Huang, M.: Health assessment of wind-turbine generator based on data. Inf. Control **47**(06), 694–701+712–713 (2018)

Fire Detection Based on Visual Image from 2010 to 2021: A Bibliometric Analysis and Visualization

Ru Xue(✉)🆔, Jingyun Hu🆔, and Yue Liu🆔

School of Information Engineering, Xizang Minzu University, Xianyang 712082, Shaanxi, China
rxue@xzmu.edu.cn

Abstract. Fire hazards are increasing, its detection technology has been innovated and developed, which has gradually garnered attention in diverse fields. To clearly know the knowledge structure of fire detection based on visuals and learn more about its development history and currently a hot concern, this paper utilizes the bibliometric method to analyze the data from 1577 pieces of research literature from 2010 to 2021, according to the records in the WOS core collection. A bibliometric analysis of this topic employing visualization software VOSviewer and CiteSpace. Primarily, CiteSpace was used to specifically analyze the classification of disciplines, sort out scholars in related fields, introduce the current mainstream core author groups, count the articles issued by different kinds of countries and institutions, and analyze the status of each country and institution. International and domestic cooperation, analysis of the most relevant journals of image-based fire detection, the subject areas of popular journals. Comprehensive analysis through VOSviewer, keyword co-occurrence was obtained analyze, and the popular research focuses, and development trends of fire detection are discussed. Finally, multiple analyses were combined to reasonably hypothesize about the future development direction of fire detection technology.

Keywords: Bibliometric analysis · Fire detection · CiteSpace · VOSviewer · Knowledge graph

1 Introduction

The emergence of fire promotes the progress of human civilization. It brings convenience to humankind but is also accompanied by severe harm. Fire refers to a disaster caused by burning out of control in time or space, which causes more than 300,000 deaths each year and is the fourth leading cause of accidental injuries globally (after road accidents, falls, and drowning) [1]. In recent years,

Supported by the Natural Science Foundation of Xizang Autonomous Region of China, "Research on Fire Detection Method Based on Convolutional Neural Network" (No. XZ202001ZR0048G).

frequent fires around the world, such as the California fire in the US, the Daliang Mountain fire in China, and the Australian wildfire, these fires will cause a large amount of greenhouse gas emissions, which are an essential factor in aggravating global warming and air pollution, as well as destroying vegetation coverage and ecological balance [2]. Timely, accurate, and effective fire detection is an essential means to control the spread of fire and reduce fire hazards. Behind this context, a clear and systematic overview of fire detection research can help scholars to have a stronger appreciation of fire detection research [3].

Scholars have been committed to researching an effective and stable fire detection method in recent decades. The earliest fire detection method was based on sensors, which sensed the intensity, range, and temperature changes of light during the firing process to determine whether a fire occurred. This method has a long detection time and a small range. It cannot be used to alarm at the early stage of the fire, nor can it be detected in large open scenes such as forest injection [4–6]. Scholars proposed to use satellite remote sensing to monitor the fire [7–9]. Satellite remote sensing technology has the edge on a comprehensive monitoring range, low cost, fast speed, and convenience for long-term dynamic monitoring. For example, L Giglio [10] proposed an improved replacement detection algorithm. With the widespread application of video surveillance technology and the rapid development of deep learning technology, fire detection technology based on computer vision has emerged as the times require. By analyzing fire images and videos, scholars proposed fire detection based on features such as shape, texture, and color [11, 12]. As fire detection methods based on feature extraction are becoming more and more mature, convolutional neural networks (CNN) have also achieved tremendous development in image classification tasks. Scholars have applied this deep learning algorithm to the research of fire detection algorithms [13].

According to the above description, there has been much-advanced research on image-based fire detection (1577 kinds of literature). Understanding and mastering the latest advances, new trends, and research hotspots will greatly benefit readers and scholars working on this research. However, traditional review articles mainly analyze and discuss algorithms, applications, and experimental effects. They fail analyze the overall and discuss it from the macro perspective. Moreover, it does not include all the papers in a period of time, only analyzes and summarizes some of them and does not provide statistical analysis. Nowadays, the growth of computer technologies brings bibliometric studies into a new age. Bibliometric analysis can visualize the state of knowledge, evolution, and emerging trends that have been applied to various professional fields from the perspective of statistics in recent years. In order to show the overall framework of this research, this paper will provide an analysis of fire detection research using maps generated by CiteSpace [15] and VOSviewer. VOSviewer can provide detailed information about the literature, such as popular research topics. CiteSpace is a tool for researchers to display network relationships, research trends, and research priorities.

To facilitate the reader in determining whether this paper contributes to his or her research, we can summarize its contributions as follows: 1) In Sect. 3, the bibliometric analysis's results are presented in six primary areas: paper output, classification analysis, analysis of co-cited journals, analysis of national and institutional collaborations, author collaboration networks and author co-citation networks, and analysis of cited references, by analyzing these categories, it helps scholars understand potential partners, cross-disciplinary research areas, countries, institutions that can further deepen collaboration. 2) In Sect. 4: research hotspots and emerging trends are summarized based on keyword co-occurrence. It helps the reader understand an important theory or concept of image-based fire detection and understand the history and latest progress in this research area. 3) In Sect. 5: we concluded the paper and prospected the image-based fire detection technology's development, helping researchers find new research opportunities and possibilities.

2   Data Source and Processing

2.1   The Sources of Data

Search related literature from Web of Science (WoS) [16] to study the development trend of image-based fire detection technology. Flames are not the only element in most fire detection based on images, so "fire detection" and "image" are regarded as the topic limit query keywords, with unlimited research directions and languages. The period time is 2010–2021.09.11, which is more classic and real-time, and this phase is the most meaningful for the development of fire detection technology research. Which is more classic and real-time, and this phase is the most meaningful for developing fire detection technology research. Adjust the search Settings to select SCI and SSCI in the WOS core library.

We use CiteSpace to remove the same article title and DOI and finally get 1577 valid papers. Select 'Full Record and Cited References' for the content of the download record [17], and the downloaded text includes the title, abstract, author, keywords, and references [18], etc.

2.2   Research Methods

According to Jim Gray's fourth paradigm: with the rapid growth of data, computers will be able to perform simulations and analyze and summarize. Citespace [19] is a widely used tool developed by Dr. Chen Chaomei used in scientific literature to identify and display new trends and new developments in scientific development. This paper uses CiteSpace to analyzes categories, authors, countries, journals, institutions, reference bursts, and keyword clustering. VOSviewer [20] is a visualization tool used to build various relationships.

3   Analysis and Discussion

3.1   Analysis of Publication Output

The amount of scientific literature published at a specific time can measure the output capacity of the subject research and the research dynamics in the field.

In order to understand the research trends of fire detection based on images, as presented in Fig. 1, Since 2010, the number of publications on fire detection research has been steadily increasing (The orange line in Fig. 1), we can divided it into two periods about the evolution of publications, the first is from 2010 to 2017, during this period, the average number of publications per year is 109, so it is the early development stage. The second period started from 2017 to 2021. At this stage, the volume of postings accounted for more than 40% of the total volume of postings, indicating that fire detection received increasing attention. The reason may be that with the warming of the climate and the accumulation of combustible materials generated by the logging ban, the degree of fire hazards has continued to increase, such as the Australian wildfire (2019), the Liang Shan fire in China (2020) and the California fire in the United States (2021), bringing immeasurable losses and harm to the world. Therefore, the related research is gradually increasing.

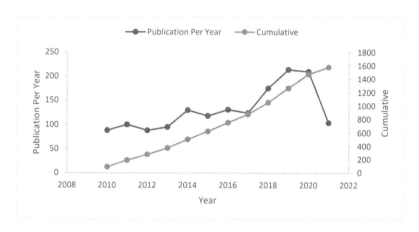

Fig. 1. The publication output of fire detection research (Color figure online)

3.2 Analysis of Categories

Analyzing the subject category of fire detection papers can reflect a specific subject's research status and development level within a given period of time. 154 subject categories were included in the fire detection literature in WoS. The top six are shown in Table 1, the top-ranked category is Engineering with citation counts of 609, the second one is Electrical and Electronic with citation counts of 431, the third is Computer Science with citation counts of 375, the 4th is Remote Sensing with citation counts of 373, the 5th is Imaging Science and Photographic Technology with citation counts of 330, the 6th is Environmental Sciences and Ecology with citation counts of 271. Subject categories's distribution showed that issues in Engineering, Electrical and Electronics, Computer Science, Remote Sensing, Imaging Science, and Environmental Sciences,

Photographic Technology, and Ecology were prioritized in research. Obviously, the research of fire detection is dominated by computer engineering disciplines, presenting an interdisciplinary phenomenon.

Table 1. Top 6 subject categories based on publication.

Rank	Subject category	Count
1	*Engineering*	609
2	*Electrical and Electronic*	431
3	*Computer Science*	375
4	*Remote Sensing* Text follows	373
5	*Imaging Sciences and Photographic Technology*	330
6	*Environmental Sciences and Ecology*	271

3.3   Analysis of Countries and Institutions

Analysis of Countries. The spatial distribution of the paper indicates the distribution of research power of the research site on a global scale, which is beneficial for scholars to study research results and conduct research cooperation [21]. The country cooperation network of fire detection research was presented in Fig. 2. Node size is positively correlated with the number of articles published, the pink outer circle represents centrality, and its thickness is proportional to the centrality value. And it can be understood that centrality represents the importance of the position occupied in the partnership, and the stronger the centrality, the more critical it is in the partnership network. The number and thickness of lines in the node are proportional to the cooperation between countries and regions.

As shown in Table 2, China produces the most academic papers, with 447 articles published in total, the second one is USA (338 articles, accounting for 21.43%), the third is India (106 articles, accounting for 6.72%), the 4th is Canada with 96 articles (accounting for 6.09%), and the 5th is South Korea (85 articles, accounting for 5.39%). It can be seen that the top ten countries have published 1437 articles in the fire detection articles studied, accounting for 91.12% of the total articles, while fire detection research from other countries accounted for 8.88%. From the perspective of centrality, the centrality of the United States, Germany, China, Australia, and Britain are all above 0.1, and they are highly relevant in international cooperation and exchanges. According to the centrality: Britain, Australia, China, Germany, USA (Sort from largest to smallest), the centrality of the US is the highest, indicating that it is vital in the international cooperation of fire detection research. In Fig. 2 that there is still a lack of cooperation among many countries. Therefore, countries should strengthen cooperation and communication.

Analysis of Institutions. Exploring the institutional characteristics in the field of fire detection can quickly understand the research pattern in this field and provide help for the integration of research resources for scientific research cooperation. As shown in Fig. 3, the top 10 most prolific publication institutions listed in Table 3. The following institutions rank among the best in this field: the Chinese Academy of Science (53 articles, centrality is 0.07, accounted for 1/4 of the number of articles published in the top ten organizations), the University of Maryland (30 articles, centrality is 0.06), Univ Sci & Technol China (21 articles, centrality is 0.02), US Forest Service (20 articles, centrality is 0.02), NASA (19 articles, centrality is 0.04), CALTECH (14 articles, centrality is 0.05), Among the top ten institutions, six were in USA, which reflects the outstanding research results of the United States in the field of fire detection. At the same time, the Chinese Academy of Science has issued many articles that show that it plays a pivotal role in fire detection research. In Fig. 3 that the cooperation between institutions has obvious limitations. There is a language barrier between countries, so there is less interaction and communication, and cooperation between institutions is more between countries. Strengthening international cooperation can lead to the sharing of research results. Therefore, international cooperation and communication between institutions should be strengthened.

Table 2. Top 10 countries based on publications.

Rank	Country	Publications	% of papers	Centrality
1	China	447	28.34%	0.18
2	USA	338	21.43%	0.39
3	India	106	6.72%	0.06
4	Canada	96	6.09%	0.06
5	South Korea	85	5.39%	0.05
6	Germany	83	5.26%	0.26
7	Italy	74	4.69%	0.06
8	Spain	72	4.57%	0.05
9	Britain	70	4.44%	0.13
10	Australia	66	4.19%	0.15

3.4   Analysis of Cited Journals

According to Bradford's law, a large number of articles on a particular subject will appear in a small number of high-quality journals, and the remaining articles will be unevenly presented in different journals. The statistical analysis of cited journals in Fig. 4, we can know the prominent output journals of current fire detection research. As indicated in Table 4, the top-ranked journal by citation

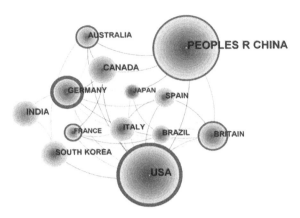

Fig. 2. The visualization map of countries participating in fire detection

counts is REMOTE SENS ENVIRON with citation counts of 494. The second one is INT J REMOTE SENS with citation counts of 412, and the third is IEEE T GEOSCI REMOTE with citation counts of 365. These journals play a key role in the research of fire detection and are the most important source of information for relevant scholars in fire science research to refer to the scientific and technological literature in this field. The h-index and citescore are essential indicators for evaluating the influence of a journal. SCIENCE has the highest h-index (1058), reflecting the biggest influence on fire detection. Analyze the subject type of the journal, remote sensing journals pay more attention to fire detection. The reason is that remote sensing technology has the advantages of dynamic real-time, update speed block, large coverage area, etc. It can detect and locate fires quickly and accurately and has an extensive application value in fire detection.

Table 3. Top 10 institutions based on publications.

Rank	Institution	Publications	Centrality	Country
1	Chinese Acad Sci	53	0.07	China
2	Univ Maryland	30	0.06	USA
3	Univ Sci & Technol China	21	0.02	China
4	US Forest Serv	20	0.02	USA
5	NASA	19	0.04	USA
6	CALTECH	14	0.05	USA
7	NOAA	14	0.02	USA
8	Concordia Uni	14	0	Canada
9	South Dakota State Uni	12	0	USA
10	Indian Inst Technol	12	0	India

Table 4. Top 7 productive journals in fire detection research: 2010–2021.

Rank	Journal	Pa	IF	CiteScore	Subject
1	REMOTE SENS ENVIRON	494	13.850	17.60	Environmental science, remote sensing
2	INT J REMOTE SENS	412	3.531	5.90	Engineering Technology, remote sensing
3	IEEE T GEOSCI REMOTE	365	8.125	8.50	Electronics and Electrical, remote sensing
4	FIRE SAFETY J	319	3.780	5.00	Civil engineering
5	REMOTE SENS-BASEL	279	5.349	6.60	Remote sensing
6	SCIENCE	276	63.714	46.8	Comprehensive
7	PATTERN RECOGN LETT	260	4.757	6.70	Computer science

Note: CiteScore: The total number of citations of papers published in the previous 3 years of the journal divided by the total number of papers published in the previous 3 years; Pa: the total publications of a journal in fire detection.

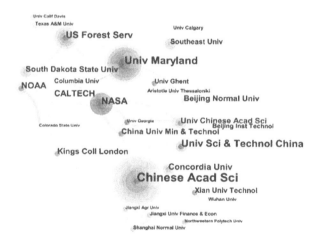

Fig. 3. The visualization map of institutions participating in fire detection

3.5   Analysis of Author and Cited Author

Analysis of Author. Doing research on authors with a large number of articles in a specific field can know their research ability and the critical role of an academic field. Use CiteSpace to draw the authors of the knowledge map of fire detection research as shown in Fig. 5, the circular nodes of different colors represent the author's different posting time, the radius of the node indicates

Fig. 4. The visualization map of journals in fire detection

the amount of the author's posting. In the author's map, we can see that the distribution of nodes is relatively scattered, but there are still scholars such as Youmin Zhang, Yongming Zhang, and Khan Muhammad at the center. Table 5 lists the ten authors and their affiliates who have published the most articles in the past twelve years. It can be seen that these author cooperation groups are all from the same institution. According to their publications, the top-ranked author by publication counts is Youmin Zhang (13 articles), followed by Yongming Zhang (12 articles) and Khan Muhammad (8 articles). As shown in Table 5, the author group centered on Youmin Zhang is all from Concordia University Montreal. They applied vision system-based unmanned aerial vehicles (UAVs) with fast maneuverability and a larger operating range to forest fire detection and introduced technologies including diagnosis and prediction, UAVs fire detection, image vibration elimination, and collaborative control [22–24]. Yongming Zhang proposed a module for real-time smoke detection. The method uses gray-level co-occurrence matrix-based texture analysis to distinguish smoke features

Table 5. Top 10 most productive authors in fire detection research.

Rank	Publications	Author	Year	Institution	Country
1	13	YOUMIN ZHANG	2015	Concordia University Montreal	Canada
2	12	YONGMING ZHANG	2010	University of Science and Technology	China
3	8	EMILIO CHUVIECO	2018	Universidad de Alcalá	Spain
4	8	CHI YUAN	2015	Concordia University Montreal	Canada
5	8	KHAN MUHAMMAD	2018	Sejong University	South Korea
6	7	XIAOBO LU	2018	Southeast University	China
7	7	SUNG WOOK BAIK	2018	Sejong University	South Korea
8	6	ZHIXIANG LIU	2015	Concordia University Montreal	Canada
9	6	JINJUN WANG	2010	University of Science and Technology	China
10	6	A ENIS CETIN	2010	Bilkent University	Ankara

Fig. 5. The visualization map of authors participating in fire detection

from other non-fire interference and then uses block processing technology to calculate texture features for each image to achieve the purpose of real-time fire detection [25]. KHAN MUHAMM proposed a dynamic channel selection algorithm for cameras based on cognitive radio networks to ensure reliable data dissemination [26].

Analysis of Co-cited Authors. Author co-citation is a crucial method to reveal the relationship between authors and the knowledge structure of the research field. Figure 6 shows the author's co-cited visualization. Table 6 lists the ten most frequently cited authors ('frequency' here refers to the citation frequencies of the 1577 papers we analyzed). The top-cited author was Toreyin BU with frequency 244, who modeled flame detection using flame features, his most cited articles [27] proposed a module for real-time fire detection by processing video data generated. The second was Giglio L with frequency 229, who uses MODIS for fire observation. His most cited article presented an automated method that uses 500-meter Moderate Resolution Imaging Spectrometer (MODIS) images combined with 1 km of MODIS active fire observations to map burning areas [28]. The third was Celik T, who modeled fire detection in different color channels. He proposed a rule-based general color model for flame pixel classification. Real time fire detection using this model in color video sequences [11]. The fourth was Chen T, who used a smoke detection system, he used two decision rules in his top cited paper: a diffusion-based dynamic characteristic decision rule and a chromaticity-based static decision rule [29]. Then, the following authors were Van D, Ko BC, Roy D, Schroeder W, Yuan F, and Chuvieco E [7,30–34].

Fig. 6. The visualization map of cited authors participating in fire detection

Table 6. Top 10 cited authors and their cited articles.

Rank	Author	Frequency	Year	Cited Articles
1	Toreyin B	244	2006	Computer vision based method for real-time fire and flame detection
2	Giglio L	229	2009	An active-fire based burned area mapping algorithm for the MODIS sensor
3	Celik T	208	2009	Fire detection in video sequences using a generic color model
4	Chen T	199	2006	The Smoke Detection for Early Fire-Alarming System Base on Video Processing
5	Van D	137	2010	Global fire emissions and the contribution of deforestation, savanna,forest, agricultural, and peat fires (1997–2009)
6	Ko B	133	2009	Fire detection based on vision sensor and support vector machines
7	Roy D	131	2008	The collection 5 MODIS burned area product — Global evaluation by comparison with the MODIS active fire product
8	Schroeder W	124	2008	Validation of GOES and MODIS active fire detection products using ASTER and ETM+ data
9	Yuan F	116	2008	A fast accumulative motion orientation model based on integral image for video smoke detection
10	Chuvieco E	114	2010	Development of a framework for fire risk assessment using remote sensing and geographic information system technologies

3.6 Analysis of Reference

In certain period, burst detection can be used to detect emergencies and research focus. Figure 7 showed the top 25 strongest references detected by CiteSpace from 2010 to 2021. The blue part represented the time interval from 2010 to 2021.

Burst detection can be divided into three stages: In the first period (2010), The paper written by Celik T contains three largest citation bursts (15.97), Ko BC (15.05), Toreyin BU (14.91). They are also the top 10 most cited authors in fire detection research. Celik T's paper burst began in 2010 and ended up in 2014. He proposed a generic color model and applied the model to color video sequences for real-time fire detection [11] Ko BC's paper burst began in 2010 and ended in 2014 too. He combined visual sensors with support vector machines (SVM) and used machine learning to study fire detection [31]. Toreyin BU applied wavelet transform to fire detection [27], the paper broke out in 2010 and ended up in 2011. Papers in this period primarily used traditional methods for fire detection analysis, such as color model, sensor detection, spectrum, spatial and temporal characteristics, etc. In the second period (2011–2016), enormous citation burst strengths originated from a paper written by Schroeder W. The burst from 2015 to 2019. He proposed a new VIIRS active fire detection algorithm [35]. In the third period (2017–2019), the largest citation burst strengths originated from the paper written by Muhammad K (8.36). Muhammad K proposed surveillance video fire detection based on a cnn and verified the applicability of CNN in CCTV surveillance systems [36]. It is worth noting that the most extended citation frequency in these documents is five years, and the shortest is two years. The reason is that those deep learning methods have the advantages of high efficiency and visualization, which can significantly improve the efficiency of fire detection.

Table 7 listed the top 10 references by frequency. References can not only reflect the academic succession relationship of the paper but also reflect the connotation and value of the paper itself. Researching cited references can help scholars understand the internal connections between authors in related fields. The most cited reference in fire detection research was Giglio L, 'The collection 6 MODIS active fire detection algorithm and fire products' [37], Giglio L was

Top 25 References with the Strongest Citation Bursts

References	Year	Strength	Begin	End	2010 - 2021
Celik T, 2009, FIRE SAFETY J, V44, P147, DOI 10.1016/j.firesaf.2008.05.005, DOI	2009	15.97	2010	2014	
Ko BC, 2009, FIRE SAFETY J, V44, P322, DOI 10.1016/j.firesaf.2008.07.006, DOI	2009	15.05	2010	2014	
Toreyin BU, 2006, PATTERN RECOGN LETT, V27, P49, DOI 10.1016/j.patrec.2005.06.015, DOI	2006	14.91	2010	2011	
Yuan F, 2008, PATTERN RECOGN LETT, V29, P925, DOI 10.1016/j.patrec.2008.01.013, DOI	2008	11.65	2010	2013	
Ho CC, 2009, MEAS SCI TECHNOL, V20, P0, DOI 10.1088/0957-0233/20/4/045502, DOI	2009	9.1	2010	2013	
Celik T, 2007, J VIS COMMUN IMAGE R, V18, P176, DOI 10.1016/j.jvcir.2006.12.003, DOI	2007	8.86	2010	2012	
Giglio L, 2009, REMOTE SENS ENVIRON, V113, P408, DOI 10.1016/j.rse.2008.10.006, DOI	2009	8.17	2010	2014	
Schroeder W, 2008, REMOTE SENS ENVIRON, V112, P2711, DOI 10.1016/j.rse.2008.01.005, DOI	2008	8.81	2011	2013	
Roy DP, 2008, REMOTE SENS ENVIRON, V112, P3690, DOI 10.1016/j.rse.2008.05.013, DOI	2008	8.81	2011	2013	
Chen J, 2010, BUILD ENVIRON, V45, P1113, DOI 10.1016/j.buildenv.2009.10.017, DOI	2010	7.27	2011	2015	
Celik T, 2010, ETRI J, V32, P881, DOI 10.4218/etrij.10.0109.0695, DOI	2010	8.83	2013	2015	
Bastarrika A, 2011, REMOTE SENS ENVIRON, V115, P1003, DOI 10.1016/j.rse.2010.12.005, DOI	2011	7.17	2013	2015	
Hansen MC, 2013, SCIENCE, V342, P850	2013	6.79	2014	2018	
Huang CQ, 2010, REMOTE SENS ENVIRON, V114, P183, DOI 10.1016/j.rse.2009.08.017, DOI	2010	6.59	2014	2015	
Schroeder W, 2014, REMOTE SENS ENVIRON, V143, P85, DOI 10.1016/j.rse.2013.12.008, DOI	2014	13.96	2015	2019	
Cetin AE, 2013, DIGIT SIGNAL PROCESS, V23, P1827, DOI 10.1016/j.dsp.2013.07.003, DOI	2013	11.96	2015	2018	
Mouillot F, 2014, INT J APPL EARTH OBS, V26, P64, DOI 10.1016/j.jag.2013.05.014, DOI	2014	6.61	2016	2019	
Giglio L, 2013, J GEOPHYS RES-BIOGEO, V118, P317, DOI 10.1002/jgrg.20042, DOI	2013	7.55	2017	2018	
Krizhevsky A, 2017, COMMUN ACM, V60, P84, DOI 10.1145/3065386, DOI	2017	7.13	2017	2019	
Simonyan K, 2014, INT C LEARN REPR, V0, P0	2014	7.76	2018	2019	
Giglio L, 2018, REMOTE SENS ENVIRON, V217, P72, DOI 10.1016/j.rse.2018.08.005, DOI	2018	8.74	2019	2021	
Muhammad K, 2018, IEEE ACCESS, V6, P18174, DOI 10.1109/ACCESS.2018.2812835, DOI	2018	8.36	2019	2021	
Yin ZJ, 2017, IEEE ACCESS, V5, P18429, DOI 10.1109/ACCESS.2017.2747399, DOI	2017	7.74	2019	2021	
Muhammad K, 2018, NEUROCOMPUTING, V288, P30, DOI 10.1016/j.neucom.2017.04.083, DOI	2018	6.71	2019	2021	
Frizzi S, 2016, IEEE IND ELEC, V0, P877, DOI 10.1109/IECON.2016.7793196, DOI	2016	6.69	2019	2021	

Fig. 7. The 25 references with the strongest citation bursts

also the top-cited author in Table 6. Remote Sensing of Environment was one of the top 5 productive journals in fire detection research in Table 4.

4   High Frequency Keywords and Trend Analysis

4.1   High Frequency Keywords

The high-frequency keywords are the core and essence of the article. The visual analysis can reflect the research's academic hotspot and development trend to a certain extent. This paper uses VOSviwer to build a keyword co-occurrence network, including the main areas of fire detection. In the map, Each color represents a different cluster, the frequency of keywords is positively related to the size of circle and the tightness of lines. Since there are 6460 keywords in total, the interface nodes are too crowded for all visualization. Therefore, the number of keyword occurrences was set to 13, and the top 103 keywords were selected for visual.

Table 7. Top 10 cited reference in fire detection.

Rank	Reference	Published	Year	Author	Frequency	Burst
1	The collection 6 MODIS active fire detection algorithm and fire products	Remote Sensing of Environment	2016	Giglio L	51	3.36
2	The New VIIRS 375 m active fire detection data product: Algorithm description and initial assessment	Remote Sensing of Environment	2014	Schroeder W	54	13.96
3	Convolutional neural network for video fire and smoke detection	IECON 2016 - 42nd Annual Conference of the IEEE Industrial Electronics Society	2016	Frizzi S	50	6.69
4	Active fire detection using Landsat-8/OLI data	Remote Sensing of Environment	2016	Schroeder W	42	5.30
5	Convolutional Neural Networks Based Fire Detection in Surveillance Videos	IEEE Access	2018	Muhammad K	41	8.36
6	A Deep Normalization and Convolutional Neural Network for Image Smoke Detection	IEEE Access	2017	Yin ZJ	38	7.71
7	Real-Time Fire Detection for Video-Surveillance Applications Using a Combination of Experts Based on Color, Shape, and Motion	IEEE Transactions on Circuits and Systems for Video Technology	2015	Foggia P	36	5.66
8	Spatio-Temporal Flame Modeling and Dynamic Texture Analysis for Automatic Video-Based Fire Detection	IEEE T CIRC SYST VID	2011	Dimitropoulos K	35	5.95
9	Early Fire Detection using Convolutional Neural Networks during Surveillance for Effective Disaster Management	Neurocomputing	2017	Khan Muhammad	33	6.71
10	The Collection 6 MODIS burned area mapping algorithm and product	Remote Sensing of Environment	2018	Giglio L	32	8.74

The visualization results are in Fig. 8, fire detection research comprises three clusters. According to the characteristics and current situation of fire detection research, the three clusters can be reduced as follows: cluster1 Algorithm improvement of fire detection (red); cluster2 the law and prevention of fire (green); cluster3 Fire area management (blue).

Cluster1 (red); The red cluster is the largest, and the largest node is fire-detection, which links 43 related keywords such as smoke detection, deep learning, model, image, and flame detection. This cluster mainly reflects fire detection methods and related image processing and recognition technologies.

Cluster2 (green); The largest node is remote sensing, mainly involving 35 keywords such as change detection, vegetation, classification, landsat, forest, and climate change. This cluster focuses on the state of fire and the loss and harm caused to the environment, ecology, and vegetation.

Cluster3 (blue): The most important node is MODIS. Associated with 19 keywords, including algorithm, validation, emission, detection algorithm, and temperature. This group mainly focuses on the cause of the fire.

Three different core clusters connect different keywords and diverge from different directions to analyze the development of image-based fire detection techniques in different fields. Includes developments in fire detection techniques, fire loss and damage, and fire characteristics. Fire damage is great and irreversible and the characteristics of fire is the focus of the development of fire detection technology, so that these three clusters form a complete fire detection technology development chain.

As shown in Fig. 8, the three clusters have different emphases and keywords. Figure 9 and Fig. 10 show the main keywords related to each other among the three clusters. In Fig. 9, the fires node in the red cluster is the core node of three cluster connectivity, fires connected to the fire-detection of the red cluster, the blue cluster of algorithm, MODIS, and the remote sensing of the green cluster, the blue cluster's MODIS and algorithm are associated with the green cluster's remote sensing and the red cluster's model. From the above analysis, it can be concluded that the keywords of the interconnection of the three clusters are mainly MODIS, fires, remote sensing, and algorithm.

Fig. 8. Network visualization map based on fire detection (Color figure online)

Fig. 9. Network part contact diagram1 (Color figure online)

Table 8. Top20 keyword of fire detection research based on the occurrence.

Rank	Keyword	Occurrence	Total link strength
1	Fire-detection	239	579
2	Fires	160	543
3	MODIS	124	548
4	Images	121	393
5	Algorithms	107	425
6	Remote sensing	101	348
7	Classification	85	285
8	Image processing	80	147
9	Smoke detection	76	211
10	Forest fires	75	227
11	Time-series	73	383
12	Wildfires	72	313
13	Convolutional neural network	70	254
14	Vegetation	67	310
15	Deep learning	66	220
16	Model	66	216
17	Change detection	61	224
18	Landsat	57	244
19	Validation	57	291
20	Flam dete	56	179

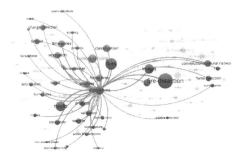

Fig. 10. Network part contact diagram2 (Color figure online)

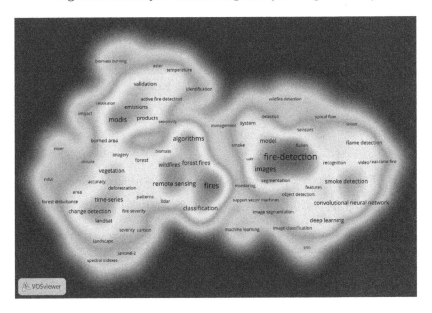

Fig. 11. Density visualization map based on fire detection

Figure 11 shows the keyword density view of fire detection, combined with Table 8 to explore the hot topics of fire detection. As shown in Table 8, The highest frequency of fire-detection is 239 times, with a total link strength of 579, followed by fires 160 total connections to 543, and the third item is MODIS 124 total contact strength of 548, which is later images, algorithms, remote sensing and so on.

The keywords selected when screening the literature are "fire-detection" and "images," so when all keywords are presented together, "fire-detection," "fires," "images" appear more often, and when selecting keyword analysis, we think about the divergence and penetration of image-based fire detection in other fields, so we choose MODIS, Remote sensing, algorithms for analysis, which appears less frequently but has more research significance.

4.2   High-Frequency Keyword Analysis

MODIS. MODIS, short for Moderate-Resolution Imaging Spectroradiometer, is a large space remote sensing instrument designed and manufactured by NASA [38]. A wide range of dynamic data can be calculated through spectral wavelength and frequency analysis [39], including changes in the atmosphere, changes in cloud cover, changes in the earth's radiation energy, and dynamic changes in the earth's surface. It is the only satellite-borne remote sensing instrument that can receive data and use it free of charge and broadcast real-time observation data to the world through the x-band [40]. Due to the emergence of MODIS, people have a higher utilization rate of image collection data in complex environments. Based on the availability of this collection data, image-based fire detection algorithms have been further improved.

As early as 2003, Giglio L proposed an improved algorithm based on the original MODIS active fire detection algorithm [33], which significantly reduced the false alarm rate [10]. MODIS data has the characteristics of complimentary, broad-spectrum, simple data reception, and high update frequency. In particular, real-time observations of the earth are of great practical value. Therefore, the proposed alternative detection algorithm makes fire detection technology has a broader development prospect.

Remote Sensing. The term "remote sensing" was coined by Evelyn of the BUREAU of Naval Research. Pruitt (Evelyn. L. Pruitt, 1960) refers to the non-contact, remote detection technology [12]. Generally refers to the use of sensors/remote sensors to detect the object's electromagnetic wave radiation and reflection characteristics through the remote sensor, such as an electromagnetic wave sensitive instrument, far away from the target and in non-contact with the target object under the condition of detecting the target object. Remote sensing technology Remote sensing can quickly observe the earth from the sky or even the space and obtain valuable remote sensing data [41,42]. With the support of MODIS and satellite equipment, the acquisition of remote sensing images has become easier than before, which has promoted the development of remote sensing technology in image processing, especially because real-time mapping can use remote sensing technology to detect many changes in the earth. Use it to prevent and control various natural disasters [43].

Fires are the most common and naturally occurring natural disasters that can be monitored and controlled by remote sensing technology. Fire will bring serious harm to the environment and ecosystem [44]. In addition to the damage to people and society, the damage to forest vegetation is irreversible [45] by applying remote sensing technology in image processing to prevent fire danger, promptly protect the environment and ecology, and reduce people's property losses.

Nowadays, image processing technology and remote sensing technology complement each other. For fire detection in a complex environment, the support of remote sensing image data and technology development is indispensable. Therefore, acquiring remote sensing data and developing remote sensing technology in image processing is vital for fire detection in a complex environment.

Algorithm. In mathematics (arithmetic) and computer science, an algorithm is a sequence of specific calculation steps defined for any definition and is often used in calculations, data processing, and automatic reasoning. In the field of fire detection, according to the different characteristics of flame, the detection algorithm includes four kinds of detection and recognition methods: flame color feature, motion feature, geometric feature, and texture feature.

The detection algorithm of the color characteristics of flame: flame has unique color characteristics. According to the different burning substances and burning degrees, the flame color is mainly distributed between red and orange to yellow and white. Most of these algorithms identify the flame by building a color resolution model to achieve the goal of fire detection.

The detection algorithm of the movement characteristics of the flame: Therefore, most of these algorithms pay attention to the dynamic changes of the flame when the flame is continuously burning in the fire video. Due to the fluidity of the air, the contour of the flame will change when it is burning, which has a jitter characteristic, and the flame is burning [46,47]. The scope will continue to expand. This type of algorithm achieves the purpose of identifying flames by monitoring changes in flame combustion.

The detection algorithm of the geometric characteristics of flame: the flame contour is unique. This algorithm mainly detects or extracts the flame contour edge to distinguish whether there is a flame in the image [48].

The detection algorithm of flame texture feature: flame texture feature refers to the flame with different characteristics in color space distribution and combination from background color similarity, the difference of texture. Most of these algorithms focus on the distribution characteristics of flame in color space, analyze the correlation between each pixel globally [49], and realize flame recognition.

Through the analysis of keywords co-occurrence network view, it can deepen the understanding of available data sources of fire detection, improve the current cognitive level of fire detection technology, have a more comprehensive view of flame characteristics and fire detection methods, and generally broaden the overall understanding of fire detection technology.

4.3   Popular Trend Analysis

Overlay the time axis in the visualization, and the size of the circle is positively related to the keyword weight, from which the change of keyword timing can be analyzed to infer the development process of fire detection technology.

Figure 12 has a timeline for Overlay visualization in the lower right corner, with the default color mapping of score values by average year of the keyword. From blue to yellow, the lighter the color, the more recent the keyword appeared. The timeline shows the keywords from 2016 to 2018. In the analysis of the trend of the time, more consideration of fire detection technology keywords in the change of time to deduce and explain the development trend of this research. In the figure, the most prominent keywords in the early 2016 years are remote

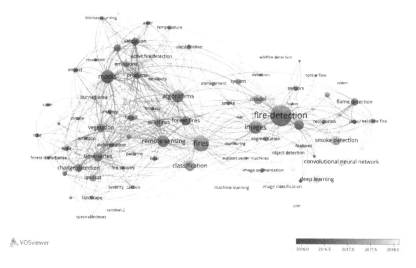

Fig. 12. Overlay visualization map based on fire detection (Color figure online)

sensing, image processing, and MODIS. It shows that the fire detection technology is now in the stage of combining remote sensing technology and image processing [50]. The fire detection technology in this stage mainly relies on the remote sensing image returned by satellite data to recognize the flame through the color characteristics and spectral frequency [51].

From 2017 to 2018, smoke detection and feature extraction keywords appeared [52]. Under normal circumstances, fires are accompanied by smoke, indicating that fire detection considers the identification of flames and gradually combines the characteristics of smoke [53], indicating that the details of fire detection are gradually changing.

The most prominent thing is that the most significant keyword change in 2018 is the convolutional neural network and deep learning [54], which indicates that fire detection technology has entered a new stage. The emergence of a convolutional neural network has achieved rapid development in computer vision. Its emergence makes image processing technology enter a new stage, and image-based fire detection has also received more attention and the extension of related applications. It starts to use deep learning models to continuously perform feature extraction and accumulation through convolutional neural networks through multiple channels [55]. Supported by today's mighty computing power, it dramatically improves the accuracy of fire image recognition and detection.

It can be seen from the change of keywords that fire detection technology has gradually changed its development focus from sensor-dependent hardware systems to algorithm-based image detection technology with the development of graphics and image technology during this decade. In addition to the shift of the center of gravity of fire detection technology, MOIDS, and Remote Sensing still account for a large proportion of fire detection technology from the node size and frequency. From the perspective of feasibility, the combined application of remote sensing image and deep learning model not only solves the problem of low accuracy of fire detection of remote sensing image in traditional image processing but also makes up the shortcoming of deep learning model requiring extensive image data in training. Therefore, it is reasonable to speculate that the future development direction of fire detection technology is to take a large number of remote sensing images as data sets, use a deep learning model for training and then predict the fire. Given many parameters in the deep learning model, the later development may focus on optimizing various models to make them more suitable for the fire field or put forward a more suitable cnn model for fire detection rely on the characteristics of flames.

5   Discussion and Future Direction

This paper systematically and intuitively summarizes the current research status of fire detection. This bibliometric study analyzes 1577 valid papers on fire detection in the WoS core corpus from 2010 to 2021. Since 2017, fire detection papers have seen a significant increase, indicating that fire detection has gradually received attention from various fields.

From the perspective of discipline analysis, engineering, electrical and electronics, computer science, remote sensing, and other disciplines are all involved, indicating that fire detection has interdisciplinary characteristics. From the perspective of national and institutional analysis and cooperation, China is the primary source country, followed by the United States, India, and Canada, which shows China's concern in fire detection. Among them, the Chinese Academy of Sciences has published many articles. The US has the highest centrality. Among the top ten institutions, the United States has six, which reflects the importance of the US in international cooperation.

Through author analysis, it is found that many authors tend to cooperate in small groups, forming several main author groups centered on Zhang Youmin, Zhang Yongming, and Muhammad Khan. The most productive author is Zhang Youmin, who proposed the application of unmanned aerial vehicles (UAVs) based on a vision system to enable fire detection with greater mobility and a more comprehensive range of forest fire detection. The top-cited author was Toreyin BU, who modeled flame detection using flame features. From the author analysis and co-cited author analysis, it can be seen that with the development of image technology, researchers continue to expand image-based fire detection technology, and more and more researchers devote themselves to this research field.

According to the analysis of cited journals, the journal REMOTE SENS ENVIRON is the most influential journal with 510 citation counts, and the subject is classified as Environmental science. Indicating that fire damage to the natural environment cannot be ignored, the progress in fire detection technology maintains the natural environment also plays a crucial role.

Use VOSviewer to analyze the fire detection literature to research hotspots and hot topics. The high-frequency vocabulary is mainly MODIS, remote sensing, algorithm, reflecting the excellent application of fire detection technology in remote sensing image data and the algorithms in image processing. Through the analysis of hot topics, it can be found that the focus of fire detection technology is gradually shifting to the algorithm of image technology. You can observe the development trend of fire detection in image processing through the overlay view. We focused on collecting fire data and detecting and recognizing flames from the beginning. However, with the development of image processing technology and the emergence of deep learning, fire detection technology gradually shifted its focus to algorithms. The algorithm has subsequently become the latest critical hot word. In summary, this paper uses CiteSpace and VOSviewer to systematically and comprehensively analyze the data of fire detection research articles from 2010 to 2021. It has a more in-depth study of fire detection.

The above multiple data analysis shows that image-based fire detection has attracted more and more attention in various fields. Image-based fire detection technology has obtained image data through MODIS equipment from the early days. Based on image data, researchers in various fields are available, and relevant detection algorithms are proposed. After developing remote sensing technology, it can be combined with image processing technology to realize fire detection.

With the proposal and development of computer hardware, deep learning models are supported by mighty computing power, which significantly improves image recognition accuracy. More mature image recognition algorithms and models are used for fire detection, especially in complex environments (remote sensing images). Previous image recognition algorithms have high false detection rates and low accuracy rates. The emergence of deep learning has made up for this aspect to a certain extent. At the same time, because of the unique environmental factors of fire detection, the use of remote sensing data is essential. In summary, the image-based fire detection technology will be used in the two directions of deep learning and remote sensing technology simultaneous development.

Based on the above analysis, this paper predicts the main development points in the field of fire detection in the future as follows:

1) In the fire warning and monitoring system, reasonable planning and layout are carried out at different levels, and specific detection methods are set for different scopes, different regions and different types of fires. Using satellite remote sensing, satellite communication, satellite navigation and other space technologies to prevent national fires; Using satellite communications to detect, locate and direct large-scale fires across the country in a timely manner; In critical areas (forest wildfires), use air patrol and Internet of Things etc. Monitoring technology can prevent and extinguish fires. For example, the identification of MODIS burn area products is often limited by the accuracy and timeliness of satellite remote sensing images. Based on the existing technology, this product improves the algorithm and combines the fire detection data with the application analysis technology (cloud computing, big data). Combined with artificial intelligence, a fire early warning and detection sys-

tem integrating fire occurrence mechanism, fire spread analysis, disaster loss and post-disaster recovery is built. Give full play to the role of new technology in fire warning and monitoring.

2) Improve the existing deep learning model and apply it to the field of fire detection: Deep learning [56] has made great progress in the field of object detection and semantic segmentation [57]. However, compared with object recognition, flame detection [58] has the following difficulties: because the flame has no obvious outline, different color sizes have different characteristics, and different environments have different flame characteristics. The accuracy of the model is affected by the fire scenario, so there is no universal fire detection model suitable for different scene fire detection. However, in the area of semantic segmentation, data sets are lacking. Manual labeling of data sets is troublesome [59], and the accuracy of data set labeling is not high. Considering that existing mature models have their own professional fields, the detection effect is the best in the original field [60]. However, when applied to the field of fire detection, the original accuracy cannot be reached. Therefore, in order to solve these problems, the existing model is improved and applied to fire detection, or specific fire detection models and algorithms are proposed, such as designing a unique feature extraction network structure and detection network according to the texture and color features of the flame, which is different from the general target detection or semantic segmentation model [62]. A fire detection model with specific characteristics is proposed [61], which is also one of the development directions of fire detection.

Meanwhile, deep learning model can be combined with remote sensing image, and remote sensing equipment can obtain a large amount of fire data [63]. The fault target in aerial images of remote sensing data is too small or the image accuracy is too low, so it is difficult to obtain a high recognition accuracy only by image processing technology. Remote sensing data sets and deep learning can achieve higher precision and accuracy through several rounds of training. Meanwhile, the deep learning model requires a large number of training data sets [64]. Therefore, for a large number of data sets, remote sensing technology can be relied on to obtain higher detection accuracy through deep learning algorithm.

In sum, CiteSpace is used to analyze the most influential authors, journals, cities, and countries in the field of fire detection. VosViewer is used to analyze the hot development direction of fire detection technology through keywords. Finally, the future development of fire detection technology is analyzed and speculated.

References

1. John, T., Nicola, C., James, H.: Improved methods for fire risk assessment in low-income and informal settlements. Int. J. Environ. Res. Public Health **14**(2), 139 (2017)
2. Brehme, C.S., Clark, D.R., Rochester, C.J., Fisher, R.N.: Wildfires alter rodent community structure across four vegetation types in southern California, USA. Fire Ecol. **7**(2), 81–98 (2011). https://doi.org/10.4996/fireecology.0702081

3. Xia, X., Yuan, F., Zhang, L.: From traditional methods to deep ones: review of visual smoke recognition, detection, and segmentation. J. Image Graph. **24**(10), 1627–1647 (2019)
4. Yu, L., Wang, N., Meng, X.: Real-time forest fire detection with wireless sensor networks. In: International Conference on Wireless Communications, vol. 2, pp. 1214–1217 (2005). https://doi.org/10.1109/WCNM.2005.1544272
5. Gutmacher, D., Hoefer, U., Woellenstein, J.: Gas sensor technologies for fire detection. Sens. Actuators, B Chem. **175**, 40–45 (2012)
6. Islam, T., Rahman, H., Syrus, M.A.: Fire detection system with indoor localization using ZigBee based wireless sensor network. In: International Conference on Informatics (2015)
7. Schroeder, W., Prins, E., Giglio, L.: Validation of GOES and MODIS active fire detection products using ASTER and ETM+ data. Remote Sens. Environ. **112**(5), 2711–2726 (2008)
8. Csiszar, I.A., Morisette, J.T., Giglio, L.: Validation of active fire detection from moderate-resolution satellite sensors: the MODIS example in northern Eurasia. IEEE Trans. Geosci. Remote Sens. **44**(7), 1757–1764 (2006)
9. Giglio, L., Schroeder, W., Justice, C.O.: The collection 6 MODIS active fire detection algorithm and fire products. Remote Sens. Environ. **178**, 31–41 (2016)
10. Giglio, L., Descloitre, J., Justice, C.O.: An enhanced contextual fire detection algorithm for MODIS. Remote Sens. Environ. **87**(2–3), 273–282 (2003)
11. Celik, T., Demirel, H.: Fire detection in video sequences using a generic color model. Fire Saf. J. **44**(2), 147–158 (2009)
12. Foggia, P., Saggese, A., Vento, M.: Real-time fire detection for video-surveillance applications using a combination of experts based on color, shape, and motion. IEEE Trans. Circ. Syst. Video Technol. **25**(9), 1545–1556 (2015)
13. Sharma, A., Kumar, H., Mittal, K.: IoT and deep learning-inspired multi-model framework for monitoring Active Fire Locations in Agricultural Activities. Comput. Electr. Eng. **93**, 107216 (2021)
14. Tian, Z., Wang, Y., Lu, J.: Bibliometric analysis of publication hot topics of smartphones in the field of health and medical services. Sci. J. Public Health **10**(3), 134–141 (2022)
15. Yi, C., Jian, M., Liu, Y.: Knowledge mapping of social commerce research: a visual analysis using CiteSpace. Electron. Commer. Res. **18**(4), 837–868 (2018). https://doi.org/10.1007/s10660-018-9288-9
16. Boyack, K., Klavans, R., Börner, K.: Mapping the backbone of science. Scientometrics **64**(3), 351–374 (2005). https://doi.org/10.1007/s11192-005-0255-6
17. Li, J., Hale, A.: Identification of, and knowledge communication among core safety science journals. Saf. Sci. **74**, 70–78 (2015)
18. Van Nunen, K., Li, J., Reniers, G.: Bibliometric analysis of safety culture research. Saf. Sci. **108**, 248–258 (2017)
19. Chen, X., Xie, H., Li, Z.: Topic analysis and development in knowledge graph research: a bibliometric review on three decades. Neurocomputing **461**, 497–515 (2021)
20. Hamidi, A., Ramavandi, B.: Evaluation and scientometric analysis of researches on air pollution in developing countries from 1952 to 2018. Air Qual. Atmos. Health **13**(12), 797–806 (2020). https://doi.org/10.1007/s11869-020-00836-4
21. Weihua, Y., Dong, X.: Visual analysis of industrial knowledge graph research based on Citespace. Remote Sens. Environ. **87**(2–3), 273–282 (2003)

22. Chi, Y., Liu, Z., Zhang, Y.: UAV-based forest fire detection and tracking using image processing techniques. In: International Conference on Unmanned Aircraft Systems (ICUAS), pp. 639–643 (2015). https://doi.org/10.1109/ICUAS.2015.7152345

23. Yuan, C., Liu, Z., Zhang, Y.: Aerial images-based forest fire detection for firefighting using optical remote sensing techniques and unmanned aerial vehicles. J. Intell. Robot. Syst. **88**(2), 635–654 (2017). https://doi.org/10.1007/s10846-016-0464-7

24. Yuan, C., Zhang, Y.: A survey on technologies for automatic forest fire monitoring, detection, and fighting using unmanned aerial vehicles and remote sensing technique. Can. J. For. Res. **45**(7), 783–792 (2015)

25. Thomson, W., Bhowmik, N., Breckon, T.P.: Efficient and compact convolutional neural network architectures for non-temporal real-time fire detection. In: 19th IEEE International Conference on Machine Learning and Applications (ICMLA), pp. 136–141 (2020). https://doi.org/10.1109/ICMLA51294.2020.0003

26. Khan, M., Jamil, A., Lv, Z.: Efficient deep CNN-based fire detection and localization in video surveillance applications. IEEE Trans. Syst. Man Cybern. Syst. **49**(7), 1419–1434 (2018)

27. Giglio, L., Loboda, T., Roy, D.P.: An active-fire based burned area mapping algorithm for the MODIS sensor. Remote Sens. Environ. **113**(2), 408–420 (2009)

28. Töreyin, B.U., Dedeoğlu, Y., Güdükbay, U.: Computer vision based method for real-time fire and flame detection. Pattern Recogn. Lett. **27**(1), 49–58 (2006)

29. Chen, T.H., Yin, Y.H., Huang, S.F.: The smoke detection for early fire-alarming system base on video processing. In: International Conference on Intelligent Information Hiding and Multimedia 2006, pp. 427–430 (2006). https://doi.org/10.1109/IIH-MSP.2006.265033

30. Roy, D.P., Boschetti, L., Justice, C.O.: The collection 5 MODIS burned area product–global evaluation by comparison with the MODIS active fire product. Remote Sens. Environ. **112**(9), 3690–3707 (2008)

31. Chuvieco, E., Aguado, I., Yebra, M.: Development of a framework for fire risk assessment using remote sensing and geographic information system technologies. Ecol. Model. **221**(1), 46–58 (2010)

32. Xu, W., Wooste, M.J., Roberts, G.: New GOES imager algorithms for cloud and active fire detection and fire radiative power assessment across North, South and Central America. Remote Sens. Environ. **114**(9), 1876–1895 (2010)

33. Kaufman, Y.J., Flynn, L.P., Kendall, J.D.: Potential global fire monitoring from EOS-MODIS. J. Geophys. Res. Biogeosci. **103**(24), 32215–32238 (1998)

34. Ko, B.C., Cheong, K.H., Nam, J.Y.: Fire detection based on vision sensor and support vector machines. Fire Saf. J. **44**(3), 322–329 (2009)

35. Wilfrid, S., Patricia, O., Louis, G.: The New VIIRS 375 m active fire detection data product: algorithm description and initial assessment. Remote Sens. Environ. **143**(1), 85–96 (2014)

36. Muhammad, K., Ahmad, J., Mehmood, I.: Convolutional neural networks based fire detection in surveillance videos. IEEE Access **6**(1), 18174–18183 (2014)

37. Giglio, L., Schroeder, W., Justice, C.O.: The collection 6 MODIS active fire detection algorithm and fire products. Remote Sens. Environ. **178**(1), 31–41 (2016)

38. Bosilovich, M.G., Robertson, F.R., Chen, J.: MERRA: NASA's modern-era retrospective analysis for research and applications. J. Clim. **24**(14), 3624–3648 (2011)

39. Gardner, R.A.: Spectral analysis of long wavelength periodic waves and applications. China's Sci. Technol. Wealth **19**(24), 71–78 (2009)

40. Venugopal, V.R.: Meteorological conditions and radio astronomy observations at X-band. J. Atmos. Sci. **20**(5), 372–375 (2010)

41. Lang, S.: Object-based image analysis for remote sensing applications: modeling reality – dealing with complexity. In: Blaschke, T., Lang, S., Hay, G.J. (eds.) Object-Based Image Analysis. LNGC, Springer, Heidelberg (2008). https://doi.org/10.1007/978-3-540-77058-9_1

42. Sun, X., Wang, B., Wang, Z.: Research progress on few-shot learning for remote sensing image interpretation. IEEE J. Sel. Top. Appl. Earth Obs. Remote Sens. **14**, 2387–2402 (2021)

43. Gm, W., Wang, B., Wang, Z.: A remote sensing surface energy balance algorithm for land (SEBAL). J. Hydrol. 212–213 (1998)

44. Xue, L., Li, Q., Chen, H.: Effects of a wildfire on selected physical, chemical and biochemical soil properties in a Pinus massoniana forest in South China. Forests **5**(12), 2947–2966 (2014)

45. Sippel, J., Siegesmund, S., Weiss, T.: Decay of natural stones caused by fire damage. Geol. Soc. Lond. Spec. Publ. **271**(1), 139–151 (2007)

46. Yu, C., Mei, Z., Xi, Z.: A real-time video fire flame and smoke detection algorithm. Procedia Eng. **62**, 891–898 (2013)

47. Hu, C., Tang, P., Jin, W.D.: Real-time fire detection based on deep convolutional long-recurrent networks and optical flow method. In: 37th Chinese Control Conference (CCC) 2018, pp. 9061–9066 (2018)

48. Qiu, T., Yan, Y., Lu, G.: An autoadaptive edge-detection algorithm for flame and fire image processing. IEEE Trans. Instrum. Meas. **61**(5), 1486–1493 (2012)

49. Liu, Z.-G., Yang, Y., Ji, X.-H.: Flame detection algorithm based on a saliency detection technique and the uniform local binary pattern in the YCbCr color space. Sig. Image Video Process. **10**(2), 277–284 (2015). https://doi.org/10.1007/s11760-014-0738-0

50. Rogan, J., Chen, D.M.: Remote sensing technology for mapping and monitoring land-cover and land-use change. Prog. Plann. **61**(5), 301–325 (2004)

51. Lu, F., Li, L., Sun, P.: Sub-critical column and capillary chromatography with water as mobile phase and flame ionization detection. J. Chin. Pharm. Sci. **10**(1), 39–41 (2001)

52. Wang, S., He, Y., Yang, H.: Video smoke detection using shape, color and dynamic features. J. Intell. Fuzzy Syst. Appl. Eng. Technol. **33**(1), 305–313 (2017)

53. Ko, B.C.: Wildfire smoke detection using temporospatial features and random forest classifiers. Opt. Eng. **51**(1), 7208 (2012)

54. Kahou, S.E., et al.: EmoNets: multimodal deep learning approaches for emotion recognition in video. J. Multimodal User Interfaces **10**(2), 99–111 (2015). https://doi.org/10.1007/s12193-015-0195-2

55. Jia, Y., Chen, W., Yang, M.: Video smoke detection with domain knowledge and transfer learning from deep convolutional neural networks. Optik Int. J. Light Electron Opt. **240**(8), 166947 (2021)

56. Fan, M., Tian, S., Liu, K.: Infrared small target detection based on region proposal and CNN classifier. Sig. Image Video Process. **15**(8), 1927–1936 (2021). https://doi.org/10.1007/s11760-021-01936-z

57. Jin, Y., Han, D., Ko, H.: TrSeg: transformer for semantic segmentation. Pattern Recogn. Lett. **148**(4), 29–35 (2021)

58. Chen, W., Chen, S., Guo, H.: Welding flame detection based on color recognition and progressive probabilistic Hough transform. Concurr. Comput. Pract. Exp. **32**(19), e5815 (2020)

59. Xia, X., Lu, Q.: Exploring an easy way for imbalanced data sets in semantic image segmentation. In: Journal of Physics: Conference Series, vol. 1213, no. 2, pp. 22003–22003 (2019)

60. Tian, Y., Chao, M.A., Kulkarni, C.: Real-time model calibration with deep reinforcement learning. Mech. Syst. Sig. Process. **165**(3), 108284 (2022)
61. Baek, J., Alhindi, T.J., Jeong, Y.S.: Real-time fire detection algorithm based on support vector machine with dynamic time warping kernel function. Fire Technol. **57**(2), 2929–2953 (2021). https://doi.org/10.1007/s10694-020-01062-1
62. Majid, S., Alenezi, F., Masood, S., Ahmad, M., Gündüz, E.S., Polat, K.: Attention based CNN model for fire detection and localization in real-world images. Expert Syst. Appl. **189**(3), 116114 (2022)
63. Wang, T., Zhang, J., Li, T.: Research on detection technology for the changes of buildings by high resolution remote sensing image. In: Journal of Physics: Conference Series, vol. 1972, no. 1, p. 012066 (2021)
64. Cao, Y., Zhou, X., Yan, K.: Deep learning neural network model for tunnel ground surface settlement prediction based on sensor data. Math. Probl. Eng. **1**, 1–14 (2021)

Real-Time Security Monitoring System for Intelligent Multi-region Transfer Platform

Rongxuan Si[1], Jing Xin[1(✉)], Seng Han[1], and Hongbo Gao[2]

[1] Xi'an University of Technology, Xi'an, China
xinj@xaut.edu.cn
[2] University of Science and Technology of China, Hefei, China
ghb48@ustc.edu.cn

Abstract. In order to realize the effective monitoring and early warning of foreign objects around the transfer platform without dead angle, this paper designs a real-time security monitoring system for intelligent multi-region transfer platform based on the YOLOv5 target detection algorithm, including a security monitoring server and a client. Firstly, the dangerous area is calibrated on the captured image, and then based on the multi-thread technology, YOLOv5 is used to detect the foreign object in multiple areas around the transfer platform, and finally the ray method is used to judge whether the foreign object invades the detection area. The practical application results of an industrial site show that the designed system can detect foreign objects (pedestrians and trolleys) in real time within the dangerous area around the transfer platform, and can also set the dangerous area range online according to the user's requirements. In addition, system can complete the detection within 0.1 s and give an alarm prompt immediately when there is an abnormality. The system has a low false alarm rate of 1% to 2%, which reduces the occurrence of foreign objects invading dangerous areas and improves the safety of the production process.

Keywords: Transfer platform · Multi-region · Monitoring system · Foreign object invasion detection

1 Introduction

With the continuous deepening of the automation degree of our country's industrial workshops and the continuous improvement of the industrial system, the level of our country's railway vehicle manufacturing industry has been continuously improved, and it has now ranked the world's leading level. However, according to the frequency of workshop accidents in China in recent years, it is easy to see that there are also many safety hazards in factory workshops. Therefore, in order to prevent safety accidents during workers' operations and to ensure the safety of workshop workers, it is especially important to ensure the stability of the working process of workshop equipment. More and more factories also pay more attention to safety issues, such as coal mines, power plants, etc. are constantly updating their own safety systems [1, 2].

© The Author(s), under exclusive license to Springer Nature Singapore Pte Ltd. 2023
Z. Yu et al. (Eds.): CIRAC 2022, CCIS 1770, pp. 305–315, 2023.
https://doi.org/10.1007/978-981-99-0301-6_23

The industrial site environment is complex. At present, in addition to the monitoring system of the equipment itself, the detection of workers on the job site and objects in the scene is also one of the most important tasks of safety detection [3, 4]. Benefiting from the continuous improvement of the performance of visual sensors [5, 6] and the rapid development of computer vision technology [7] in recent years, security detection systems at this stage most often use cameras for monitoring, and then use computer vision technology to obtain data from the extract information from images [8].

The transfer platform is a large-scale special equipment used in the manufacture and maintenance of railway vehicles. Its main function is to perform parallel rail transfer operations between different tracks [9]. During the operation of the transfer platform, there will be dangerous areas around it. If there are people or objects within this range, it will threaten the personal safety of the personnel and affect the normal workshop work efficiency. At this stage, object detection within a fixed range can be divided into two sub-tasks: target detection and target ranging. The commonly used methods are to use target detection and semantic segmentation in computer vision to obtain targets from images obtained by cameras [10–12], and then use binocular ranging [13–15] or add auxiliary equipment for ranging (infrared ranging, ultrasonic ranging [16], three-dimensional light detection ranging [17]) and other methods to obtain the distance information of the target. However, the application of the above-mentioned existing mainstream ranging methods in actual industrial sites still faces many major challenges. For example, for visual ranging methods, it is necessary to obtain the internal and external parameters of the camera. In the actual industrial scene environment, due to the movement of industrial equipment, the internal and external parameters of the camera cannot be maintained stably and may change, and the camera parameters need to be adjusted many times. Especially the binocular ranging method has disadvantages such as large system volume and low measurement speed. For the method of adding an auxiliary ranging module, it is also necessary to lay lines for the new ranging module, which increases the system cost. On the other hand, since the dangerous area of the scene environment is relative to the transfer platform itself, even if the position of the target to the ranging sensor can be accurately calculated, in practice, converting the coordinates of the object under the sensor to the world coordinates will increase the error.

In view of the above problems, this paper designs a set of real-time security monitoring system for intelligent multi-region transfer platform. During the working process of the transfer platform, it monitors whether there are safety hazards in the surrounding area of the moving platform in real time. According to the location of the foreign objects of the transfer platform, the system divides the surrounding area of the transfer platform into three areas: the safe area, the alarm area and the break area. Foreign objects are allowed to walk in the safe area. If they enter the alarm area, the alarm device will be triggered to prompt the foreign objects to leave the area. If foreign objects enter the break area, the transfer platform will stop working.

The main contributions of this paper are summarized as follows:

- Multi-region target detection is realized by multi-thread technology combined with YOLOv5, which meets the detection accuracy and real-time requirements of industrial sites.
- The two-point coordinate combined with the ray method are used to judge whether the foreign object invades the dangerous area, which can meet the requirements of the false alarm rate of industrial site.

The writing arrangement of this paper is as follows: Sect. 2 briefly introduces the framework of the system proposed in this paper, and explains basic theory involved in constructing the system; Sect. 3 gives the experimental results and analysis in real scenarios. Finally, a summary is made.

2 System Overview

This section mainly introduces the topology structure, main function modules and related algorithm principle of the designed real-time security monitoring system for intelligent multi-region transfer platform.

2.1 System Composition

This system is mainly composed of industrial camera, monitoring industrial computer, client and PLC. The system topology diagram is shown in Fig. 1. The main functions of the system include image acquisition, storage and display, image transmission, foreign object intrusion detection and alarm. The system transmits the collected images to the monitoring industrial computer, and uses the YOLOv5 target detection algorithm combined with the ray method to achieve foreign object intrusion detection and alarm functions in dangerous areas. The real-time security monitoring system for intelligent multi-region transfer platform designed in this paper includes a multi-channel video image acquisition module, an early warning area division module, a target detection module, an intrusion judgment module and an early warning module. Its functional module block diagram is shown in Fig. 2.

The main function of the designed security monitoring system of the transfer platform is foreign object intrusion detection and alarm, that is, when a certain camera detects a foreign object within the alarm range, a frame will flash above the corresponding camera canvas, and at the same time, the text alarm area will display people or obstacles in the corresponding position of the camera to remind the operator and worker pay attention to safety; when foreign objects are detected within the braking range, the text alarm area will not display the detection information, but directly transmit the braking signal to the PLC for emergency braking to avoid equipment damage and personal injury. Among them, the multi-channel video image acquisition module is built to acquire images from surveillance cameras and providing data sources for intrusion detection algorithms.

Because this system needs to realize the video collection of multiple cameras, it uses multi-threading technology to obtain multi-channel video in real time. The calibration

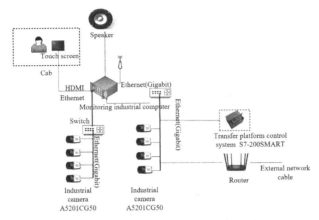

Fig. 1. Security monitoring system topology diagram.

process of different dangerous areas in the early warning area division module is to first capture images of dangerous areas in line with the actual scene division, and then calibrate the dangerous areas on the image information, thus the calibration of different dangerous areas can be achieved. In this system, the working area of the transfer platform is divided into safety area, alarm area and brake area, and its schematic diagram is shown in Fig. 3. The adjustable range of the braking area distance is 0.5–1.0 m, and the adjustable range of the alarm area is 1.0–5.0 m. The target detection module and the foreign object intrusion judgment module are the key parts of the whole system. The algorithm implementation of these two modules will be described in detail later. The early warning module is the output part of the system, which is responsible for analyzing the results detected by the system and feeding back the results to the staff in real time, and the voice reminds the staff to deal with it in time.

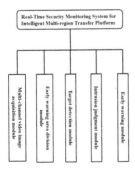

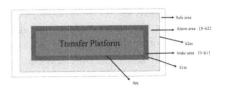

Fig. 2. Block diagram of the functional modules of the safety monitoring system.

Fig. 3. Schematic diagram of the division of the transfer platform area. The red area is the braking area (0.5 ≤ h1 ≤ 1.0 m), the yellow area is the alarm area (1.0 ≤ h2 ≤ 5.0 m), and the white area is the safe area. (Color figure online)

2.2 Implementation Principle of Main Functional Modules

The core modules of this system are the target detection module and the foreign object intrusion judgment module. The algorithm implementation principle is as follows:

Object Detection Module

Image Acquisition. In order to realize all-round security monitoring without dead ends around the transfer platform equipment, after analyzing and calculating the actual scene, we adopted the deployment method of installing two cameras at each of the four corners of the transfer platform, and those cameras are installed at the position of the gantry with a height of 2.5 m. We choose the model A5201CG50 industrial camera, as shown in Fig. 4. The 4 camera lenses installed on the long side of the gantry are 8 mm, and the 4 camera lenses on the narrow side are 12 mm. According to the on-site environment, we adjust the installation angle of the camera and the focal length of the camera to determine the field of view of the camera, and at the same time ensure a clear field of view, so that the camera can see the area 5 m in front of another camera in the same direction. The effective coverage distance of the final camera is greater than 34 m, which can cover the span of the equipment and meet the requirements of the camera's all-round field of view coverage.

Object Detection. Since the position of the camera has an oblique angle, the captured results will be distorted, so the algorithm is required to have good robustness. On the other hand, in order to provide the detection result to the alarm module in time, the algorithm should have a fast image processing function. The YOLO series [18, 19] is a single-stage fast target detection algorithm based on deep learning. Compared with the two-stage algorithm [20–22], the YOLO algorithm treats the target detection problem as a regression problem, which speeds up the detection speed of the algorithm [23, 24]. Therefore, this system selects the YOLOV5 algorithm based on deep learning, and trains it so that it has the ability to detect pedestrians and obstacles.

The YOLOv5 network is mainly composed of Backbone network, Neck network and Prediction network. The Backbone network is used to aggregate and form image features at fine-grained levels of different images, and is composed of a multi-layer convolutional neural network including numerous modules. Neck network is a series of feature fusion networks that combine top-down and bottom-up to combine image features, so that the network can well identify the same object of different sizes and scales. The Prediction network is used for the final reasoning and detection. Anchor boxes are applied to the feature map output by the Neck network, and the output contains the target object's class probability, the object's score, and the vector of the bounding box position. The input-output mapping relationship of the YOLOv5 algorithm is shown in Fig. 5. After the image is input into the YOLOv5 network, the output tensor corresponding to the image is obtained through the Backbone network, the Neck network and the Prediction network, including the coordinate information of the candidate frame (x, y, w, h), the confidence P of each candidate box and the probability value of the category.

Fig. 4. Surveillance camera, model A5201CG50.

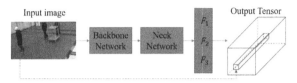

Fig. 5. YOLOv5 algorithm target detection forward process. The red cell represents the class probability of the target object, the object's score and the vector of the bounding box position. Where F is the output of the prediction network, representing the feature maps at different down sampling rates. (Color figure online)

Foreign Object Intrusion Judgment Module. The coordinates of the two ends of the bottom edge of the rectangular frame obtained by target detection are the key factors in determining the position of the object. Whether the object is in a certain area can be judged by the coordinates of the two ends of the bottom edge of the rectangular frame of the object. By detecting the coordinates of the two points of the target, the system uses the ray method [25] judging whether the coordinates are inside the dangerous area to realize the judgment of foreign object area intrusion. The implementation principle is shown in Fig. 6, in which the black box is the rectangular box obtained by the target detection algorithm, and the two points A and B are the coordinates of the two points at the bottom of the rectangular box. When two points A and B are in the braking area, it is determined that a foreign object has invaded the braking area, and the camera will capture the intrusion picture and remind the staff to brake urgently; when both points A and B are not in the braking area, as long as there is one point in the alarm area when it is determined that it is a foreign object intruding into the alarm area, the camera will capture the intrusion picture and remind the staff to pay attention to safety. When both points A and B are not in the braking area and the alarm area, it is safe, and the transfer platform works normally.

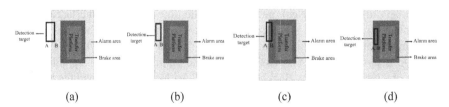

(a)   (b)   (c)   (d)

Fig. 6. Two-point coordinate judgment area intrusion diagram. (a) The target partially enters the alarm area. (b) The target completely enters the alarm area. (c) The target partially enters the brake area. (d) The target enters the brake area completely.

3 Experimental Results

In order to verify the effectiveness and reliability of the designed system, a detection data set for transfer platform monitoring system is built and the target detection experiments are firstly conducted on the built data set, and then the whole monitoring system performance test experiments are conducted on the practical application on-site environment.

3.1 Model Training on Self-built Dataset

In this system, a pedestrian detection dataset is first established, and then the YOLOv5 pedestrian detection algorithm in the platform is trained. In order to better adapt to the on-site environment, we adopt the data mixing method, after labeling the on-site pictures collected in the workshop under labeling, mix them with the extracted person category data set in the COCO data set. Finally, a dataset of 11064 samples is obtained, including two categories of pedestrians and trolleys. The dataset is then randomly divided into training sets and test sets.

Our system trains the model under the ubuntu operating system, the CPU is Intel(R) i9-10850K, and the GPU is NVIDIA GeForce RTX 3060, the programming language is Python.

Using the above dataset to iteratively train the YOLOv5 algorithm, the optimal weight of the network for pedestrian and trolley detection can be obtained. The training results show that the model trained with YOLOv5s performs well, and the mAP value reaches 93.0% when the IOU is 0.5. Then it was tested on the validation set. When the IOU was 0.5, the mAP reached 87.7%. The pedestrian and trolley detection results in the validation set are shown in the Fig. 7. It can be seen from the Fig. 7 that after being processed by the algorithm of YOLOv5, almost all targets in the sample can be detected, and the occluded targets and targets with different lighting environments can be accurately detected. The test results show that the model meets the requirements of the system and can accurately detect pedestrians and obstacles.

Fig. 7. Detection results in the validation set. The training effect of the model was verified on the constructed mixed data set, including the original COCO data and the industrial field data. The verification results show that it can also accurately identify pedestrian and obstacle targets with occlusions and missing in industrial sites.

3.2   On-Site Environmental Testing

In order to verify the performance of the real-time security monitoring system for intelligent multi-region transfer platform designed in this paper, the experiment uses 8 industrial cameras A5201CG50 to simultaneously monitor the four areas around the transfer station equipment for a long time. The monitoring video frame rate is 24 frames per second. The camera resolution is 1280×720. The tester walks around the transfer platform and simulates the behavior of pedestrians intruding into the area. Figure 8 shows the detection result of the scene images collected by four cameras at a certain time after being processed by the detection algorithm. At this time, the braking distance is 0.5 m, and the early warning distance is 5.0 m. Points A and B in Fig. 8 (a) and (b) are the two ends of the bottom edge of the pedestrian detection frame. Since points A and B are both in the early warning area at this time, it is determined that a person has invaded the early warning area, and the server sends the client and voice alarm module an alarm signal to remind operators and staff to pay attention to safety; points A and B in Fig. 8(c) and (d) are the two ends of the bottom edge of the trolley detection frame, and points C and D are the two ends of the bottom edge of pedestrian detection frame, points A, B, and D in Fig. 8 (c) are all in the early warning area, so it is determined that pedestrians and trolley invade the early warning area. In Fig. 8 (d), point A is in the braking area, and points B and C are in the early warning area, so it is determined that the trolley invades the braking area, the server sends a braking signal to the PLC, and the transfer platform stops working.

The client interface designed by this system is shown in Fig. 9, including the alarm information area, the text information prompt area, the image information display area and the operation button area. Figure 9(a) is the system login interface, with administrator-level and operator-level login rights; Fig. 9(b) is the system parameter setting interface, which can manually set the early warning distance of 8 cameras and the braking distance when the transfer platform is working. When the system detects that foreign object has entered the early warning area, the server sends an alarm signal, and the client interface obtains the alarm information through real-time refresh, displaying information consistent with the real alarm situation.

| (a) | (b) | (c) | (d) |

Fig. 8. On-site environmental testing results. (a) Pedestrian is in the warning area. (b) Pedestrian is in the warning area. (c) Pedestrian and trolley are in the warning area. (d) Pedestrian is in the warning area, trolley is in the warning area.

False Alarm Rate Analysis. In order to test the false alarm rate of this system, we randomly selected 100 alarm results for each of 8 cameras, and the results are shown in Table 1.

(a)   (b)

Fig. 9. Client interface. (a) Login interface. (b) System parameter setting interface.

Table 1. Alarm test results.

	Number of correct alarms	Number of false alarms
Camera 1	99	1
Camera 2	99	1
Camera 3	98	2
Camera 4	99	1
Camera 5	99	1
Camera 6	99	1
Camera 7	98	2
Camera 8	98	2

It can be seen from the test results that the false alarm rate of the method in this paper is 1% in the forward direction of the transfer platform, and 2% on both sides of the narrow side of the transfer platform. However, the false alarm rate generated at this time belongs to the early alarm before the foreign object has reached the detection area, which meets the requirements of the false alarm rate of actual production.

Real-Time Analysis. This system has high requirements for the real-time performance. The real-time performance includes real-time collection of monitoring data from the front end of the camera and display the monitoring image on the client. It also includes emergency handling capabilities for intrusion behaviors. Real-time early warning of the intrusion behavior, and timely remind the staff to deal with it accordingly. Through the real-time test of the data update time, data transmission time and alarm response time of the security monitoring system, multiple timing tests are performed on the data, and the test results are the average of multiple timing data. The results are shown in Table 2, where the data update time includes the multi-channel image acquisition time and the time required to obtain the alarm information from the intrusion detection module, and the data transmission time refers to the sending of images and alarm data from the server to the client to display images and alarm information. The alarm response time refers to the time required from the monitoring server sending the alarm signal to the PLC receiving the alarm signal.

Table 2. System response time

	Data update	Data transmission	Alarm response
System response time(s)	0.081	0.01	0.001

The test results show that when the foreign object is in the dangerous area, the system can generate an alarm signal within 0.1 s, which can ensure the real-time performance of the production process.

From the experimental results of the data set and the actual operation results in the field, it can be seen that this system can detect and alarm in real time whether there are foreign objects such as pedestrians and trolleys intruding in the dangerous area during the moving process of the transfer platform equipment, and can be used to assist the safe operation of the transfer platform.

4 Conclusion

In this paper, according to the characteristics of the operation environment of the transfer platform, a set of real-time security monitoring system for intelligent multi-region transfer platform is designed. The test results show that the system meets the on-site safety requirements and can effectively prevent casualties and equipment damage in the dangerous area during the transfer process. It has been deployed and applied in the real scenarios.

Acknowledgment. This work is supported by the Chinese National Natural Science Foundation (Grant No. 61873200, U20A20225, U2013601), Provincial Key Research and Development Program(Grant No. 2022-GY111,202004a05020058), the Natural Science Foundation of Hefei (Grant No. 2021032), Xi'an Science and Technology Plan Project (Grant No. 22GXFW0070) and the CAAI-Huawei MindSpore Open Fund.

References

1. Chen, X.: Design of coal mine safety monitoring system logical control automatic detection device. Mine Autom. **48**(6), 154–158 (2022)
2. Zeke, L.I., Zewen, C.H., Chunyan, W.A., Zhiguang, X.U., Ye, L.I.: Research on security evaluation technology of wireless access of electric power monitoring system based on fuzzy. In: CCET, pp. 318–321 (2020)
3. Ma, Y., Li, T., Xu, D., Yu, C.: Action recognition for intelligent monitoring. Image Graph. **24**(2), 0282–0290 (2019)

4. Zhao, X.: Research and implementation of face recognition in remote intelligent monitoring system. In: ICOSEC, pp. 1013–1016 (2021)
5. Kumar, S.: A novel camera system for computer vision. In: ISOCC, pp. 29–30 (2021)
6. Chen, Y., Zhou, F., Sun, J., Sun, P., Liu, Y.: A novel mirrored binocular vision sensor based on spherical catadioptric mirrors. IEEE Sens. J. **21**(17), 18670–18681 (2021)
7. Zhang, X., Xu, S.: Research on image processing technology of computer vision algorithm. In: CVIDL, pp. 122–124 (2020)
8. Purohit, M., Singh, M., Yadav, S., Singh, A.K., Kumar, A., Kaushik, B.K.: Multi-sensor surveillance system based on integrated video analytics. IEEE Sens. J. **22**(11), 10207–10222 (2021)
9. Liu, Z.: Design of 180t heavy-duty rotary crane platform. Rail Transit Equip. Technol. **28**(2), 18–21 (2020)
10. AlZaabi, A., Abi Talib, M., Nassif, A.B., Sajwani, A., Einea, O.: A systematic literature review on machine learning in object detection security. In: ICCCA, pp. 136–139 (2020)
11. Zhao, X., Zhang, Q., Zhao, D., Pang, Z.: Overview of image segmentation and its application on free space detection. In DDCLS, pp. 1164–1169 (2018)
12. Noman, M., Stankovic, V., Tawfik, A.: Object detection techniques: overview and performance comparison. In ISSPIT, pp. 1–5 (2019)
13. Yang, J., Wang, C., Wang, H., Li, Q.: A RGB-D based real-time multiple object detection and ranging system for autonomous driving. IEEE Sens. J. **20**(20), 11959–11966 (2020)
14. Chen, Y., Zhou, F., Zhou, M., Zhang, W., Li, X.: Pose measurement approach based on two-stage binocular vision for docking large components. Meas. Sci. Technol. **31**(12), 125002 (2020)
15. Huang, L., et al.: Obstacle distance measurement based on binocular vision for high-voltage transmission lines using a cable inspection robot. Sci. Prog. **103**(3) (2020). 0036850420936910
16. Shao, Z., Peng, Y., Pala, S., Liang, Y., Lin, L.: 3D ultrasonic object detections with > 1 meter range. In MEMS, pp. 386–389 (2021)
17. Zhao, X., Sun, P., Xu, Z., Min, H., Yu, H.: Fusion of 3D LIDAR and camera data for object detection in autonomous vehicle applications. IEEE Sens. J. **20**(9), 4901–4913 (2020)
18. Redmon, J., Divvala, S., Girshick, R., Farhadi, A.: You only look once: unified, real-time object detection. In CVPR, pp. 779–788 (2016)
19. Redmon, J., Farhadi, A.: YOLO9000: better, faster, stronger. In: CVPR, pp.6517–6525 (2017)
20. Girshick, R.: Fast R-CNN. In: Proceedings of the IEEE International Conference on Computer Vision. In ICCV, pp. 1440–1448 (2015)
21. Ren, S., He, K., Girshick, R., Sun, J.: Faster R-CNN: towards real-time object detection with region proposal networks. TPAMI **39**(6), 1137–1149 (2017)
22. He, K., Gkioxari, G., Dollár, P., Girshick, R.: Mask R-CNN. In Proceedings of the IEEE International Conference on Computer Vision. In ICCV, pp. 2961–2969 (2017)
23. Jiao, L., et al.: A survey of deep learning-based object detection. IEEE Access **7**, 128837–128868 (2019)
24. Fu, M., Deng, M., Zhang, D.: Survey on deep neural network image target detection algorithms. Comput. Syst. Appl. **31**(7), 35–45 (2022)
25. Jiang, P., Liu, M.: Improved ray method to judge the relation of point and polygon including simple curve. Sci. Surv. Mapp. **34**(5), 220–222 (2009)

Autonomous Object Tracking System of UAV Based on Correlation Filtering

Jing Xin[1], Pengyu Yue[1], Hongbo Gao[2(✉)], Jia Zhao[1], Le Wang[1], and Jiale Han[3]

[1] Xi'an University of Technology, Xi'an, China
[2] University of Science and Technology of China, Hefei, China
ghb48@ustc.edu.cn
[3] Shaanxi Key Laboratory of Integrated and Intelligent Navigation, The 20th Research Institute of China Electronics Technology Corporation, Xi'an 710068, China

Abstract. Aiming at the problem of UAV autonomous object tracking under the condition of limited computing resources, this paper combines the high-speed Kernel Correlation Filter (KCF) tracking algorithm with UAV motion control to construct a vision-based UAV autonomous object tracking system. Firstly, the RGB data is captured through the UAV on-board camera and transmitted to the control terminal; After calibrating the initial frame of the tracked object, the control terminal uses KCF algorithm to predict the position of the tracked object at the subsequent time; Then, the relative position of the UAV to the object is estimated based on visual tracking results; Finally, the relative position of the UAV and the object is used to calculate the movement control amount of the UAV. The experimental results show that the vision-based UAV autonomous object tracking system constructed in this paper can achieve fast and robust UAV autonomous object tracking and relative position maintenance with CPU support and low memory usage.

Keywords: Unmanned aerial vehicles · Autonomous visual tracking · Limited computing resources · KCF

1 Introduction

Unmanned aerial vehicle (UAV) has been widely used in military and civil fields for its intelligence, autonomy, small size and flexibility. Vision based UAV object tracking can used in complex and variable unstructured scenes, high real-time and robust vision-based UAV object tracking technology is the key to achieve the autonomous mission [1].

Visual object tracking refers to the feature extraction of moving object in the region of interest, calculating the current and subsequent motion states of the object. In recent years, object tracking technology has received extensive attention [2–7]. However, object tracking methods still face many challenging problems, such as ambient light changes, similar objects, occlusion, deformation, rotation, out of field of view, scale changes, and so on. These methods can be divided into classical algorithms [3], filtering algorithms [4, 5] and deep learning algorithms [6, 7]. Aiming at the difficulties of object tracking of UAV, Nam [8]. Put forward a novel tracker SiamDMV based on memory and

Z. Yu et al. (Eds.): CIRAC 2022, CCIS 1770, pp. 316–326, 2023.
https://doi.org/10.1007/978-981-99-0301-6_24

Siamese network, and comprehensively evaluated the tracker on related datasets. The method can effectively deal with challenges such as appearance change and occl-usion of the tracked target object. In addition, temporal regularization was introduced into DCF to weaken the influence of boundary effects and illumination changes on the object tracking process, and good tracking accuracy is obtained with low computational cost [9]. Siamese Transformer Pyramid Networks (SiamTPN) is proposed to solve the problem that trackers can't be applied to mobile platforms with limited computing resources under complex architecture [10]. However, the above work is based on the UAV dataset and has not been applied to the UAV physical object. To solve the problem, Chakrabarty et al. [11] combined a CMT tracking algorithm with a UAV platform, and completed the relative distance keeping and real-time tracking of the UAV and the tracked object in an indoor environment [12]. However, when the object is lost, the UAV begins to hover or land, and it can no longer track the object. Wesam et al. [13] used the particle filter method of a multi-feature fusion scheme for object tracking, which had a higher tracking success rate. Li et al. [14] combined the Spatio-temporal regularized correlation filter with UAV, and the experimental test showed good performance results.

With the increasing development of object tracking technology, the tracking algorithm based on the discriminant model of regression method became popular, and correlation filtering becomes a popular tracking algorithm framework. Henriques et al. [3] proposed a closed-form classification method to deal with the problem of redundant training data in the application of discriminative classifiers in the field of object tracking. At the same time, Gaussian kernel function was used for training and detection, which greatly improved the tracking effect. Henriques [4] introduced the feature of Histogram of Oriented Gradients (HOG) and proposed a high-speed Kernel Correlation Filter, which effectively improved the performance of the algorithm. Unlike the deep learning algorithm, the correlation filtering algorithm does not need GPU acceleration, and has higher tracking accuracy than the traditional classical algorithm, and its calculation mode is in the frequency domain, which greatly improves the speed of the algorithm.

In view of the above difficulties in object tracking of UAV, KCF algorithm [4, 15] in the correlation filtering framework is selected and applied to the real UAV for achieving the autonomous object tracking task of the UAV in this paper. The main contribution of this paper is to build an autonomous object tracking system for UAV, and combine the object tracking algorithm (KCF) with the UAV movement to maintain the relative position between the UAV and the tracked object. This system does not need GPU acceleration, and the UAV can autonomously and accurately track the object when the illumination changes and similar objects interfere. The contribution of this paper is to build an autonomous object tracking system for UAVs that is applicable to low computing resources and low memory usage conditions. Experimental results show that UAVs can robustly track object and maintain relative positions using vision in real time.

2 Autonomous Object Tracking of UAV System

In this paper, we combine the KCF method of correlation filtering with the UAV control to build the UAV autonomous object tracking system. The system can complete the autonomous object tracking task of UAV based on high-speed visual feedback without GPU. The UAV terminal adopts the DJI's Tello UAV, and the ground control terminal adopts the notebook computer with the Windows10 system and Intel Core i5 processor.

The overall block diagram of the system is shown in Fig. 1. The UAV terminal and the ground control terminal are connected and communicated through the LAN (Local area network). The UAV terminal takes the video stream from the first angle of view through the onboard camera, and uses the LAN to transmit the RGB image to the ground control terminal. When the ground control terminal receives RGB image transmission, the ground control terminal selects the tracking object in the initial frame and uses the KCF algorithm to track the object.

Fig. 1. Schematic UAV object tracking system.

The main steps of the tracking algorithm are as follows:

Step 1: to extract the features of the collected initial frame image and multiply it by the permutation matrix many times for obtaining the cyclic matrix of the object image block.

In the object tracking task, positive samples are generally obtained only in the object location box provided in the initial frame. It uses the vector $x = \{x_1, x_2, x_3, \ldots, x_n\}$ to represent the image block of the object. Multiply the image block x of the object multiple times by the permutation matrix to obtain multiple cyclic shifted sample vectors, that is, the cyclic matrix of x, expressed as $C(x)$.

$$X = C(x) = \begin{bmatrix} x_1 & x_2 & x_3 & \cdots & x_n \\ x_n & x_1 & x_2 & \cdots & x_{n-1} \\ x_{n-1} & x_n & x_1 & \cdots & x_{n-2} \\ \vdots & \vdots & \vdots & \ddots & \vdots \\ x_2 & x_3 & x_4 & \cdots & x_1 \end{bmatrix} \tag{1}$$

The above cyclic matrix represented in the time domain is transformed into the complex domain by Fourier transform. Let F represents the Fourier transform matrix, $diag$ represents diagonalization, and $\hat{x}$ represents the sample signal in the frequency domain. The transformed cyclic matrix expression is shown in (2):

$$X = F diag(\hat{x}) F^H \tag{2}$$

Step 2: to train the filter w by using the ridge regression model through minimizing the error between the estimated value $f(z) = w^T z$ and the object y_i, as shown in (3).

$$\min_{w} \sum_i (f(x_i) - y_i)^2 + \lambda ||w||^2 \tag{3}$$

Next, we can express w in the form of matrix, calculate the derivative and convert it to the complex domain to obtain the following formula:

$$w = (X^T X + \lambda)^{-1} X^H y \tag{4}$$

In (4) λ is the regularization coefficient. Each row of $X = [x_1, x_2, \ldots, x_n]^T$ represents the sample vector used for training, and X^H represents the complex conjugate transpose matrix.

Substitute (2) into (4) to obtain filter w in complex domain, as (5):

$$\hat{w} = diag(\frac{\hat{x}^*}{\hat{x}^* \otimes \hat{x} + \lambda})\hat{y} \tag{5}$$

Step 3: Using kernel function to predict the object location.

After the reliable template filter is obtained, the kernel function is introduced to detect and locate the object.

$$k^Z = C(k^{xz}) \tag{6}$$

where k represents the kernel function, x represents the training samples obtained from the previous frame, and z represents the candidate samples sampled from the current frame. Then, the regression function of candidate samples can be obtained, which is transformed into the complex domain and expressed as (7), where α represents the regression coefficient.

$$\hat{f}(z) = \hat{k}^{xz} \otimes \hat{\alpha} \tag{7}$$

$\hat{f}(z)$ is the position of the object in the image estimated by the KCF algorithm. The ground control terminal transmits the output tracking object position to the UAV terminal through LAN. The UAV estimates the relative position between itself and the object through the visual tracking results, and generates the corresponding back and forth, left and right, up and down movements according to the relative position with the tracking object, as follows.

When the tracked object moves backward and forward, the UAV determines whether to move backward and forward according to the bounding box area greater than or less than the threshold range, as shown in (8).

$$\begin{cases} GoBackward & if \ Area > Th_1 \\ GoForward & if \ Area < Th_2 \\ Hover & if \ Th_2 < Area < Th_1 \end{cases} \tag{8}$$

where, $Area$ represents area of the box, Th_1 and Th_2 represent the maximum threshold and minimum threshold, respectively.

When the tracked object rotates left and right, moves upward and downward, the UAV determines whether to generate left and right rotation and up and down motion according to the position of the bounding box, as shown in (9).

$$
\begin{cases}
GoLeft & if \ x < \frac{framewidth}{2} - deadzone \\
GoRight & if \ x > \frac{framewidth}{2} + deadzone \\
GoUp & if \ y < \frac{frameheight}{2} - deadzone \\
GoDown & if \ y > \frac{frameheight}{2} + deadzone \\
Hover & otherwise
\end{cases}
\tag{9}
$$

where x and y respectively represent the abscissa and ordinate of the center point of the bounding box, *framewidth* and *frameheight* respectively represent the width and height of the RGB image, where *otherwise* represents the tracked object is in the dead zone, that is, the *Area* of the bounding box meets $Th_2 < Area < Th_1$, and the coordinates of the center point of the bounding box meet $\frac{framewidth}{2} + deadzone \geq x \geq \frac{framewidth}{2} - deadzone, \frac{frameheight}{2} - deadzone \geq y \geq \frac{frameheight}{2} - deadzone$.

Here, the dead zone is defined as the input signal range when the corresponding output of the UAV system is zero. Specifically, when the target is in the cube area in space, it is considered that the relative position between the UAV and the tracked target remains unchanged, and the UAV has no motion control command and remains hovering.

Finally, the UAV realized the vision-based UAV object tracking relative position maintenance through the above system, and completed the real-time and robust UAV object tracking.

3 Experiment

In order to verify the effectiveness of the developed UAV object tracking system, two groups tracking experiments are conducted on the DJI's Tello UAV shown in Fig. 2. And we tested the proposed system under the i7-9750 H CPU. The total memory usage of the vision-based UAV autonomous object tracking system is only 121 Mb. In the following experiment: the calculation of the object tracking algorithm, relative position estimation, and UAV motion control takes a total of 18 ms. This is much higher than the UAV frame rate (30 Fps), which meets the real-time requirements.

Fig. 2. DJI's Tello UAV.

The tracking experiment results are shown in Figs. 3, 4, 5, 6, 7, 8 and 9, where subfigure a, b, c, d, e of each figure represents the key frame of the tracking video. In the experiment, the people are regarded as the tracked object, and the object in the black oval box is DJI's Tello UAV. In order to represent the position and posture of the UAV clearly during tracking, a three-dimensional coordinate system is set up on the UAV. The red arrow denotes the positive direction of the UAV.

3.1 Object Simple Movement

The purpose of the experiment is to verify the effectiveness of the proposed UAV visual tracking system. The tracked object makes a simple movement, and the UAV generates the corresponding command to follow, maintain its position relative to the tracked object. In the experiment, the tracked object is marked using a rectangular box in the initial frame. The tracking results are shown in Figs. 3, 4, 5, 6, 7 and 8.

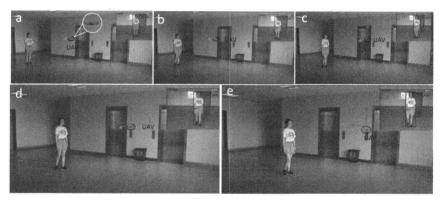

Fig. 3. Object is moving close to the UAV.

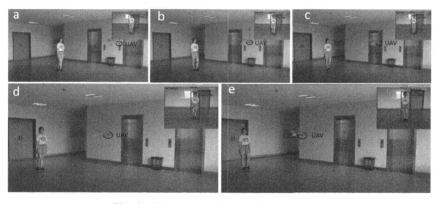

Fig. 4. Object is moving away from the UAV.

Figure 3 shows the UAV tracking results when the object is moving close to the UAV. When the tracked object continues to move forward from its current position, the distance between the tracked object and the UAV gradually decreases, and the bounding box area of the tracked object becomes larger. When the bounding box area is greater than the maximum threshold value, the UAV generates backward motion, as shown in Fig. 3a, b. During the backward movement of the UAV, the distance between the UAV and the tracked object gradually increases, so that when the bounding box area is within the threshold range of the set threshold, the UAV will no longer move backward and remain hovering, as shown in Fig. 3c. When the distance between the UAV and the tracked object decreases again, the UAV generates backward motion again, as shown in Fig. 3d, e.

Figure 4 shows the UAV tracking results when the object is moving away from the UAV. The tracked object moves backward from its current position. When the bounding box area is less than the threshold range, the UAV generates forward motion, as shown in Fig. 4b, c, d; When the bounding box area is within the threshold range, the UAV remains hovering, as shown in Fig. 4a, e.

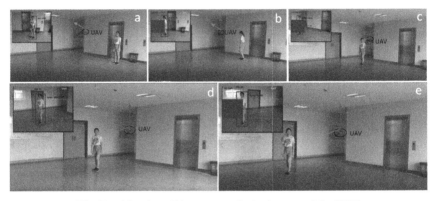

Fig. 5. Object is walking counterclockwise around the UAV.

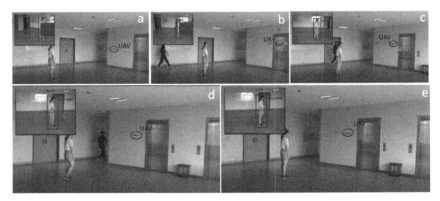

Fig. 6. Object is walking clockwise around the UAV.

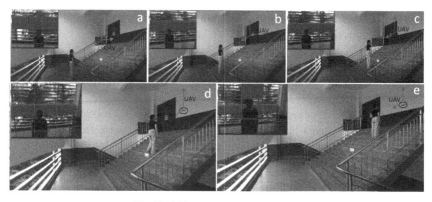

Fig. 7. Object is upward movement

Fig. 8. Object is downward movement.

Figures 5 and 6 shows the UAV tracking results when the object is walking around the UAV. When the tracked object rotates left and right, the UAV determines whether to generate left-right rotation movement according to the abscissa position of the center point of the box. When the tracked object rotates and moves left or right continuously in the current position, the abscissa position of the center point leaves the dead zone, and the UAV generates left motion or right motion, as shown in Figs. 5b, c, e and 6a, b respectively. Otherwise, the UAV will remain hovering within the dead zone, as shown in Fig. 5a, d and 6c, d, e.

When the tracked object moves upward and downward, the UAV determines whether to generate up and down motion according to the ordinate position of the center point. When the tracked object continues to climb up or down the stairs from its current position, the longitudinal coordinate position of the central point of the bounding box leaves the dead zone, and the UAV tracks the tracked object to generate upward or downward movement, as shown in Figs. 7e and 8c respectively. When the tracked object continues to climb the stairs, the UAV will also generate backward and forward movements, as shown in Fig. 7a, c and 8b, d respectively. When the UAV is within the dead zone, the UAV remains hovering, as shown in Figs. 7b, d 8a, e.

During the UAV tracks the object, the tracking results shown in Fig. 6b, c, d show that similar objects interfere around the tracked object, and the results shown in Figs. 7 and 8 show that the UAV tracks the object in the backlight scene with changing illumination, and the UAV can accurately track the object.

To sum up, the designed UAV system can complete the robust object tracking in different motion states in the presence of background interference and backlight conditions.

3.2 Object Complex Motion

The purpose of this experiment is to verify that the UAV can accurately track the object when the tracked object makes complex movements. The UAV will calculate the relative position of itself and the target object through the bounding box. When the target object moves, the UAV generates the speed command according to the relative position changes to achieve object tracking in complex environments.

Fig. 9. Experimental diagram of complex object motion.

We tested the algorithm in scenes with lighting changes and similar background interference. The tracked target object moves from a low-light indoor environment to a high-light outdoor environment. During the experiment, the tracked object moves randomly and continuously. As shown in Fig. 9a, the UAV and the tracked object are in the dead zone and remain hovering; Fig. 9b shows that the UAV follows the object to generate downward motion; Fig. 9c and e show that when the tracked object continues to move forward, the distance between the two gradually increases, and the UAV generates forward motion; Fig. 9d shows that the tracked object moves to the right, and the UAV generates a right motion accordingly.

Two groups of experiments show that the proposed UAV object tracking system can track accurately and in real time when the tracked object moves back and forth, left and right, rotation, up and down, even there are similar object interference and illumination changes. Experimental results show that the designed UAV system can achieve the real-time and robust UAV autonomous object tracking.

4 Conclusion

In this paper, a high-speed Kernel Correlation Filter (KCF) tracking algorithm is combined with UAV motion control, and an autonomous object tracking system for UAV is designed. Experiments show that this system can achieve autonomous real-time tracking of highly robust UAVs only with the support of CPU with low memory usage. In the future, we will consider using the redetection mechanism to further deal with the problem of the object disappears in the FOV of the UAV during the tracking.

Acknowledgment. This work is supported by the Chinese National Natural Science Foundation (Grant No. 61873200, U20A20225, U2013601), Provincial Key Research and Development Program (Grant No. 2022-GY111, 202004a05020058), Xi'an Science and Technology Plan Project (Grant No. 22GXFW0070), the Natural Science Foundation of Hefei (Grant No. 2021032), and the CAAI-Huawei MindSpore Open Fund.

References

1. Wu, X., Li, W., Hong, D., Tao, R., Du, Q.: Deep learning for unmanned aerial vehicle-based object detection and tracking: a survey. IEEE Geosci. Remote Sens. Mag. **10**(1), 91–124 (2021)
2. Gong, Z., Gao, G., Wang, M.: An adaptive particle filter for target tracking based on double space-resampling. IEEE Access **9**, 91053–91061 (2021)
3. Henriques, J.F., Caseiro, R., Martins, P., Batista, J.: Exploiting the circulant structure of tracking-by-detection with kernels. In: Fitzgibbon, A., Lazebnik, S., Perona, P., Sato, Y., Schmid, C. (eds.) ECCV 2012. LNCS, vol. 7575, pp. 702–715. Springer, Heidelberg (2012). https://doi.org/10.1007/978-3-642-33765-9_50
4. Henriques, J.F., Caseiro, R., Martins, P., Batista, J.: High-speed tracking with kernelized correlation filters. IEEE Trans. Pattern Anal. Mach. Intell. **37**(3), 583–596 (2015)
5. Danelljan, M., Häger, G., Khan, F.S., Felsberg, M.: Discriminative scale space tracking. IEEE Trans. Pattern Anal. Mach. Intell. **39**(8), 1561–1575 (2017)
6. Marvasti-Zadeh, S.M., Cheng, L., Ghanei-Yakhdan, H., Kasaei, S.: Deep learning for visual tracking: a comprehensive survey. IEEE Trans. Intell. Transp. Syst. **23**(5), 3943–3968 (2022)
7. Xu, Y., Wang, Z., Li, Z., Ye, Y., Yu, G.: SiamFC++: towards robust and accurate visual tracking with target estimation guidelines. In: Proceedings of the AAAI Conference on Artificial Intelligence, pp. 12549–12556 (2020)
8. Nam, G., Oh, S.W., Lee, J., Kim, S.J.: DMV: visual object tracking via part-level dense memory and voting-based retrieval. ArXiv, abs/2003.09171 (2020)
9. Elayaperumal, D., Joo, Y.H.: Aberrance suppressed spatio-temporal correlation filters for visual object tracking. Patt. Recognit. **115**, 107922 (2021)
10. Xing, D., Evangeliou, N., Tsoukalas, A., Tzes, A.: Siamese transformer pyramid networks for real-time UAV tracking. In: 2022 IEEE/CVF Winter Conference on Applications of Computer Vision (WACV), pp. 1898–1907 (2022)

11. Chakrabarty, A., Morris, R.A., Bouyssounouse, X., Hunt, R.: Autonomous indoor object tracking with the Parrot AR.Drone. In: 2016 International Conference on Unmanned Aircraft Systems (ICUAS), pp. 25–30 (2016)
12. Nebehay, G., Pflugfelder, R.P.: Clustering of static-adaptive correspondences for deformable object tracking. In: 2015 IEEE Conference on Computer Vision and Pattern Recognition (CVPR), pp. 2784–2791 (2015)
13. Askar, W.A., Elmowafy, O., Youssif, A.A., Elnashar, G.A.: Optimized UAV object tracking framework based on Integrated Particle filter with ego-motion transformation matrix. In: MATEC Web of Conferences. EDP Sciences (2017)
14. Li, Y., Fu, C., Ding, F., Huang, Z., Lu, G.: AutoTrack: towards high-performance visual tracking for UAV with automatic spatio-temporal regularization. In: IEEE/CVF Conference on Computer Vision and Pattern Recognition (CVPR), pp. 11920–11929 (2020)
15. Xu, L., Luo, H., Hui, B., Chang, Z.: Real-time robust tracking for motion blur and fast motion via correlation filters. Sensors (Basel, Switzerland) **16**(9) (2016)

A Vision-Based Rail Alignment Detection Algorithm for the Transfer Platform

Jie Wang, Jing Xin$^{(\boxtimes)}$, Yangguang Hou, and Shangbin Jiao

Xi'an University of Technology, Xi'an 710048, People's Republic of China
xinj@xaut.edu.cn

Abstract. Transfer platform equipment is often used to transport the Electric Multiple Units (EMU). When the EMU moves up and down the transfer platform, the rail on the transfer platform needs to be precisely aligned with the ground rail. This process is called as rail alignment. Due to the drastic change of illumination on the real industrial environment, both the recognition rate of the ground rail number and the rail detection accuracy are low. Aiming at this problem, this paper proposes a vision-based rail number recognition and rail detection algorithm. Firstly, the intelligent optical character recognition (OCR) visual recognition technology is used to recognize the rail number, and recognition results is used to judge whether the transfer platform has reached the target rail. When reaching the target rail, the improved Line Segment Detector (LSD) linear detection algorithm is used to detect the rail, and the specific position of the target rail in the image is obtained. Finally, combined with the camera calibration results, the physical distance information between the target rail and the rail on the transfer platform is obtained. In addition, the recognition accuracy of the ground rail number exceeds 95% at the low-speed motion of the camera (6.243 m/min), and also exceeds 80% at the high-speed motion (21.536 m/min). The average value of the rail alignment detection accuracy is 5.6 mm, and the accuracy requirement of rail alignment task is 10 mm on the real industrial environments, which meets the high-precision rail alignment task requirements for the transfer platform.

Keywords: Transfer Platform · Rail Alignment · Rail Detection · Rail Number Recognition

1 Introduction

With the rapid development of China's railway vehicle manufacturing industry, the railway vehicle manufacturing industry has been at the international leading level and has gradually entered the international market. It has been exported to many countries in the world, such as Russia, Kazakhstan, Brazil, Australia, Mozambique and other countries [1]. The transfer platform is a large-scale special non-standard equipment, which is used for the parallel transferring vehicles between different rails in the manufacturing and maintenance process of railway vehicles [2].

© The Author(s), under exclusive license to Springer Nature Singapore Pte Ltd. 2023
Z. Yu et al. (Eds.): CIRAC 2022, CCIS 1770, pp. 327–338, 2023.
https://doi.org/10.1007/978-981-99-0301-6_25

When the EMU moves up and down the transfer platform, the rail on the transfer platform needs to be fully aligned with the rail on the ground. Currently, the aligning of the rail on the transfer platform is mainly operated manually. Due to design defects, operation and maintenance, etc., the rail alignment accuracy is relatively low [3]. This seriously affects the efficiency of getting on and off the transfer platform. So, it is necessary to design a fast and high precision vision-based detection algorithm for transfer platform rail aligning.

Linear detection is the key technology to realize the automatic rail alignment. The traditional linear detection methods will have over-detection and under-detection problems in the actual application process, and the detection accuracy is also insufficient [4]. To realize the accurate detection of the rail, it is important to extract the rail line well [5]. There are three kinds of image line segment detection, namely, Hough transform method, edge connection method, and Gradient-based method [6]. The Hough transform method is difficult to determine the line segment endpoints, and Almazan et al. [7] combined the global accumulation method in Hough with the perceptual combination method of the image, which finally improved the detection results. The edge connection method generates lines by fitting the edges of the lines. Akinlar et al. [8] proposed a fast line detection algorithm based on edge pixel chains. Lu et al. [9] considered that information would be lost during edge detection, so they proposed an adaptive parameter Canny algorithm to extract edges.

The edge-based method needs to be able to extract the edge well, but there is always a loss of the image information in edge extraction. The image gradient-based methods extract straight lines by using similar gradient directions in local regions. Therefore, researchers put forward a variety of improved line segment detectors (LSD) [10–12] to improve the accuracy and robustness of straight line detection. However, the above methods will detect all the straight lines in the image, and does not involve screening out straight lines that meet the conditions from multiple straight lines. Under the influence of factors such as drastic changes in light and complex on the real industrial environments of the transfer platform, how to accurately detect and screen out the rail is a problem that needs to be solved in this paper.

Aiming at this problem, this paper proposes a vision-based rail alignment detection algorithm for the transfer platform, including rail number recognition and rail detection. The proposed algorithm improves the recognition rate of ground rail numbers and the accuracy of rail detection in spite of the drastic change of illumination on the real industrial environments.

The rest of this paper is organized as follows; Sect. 2 describes the principle of the proposed algorithm. The experimental results and performance analysis are presented in Sect. 3. Finally, summary and possible improvements as future works are given in Sect. 4.

2   Algorithm

In this paper, a vision-based rail alignment detection algorithm for the transfer platform is proposed, including rail number recognition and rail detection. Figure 1 shows a transfer platform on the real industrial environments, in which the yellow area is transfer platform device. And the middle is the moving area of the transfer platform. When the rail alignment task is performed, the image is captured on the real industrial environments through the designed online image acquisition system. The rail number in the image is recognized by the vision-based rail number recognition algorithm, and the recognition results is used to judge whether the transfer platform has reached the target rail. When the transfer platform reaches the target rail, the ground rail is detected by a vision-based rail line detection algorithm. Once the transfer platform rail and the ground rail are accurately aligned, which shown in Fig. 2, the rail alignment task is completed.

In the next section, three main parts of rail alignment detection algorithm will be described in detail. They include online image acquisition, rail number recognition based on intelligent OCR and rail detection based on improved LSD straight line detection.

Fig. 1. A transfer platform on the real industrial environments

Fig. 2. Schematic of the rail alignment

2.1 Online Image Acquisition

In order to realize the acquisition of images on the real industrial environments, an image acquisition system is designed in this paper. Figure 3 shows a schematic diagram of camera layout, in which the yellow region represents the transfer platform, and both ends of the transfer platform are the rail numbers and rails that need to be detected. The installation position of the alignment camera is F9 in Fig. 3. The alignment camera is used to capture the current rail images in the real industrial environments when the transfer platform moves left and right. After that, the captured rail images will be transmitted to the rail alignment server for rail number recognition and rail detection in the real industrial environments. The rail alignment camera used in this system is Huarui A7500MG20, which is a 5-megapixel color camera. In order to be able to see the rail and rail number in the camera's field of view at the same time, the camera was installed at 5.5 m above the ground rail, and the installation angle was obliquely forward. The field of view of the camera is 1.5 m × 1.7 m, and the real distance corresponding to an average single pixel is 0.65 mm. The images collected by the device can meet the requirements of high-precision detection.

Fig. 3. Schematic diagram of camera layout.

2.2 Rail Number Recognition

In the actual EMU production task, the recognition of target rail number is an indispensable task, which can help the transfer platform to accurately reach the target rail in the moving process. The common OCR character recognition algorithm can effectively solve this problem.

OCR commonly known as optical character recognition. The whole process of the traditional OCR algorithm [13] is shown in Fig. 4. In some cases where the environment is better and the text is more standardized, traditional OCR can also be well recognized. However, the traditional OCR algorithm is subject to much manual intervention. It is necessary to introduce manual intervention in the above-mentioned links, and it is difficult to achieve end-to-end training. Therefore, the recognition effect is poor in some complex environments and large interference.

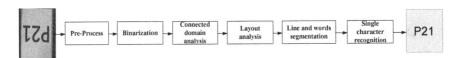

Fig. 4. Flow chart of traditional OCR technology.

In the real industrial environments, the sunlight often changes drastically. In some camera angles of view, the rail number will be reflected, which leads to the deterioration of the traditional OCR recognition effect. Figure 5 shows an original image of the rail number, which is collected using the rail alignment camera in the real industrial environments.

Therefore, in order to realize the accurate recognition of the rail number, it is necessary to preprocess the image in the real industrial environments. Preprocessing is the first step in OCR recognition, which is used for image enhancement [14]. For images with bending deformation, Ma [15] et al. proposed the DocUNet algorithm, which uses a learning-based method to restore distorted document images to flat images. For low-resolution images, super-resolution image reconstruction is generally used, for example, sparse expression is adopted for super-resolution image reconstruction [16].

In this paper, the color enhancement of the rail number image is carried out, and then it is mapped to the HSV (Hue Saturation Value) color space to extract rail number for threshold segmentation. Figure 6 shows the result of the rail number after preprocessing, respectively. It can be seen that the rail numbers are completely extracted after the image is preprocessed.

Fig. 5. Original rail number.   **Fig. 6.** Preprocessing result of rail number.

In view of the excellent feature extraction ability of deep learning, a variety of deep learning models are applied to OCR technology [17–20], among which the design of network model is the key point. In the EAST algorithm [17], its network model is a fully convolutional neural network, which directly returns the outline of the text target region on the entire image target, and finally outputs the text prediction at each position. In 2018, liu et al. proposed a Pixel-based algorithm FOTS [18], which combined text detection and text recognition, and proposed an end-to-end trainable network. Li et al. combined Pixel-based and Anchor-based, and proposed the Pixel-Anchor algorithm [19], which combined the advantages of Pixel-based and Anchor-based, and improved the performance of the recognition network by dilated spatial pyramid pooling.

Therefore, in this paper the traditional manual method is replaced with a DL_based intelligent OCR algorithm [20]. The preprocessed results are used as input into the Resnet and SLTM models, which improves the recognition rate of the OCR algorithm. Figure 7 shows the flow chart of the rail number recognition based intelligent OCR recognition.

The rail number recognition algorithm can be mainly divided into three steps. The first step is to capture the rail number image, which is the input of the entire intelligent OCR algorithm. The second step is to pre-process the image for improving the accuracy of subsequent intelligent OCR recognition. By analyzing the acquired images, it can be concluded that the color of the rail number is clearly distinguished from the surrounding environment, so the rail number can be extracted by color difference. The third step is to input the preprocessed image into the intelligent OCR recognition algorithm to identify the rail number.

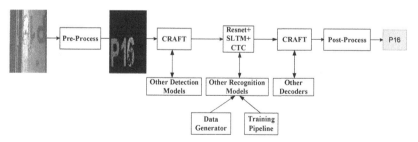

Fig. 7. The flow chart of the rail number recognition based intelligent OCR recognition.

2.3 Rail Detection

LSD algorithm involves two basic concepts: gradient and image baseline (Level-line). Firstly, LSD calculates the angle between each pixel and the reference line to construct a level-line field. Then, the pixels with approximately the same orientation in the field are merged using a region growing algorithm to obtain a series of line support regions. Finally, straight line segments are extracted through merging the pixels in these regions, and error is controlled based on "Contrario model" and "Helmholtz principle" [21]. Figure 8(a), (b) shows the original rail image and the result of LSD line detection in the real industrial environments, respectively.

As can be seen in Fig. 8, in the real industrial environments, the rail and the gasket are tightly combined. And the gasket exists in the form of small squares. The traditional straight line detection algorithm is easy to misidentify the rail and the concave edge. In addition, the complexity of the gasket also makes the algorithm unable to completely segment the rail. In order to realize the accurate detection of the rail, an improved LSD straight line detection algorithm is proposed.

If the entire image is processed, the performance of subsequent rail detection and extraction will inevitably be reduced. Therefore, it is particularly important to extract the rail and washer region accurately and to quickly recognize [22, 23]. Firstly, the current RGB image is mapped to the HSV color space through HSV threshold segmentation [24]. The gasket region could be detected using the color difference between the gasket and the surrounding region, so as to determine the rough region of the rail in the current image. Figure 9 shows the extraction result of rail region, in which Fig. 9(a) is the original image, and Fig. 9(b) is the rail region image after threshold segmentation. Then, LSD straight line detection algorithm is applied in the rail region after threshold segmentation, and the straight line that meets the slope and length requirements in the region can be detected. Finally, the straight line is screened using principal component analysis [25], and the qualified rail is therefore screened out. Figure 10 shows the block diagram of the improved LSD line detection algorithm.

| (a) | (b) | (a) | (b) |

Fig. 8. Original rail image and LSD straight line detection results.

Fig. 9. The extraction result of rail region.

As shown in Fig. 10, the rail detection algorithm is mainly divided into five steps. The first step is collect the image offline through the camera. The second step is to crop out the fixed rail region in the image according to the approximate position information of the fixed rail in the image to obtain the rail region clipping map. The third step extracts the rail region. The fourth step extracts the straight line in the rail region through the LSD line detection algorithm. The fifth step is to screen out suitable straight lines by principal component analysis. Finally, the rail inspection results of the field image are obtained.

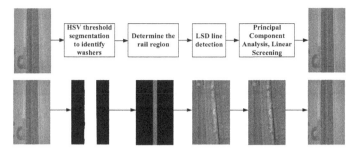

Fig. 10. Block diagram of improved LSD line detection algorithm

3 Experiment

In this section, several groups experiment of the rail number recognition and rail detection are conducted to verify the validity of the rail number recognition algorithm and rail detection algorithm proposed in this paper. The online image acquisition system constructed in the Sect. 2.1, is used to collect 1200 valid images of 26 rail numbers in the real industrial environments. Among them, 520 images are used for rail detection, and 680 images are used for rail number recognition. Finally, combined with the camera calibration results, the real distance information obtained by the rail detection algorithm is obtained.

3.1 Camera Calibration

The physical distance information between the fixed rail on the transfer platform and the target rail is the key control quantity required to realize the automatic rail alignment of the transfer platform. Only the pixel distance between the fixed rail and the target rail is obtained through image detection, and needs to be converted into the actual physical distance. Therefore, the following camera calibration process is designed to obtain the mapping relationship between the pixel distance and the actual physical distance in the entire camera field of view. The checkerboard is placed in the upper left, middle left, lower left, upper right, middle right, lower right areas in sequence. The placement covers the entire camera field of view. A total of six calibration images are collected, as shown in Fig. 11 (The size of the checkerboard used is 12×17, and the distance between the corners is 2 cm).

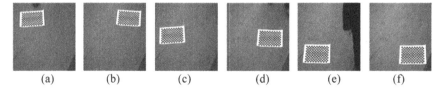

(a)   (b)   (c)   (d)   (e)   (f)

Fig. 11. Checkerboard layout diagram

Next, the six calibration maps are calibrated, and the pixel coordinates of each corner of the checkerboard in the image are obtained using the corner detector. According to the checkerboard size, the ratio of the pixel distance at each corner to the real distance can be obtained. The proportional values at each corner are fitted on a plane, and finally the mapping relationship between the real distance and the pixel distance in the entire camera field of view is obtained as shown in Fig. 12.

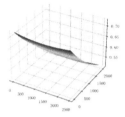

Fig. 12. Pixel distance and true distance mapping ratio

3.2 Recognition Results and Analysis of Rail Numbers

In order to verify the recognition effect of the rail number, several experiments are carried out on a video of the moving transfer platform working in the real industrial environments. The video includes a total of 26 rail numbers from P1 to P26, and a total of 1416 images, of which there are a total of 680 valid images with complete rail numbers. During the low-speed movement of the camera, approximately 90 valid images can be collected for each rail number. During the high-speed movement of the camera, approximately 20 valid images can be collected for each rail number. Table 1 shows the recognition results of P1—P10 rail numbers.

The operation of the transfer platform is divided into high speed state and low speed state, and the effective images (i.e. the images with complete rail number) that appear during the operation of the transfer platform are counted, the algorithm is judged by the correct recognition accuracy.

It can be seen from the Table 1 that the recognition accuracy is above 95% under the low-speed motion of the camera (6.243 m/min). When the camera moves at a high speed (21.536 m/min), some blurred images appear due to the camera moving too fast, resulting in a recognition error, but the final recognition accuracy of the rail number is also above 80%. The recognition accuracy of the rail number meet the requirement of the automatical rail alignment task on the real industrial environments.

3.3 Rail Detection Results and Analysis

The improved LSD straight line detection algorithm proposed in this paper is used to detect the rails on the real industrial environments. There are 26 rails in total, and 20 images are collected for each rail, a total of 520 images are used for verify rail detection algorithm. Figure 13 shows the detection results of rail at P1, P7, P8, and P26. The green line in the image is the final screened rail side line. It can be seen that the green line,

Table 1. Recognition result of rail numbers

rail number	Valid images that appear during the relocation process	Number of correct recognition	Recognition rate
P1	95	93	97.9%
P2	90	87	96.7%
P3	25	22	88%
P4	20	17	85%
P5	20	18	90%
P6	23	20	86.9%
P7	19	18	94.7%
P8	23	20	86.9%
P9	24	20	83.3%
P10	21	18	85.7%

which represent the detection results of the rail, almost completely coincides with the side edge of the rail.

It can be seen from the Fig. 13 that the improved LSD straight line detection algorithm can effectively detect the two side edges of the rail in the different rail number, different regions of the image (left, right, middle).

When the fixed rail on the transfer platform is completely aligned with the ground target rail, the pixel distance between the target rail and the fixed rail in the image can be calculated by comparing the line along the side of the target rail and the line along the side of the fixed rail (as shown in Fig. 14). Combined with the camera calibration results in Sect. 3.1, the pixel distances can be converted into real physical distances.

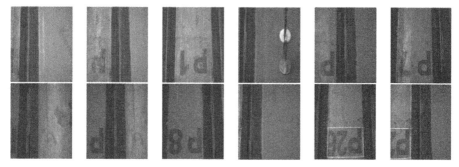

Fig. 13. The result of rail detection (The green line in the image is the final screened rail side line)

In the experiment, 520 images are used to verify the rail detection performance, performance analysis of the algorithm is shown in Table 2. The ground truth data is obtained by the actual manual measurement. The maximum error of the distance is 15 mm, and the minimum error is 0.1 mm, and the average error is 5.6 mm, and the average running time of a single image is 80 ms.

The maximum error of the distance is 15 mm.The specific reasons for the error are as follows: there are 26 rails in the site, and there are two rails where the washers side edge are severely worn. There is a gap between the worn washers and the rail If the detection results of the washer side edge in the image are more robust, the washer side edge line will be misjudged as the rail side edge line, leading to an increase in distance error. This kind of misjudgment can be improved from two aspects: algorithm maintenance and hardware maintenance. The interference caused by the edge of worn gasket can be removed by timely replacing the rail gasket and eliminating the gap. Generally, the difference of gray level features between the images on both sides of the rail side is obviously greater than that of the images on both sides of the gasket side. The gray level difference value of both sides of the side line detected by the algorithm is obtained by establishing an appropriate gray level difference model on both sides of the straight line, and an appropriate threshold is set to eliminate the misjudged gasket side line.

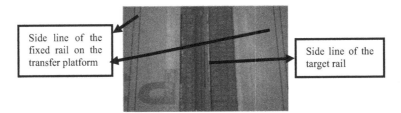

Fig. 14. Schematic diagram of rail side line

It can be seen from the Table 2 that the proposed rail detection algorithm meets the rail detection accuracy requirements (<10 mm) and real-time requirements (<100 ms) of rail alignment tasks on the real industrial environments.

Table 2. Algorithm performance analysis

Maximum measurement error/mm	Minimum measurement error/mm	Average error/mm	Single image algorithm running time/ms
15	0.1	5.6	80

4 Conclusion

In this paper, a vision-based rail number and rail detection algorithm is proposed for the automatic rail alignment system of the transfer platform. It can realize the recognition of the rail number and the detection of the rail on the real industrial environments. The rail number recognition algorithm can adapt to the complex environment of the real industrial, and can also ensure a good rail number recognition accuracy when the camera moves at a high speed (21.536 m/min). In the case of slow speed (6.243 m/min), the accuracy rate is at least 90%. So the recognition effect is good. The average distance error of the transfer platform rail and the ground rail after aligning is within 10 mm, the rail detection algorithm can make the rail alignment accuracy of the transfer platform reach millimeter level when it is moving. Which meets the requirements of the high-precision rail alignment task of the transfer platform.

As future works, in order to improve the adaptability of the algorithm proposed on the real industrial environments, the proposed rail alignment detection algorithms will be further extended into two aspects:

(1) During the moving process of the transfer platform on the real industrial environments, there will be a camera shake problem, which will affect the rail alignment error in actual production. It is necessary to design an anti-shake rail straight line detection algorithm.
(2) There are some special rails on the real industrial environments (multiple sets of rails coexist), in order to improve the adaptability of the algorithm, it is realized by adding labels to assist the recognition based on the original improved LSD line detection.

Acknowledgment. This work is supported by the Shaanxi Provincial Key Research and Development Program (Grant No. 2022-GY111), Xi'an Science and Technology Plan Project (Grant No. 22GXFW0070), and Chinese National Natural Science Foundation (Grant No. 61873200).

References

1. Chu, F., Zu, X.: Research and design for transfer plat-form with multi track. Equipment Manufact. Technol. **43**(08), 182–184 (2015)
2. Liu, Z.: Design of 180t heavy-duty rotary crane platform. Rail Transit Equipment Technol. **28**(02), 18–21 (2020)
3. Guo, T.: The new migrating machine. Coal Min. Mach. **25**(03), 97–98 (2004)
4. Grompone von Gioi, R., Jakubowicz, J., Morel, J.M., Randall, G.: On straight line segment detection. J. Math. Imaging Vis. **32**(3), 313–347 (2008)
5. Micusik, B., Wildenauer, H.: Descriptor free visual indoor localization with line segments. In: Proceedings of the IEEE Conference on Computer Vision and Pattern Recognition, pp. 3165–3173 (2015)
6. Zheng, X., Zhong, B.: Overview and evaluation of image straight line segment detection algorithms. Comput. Eng. Appl. **55**(17), 9–19 (2019)
7. Almazan, E.J., Tal, R., Qian, Y., Elder, J.H.: MCMLSD: a dynamic programming approach to line segment detection. In: Proceedings of the IEEE Conference on Computer Vision and Pattern Recognition, pp. 2031–2039 (2017)
8. Akinlar, C., Topal, C.: EDLines: a real-time line segment detector with a false detection control. Patt. Recogn. Lett. **32**(13), 1633–1642 (2011)
9. Rick Chang, J., Li, C., Poczos, B., Vijaya Kumar, B.V.K., Sankaranarayanan, A.C.: One network to solve them all--solving linear inverse problems using deep projection models. In: Proceedings of the IEEE International Conference on Computer Vision, pp. 5888–5897 (2017)

10. Von Gioi, R., Jakubowicz, J., Morel, J.M., Randall, G.: LSD: a fast line segment detector with a false detection control. IEEE Trans. Patt. Anal. Mach. Intell. **32**(4), 722–732 (2010)
11. Salaün, Y., Marlet, R., Monasse, P.: Multiscale line segment detector for robust and accurate SfM. In: 2016 23rd International Conference on Pattern Recognition (ICPR), pp. 2000–2005. IEEE (2016)
12. Luo, W., Cheng, Y., Li, Y., Wen, P.: Line segment detection algorithms towards high resolution color image. Microelectron. Comput. **46**(12), 25–30 (2017)
13. Li, C., Li, X.: Intelligent book recognition system based on Chinese OCR model. Comput. Knowl. Technol. **17**(28), 20–22 (2021)
14. Wang, K., Yang, F., Jiang, S.: An overview of optical character recognition. Comput. Appl. Res. **37**(S2), 22–24 (2020)
15. Ma, K., Shu, Z., Bai, X., Wang, J., Samaras, D.: DocUNET: document image unwarping via a stacked U-Net. In: Proceedings of the IEEE Conference on Computer Vision and Pattern Recognition, pp. 4700–4709 (2018)
16. Yang, J., Wright, J., Huang, T., Ma, Y.: Image super-resolution as sparse representation of raw image patches. In: 2008 IEEE Conference on Computer Vision and Pattern Recognition, pp. 1–8. IEEE (2008)
17. Zhou, X., et al.: EAST: an efficient and accurate scene text detector. In: Proceedings of the IEEE Conference on Computer Vision and Pattern Recognition, pp. 5551–5560 (2017)
18. Liu, X., Liang, D., Yan, S., Chen, D., Qiao, Y., Yan, J.: FOTS: fast oriented text spotting with a unified network. In: Proceedings of the IEEE Conference on Computer Vision and Pattern Recognition, pp. 5676–5685 (2018)
19. Li, Y., et al.: Pixel-anchor: a fast oriented scene text detector with combined networks. arXiv preprint arXiv:1811.07432(2018)
20. Wang, D.: Applied research on artificial intelligence OCR technology. Electron. Softw. Eng. **11**(01), 122–125 (2022)
21. Cao, Y., He, T., Liu, L.: Rail surface boundary extraction based on improved LSD line detection algorithm. J. East China Jiaotong Univ. **38**(03), 95–101 (2021)
22. Zhang, H., Jin, X., Wu, Q., Wang, Y., He, Z., Yang, Y.: Automatic visual detection system of railway surface defects with curvature filter and improved Gaussian mixture model. IEEE Trans. Instrum. Meas. **67**(7), 1593–1608 (2018)
23. Kai, W., Guicang, Z.: Research on image edge detection based on improved ant colony algorithm. Comput. Eng. Appl. **53**(23), 171–176 (2017)
24. Xu, J., Qu, H., Zhang, Z., Wang, J.: Color texture image retrieval based on multi-feature Fusion in HSV space. Comput. Dig. Eng. **49**(11), 2342–2347 (2021)
25. Xu, J., Yang, Y., Liu, M., Yang, B.: Principal component analysis is used to identify adhesive steel defects in infrared image sequences, Indust. Buildings **52**(S1), pp. 496–500+205 (2022)

Construction and Practice of "Three 'Wholes' and Six 'Integrations'" Intelligent Robot Education System

Duanling Li[1,2(✉)], Hongyu Ma[1], Ran Wei[1], Dehui Zhang[2], and Fujun Liang[3]

[1] Beijing University of Posts and Telecommunications, 10 Xi Tu Cheng Road, Haidian District, Beijing 100876, China
Duanlingli@bupt.edu.cn
[2] Shaanxi University of Science and Technology, Weiyang District, Xi'an 712000, China
[3] Machinery Industry Information Institute, Beijing 100037, China

Abstract. In recent years, the number of universities successfully applying for robot engineering has increased year by year, however, the educational resources of most universities can't fulfill the learning needs of such a highly interdisciplinary subject. In order to solve several outstanding problems commonly existed in the practical education of intelligent robots, this paper puts forward the concept of "three 'wholes' and six 'integrations'" to build a complete system and institutional mechanism system of practical education for innovation and entrepreneurship, to cultivate students' two abilities of "practice" and "innovation and entrepreneurship". The methods may solve some problems in the practical intelligent robot's education of entrepreneurship and innovation, aiming to help to form a virtuous circle system like an ecosystem. This will help college teachers to build a complete education system, which is conducive to cultivating high-quality talents who are better at innovation and entrepreneurship. This paper has four innovations: orientation, systematization, modularization and achievement.

Keywords: Three "wholes" and six "integrations" · Practice · Innovative · Entrepreneurship

1 Introduction

In order to improve the robot industry structure and achieve industrial upgrading, China launched a series of related industrial policies from 2013 to 2016. For instance, in 2013, the Ministry of Industry and Information Technology issued the policy "Guiding Opinions on Promoting the Development of Industrial Robots"; In 2015, the State Council issued the policy "Made in China 2025"; In 2016, the Ministry of Industry and Information Technology, the National Development and Reform Commission and the Ministry of Finance issued the policy "Robot Industry Development Plan (2016–2020)". With the government's strong support for the transformation and upgrading of traditional industries, the industrial robot market continues to grow, and the personal/family service

Z. Yu et al. (Eds.): CIRAC 2022, CCIS 1770, pp. 339–348, 2023.
https://doi.org/10.1007/978-981-99-0301-6_26

robot market is driven to grow rapidly. Moreover, the concept of robots and the popularity of market participation is consistently rise. The development of robot technology in industry and its application in life service field urgently need a large number of robot engineering professionals.

2 Review of Related Research

"Robotic Engineering Major" is an emerging major established in response to national construction needs and international development trends. In 2016, it was approved by the Ministry of Education as an emerging undergraduate major and included in the enrollment plan. This major is an interdisciplinary frontier subject, which takes the robot science and technology problems involved in control science and engineering, mechanical engineering, computer science and technology, biomedical engineering and cognitive science as the research objects, which comprehensively applies the theories, methods and technologies of natural science, engineering technology, social science, humanities and other related disciplines to study the intelligent perception of robots, optimal control and system design, man-machine interaction mode and other academic issues. Students majoring in robot engineering have the characteristics of thick foundation, wide caliber, emphasis on practice and innovation. They have the ability of team organization, coordination and comprehensive application of what they have learned, while having the professional advantage of mastering multidisciplinary basic theories.

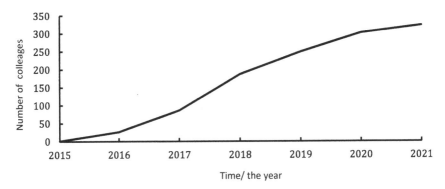

Fig. 1. The number of universities that successfully applied for robot engineering major

In recent years, the number of colleges successfully applying for robot engineering has increased year by year (shown in Fig. 1), however, the proportion of robotics engineering majors offered is not high among the majors offered by the majority of domestic universities, while it can't fulfill the students' learning needs for intelligent robots, which is a highly interdisciplinary subject. Therefore, the original traditional technology, cultivation environment and objectives need to be reformed and optimized [1]. The adoption of current engineering interdisciplinary and innovative teaching, which is directly reflected in relying on and developing digital systems and open-source software, is to ensure and promote the training and development of undergraduate robotics engineering technology and innovative talents [2]. In the construction process of robot direction, not only the spiral teaching and gradual teaching are required, but also the curriculum system should be based on digital and intelligent system technology. It is necessary to reasonably organize the teaching contents such as science and engineering foundation, major professional foundation, robot technology foundation, advanced application of robot engineering and comprehensive design knowledge, which infuses students' foundation, expansion and discussion. In the course content and experiment, we should fully tap the ideas, means and practices of using open-source hardware and software resources that gather the wisdom of the global elite.

There are several outstanding problems in the practice education of intelligent robots:

(1) Lack of a complete system, the number of training bases is small and the quality is unstable [3]. Therefore, students' practical opportunities and internship time become less.

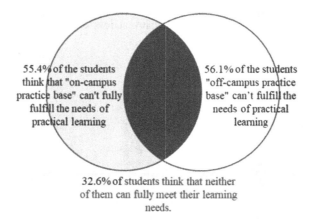

55.4% of the students think that "on-campus practice base" can't fully fulfill the needs of practical learning

56.1% of the students "off-campus practice base" can't fulfill the needs of practical learning

32.6% of students think that neither of them can fully meet their learning needs.

Fig. 2. The satisfaction of students' training base

Domestic surveys show that 55.4% and 56.1% of the students think that "on-campus practice base" and "off-campus practice base" can't fully fulfill the needs of practical learning (shown in Fig. 2), which also shows that colleges and universities haven't fully connected theory with practice [4]. Furthermore, students will have less understanding of future jobs and industrial chains. Moreover, they have poor practical ability to solve practical problems.

(2) Lack of innovative inspiration and creative realization carrier, the students' interest is in low level. As a result, they do not have a strong enough sense and interest of innovation and entrepreneurship [5].

The following Table 1 shows that only 42.3% of the students agree that "they have made a preliminary plan for their career through four years of study", 64.2% of the students think that they have not fully mastered the basic knowledge of employment and entrepreneurship, and only 44.3% of the students think that colleges can entirely carry out various innovation and entrepreneurship competitions.

Table 1. The students' recognition of teaching quality in school

Form	Agree (%)	Disagree (%)
Have a preliminary career plan	57.7	42.3
Master the basic knowledge	64.2	35.8
Carry out various competitions	55.7	44.3

(3) On-campus teachers do not have enough practical experience in industry and entrepreneurship [6]. The construction of teaching staff pays more attention to the requirements of academic qualifications, scientific research and classroom theoretical teaching level, which may invest less energy in effectively guiding students.

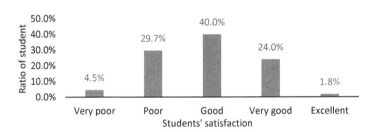

Fig. 3. Students' satisfaction with teachers' innovative spirit

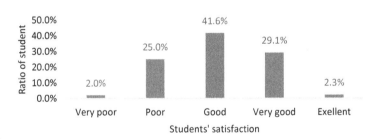

Fig. 4. Students' satisfaction with teachers' teaching methods

According to the questionnaire of nearly 500 students, about 66.0% of the students are satisfied with the innovative spirit of the teachers (shown in Fig. 3), about 73.0% are

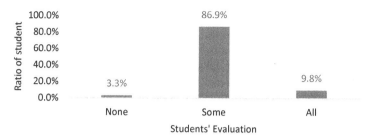

Fig. 5. Students' Evaluation of Innovative Teachers in Teaching

satisfied with the teaching methods of the teachers (shown in Fig. 4), and about 87% think that only some teachers are innovative teachers (shown in Fig. 5). Obviously, the innovative spirit and teaching methods of teachers in some universities still need to be further promoted and improved [7].

This paper will further promote the reform of education and teaching through the exploration of the dual-innovation education system, and inject new kinetic energy and vitality into education and practice, so as to help college teachers to build a complete education system, which is conducive to cultivating high-quality talents who are better at innovation and entrepreneurship.

3 Research Approach

3.1 Basis of Topic Selection

In order to fulfill the students' learning needs for such a highly interdisciplinary intelligent robot, it is necessary to reform and optimize the technology, environment and teaching objectives, which can enhance students' learning interest, increase their practical ability and cultivate their innovative and entrepreneurial ability.

3.2 Research Process

With the common problems in the practice teaching of innovation and entrepreneurship, our research group has made a long-term research on the current situation considering the shortage of training experience and teaching resources. Through the whole cultivation coverage of students' practical ability and innovation and entrepreneurship, the whole chain of double-innovation practical education of "finding problems-inspiring inspiration-improving ability-realizing creativity", the whole process of "the swallow opportunity in freshman year—the college students' innovation project in the second year –deepen the improvement of the project in junior year—the graduation project in senior year" is based on the idea and practice of " three 'wholes' and six 'integrations'", which includes interdisciplinary integration, teaching and research integration, inter-college integration, college-enterprise integration, integration at home and abroad, as well as online and offline integration, thereby building a rounded system and institutional mechanism system of double-innovation practical education, and strive to cultivate students' ability of " practice" and " innovative entrepreneurship"[8].

Reverse Design, Revise the Training Plan, and Implement the Training Goal of Innovation and Entrepreneurship. In recent years, all majors are built according to the requirements of engineering education professional certification, which includes: student-centered educational philosophy, the educational orientation of OBE [9], as well as continuous quality culture. According to the concept of OBE, the three elements of expected learning outcomes—implementation of teaching—evaluation of learning outcomes should form a closed loop of educational process.

According to the needs of professional certification, this paper designs the talent training objectives according to the professional characteristics, and defines what the results are. After the goal is formulated, it still needs to be further decomposed into graduation requirements, and then further decomposed into the whole curriculum system, and the curriculum goal is refined into six-dimensional goals according to the theory of "meaningful learning". The basic logic of the theory of "meaningful learning" is to make students have psychological cognition of the new knowledge they have acquired and consider that the learning content is meaningful. Students' recognition will be transformed into learning motivation. Instead of instilling "value" directly, teachers should explain value from professional knowledge. Only when students learn knowledge and know how to apply it, they should integrate multi-disciplinary knowledge while solving practical problems, thus forming the awareness and learning ability of active learning [10]. These goals can be achieved by organizing different teaching activities, different teaching contents and different assessment methods. This is the way to cultivating talents through the talent training programs and curriculum syllabuses, and it is also the requirement to return to the education common sense and education responsibility.

Build a Carrier of Innovation and Entrepreneurship Ability Training with "Full Coverage, Full Chain, and Full Process". The "comprehensive design and innovative exploration experiments" can realize the full coverage of students' ability of practice, innovation and entrepreneurship. Moreover, they can foster students' innovative and entrepreneurial ability, and realize their "whimsical" creativity and dreams. The whole process of cultivating the students' ability is realized by " the swallow opportunity in freshman year—the college students' innovation project in the second year –deepen the improvement of the project in junior year—the graduation project in senior year ", and students are encouraged to participate in innovative and entrepreneurial projects, so as to cultivate creative problem-solving ability and teamwork spirit, to realize the whole chain of practice education with "finding problems-inspiring inspiration-improving ability-realizing creativity", to organize "academic associations" to cultivate students' innovative thought and inspire students' innovative inspiration, and to hold innovative and entrepreneurial activities every year.

According to the process from conception to realization of a robot project, this paper progressively introduces the components of robot system, structural design, mathematical model, driving mechanism, simulation analysis, control method, sensing technology, information fusion, trajectory planning and practical application, etc. Meanwhile, students can participate in the corresponding projects according to the learning progress. Students' participation in the project cannot be limited to the main structure design of the robot, the research of control algorithm or the realization of robot vision. With the cooperation of each group of students, the basic design of intelligent robot can be finally completed, thus it can perform some simple tasks. In the whole process of the completion of the project, the situation of students' learning will be reflected. Furthermore, it will cultivate students' practical ability, teamwork ability and other abilities.

Based on the Project, Promote Six Integrations and Build a Practical Ability Training Mode. With the goal of "cultivating top-notch talents for innovation and entrepreneurship in intelligent robots", this paper is based on disciplines, adopts diversified training models, flexible management models and personalized training programs to stimulate students' desire for exploration, tap students' innovative potential, and cultivate high-quality innovative and entrepreneurial talents. By the "six-integration" education mode of interdisciplinary integration, teaching and research integration, inter-school integration, school-enterprise integration, integration at home and abroad as well as online and offline integration, we can cultivate compound top-notch innovative talents.

During the teaching process of the courses involved in this paper, teachers can add their latest scientific research achievements to it, which can not only help students understand the latest research trends and hot spots in this field, but also encourage interested students to combine with teachers' research direction by participating in the project, so as to promote and realize the talent training mode of "project-based teaching".

The teachers actively carried out offline classroom teaching activities. During the holidays, massive open online course studies such as *System Design Innovation and Robot Practice* and *Charming Robot* were arranged, daily sharing activities were organized, and the projects were grouped in advance. According to the combination of personal interests and teachers' scientific research projects, every student selected a topic and set up a college students' innovation project, so that they could fully study the course with problems in purpose and find solutions to the project from the course.

In order to foster the practical ability of students in the direction of intelligent robots, we should create a good experimental site and training conditions, and build a perfect innovation and entrepreneurship cultivation system. In view of the limited training base and equipment in our university, our team has jointly applied for two collaborative education projects of the Ministry of Education with some enterprises, and the intelligent robot training base is under construction.

Our team tried to invite famous lecturers to broaden students' horizons. The online lecture adopts the new form of "online development and participation in many places". Professor Sun Lining, who is honored *National outstanding youth*, Dean of School of Mechanical and Electrical Engineering of Soochow University, and Dr. Zhang, who is honored *Academician of Hamburg Academy of Sciences*, expert of the *National Thousand Talents Program*, Distinguished Visiting Professor of Tsinghua University, have been invited to jointly give academic lectures. "Listening to the teacher from a distance is thought to be worthy of live up to the most beautiful March." Under the COVID 19 epidemic situation, many students gathered in the online class and enjoyed the frontier lectures of intelligent robot technology, which reflected everyone's desire for knowledge and responsibility for the present. The lecture also inspired the patriotic enthusiasm of the students and reflected the determination of Chinese people all over the world to unite and overcome the difficulties together. One classmate said: I was deeply touched by a remark made by Professor Zhang "Apart from material assistance, we scientists, young people and professors in artificial intelligence and robot research and development, I think what are the important roles we play here ..." From Professor Zhang, I saw my mission and sense of responsibility as a scientific and technological worker. No matter where I am, I should make my own contribution to my "root".

Various forms of teaching and evaluation modes to enhance students' innovative and entrepreneurial ability. During the COVID 19 epidemic, students are not permitted go back to school. In order to eliminate students' anxiety and laziness, our team contacted students one month in advance, established a course QQ group, and launched daily sharing activities in the group. Every day, students took turns to share the cutting-edge technology and the latest hot spots related to the course. Some students said that the "daily sharing" has benefited the most in half a semester. The shared information allows students to understand the industry dynamics, to know what the advanced or popular development direction is, and to what extent it develops, which is of great help to our study direction and even our life planning, and lets us know what direction to work towards. It allows us know the top level in the industry, making clear the gap between ourselves and the top talents in the industry, and keep awe forever, so that we will not rest on our laurels. At the same time, sharing information is a collision of ideas. Everyone likes different directions and fields. Sharing with each other allows us to learn from each other and complement our knowledge blind spots.

How to evaluate the effectiveness of the course? This is a hot topic that many universities are concerned about at present. Universities need to foster and improve students' knowledge, ability and personality. The education that students receive at campus mainly takes knowledge as the carrier, cultivates students' abilities in all aspects, and then shapes their personality through the learning of ideological and political education in curriculum [11]. However, ten or twenty years after graduation, students will find that what determines whether a student's career can reach a high level is personality and character at the first rank, work ability at the second rank, but knowledge at the third rank. The ultimate purpose of the course is to influence students' personality [12]. The evaluation of its effectiveness should not be limited to a certain semester, but should be made in the longer-term development of graduates.

According to reports, after a series of explorations and summaries, Tongji University has established a "three-circle" curriculum ideological and political education mode with the first classroom professional curriculum as the core, the second classroom speculative and practical platform as the extension, and the subject culture as the environmental infiltration. Specifically, first of all, based on the first class, college teachers need to prepare for the ideological and political work of specialized courses. Next, by social practice, professional practice and other second classes, students go down to the grass-roots level and realize the value of this major to society. Finally, as to the third circle, students are requires to understand the connotation of discipline culture, and inherit the excellent qualities of our ancestors. Three circles are wrapped together to achieving the goal of educating people. Therefore, it is also necessary to conduct an all-round and multi-dimensional evaluation of the education system.

In the course of robotics, our team insists on diversified assessment and strict assessment. In the way of assessment, we set up inquiry assessment of homework and final report assessment. Moreover, the teachers will comprehensively consider the usual process and the final results.

In the inquiry-based homework, divergent design questions are put forward, so that students can think based on the foundation and improve their design ideas. For example, in the image recognition part, students' ability to analyze and solve problems is trained by setting coin recognition tasks.

There are various forms of homework, such as research report, lecture propaganda copy, lecture summary, project report, project oral defense and so on, which can comprehensively improve students' ability and engineering literacy.

In the final report-style assessment, the students' mastery of knowledge and ability is examined by systematically designing questions. By the overall design, students can reflect the understanding of robot design, development and application capabilities. Further, we will analyze the corresponding goal achievement degree and collect students' feedback on the learning effect.

Students are encouraged to participate in innovative and entrepreneurial projects to test the teaching achievements and learning ability. Last year, seven groups of students participated in the *Capital University Students Mechanical Innovation Design Competition* and won two first prizes and five second prizes. One article has been accepted by the international conference, one article has been published in WeChat official account, two articles have been written for submission, and one patent has been applied for successfully.

4 Conclusion

To improve the innovative practice ability of college students majoring in intelligent robots, we should create a good experimental site and training conditions, build a perfect innovation and entrepreneurship cultivation system, and form a virtuous circle system like an ecological system. This paper has the following innovations:

Orientation. With the rapid development of the robot industry, the demand for talents in the market and students' interest in robots are also growing. Considering the cross-integration of multi-specialties, it is necessary to optimize the curriculum, build a robot characteristic training base, and cultivate talents who is in short supply in society.

Systemization. Construct the whole process of talent cultivation of "training goal formulation—teaching plan revision—curriculum construction—innovation and entrepreneurship projects and competition guidance-teaching quality evaluation", and put the practical education mode of "joint training of talents by colleges and industries" and "learning based on practical problems and practical projects" into practice.

Modularization. According to the process from conception to realization of a robot project, a robot general education course is established, including robot structure design module, intelligent control module, intelligent perception and comprehensive application module, which will gradually become a "golden course" and serve as a model for robot education. On the basis of robot system knowledge and practical training, each professional team participates in by mutual cooperation, which well fulfills the requirements of new engineering talents training.

Achievement. By participating in related science and technology project competitions, it is necessary to cultivate students' working ability, innovative consciousness and ability, team cooperation ability, ability to learn new knowledge quickly, analytical writing ability, etc.

Acknowledgment. This study was co-supported by the National Natural Science Foundation of China (Grant No. 52175019), Beijing Natural Science Foundation (Grant No. 3212009 and No.L222038).

References

1. Liu, Y.F, Yang, Y.Q., Han, L.Y.: Research on the cultivation path of college students' innovation and entrepreneurship ability under the background of new engineering. Theoret. Res. Pract. Innov. Entrepreneurship **002**(006), 118–119,126 (2019)
2. An, J., Mu, H.R.: The exploration and practice of innovation and entrepreneurship education in robotics courses. Educ. Teach. Forum **406**(12), 274–275 (2019)
3. Wang, X.: Research on cultivation of college students' innovation and entrepreneurship ability based on robot practice base. Theoret. Res. Pract. Innov. Entrepreneurship **3**(16), 176–177,188 (2020)
4. Zhao, Z.: Research on strategic management of training quality of engineering talents in colleges and universities. Dalian University of Technology (2019)
5. Li, T.J.: Research on the integration of robot-oriented innovation and entrepreneurship education and mechanical and electrical professional education. Educ. Teach. Forum **8**, 37–38 (2018)
6. Deng, Z.H., Liu, M.: Research and practice of college students' innovation and entrepreneurship in the field of robot technology application. Comput. Telecommun. **000**(011), 11–13 (2019)
7. Yuan, C.: Sociological analysis of innovative talents cultivation in colleges and universities. Huazhong Normal University (2014)
8. Zhang, R., Ma, N., et al.: Research on Beijing-Tianjin-Hebei collaborative development and innovative education model of applied universities—taking the development and application of robotic innovation and entrepreneurship ecosystem in Beijing union university as an example. Connecting Beijing-Tianjin—— Proceedings of the Coordinated Development of Xiong'an New Area and Beijing-Tianjin-Hebei. Langfang Society of Applied Economics (2017)
9. Jia, B., Chen, X.D., Li, H.: Construction and practice of professional learning achievement evaluation system under the concept of OBE. Sci. Educ. J. **8** (2017)
10. Luo, L.: Innovation and entrepreneurship education reform of industrial robots in higher vocational colleges based on innovation and entrepreneurship platform
11. Xi, J.P.: Xi Jinping emphasized at the National Conference on Ideological and Political Work in Colleges and Universities: Putting ideological and political work through the whole process of education and teaching to create a new situation for the development of my country's higher education. People's Daily, 12–09–2016
12. Jin, L.H., Gao, Z.: Some reflections on "Course Ideology and Politics". Mod. Vocat. Educ. (18) (2017)

A Classification Framework Based on Multi-modal Features for Detection of Cognitive Impairments

Sheng Chen[1], Haiqun Xie[2], Hongjun Yang[1], Chenchen Fan[1], Zengguang Hou[1(✉)], and Chutian Zhang[1,3]

[1] Institute of Automation, Chinese Academy of Sciences, Beijing 100190, China
{chensheng2016,hongjun.yang,fanchenchen2018,zengguang.hou}@ia.ac.cn
[2] The First People's Hospital of Foshan, Guangdong 528010, China
[3] Macau Institute of Systems Engineering, Macau University of Science and Technology, Macau, China
2109853PMI30005@student.must.edu.mo

Abstract. Mild cognitive impairment (MCI) is the preliminary stage of dementia, and has a high risk of progression to Alzheimer's disease (AD) in the elderly. Early detection of MCI plays a vital role in preventing progression of AD. Clinical diagnosis of MCI requires many examinations, which are highly demanding on hospital equipment and expensive for patients. Electroencephalography (EEG) offers a non-invasive and less expensive way to diagnose MCI early. In this paper, we propose a multi-modal fusion classification framework for MCI detection. We collect EEG data using a delayed match-to-sample task and analyze the differences between the two groups. Based on analysis results, we extract Power spectral density (PSD), PSD enhanced, Event-related potential (ERP) features in EEG signal along with physiological features and behavioral features of the subjects to classify MCI and healthy elderly. By comparing the effect of different features on classification performance, we find that the time-domain based ERP features are better than the frequency-domain based PSD or PSD enhanced features to overcome inter-individual differences to distinguish MCI, and these two features have good complementarity, fusing ERP and PSD enhanced features can greatly improve the classification accuracy to 84.74%. The final result shows that MCI and healthy elderly can be well classified by using this framework.

Keywords: Mild cognitive impairment · EEG · Machine learning

1 Introduction

Over 46 million people were living with dementia worldwide, this number is estimated to increase to 131.5 million by 2050 [1], AD accounts for about 60% of all dementia cases, it can be well treated only when the diagnostic and therapeutic

Z. Yu et al. (Eds.): CIRAC 2022, CCIS 1770, pp. 349–361, 2023.
https://doi.org/10.1007/978-981-99-0301-6_27

envelope falls back to an early prodromal stage [2,3]. The neurological state prodromal to AD is known as MCI. 10% to 15% of patients who have been diagnosed with MCI will convert to AD per year [4]. Early detection of MCI becomes one of the key measures to prevent AD. Neuroimaging provides an effective basis for the diagnosis and progression of MCI, but many of the neuroimaging methods (e.g., MRI, PET) of detecting MCI are expensive, invasive, and require specialized expert analysis to get the results. Due to the high cost and the limitations of hospital condition, many people who suffer from MCI cannot been diagnosed at the early stage and intervened effectively, which increases the risk of progression to AD. Therefore, it is necessary to find an affordable, convenient and fast way to detect MCI.

EEG is a technique that measures biometric data from the human brain, which can be decoded to understand underlying physical and psychological status [5]. It has the characteristics of high temporal resolution, non-invasive, wearable and portable, and has been wildly used as a true neuroimaging method for clinical diagnosis of diseases [6]. Cosimo et al. [7] developed an original multi-modal features extraction methodology based on continuous wavelet transform and bispectrum analysis of EEG recordings. Ieracitano et al. [8] extracted some statistical coefficients from average Time-Frequency Map related to a 19-channels EEG epoch, and fed them into a Multi-Layer Perceptron to differentiate EEG segments of patients affected by neurological disorders. Eduardo et al. [9] extracted relative power, spectral entropy and Hjorth complexity and implemented a self-driven analysis pipeline to discriminate the AD, MCI and healthy people. Burcu et al. [7] extracted discrete wavelet transform, PSD and coherence features and used bagged trees to classify AD, MCI and healthy elderly. Khatun et al. [10] extracted 590 features from the ERP of the single-channel EEG data obtained from Fpz location, and used SVM and LR to classify 15 MCI and 8 healthy elderly. Mesut et al. [11] showed that permutation entropy is an effective neuro-marker for discrimination of AD, and demented EEG shows less complex patterns compared with control group.

Various features were used in existing studies including time domain, frequency domain, and time-frequency domain features. These studies show that different features have a great effect on the classification, so it is very meaningful to find a feature that can distinguish MCI well. In addition, different experimental paradigms were used when collecting EEG signals. Most studies use EEG data collected from participants in resting state with eyes closed or eyes open [7,8,11–13]. The advantage of this is that it is more convenient to measure EEG signals and does not require complicated operations and too much cooperation from the participants, especially for AD patients with severe symptoms, it will take too much time and energy to let them cooperate. Other studies employed a characteristic experimental paradigm to acquire EEG signals, In [10], participants need to receive a sound stimulus when collecting EEG signals, and they were asked to quickly differentiate it with a binary response; Timothy et al. [14] compared the effects of EEG signals collected from eyes closed resting state and short term memory task on identifying MCI, showing that short term memory task condition have better performance compared to eyes closed condition. In addition, some features can only be extracted when there is a corresponding paradigm, because these features do not exist in the resting state, such as ERP features [10,15]. Therefore, when classifying the more difficult tasks (MCI vs HC), a paradigm of cognitive tasks will have certain advantages.

The performance varies widely in the existing studies due to the small size of samples [16]. In the task of distinguishing between MCI and healthy elderly, some studies can only achieve 76.47% accuracy [12], but other studies can reach as high as 96.5% accuracy [7]. Although the features they extracted and the machine learning methods they used are different, the more important reason is that the ways they split the dataset are different. Some studies used an epoch as a sample to train the model and the final result was at the epoch level, while others calculated the accuracy from the individual level. For the way of using an epoch as a sample, it is easy to cause data leakage, because an individual can only have one label (dementia or normal), these epochs are actually strongly correlated. Therefore, it makes more sense to train the model across individuals. Since the EEG of different individuals vary greatly, it is meaningful to find features that are less affected by individual differences.

The major contributions of this paper can be summarized as follows:

- We compare the effects of different features on the model, and find that the features extracted from the latency period in the ERP perform better than other features.
- The time domain feature ERP and the frequency domain feature PSD have good complementarity, and the fusion of the two features can significantly improve the performance.
- Using a single-channel EEG data can also perform not much worse than using multi-channel, it can achieve an accuracy of 76.26%.

2 Methodology

2.1 EEG Data Recording and Data Preprocessing

EEG data were recorded in the First People's Hospital of Foshan, including 59 participants with 32 MCI patients and 27 healthy control (HC), the diagnosis results were obtained by experts based on a comprehensive analysis of the patient's MRI images, cerebrospinal fluid assays, and neuropsychological scale. All the participants were informed in advance of the purpose of the research and signed the Informed Consent Form. EEG data were recorded using a dry electrode EEG device (Wearable Sensing, DSI-24), with 19 channels and sampling with the frequency 300 Hz.

Delayed Match-to-Sample (DMS) Task: Inspired by the research in [15], we use a DMS task to classify MCI and HC. In this task, participants need to press the button as we required, the details process of the DMS task are shown in Fig. 1. The images are taken from Snodgrass and vanderwart [17], the entire process is performed using E-prime software, we use the software to label

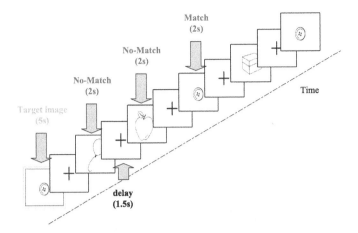

Fig. 1. The flow of the delayed match-to-sample task. A target image with green border appears for 5 s. After 1.5 s delay, five test images that last for 2 s appear in sequence, participants need to judge whether each the image matched or do not match the target image by pressing the left or right button. The target image of each trial is different, and half of the test images are limited to matched images. Each participant preform 30 trials. (Color figure online)

different stimuli tasks and get the reaction time of the participant pressing the button. There are two different stimuli in DMS task, one for the appearing image is same as target image, the other one for the appearing image is different with the target image. We exclude the EEG signals of that participants failed to respond correctly according to the rules, considering that those signals are not well categorized as to which stimuli it is.

Data Preprocessing and Analysis: For each participant's EEG signal, we firstly locate the channels, and select A1 and A2 as reference channel. Then, we filter EEG signal with a 0.5 Hz–70 Hz filter and extract the EEG signal of the 2 s time period when the participant judge the images as an epoch. Next, we manually delete some obvious bad segments, and use independent component analysis (ICA) to remove eye movement artifacts. Finally, we delete extreme values greater than 150 μV and get the final preprocessed EEG signal.

We perform a group analysis of MCI and HC in the frequency domain, the result is shown in Fig. 2(a). In δ and θ band, some channels have higher amplitude in MCI group and other channels have higher amplitude in HC group. But in α band, the amplitudes of all channels in the MCI group are higher than or equal to the HC group, on the contrary, the amplitudes of all the channels in the HC group in β band are higher than or equal to those in the MCI group. This indicates that MCI may be due to insufficient amplitude in β band on the F4-C4 channel, and is compensated by the amplitude in α band on the other channels. This conclusion is consistent with the study [18] that slowing of EEG rhythms is a remarkable symbol in MCI patients. In addition, we subtract the ERP of the match task from the non-match task, and obtain the amplitude difference between the match and non-match tasks

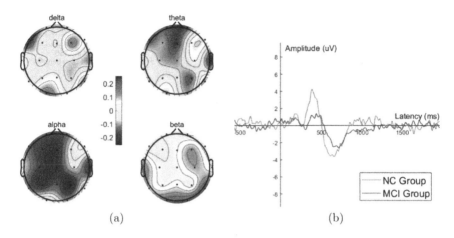

Fig. 2. (a) The difference between the topography of each band in the MCI group and the HC group; (b) The amplitude difference of the match and non-match tasks between MCI group and HC group on F3 channel.

for the HC group and the MCI group, result is shown in Fig. 2(b), we find that the differences are mainly in the frontal region and the time period is mainly concentrated in the period of 300 ms–600 ms after the test images appear. Therefore, we focus on this time period when extracting features, and use this difference to extract features to distinguish MCI from HC.

2.2 Feature Extraction

In this paper, we extract the following features to train model:

PSD Features: Power spectral density is widely used in EEG signal processing, the power of EEG in a specific band can calculated by integrating over positive and negative frequencies [19]. The finite time power spectral density is defined as

$$e^{jw} = \frac{1}{2\pi N} |\sum_{n=1}^{N} x(n)e^{-jwn}|^2 \tag{1}$$

PSD Enhanced Features (PSDE): Considering the EEG signal vary greatly in a short time in the DMS task. The conventional calculation method of PSD is to divide the EEG into many overlapping epochs, and then calculate the average of all these epochs to get the final value. Purely PSD features will miss some temporal information. To overcome this shortcoming, we calculate the value of PSD every 300 ms, and use the PSD of different time periods as features to input to the classifier. Therefore, we gain a total of 20 features for 5 time periods in 4 frequency bands, the computational methods is as Fig. 3.

ERP Features: ERPs are scalp-recorded voltage fluctuations that measure brain response to a time-locked event [20]. This specific activity average EEG

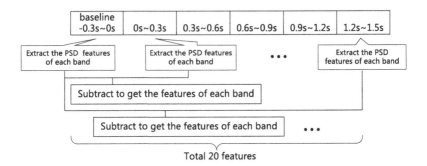

Fig. 3. Computational methods for PSDE features in DMS task

Table 1. Physiological information quantification standard

Age	Value	Education level	Value
55–60	1	Primary education	1
60–65	2	Secondary education	2
65–70	3	Higher education	3
70–75	4		
75–	5		

across many trials together and enhance the task related activity while minimizing or canceling unwanted activity. The main types of features extracted from ERP waveforms are evoked voltage and latency duration under different events. As analysis in above section, we have found that the characteristics in the period of 300 ms–600 ms after stimulus occurrence are significant, we extract 4 features from ERP, which are the amplitude difference between the mean value and max value of the match and non-match tasks, the time difference between the maximum value and minimum value of the match and non-match tasks.

Physiological Features (PF): Physiological characteristics such as age and education level also provide evidence for the diagnosis of dementia, these information can be obtained easily. We quantify these features using fixed width packing method, the quantification method in this paper is shown in the Table 1. Afterwards, these features are zero-score normalized and fed to model.

Behavioral Features (BF): When the participants were doing the DMS task, the E-prime software recorded some behavioral information of the participants, including information on whether the participants responded correctly in each epoch, whether the participants responded within the specified time (2 s) in each epoch, and the time participant pressed the button after seeing the test image. We calculate the participant's correct rate, missing rate and average reaction time and extract these information as behavioral features.

2.3 Model Training

Different data split methods have a great impact on final result of the classifier [21], in order to avoid data leakage, we treat each subject as a sample, each individual has multiple epochs, and we take their average as a feature representing the individual. Considering dataset is relatively small, to make full use of the data, we leave one subject out as test set, the remaining subjects are divided into the training set and the validation set according to the 5-fold cross-validation method to select the hyperparameters of the model. We gain models whose number is equal to the number of participants at the end, and count the number of model which correctly distinguish the leave-out subject's label. The ratio of the correct classification models to all models is used as the average accuracy of the specific classifier. The following three different classifiers are used in this paper:

Support Vector Machine (SVM): SVM uses kernel functions to map features to high-order dimensions and find an optimum hyperplane for classification [22]. In this paper, we use a grid search method on the validation set, try different parameters for the linear kernel C (from 10^{-4} to 10) and different parameters C (from 10^{-1} to 100) and σ (from 10^{-5} to 10^{-1}) for the radial basis function(RBF) kernel, to find the best kernel function and corresponding parameters on validation set, and use it to test its effect on the test set.

K-Nearest Neighbor (KNN): The Minkowski distances is use as distance metric, and weights coefficient is chosen as "distance" to reduce the impact of sample imbalance problems, we try different values for the number of neighbors (from 1 to 11) on validation set, and use the best value for the test set.

Decision Tree (DT): We construct decision trees for two cases, one with criterion function for the gini impurity and the other for the Shannon information gain. Grid search method is used on validation set to select maximum depth of the tree and maximum features.

The evaluation metrics including accuracy (Acc), sensitivity (Sen) and specificity (Spe), we also calculate the average accuracy of the models on the validation set (Vali Acc), which will be compared to the average accuracy (Test Acc) on the test set to judge whether the trained model is overfitting.

3 Results

3.1 The Effect of Different Features on a Single Channel

The performance of different bands of PSD and PSDE features is shown in the Table 2, the accuracy in the table is based on SVM. We can see that the overall classification accuracy is not satisfying, and using the features of multiple frequency bands is sometimes not necessarily better than that of a single frequency band. θ and α band perform better. The performance of PSDE feature is better than PSD feature on the whole, it may account for that PSDE feature contain the frequency information of the task in different time periods, in other

Table 2. The performance of different bands of frequency domain features.

Extraction method	Acc (%)				
	δ	θ	α	β	All band
PSD	66.26	62.71	67.80	66.67	66.26
PSDE	66.10	69.49	71.18	64.40	66.10

Table 3. The performance of ERP features.

Features	Channel	Vali Acc (%)	Test Acc (%)	Sen (%)	Spe (%)
ERP (voltage)	F7	64.14	71.18	75.00	66.67
ERP (latency)	Fz	74.39	74.57	71.88	77.78
ERP (all)	F3	72.81	71.18	75.00	66.67

words, it also provides part of the time information. However, the performance of PSDE feature using all frequency band drops significantly, it means that too many unimportant features can interfere with the model, and it is necessary to simplify features.

As can be seen from Table 3, the ERP latency features perform better than voltage features. It may account for that individual differences might have a greater impact on voltage than cognitive impairment, and the latency can better reflect the cognitive and executive status of the participants. However, the performance reduces if using both of the voltage features and latency features, which means that there is a phenomenon of feature redundancy, more features will not necessarily improve the effect. By comparing with PSDE features, ERP features perform better than the frequency domain features, indicating that time information has greater significance for distinguishing MCI.

3.2   The Effect of Using Multiple Channels

We set up several channel sets, which are symmetrical to the left and right brain and mainly focus on the frontal and parietal lobes. We calculate the accuracy on multiple channel, the result is shown in Table 4. We can see that the performance of ERP in the case of multiple channel is better than that of single channel, and the accuracy rate increases to 74.57%. The channels with good performance are mainly concentrated in the frontal and parietal lobes, and it is consistent with the study of [15,23]. But the frequency domain features do not perform well with multiple channel, sometimes even worse than with a single channel. Since the classifier is a simple model, it is not strong enough to eliminate the influence of useless channel information, so it performs particularly poor on PSDE features that extract 20 features per channel.

Table 4. The performance using multiple channels

Features	Channel	Vali Acc (%)	Test Acc (%)	Sen (%)	Spe (%)
PSD	Cz-P3-P4	66.15	62.71	62.50	62.96
PSDE	Fz-C3-C4	63.61	61.02	71.88	77.78
ERP	F3-C3-Fz-Cz-F4-C4	72.22	74.57	75.00	74.07

Table 5. The performance of multiple features and multiple channels

Features	Channel (ERP)	Channel (PSD)	Vali Acc (%)	Test Acc (%)
ERP+BF	C3	\	73.93	72.88
ERP+PF	F3	\	72.22	74.58
PSDE+BF	\	Fp2	68.92	71.18
PSDE+PF	\	C3	68.31	72.88
ERP+PSD	Fz	Fz	**76.04**	**76.27**
ERP+PSDE	F3, F4, Cz, Fp1, Fp2	Fp1, Fp2	78.20	81.35
ERP+PSDE+PF	Fp1	C4	**85.44**	**84.74**
ERP+PSDE+PF+BF	Fz	F3, F4, Cz, F1, Fp2	78.20	76.27

3.3 Feature-Level Fusion of Multiple Features and Multiple Channels

We fuse different EEG features at the feature-level, as well as other features, including PF and BF. The result is shown in Table 5. It can be seen from the table that the channels with good performance are concentrated at the frontal and parietal lobes, and the fusion of various features can improve the accuracy of classification. Among them, the accuracy of ERP features plus PF increases to 74.58%, but the improvement of ERP features plus BF is not obvious. The same phenomenon also occurs in the PSDE feature. This indicates that the complementarity of BF to the features of ERP and PSDE is not as strong as that of PF, and the effectiveness of PF is consistent with the fact that some physiological information can provide reference for clinical diagnosis. In addition, the accuracy rate of the ERP feature plus the PSDE features greatly increases to 81.35%, which may account for that there is no frequency information in the ERP feature, and frequency information is just provided in the PSDE features, including both time domain information and frequency domain information can greatly improve performance. One interesting thing is that we find the accuracy of using only one single channel (Fz) can still reach 76.27%, it is not much lower than that of using multiple channels. The reason for the good effects of the Fz channel may be that the Fz is located in the center of the brain, it can comprehensively reflect the overall condition of the brain. This makes great sense in practical application, we can diagnose dementia by measuring EEG signals in just one channel of the brain, that can reduce many problems during measurement and greatly reduce measurement costs.

3.4   Model Performance Evaluation

Figure 4 shows the accuracy of different classifiers using different features. As can be seen from the figure, the accuracy of different classifiers using the same feature is not much different, the performance of SVM is better overall. Different features have a greater impact on the classification result, using more features can improve accuracy, especially after using the ERP and PSDE features at the same time, the improvement is obvious.

As can be seen from the Tables 3, 4 and 5, the accuracy of the validation set is not much different from the accuracy of the test set, which means that the model is not overfitting, but in some cases, the accuracy of the validation set is lower than that of the test set accuracy. This phenomenon means that in the training process, the hyperparameters only need to be within a certain range. Because the distribution of the validation set and test set data itself is different, the hyperparameters that are optimal in the test set are not necessarily suitable for the test set. Thus, it is more important to extract a feature that can reflect the difference between MCI and HC. By comparing the difference in the accuracy of the validation set and the test set on different features, we find that the accuracy of the validation set containing ERP features is mostly slightly higher or very close to the accuracy of the test set, the models containing only frequency domain features often have lower accuracy on the validation set than the test set, which also shows that ERP is more stable in distinguishing MCI than PSD, and is less affected by individual differences.

Based on the result of Table 5, we select the ERP features of Fp1 channel and PSDE features of C4 channel, along with PF features, to explore the effect of different hyperparameter values on the SVM classifier, the result is shown in Fig. 5. It can be seen from the Fig. 5(a) that as the value of C increases, the accuracy of the model first rises to a value around 77.97% and then decreases, and the highest accuracy is obtained when C is around 0.002. The best model has a small value of C, which means the model has a greater tolerance for errors and good generalization performance. Comparing Fig. 5(a) and Fig. 5(b), it can be seen that the accuracy of using RBF kernel is higher than using linear kernel, it can achieve the highest accuracy of 84.74%, but the optimal hyperparameter of the RBF kernel are a relatively large C and a small γ. After the C value exceeds 10, the model gradually overfits as the C value increases, and the accuracy of the model decreases. On the other hand, a relatively small γ value can ensure that the model has better robustness. Due to the large individual differences of EEG signals, the selection of hyperparameters tends to sacrifice some accuracy to prevent model overfitting.

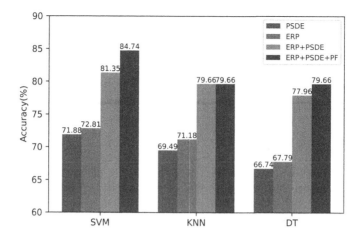

Fig. 4. Comparison of the accuracy of different classifiers using different features

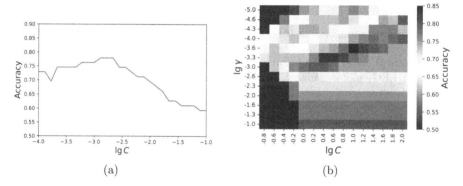

Fig. 5. (a) The effect of different C values on SVM with linear kernel; (b) The effect of different C and γ values on SVM with RBF kernel.

4 Conclusion

In this work, we collect EEG signals of MCI and HC in the DMS task, and compare the effects of different features and different classifiers on distinguishing MCI and HC. We find that ERP features can better distinguish MCI. In addition, we find that using a variety of different modal features can improve the performance of the model, especially fusing ERP features and PSDE features can significantly improve the accuracy, but fusing a higher number of channels does not necessarily improve the results, channels with good performance are mainly concentrated in the frontal region. In the case of using SVM classifier by fusing ERP, PSDE and PF features, our final result is that the classification accuracy of selecting a specific set of channels can achieve 84.74%, and selecting only one single channel (Fz) can still reach 76.26%. We believe that our work will have great significance for the future application of EEG in detecting MCI.

Funding. This work was supported in part by the National Key R&D Program of China (Grant 2018YFC2001700), National Natural Science Foundation of China (Grants 62073319, U1913601, 61720106012), Beijing Sci&Tech Program (Grant Z211100007921021), Alliance of International Science Organizations (ANSO) Collaborative Research Project (Grant ANSO-CR-PP-2020-03), and by the Strategic Priority Research Program of Chinese Academy of Science (Grant XDB32040000).

References

1. Prince, M.J., Wimo, A., Guerchet, M.M., Ali, G.C., Wu, Y.T., Prina, M.: World Alzheimer report 2015-the global impact of dementia: an analysis of prevalence, incidence, cost and trends (2015)
2. Karakaya, T., Fußer, F., Schroder, J., Pantel, J.: Pharmacological treatment of mild cognitive impairment as a prodromal syndrome of Alzheimer's disease. Curr. Neuropharmacol. **11**(1), 102–108 (2013)
3. Robinson, L., Tang, E., Taylor, J.P.: Dementia: timely diagnosis and early intervention. BMJ **350**, 1–6 (2015)
4. Breton, A., Casey, D., Arnaoutoglou, N.A.: Cognitive tests for the detection of mild cognitive impairment (MCI), the prodromal stage of dementia: meta-analysis of diagnostic accuracy studies. Int. J. Geriatr. Psychiatry **34**(2), 233–242 (2019)
5. Altaheri, H., et al.: Deep learning techniques for classification of electroencephalogram (EEG) motor imagery (MI) signals: a review. Neural Comput. Appl. 1–42 (2021). https://doi.org/10.1007/s00521-021-06352-5
6. Biasiucci, A., Franceschiello, B., Murray, M.M.: Electroencephalography. Curr. Biol. **29**(3), R80–R85 (2019)
7. Ieracitano, C., Mammone, N., Hussain, A., Morabito, F.C.: A novel multi-modal machine learning based approach for automatic classification of EEG recordings in dementia. Neural Netw. **123**, 176–190 (2020)
8. Ieracitano, C., Mammone, N., Bramanti, A., Marino, S., Hussain, A., Morabito, F.C.: A time-frequency based machine learning system for brain states classification via EEG signal processing. In: 2019 International Joint Conference on Neural Networks (IJCNN), pp. 1–8. IEEE (2019)
9. Perez-Valero, E., Lopez-Gordo, M.Á., Gutiérrez, C.M., Carrera-Muñoz, I., Vílchez-Carrillo, R.M.: A self-driven approach for multi-class discrimination in Alzheimer's disease based on wearable EEG. Comput. Methods Programs Biomed. **220**, 106841 (2022)
10. Khatun, S., Morshed, B.I., Bidelman, G.M.: A single-channel EEG-based approach to detect mild cognitive impairment via speech-evoked brain responses. IEEE Trans. Neural Syst. Rehabil. Eng. **27**(5), 1063–1070 (2019)
11. Şeker, M., Özbek, Y., Yener, G., Özerdem, M.S.: Complexity of EEG dynamics for early diagnosis of Alzheimer's disease using permutation entropy neuromarker. Comput. Methods Programs Biomed. **206**, 106116 (2021)
12. Ruiz-Gómez, S.J., et al.: Automated multiclass classification of spontaneous EEG activity in Alzheimer's disease and mild cognitive impairment. Entropy **20**(1), 35 (2018)
13. Durongbhan, P., et al.: A dementia classification framework using frequency and time-frequency features based on EEG signals. IEEE Trans. Neural Syst. Rehabil. Eng. **27**(5), 826–835 (2019)

14. Timothy, L.T., Krishna, B.M., Nair, U.: Classification of mild cognitive impairment EEG using combined recurrence and cross recurrence quantification analysis. Int. J. Psychophysiol. **120**, 86–95 (2017)

15. Li, J., et al.: A cognitive electrophysiological signature differentiates amnestic mild cognitive impairment from normal aging. Alzheimer's Res. Ther. **9**(1), 1–10 (2017). https://doi.org/10.1186/s13195-016-0229-3

16. Yang, S., Bornot, J.M.S., Wong-Lin, K., Prasad, G.: M/EEG-based bio-markers to predict the MCI and Alzheimer's disease: a review from the ML perspective. IEEE Trans. Biomed. Eng. **66**(10), 2924–2935 (2019)

17. Snodgrass, J.G., Vanderwart, M.: A standardized set of 260 pictures: norms for name agreement, image agreement, familiarity, and visual complexity. J. Exp. Psychol. Hum. Learn. Memory **6**(2), 174 (1980)

18. Jeong, J.: EEG dynamics in patients with Alzheimer's disease. Clin. Neurophysiol. **115**(7), 1490–1505 (2004)

19. Unde, S.A., Shriram, R.: Coherence analysis of EEG signal using power spectral density. In: 2014 Fourth International Conference on Communication Systems and Network Technologies, pp. 871–874. IEEE (2014)

20. Herrmann, C.S., Knight, R.T.: Mechanisms of human attention: event-related potentials and oscillations. Neurosci. Biobehav. Rev. **25**(6), 465–476 (2001)

21. Wen, J., et al.: Convolutional neural networks for classification of Alzheimer's disease: overview and reproducible evaluation. Med. Image Anal. **63**, 101694 (2020)

22. Pisner, D.A., Schnyer, D.M.: Support vector machine. In: Machine Learning, pp. 101–121. Elsevier (2020)

23. Mamani, G.Q., Fraga, F.J., Tavares, G., Johns, E., Phillips, N.D.: EEG-based biomarkers on working memory tasks for early diagnosis of Alzheimer's disease and mild cognitive impairment. In: 2017 IEEE Healthcare Innovations and Point of Care Technologies (HI-POCT), pp. 237–240. IEEE (2017)

Intelligent Security Video Surveillance System Based on GCN

Yue Min[1], Ruining Chen[1], Dunjun Li[1], Duanling Li[2(✉)], and Zhiqing Wei[3(✉)]

[1] School of Computer Science, Beijing University of Posts and Telecommunications, Beijing 100876, China
{minyue,ruiningchen,ldj}@bupt.edu.cn
[2] School of Modern Post (School of Automation), Beijing University of Posts and Telecommunications, Beijing 100876, China
duanlingli@bupt.edu.cn
[3] Key Laboratory of Universal Wireless Communications, Ministry of Education, Beijing University of Posts and Telecommunications, Beijing 100876, China
weizhiqing@bupt.edu.cn

Abstract. As the competitive focus of video surveillance technology, intelligent system that recognizes abnormal human behavior for home security is increasingly in demand. We propose a framework aiming to take a holistic approach to analyze human behavior. When abnormal behavior is detected, users can receive alert through SMS. Moreover, database is involved to record abnormal behavior for view and search later on. This framework is developed by integrating state-of-art advancements and technologies in human skeleton recognition, human behavior recognition and data augmentation. Our system has been tested and proven to work well. It's promising that this framework can conduce to the improvement of living standard in home security monitoring.

Keywords: Intelligent surveillance · Graph convolutional neural network · Data augmentation · Activity recognition

1 Introduction

According to the statistics of China Statistical Yearbook, the proportion of criminal cases of theft filed by public security organs in all criminal cases from 2013 to 2019 is 68.30%, 67.83%, 67.96%, 66.97%, 63.10%, 54.97% and 46.44% in order, accounting for more than 62% of the total criminal cases, which is the largest number of all criminal cases, and the most representative cases of property invasion [9].

A variety of methods emerged targeted at social problems such as high crime rates, low crime detection rates and insufficient police force. For example, smart

This work was supported in part by the Beijing Municipal Natural Science Foundation under Grant L192031, and in part by the National Key Research and Development Program of China under Grant 2020YFA0711302.

Z. Yu et al. (Eds.): CIRAC 2022, CCIS 1770, pp. 362–373, 2023.
https://doi.org/10.1007/978-981-99-0301-6_28

door locks replace the conventional mechanical key authentication unlocking method with digital authentication unlocking method, it focuses on simplify the process of occupant unlocking, and as the initial link of the whole house Internet of things to improve the intelligence of the furniture. However, in terms of security, the smart door lock only achieves the prevention of offender opening the lock through the mechanical part of the lock, but not preventing theft. In addition, it does not have a monitoring function and cannot record criminal evidence of the wrongdoer after being stolen.

With the deepening of social information, monitoring system is constantly expanding its coverage, but people are no longer satisfied with the traditional video surveillance screen that can only be watched without any intelligent function. Instead, As the competitive focus of video surveillance technology, there is an emergent need for an intelligent system that recognizes suspicious human behavior. Moreover, SMS alerts, cell phone alerts and other functions are expected.

We propose a framework aiming to take a holistic approach to study, track, monitor, and analyze human behavior. This framework is developed by integrating the state-of-art advancements and technologies in human skeleton recognition, human behavior recognition and data augmentation. It's promising that this framework can contribute to lead to a life style of high standard.

In summary, the main contributions of our work are summarized as follows:

- To the best of our knowledge, this paper is the first to apply Openpose [3], VideoPose3D [10], PoseAug [6] and ST-GCN [18] comprehensively to construct an end-to-end framework for home security systems.
- We have systematically implemented a intelligent monitoring system capable of storing abnormal video properly and sending alerts to users in an accurate and timely manner.
- We review the related topics and methods included in monitoring system, human skeleton recognition, human action recognition based on GCN and graph data augmentation.

2   Related Work

To ensure human safety, there is a growing demand for intelligent video surveillance systems that can detect dangerous situations for various scenarios. For specific ones mentioned above, there are various video surveillance systems designed for it. For example, systems that are designed for public scenes aim at predicting dangerous or risky events, while systems applied in private scenes focus on a rather simple task, like remote access and video storage [5].

The past methods of intruder detection are generally based on proximity sensors [12] or Hall sensors [4]. With the development of the field of computer vision, the innovation and improvement of theories such as artificial intelligence, model recognition, image processing and deep learning tools, the analysis of abnormal behavior of crowds based on video has become a research direction of great interest in the field of computer vision.

In the field of human behavior recognition, there are multiple traditional approaches. For example, [8] used particle systems and particle advection to represent behavior for feature extraction and achieves better results in describing the crowd flow patterns in real-time scenes. However, the traditional optical flow method, due to the problem of changing real-time scenes and unstable crowd structure, performs poorly in describing temporal correlation as well as describing the temporal and spatial properties of the motion flow. In [13], Wang et al. proposed a way to detect abnormal events based on movement information of video sequence and Hidden Markov model. Nevertheless, the generalization ability of the system is poor, and the model needs to be reclassified and retrained for different scenarios in order to identify and detect abnormal behavior of the crowd.

However, with the continuous development in the field of computer vision, researchers have incorporated deep learning algorithms into abnormal behavior recognition and detection. Deep learning has become a recent research hot spot due to its supreme feature extraction effect and excellent data fitting ability to achieve high detection accuracy. There has been some prior research in this area, including dual-stream neural network [14,19], pulse-linear stream convolutional neural network [16] and generalized regression neural network [1,17].

3   Tasks

The development of a successful home security monitoring system is not an easy task, there needs to develop a scientific, rational and practical engineering approach. Home security monitoring is different from the general system, it is a variety of hardware environments and software constitutes a complex technical system. Moreover, its development process not only involves engineers and users, but also the integrated use of management science, information science, computer and communications technology. Therefore, the development of home security monitoring systems can be categorized as complex system engineering. The proposal of this project needs to start from a system perspective, with the use of engineering tools, organization and coordination of deliberate analysis, design and implementation of the process.

Through elaborate research and study, home security monitoring system needs are mainly summarized to be reflected in three areas stated as follows.

1. Danger alert: Intelligent monitoring requires timely abnormality sensing and effective alarming. In this part of abnormality sensing, this project proposes a new composite alarm method by incorporating multiple alarm methods into the scope of detecting abnormality together with the system design.
2. Suspicious video queries: Intelligent monitoring requires the retention of video records in order to provide materials for later inquiries and forensics. At the same time, users need to be able to accurately and quickly find what they need among the many video files. This requires the system to provide information such as the time of recording and the cause of alarm at the same

time. The project is designed to mark suspicious faces and abnormal behavior to facilitate quick search.

3. User-friendly UI interface: Users can turn on and off the security monitoring system at any time, receive and process alarm signals, and easily set some key parameters of the security monitoring system. Later on, users can easily retrieve and view all existing video and alarm information.

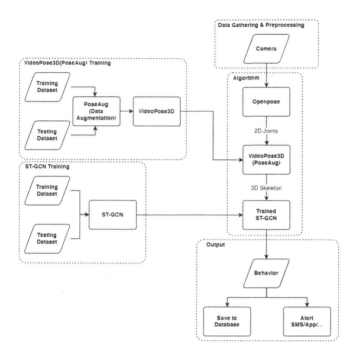

Fig. 1. Structure of surveillance system

4   System Design

On top of the requirements put forward, focusing on the rapid development of future home security systems, drawing on the successful experience of various home monitoring programs, following the rapid development of science and technology, in line with the new economic development needs, this project put forward of a set of targeted and perfect demand analysis program.

The overall general architecture of the project is presented in Fig. 1.

4.1   System Structure

Data Gathering. This is the first step for the system. We acquire complex surrounding information at high frame rate and high resolution from camera. Other than camera video data acquisition, this step also includes the functions camera working parameters adjustment, video image transmission, etc.

Data Preprocessing. After the video image acquisition is obtained, these images are often disturbed by noise, or due to the influence of lighting, the brightness and color of the image will be underexposed or overexposed, at this time, if the video image is directly handed over to the subsequent module for processing, it will increase the difficulty of processing. Therefore, the video image is often pre-processed first, the noise is filtered out, and the brightness and color degree are rectified to a reasonable range, and the technical goal of image pre-processing is responsible for some such processing. Video image pre-processing results will directly affect the results of the subsequent steps, and is also a very important pre-processing link in intelligent video surveillance.

Joint Point Detection. As shown in Fig. 2, the human joint points can be characterized by 18 key points, including nose, neck, shoulder, elbow, etc. For a video sequence, skeleton data is denoted as set $V = \{v_{i,j} | i = 1, ..., N; j = 1, ..., T\}$, where $v_{i,j}$ represents i^{th} joint vector in j_{th} frame. After inputting the pre-processed 2D color image, a set of feature maps are extracted from the original image by CNN. Moreover, in [3], Part Confidence Maps and Part Affinity Fields(PAF) respectively can be obtained through further application of CNN. For two candidate part locations d_{j1} and d_{j2}, the confidence in their association is measured through:

$$E = \int_{u=0}^{u=1} L_c(p(u)) \cdot \frac{d_{j2} - d_{j1}}{\|d_{j2} - d_{j1}\|_2} \tag{1}$$

where $p(u)$ interpolates the position of the two body parts d_{j1} and d_{j2}. If a point p lies on the limb, the value at $L_c(p)$ stands for a unit vector that points from $j1$ to $j2$;

Skeleton Connection. Intuitively, human skeleton shows up as an isomorphic graph with joints as nodes and joint connections as edges. The natural association among joints is presented in Table 1.

Furthermore, to take the temporal movement into consideration, joints in every frame can be associated with the temporal domain. Consequently, the human skeleton can be restated as graph-based data comprises both spatial and temporal information. In this way, human activity recognition is reduced to a graph learning problem.

To be more specific, take ST-GCN [15] as an example. It generates the spatial temporal graph in two stages. First, according to the connectivity of human body

Table 1. Human body structure joint point connection set description

Joint point connection	Description	Joint point connection	Description
(0,1)	Hip - Right Hip	(8,9)	Thorax - Head
(0,4)	Hip - Left Hip	(8,10)	Thorax - Left Shoulder
(0,7)	Hip - Spine	(8,13)	Thorax - Right Shoulder
(1,2)	Right Hip - Right Knee	(10,11)	Left Shoulder - Left Elbow
(2,3)	Right Knee - Right Foot	(11,12)	Left Elbow - Left Wrist
(4,5)	Left Hip - Left Knee	(13,14)	Right shoulder - Right Elbow
(5,6)	Left Knee - Left Foot	(14,15)	Right Elbow- Right Wrist
(7,8)	Spine - Thorax		

structure, the joints within one frame are connected. Then each joint will be connected to the same joint in the consecutive frame to form temporal relations. Finally, the human skeleton is reduced to a graph presented in Fig. 3.

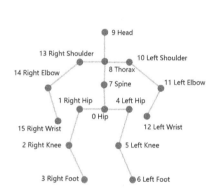

Fig. 2. Human skeleton

Fig. 3. Space-time skeleton diagram

Data Augmentation. GCNs need a large amount of graph data support. However, there are limited number of annotated samples and limited number of neighbors. Additionally, current GCN methods face the challenge of poor robustness, which leads to the risk of over-fitting phenomena and vulnerability to attacks. To address this issue, research on spoofing countermeasures has gained attention to protect GCN from such attacks. Therefore, graph data augmentation enjoys widespread use in modern graph-based machine learning.

On graph-level tasks, GDA techniques aim at generating extra data for training with known labels from the input training data. Broadly speaking, we can distinguish between four classes of geometric learning problems, namely, feature modification, structure augmentation, sub-graph sampling and hybrid.

To address the problem of Human pose estimators suffering poor generalization performance to new data sets, data augmentation is introduced in the training step of this system to eliminate the limited diversity of pose pairs in the training data.

Human Behavior Recognition. Human behavior is then recognized based on the extracted dynamic skeleton information. However, conventional convolution neural networks is applied to Euclidean structure, hence can not directly applied in the non-Euclidean structure of the skeleton data. [2] proposed that Geometric deep learning a way to generalize structured deep neural models to non-Euclidean domains, which makes possible the application on the graph. In light of that, GCN is widely used in human-skeleton-based behavior recognition. [18] proposed a new deep learning method called the Spatial-Temporal Graph Convolutional Network (ST-GCN), which is based on the graph representation of skeletons, which has a great performance. ST-GCN comprises many GCN layers, each layer consisting of a spatial convolution and a temporal convolution operation. These layers are able to jointly model the spatiotemporal feature.

Video Clip Storage. In order to store video clips containing suspicious behavior for subsequent viewing, we have adopted the general practice of the video surveillance industry, which is storing video clips in a database. There are several ways to implement it, such as using `BLOB` data in SQL databases, using MongoDB's `GridFS`, or storing video file paths and their corresponding information in database. Taking database performance and other factors into account, the method of storing video file paths is used in the system.

There are multiple optional databases available. They can be generally sorted into two categories, which are SQL databases and NoSQL databases. SQL databases are based on tables that have fixed structures, while NoSQL databases use a variety of models for storing data, from key-value to documents. It's widely acknowledged that SQL databases are more suitable for data that has fixed structure and NoSQL databases can handle data without a fixed structure more easily and efficiently [7]. Considering that the data to be stored has a relatively fixed format, SQL has a better performance in this case, SQL is finally chosen as the database of this system. Taking personal data privacy into consideration, the database and video files are stored locally, but it's also possible to adapt this system for server storage, allowing convenient application in different scenarios. The structure of database is shown in Fig. 4.

Alarm and Enforcement. This module is responsible for issuing alarms for threatening actions. The system can directly drive away intruders through active defense systems such as loudspeakers, while also providing software interfaces for other alarm methods, such as SMS, mobile applications and so on.

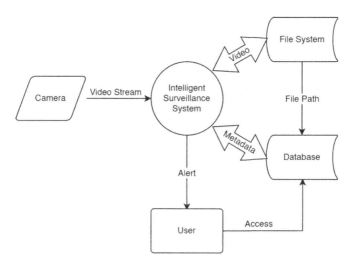

Fig. 4. Structure of database

4.2 Implementations

In this section, we present the overall implementation of our system.

First, we train both VideoPose3D [10] and ST-GCN [15] on NTU RGB+D Cross View dataset [11] to acquire relevant features for generating 3D joint points from 2D joint points and action classification. For VideoPose3D, we apply PoseAug [6] in training for data augmentation to enhance the robustness of our model.

Fig. 5. Information about video data

Fig. 6. Detection result

Then, we apply our pre-trained model to test dataset. Many surveillance view video were also recorded for testing. The basic information about the collected video data is shown in Fig. 5. The 2D joint points are detected from RGB video stream through Openpose [3]. Then, 2D joint points are processed by Video-Pose3D to get 3D joint points. The 3D joint points are later connected to form human skeleton in the form of graph. Taking the graph data as input, human behavior is recognized through ST-GCN [15] which takes both spatial and temporal information into consideration.

For abnormal behavior recognition, We analyzed and extracted the action categories contained in security-threatening behaviors. If such actions are identified from the input video, and the number of occurrences and the total duration exceed the threshold, it is considered that there has been abnormal behavior.

When abnormal behavior is detected, the corresponding video is tagged and stored in the database for subsequent viewing or retained as evidence of the crime. At the same time, automatic alarms are accessed to send alert messages to users.

(a) SMS message   (b) Email message

Fig. 7. Alert message

5   Performance

The system was tested on the NTU RGB+D Cross View dataset and obtained an accuracy of 86.50%. In our tests with recorded surveillance view video, all abnormal behaviors are successfully detected by our system, which is shown in Fig. 6.

In order to present the users with accurate and timely emergency alert, detected abnormal message is sent with SMS and Email. It is shown in Fig. 7 that this function performs well and can send alerts to users accurately and timely.

Through the use of the database, the system successfully realized manual video recording and suspicious behavior automatic video recording with safe storage and efficient query. The system provides stored video data to users in the form of interfaces, users can query, modify, and export videos through the application. These videos can be used by users to confirm threats or as leads in case investigations. Example of data stored in database is shown in Fig. 8.

▽· WHERE		≡· ORDER BY	
🔢 time ⇕ 🔢 type	⇕	🔢 path	⇕
1 1660995387 Manual		~/video/1660995387.mp4	
2 1660897726 Intrude Intention		~/video/1660897726.mp4	
3 1660563732 Manual		~/video/1660563732.mp4	

Fig. 8. Structure of database

The system is also dedicated to proposing excellent UI design interfaces that can be easier for users to operate and understand. A clear UI interface enables users to easily master every step of the software so that they can operate proficiently, which can enhance the user experience. The designed UI interface is shown in Fig. 9.

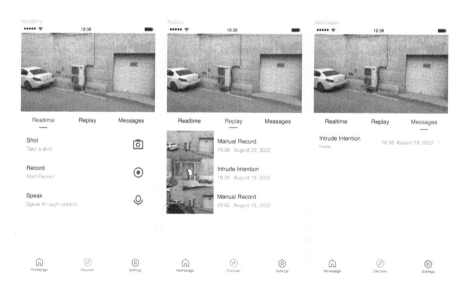

Fig. 9. User interface

6 Conclusion

In this paper, first, we provide a comprehensive overview of relative methods related to video surveillance system. Then, we analyze the main requirements of users and present the main tasks on top of them. Moreover, we provide an intelligent video surveillance system for human behavior recognition. We take the original video as input and output human behavior recognition results. Future work can be extended to involve more powerful algorithm and combining more state-of-art graph data augmentation methods.

Acknowledgement. This study was co-supported by the National Natural Science Foundation of China (Grant No. 52175019), Beijing Natural Science Foundation (Grant No. 3212009 and No.L222038).

References

1. Aradhya, V., Mahmud, M., Guru, D., Agarwal, B., Kaiser, M.S.: One-shot cluster-based approach for the detection of COVID-19 from chest X-ray images. Cogn. Comput. **13**(4), 873–881 (2021)
2. Bronstein, M.M., Bruna, J., LeCun, Y., Szlam, A., Vandergheynst, P.: Geometric deep learning: going beyond euclidean data. IEEE Signal Process. Mag. **34**(4), 18–42 (2017)
3. Cao, Z., Hidalgo, G., Simon, T., Wei, S.E., Sheikh, Y.: OpenPose: realtime multi-person 2D pose estimation using part affinity fields. arxiv 2018. arXiv preprint arXiv:1812.08008 (2018)
4. Chilipirea, C., Ursache, A., Popa, D.O., Pop, F.: Energy efficiency and robustness for IoT: building a smart home security system. In: 2016 IEEE 12th International Conference on Intelligent Computer Communication and Processing (ICCP), pp. 43–48. IEEE (2016)
5. Elharrouss, O., Almaadeed, N., Al-Maadeed, S.: A review of video surveillance systems. J. Vis. Commun. Image Represent. **77**, 103116 (2021). https://doi.org/10.1016/j.jvcir.2021.103116. https://www.sciencedirect.com/science/article/pii/S1047320321000729
6. Gong, K., Zhang, J., Feng, J.: PoseAug: a differentiable pose augmentation framework for 3D human pose estimation. In: Proceedings of the IEEE/CVF Conference on Computer Vision and Pattern Recognition, pp. 8575–8584 (2021)
7. Han, J., Haihong, E., Le, G., Du, J.: Survey on NoSQL database. In: 2011 6th International Conference on Pervasive Computing and Applications, pp. 363–366. IEEE (2011)
8. Li, C.L., Hao, Z.B., Li, J.J.: Abnormal behavior detection using a novel behavior representation. In: The 2010 International Conference on Apperceiving Computing and Intelligence Analysis Proceeding, pp. 331–336. IEEE (2010)
9. National Bureau of Statistics of China: China statistical yearbook 2020. China Statistical Publishing House (2020)
10. Pavllo, D., Feichtenhofer, C., Grangier, D., Auli, M.: 3D human pose estimation in video with temporal convolutions and semi-supervised training. In: Conference on Computer Vision and Pattern Recognition (CVPR) (2019)

11. Shahroudy, A., Liu, J., Ng, T.T., Wang, G.: NTU RGB+D: a large scale dataset for 3D human activity analysis. In: Proceedings of the IEEE Conference on Computer Vision and Pattern Recognition, pp. 1010–1019 (2016)
12. Shahzad, F.: Low-cost intruder detection and alert system using mobile phone proximity sensor. In: 2017 International Conference on Innovations in Electrical Engineering and Computational Technologies (ICIEECT), pp. 1–5. IEEE (2017)
13. Wang, T., et al.: Abnormal event detection based on analysis of movement information of video sequence. Optik **152**, 50–60 (2018)
14. Xu, N., et al.: Dual-stream recurrent neural network for video captioning. IEEE Trans. Circuits Syst. Video Technol. **29**(8), 2482–2493 (2018)
15. Yan, S., Xiong, Y., Lin, D.: Spatial temporal graph convolutional networks for skeleton-based action recognition. In: Thirty-Second AAAI Conference on Artificial Intelligence (2018)
16. Yang, B., Zhang, H.: A CFAR algorithm based on Monte Carlo method for millimeter-wave radar road traffic target detection. Remote Sens. **14**(8), 1779 (2022)
17. Yavuz, E., Kasapbaşı, M.C., Eyüpoğlu, C., Yazıcı, R.: An epileptic seizure detection system based on cepstral analysis and generalized regression neural network. Biocybern. Biomed. Eng. **38**(2), 201–216 (2018)
18. Yu, B., Yin, H., Zhu, Z.: Spatio-temporal graph convolutional networks: a deep learning framework for traffic forecasting. arXiv preprint arXiv:1709.04875 (2017)
19. Zhao, Z., Li, R.: Bayesian cellular automata fusion model based on dual-stream strategy for video anomaly action detection. Pattern Recognit Image Anal. **31**(4), 688–698 (2021)

A Single-Cell Imputation Method Based on Mixture Models and Neural Networks

Aimin Li[(⊠)], Junjie Niu, Siqi Xiong, and Fengqing Dang

School of Computer Science and Engineering, Xi'an University of Technology, Xi'an, China
liaiminmail@gmail.com

Abstract. In the field of single-cell sequencing, single-cell imputation has always been an important research direction. In the single-cell matrix, there are not only zeros that are truly expressed, but also many non-zero items whose expression values are too low to become zeros. The latter phenomenon is called 'Dropout'. In the past, old imputation models often considered the connection between cells and ignored the role of highly expressed genes. To address this difficulty, we introduced a new imputation method that uses a mixture model to Identify highly expressed genes, which are then fed into the neural network imputation model. The high-expressed genes are used as datasets to learn and train the model, and the predicted results are outputted and interpolated into the corresponding low-expressed models. The comparative evaluation of human datasets and mouse datasets shows that this method can effectively identify dropout in cells. Value, strengthen the clustering between cell populations, and improve the ability of differential expression analysis.

Keywords: Single-cell sequence · Impute · Statistics · Neural networks

1 Introduction

Single-cell sequencing refers to the amplification and sequencing of the transcriptome or genome at the single-cell level to detect single-cell data from multiple omics, transcriptomics, epigenomics, and proteomics. However, when single cells are isolated and then sequenced separately, the throughput is very low, which is mainly limited by cost. As the number of single cells to be tested increases, the cost of sequencing will increase almost linearly. To overcome this difficulty, barcode single-cell identification methods have been adopted in recent years. Its main idea is to add a unique DNA sequence to each cell, so that when sequencing, the sequence with the same tag is regarded as from the same cell. With this strategy, the information of hundreds or thousands of single cells can be measured by building a library at one time. There will be many zero values in the cell-gene matrix formed after each library establishment, which will affect downstream analysis. The zeros may be really unexpressed or they may be too small to express, and the two may have different effects on the results. Single-cell imputation technology emerged as the times require and can be used to effectively solve the above problems [1]. There are many downstream analysis methods that can be used to evaluate the quality

Z. Yu et al. (Eds.): CIRAC 2022, CCIS 1770, pp. 374–383, 2023.
https://doi.org/10.1007/978-981-99-0301-6_29

of the imputation results, such as clustering, normalization, differential expression, etc., among that clustering analysis is the most used.

The current impute algorithms can be divided into model-based impute algorithms, smoothing-based impute algorithms, and neural network-based impute. In 2018, Professor Li proposed an impute algorithm based on statistical models, ScImpute [2]; In 2019, Professor Arisdakessian proposed a neural network-based impute method, which uses a deep neural network to learn the distribution law. A big step forward in interpolation efficiency [3]; In 2021, Professor Wang introduced a new learning framework that combines statistical models, graph neural networks, clustering between cells, and imputation at the same time, integrating three auto-encoders to cluster.Using the end of clustering as the termination condition, imputation based on the existing relationship between cells [4]; In 2021, Professor Rao invented the algorithm GraphSCI [5] based on graph convolution and auto-encoder, which also uses clustering and graph convolution to extract The features are interpolated with the statistical model ZINB, and finally the relationship between genes and genes and between cells and cells can be obtained. SDImpute also uses the similarity between genes to automatically identify Dropout events, followed by imputation, which is a great tool for expressing cellular heterogeneity [6].

In the past, the algorithm considered more the correlation between genes and the similarity between cells and cells, which were used as the basis for inference and subsequently used for imputation. However, they did not consider the usefulness of extracting highly expressed genes to the algorithm. More importantly, the use of neural networks to speed up the learning rate is also beneficial to the imputation results. Therefore, we provide a new imputation method, which uses a statistical model to screen out highly expressed genes, uses highly expressed genes as the data set training model, corrects the parameters in the network, takes the low expression genes as the input after the training, outputs the gene expression value predicted by the network, and impute the final results into the original expression matrix. According to the comparative evaluation of the human data set, This method can effectively identify the missing values in cells.

2 Related Work

2.1 Mixture Model

A mixture model is a combination of several different models to form a new model. In statistics, a mixture model represents a probability model of the existence of subgroups in a large group. Generally speaking, a mixture model fits a mixture distribution that represents the probability distribution of the observations in the large group. In this experiment, we represented the dropout part in single cells as a gamma distribution and the non-dropout part as a Normal distribution [7].

2.2 Normal Distribution

The normal distribution, also known as the Gaussian distribution, is a very important probability distribution in the fields of mathematics, physics and engineering, and has a significant influence in many aspects of statistics. If the random variable X obeys a normal distribution with mathematical expectation of μ and a variance of ∂^2, , denoted as $N(\mu, \partial^2)$. Its probability density function is the expected value of the normal distribution μ determines its position, and its standard deviation ∂ determines the magnitude of the distribution [8]. Normal distribution is the standard normal distribution when $\mu = 0$, $\partial = 1$.

$$f(x) = \frac{1}{\sqrt{2\pi}} \exp\left(-\frac{(x-\mu)^2}{2\partial^2}\right) \tag{1}$$

The normal distribution is widely used in medical phenomena, such as the height of the population, the number of red blood cells in the blood, the amount of hemoglobin, cholesterol, etc., as well as random errors in experiments, which are presented as normal or approximately normal distribution. We marked normal non-deleted cells with a normal distribution curve in single-cell sequencing.

2.3 Gamma Distribution

Gamma distribution is a continuous probability function of statistics, and it is a very important distribution in probability statistics. The problem solved by gamma distribution is "how long does it take for n random events to occur", which can be regarded as n The sum of exponentially distributed independent random variables [9].

$$f_x(x) = \begin{cases} \frac{\lambda^\alpha x^{\alpha-1} e^{-\lambda x}}{\Gamma(\alpha)}, & x > 0 \\ 0, & x \leq 0 \end{cases} \tag{2}$$

The parameter α is called the shape parameter, and β is called the inverse scale parameter. When $\alpha = 1$, it becomes an exponential distribution.

2.4 EM

Expectation maximum algorithm is a kind of optimization algorithm that performs maximum likelihood estimation through iteration, and is usually used as a probability model for dropout data for parameter estimation. The EM algorithm is widely used to deal with dropout value in data, as well as parameter estimation for many machines learning algorithms, including Gaussian mixture models and hidden Markov models. The standard computational framework of the EM algorithm consists of alternating E-steps and M-steps [10].

1. E-Step: Using the existing estimates of the hidden variables, calculate their maximum likelihood estimates.

$$Q(z) = p(z|x; \theta) \tag{3}$$

2. M-step: Maximize the maximum likelihood value obtained in E step to calculate the value of the parameter.

$$\theta = argmax\theta \sum_z Q_i(z) log \frac{p(z, x; \theta)}{Q(z)} \tag{4}$$

The convergence of the algorithm ensures that the iterations at least approach local maxima.

3   Method

The method is based on deep learning, implemented using Tensorflow, and has the following five steps: preprocessing, identifying highly expressed genes, network architecture, computing imputation and evaluating (see Fig. 1).

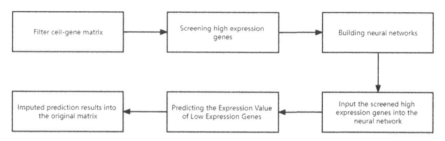

Fig. 1.   Single cell sequencing impute process

3.1   Preprocessing

The preprocessing is to eliminate the influence of Unrelated cells and low-quality cells on the experiment and avoid introducing too much noise to the downstream analysis. During the sampling phase, many unrelated cells may be involved. For example, dead cells may be incorporated into the DNA library during construction; Multiple cells are captured in the same GEM; The low coverage and capture rate of transcripts lead to the undetectable expression of some genes; These will affect our final analysis results. Therefore, before analyzing the counting matrix, we need to conduct quality control on cells to remove low-quality cells as much as possible.

The first step of pretreatment is filtering. The original input matrix is the cell-gene matrix, which is composed of gene expression levels of multiple cell samples. Each row in the two-dimensional matrix represents the expression level of a gene in different cell samples, and each column represents the expression level of each gene in a cell sample. The higher the value in the matrix, the stronger the correlation between the cell and the current genome, and the more valuable the value is. On the contrary, genes with low values have little reference value and need to be eliminated [11]. Traverse the whole matrix. If there are less than 200 genes expressing numerical values in a cell sample, filter the cell sample, that is, delete the column from the two-dimensional matrix. If the number of cells with a gene expression value is less than 3, the gene will be filtered out, that is, the row will be deleted from the two-dimensional matrix. After deleting some ineligible genes and cells, the cell gene matrix is still a two-dimensional matrix. Each row is a genome, and each column is a cell sample. The value is the gene expression level in the cell. This matrix is called count matrix.

The second step is to screen out mitochondrial genes. In the process of cell isolation, single-cell sequencing occasionally causes cell damage or library preparation failure, which often introduces some low-quality data [12]. It is manifested as cellular expression, decreased gene expression or increased proportion of mitochondrial genes. If these damaged rows or columns are not removed, it may have an impact on downstream analysis results. So be sure to remove these low-quality rows and columns before analyzing them.

The filtered expression values are normalized. We use TPM processing [13], that is, the number of transcripts per million mapped reads per kilobase of transcripts will first normalize the gene length, and then normalize the sequencing depth. The formula is $TMP_i = 10^6 * \frac{n_i/l_i}{\sum_j n_i/l_i}$. This method is more suitable for comparing repeated samples within a group and comparing samples within a group. The highly expressed genes were then identified using a gamma-normal model.

3.2 Identify Highly Expressed Genes

The reason for identifying highly expressed genes is that most cells express similar genes among different cells, and only a few genes express differently. The purpose of feature selection is to screen out characteristic genes to represent the main differences in data [14].

The first step is cluster, define cells as nodes and gene expression values in cells as eigenvalues for k-means clustering. The European distance is used to measure the similarity of gene expression in cells, and cells with similar eigenvalues are gathered together as a cell subgroup. In the second step, the gamma normal mixture model is used to distinguish high expression genes from low expression genes. The gamma model is used to count the cell subsets with more missing values, and the normal model is used to count the cell subsets with less missing values. The identified high expression genes will be preserved. We default k for 5.

$$c^{(i)} := argmin_j \left|\left|x^{(i)} - \mu_j\right|\right|^2 \tag{5}$$

After getting the clustering results, we can get the neighboring cells of each cell in the count matrix, and then screen for the highly expressed genes. Since the zero values in the matrix are not necessarily all from the dropout phenomenon, we build a statistical model to judge whether these zero values are really missing. The deletion rate needs to be counted in advance to determine the highly expressed genes.

We used two statistical models to determine expression content, and non-zero values can be counted using a gamma-normal mixed model. The part with large dropout value is counted by the gamma model, that is, the low-expression gene is counted, and the part with small missing value is determined by the normal model, that is, the high-expressed gene [15]. Each cluster will have a separate mixture model. The expression value content is given according to the statistical model, and the default cutoff threshold is 0.5. Gamma distribution and normal distribution are

$$f(X, \alpha, \beta) = \frac{\beta^\alpha}{\Gamma(a)} X^{\alpha-1} e^{-\beta x} \tag{6}$$

$$f\left(X, \mu, \sigma^2\right) = \frac{1}{\sigma\sqrt{2\pi}} e^{-\frac{(X-\mu)^2}{2\sigma^2}} \tag{7}$$

Assuming that the probability of low gene distribution in a cluster is ρ, then the density function of genes x_i in each cluster satisfies:

$$f\left(x_i, \alpha, \beta, \mu, \sigma^2\right) = (1 - \rho)\frac{\beta^\alpha}{\Gamma(a)} x_i^{\alpha-1} e^{-\beta x} + \rho \frac{1}{\sigma\sqrt{2\pi}} e^{-\frac{(x_i-\mu)^2}{2\sigma^2}} \tag{8}$$

where is the input count matrix library, is the probability of gene deletion in a single cell, k is the cluster size, and are the shape parameter and inverse scale parameter of the gamma distribution, respectively. Are the mean and variance of the normal distribution, respectively. The maximum expectation of the gamma-normal model was derived using the EM algorithm. EM iterates until the end of the update, and selects a threshold of 0.5. If the final result is greater than 0.5, it is called a high-expressed gene, otherwise it is a low-expressed gene.

3.3 Network Architecture

Each cluster uses a new neural network based on the previously clustered clusters. We put the selected high expression genes in each cluster into neural network training in blocks. The input layer is 512 neurons, and each 512 neurons are trained as a group in batches. Repeat iteration until all gene training is completed. The network cannot be set too deep, which may lead to smooth nodes due to over fitting [16].

There are five layers in the network architecture. The specific neural network model is shown in Fig. 2. The first layer is the input layer containing 512 neural nodes, the second layer is the full connection layer, the activation function is ReLu, include 256 cell node and the third layer is the Dropout layer. After trying, we chose the dropout rate of 20%. The purpose of adding the second layer of activation function and the third layer of Dropout layer is to reduce the interdependence between parameters and ease the occurrence of over fitting problems. The fourth and fifth layers are still full connection layers with 512 cell nodes (see Fig. 2). The purpose of adding these two layers is to better increase the connection between cells and map the learned features to the global sample space. The loss function uses mean square error (MSE) to reduce the error between the input layer and the output layer, genes with higher expression values have higher weight. Among the highly expressed genes, 95% of the data are used as training sets and 5% as test sets. We set the initial learning rate of the network to 0.0001, and each epoch cycle will automatically modify the learning rate. The optimizer is Adam. The screened high expression genes are input into the training parameters of the neural network, and the output results are the expression values that should be reflected by the low expression genes. Finally, replace the result in the original matrix.

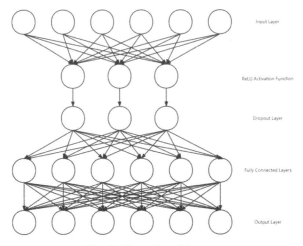

Fig. 2. Network architecture

3.4 Impute

In single cell sequencing, the function of impute is to supplement the value of gene expression that is not expressed due to accidental fragmentation during library construction. This facilitates the subsequent analysis of single cell sequencing data and improves the accuracy of subsequent analysis results.

Firstly, the screened high expression genes are divided into training sample data set and test sample data set, and the neural network model is trained using the training sample data set to obtain the prediction model. Secondly, the low expression genes in the cluster are input into the trained prediction model to obtain the prediction results. Finally, the expression value of the low expression gene in the original matrix is replaced by the prediction result, and a whole line of genes is replaced. The original matrix has many zero values, which are significantly reduced after replacement, facilitating downstream analysis.

3.5 Evaluate

PCC. The Pearson correlation coefficient is widely used to measure the degree of correlation between two variables, and its value is between -1 and 1. The Pearson correlation coefficient between two variables is defined as the quotient of the covariance and standard deviation between the two variables, which can be used to measure the degree of correlation between two things, which can be regarded as the difference between the imputed gene and the original gene. Correlation [17].

$$Corr = \frac{Cov(X(gene), X_{method}(gene))}{Var(X(gene)) * Var(X_{method}(gene))} \tag{9}$$

where X is the input matrix, Cov is the covariance matrix and Var is the variance.

MSE. Mean squared error is a more convenient method to measure the "average error". MSE can evaluate the degree of change in the data. The smaller the value of MSE, the better accuracy of the prediction model in describing the experimental data [18].

$$MSE = \sum (X(gene) - X_{method}(gene))^2 \tag{10}$$

4   Experiment

4.1   Data Set

We select four datasets selected in this paper, two mouse datasets and two human datasets, those public datasets on the Internet. The mouse datasets can be downloaded from the GEO database as GSE67602 (mouse epidermal single cell) and GSE60361 (mouse cerebral cortex single cell). This database is a public repository for various high-throughput experimental data. Human datasets are Jurkat and 293T, both of which can be downloaded from the official website of 10X Genomes.

4.2   Preprocessing Results

After getting the data set and performing preprocessing filtering, many irrelevant genes and dead cells in the original matrix will be screened out. Table 1 shows the comparison of the number of cells and genes in the four data sets before and after screening. The experimental results showed that the number of cells was basically unchanged, and the number of genes was significantly reduced. We call the screened cell gene matrix the counting matrix.

Table 1. Comparison before and after data filtering

Data Set	Before filtering	After filtering
Jurkat	3258×26024	3258×15269
293T	2885×32738	2885×16316
GSE60361	3005×16382	3005×15602
GSE67602	1442×16383	1442×13001

4.3   Imputation Results

This experiment is compared with the DeepImpute algorithm, and two evaluation indicators, Pearson correlation coefficient and mean square error, are compared. Table 2 shows that after using this method, the Pearson correlation coefficient is significantly improved, and the correlation of the impute results is significantly improved; the mean square error is also reduced accordingly.

Table 2. Data impute results

DataSet	Corr	DeepImpute Corr	MSE	DeepImpute MSE
JurKat	0.91	**0.92**	**0.13**	0.14
293T	**0.92**	0.91	**0.122**	0.124
GSE60361	**0.83**	0.81	**0.12**	0.16
GSE67602	**0.87**	0.77	**0.15**	0.23

5   Conclusion

This paper introduces a method based on hybrid imputation of statistical models and neural networks. The experimental results show that there are obvious advantages to use this method. Not only is the imputation effect better, but it is also beneficial for downstream analysis. According to the experimental results, it can be seen that the efficient extraction of highly expressed genes is crucial for subsequent imputation work. The extraction based on the statistical model can obtain more accurate highly expressed genes, which provides a good start for subsequent imputation. The interpolation method based on neural network can effectively learn the characteristics of highly expressed genes, showing higher accuracy and calculation speed during interpolation, and reducing memory consumption. However, due to the problem of network depth, it can also be trained more fully. If the overfitting problem can be effectively solved, the interpolation results can be further broken through.

Funding.   This work was supported by Science Basic Research Program of Shaanxi (Program no. 2021JM-347).

References

1. Usoskin, D., et al:. Unbiased classification of sensory neuron types by large-scale single-cell RNA sequencing. Nat. Neurosci. **18**, 145 (2015). Nature Publishing Group
2. Li, W.V., Li, J.J.: An accurate and robust imputation method scImpute for single-cell RNA-seq data. Nat. Commun. **9**, 997 (2018)
3. Arisdakessian, C., Poirion, O., Yunits, B., et al.: DeepImpute: an accurate, fast, and scalable deep neural network method to impute single-cell RNA-seq data. Genome Biol. **20**, 211 (2019)
4. Wang, J., Ma, A., Chang, Y., et al.: scGNN is a novel graph neural network framework for single-cell RNA-Seq analyses. Nat. Commun. **12**, 1882 (2021)
5. Rao, J., Zhou, X., Lu, Y., Zhao, H., Yang, Y.: Imputing single-cell RNA-seq data by combining graph convolution and autoencoder neural networks. iScience **24**(5), 102393 (2021). ISSN 2589-0042, https://doi.org/10.1016/j.isci.2021.102393
6. Qi, J., Zhou, Y., Zhao, Z., Jin, S.: Correction: SDImpute: a statistical block imputation method based on cell-level and gene-level information for dropouts in single-cell RNA-seq data. PLOS Comput. Biol. **18**(1), e1009770 (2022)
7. Phoong, S.Y., Khek, S.L., Phoong, S.W.: The bibliometric analysis on finite mixture model. SAGE Open (2022). https://doi.org/10.1177/21582440221101039

8. Ahsanullah, M., Kibria, B.M.G., Shakil, M.: Normal distribution. In: Normal and Student's t Distributions and Their Applications. Atlantis Studies in Probability and Statistics, vol. 4. Atlantis Press, Paris (2014). https://doi.org/10.2991/978-94-6239-061-4_2

9. Stacy, E.W., Mihram, G.A.: Parameter estimation for a generalized gamma distribution. Technometrics 7(3), 349–358 (1965). https://doi.org/10.1080/00401706.1965.10490268

10. Ng, S.K., Krishnan, T., McLachlan, G.J.: The EM algorithm. In: Gentle, J.E., Härdle, W.K., Mori, Y. (eds.) Handbook of Computational Statistics, pp. 139–172. Springer, Heidelberg (2012). https://doi.org/10.1007/978-3-642-21551-3_6

11. Gayoso, A., Lopez, R., Xing, G., et al.: A Python library for probabilistic analysis of single-cell omics data. Nat. Biotechnol. 40, 163–166 (2022). https://doi.org/10.1038/s41587-021-01206-w

12. Batut, B., Hotz, H.-R., Tekman, M.: Clustering 3K PBMCs with Scanpy (Galaxy Training Materials) (2021). https://training.galaxyproject.org/archive/2021-11-01/topics/transcriptom ics/tutorials/scrna-scanpy-pbmc3k/tutorial.html. Accessed 14 Jul 2022

13. Qiu, X., Hill, A., Packer, J., et al.: Single-cell mRNA quantification and differential analysis with Census. Nat. Methods 14, 309–315 (2017). https://doi.org/10.1038/nmeth.4150

14. Anowar, F., Sadaoui, S., Selim, B.: Conceptual and empirical comparison of dimensionality reduction algorithms (PCA, KPCA, LDA, MDS, SVD, LLE, ISOMAP, LE, ICA, t-SNE). Comput. Sci. Rev. 40, 100378 (2021). ISSN 1574-0137, https://doi.org/10.1016/j.cosrev.2021.100378

15. Ghazanfar, S., Bisogni, A.J., Ormerod, J.T., Lin, D.M., Yang, J.Y.H.: Integrated single cell data analysis reveals cell specific networks and novel coactivation markers. BMC Syst. Biol. 10, 11 (2016)

16. Zeng, Y., Zhou, X., Rao, J., Lu, Y., Yang, Y.: Accurately clustering single-cell RNA-seq data by capturing structural relations between cells through graph convolutional network. In: 2020 IEEE International Conference on Bioinformatics and Biomedicine (BIBM), pp. 519–522 (2020). https://doi.org/10.1109/BIBM49941.2020.9313569

17. Benesty, J., Chen, J., Huang, Y., Cohen, I.: Pearson correlation coefficient. In: Cohen, I., Huang, Y., Chen, J., Benesty, J. (eds.) Noise Reduction in Speech Processing, pp. 1–4. Springer, Heidelberg (2009). https://doi.org/10.1007/978-3-642-00296-0_5

18. Tuchler, M., Singer, A.C., Koetter, R.: Minimum mean squared error equalization using a priori information. IEEE Trans. Signal Process. 50(3), 673–683 (2002). https://doi.org/10.1109/78.984761

A Novel Community Detection Algorithm Based on Deep Learning Algorithm

Lili Wu, Rong Fei[✉], and Yuxin Wan

School of Computer Science and Engineering, Xi'an University of Technology, Xi'an 710048, China
annyfei@xaut.edu.cn

Abstract. With the extremely rapid growth of data scale, feature reduction in communities is gradually gaining attention. Community detection methods based on deep learning can discover deep network information and complex relationships, and better handle high-dimensional data. In this paper, we apply deep learning to community detection by using a deep sparse autoencoder to reduce the dimension of the input matrix of the network graph and extract data features from it, and continuously reduce the reconstruction error until the optimal solution is found to achieve the classification of communities. The community results obtained from K-means clustering using adjacency matrix directly, K-means clustering using the similarity matrix, K-means clustering using the feature matrix after dimensionality reduction by the autoencoder, and K-means clustering using the feature matrix after dimensionality reduction by the sparse autoencoder are compared. Experiments on Strike, Football and Karate network datasets were conducted to test the community detection results under the above four methods, and the detection results were analyzed using three evaluation metrics, such as NMI. In addition to hop count threshold, there are parameters such as decay factors that have an impact on the community detection results, so control variate method is used to explore effect on experiments when the parameters take various values.

Keywords: Community detection · Deep sparse autoencoder · Deep learning · K-means

1 Introduction

Community detection techniques can discover subcommunity groups from complex and large sets of networks. With data and information fast growing in recent years, feature dimension reduction in communities has also received increasing attention, and community detection based upon deep learning can discover deep network information and complex relationships to better handle high-dimensional data.

Some community detection methods use graph theory, in which the nodes in the graph are divided into multiple subgraphs with different properties in the form of mutual exclusion, and two of the most well-known and effective methods are the Kernighan-Lin (KL) algorithm [1] and the Fiduccia-Mattheyses (FM) [2] algorithm. Among community detection algorithms based on modularity optimization, extreme value optimization, simulated annealing, spectral clustering and genetic algorithms are the main ways to construct modularity optimization for the study of communities, where modularity is proportional to the density of node edges within the community, where the Louvain algorithm [3] optimizes the partitioning of communities by maximizing the modularity of the whole community.

K-means [4] is a kind of clustering method which is usually applied to community detection. It directly uses adjacency matrix for clustering, thus ignoring the indirect relationships between nodes, and the accuracy needs to be improved. With the gradual expansion of the scale of social networks and the gradual increase of data dimensionality, this poses a great challenge to the algorithms using clustering methods for community detection. Deep learning [5] is able to learn the trend changes of data, especially nonlinear data, and by constructing a multi-layer networks [6–8] model, different expressions of the data are learned so as to achieve the purpose of downscaling and extracting features.

In this paper, we construct a deep spare autoencoder [9] to implement community detection, firstly, we propose the definition of s-hop number, derive the similarity matrix from the inter-node similarity calculation formula, dimensionality reduction and feature extraction for high-dimensional data rows, and use K-means method for clustering, and obtain the clustering results with high accuracy.

2 Preface

2.1 Matrix Preprocessing

The sets of nodes and edges of network graph $G = (V, E)$ are, respectively, $V = \{v_1, v_2, \ldots, v_n\}$ and $E = \{e_1, e_2, \ldots, e_n\}$, and all neighboring nodes of node u form the set N(u). $A = [a_{ij}]_{n \times n}$ is adjacency matrix which shows the connectivity between nodes in graph G. If v_i is connected to v_j by an edge, then $a_{ij} = 1$, and conversely, then $a_{ij} = 0$.

Definition 1 (s-hop): A node u can reach node v after s-hops (s-hops) if it can form a path between node u and node v after at least s-hops.

Definition 2 (node similarity): The similarity between nodes u and v can be calculated using Eq. (1).

$$Sim(u, v) = e^{\sigma(1-s)} \tag{1}$$

where node u arrives at node v after s-hop, $s \geq 1$. σ is called the decay factor, $\sigma \in (0, 1)$. The similarity among nodes is inversely associated to number of hops. Decay factor σ can measure the change of similarity, the larger the decay factor σ is, the faster the similarity relationship between nodes decays.

The similarity values between any two nodes are calculated by the above formula (1), then the matrix $X = [x_{ij}]_{n \times n}$ consisting of these similarity values is the similarity matrix.

2.2 Deep Sparse Autoencoder

Autoencoder is unsupervised and it can encode data efficiently to get the eigenvalues of the data and achieve dimensionality reduction.

Figure 1 is Autoencoder's structure. It includes encoder and decoder. Encoding refers to the processing of inputting data to the input layer and then reaching hidden layer. Firstly, original data is input into the encoder for dimensionality reduction, and the output from the encoder is then used as the input of the decoder, and it is necessary to make the input data have the same dimensionality as the output data. Finally, the reconstruction error is calculated by comparing the original data with the output result, and then the weight matrix is automatically adjusted using the back propagation algorithm. Keep counting the error and then end if number of loops or the reconstruction error is smaller than the given range.

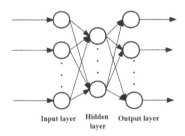

Input layer   Hidden   Output layer
                layer

Fig. 1. Autoencoder

The process is described in detail below.

Similarity matrix is the input matrix and the encoding $h_i \in R^{d \times 1}$ is obtained by (2).

$$h_i = s_f(Wx_i + p) \tag{2}$$

The input h_i is sent to the decoding layer and the decoding result $x_i' \in R^{n \times 1}$ is obtained as input information according to (3).

$$x_i' = s_g(\widetilde{W} h_i + q) \tag{3}$$

Through training, the parameters $\theta = \{W, \widetilde{W}, p, q\}$ are automatically adjusted to continuously reduce the reconstruction error of x_i and x_i' to minimize, it is as (4).

$$\min_{W, \widetilde{W}, p, q} imize \sum_{i=1}^{n} \left\| s_g(\widetilde{W} s_f(Wx_i + p) + q) - x_i \right\|_2^2 \tag{4}$$

To reduce the matrix computation error, it is necessary to add sparsity restrictions and introduce KL scatter, it is as (5).

$$\sum_{j=1}^{d} KL\left(\rho||\frac{1}{n}\sum_{i=1}^{n}h_i\right) \tag{5}$$

Finally, the reconfiguration error of the constructed autoencoder is as (6).

$$L(\theta) = \sum_{i=1}^{n}\left\|s_g(\widetilde{W}\,s_f(Wx_i+p)+q) - x_i\right\|_2^2 + \alpha\sum_{j=1}^{d}KL\left(\rho||\frac{1}{n}\sum_{i=1}^{n}s_f(Wx_i+p)\right) \tag{6}$$

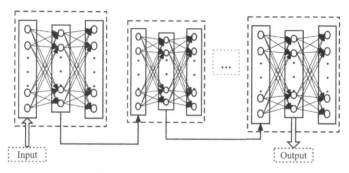

Fig. 2. Deep sparse autoencoder

In Fig. 2, deep sparse autoencoder is made of multiple layers of sparse autoencoders. The data is first input to the first layer, trained and then the output of hidden layer is input to the next layer. Finally, output of the last layer is the data after descending and extracting features.

2.3 CDDLA

The flow of the CDDLA (a novel community detection algorithm using deep learning) is given in Table 1. And CDDLA uses deep sparse autoencoder to dimensionality reduction and extract feature from similarity matrix, and then uses k-means to get community results.

Table 1. CDDLA algorithm

Algorithm 1: CDDLA

Input: adjacency matrix,
      k (number of communities),
      S (hop count threshold),
      σ (decay factor),
      T (number of layers of sparse autoencoder),
      d (number of nodes per layer)

Output: community division result

1 :   **FOR** each x **in** V

2 :   initialize each node to an unvisited state, $Queue = \Phi$ and hop set $D = \Phi$

3 :   mark x as in-access and hop count of x equal to 0, write x and hop count 0 to D, push x into the Queue

4 :   **WHILE** $Queue \neq \Phi$

5 :   remove node u from the $Queue$

6 :   **FOR** each v **in** N(u)

7 :   **IF** v is unvisited **and** u is in (S-1)-hop of x

8 :   set v to accessing status

9 :   calculate number of hops from x to v which is number of hops from x to u to add 1

10 :   write v and number of hops from x to v to D, add v to $Queue$

11 :   **End**

12 :   **End**

13 :   set u to end of visit status

14 :   **End**

15 :   **FOR** each v **in** V

16 :   calculate the similarity of x and v according to the set of hop counts D

17 :   **End**

18 : **End**

19 : get similarity matrix X, $X^{(1)} = X$

20 : **FOR** j=1 **to** T

21 :   create a sparse autoencoder

22 :   input feature matrix $X^{(j)}$

23 :   train the sparse autoencoder by the optimizing formula (6)

24 :   obtain the representation of the hidden layer $H^{(j)}$, $X^{(j+1)} = H^{(j)}$

25 : **End**

26 : run k-means and cluster to get the resultant community

3 Evaluation Criteria

Three of the more used criteria for evaluating the division results of community detection algorithms are Fsame, NMI, and Q. Among them, Fsame and NMI are commonly used community evaluation criteria to analyze community detection results.

For the three evaluation criteria: the larger the value of Fsame indicates that the intersection between the divided result community and the real community is larger and the clustering result is better; the closer NMI is to 1, the higher the degree of concordance between the resultant community and the real community; the larger the Q modularity, the better the community detection results.

3.1 Evaluation Criteria Fsame

Fsame is calculated by the formula (7).

$$F_{same} = \frac{1}{2n} \left(\sum_{i=1}^{k} \max_{j} \left| C_i \cap C'_j \right| + \sum_{j=1}^{t} \max_{j} \left| C_i \cap C'_j \right| \right) \tag{7}$$

where counts of nodes of G is n, counts of true communities is t and the counts of real communities is represented by k.

3.2 Evaluation Criteria NMI

NMI is calculated by the formula (8).

$$NMI = \frac{-2 \sum_{ij} N_{ij} \log \frac{N_{ij} N_t}{N_{i.} N_{.j}}}{\sum_{i} N_{i.} \log \frac{N_{i.}}{N_t} + \sum_{j} N_{.j} \log \frac{N_{.j}}{N_t}} \tag{8}$$

where counts of communal nodes between C_i and C'_j is expressed by N_{ij}.

3.3 Evaluation Criteria Q

Q is calculated by (9).

$$Q = \sum_{i=1}^{k} \left(\frac{E_i^{in}}{m} - \left(\frac{2E_i^{in} + E_i^{out}}{2m} \right)^2 \right) \tag{9}$$

where edges within community C_i is E_i^{in}, edges external to community C_i is E_i^{out}, and total number of edges of graph G is m.

4 Experiment

4.1 Experiment Description

Relu is activation function for encoding layer, sigmoid is activation function for decoding layer and loss function is binare_crossentropy, which are all built-in functions of Keras and can be called directly by importing the Keras library.

Three datasets were used in the experiment and described in Table 2. Among them, Strike is the communication network of sawmill workers about the strike topic, Football is the matchup relationship network of 2006 NCAA soccer game, from which we select

Table 2. Dataset information

Dataset	Count of nodes	Count of edges	Count of communities
Strike	24	38	3
Karate	34	78	2
Football	180	788	11

some data, and the Karate [10] dataset describes the friendship between 34 individuals in American college karate clubs in the 1970s.

In the dataset comparison experiments, four comparison experiments were made on these three datasets to evaluate the resultant communities got by clustering using three evaluation metrics, Fsame, NMI and Q, respectively. These four methods are as follows.

CDDLA-adjacency matrix: it refers to K-means clustering directly using the adjacency matrix for network graph.

CDDLA-similarity matrix: it refers to K-means clustering using the similarity matrix of graph.

CDDLA-autoencoder: it refers to taking the similarity matrix into the autoencoder, performing dimensionality reduction to obtain the feature matrix, and then using K-means clustering.

CDDLA-sparse autoencoder: it means taking the similarity matrix into the sparse autoencoder, getting reduced-dimensional feature matrix, and then using K-means clustering.

During the dataset parameter experiments, not only hop count threshold but also decay factor, even layers of deep sparse autoencoder all have an effect on the experimental results, and experiments were executed with various parameter taking values to find their effect.

4.2 Dataset Comparison Experiments

The comparison experiments on the Strike dataset are as follows.

CDDLA-adjacency matrix: Fsame is 0.9167, NMI is 0.8213, Q is 0.4733.

CDDLA-similarity matrix: Fsame is 0.8333, NMI is 0.6750, and Q is 0.3438.

Table 3. CDDLA-autoencoder on Strike dataset

Group number	Fsame	NMI	Q
The first group	0.6857	0.4304	0.1243
The second group	0.7083	0.3566	0.1592
The third group	0.6875	0.3832	0.1915
The fourth group	0.7083	0.4037	0.1652
The fifth group	0.7291	0.3902	0.1783

Table 4. CDDLA-sparse autoencoder on Strike dataset

Group number	Fsame	NMI	Q
The first group	0.7083	0.4651	0.3217
The second group	0.8125	0.6179	0.2621
The third group	0.7292	0.3923	0.2739
The fourth group	0.7917	0.5658	0.3231
The fifth group	0.7708	0.5641	0.2469

CDDLA-autoencoder: five randomly selected groups of results were assessed and Table 3 shows the results.

CDDLA-sparse autoencoder: five sets of clustering results are randomly taken for evaluation, and Table 4 shows the results.

From the above experimental results, it is obvious that the best community detection results are obtained from the CDDLA-adjacency matrix among the four methods, where Fsame reaches 0.9167, NMI is 0.8213, and Q is 0.4733, while in the CDDLA-similarity matrix, the values of the three evaluation criteria are smaller than the first method, because the two parameters of hop count threshold and decay factor in the experiment have an effect on the similarity between nodes; and the results of the latter two methods are not better than the former two methods, which is because, Strike dataset is small, and autoencoder is more effective in downscaling and feature extraction for high-dimensional data, so for small dataset like Strike a better clustering result can be gained by using adjacency matrix directly.

The comparison experiments on the Football dataset are as follows.

CDDLA-adjacency matrix: Fsame is 0.4556, NMI is 0.3928, and Q is 0.1409.

CDDLA-similarity matrix: Fsame is 0.9944, NMI is 0.9889, and Q is 0.5090.

CDDLA-autoencoder: five sets of clustering results were randomly taken for evaluation, and Table 5 are the results.

Table 5. CDDLA-autoencoder on Football dataset

Group number	Fsame	NMI	Q
The first group	0.9056	0.8728	0.4202
The second group	0.9250	0.9060	0.4397
The third group	0.8528	0.8178	0.3588
The fourth group	0.9500	0.9245	0.4726
The fifth group	0.8889	0.8535	0.3949

CDDLA-sparse autoencoder: five randomly selected groups of results were assessed and results are given in Table 6.

Table 6. CDDLA-sparse autoencoder on Football dataset

Group number	Fsame	NMI	Q
The first group	0.8611	0.8209	0.3602
The second group	0.8611	0.8022	0.3659
The third group	0.8250	0.7927	0.3196
The fourth group	0.8917	0.8569	0.3886
The fifth group	0.9028	0.8497	0.4024

In the experimental results on Football dataset, it is not like the best community detection result obtained by CDDLA-adjacency matrix on Strike dataset, instead the community detection result obtained by this method is the worst, while the community detection result obtained by both CDDLA-autocoder and CDDLA-sparse autocoder is better with the value of Fsame around 0.9000, NMI around 0.8500 and Q around 0.4000. This is because the Football dataset is much larger than the Strike dataset, and the autoencoder can reduce and extract features from the high-dimensional data to get better community detection results.

The comparison experiments on the Karate dataset are as follows.

CDDLA-adjacency matrix: Fsame is 0.8823, NMI is 0.4764, Q is 0.2813.

CDDLA-similarity matrix: Fsame is 0.8324, NMI is 0.4765, and Q is 0.2813.

CDDLA-autoencoder: five sets of clustering results are randomly taken for evaluation, and you can see the results in Table 7.

CDDLA-sparse autoencoder: five sets of clustering results are randomly taken for evaluation, and Table 8 shows the results.

Table 7. CDDLA-autoencoder on Karate dataset

Group number	Fsame	NMI	Q
The first group	0.7647	0.2385	0.2031
The second group	0.8235	0.3340	0.2680
The third group	0.7942	0.2848	0.1728
The fourth group	0.7647	0.2616	0.1851
The fifth group	0.8236	0.3631	0.2354

On the Karate dataset, the values of evaluation criteria of the community detection results obtained by the four methods do not differ much, while the overall CDDLA-sparse autoencoder method has Fsame around 0.8500, NMI around 0.4000, and Q around 0.25, which is due to the small size difference between the Karate and Strike datasets.

Table 8. CDDLA-sparse autoencoder on Karate dataset

Group number	Fsame	NMI	Q
The first group	0.7941	0.2847	0.2300
The second group	0.7941	0.3098	0.1814
The third group	0.8824	0.4765	0.2813
The fourth group	0.8529	0.4231	0.2620
The fifth group	0.8236	0.3380	0.2307

4.3 Dataset Parameter Experiments

The parameter experiments on the Strike dataset are as follows.

Hop count threshold: on the Strike dataset, layers for deep sparse autoencoder is [16-8], and decay factor is 0.5 to study the influence of various hop count thresholds on community detection results.

Decay factor: On the Strike dataset, layers of the deep sparse autoencoder is [16-8], and hop threshold is 3 to investigate the effect of different decay factors.

Since the Strike dataset is small and there are only 24 nodes and 38 edges, it is optimal to make layers for encoder [16-8].

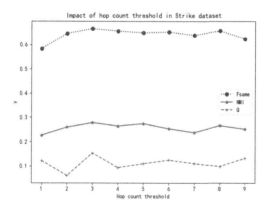

Fig. 3. Impact of hop count threshold in Strike dataset

In Fig. 3, hop count threshold is different, evaluation criteria Fsame around 0.6500 fluctuates, NMI varies around 0.2500, Q fluctuates above and below 0.1000, and the optimal hop count threshold is 3, when Fsame is maximum 0.6820, NMI is maximum 0.2900, and Q is maximum 0.1857.

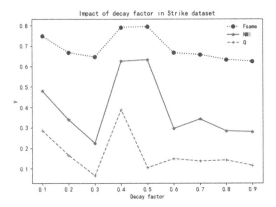

Fig. 4. Impact of decay factor in Strike dataset

In Fig. 4, the decay factors are different values, and the evaluation criterion Fsame is stable around 0.7000, and NMI and Q fluctuate more, with NMI varying around 0.4000 and Q fluctuating above and below 0.2000. The best decay factor is 0.5, and although the Q value is not the largest at this time, both Fsame and NMI are the largest, with Fsame at 0.7958, NMI at 0.6325, and Q at 0.1200.

The parameter experiments on the Football dataset are as follows.

Hop count thresholds: various hop count thresholds is studied on the Football dataset with a deep sparse autoencoder with layers [128-64] and a decay factor of 0.5.

Decay factor: On the Football dataset, layers of the deep sparse autoencoder is [128-64], and let hop threshold equal to 1 to analyze the effect of different decay factors.

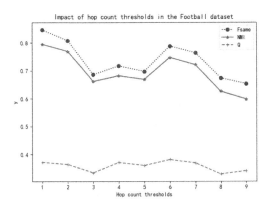

Fig. 5. Impact of hop count threshold in Football dataset

In Fig. 5, with the change of hop count threshold, the changes of evaluation criteria Fsame and NMI are relatively consistent, they both fluctuate up and down around 0.7000, while Q fluctuates around 0.3500. The maximum Fsame is 0.8750 and the maximum Q is 0.3600 when the hop count threshold is 1.

In Fig. 6, the variation of evaluation criteria Fsame and NMI is relatively consistent, they both fluctuate up and down around 0.6500, while Q fluctuates around 0.3000. When the decay factor is 0.4, the maximum Fsame is 0.7350 and Q is 0.3250.

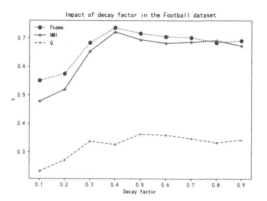

Fig. 6. Impact of decay factor in Football dataset

The count of encoder layers: on the Football dataset, hop count threshold is 1 and decay factor is 0.4 to study the effect of layers of deep sparse autoencoders, and number for nodes per layer is [128, 100, 80, 64] in order in the experiment.

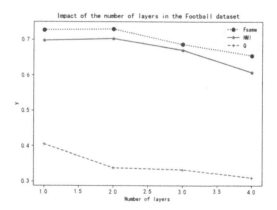

Fig. 7. Impact of the number of layers in the Football dataset

In Fig. 7, as layers are changed from 1 to 4, the evaluation criteria Fsame and NMI change consistently; they both fluctuate up and down around 0.7000, while Q fluctuates around 0.3500. When the optimal number of layers is 2, the maximum Fsame is 0.7650 and Q is 0.3450.

From the values of these evaluation indexes, it can be concluded that the community detection results obtained when encoder has two layers and per layer respectively has 128 nodes and 64 nodes, are better.

4.4 Visualization Experiments

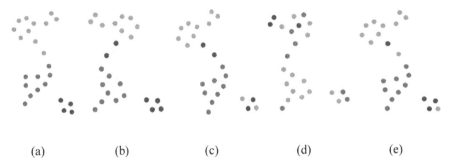

<table>
<tr><td>(a)</td><td>(b)</td><td>(c)</td><td>(d)</td><td>(e)</td></tr>
</table>

Fig. 8. (a) Real communities (b) CDDLA-adjacency matrix (c) CDDLA-similarity matrix (d) CDDLA-autoencoder (e) CDDLA-sparse autoencoder

The (a) picture in Fig. 8 shows the real subcommunities of the Strike dataset, and in the (b) picture there is two node with wrong division, so the CDDLA-adjacency matrix method has better division results for the small dataset; in the (c) picture four nodes are divided into wrong subcommunities, because in the CDDLA-similarity matrix method, the choice of hop count threshold affects the similarity between nodes; in the (d) and (e) picture, the CDDLA-sparse autoencoder method gets better community division results, indicating that increasing the KL sparsity limit has a certain effect on the division results. Moreover, on larger datasets such as Football, the resultant communities obtained by CDDLA-sparse autoencoder are the closest to the real communities.

5   Conclusions

The community detection results of K-means methods under four CDDLA-based approaches were experimented upon the Strike, Football, and Karate datasets, respectively, and by using three evaluation criteria a conclusion is gained that the community results on some larger datasets by using CDDLA-sparse autoencoder method were greater, which implies that better community results were obtained by using deep sparse autoencoder. In the parametric experiments, optimal values of the parameters are: a hop count threshold of 3, a decay factor of 0.5, and a number of layers of [16-8] on the Strike dataset, and a hop count threshold of 1, a decay factor of 0.4, and a number of layers of [128-64] on the Football dataset.

References

1. Kernighan, B.W., Lin, S.: An efficient heuristic procedure for partitioning graphs. Bell Syst. Tech. J. **49**(2), 291–307 (1970)
2. Fiduccia, C.M., Mattheyses, R.M.: A linear-time heuristic for improving network partitions. In: 19th Conference on Design Automation. ACM (1982)

3. Meo, P.D., Ferrara, E., Fiumara, G., et al.: Fast unfolding of communities in large networks (2008)
4. Schaeffer, S.E.: Graph clustering. Comput. Sci. Rev. **1**(1), 27–64 (2007)
5. Su, X., et al.: A comprehensive survey on community detection with deep learning. IEEE Trans. Neural Netw. Learn. Syst. **2022**, 21 (2022)
6. Bengio, Y., Courville, A., Vincent, P.: Representation learning: a review and new perspectives. IEEE Trans. Pattern. Anal. Mach. Intell. **35**(8), 1798–1828 (2013)
7. Schmidhuber, J.: Deep learning in neural networks: an overview. Neural Netw. **61**, 85–117 (2015)
8. Lecun, Y., Bengio, Y., Hinton, G.: Deep learning. Nature **521**(7553), 436 (2015)
9. Jing-Wen, S., Chao-Kun, W., Xin, X., Xiang, Y.: Community detection algorithm based on deep sparse autoencoder. J. Softw. **28**(3), 648–662 (2017)
10. Zachary, W.W.: An information flow model for conflict and fission in small groups. J. Anthropol. Res. **33**, 452–473 (1977)

Bearing Small Sample Fault Diagnosis Based on DCGAN and CNN

Miao Gao, Xinhong Hei[(⊠)], and Kuan Zhang

School of Computer Science and Engineering, Xi'an University of Technology, Xi'an 710048, China
heixinhong@xaut.edu.cn

Abstract. It is suggested to use deep convolutional generative adversarial networks and convolutional neural networks to diagnose faults in small samples of bearings. The CWRU bearing dataset is pre-processed with data and used as input to DCGAN, which is trained in DCGAN. When the number of training sessions reaches the experimentally set number, the training is stopped and the samples generated by the generator are mixed with the original samples and used as input to CNN, on which the classification model is trained to achieve fault classification. Comparative studies were carried out on the dataset of taken bearings to show the efficacy of the suggested method. The findings demonstrate how well the suggested diagnosis approach diagnoses bearing faults while outperforming competing algorithms and models.

Keywords: Small samples · DCGAN · CNN · Fault diagnosis

1 Introduction

Rolling bearings as a basic component of rotating machinery and equipment, widely used in a variety of mechanical equipment, its normal state or not directly affect the normal operation of mechanical equipment, rotational machine failure is one of the primary causes of rolling bearing failure [1]. Consequently, the technology of machinery and equipment fault diagnostics includes rolling bearing problem diagnosis, rolling bearing fault diagnosis is an important element of machinery and equipment fault diagnosis technology [2, 3].

Researchers from both local and foreign countries have conducted a significant amount of study on the topic. Literature [4] uses TCGAN to expand the sample size and then establishes a semi-supervised model to achieve fault sample classification; literature [5] discusses a GAN model CSGAN based on CGAN and SGAN and gives a specific design, which solves the drawback that CGAN can only discriminate true-false but not classification and SGAN needs to discriminate true-false and discriminate classification at the same time; A bearing defect diagnostic approach based on adaptive normalized SCAN of a one-dimensional vibration signal is suggested in the literature [6]. However, the simulation data generated by the SCAN is not controllable; Using a conditional deep convolutional adversarial network generation model, literature [7] suggests an imbalanced fault diagnostic technique that can increase fault diagnosis accuracy; A limited sample failure diagnostic approach for bearings is proposed in the literature [8] and is based on information-generating adversarial networks and convolutional neural networks, where the vibration signal undergoes a short-time Fourier transform to make better use of time-domain and frequency-domain information and facilitate infoGAN processing.

The problem of limited sample data in bearing defect diagnostics has been successfully resolved using the aforementioned technique. Because its input is one-dimensional data, it does not fully learn the image generation ability of GAN variant and takes into account the poor effect of convolutional neural network directly processing signal generated by a single-dimensional vibration and the powerful extraction ability of CNN to image data. In order to create a two-dimensional picture signal from a single-dimensional vibration signal, the modified image data is utilized as the input for the whole network [4]. In order to solve the issue of limited sample data, this research suggests a limited sample bearing fault diagnostic approach based on Deep Convolutional Generative Adversarial Network (DCGAN) and Convolutional Neural Network (CNN). The original data set is pre-processed and converted into a two-dimensional grey-scale image, which is used as the input of DCGAN for adversarial training to increase the training set and build a CNN bearing fault diagnostic technique. The test results demonstrate that the model is more stable and produces higher quality samples under unbalanced scenarios, and that the method has good fault diagnosis capabilities.

2 Principle and Objective Function of DCGAN

DCGAN is an improved GAN model that combines the CNN and the original GAN into one, using deep convolutional neural networks for both the generative and discriminative networks [9]. DCGAN improves the stability of the base GAN and the quality of the generated results. Its convolutional layer extracts features and generates close to realistic images. A generator(G) and a discriminator(D) make up the DCGAN model. The basic principle of DCGAN is simple. In the field of image generation, for example, while D is in charge of determining if the created images and the actual data set are true or false, G receives a random sequence produced according to a specific posterior distribution as noise and creates images that are as similar to the actual data as feasible. The two have opposing aims, thus constituting a process of playing each other, with the generator and discriminator updated by the result of TRUE OR FALSE. The basic schematic of DCGAN is shown in Fig. 1.

The objective function of a DCGAN is a minimization maximization process with the following objective function [10]:

$$\min_G \max_D V(D, G) = E_{x \sim P_{data}(x)}\left[\log D(x)\right] + E_{z \sim P_z(z)}\left[\log(1 - D(G(z)))\right] \quad (1)$$

The equivalent $V(G, D)$ here indicates the degree of difference between the true and generated samples. The equivalent $\max_D V(G, D)$ means to fix the generator G in such a way that the discriminator can maximise, as far as possible, whether the samples come from real data or generated data. The latter part is then seen as a whole order. Let

$L = \max\limits_{D} V(G, D)$, the equation $\min\limits_{G} L$ here is used to obtain a generator G conditional on a fixed discriminator D. This G requires the ability to minimise the difference between the true and generated samples. Through the min max gaming process described above, ideally the generated distribution will converge to the true distribution.

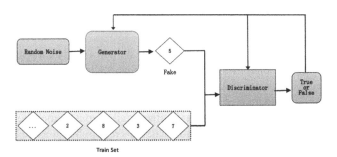

Fig. 1. Basic schematic diagram of DCGAN

3 Bearing Fault Diagnosis Method Based on DCGAN and CNN

For the bearing fault problem under small sample data, a DCGAN and CNN-based bearing small sample flaw diagnosis technique is suggested, the process is as follows: firstly, data pre-processing is performed on the adopted dataset to convert the 1D data into 2D grayscale images, then it is used as the input of DCGAN, and training is performed in DCGAN to enhance the imbalance data of these small samples, the training is terminated when the amount of training data sessions equals the empirically determined amount of sessions, and as input to the CNN, the generator's samples are combined with the original data samples, and the CNN is then trained with these samples, and then the data from the test samples are input into the trained CNN model for fault classification and outputting the results, as depicted in Fig. 2 for the whole experiment's algorithmic framework.

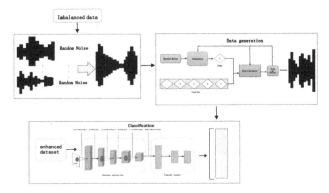

Fig. 2. Algorithm structure diagram

3.1   Generate Sample Data Using DCGAN

To resolve this issue of fault classification under unbalanced data, this work uses DCGAN to enhance the sample size and improve the precision of fault data classification. A schematic representation of the DCGAN's generator is provided in Fig. 3. The random noise is first generated as input to the input layer, which can be found through the diagram, and after being fed, it passes through a fully connected layer, followed by a process of upsampling, which uses a transposed convolutional layer, after which it is back-propagated and this data is processed for the next layer using the activation function ReLU. The output of the final layer is the transposed convolution layer and these outputs are passed through the activation function Tanh, resulting in a final grey-scale map of 64 * 64 pixels.

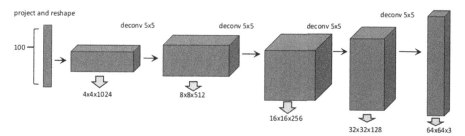

Fig. 3. Generator block diagram of DCGA

Figure 4 depicts a schematic representation of the discriminator's structure in a DCGAN. In the procedure employed to address the issue, the convolution kernel of this network is required to be 5 * 5. To extract the same features from different pictures, the convolution kernel serves as an extractor. The network's input layer receives as input a 64 × 64 greyscale image, which is then downsampled, back-propagated and processed using a non-linear activation function, LeakyReLU, to serve the next layer. This is then turned into a one-dimensional vector, a process using Flatten, and finally it is only necessary to determine the truth of the image, using a fully connected layer to do this.

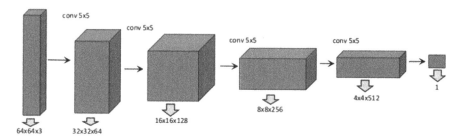

Fig. 4. Discriminators block diagram of DCGAN

3.2 Fault Classification Using CNN

The ReLU function was utilized as the activation function in this experiment. The mechanism of activation ReLU plays a significant role in neural networks, it has many features, such as it makes the whole training process fast and easy, in addition, it is also characterized by non-linearity, which makes it much more capable of integrating information, and it converges quite fast in stochastic gradient descent compared to other activation functions [11]. A schematic diagram of the CNN model used in this experiment is shown in Fig. 5.

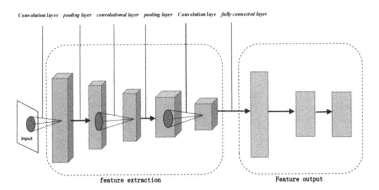

Fig. 5. The structure of CNN used in this experiment

As shown in Table 1, the information about the relevant parameters of the CNN structure used in this experiment.

Table 1. CNN structure and parameter information used in this experiment

Layer name	Quantity of convolution kernels	Quantity of convolution kernels	Pooling domain size	Step size
Input layer	–	–	–	–
Convolutional layer	32	3 * 3	–	1
Max pooling layer	–	–	2 * 2	2
Convolutional layer	64	3 * 3	–	1
Max pooling layer	–	–	2 * 2	2

(*continued*)

Table 1. (*continued*)

Layer name	Quantity of convolution kernels	Quantity of convolution kernels	Pooling domain size	Step size
Convolutional layer	64	3 * 3	–	1
Fully connected layer	–	–	–	–
Output layer	–	–	–	–

Table 2 below shows the model parameters for the CNN used in this experiment.

Table 2. Parameters of the CNN model used in this experiment

Training parameters	Parameters
Training rounds	100
Learning rate	0.01
Loss function	Cross-entropy loss
Optimization function	Gradient descent

4 Experiments

The CWRU Bearing Data Center website served as the source for the experimental data, where the motor shaft of the apparatus was supported with a test bearing and the single point of failure it discloses was generated by an EDM technique. The test selected in this paper is the fault data of the drive end of 12 kHz. Nine different fault data and one normal data were taken at a motor speed of 1797 r/min. As shown in Table 2, there are 9 kinds of fault data, and Table 3 is a normal data. According to 70% and 30%, the data set was split into a training set and a validation set. The samples from the training set were put into DCGAN for adversarial training.

4.1 Training and Synthetic Sample Generation Experiments for DCGAN Models

In conducting this experiment, the data set shown in Tables 3 and 4 was taken as an example of ten different states of drive end bearing data and initially, while training was still ongoing, the experiment's iteration count was set at 100. The data pre-processing was then carried out and the data used was 1D data, but as the 1D fault diagnosis method could not fully learn from the GAN machine variant image generation, the insufficient diversity and quality of the samples that were produced and the effective extraction of

Table 3. Nine kinds of fault data taken in the experiment

Fault diameter	Motor load horsepower	Motor approximate speed (r/min)	Inner ring failure	Rolling element failure	The relative position of the outer ring conforms to the area
0.1778 mm	0	1797	IR007_0 (105.mat)	IR007_0 (118.mat)	IR007_0 (130.mat)
0.3556 mm	0	1797	IR007_0 (169.mat)	IR007_0 (185.mat)	IR007_0 (197.mat)
0.5334 mm	0	1797	IR007_0 (209.mat)	IR007_0 (222.mat)	IR007_0 (234.mat)

Table 4. A normal data taken in the experiment

Motor load (horsepower)	Motor approximate speed (r/min)	Normal base data
0	1797	Normat_0 (97.mat)

picture data by convolutional neural networks, the original 1D data was considered to be converted to a 2D grey scale map. The process is as follows: take any 1000 non-repeating starting points from the original 1D data points, and 4096 points from these 1000 starting points, making a total of 1000 * 4096 1D data, and then transform them into 64 * 64 images, and finally normalize these data again to obtain a grey-scale map and then put them into DCGAN for training. For this experiment, there will be 100 training sessions.

To demonstrate the conflict that arises during the generative adversarial network's training, as shown in Fig. 6, it is the loss curve of the generator and discriminator in this experiment's training of the DCGAN network for a specific failure type. From the diagram, it can be seen that the curves of the generator and the discriminator have been constantly oscillating, that is, playing games with each other.

The experiment involved taking the grey scale maps of the outcomes of the first, 44th, 73rd, and 100th iterations after the original grey scale map was fed into the DCGAN for training. After the 44th iteration, the greyscale graph is clearly different but still very different from the original image; after the 73rd iteration, the greyscale graph is gradually getting closer to the original image; and the outcome of 100 iterations demonstrates that it is very close to the original image (Fig. 7).

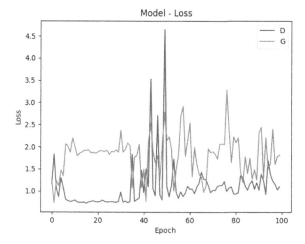

Fig. 6. A certain type of fault in the DCGAN network discriminator and generator loss curve

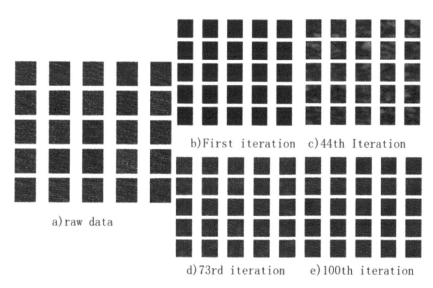

Fig. 7. Synthesis of new samples using DCGAN process

The above-mentioned images generated by the generator during the training of DCGAN, compared with the original images, generated two-dimensional grayscale images that were similar to, but not identical to, the real grayscale images, which can indicate that the DCGAN model is able to learn both effective features and high caliber and variety of the learning process's generated data. In the case that the original samples for the experiment were not sufficient, new samples were generated by training DCGAN, and these samples would raise the sample dataset's sample size, and training the classification model afterward would enhance the model's capacity for classification.

4.2 CNN-Based Fault Classification

The DCGAN is used to increase the data set. The CNN classification model's input is combined with the extended data and the original data. The experiment is run to obtain the quality change map for the CNN training and validation sets with the number of iterations, as shown in Fig. 8. The graph demonstrates that when the amount of iterations rises, both the training set's and the validation set's efficiency grow. The precision of the two varies substantially at the start of the iteration, and there have been around 30 direct iterations. The correctness of the training dataset is always higher than that of the validation set during the entire method, and the quality of the training set and validation set often differ only little.

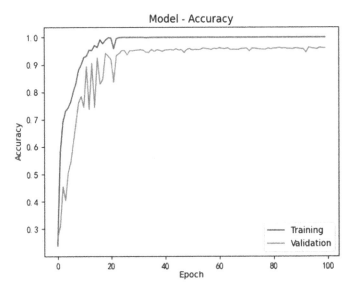

Fig. 8. Variation of CNN training set and validation set accuracy with the number of iterations

Figure 9 below shows the variation in loss value caused by a CNN model's training process's increased iterations. The figure shows that as the number of iterations rises, the losses for both the training set and the validation set steadily decrease. At the beginning of the iteration, the loss of the two changes relatively large, especially the test set fluctuates significantly between the number of iterations 10–20, and the loss of them tends to be flat after the number of iterations 20, and Throughout the whole procedure, the loss on the test set is always greater than the loss on the training set.

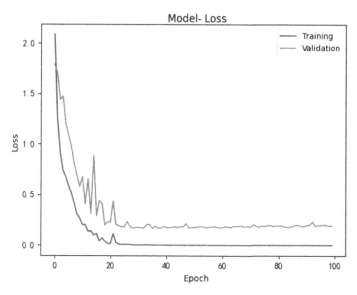

Fig. 9. Changes in loss values during CNN model training

A common way to evaluate accuracy is to use the confusion matrix, which is expressed in n rows and n columns. When it comes to image categorization accuracy, user accuracy, mapping accuracy, and overall accuracy are all significant criteria. The confusion matrix, in unsupervised learning, is a visualisation technique used to direct learning in supervised learning. The classification results are primarily contrasted with the real measurements and then expressed within the confusion matrix when evaluating the accuracy of an image. By contrasting each measured picture constituent's kind and placement with how those elements appear in the recognized image, the confusion matrix is constructed.

Figure 10 below shows the confusion matrix diagram for the 10 sample categories used in this experiment, each row in this diagram represents the true sample labels and each column represents the predicted sample labels, taking the first row as an example, representing the true samples labelled as category 0. After classification and prediction by classifier, the first square number is 132, indicating that 132 samples with real sample label of 0 are correctly predicted as label 0, two samples are incorrectly classified as belonging to group 3, one sample as belonging to category 4, and two samples as belonging to category 8. For label 0 in this confusion matrix, the larger the number in the first small square the better, and the smaller the number in the other small squares the better. The amount of the items on the diagonal should be as high as possible, and the number of the components in the other locations should be as low as possible. Figure 10 demonstrates that this experiment's classification results are accurate.

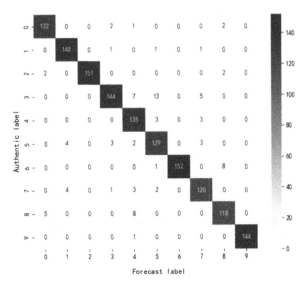

Fig. 10. Confusion matrix plot for ten sample categories

Table 5 below shows the values of the different evaluation indicators for the 10 categories of this experiment, with precision, recall and F1 indicators. The classification outcomes of this experiment may be found to be still quite good, with relatively high values for each of the evaluation indicators.

Table 5. The value of different evaluation indicators

Data category	Precision	Recall	F1-score
0	0.96	0.95	0.96
1	0.98	0.95	0.96
2	0.97	1.00	0.99
3	0.85	0.95	0.90
4	0.96	0.86	0.91
5	0.91	0.87	0.89
6	0.94	1.00	0.97
7	0.92	0.91	0.92
8	0.90	0.91	0.90
9	0.97	0.98	0.98

4.3 Comparison of the Results of Different Methods

During this test, a new sample data set is trained and synthesized by DCGAN model. When CNN is used to classify bearing fault data, the goal is to increase classification accuracy. A relative experiment is conducted to confirm the viability of this technology for bearing limited sample fault diagnostics. The comparison experiments were DCGAN + KNN and GAN + CNN, where DCGAN and GAN were used for data enhancement and KNN and CNN for data classification respectively. Table 6 clearly shows that the DCGAN + CNN method outperforms the other three methods for each assessment criteria, supporting the viability of the strategy proposed in this study.

Table 6. Contrast of the outcomes of different methods

Experimental method	Precision/%	Accuracy/%	Recall/%	F1-score/%
DCGAN + CNN	94.03	93.98	93.94	93.91
DCGAN + KNN	90.94	85.70	85.70	86.62
GAN + CNN	86.59	89.62	88.16	87.49

5 Conclusion

A novel DCGAN, is used in the fault classification module to expand the original imbalanced fault data, reduce the imbalance of the fault data samples, and use the expanded data for subsequent classification tasks.

It is suggested to use DCGAN data augmentation to classify faults. The data is expanded by DCGAN, and the new data set is used as a new feature vector using multiple methods for feature extraction, after which a convolutional neural network is used to train the classifier, effectively improving the classification of unbalanced fault data.

References

1. Li, H., Liu, T., Wu, X., Chen, Q.: Research on bearing fault feature extraction based on singular value decomposition and optimized frequency band entropy. Mech. Syst. Signal Process. **118**, 477–502 (2019)
2. Jiang, W., Zhou, J., Liu, H., Shan, Y.: A multi-step progressive fault diagnosis method for rolling element bearing based on energy entropy theory and hybrid ensemble auto-encoder. ISA Trans. **87**, 235–250 (2019)
3. Wang, Y., Liu, D., Wang, Y.: Rolling bearing fault diagnosis with GSA-VMD and adaptive CNN. Modular Mach. Tool Autom. Manuf. Tech. **2022**(07), 85–89 (2022)
4. Cao, S.: Generative adversarial network based methods for rolling bearing fault diagnosis. Huazhong University of Science and Technology, Wuhan (2019)
5. Fan, X., Liu, X.: Application of generative adversarial nets in bearing fault diagnosis. Mech. Sci. Technol. Aerosp. Eng. 1–8 (2022)

6. Zhao, D., Liu, F., Meng, H.: Bearing fault diagnosis based on the switchable normalization SSGAN with 1-D representation of vibration signals as input. Sensors **19**(9), 2000 (2019)

7. Luo, J., Huang, J., Li, H.: A case study of conditional deep convolutional generative adversarial networks in machine fault diagnosis. J. Intell. Manuf. **32**, 407–425 (2020)

8. Yang, Q., Lu, J., Tang, X., Sheng, X., Yang, R.: Bearing small sample fault diagnosis based on InfoGAN and CNN, vol. 42, no. 11, pp. 235–240 (2021)

9. Zhi, Y., Gao, Y., Chen, Y.: A simulation method of underwater acoustic data based on DCGAN, vol. 45, no. 06, pp. 10–12 (2021)

10. Zhang, X., Zhou, Y., Zeng, D., Peng, F., Zhao, S.: DCGAN bearing fault diagnosis method under unbalanced samples. Mech. Sci. Technol. Aerosp. Eng. **41**(01), 9–15 (2022)

11. Li, H., Tian, Y., Zhang, C., Zhang, S., Atkinson, P.M.: Temporal sequence Object-based CNN (TS-OCNN) for crop classification from fine resolution remote sensing image time-series. Crop J. **10**(05), 1507–1516 (2022)

AFER: Automated Feature Engineering for Robotic Prediction on Intelligent Automation

Yongxuan Wu[1] and Xun Han[2,3]($\boxtimes$)

[1] Faculty of Computing, Harbin Institute of Technology, Harbin 150001, China
[2] Intelligent Policing Key Laboratory of Sichuan Province, Luzhou 646000, China
`hldwxhx@163.com`
[3] Department of Transportation Management, Sichuan Police College, Luzhou 646000, China

Abstract. With the wide application of robots in industry, the advantages of robot process automation (RPA) are impressive in accuracy and efficiency. However, RPA only allows the defined task orientation to be driven by the process due to its mechanically repeated rules, which results in the inability of traditional robots to do complex data extraction and prediction regression, lacking flexibility and robustness. Intelligent automation (IA), the integration of machine learning and RPA, emerges as the times require. IA enables robots to have the ability to recognize and analyze data, so that they can learn and make decisions independently. However, IA relies heavily on data training and lacks features of high quantity and quality. Considering the probability of human error and extremely costly in time of traditional feature engineering, we attempt to apply automated feature engineering on IA to solve this problem, which liberates massive and monotonous manual work. In this paper, we proposed an approach named AFER, an elastic net regression based automatic feature engineering algorithm, which can automatically generate and select a large number of informative and essential features with underlying relationship and different information. We conducted exact experiments to demonstrate its certain stability and outstanding performance in robotic predictive models.

Keywords: Automated feature engineering · Intelligent automation · Robot process automation

1 Introduction

With the wide application of robots in industry, robot process automation is impressive in terms of accuracy, efficiency, ease of operation and reduction of labor. However, from the perspective of traditional design, RPA [1–3] has some limitations in application:

1. It requires manual intervention, and the existing RPA cannot independently complete the whole set of process tasks. Although it is conceivable to manually code a complete and error free algorithm process, it is almost impossible to achieve this.

Z. Yu et al. (Eds.): CIRAC 2022, CCIS 1770, pp. 411–424, 2023.
https://doi.org/10.1007/978-981-99-0301-6_32

2. Lack of flexibility. If there is no manual error correction, it is easy to make mistakes or even stop when encountering behaviors that the robot cannot recognize. This also means that whenever there is any change, the algorithm needs to be modified and updated.

Now, under the integration of machine learning and artificial intelligence, RPA has made a new breakthrough - intelligent automation (IA) [4–7]. IA enables robots to have the ability of data cognition and analysis, and can independently learn and make decisions, which has made new breakthroughs in RPA analysis and automatic scheduling, error handling, medical robots and automatic driving [8–10]. IA has changed from process driven by traditional RPA to data driven, and training data has become the core component of IA. This also means that all indicators of IA are heavily dependent on data and characteristics [11]. Therefore, how to generate and select features has become extremely important, but traditional feature engineering is not competent for this work due to its time consumption and human errors, so automatic machine learning gives us the answer to this problem.

In general, to build a scalable and stable machine learning system, the following steps are usually required in sequence: data cleaning, data preprocessing, feature engineering, model tuning and model evaluation, etc. It is universally acknowledged that the quality of feature space largely determines the performance of machine learning system [12]. Therefore, feature engineering which determines the upper limit of performance plays the most essential role in machine learning pipeline.

However, traditional feature engineering not only calls for the substantial manual effort and experienced domain experts to participate in generating and selecting features, which is usually task-specific, monotonous and involving an endless trial and error process, but also is extremely time-consuming, which makes impracticable to perform feature engineering manually in all of scientific research and industrial tasks with the booming demand for machine learning techniques. Therefore, Automatic Feature Engineering emerges as the times require, which is a significant topic of automatic machine learning (AutoML) [13–16]. The development of automatic feature engineering not merely liberates experts from massive and monotonous manual work, but improves the stability and scalability of machine learning systems.

Several studies have been conducted on this topic. Majority of methods follow the standard generation-selection procedure [17–19] to perform automatic feature engineering. However, there are some intractable problems in the process of implementation and evaluation. On the one hand, this strategy generates features by implementing predefined operators or functions, but the particular operator is biased to the particular feature space. It is arduous to distinguish which of the universal or specific operators will perform better. If a particular operator is always used in a particular feature space, it will not only become complex, but also lead to over fitting. On the other hand, these methods invariably apply all transformations to the given dataset to generate all legal features in the feature generation step and select a subset from them in the feature selection step. Therefore, the time and space complexity are terribly high, which makes it impracticable for tasks with high feature dimension or large data size.

In this paper, we propose a method named AFER (**A**utomated **F**eature **E**ngineering for **R**obotic Prediction on Intelligent Automation), which includes typical generation-selection procedure to generate high-quality features, to alleviate the problems of the traditional feature engineering. The contributions are summarized as follows:

- In the feature generation step, we use the distance correlation coefficient to filter the relevant feature pairs, and then use elastic net regression to mine the prominent variations and underlying information between the feature pairs relatively completely to generate more effective and informative new features.
- In the feature selection step, we use the regularized regression based recursive feature elimination algorithm to select the features with high weight by continuously constructing the elastic network regression model.
- We have experimentally demonstrated the virtues of our method on a great quantity of datasets and multiple classification algorithms. Our method achieves an average 2.27% improvement in the prediction accuracy, compared with the original feature space. This proves that our work is effective in Robotic Prediction.

The rest is organized as follows: Sect. 2 reviews the related work; Sect. 3 explains the problem definition of our method; Sect. 4 details our description of AFER and analyses some advantages of the model; Sect. 5 lists the detail of datasets, evaluates the accuracy of the model, the relative importance comparison of new features with original features and elastic network regression analyses; Sect. 6 states the conclusion and future work.

2   Related Work

From the perspective of how to construct new features, the current mainstream automated feature engineering model methods can be roughly divided into three categories, which includes expansion-reduction approach, evolution-centric approach and performance-based exploration approach.

Expansion-reduction approach. Given a supervised learning dataset, a simple method is to directly apply all transformation methods to the given dataset and sum all the resulting features. It will result in a large number of features, only a few of which might be valuable and useful to the target classifier. Therefore, it is necessary to reduce the dimension of features in order to avoid dimensional disasters and improve model performance. The automatic feature engineering system based on the expansion and reduction method usually constructs the predefined operation function or uses the regression method to generate features. Kanter [20] proposed deep feature synthesis. The expansion process uses a set of predefined operation functions to connect tables and construct new features. The reduction process uses truncated singular value decomposition for feature selection. But the calculation time of this method is very long. Some other work attempt to analysis the correlation between feature pairs by regression to generate features. The expansion process of Autolearn [21] is to generate relevant features through regression analysis of feature pairs, and the reduction process is to select the newly generated features through stability selection and information gain algorithm. LBR [22] improves the above method. In the expansion process, features are classified based on labels to consider the information of feature pairs. In the reduction process, the maximum information coefficient is used for feature screening, but it still cannot avoid the defect of excessive computational resource and time cost in the regression fitting process.

Evolution-centric approach. Compared with the above method, only a small number of high-quality features are generated in each iteration, and the evolutionary feature space is iterated continuously. Although this method is more scalable than expansion-reduction, it is also slower because it involves the continuous evaluation of the model. FICUS [23] is the earlier classic work of this approach. The expansion process is to transform the original features through predefined operation functions to form a potential candidate feature space. The reduction process uses information gain guided beam search to automatically screen the best feature space. ExploreKit [24] proposes an automatic feature engineering framework that uses scalable multi-level operators to generate features, sort multi-dimensional information and iterate. This framework generates a large number of legal features through the combination of multi-level operators in the existing feature space. Then the features are put into the classification model one by one according to the ranking from high to low until they are higher than the threshold.

Performance-based exploration approach. The basic framework of the approach guided search is to use the hierarchical structure of heterogeneous transformation graph. The nodes of graph represent different forms of data sets obtained by applying transformation functions to datasets. The process of data set transformation is to apply all transformation functions to all possible features and generate multiple additional features, and then select, train and evaluate optional features. RAAF [25] optimized the exploration method and used the simulated annealing heuristic to optimize the extreme consequences of over fitting caused by performance guided search. Khurana [26] uses Q-learning on graph to support fine-grained and efficient exploration of feature engineering. This method can also apply knowledge from existing data sets to new data sets. CAFEM [27] uses the method of double depth Q-learning to explore on the basis of the heterogeneous transformation graph, estimates the state action value through the depth neural network and obtains the next step through the greedy method.

The existing automatic feature engineering has shortcomings in time complexity and accuracy, and some methods also need to be improved in scalability and stability. In this paper, we try to use elastic network regression to further mine the underlying information between features.

3 Problem Definition

Consider a robotic predictive model task under supervised learning, which can be defined as $S_1 = \langle D, L, m \rangle$. $D = \langle F, y \rangle$ is a given dataset with d features $F = \{f_1, f_2 \ldots f_d\}$ and n labels $y = \{y_1, y_2 \ldots y_n\}$. Consider a classification algorithm $\mathbf{L}$ applicable to the label vector y, and the performance metric $\mathbf{m}$ of the algorithm. Use $A_L^m(F, y)$ represents the performance of the predictive model of the machine learning task. Now consider a set of transformation functions $T = \{t_1, t_2 \ldots t_k\}$, when transformation is used for features F, the process can be expressed as: $F_{new} = T(F_{given})$.

The process of Automatic Feature Engineering is to predefine or learn a set of feature generation function $T = \{t_1, t_2 \ldots t_k\}$ to generate new feature space F_{new} based on the given features F_{given}. The goal of Automatic Feature engineering is to maximize the performance of the model: $\arg\max A_L^m(F_{given} \cup F_{new}, y)$.

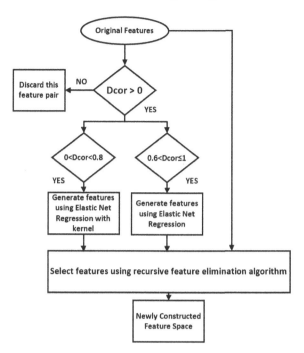

Fig. 1. The overview of AFER

4 Method

4.1 Principle of AFER'S Design

For robotic prediction, we need a stable and efficient automatic feature engineering algorithm. But in the majority of prior literature, the generation-selection based strategy generates features by a set of experience dependent predefined operators. The typical disadvantage of this strategy is that it is impractical to predefine each appropriate set of operators for each specific dataset.

In this paper, instead of predefined operators, we use elastic network regression, to mine correlated and different information between feature pairs to generate and select features. The motivation and intuition of AFER is that the relationship and information between feature pairs might be vary for each class. Although there is no guarantee that the relevant information of each feature pair can mine effective and significant differences, it can be reasonably expected that different and excellent underlying information can always be obtained in the regression mining process of a large number of feature pairs. At the same time, with the application of elastic network regression, this mining method will also tend to be stable. Therefore, we will not use too much effort to train elastic network regression, but merely as a stable regression tool to ensure stability and scalability.

- Use elastic network regression to fit feature pairs can be effective and stable to construct effective and different features.
- Elastic network regression based recursive feature elimination algorithm to filter the features will make the model more efficient and avoid dimensional disasters.

4.2 The Mechanics of AFER

In this paper, we determine to apply elastic network regression in generation-selection procedure to fit feature pairs with correlation and select informative features. As shown in Fig. 1, our proposed method AFER, has the following two major steps:

- **Feature generation:** Filter out the uncorrelated feature pairs and divide the pairs into linear or non-linear relationship by distance correlation [28]. Transform the filtered feature space by mining the prediction and difference between the feature pairs with correlation using elastic network regression to generate new features.
- **Feature selection:** Prune the fusion of newly generated feature space and ordinary feature space using the regularized regression based recursive feature elimination by continuously constructing the elastic network regression model.

Feature Generation: The relationship between feature pairs is divided into linear or non-linear by distance correlation. At the same time, distance correlation can discard the independent feature pairs. Distance correlation is a method to calculate whether there exists a relationship between a feature pair, which means that the two features are not independent. The reason for using the distance correlation coefficient is mainly the following outstanding advantages:

- Distance correlation overcome the defects of Pearson, Spearman and Kendall correlation. Distance correlation has the ability to capture all the types of linear and nonlinear relationships and strictly and accurately judge the independence between features by the result is 0.
- Distance correlation is superior to other methods for judging linear or non-linear. It can cover all functional relationships in a balanced way and give approximately similar results under different types of noise.
- The linear relationship of distance correlation is between 0.7 to 1 and the non-linear relationship of distance correlation is 0 to 0.7. Moreover, in order to overcome the defect that the distance correlation is unstable at the edge, the non-linear limit is relaxed between 0 to 0.8 and the linear limit is relaxed between 0.6 to 1.

The distance correlation between u and v can be expressed as $dcorr(u, v)$. When $dcorr(u, v) = 0$ exists, u and v are independent of each other. The bigger $dcorr(u, v)$, the stronger the correlation between u and v. The dimensions of u and v are be represented as d_u and d_v. The formula of distance correlation is expressed as:

$$\hat{d}corr(u, v) = \frac{\hat{d}cov(u, v)}{\sqrt{\hat{d}cov(u, u)\hat{d}cov(v, v)}} \tag{1}$$

$\hat{d}cov(u, v)$ can be calculated as $\hat{d}cov^2(u, v) = \widehat{S_1} + \widehat{S_2} - 2\widehat{S_3}$. $\widehat{S_1}$, $\widehat{S_2}$ and $\widehat{S_3}$ can be calculated as follows.

$$\widehat{S_1} = \frac{1}{n^2} \sum_{i=1}^{n} \sum_{j=1}^{n} u_i - u_{jd_u} v_i - v_{jd_v} \tag{2}$$

$$\widehat{S_2} = \frac{1}{n^2} \sum_{i=1}^{n} \sum_{j=1}^{n} u_i - u_{jd_u} \frac{1}{n^2} \sum_{i=1}^{n} \sum_{j=1}^{n} v_i - v_{jd_v} \tag{3}$$

$$\widehat{S_3} = \frac{1}{n^3} \sum_{i=1}^{n} \sum_{j=1}^{n} \sum_{l=1}^{n} u_i - u_{ld_u} v_i - v_{ld_v} \tag{4}$$

About $\hat{d}cov(u, u)$ and $\hat{d}cov(v, v)$ can be calculated by the same calculation method as above. After filtering and classification of distance correlation, the feature pairs are divided into linear pool and non-linear pool. The next step is the regression fitting of feature pairs to generate new features.

Regression is usually the key tool to analyze the relationship between two variables. In this work, the two variables are the two features of the feature space. We use regularized regression to mine the relationship between the two features to generate new features. The advantage of regularized regression algorithm is that it can prevent over fitting and improve generalization ability.

In this work, we use elastic net regression to fit linear feature pairs and elastic net regression with polynomial kernel to fit non-linear feature pairs. The well-known regularization regression methods are ridge regression and lasso regression, which have different characteristics. At this time, it is intuitive to figure out that if the two regularization regression methods are combined, the benefits of the two methods may be combined to generate more informative features. This regularized regression algorithm is called elastic network regression. The cost function of elastic network regression combines the two regularized regression methods through two parameters to control the size of punishment items, which ensures the stability and accuracy of the model in regression fitting feature pairs.

$$\min_{\omega} \frac{1}{2n} \|X\omega - y\|_2^2 + \alpha\rho\|\omega\|_1 + \frac{\alpha(1 - \rho)}{2} \|\omega\|_2^2 \tag{5}$$

Moreover, in this model, elastic network regression is just a tool to mine the correlation and difference between feature pairs, thus no more multi parameter optimization will be done for elastic network regression, and only the default parameter configuration will be used.

Elastic network regression with kernel is a combination of elastic network regression with the kernel trick, which is an extension that can learns a linear regression in the space induced by the respective kernel and data. In the case of non-linear kernels, it corresponds to the non-linear function in the original space.

Each pair of correlated features (F_i, F_j) will generate two new sorts of features:

- First sort of generated feature is the prediction. It is constructed by fitting regression F_i on F_j for every pairs with correlation. This new feature is named as $F_{prediction}$. Moreover, regressing F_i on F_j and regressing F_j on F_i are different, which will generate respective new feature. In theory, the new features contain the underlying and valuable information, which is hidden in the linear and non-linear feature pairs. However, the new feature sometimes just replicates the original feature, but the majority of new features are different from original features and performs brilliantly.
- Second sort of generated feature is the difference. It is generated by making the difference of the original feature F_j with the $F_{prediction}$, which is stated as $F_{difference}$, obtained by $F_j - F_{prediction}$. The first sort of feature means the prediction, which may be different from the original feature. This sort of feature endeavor to apprehend the difference, which implies the variation between the original feature and prediction feature.

The feature generation step discovers the correlated feature pairs through distance correlation and generates the informative and diversified features through elastic net regression, which captures the prominent relationship and difference. The newly generated relatively perform brilliantly in predictive model, but new feature space still exists a large number of invaluable features, which may result in reduction of accuracy and dimensional disaster. Therefore, a stable and efficient feature selection algorithm must be indispensable.

Feature Selection: All the new features, generated in the previous step, may exist several of unimportant features. We attempt to use the regularized regression based recursive feature elimination to select the top performing features by continuously constructing the elastic network regression model, which remarkably elevates the classification accuracy of the prediction model. The recursive feature elimination algorithm plays two significant roles in the feature selection step. On the one hand, it elevates the performance and prevents overfitting. On the other hand, it can decrease the number of features so as to avoid dimension disaster. Furthermore, it should be noted that feature selection process is employed over the combination of newly generated features and original features.

The core point of recursive feature elimination is to decrease the dimension of features to select the needed features by recursion. Firstly, give each feature a weight, and then train them on the predefined model. Secondly, after obtaining the weight of the features, discard the feature with the smallest absolute weight. Thirdly, recursion continues until the number of remaining features reaches the threshold. The stability and efficiency of this method largely depend on what the underlying model is during recursion. For instance, if recursive feature elimination uses non-regularized regression, the algorithm will become unstable. On the contrary, if it uses regularized regression, it will usually become stable and efficient. Therefore, we use elastic network regression as the underlying model of recursive feature elimination.

As described above, elastic network regression can learn a sparse model similar to lasso regression, while retaining ridge regression's regularization property. It combines the advantages of the two, which is especially suitable for occasions where multiple features are related to each other. When multiple excellent but highly related features are coherent, lasso regression may choose only one of them at random, while ridge regression will choose all the features. When multiple features are related to another feature. Elastic network regression will be extraordinarily useful and stable.

5 Experiments

5.1 Dataset

We evaluated AFER on 6 classification datasets, taken from the UC Irvine repository [29]. There characteristics are shown in Table 1.

Table 1. Characteristics of 6 datasets

Dataset Name	Label	Features	Size
Sonar	2	60	208
Ionosphere	2	34	351
Haberman	2	3	306
E. coli	8	7	336
Wine	3	13	178
Abalone	3	7	4177

5.2 Experimental Setup

We evaluate 6 classification algorithms (CLF) to validate our model: K-Nearest Neighbour (KNN), Logistic Regression (LR), SVM, Random Forest (RF), Decision Tree (DT) and Adaboost (AB).

We compared our model with original dataset and 3 other automatic feature engineering methods, including TFC, ExploreKit and AutoLearn. The evaluation performance are measured in terms of classification accuracy on original dataset and the new datasets constructed by 3 other automatic feature engineering methods and AFER. The accuracy is shown in Table 2.

5.3 Evaluation Comparison

Table 2 show the classification accuracy of 6 classification algorithms in original datasets and 4 automatic feature engineering methods. We achieved 2.27% improvement of classification accuracy more than the original feature space, in all 6 datasets and 6 classification algorithms, which confirms that AFER can automatically generate and select a great deal of informative and important features with underlying relationship and different information.

5.4 Feature Analysis

We compared the importance of original features with generated features in Fig. 2. Here, the ordinate means the relative importance, which is measured by an algorithm, whose implementation in [30]. Illustrations show that the part of new features constructed by AFER have the more relative importance than the original features, which demonstrates our model achieved the expected goal.

5.5 Regression Demonstration

We analyzed the regression fitting process of the correlated feature pairs in Fig. 3, which are relatively perfect linear and nonlinear regression fitting diagrams. It shows the prediction features mine the correlation of feature pairs and difference features search the underlying variation between the original feature and the prediction feature.

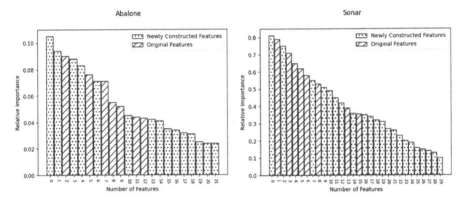

Fig. 2. The feature relative importance of Abalone and Sonar Datasets

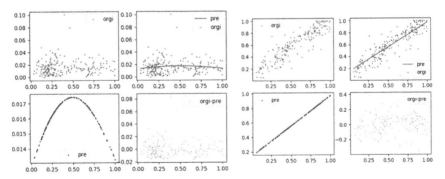

Fig. 3. The regression of non-linear feature pairs and linear feature pairs

Table 2. Classification accuracy on 6 datasets

Dataset	CLF	ORIG	TFC	EK	AL	AFER
Sonar	KNN	78.35	81.48	82.40	**83.19**	81.51
	LR	77.42	78.12	78.73	**79.00**	78.45
	SVM	73.54	74.54	76.11	**77.30**	75.32
	RF	73.55	**81.00**	47.40	77.87	76.89
	DT	75.01	74.23	74.96	**75.02**	74.87
	AB	**80.74**	80.00	53.95	78.83	79.32
Haberman	KNN	71.89	70.00	**72.27**	68.68	68.89
	LR	74.19	72.07	74.52	**76.16**	75.34
	SVM	74.18	73.97	75.37	75.82	**75.89**
	RF	68.63	68.91	**69.98**	65.34	66.43
	DT	66.65	66.09	**67.23**	66.34	66.65
	AB	70.25	71.19	**72.17**	69.93	70.34
Wine	KNN	67.93	74.89	83.40	**93.84**	89.91
	LR	95.52	96.89	95.12	**98.30**	97.23
	SVM	83.03	88.14	90.82	**98.31**	96.76
	RF	96.07	96.68	90.00	**97.20**	96.98
	DT	91.57	91.79	92.45	**93.22**	92.76
	AB	85.82	**88.12**	62.80	84.71	85.12
Ionosphere	KNN	84.31	84.66	**85.97**	83.46	84.21
	LR	87.44	87.26	87.67	**87.95**	87.76
	SVM	87.44	86.71	**88.01**	84.30	85.12
	RF	93.15	91.65	**93.97**	92.30	92.21
	DT	88.32	87.12	88.12	**88.59**	88.34
	AB	92.02	90.94	90.31	**92.43**	91.87
E. coli	KNN	86.59	**88.42**	**88.42**	84.82	85.23
	LR	75.88	78.23	82.83	**87.19**	86.98
	SVM	85.71	85.71	**86.30**	**86.30**	86.21
	RF	82.73	83.46	85.12	**86.59**	85.89
	DT	79.74	76.32	**80.34**	76.48	78.85
	AB	62.47	63.54	**65.75**	**65.75**	65.34
Abalone	KNN	**23.27**	21.64	23.09	22.71	22.23
	LR	24.61	23.69	24.79	**26.50**	25.25

(*continued*)

Table 2. (continued)

Dataset	CLF	ORIG	TFC	EK	AL	AFER
	SVM	25.71	25.64	25.68	**26.07**	25.23
	RF	22.91	18.78	**23.18**	22.21	22.11
	DT	19.27	19.00	19.29	**19.41**	19.35
	AB	20.61	19.10	**21.12**	20.61	20.82

6 Conclusion and Future Work

In this work, in order to optimize the traditional RPA to data-driven IA, we propose to use automated feature engineering to solve the problem of feature shortage in robot prediction. AFER can automatically generate and select a large number of informative and essential features with underlying relationship and different information. The elastic network regression is applied to both the feature generation step and the feature selection step, which demonstrates its appropriate stability and superior performance. In future work, we intend to extend our method with reinforcement learning for Robotic Prediction on Intelligent Automation.

Funding. This paper was funded by Independent Project of Intelligent Policing Key Laboratory of Sichuan Province (No. ZNJW2022ZZZD001).

References

1. Aguirre, S., Rodriguez, A.: Automation of a business process using robotic process automation (RPA): a case study. In: Figueroa-García, J.C., López-Santana, E.R., Villa-Ramírez, J.L., Ferro-Escobar, R. (eds.) WEA 2017. CCIS, vol. 742, pp. 65–71. Springer, Cham (2017). https://doi.org/10.1007/978-3-319-66963-2_7
2. Syed, R., et al.: Robotic process automation: contemporary themes and challenges. Comput. Ind. **115**, 103162 (2020)
3. Ivančić, L., Suša Vugec, D., Bosilj Vukšić, V.: Robotic process automation: systematic literature review. In: Di Ciccio, C., et al. (eds.) BPM 2019. LNBIP, vol. 361, pp. 280–295. Springer, Cham (2019). https://doi.org/10.1007/978-3-030-30429-4_19
4. Jha, N., Prashar, D., Nagpal, A.: Combining artificial intelligence with robotic process automation—An intelligent automation approach. In: Ahmed, K.R., Hassanien, A.E. (eds.) Deep Learning and Big Data for Intelligent Transportation. SCI, vol. 945, pp. 245–264. Springer, Cham (2021). https://doi.org/10.1007/978-3-030-65661-4_12
5. Rajawat, A.S., Rawat, R., Barhanpurkar, K., Shaw, R.N., Ghosh, A.: Robotic process automation with increasing productivity and improving product quality using artificial intelligence and machine learning. In: Artificial Intelligence for Future Generation Robotics, pp. 1–13. Elsevier (2021)
6. Reddy, K.N., Harichandana, U., Alekhya, T., Rajesh, S.: A study of robotic process automation among artificial intelligence. Int. J. Sci. Res. Publ. **9**(2), 392–397 (2019)
7. Chakraborti, T., et al.: From robotic process automation to intelligent process automation. In: Asatiani, A., et al. (eds.) BPM 2020. LNBIP, vol. 393, pp. 215–228. Springer, Cham (2020). https://doi.org/10.1007/978-3-030-58779-6_15

8. Martins, P., Sá, F., Morgado, F., Cunha, C.: Using machine learning for cognitive Robotic Process Automation (RPA). In: 2020 15th Iberian Conference on Information Systems and Technologies (CISTI), pp. 1–6 (2020)
9. Leno, V., Dumas, M., La Rosa, M., Maggi, F.M., Polyvyanyy, A.: Automated discovery of data transformations for robotic process automation. arXiv preprint arXiv:2001.01007 (2020)
10. Huang, F., Vasarhelyi, M.A.: Applying robotic process automation (RPA) in auditing: a framework. Int. J. Acc. Inf. Syst. **35**, 100433 (2019)
11. Agostinelli, S., Marrella, A., Mecella, M.: Research challenges for intelligent robotic process automation. In: Di Francescomarino, C., Dijkman, R., Zdun, U. (eds.) BPM 2019. LNBIP, vol. 362, pp. 12–18. Springer, Cham (2019). https://doi.org/10.1007/978-3-030-37453-2_2
12. Hastie, T., Tibshirani, R., Friedman, J.H.: The Elements of Statistical Learning: Data Mining, Inference, and Prediction, vol. 2. Springer, New York (2009). https://doi.org/10.1007/978-0-387-84858-7
13. Waring, J., Lindvall, C., Umeton, R.: Automated machine learning: review of the state-of-the-art and opportunities for healthcare. Artif. Intell. Med. **104**, 101822 (2020)
14. Hutter, F., Kotthoff, L., Vanschoren, J.: Automated Machine Learning: Methods, Systems, Challenges. Springer, Cham (2019). https://doi.org/10.1007/978-3-030-05318-5
15. Yao, Q., et al.: Taking human out of learning applications: a survey on automated machine learning. arXiv preprint arXiv:1810.13306 (2018)
16. Truong, A., Walters, A., Goodsitt, J., Hines, K., Bruss, C.B., Farivar, R.: Towards automated machine learning: evaluation and comparison of AutoML approaches and tools. In: 2019 IEEE 31st International Conference on Tools with Artificial Intelligence (ICTAI), pp. 1471–1479 (2019)
17. Khurana, U., Turaga, D., Samulowitz, H., Parthasrathy, S.: Cognito: automated feature engineering for supervised learning. In: 2016 IEEE 16th International Conference on Data Mining Workshops (ICDMW), pp. 1304–1307 (2016)
18. Shi, Q., Zhang, Y.-L., Li, L., Yang, X., Li, M., Zhou, J.: SAFE: scalable automatic feature engineering framework for industrial tasks. In: 2020 IEEE 36th International Conference on Data Engineering (ICDE), pp. 1645–1656 (2020)
19. Fan, W., et al.: Generalized and heuristic-free feature construction for improved accuracy. In: Proceedings of the 2010 SIAM International Conference on Data Mining, pp. 629–640 (2010)
20. Kanter, J.M., Veeramachaneni, K.: Deep feature synthesis: towards automating data science endeavors. In: 2015 IEEE International Conference on Data Science and Advanced Analytics (DSAA), pp. 1–10 (2015)
21. Kaul, A., Maheshwary, S., Pudi, V.: AutoLearn—Automated feature generation and selection. In: 2017 IEEE International Conference on Data Mining (ICDM), pp. 217–226 (2017)
22. Wang, M., Ding, Z., Pan, M.: LbR: a new regression architecture for automated feature engineering. In: 2020 International Conference on Data Mining Workshops (ICDMW), pp. 432–439 (2020)
23. Markovitch, S., Rosenstein, D.: Feature generation using general constructor functions. Mach. Learn. **49**(1), 59–98 (2002)
24. Katz, G., Shin, E.C.R., Song, D.: ExploreKit: automatic feature generation and selection. In: 2016 IEEE 16th International Conference on Data Mining (ICDM), pp. 979–984 (2016)
25. Ladeira, L.Z., Borro, L.C., Violato, R.P.V., Bonadia, G.C.: RAAF: resource-aware auto featuring. In: 2021 55th Annual Conference on Information Sciences and Systems (CISS), pp. 1–6 (2021)
26. Khurana, U., Samulowitz, H., Turaga, D.: Feature engineering for predictive modeling using reinforcement learning. In: Proceedings of the AAAI Conference on Artificial Intelligence, vol. 32, no. 1 (2018)

27. Zhang, J., Hao, J., Fogelman-Soulié, F.: Cross-data automatic feature engineering via meta-learning and reinforcement learning. In: Lauw, H.W., Wong, R.-W., Ntoulas, A., Lim, E.-P., Ng, S.-K., Pan, S.J. (eds.) PAKDD 2020. LNCS (LNAI), vol. 12084, pp. 818–829. Springer, Cham (2020). https://doi.org/10.1007/978-3-030-47426-3_63

28. Székely, G.J., Rizzo, M.L., Bakirov, N.K.: Measuring and testing dependence by correlation of distances. Ann. Stat. **35**(6), 2769–2794 (2007)

29. Asuncion, A., Newman, D.: UCI machine learning repository, Irvine, CA, USA (2007)

30. Pedregosa, F., et al.: Scikit-learn: machine learning in Python. J. Mach. Learn. Res. **12**, 2825–2830 (2011)

Design of an Improved Process Mining Algorithm for Manufacturing Companies with Industrial Robots

Baiwei Zhao[1] and Xun Han[2,3(✉)]

[1] Faculty of Computing, Harbin Institute of Technology, Harbin 150001, China
[2] Intelligent Policing Key Laboratory of Sichuan Province, Luzhou 646000, China
hldwxhx@163.com
[3] Department of Transportation Management, Sichuan Police College, Luzhou 646000, China

Abstract. Industrial robots are gradually being used in the field of intelligent manufacturing, but there are still some problems in the transparency of production processes and product quality control. Using process mining technology, analyzing the collected log information in the robot production process is a solution to these problems. In recent years, the conformance checking in process mining has developed rapidly, and many conformance checking algorithms have been proposed. However, not all algorithms are suitable for real intelligent manufacturing scenarios. Aiming at the problem that the Log Skeleton algorithm proposed in recent years cannot accurately express the process model in the manufacturing process, an improved scheme of the Log Skeleton algorithm is proposed, and an improved conformance checking scheme based on the algorithm is designed to make it more suitable for practice. The performance of the improved algorithm in the actual manufacturing environment is verified by experiments. Experiments show that the improved scheme proposed in this paper improves the application value of the Log Skeleton algorithm in the actual production environment.

Keywords: Industrial robots · Process mining · Manufacturing

1 Introduction

With the increasing maturity of robot technology, the application scenarios of industrial robots in the manufacturing industry are becoming more and more abundant [1]. At present, the wide application of industrial robots faces two main problems: how to make the production process transparent and how to control the quality of intelligent manufacturing products. A log system adapted to robots is introduced into the production process, and these problems can be effectively solved by scientifically analyzing the collected log.

When a robot is used in a manufacturing enterprise, the complete production process needs to be determined and input first. The efficiency of the production process directly determines the work efficiency of the robot. To ensure future competitiveness, most companies need to optimize the effectiveness of their manufacturing processes and

© The Author(s), under exclusive license to Springer Nature Singapore Pte Ltd. 2023
Z. Yu et al. (Eds.): CIRAC 2022, CCIS 1770, pp. 425–437, 2023.
https://doi.org/10.1007/978-981-99-0301-6_33

increase the efficiency of the processes to reduce the energy consumption of robots [2]. The optimization of this process requires a deep understanding of one's own manufacturing process. However, in most manufacturing companies, the process flow is often too idealized in design and has no practical reference. In order to put forward more precise and practical optimization suggestions for intelligent manufacturing robots, it is necessary to analyze the real business process operation mode [3].

The proposal and development of process mining (Process Mining) technology can discover the real operation mode of the business process, and use the production process analyzed from the log system for the input of intelligent manufacturing robots, which can solve this basic production efficiency and energy consumption problem [4]. On the other hand, we can diagnose the production process using process mining, propose optimization suggestions for the production process of industrial robots, analyze possible problems or screen out products that may have problems, and further improve the intelligence of manufacturing enterprises degree of chemistry and the overall quality of the product.

The structure of this paper is arranged as follows: Sect. 2 introduces the related work, Sect. 3 introduces data pre-processing scheme before the algorithm, mainly including the screening of the complete process and a simple data cleaning scheme. Section 4 briefly introduces the Log Skeleton algorithm and analyses and improves the algorithm. Section 5 designs experiments to verify the performance of the improved algorithm. Section 6 states the conclusion and future work.

2 Related Work

Process Mining, as a data-driven method, obtains process knowledge from event logs of information systems, and discovers, monitors, and improves actual system behavior patterns [5].

It automatically discovers business processes and many additional process enhancement techniques. The research direction of process mining mainly has three aspects: process discovery, conformance checking and process enhancement. At present, process mining has been initially applied in the medical and financial fields [6–9]. At the same time, it has also attracted much attention in the field of manufacturing. Most foreign scholars believe that process mining will provide an opportunity for the intelligence of the manufacturing industry. The literature [10–17] initially introduces the application prospects of process mining in the manufacturing industry. Reference [18] and [19] respectively analyze the application cases in terms of measuring product quality and predicting workload in manufacturing processes. Reference [20] and [21] propose that for small and medium-sized manufacturing enterprises, process mining is used to predict process performance. End Time. Through the consistency inspection technology in process mining, abnormal processes in the production process of manufacturing enterprises can be diagnosed, and the quality of products and the efficiency of production can be improved. Nowadays, more and more manufacturing enterprises improve their production processes through the conformance checking algorithm. At the same time, [22] proposed an intelligent production process log collection scheme oriented to the conformance checking algorithm. The literature [23]and [24] introduce a process evaluation scheme for the application of consistency inspection technology in the production process of manufacturing enterprises. Reference [25] analyzes the manufacturing process in terms of data flow and running time, and diagnoses abnormal processes that deviate from the model.

3   Log Data Preprocessing

When analyzing and processing log data, the collected log data needs to be preprocessed first. On the one hand, the collection of logs is often all log information within a time interval from a certain start time to a certain collection time. This truncated collection method may collect processes that do not completely end and processes that have started before the start time of the log. These incomplete processes will cause the process model simulated by the algorithm to be incomplete. Error messages are generated when performing s or process diagnostics. On the other hand, in the manufacturing field, the data collected in the harsh environment, such as high-temperature steelmaking environment or other harsh environments, is often missing, so it is very necessary to clean up log data. This Section will introduce the Data preprocessing scheme.

Due to the characteristics of the production process of manufacturing enterprises, that is, the usual process is often an established process plan. Usually, in this case, the complete process can be screened by directly obtaining the process information, and the user can specify the start and end of the input process. Activities, the screening process is carried out for the scheme of starting activities and ending activities set by the user. This solution is relatively simple, but this solution has strong requirements on the user's familiarity with the process model. The complete process screened out by this solution has strong interpretability and can complete the process selection very accurately (Fig. 1).

Algorithm 1 Event Based Full Trace Select Algorithm

Input: Log Contains Unfinished Traces,Begin Event be,End Event ee
Output: Finished Traces in Log
  Initialization: $res = \{\}$
  for all Trace in Log **do**
    if be in trace and ee in trace **then**
      res.add(event)
    end if
  end for
  return res

Fig. 1. Event based full trace select algorithm

Although a relatively simple and efficient screening scheme is proposed above, which requires users to have a relatively accurate understanding of their own process models, but usually most enterprises do not have a relatively transparent understanding of their own production process models. This is also one of the application fields of process mining in the manufacturing industry. When faced with this black box model, how to more accurately judge whether the process has ended is a problem that needs to be solved.

In this paper, a process screening scheme based on process heartbeat is proposed. The process whose distance from the collection time exceeds a certain heartbeat time interval is selected as the completed process. In this paper, the detection time is dynamically adjusted to improve the efficiency and accuracy of screening. First, a longer detection time interval is initialized, a series of end processes are selected, and then the information of these end processes is used to predict and estimate a complete process in the entire model. The duration of the interval to dynamically update the detection time (Fig. 2).

Algorithm 2 Full Traces Select Algorithm

Input: Log Contains Unfinished Traces,Default timebreak:N,windowsSize:k
Output: A Log contains only finished traces
  Initialization: $time = N, w = 0, res = []$
  while w less than k **do**
    get trace in [startTimestamp+time,endTimestamp-time]
    if trace in res **then**
      time = time / 2
    else
      k++,res.add(trace)
    end if
  end while
  time = time.avgTime
  for all trace in [startTimestamp+time,endTimestamp-time **do**
    if trace not in res **then**
      res.add(trace)
    end if
  end for
  return res

Fig. 2. Full traces select algorithm

Batch processing activities are often an inevitable part of the production process in the manufacturing industry. It may be a production step that needs to be carried out in parallel in a fixed production process, or it may appear in the management process model or ERP system of an enterprise. Production orders that are complex or require a large production volume may need to distribute production tasks to different production workshops. In this case, batch operations will be generated in the log data.

Batch operations have a serious impact on the mining and analysis of process patterns. Some normal process models may have some short self-cycles. For example, when manufacturing, the manufactured products often require multiple rounds of quality inspection, and only qualified products can be shipped out after multiple rounds of inspections. Such self-loops are very common in most process models, but the emergence of batching can generate a series of other self-loops in the process model. This kind of self-loop can lead to the behavior of the algorithm based on the sequence of events. The mode is disrupted, causing these behavioral modes to lose their original logical meaning. On the other hand, in the face of this batch mode, due to the inability to determine the limit of the number of batch operations in the process, it will lead to some statistical processes. The characteristics of the frequency of occurrence of activities cannot play a role. In these cases, it will lead to insufficient performance of the process model based on the event behavior pattern, or even inaccurate subsequent diagnosis information due to the insufficient performance of the process model and incorrect diagnostic information (Fig. 3).

Algorithm 3 Batch Analysing Algorithm

Input: Log
Output: Batch Events in Log
  Initialization: $res = \{\}$
  for all Trace in Log **do**
    get frequency of all event
    for all Event in Trace **do**
      if frequency of event changes **then**
        res.add(event)
      end if
    end for
  end for
  return res

Fig. 3. Batch analyzing algorithm

4   Method

4.1   Log Skeleton Algorithm

The Log Skeleton algorithm [26] was originally used for process discovery. The general idea in the academic community at that time was that "a model with strong performance should have a higher fitness index", that is, it can accurately determine whether the trace in the log data is generated by the model. The Log Skeleton algorithm believes that a model that can accurately complete the classification task of log data has stronger model expression capabilities. Log Skeleton represents the process model by capturing the relationship between activities in log data: Equivalence (activity that occurs with the same frequency in all log traces), always after, always before, directly follow and never together. The core of the Log Skeleton algorithm is more like a classification task, and the results of the algorithm are like extracting the common characteristics of all process events in the log. The pseudo code of the algorithm is shown in the following figure (Fig. 4).

When dealing with real complex production environments, in order to ensure the efficiency of the algorithm, we make some small improvements to the algorithm.

Algorithm 4 Log Skeleton Algorithm

Input: Log
Output: Process Models Represented by Behavioral Patterns
  Initialization: $res = []$
  for all Trace in Log **do**
    get equivalence patterns from Trace
    get always_after patterns from Trace
    get always_before patterns from Trace
    get never_together patterns from Trace
    get directly_follow patterns from Trace
    res = combine behavioral patterns
  end for
  return res

Fig. 4. Log skeleton algorithm

4.2 Improvement for Log Skeleton

In most actual production processes, there is such a situation: the emergence of a self-circulating structure, it is possible that in the process model, for a certain event, its activities are often formed with this series of self-circulation, and this self-circulation may It is a repeating cycle of itself, or it may be a repeating cycle of multiple itself, that is, the cycle structure of these cycles is not only composed of a log activity, a simple loop body may be composed of two or more events. In this case, it is not accurate enough to use the frequency interval of event occurrence as the expression form of the process model. Therefore, in the improved Log Skeleton algorithm in this paper, the number of occurrences of all self-loop structures will be counted to represent the process model. Although this change is small, the actual results show that in the real data set, this improvement has a great impact on the expressive ability of the algorithm.

Another small improvement to the algorithm is mainly for the simplification of log behaviour patterns with relatively repetitive functions in the algorithm. As mentioned above, when the Log Skeleton algorithm expresses the model, the selected log behaviour mode includes two modes with repeated functions, namely always_after and always_before. We can easily conclude that the behaviour patterns of these two events have the same effect in the actual application process. For process events A and B, if A and B satisfy the always_after relationship, then B and A must satisfy the always_before relationship. For these relational patterns with repeated functions, the improved algorithm is pruned to reduce the load of the algorithm.

In this paper, in order to ensure as much as possible to fit the various cooperative relationships existing in the real process, in addition to retaining the equivalence in the original algorithm, a new behaviour mode cooperation is defined, of which the latter is a relatively loose constraint relationship. Together, these two behavioural patterns simulate synergies in real processes. For events A and B, if events A and B meet the following condition (1), A and B are considered to meet the cooperation behaviour mode:

$$\exists\, trace\ in\ Log,\ AB\ not\ in\ never\_together \qquad (1)$$

As mentioned above, there are some event behaviour patterns with replaceable relationships in the production log data of manufacturing enterprises. These events are not completely mutually exclusive in nature, and these events are behaviour patterns that cannot be discovered in Log Skeleton. These behaviour patterns are mainly generated in the intelligent process of the manufacturing industry. As mentioned above, the production process of the manufacturing industry is usually generated through the fusion relationship between multiple levels. In this case, if the behaviour pattern is to be used to express the process model, the analysis and mining of this relationship is very meaningful. Therefore, in this paper, the expression effect of Log Skeleton between this influence model is optimized. A behaviour pattern for non-mutually exclusive replaceable relations is proposed. In the improved algorithm, if event A and event B satisfy the following relationship (2) and (3), it means that there is a non-exclusive alternative relationship between event A and event B:

$$A.\, directlyfollow \ = \ B.\, directly\, follow \tag{2}$$

$$\forall C,\ if\ A \in C.\ directlyfollow\ then\ B \in C.\ directlyfollowB \tag{3}$$

4.3 Conformance Checking

Usually, when performing conformance checking, it is not only necessary to locate and analyze the problems existing in the trace; on the other hand, it is necessary to judge the degree of fit between the process models for a specific trace. When quantifying the fitting degree between the process model and the trace, a common way is to simply take the proportion of these log event relation tuples with differences in the whole model. When testing with some widely used data in academia, this scheme can often achieve very satisfactory results, but when we use the same scheme to test the consistency of log data collected in these real production processes, found that because the real process is often more complex, there are a large number of activities with different names in a process model, and these activities often show great differences in the frequency of occurrence, such as the design in the model generated by the enterprise resource planning system of an enterprise. There are many activities in the behavioral events at multiple levels, but some activities appear less frequently in a single process. These are mostly decision-making behavioral activities. At the same time, there are other activities such as production pipeline activities in the log which often appears in large numbers. When we are diagnosing the process of the enterprise, there may be problems with these activities, but when there are problems in the activities at different levels, the impact on the enterprise is not equivalent. The negative impact of the process is more serious, so this kind of statistical analysis scheme that treats all problems equally is often unreasonable. Therefore, this paper proposes an activity weighting scheme based on the frequency of events in the log. For those activities that occur less frequently in the process, most of which are log information generated by higher-level decision-making systems. When these activities show deviations from the process model, more attention should be paid to troubleshooting. Therefore, for these activities with less frequent occurrences, we need to ensure that it will have a greater impact on the quantification of the fitting degree.

Therefore, we design a measure to define the weight of log events based on the occurrence frequency of events in the log. The realization of this measure ensures the reliability of the process diagnosis results, and at the same time provides a stronger reference for these diagnosis results. Actually, these costs should be provided by the user and is inversely proportional to the frequency of events (Fig. 5).

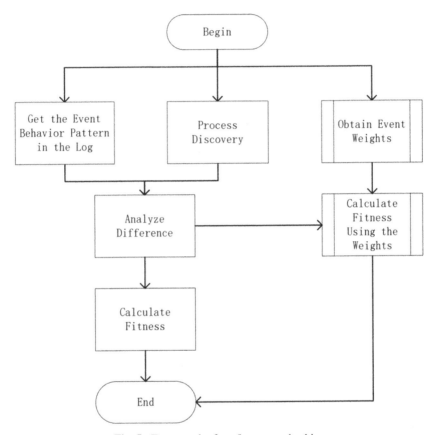

Fig. 5. Framework of conformance checking

5 Experiments

5.1 Dataset

This experiment mainly aims at the data sets commonly used in academia and the log data collected from the real manufacturing process obtained from the cooperative enterprises, and analyzes the performance of the improved algorithm by comparing different algorithms. The experiment is mainly designed from two aspects. The main goal is to verify the improved model expression ability and the ability to screen abnormal processes when applied to conformance checking. When verifying the expressive ability of the process model, these data are divided mainly according to the data set provided by BPIC (Table 1).

Table 1. Dataset from BPIC

Dataset	Traces	Events
Prepaid travel cost	2099	18246
Domestic declarations	10500	56437
Requests for payment	6886	36796
International declarations	6449	72151
Travel permits	7065	86581

5.2 Dataset Partition

As mentioned earlier, the data sets provided by BPIC are simple, and the average number of events contained in a trace is small. Due to the simplicity of these data sets, the model is derived by dividing the data set, part of which is used for process discovery, and the expressive ability of the model is judged by the process model's ability to identify the remaining data. When verifying the diagnostic ability of the algorithm, it is based on the real production process data, and through division, one part is used for process discovery, and the remaining part is damaged to the process integrity to ensure that the two parts cannot be derived from the same process model. The abnormal diagnosis ability of the algorithm is represented by analyzing the ability of the process model to discriminate these abnormal processes. In the face of the data set provided by BPIC, some algorithms commonly used in academic research are used for comparative analysis. However, when processing log data of manufacturing production process, some algorithms have serious time-consuming problems and lack any practical value. Different comparison algorithms are selected for the data sets. When comparing the expression ability of process models, by dividing the data set, part of it is used for "training", that is, used for process discovery to generate process models, and part of it is used to detect the expressive ability of the obtained process. The indicators used here are fitness indicators mentioned earlier are in full compliance as the evaluation criteria (Table 2).

5.3 Experimental Setup

In the experiment, for the relatively simple data set provided by BPIC, the comparison algorithms used are mainly the Token Based Replay algorithm [27], the Alignment algorithm, and an Alignment algorithm whose performance is improved by dividing the model [28]. These algorithms are all based on Petri Net, a model expression scheme for conformance checking. The Petri Net model in this experiment is derived from the inductive miner [29], while the algorithm in this paper is expressed based on the log event behavior model. However, when processing the data of the real production process, due

Table 2. Dataset partiton results

Dataset	Discovery	Conformance checking
Prepaid travel cost	1500	599
Domestic declarations	7000	3500
Requests for payment	5000	1886
International declarations	5000	1449
Travel permits	5000	2065
Manufacturing log data	5000	1322

to the complex process model, the search space faced by the Alignment algorithm is very complex. As a result, the Alignment algorithm often runs too slowly in the actual application process and has no application space. Therefore, in the manufacturing process Data, through repeated experiments and Token Based Replay algorithm for comparative analysis. The comparison algorithms in the experiment are all from pm4py [30], an open source python library.

5.4   Results and Analysis

Table 3 mainly shows the results of the first set of experiments, which are mainly used to detect the expressive ability of the model from the BPIC dataset. The results of the second set of experiments are shown in Table 4. This set of experiments was carried out on the log of the manufacturing enterprise to test the performance of the conformance checking scheme.

Table 3. Results on BPIC dataset

Dataset	Token based replay	Improved log skeleton	Alignment	Log skeleton
Prepaid travel cost	599	582	599	524
Domestic Declarations	3500	3498	3500	3327
Requests for payment	1884	1882	1882	1796
International Declarations	1449	1447	1448	1287
Travel permits	2059	2053	2058	1753

Table 4. Results on manufacturing log

	Test1	Test2	Test3	Test4	Test5
Log skeleton	1233	1229	1231	1227	1235
Token Based replay	1296	1285	1289	1292	1292
Improved log skeleton	1297	1292	1294	1301	1295

It can be seen from the above results that the performance of the Log Skeleton algorithm before optimization is not ideal in the experiment based solely on the experimental results, but the algorithm after the improvement scheme has improved the screening ability of these abnormal processes, which has surpassed the currently commonly used Token Based Replay algorithm. The results show that on some relatively simple data sets, the improved algorithm has a strong model expression ability, and the expression ability of the obtained model can reach the approximate effect of the most accurate inductive miner algorithm. On the other hand, when using the event behavior pattern obtained by the improved algorithm for conformance checking, the improved algorithm has surpassed the currently widely used Token Based Replay algorithm. The improved algorithm not only has stronger model expression ability, but also can make more accurate enterprise process diagnosis results based on this model.

6   Conclusion and Future Work

This paper mainly analyzes, improves, and verifies the performance of the Log Skeleton algorithm in the actual production log data. First, the real process data is different from the data set used in academic research. The former is all process-related information in the log collection interval. Among these processes, many processes have not ended or have started before the collection. This kind of unfinished process And because of the missing process in the collection process, etc., and the latter contains some complete log processes. Therefore, the preprocessing module of process data is firstly proposed in this paper, which mainly includes the screening of complete processes and the cleaning plan of problematic processes. Then the paper analyzes the traditional Log Skeleton algorithm. First, according to some prior knowledge, it analyzes and introduces the physical meaning of the event behavior pattern statistics of the Log Skeleton algorithm. It mainly improves the expression of the synergistic relationship. The expression of the model is obtained, and the expression of the model is refined by adding the scheme of the event behavior pattern. A more accurate and practical conformance checking scheme based on Log Skeleton algorithm is proposed. The frequency of events in the log is used to introduce the degree of influence of different events on the diagnosis results, and this scheme of increasing the weight of events improves the referentiality of the quantified results obtained by the conformance checking algorithm. This paper expands and analyzes the Log Skeleton algorithm commonly used in academic research, optimizes the expression form of the Log Skeleton algorithm for the process model, and proposes a more rigorous and more in line with the actual production process. It can also play a more objective role in the real business process. As mentioned above, the Log Skeleton algorithm has advantages which other algorithms do not have in a distributed environment. The follow-up research direction can be the implementation and optimization of the Log Skeleton algorithm in a distributed environment, which can improve the performance of the log system. Analytical efficiency. On the other hand, in recent years, many approximate conformance checking algorithms and online conformance checking algorithms have been proposed. In different application scenarios, different algorithms have different requirements. Currently, online conformance checking algorithms are favored. It is also the development direction of subsequent conformance checking algorithms.

Funding. This paper was funded by Independent Project of Intelligent Policing Key Laboratory of Sichuan Province (No. ZNJW2022ZZZD001).

References

1. Karabegović, I., Karabegović, E., Mahmić, M., Husak, E.: Implementation of industry 4.0 and industrial robots in the manufacturing processes. In: Karabegović, I. (eds.) NT 2019. LNNS, vol. 76, pp. 3–14. Springer, Cham (2020). https://doi.org/10.1007/978-3-030-18072-0_1
2. Brossog, M., Bornschlegl, M., Franke, J.: Reducing the energy consumption of industrial robots in manufacturing systems. Int. J. Adv. Manuf. Technol. **78**(5) (2015)
3. Yamada, A., Takata, S.: Reliability improvement of industrial robots by optimizing operation plans based on deterioration evaluation. Cirp Ann. **51**(1) (2002)
4. Zhang, M., Yan, J.: A data-driven method for optimizing the energy consumption of industrial robots. J. Clean. Prod., 285 (2021)
5. Van Der Aalst, W.: Process mining. Commun. ACM **55**(8), 76–83 (2012)
6. Rojas, E., et al.: Process mining in healthcare: a literature review. J. Biomed. Inform. **61**, 224–236 (2016)
7. Asare, E., Wang, L., Fang, X.: Conformance checking: workflow of hospitals and workflow of open-source EMRs. IEEE Access **8**, 139546–139566 (2020)
8. Siek, M., Mukti, R.M.G.: Business process mining from e-commerce event web logs: conformance checking and bottleneck identification. In: IOP Conference Series: Earth and Environmental Science, vol. 729, no. 1, p. 012133. IOP Publishing (2021)
9. Dunzer, et al.: Conformance checking: a state-of-the-art literature review. In Proceedings of the 11th International Conference on Subject-Oriented Business Process Management, pp. 1–10 (2019)
10. Stefanovic, D., Dakic, D., Stevanov, B., Lolic, T.: Process mining in manufacturing: goals, techniques and applications. In: Lalic, B., Majstorovic, V., Marjanovic, U., von Cieminski, G., Romero, D. (eds.) APMS 2020. IAICT, vol. 591, pp. 54–62. Springer, Cham (2020). https://doi.org/10.1007/978-3-030-57993-7_7
11. Mahendrawathi, E.R., et al.: Analysis of production planning in a global manufacturing company with process mining. J. Enterp. Inf. Manag. (2018)
12. Bettacchi, A., Polzonetti, A., Re, B.: Understanding production chain business process using process mining: a case study in the manufacturing scenario. In: Krogstie, J., Mouratidis, H., Su, J. (eds.) CAiSE 2016. LNBIP, vol. 249, pp. 193–203. Springer, Cham (2016). https://doi.org/10.1007/978-3-319-39564-7_19
13. Son, S., et al.: Process mining for manufacturing process analysis: a case study. In: Proceeding of 2nd Asia Pacific Conference on Business Process Management, Brisbane, Australia (2014)

14. Mahendrawathi, E.R., Astuti, H.M., Wardhani, I.R.K.: Material movement analysis for warehouse business process improvement with process mining: a case study. In: Bae, J., Suriadi, S., Wen, L. (eds.) AP-BPM 2015. LNBIP, vol. 219, pp. 115–127. Springer, Cham (2015). https://doi.org/10.1007/978-3-319-19509-4_9

15. Wilhelm, Y., Schreier, U., Reimann, P., Mitschang, B., Ziekow, H.: Data science approaches to quality control in manufacturing: a review of problems, challenges and architecture. In: Dustdar, S. (eds.) SummerSOC 2020. CCIS, vol. 1310, pp. 45–65. Springer, Cham (2020). https://doi.org/10.1007/978-3-030-64846-6_4

16. Brundage, M.P., et al.: Using graph-based visualizations to explore key performance indicator relationships for manufacturing production systems. Procedia Cirp **61**, 451–456 (2017)

17. Duong, L.T., Travé-Massuyès, L., Subias, A., Roa, N.B.: Assessing product quality from the production process logs. Int. J. Adv. Manuf. Technol. **117**(5–6), 1615–1631 (2021). https://doi.org/10.1007/s00170-021-07764-2

18. Park, M., Song, M., Baek, T.H., Son, S., Ha, S.J., Cho, S.W.: Workload and delay analysis in manufacturing process using process mining. In: Bae, J., Suriadi, S., Wen, L. (eds.) AP-BPM 2015. LNBIP vol. 219, pp. 138–151. Springer, Cham (2015). https://doi.org/10.1007/978-3-319-19509-4_11

19. Stertz, F., Mangler, J., Scheibel, B., Rinderle-Ma, S.: Expectations vs. experiences – process mining in small and medium sized manufacturing companies. In: Polyvyanyy, A., Wynn, M.T., Van Looy, A., Reichert, M. (eds.) BPM 2021. LNBIP, vol. 427, pp. 195–211. Springer, Cham (2021). https://doi.org/10.1007/978-3-030-85440-9_12

20. Ruschel, E., Loures, E.D.F.R., Santos, E.A.P.: Performance analysis and time prediction in manufacturing systems. Comput. Ind. Eng. **151**, 106972 (2021)

21. Seiger, R., et al.: Towards IoT-driven process event log generation for conformance checking in smart factories. In: 2020 IEEE 24th International Enterprise Distributed Object Computing Workshop (EDOCW), pp. 20–26. IEEE (2020)

22. Farooqui, A., et al.: Towards data-driven approaches in manufacturing: an architecture to collect sequences of operations. Int. J. Prod. Res. **58**(16), 4947–4963 (2020)

23. Ehrendorfer, M., et al.: Conformance checking and classification of manufacturing log data. In: 2019 IEEE 21st Conference on Business Informatics (CBI), vol. 1, pp. 569–577. IEEE (2019)

24. Van der Aalst, W., Adriansyah, A., van Dongen, B.: Replaying history on process models for conformance checking and performance analysis. Wiley Interdiscip. Rev. Data Min. Knowl. Discov. **2**(2), 182–192 (2012)

25. Park, M.J.: Conformance checking for manufacturing processes using control-flow perspective and time perspective (2015)

26. Verbeek, H.M.W., Medeiros de Carvalho, R.: Log skeletons: a classification approach to process discovery. arXiv preprint arXiv:1806.08247 (2018)

27. Berti, A., van der Aalst, W.M.P.: Reviving token-based replay: increasing speed while improving diagnostics. In: ATAED@ Petri Nets/ACSD, pp. 87–103 (2019)

28. Lee, W.L.J., et al.: Recomposing conformance: closing the circle on decomposed alignment-based conformance checking in process mining. Inf. Sci. **466**, 55–91 (2018)

29. Leemans, S.J., Fahland, D., Van Der Aalst, W.M.: Process and deviation exploration with inductive visual miner. BPM (demos) **1295**(8) (2014)

30. Berti, A., Van Zelst, S.J., van der Aalst, W.: Process mining for python (PM4Py): bridging the gap between process-and data science. arXiv preprint arXiv:1905.06169 (2019)

Mine-Microseismic-Signal Recognition Based on Meta-learning

Xiangqi Han, Zedong Lin[✉], Xiaoying Jiang, and Shanyou Song

College of Computer Science and Engineering, Shandong University of Science and
Technology, Qingdao 266590, China
zedonglin@163.com

Abstract. The mine management robot must have the ability to identify microseismic signals from collected data. Classical deep learning models are more
susceptible to overfitting when dealing with small samples. To address this issue,
this paper proposes two meta-learning-based methods to identify microseismic
signals in mines. First, a set of wavelet basis functions is used to transform the
microseismic and blast signals to generate 2D feature maps of wavelet coefficients.
Then, two models based on convolutional neural networks were constructed using
MAML and ANIL. Finally, comparative experiments of the two methods are conducted on a real data set. The experimental results show that the proposed methods
in this paper have good performance in terms of efficiency and accuracy.

Keywords: Management robot · Small samples · Microseismic signal · Blast
signal · MAML · ANIL

1 Introduction

In recent years, along with the rapid development of industry, China's coal resources are
consumed in large quantities, and the shallow coal reserves have been slowly depleted.
The mining of coal resources can only be extended deeper. The disasters such as rock
explosions, large roof collapses and mine earthquakes seriously threaten the lives of
workers and the safe mining of coal resources [1]. How to carry out effective early
warning of mine hazards is a pressing challenge for safe mining [2]. The microseismic
monitoring technology represented by the measurement robot realizes continuous and
real-time monitoring of microseismic events [3, 4], which provides strong support for
mine disaster early warning [5, 6]. The measurement robot is subject to interference
from vibration signals generated by blasting operations and various background noises
in the process of monitoring microseismic signals. Therefore, how to accurately and
effectively identify the signals is the key to the further application of microseismic
monitoring technology [7, 8].

2 Related Work

Researches on the identification of microseismic signals in mines are divided into two
parts: parametric analysis and traditional machine learning.

© The Author(s), under exclusive license to Springer Nature Singapore Pte Ltd. 2023
Z. Yu et al. (Eds.): CIRAC 2022, CCIS 1770, pp. 438–445, 2023.
https://doi.org/10.1007/978-981-99-0301-6_34

Parametric analysis investigates the differences between mine signal characteristics to identify microseismic signals. Malovichko et al. [9] used maximum likelihood to identify microseismic and blast signals using the event occurrence time, radiation pattern, and the energy difference between the decomposed low-frequency band and high-frequency band as features. Zhao et al. [10] used Fisher discriminant analysis to identify microseismic signals based on their trend line slope values as well as peak coordinates. Zhu et al. [11] established a joint multi-channel intra-waveform identification method based on the characteristics of the source and monitoring points, such as the relationship between distance and amplitude, distance difference and time difference. This approach relies on manually defined features whose extraction is a very tedious task.

Some literatures use traditional machine learning for the identification of microseismic signals. Shang et al. [12] first decomposed signals using the Empirical Mode Decomposition (EMD), used Singular Value Decomposition (SVD) to obtain the singular values of each component, then used support vector machines to classify the microseismic and blast signals. Dong et al. [13] used neural networks to identify microseismic signals, which made the accuracy of identification further improved. However, the method requires a large amount of data for the model to achieve better results. Zhao et al. [14] also designed a neural network model to recognize nine types of mine signals.

Although the existing methods have achieved some results in microseismic signal recognition, the accuracy still needs further improvement in small samples. To address the problem, this paper proposes a meta-learning-based method for microseismic signal identification in small samples. The main contributions are as follows:

1. First, two convolutional neural network-based models were constructed using MAML and ANIL to solve the problem of mine microseismic signal recognition under small samples.
2. Second, the effects of different types of recognition tasks on the accuracy and efficiency of the two models were explored.
3. Finally, experiments were conducted on the models constructed in this paper using a real dataset to verify the effectiveness of the proposed method.

3   Wavelet Packet Decomposition

Wavelet packet decomposition is a method of multi-scale decomposition of original signals using wavelet basis functions (WBFs), which enables finer mining of the time-domain and frequency-domain features of signals [15]. A signal is decomposed using WBFs. The signal S(t) is first decomposed into a high-frequency part D_1 and a low-frequency part A_1, and then a similar decomposition is performed on D_1 and A_1. DD_2 and DA_2 are the high-frequency and low-frequency parts of D_1 respectively. The same process is used to decompose A_1. The entire decomposition process neither contains irrelevant and redundant information nor omits any critical information.

The formalization of the wavelet packet decomposition of the signal S(t) is defined as follows:

$$S(t) = \sum_{j=0}^{2^{i-1}} f_{i,j}(t_j) = f_{i,0}(t_0) + \ldots + f_{i,2^{i-1}}(t_{2^{i-1}}) \tag{1}$$

where $f_{i,j}(t_j)$ represents the j-th component of the i-th layer of the signal S(t), $j = 0, 1, 2, \ldots, 2^{i-1}$ ($i = 1, 2, 3, 4, 5, \ldots$). Each layer decomposes the signal of the previous layer into two parts, low frequency and high frequency, so that there are 2^i sub-signals in layer i.

4 Meta-learning

Meta-learning, also called learning to learn, aims to allow a model to be trained through a number of tasks so that the model can have the ability to learn as humans do. In addressing small-sample learning, meta-learning improves the reliance of traditional machine learning on large amounts of labeled data when performing training. Small-sample learning has become a prominent application of meta-learning in the field of supervised learning [16].

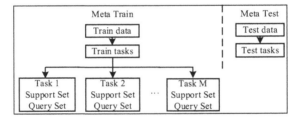

Fig. 1. Schematic diagram of meta-learning

As shown in Fig. 1, meta-learning can be divided into two phases: meta-training and meta-testing. In the meta-training phase, firstly, N classes are randomly selected in the training dataset, and K samples are taken from each class as Support Set to temporarily update the parameters of the model. Then a batch of samples are taken from the remaining data following the same process as Query Set, which is used to really tune the parameters of the model. The generalization ability of the model under different classification tasks is explored in this way. In the meta-testing phase, the model's generalization ability is evaluated using a test dataset to validate the model's performance when a new classification task is performed. Meta-learning requires the model to learn how to classify from N × K samples, often referred to as the N-way, K-shot classification problem [17].

5 MAML

MAML (Model-Agnostic Meta Learning) is a very important approach in solving small-sample problems, which is not limited by the structure of the model [18]. MAML does not require a large number of samples to learn effectively for a new task. Therefore, MAML alleviates the requirement of a large number of training samples for deep learning models and achieves better results in dealing with small-sample problems.

MAML learning process is as follows:

1. Initialize the parameters θ of the model $f(\theta)$;
2. Train the small sample classification task T according to 3 and 4;
3. Inner loop: construct Support Set by randomly selecting samples in the training dataset to train $f(\theta)$, obtain temporary θ';
4. Outer loop: construct Query Set to train $f(\theta')$ with randomly selected samples in the training dataset, really update θ;
5. Repeat 2, 3 and 4 until all tasks are trained to obtain the final parameter $\hat{\theta}$;
6. Construct a test task set in the test dataset to evaluate the performance of $f(\hat{\theta})$.

MAML is characterized by dividing the optimization process into inner and outer loops. The optimal parameters $\{\theta_1, \theta_2, \ldots\ldots, \theta_i\}$ for a batch of subtasks are obtained by the inner loop. The outer loop obtains the parameters $\hat{\theta}$ that can be quickly adapted to a new task by fine-tuning the optimal parameters θ.

6 ANIL

Raghu et al. [19] found that feature reuse is an important factor for effective MAML and proposed ANIL (Almost No Inner Loop).

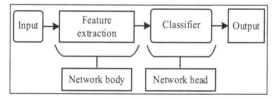

Fig. 2. ANIL diagram

As shown in Fig. 2, MAML and ANIL contain two modules, the main body, and the head. The main body is generally a feature extraction network and the head consists of a fully connected network. In the outer loop, both methods update the parameters of the entire model. In the inner loop, unlike MAML, ANIL updates only the head. There is no need to update the main body, making ANIL update significantly fewer parameters during the inner loop and improving efficiency.

7 Experimental Evaluation

A real dataset is used to evaluate the convolutional neural network recognition models based on MAML and ANIL. The experiments mainly include 1) the difference in recognition accuracy between the two models on different recognition tasks, 2) the difference in recognition accuracy between the two models under the same recognition task, and 3) the difference in efficiency between the two models under the same recognition task.

The experimental environment is as follows: CPU: Intel(R) Xeon(R) CPU E5-2690 v4 @ 2.60 GHz; GPU: Tesla M10; Python version: 3.8.2; PyTorch version: 1.8.1.

7.1 Dataset Preprocessing

400 microseismic signals and 400 blast signals are collected from a coal mine and divided into the training set and the testing set according to 4:1. A set of WBFs are used to decompose the mine signals and finally generate feature maps as input to the model.

An 8-layer decomposition of the mine signal is performed using a WBF to obtain 256 sub-bands. The length of each sub-band is 256. Finally, a mine signal is transformed into a feature map of size 256 × 256. The feature map is normalized as follows:

$$X = \frac{X_i - X_{min}}{X_{max} - X_{min}} \tag{2}$$

where X_i is a pixel of the feature map, X_{min} is the minimum value of pixels in this map, and X_{max} is the maximum one.

Different WBFs exhibit different characteristics of the signal. Double orthogonality and tight support are the two most important factors affecting wavelet packet decomposition. As shown in Table 1, according to these two factors, this paper uses 32 different WBFs to decompose signals, which improves the diversity of samples.

Table 1. WBFs used in this paper

Type	WBFs
Haar	haar
Daubechies	db1, db2, db3, db4, db5, db6
Biorthogonal	bior1.1, bior1.3, bior1.5, bior2.2, bior2.4, bior2.6
Coiflets	coif1, coif2, coif3, coif4, coif5, coif6
Symlets	sym2, sym3, sym4, sym5, sym6, sym7
Dmeyer	demy
ReverseBior	rbio1.1, rbio1.3, rbio1.5, rbio2.2, rbio2.4, rbio2.6

7.2 Model Architecture

The architecture of the recognition model proposed in this paper is shown in Fig. 3. The main body contains four convolutional modules: a convolutional layer, a BN layer, a ReLu activation function, and a pooling layer. The head is a linear fully connected layer.

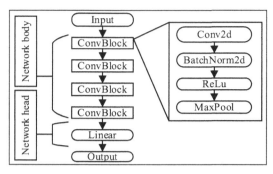

Fig. 3. Model architecture

7.3 Results Analysis

To compare the accuracy of MAML-based and ANIL-based models on the same recognition task, several small-sample recognition tasks were used for comparative analysis. The comparison in recognition accuracy is shown in Fig. 4.

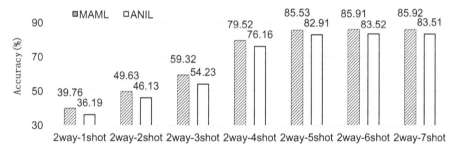

Fig. 4. Accuracy comparison

The following conclusions can be drawn from Fig. 4. 1) The recognition accuracy of the two models increases as the sample numbers K of class increases, but their differences are not significant. 2) With only 4 samples, the recognition accuracy of the two models is already high, which shows the effectiveness of methods proposed in this paper.

The two models were trained for 1000 rounds on different tasks with sample sizes K of 5, 6, and 7, respectively. The training elapsed time is shown in Fig. 5.

The following conclusions can be drawn from Fig. 5. 1) The training time of two models increases as the sample numbers K of class increases, but the increment of ANIL is not large. The reason is that ANIL only updates the head in the inner loop making the computational effort significantly lower. 2) For the same recognition task, the training time of the ANIL-based model is significantly less compared to the MAML-based one.

8 Conclusions

In this paper, we propose two meta-learning-based methods for small-sample microseismic signal identification. First, data enhancement of small-sample signals is achieved by

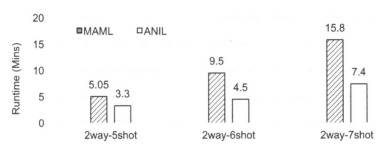

Fig. 5. Runtime comparison

decomposing microseismic and blast signals using a set of WBFs. Then, small-sample microseismic signal recognition models are constructed based on MAML and ANIL respectively. Finally, the performance of the two models for microseismic signal recognition under small samples is compared using a real dataset. The MAML-based model is used for scenarios where recognition accuracy is very critical. The ANIL-based model runs more efficiently with little loss of accuracy.

Acknowledgements. This work was supported in part by the Taishan Scholars Program of Shandong Province (No. ts20190936), Excellent Youth Innovation Team Foundation of Shandong Higher School (No. 2019KJN024), National Coal Indus-try Higher Education Major Research Project (No. 2021MXJG004).

References

1. Cheng, T., Yi, Q., Wu, Y.: Application of improved EWT_MPE model in feature extraction of mine microseismic signal. Vib. Shock (2021)
2. Yi, Q.: Research on Feature Extraction and Automatic Classification of Mine Microseismic and Blasting Vibration Signals. Jiangxi University of Science and Technology (2021)
3. Cheng, H., Zhao, H., Xu, J.: Study on floor heave mechanism and control technology of roadway based on slipline field theory. J. Min. Sci. Technol.. **6**(3), 314–322 (2021)
4. Jiang, F., Yin, Y., Zhu, Q.: Feature extraction and classification of mining microseismic waveforms via multi-channels analysis. J. China Coal Soc. **39**(2), 229–237 (2014)
5. Ma, C., Li, T., Zhang, H.: A method for numerical simulation based on microseismic information and the interpretation of hard rock fracture. J. Appl. Geophys. (2019)
6. Gong, F., Si, X., Li, X.: Experimental investigation of strain rock burst in circular caverns under deep three-dimensional high-stress conditions. Rock Mech. Rock Eng. **52**(4) (2018)
7. Xie, X., Ye, G., Liu, J.: On control of accuracy and stability of microseismic location in a mining scale. Chin. J. Geotech. Eng. **36**(5), 899–904 (2014)
8. Zhang, X., Jia, R., Lu, X.: Identification of blasting vibration and coal-rock fracturing microseismic signals. Appl. Geophys. **15**(02), 134–143+218 (2018)
9. Malovichko, D.: Discrimination of blasts in mine seismology; proceedings of the deep mining 2012. Australian Centre for Geomechanics, Perth, F (2012)
10. Zhao, G., Ma, J., Dong, L.: Pattern recognition of mine microseismic and blasting signals based on waveform onset characteristics. Chin. J. Nonferrous Metals (Engl. Ed.) **10**, 3410–3420 (2015)

11. Zhu, Q., Jiang, F., Wang, C.: Optimization of microseismic wave automatic pickup and multi-channel joint positioning. J. Coal **38**(03), 397–403 (2013). https://doi.org/10.13225/j.cnki.jccs.2013.03.002

12. Shang, X.: Feature extraction and classification method of mine microseismic and blasting signals based on EMD_SVD. Chin. J. Geotech. Eng. **38**(10), 10 (2016)

13. Dong, L., Tang, Z., Li, X.: Identification method of microseismic and blasting events based on convolutional neural network and original waveform. J. Cent. South Univ. Engl. Ed. **27**(10), 12 (2020)

14. Zhao, H., Liu, R., Liu, Y.: Research on classification and identification of mine microseismic signals based on deep learning method. J. Min. Sci. **7**(2), 9 (2022)

15. Song, G., Liu, T., Wang, C.: Research on the application of wavelet analysis in microseismic signal processing. Shandong Sci. **24**(03), 64–68+74 (2011)

16. Liu, Y.: Research on a Generic Computational Tool for Two-Layer Optimization Oriented to Meta-Learning. Dalian University of Technology (2021). https://doi.org/10.26991/d.cnki.gdllu.2021.002187

17. Xu, C., Sun, Y., Li, G.: Research on small sample commodity image classification based on depth metric learning. J. Chongqing Univ. Technol. (Nat. Sci.) **34**(09), 209–216 (2020)

18. Finn, C., Abbeel, P., Levine, S.: Model-agnostic meta-learning for fast adaptation of deep networks. In: International Conference on Machine Learning. PMLR (2017)

19. Raghu, A., Raghu, M., Bengio, S.: Rapid learning or feature reuse? Towards understanding the effectiveness of MAML. CoRR, abs/1909.09157 (2019)

A Positioning Optimization Method for Anti-underwater Vehicle

Jiajing Wang[(✉)], Zhu Kou, Xiangtao Zhao, and Dongtian Guo

Dalian Naval Academy, Dalian 116018, China
601770950@qq.com

Abstract. Underwater vehicle poses a threat to underwater safety due to the small target and low radiation noise. The high sensitivity fiber-optic hydrophone is an advanced early warning detector, it can improve the efficiency of anti-underwater vehicle warfare. The phase generated carrier (PGC) demodulation technology is widely used in interferometric fiber-optic hydrophones because of its high sensitivity, wide dynamic range, and high phase measurement accuracy. An ellipse fitting optimization method based on least squares is proposed in this paper to solve the non-linear error in the PGC demodulation process to improve the system demodulation accuracy. The experimental results show that compared with the previous demodulation, after using the least-squares ellipse fitting optimization, the relative amplitude and harmonic suppression ratio of the same frequency are greatly improved, the demodulation accuracy is effectively enhanced, and the positional accuracy to detecting underwater vehicle is increased.

Keywords: Anti-underwater vehicle · Fiber-optic hydrophone · PGC demodulation · Nonlinear optimization · Ellipse fitting

1 Introduction

With the development of robot technology, more and more underwater vehicles are involved in underwater attack tasks, so how to counterattack underwater vehicle has become a new topic. The first step of anti-underwater vehicle is to detect. However the underwater vehicle has a small target and low radiation noise of motion, the high sensitivity detector is needed. The fiber-optic hydrophone can easily percept of weak signal, it is suitable for detection of underwater vehicle. So layout arrays using fiber-optic hydrophone could realize the target positioning to underwater vehicle.

Fiber-optic hydrophone is a subaqueous sound sensor which is built on optical fiber and optoelectronics. By high sensitivity fiber optic interferential measurement, a water sound signal is converted to a optic signal, then sent it to the signal processing system to pick up the sound signal information. The phase generated carrier (PGC) demodulation technology is widely used in interferometric fiber-optic hydrophones because of its high sensitivity, wide dynamic range, and high phase measurement accuracy. The PGC demodulation technology realizes the demodulation due to the phase difference caused by changing two channels of optical signals. The commonly used methods include differential cross multiplication (PGC-DCM) [1] and arctangent (PGC-Arctan) algorithm.

The method used in this paper is the arctangent algorithm. The traditional PGC-Arctan demodulation algorithm is still affected by the modulation depth. When the modulation depth fluctuates, the demodulation result will produce nonlinearity and cause severe harmonic distortion [2]. The traditional PGC-Arctan algorithm also does not consider the accompanying amplitude modulation and system noise caused by the internal modulation. Moreover, the two demodulated signals contain non-orthogonal nonlinear errors. The graph that is drawn by the discrete points of the two signal outputs changes from a circle to an ellipse. Therefore, this paper proposes a nonlinear optimization method of ellipse fitting based on least squares. By means of the nonlinear optimization algorithm of least squares, the corresponding ellipse parameters are fitted. Then the orthogonal data after nonlinear optimization is demodulated by the PGC-Arctan algorithm, which can solve the problem of spurious amplitude modulation. By comparing the direct demodulation and the least squares algorithm, the effectiveness of the proposed method for nonlinear error correction in the PGC demodulation process is verified.

2 Theory

This paper adopts the Mach-Zehnder interferometric fiber-optic hydrophone. There are two PGC modulation ways, including internal and external modulations. The light intensity expression of the interference output signal channel obtained by internal modulation is as follows:

$$S = (1 + m \cos \omega_0 t)(A + B \cos[C \cos \omega_0 t + \varphi(t)]) \tag{1}$$

where T and U are constants, which are directly proportional to the power of the light source, $C \cos \omega_0 t$ is a frequency-doubled carrier signal, and $\kappa(t)$ is the phase changes caused by the changes in external physical quantities [3]. The term $(1 + m \cos \omega_0 t)$ is caused by the parasitic amplitude modulation, and m is the associated amplitude modulation index. At this time, the outputs of the two filters are:

$$S_1 = \frac{Tm}{2} + \frac{Um}{2}[J_0(C) - J_2(C)] \cos \kappa(t) - UGJ_1(C) \sin \kappa(t) \tag{2}$$

$$S_2 = \frac{Um}{2}[J_3(C) - J_1(C)] \sin \kappa(t) - UGJ_2(C) \sin \kappa(t) \tag{3}$$

In Eqs. (2) and (3), $J_i(C)$ is the Bessel's functions of the i order. G is the amplitude value. Then the output of the ratio of S_1 to S_2 is no longer linear, and the traditional PGC-Arctan demodulation scheme is not applicable. Therefore, this paper proposes an ellipse fitting algorithm based on least-squares to solve the problem of the nonlinear error caused by associated amplitude modulation. Based on the PGC-Arctan demodulation method, a pair of orthogonal signals is obtained by ellipse fitting and the least-square nonlinear optimization on the two of low-pass filtered signals. The principle block diagram of the algorithm is shown in Fig. 1.

The following part is the specific implementation of the algorithm. The final general expressions of the nonlinear error can be obtained by trigonometric transform on Eqs. (2)

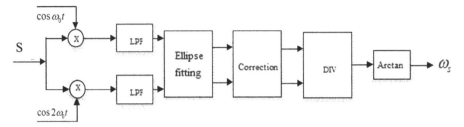

Fig. 1. The PGC demodulation method proposed in this paper.

and (3), which are as follows:

$$S_x = h + t\cos[\kappa(t)]$$
$$S_y = k + u\cos[\kappa(t) - \delta]$$
(4)

In Eq. (4), S_x and S_y are the two channels of observed signals, and the nonlinear error in the equation is calibrated by an ellipse fitting algorithm to achieve the following expression:

$$S_x = \cos[\kappa(t)]$$
$$S_y = \sin[\kappa(t)]$$
(5)

Equation (5) can be organized to:

$$\frac{(S_x - h)^2}{t^2} + \frac{(S_y - k)^2}{u^2} - 2\cos\delta(S_x - h)(S_y - k)/tu = \sin^2\delta$$
(6)

The known standard ellipse equation is:

$$x^2 + Uxy + Cy^2 + Dx + Ey + F = 0$$
(7)

The parameters $h, k, t, u,$ and δ can be obtained by comparing Eq. (6) and Eq. (7), as shown in Eq. (8):

$$\begin{cases} h = (2CD - UE)/(U^2 - 4C) \\ k = (2E - UD)/(U^2 - 4C) \\ t = [(h^2 + k^2C + hkU - F)/(1 - U^2/4C)]^2 \\ u = (t^2/C)^{\frac{1}{2}} \\ \delta = \cos^{-1}[-U/2\sqrt{C}] \end{cases}$$
(8)

The parameters that the ellipse fitting calibration algorithm needs to calculate are the ellipse parameters $U, C, D, E,$ and F [4]. This paper obtains the data $M = \{S_x; S_y\}_n$ through measurement. Then n groups of ellipse equations can be obtained by substituting them into Eq. (7), and the ellipse parameters $U, C, D, E,$ and F can be obtained by using the least-squares method to optimize these n groups of equations. The residual can be acquired by substituting the data points $\{S_x; S_y\}$ into the ellipse equation, which is as follows:

$$S_{xi}^2 + US_{xi}S_{yi} + CS_{yi}^2 + DS_{xi} + ES_{yi} + F = r_i \tag{9}$$

Using the nonlinear optimization principle of the least-squares method, the residual sum of the squares is calculated as:

$$P = \sum_{i=1}^{n} r_i^2 \tag{10}$$

To obtain the ellipse parameters that are infinitely close to the observed values, the minimum value of Eq. (10) is taken. Thus, the following equation should be satisfied:

$$\frac{\partial P}{\partial u_i}\bigg|_{i=1}^{5} = 0, \quad u_i = U, C, D, E, F \tag{11}$$

Equation (11) is expanded to:

$$
\begin{bmatrix} U \\ C \\ D \\ E \\ F \end{bmatrix} =
\begin{bmatrix}
\sum_{i=1}^{N} Sx_i^2 Iy_i^2 & \sum_{i=1}^{N} Sy_i^3 Ix_i & \sum_{i=1}^{N} Sx_i^2 Iy_i & \sum_{i=1}^{N} Sx_i Iy_i^2 & \sum_{i=1}^{N} Sx_i Iy_i \\
\sum_{i=1}^{N} Sy_i^3 Sx_i & \sum_{i=1}^{N} Sy_i^4 & \sum_{i=1}^{N} Sx_i Iy_i^2 & \sum_{i=1}^{N} Sy_i^3 & \sum_{i=1}^{N} Sy_i^2 \\
\sum_{i=1}^{N} Sx_i^2 Sy_i & \sum_{i=1}^{N} Sx_i Sy_i^2 & \sum_{i=1}^{N} Sx_i^2 & \sum_{i=1}^{N} Sx_i Sy_i & \sum_{i=1}^{N} Sx_i \\
\sum_{i=1}^{N} Sx_i Sy_i^2 & \sum_{i=1}^{N} Sx_i Sy_i^2 & \sum_{i=1}^{N} Sx_i Sy_i^2 & \sum_{i=1}^{N} Sy_i^2 & \sum_{i=1}^{N} Sy_i \\
\sum_{i=1}^{N} Sx_i Sy_i & \sum_{i=1}^{N} Sy_i^2 & \sum_{i=1}^{N} Sx_i & \sum_{i=1}^{N} Sy_i & N
\end{bmatrix}^{-1}
\left(-\begin{bmatrix}
\sum_{i=1}^{N} Sx_i^3 Sy_i \\
\sum_{i=1}^{N} Sx_i^2 Sy_i^2 \\
\sum_{i=1}^{N} Sx_i^3 \\
\sum_{i=1}^{N} Sx_i^2 Sy_i \\
\sum_{i=1}^{N} Sx_i^2
\end{bmatrix}\right) \tag{12}
$$

The ellipse parameters $U, C, D, E,$ and F, obtained from Eq. (12), are substituted into Eq. (8) to calculate the parameters $h, k, t, u,$ and δ. Then, by replacing the parameters $h, k, t, u,$ and δ into Eq. (4), the interference signal after calibration can be achieved as shown in Eq. (13):

$$
\begin{cases}
S_x' = (S_x - h)/t = \cos[\kappa(t)] \\
S_y' = \dfrac{[(S_y - k)/u - \cos\kappa(t)\cos\delta]}{\sin\delta} = \sin[\kappa(t)]
\end{cases} \tag{13}
$$

where the data points $\{S_x'; I_y'\}$ are the two calibrated orthogonal interference signals.

3 Simulation

In order to analyze and verify the proposed method, relevant numerical simulations are carried out.

3.1 Simulation and Discussion of Associated Amplitude Modulation Index *M*

In this paper, the associated amplitude modulation index *m* is simulated from 0 to 0.3 by stepping of 0.05. Then, the output data before and after ellipse fitting are compared to determine whether the ellipse fitting algorithm based on the least-squares can calibrate the nonlinear error caused by the associated amplitude modulation, and its optimization effect is verified. Figure 2 shows the variation results of the relative amplitude difference RAE, the harmonic suppression ratio HSR and the phase noise with the associated amplitude modulation index *m*.

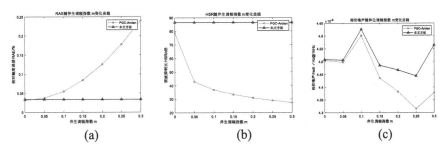

Fig. 2. Influence of the associated amplitude modulation index *m* on demodulation: (a) variation curve of RAE with m, (b) variation curve of HSR with m, and (c) variation curve of phase noise with *m*.

As shown in Fig. 2, with the increase in the parasitic amplitude modulation index, the RAE and HSR of the proposed method are basically stable at 0.03% and −87 dB, respectively, which meets the requirements of the index. However, the performance of the PGC-Arctan demodulation deteriorates sharply with the increase in the associated amplitude modulation, and the HSR even drops by 30 dB, so the demodulation function cannot be realized. In Fig. 2 (c), with the increase in the parasitic amplitude modulation index m, the phase noises of the two algorithms have a slight change, both of which are less than 3×10^{-8} rad/Hz@1 kHz. However, the phase noise of the method in this paper is always higher than the PGC-Arctan demodulation, indicating that with the increase in the associated amplitude modulation index, the proposed method will increase the noise of some frequency points in the range of 1 kHz. However, this defect is negligible due to its relatively small value.

3.2 Simulation and Discussion of Two-Channel Signal Carrier Amplitude Ratio G_p/H_p

In this paper, the two-channel signal carrier amplitude ratio G_p/H_p is simulated from 1 to 10 by stepping of 1, and the output data before and after ellipse fitting are compared to determine whether the ellipse fitting algorithm based on the least-squares can calibrate the nonlinear error caused by the amplitude deviation degree of the two-channel carriers, and its optimization effect is verified. Figure 3 shows the variation results of RAE, HSR, and phase noise with the carrier amplitude ratio G_p/H_p of the two signals.

In Fig. 3 (a) and (b), with the increase in the amplitude ratio of the two signals, the RAE of the proposed technique is basically stable at 0.001%, and the HSR is stable at −87 dB, which fully meets the index requirements. However, the performance of PGC-Arctan demodulation deteriorates with the increase in the amplitude ratio of the two signals, and the demodulation function cannot be realized. As can be seen in Fig. 3(c), with the increase in the amplitude ratio of the two signals, the phase noise of the method in this paper is basically unchanged and less than 3×10^{-8} rad/Hz@1 kHz. However, the phase noise of the PGC-Arctan demodulation has always been growing with the maximum value exceeding 1.8×10^{-8} rad/Hz@1 kHz, indicating that with the increase in the amplitude ratio of the two signals, the method in this paper can effectively reduce the phase noise power and realize the optimization of nonlinear data.

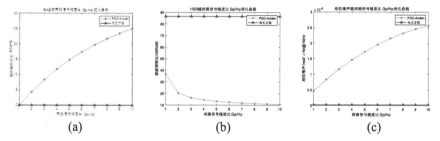

Fig. 3. Influence of two-channel signal carrier amplitude ratio G_p/H_p on demodulation: (a) variation curve of RAE with G_p/H_p, (b) variation curve of HSR with G_p/H_p, and (c) variation curve of phase noise with G_p/H_p.

3.3 Simulation and Discussion of the Phase Difference K Between the Local Carrier and the Phase Carrier

In this paper, the phase shift K of the local carrier and the phase carrier is simulated from 0 to $\pi/4$ by stepping of $\pi/32$. The output data before and after ellipse fitting are compared to determine whether the ellipse fitting algorithm based on the least-squares can calibrate the nonlinear error caused by the phase shift between the local carrier and the phase carrier and its optimization effect is verified. Figure 4 shows the variation results of RAE, HSR, and phase noise with the phase shift ϕ between the local carrier and the phase carrier.

It can be seen from Figs. 4(a) and (b) that with the increase in the phase shift between the local carrier and the phase carrier, the RAE of the proposed method is basically stable at 0.001%, and the total harmonic distortion is stable at −87 dB, which fully meets the requirements of the index. However, the performance of PGC-Arctan demodulation deteriorates sharply with the increase in the phase shift between the local carrier and the phase carrier, and the RAE exceeds 0.2%. Hence, the demodulation function cannot be realized. As can be seen from Fig. 4(c), with the increase of the phase shift between the local carrier and the phase carrier, the phase noise of both demodulations has some deterioration. When the phase shift is less than $5/32\pi$, the phase noise of both methods

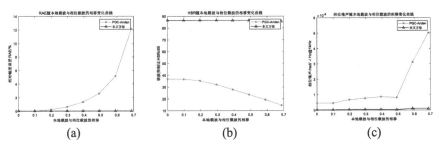

Fig. 4. Influence of the phase shift K between the local carrier and the phase carrier on demodulation: (a) variation curve of RAE with K, (b) variation curve of HSR with K, and (c) variation curve of phase noise with K.

is very small. When the phase shift is less than $5/32\pi$, the proposed method in this paper is clearly better than the PGC-Arctan demodulation, which proves that the proposed approach can effectively suppress the phase noise.

4 Conclusions

Aiming at the fluctuation of modulation depth in PGC demodulation and the associated amplitude modulation caused by internal modulation, this paper proposed an ellipse fitting method based on the least-squares and the traditional PGC-Arctan demodulation method to optimize the nonlinear error. Besides, three groups of data simulations compared the proposed method with the PGC-Arctan demodulation method. The conclusions are: (1) With the increase in the associated amplitude modulation index, the method in this paper performs well in various indicators. It can effectively solve the problem of the nonlinear error caused by the associated amplitude modulation. (2) With the increase in the amplitude ratio of the two signals, the method in this paper can effectively reduce the phase noise power and realize the optimization for the nonlinear data. (3) Considering that the signal in the actual environment of the military field usually contains ocean and polarization noises, the proposed method can eliminate the influence caused by noises. (4) When the relevant parameters fluctuate, the presented method can correctly calibrate the relevant parameters with relatively good stability and effectively reduce the amplitude distortion.

In summary, the method proposed in this paper can effectively calibrate the non-orthogonal data and realize the nonlinear optimization, which helps to improve the PGC demodulation performance of the fiber-optic hydrophones, and effectively improve the locating and detecting capability of anti-underwater vehicle.

References

1. Han, C., Cao, J., Liu, X.: Research on the frequency characteristic of LPF in fiber-optic hydrophone system with PGC demodulation. Appl. Sci. Technol. **35**(5), 23–27 (2018)
2. Zhang, A., Wang, K., He, B.: Research on PGC demodulation algorithm of interference fiber sensor. Electro Opt. Technol. Appl. **28**(6), 49–53 (2013)

3. Cai, H., Ye, Q., Wang, Z.: Progress in research of distributed fiber acoustic sensing techniques. J. Appl. Sci. **36**(1), 41–58 (2018)
4. Shi Q.: The stability and consistency analysis of optical seismometer system using phase generated carrier in field application. In: The International Society for Optical Engineering, pp. 75081M–75081M-9. Proceedings of SPIE, Shanghai (2009)

Correction to: Intelligent Detection of Stratigraphy Boundary Based on Deep Learning

Qin Zhao, Tilin Wang, Yanming Liu, Mingsong Yang,
Xiaojuan Ning, and Xinhong Hei

Correction to:
Chapter "Intelligent Detection of Stratigraphy Boundary
Based on Deep Learning" in: Z. Yu et al. (Eds.):
***Intelligent Robotics*, CCIS 1770,**
https://doi.org/10.1007/978-981-99-0301-6_9

In the originally published chapter 9 the acknowledgement section was erroneously omitted. This has been corrected and acknowledgement has been added at the end of the paper.

The updated original version of this chapter can be found at
https://doi.org/10.1007/978-981-99-0301-6_9

Author Index

© The Editor(s) (if applicable) and The Author(s), under exclusive license
to Springer Nature Singapore Pte Ltd. 2023
Z. Yu et al. (Eds.): CIRAC 2022, CCIS 1770, pp. 455–456, 2023.
https://doi.org/10.1007/978-981-99-0301-6

Printed in the United States
by Baker & Taylor Publisher Services